SCRAMBLE!

SCRAMBLE!

The dramatic story of a young
fighter pilot's experiences during the
Battle of Britain & the Siege of Malta

TOM NEIL
INTRODUCTION BY JAMES HOLLAND

AMBERLEY

To my wife, who also served, and who was much more capable on the ground than ever I was in the air; and my three sons, who should at least know something of these events.

The illustrations are copyright of the author unless otherwise stated. Illustrations 74 & 75 © Jonathan Reeve. The publishers would like to thank David Reeve for his assistance in the publication of this book.

This edition first published 2015

Amberley Publishing
The Hill, Stroud
Gloucestershire, GL5 4EP

www.amberley-books.com

Copyright © Tom Neil 2015

The right of Tom Neil to be identified as the Author of this work has been asserted in accordance with the Copyrights, Designs and Patents Act 1988.

ISBN 978 1 4456 4951 1 (hardback)
ISBN 978 1 4456 4952 8 (ebook)

British Library Cataloguing in Publication Data.

A catalogue record for this book is available from the British Library.

Typeset in 11pt on 14.5pt Sabon.
Typesetting by Amberley Publishing.

Printed in the UK.

Contents

Introduction
by James Holland

On a wonderfully warm and summery July evening back in 2007, the Battle of Britain Fighter Association held their Sunset Dinner at Bentley Priory in Stanmore in north-west London. This lovely Georgian mansion, perched on a hill overlooking much of the city, was the former Headquarters of RAF Fighter Command. It was from where Air Chief Marshal Sir Hugh Dowding had created the world's first fully co-ordinated air defence system in the late 1930s; it was also where he had commanded the Battle of Britain. And once the Luftwaffe had been beaten and the invasion scare had diminished, the house continued to be the base of Fighter Command for the rest of the war, and beyond that, remained one of the RAF's principal command posts. Now, however, more than sixty years after the end of the war, it was about to be sold off by the MOD.

The Battle of Britain Fighter Association was open to any pilot or aircrew who had flown in the battle, and in the years that followed the war, Bentley Priory was regularly used as a venue for gatherings. It was, in many ways, the spiritual home of these men, so the Sunset Dinner was bound to be a particularly poignant evening. Many of The Few had long since departed, but there were a good number there that evening, and not least Tom Neil, who, although recovering from a hip replacement and temporarily in a wheelchair, was in good spirits. Certainly, with his thick wave of white hair and mischievous eyes, and looking impeccable in his black tie and row of medals, he still managed to cut a dash and sit ramrod straight, even though he was a few days shy of eighty-seven.

Many who lived through the war years had extraordinary experiences and performed incredible feats of valour, and this was certainly true of Tom, who finished the war with no less than fourteen aerial victories to his name. This made him almost a triple ace, and to put this in some perspective, less than five percent of fighter pilots scored the magic five required to become an ace. Those who shot down more than ten were considerable fewer than that; Tom has fourteen to his name, putting him amongst the most successful Allied fighter pilots of the war. As I write this, he is Britain's highest-scoring living ace.

He was also twice awarded the Distinguished Flying Cross, given for valour, as well as an Air Force Cross and the US Bronze Star. None of these medals were handed out lightly. He flew throughout the Battle of Britain, in the Siege of Malta, and in June 1944, whilst serving with the Americans, was among the very first fighter pilots to land back in France. Later, he continued to put himself in the face of danger by becoming a test pilot - a notoriously hazardous and often lethal occupation.

I had first met Tom some years before while I was researching the Siege of Malta. He had been a Hurricane pilot out there in 1941 and so had suggested I visit him at his home in Norfolk. His wife, Eileen, was every bit as charming as he, and they both still had wonderfully sparky banter with each other. Tom was 'Neil' whenever she was attempting to be stern with him; she, on the other hand, was 'Flight Officer' – a reference not only to her days in the WAAF during the war, but also to her lower rank than his own.

In all my conversations, Tom has never been anything other than sparkling company. Like many from that greatest generation, he is always self-effacing, and the humour is never far away; the glint of amusement can usually be seen in his eyes. He is also always erudite and perceptive. These traits, combined with my own awe for his achievements, make him sensationally good company. Time with Tom is always a treat.

At Bentley Priory that evening in July 2007, there were drinks and then we were ushered out onto the balcony to watch the Battle of Britain Memorial Flight perform a fly-past. One Hurricane and one Spitfire flew over then began twirling and dancing around the sky and I then glanced down to see Tom, still in his wheelchair, stuck behind one of the famous stone pillars and unable to see anything of this display.

'Do you want me to move you?' I asked him.

Tom's eyes twinkled. 'Don't worry,' he said. 'I know what they look like.'

That was certainly true enough, and by the time he left Malta in December 1941, he had seen enough of Hurricanes to last him a lifetime. There is no doubt that it was a fine fighter aircraft in its day and performed very well during the Battle of Britain, but even by 1940, it was becoming obsolescent. By the time Tom arrived on Malta in the summer of 1941, it was being woefully outclassed by the latest Messerschmitt 109s. Tom and his beleaguered colleagues, stuck on that island battling overwhelming enemy bombers and fighters, as well as intense heat, mosquitoes, dysentery and insufficient supplies of food and drink, needed the latest Spitfire Mk Vs, which at the time were filling squadrons back home in Britain with some abundance. This was blindingly obvious to all the pilots, but as far as Tom was concerned, not enough was being done to get them to Malta. So angry and frustrated was he that when the Air-Vice Marshal Lloyd, the Air Officer Commanding, Malta, suggested a bad workman blamed his tools, Tom got very near to punching him in the face. Tom left the island with a sense of enormous relief that he was still alive - it was a miracle that he was – and with the determination never to set foot on Malta ever again.

That didn't happen. Age mellowed him and he has since returned to the island numerous times, and, of course, has written his wonderfully honest and vivid account of his time there during the war. His chapters about Malta, as with the rest of his writing, are suffused with his own voice; reading his words, one can hear him saying them.

If Tom has spent much of his retirement thinking and writing about those wartime years, it is hardly surprising. He was just eighteen when he joined the RAF Volunteer Reserve and still only nineteen for much of the Battle of Britain. Most young men in Britain today spend their late teens and early twenties living a life free of most responsibilities; when I look back on my own life as a young adult it is embarrassing how feckless and hopeless I was. Yet Tom was flying for his life, and for Britain's future. The responsibility on his shoulders was enormous. Being involved in the biggest global conflict in the history of the world, and to have seen what he witnessed, unquestionably had a profound and lasting effect.

Time, however, has given him the chance to analyse his experiences and it is this, coupled with rare writing skills, that have combined to make *Scramble* such an enthralling and compelling read. The young man he once was leaps off every page, but there is wisdom and perspective there too. We feel the immediacy of his experiences, but we also know a lifetime's wisdom is infusing those memories.

Nor is there any drum-beating or nostalgic glorification of the past, which helps make his book stand out from many other wartime memoirs. Rather, he is quick to criticise where he believes it due and equally happy to apportion praise when he believes it to be deserved. It was Tom, for example, who first alerted me to the fact that the Spitfire in 1940 was not necessarily the finest fighter in the world. Rather, he was adamant that accolade belonged to the Messerschmitt 109. 'The 109 could do the three things needed in air-to-air combat better than any other aircraft at the time,' he said. 'It could climb quicker than any other plane, had a combination of cannons and machine-guns that had fifty-five seconds' of ammunition, and could dive out of the way quicker than the Spitfire.' In contrast, he pointed out, Spitfires and Hurricanes had just 14.7 seconds' of ammunition. He was in his ninetieth year when he told me that, and did so with the well-reasoned lucidity and detail of a man half his age. Air-to-air fighting, he told me, was not about fancy manoeuvres and out-turning your enemy; if your plane could climb, dive and pack a bigger punch than the opposition, that was enough.

It was also Tom who pointed out the Luftwaffe simply never had enough bombers in 1940. Most Battle of Britain veterans remember the terrible sense of being perpetually and hopelessly outnumbered, but Tom told me about flying from North Weald on 3 September 1940, which showed how he had rationally analysed his experiences in a way most in his shoes never had. That day, he and eleven others from 249 Squadron took off in their Hurricanes only to see the airfield come under attack and disappear under a mass of smoke and debris. He wondered how was ever going to get back down again, but then cheerfully explained that not only he but all the squadron touched down again safely by simply dodging the potholes. 'You need an awful lot of bombs,' he said, 'to knock out an entire grass airfield.'

It seems incredible that before so very long, that extraordinary generation will be gone; they are fading fast. We are lucky, however, very lucky, that someone as exceptional as Tom has written about his wartime experiences. Not only is his adventure a thrilling read, it is also one told in a very distinct and entertaining voice. Long years after the last of the wartime pilots has finally departed, Tom will continue to be with us. We will be able to read this remarkable book and hear him still.

James Holland, May 2015

Author's Note

In 1980, or thereabouts, having spent many years writing about my war experiences as a fighter pilot in the Second World War, and having them published in various aviation magazines, I was invited by the publishers *William Kimber* to provide material for a book about my flying in the Royal Air Force throughout the three year period, 1938 to 1941. As this would involve writing about my flying training, before and during the war, the Battle of Britain and the Siege of Malta, it was immediately apparent that in order to do justice to all three events, a lengthy book would result.

As anticipated, the volume of the original offering was so large that the publisher felt it necessary to recommend that three books should eventually be made, the first being about the Battle of Britain and entitled *Gunbutton to Fire,* and the two others, with separate titles, to be published at a later date. Sadly, *William Kimber* went out of business before these arrangements could be finalized, and books two and three were later produced elsewhere.

As all three books have sold well over the years and are still greatly in demand, and because there are so few of us veterans of the Battle of Britain and Siege of Malta left to write of their experiences, I thought it appropriate that the original three books should be offered once more to the public under the single, separate title, 'SCRAMBLE!'

The material in this book is as I wrote it many years ago, and although there have been some recent amendments and additions, I hope it will be seen as forming a true account of what it was like to be a fervently patriotic youth, born in 1920, brought up in the shadow of Hitler's Germany, and gifted with that rarest of privileges - that of being an RAF fighter pilot during the Second World War.

Much of my writing at the time was based, among other official documents, on many hundreds of letters sent to my parents over those early wartime years, correspondence lovingly preserved by them until their death in the 1970s, then inherited by me.

Such memories are now beyond price. Of the 3,000 young officer and NCO pilots who took an active part with me in the Battle of Britain, fewer than 20 remain, our average age in 2015 being at least 96. Sadly, but inevitably, we shall all soon drift into oblivion.

For this reason, I feel it vital for our nation's history and future existence, that those boyhood companions of mine who fought with me, sacrificed their lives or were crippled mentally as well as physically by their ordeals, should be remembered fondly with pride and gratitude and granted the greatest possible honour and respect.

This then is part of the story of those early years and on each of their tombstones should be written, 'He offered his life and set a splendid example!'

1

Early Days

I was born in Liverpool on Bastille Day, 1920, or more precisely, Bootle, which is the northern suburb of that city.

1920 was a vintage year for us males as mother nature, with the enthusiastic cooperation of three million servicemen returning from the Flanders trenches and beyond in 1919, strove to correct the imbalance of the sexes brought about by the catastrophic casualties of the First World War.

Although even then an area in decline, for me, growing up in Liverpool during the momentous inter-war years of the '20s and '30s was unquestionably special. Being typical of many thousands of young men who fought in the air throughout the Second World War, my upbringing and the opinions I held at that time may therefore be worthy of mention. Such information, too, will make rather more sense of some of the events I will later describe.

As I write, Bootle is a remarkably unfunny town, being a victim of the postwar 'Liverpool sickness' and the seemingly endless depressions that are a feature of that dismal malady. During much of my childhood, the Liverpool docks – most of them in Bootle – were tangible evidence of Britain's far-flung Empire and maritime might throughout much of the nineteenth and twentieth centuries. Until about 1927, they were packed tight with Cunard and White Star ocean liners – the *Aquitania*, *Mauritania*, *Berengaria*, *Olympic*, *Doric*, even, for the briefest period, the doomed *Titanic* – whose massive red or cream funnels towered above the overhead railway and bustling dockside streets. Now, alas, the railway has gone and those once busy wharfs and basins are mostly empty, their silent warehouses accommodating, at best, collections of twentieth-century art and other manifestations of the 'new prosperity' and at worst, the decaying rubbish of a forgotten era of plenty. Fifty and more years later, it is still with pain and sadness that I recall witnessing the precipitate continuance of Liverpool's tragic decline when, in May, 1941, in the act of boarding His Majesty's aircraft carrier *Furious*, which was to take my aeroplane and me to the Middle East, I saw much of that once thriving area reduced to rubble and ashes after seven nights of continuous bombing, a score or more ships burning, listing or sunk, their innards bleeding into the flotsam littered dark green bile of the basins, a hundred warehouses shattered, and the tall-walled Tate and Lyle repositories bubbling with crimson globules of flame and crumbling to dust amid the sweet, dark odour of burning sugar. In the fog, smoke and stench of that late morning of 8 May, 1941, I saw the gutters running with the lifeblood of Liverpool.

Although difficult to imagine now, even in my childhood, the northern parts of Bootle were full of splendid Edwardian houses with attics and basements, demure housemaids in frilly caps, and four-acre gardens. There was then a profusion of apple orchards on what was later the site of the municipal girls' Secondary School on Breeze Hill, that particular road, together with a dozen others named after Oxbridge Colleges – Merton, Balliol, Trinity, Downing, Gonville and more – serving to emphasis the 'superior' nature of the area.

At the bottom of Breeze Hill stood – and still stands – the Parish Church of Christ – another touch of Oxbridge – where, between the ages of ten and thirteen, I was a choirboy. There were sixteen of us at the time, an artful, smirking bunch, brimful of monkey tricks, all of us rigid with piety in stiff Eton collars, bow-ties, and surplices so white and starched that we crackled like static whenever we moved. Our rascality was further masked by faces so angelic that, as a group, we could have raised millions for the starving poor had someone had the nous to recognise our enormous potential.

The incumbent then was the Reverend Edward Mason, M.A., a small, circular, bald-headed gentleman with the wild eyes of a zealot which glared tiger-like from a thicket of Dennis Healey eyebrows. A powerhouse of holy energy, he surged around his parish like a cyclone, bludgeoning his flock with the word of God. His sermons were never less than twenty-five minutes in length and woe betide anyone who took refuge in a quiet nap. Among his parishioners, opinions were unanimous: if the Lord had had the Reverend Mason on his side instead of Peter, John, and one or two others of his layabout disciples, Christianity might have taken an altogether different course.

Mainly to indulge my mother, I endured my stint as choirboy – two services each Sunday and every Thursday night choir practice – until my voice showed signs of breaking. We were paid one (old) penny per service, with nothing for the practices, and like sixteen Oliver Twists, would line up solemnly for our dibs at the end of each quarter – all of two shillings each (about ten pence in present day money).

Alas, it is sad to see the place now. When last I visited it, the bells were silent, the building battle-scarred, the gold-tipped ornamental gates gone, and the surrounds seedy and unkempt. With a little imagination, it appeared only one step removed from it's seemingly inevitable fate – a bingo hall.

I mention this as in 1932, when I was still a member of the choir, it was a fellow chorister who introduced me to that splendid magazine, *Popular Flying* and, in hoarse whispers between surreptitiously munching our liquorice Pontefract cakes and tuppenny Mars bars in the choir stalls, we would excitedly compare the top speeds of Bristol Bulldogs and Hawker Furys and discuss what was happening in the fascinating world of aviation – which was a great deal. In the early 30s, the whole nation was agog with news of Britain's Schneider Trophy successes, several much publicised solo flights to Australia and South Africa in tiny 'phut-phut' aeroplanes, thrilling air races all over the world, and hair-raising trips across the Atlantic and Pacific oceans in 'planes totally unsuited to traversing anything wider than the Thames estuary. The names of Amy Johnson, Jim Mollison, Amelia Earhart, Wiley Post, Kingsford Smith, Tommy Rose and a score of others, were constantly in the headlines of the national press, as was a library photograph of four Hawker Hart light bombers in formation, which was trotted out ad nauseum whenever the newspapers wished to make known that the RAF had again been in action against some recalcitrant Afridis on the North West Frontier of India, or the beastly Kurds in present-day Iraq. Britons everywhere of the Kipling genre, slapped their thighs with swagger canes and with stiff upper lips and not much else, policed and administered most of the world in those days – and did it very well – and there were, and remain, many luridly naughty songs, sung to this day in RAF officers' messes the world over, about what happened to those unfortunate pilots in Bristol Fighters, Fairey Gordons, Westland Wapitis, et al, who were obliged to force-land among the razor-sharp knives of the tribesmen's ladies.

Yes, aviation was the thing of the decade, even before rearmament had gathered pace in Great Britain and, with it, in 1935, the appearance of many new military aircraft including the prototypes of those magnificent fighters, the Hawker Hurricane and Supermarine Spitfire. 300-plus miles per hour, for heaven's sake! Wow! Incredible! And eight machine guns instead of the usual two! Eight, if you please! Whatever next?

It was also in 1932 that my parents had reason to visit London – an event in itself as to me the capital city was as remote as Kathmandu – and I found myself one day at Croydon Aerodrome, which was London's main airport throughout the 1930s. I had stood there in petrified awe, watching flat-chested ladies in plant-pot hats – it was then the so-called flapper period with boyish figures definitely in vogue – positively round-shouldered under the weight of diamonds and mink, most of them smoking cigarettes affixed like spears to long Tallula Bankhead holders – I had never seen ladies smoke in public before – all waiting to board the several giant four-engined leviathans of the air whose engines were coughing and clattering like castanets on the tarmac outside.

Those aircraft, I came to know later, were Handley-Page 42s of Imperial Airways, huge individually-named four-engined biplanes which, on a good day and a stiff wind from the rear, could work up to an electrifying 90 mph on their twice daily dash to Le Bourget, Paris. For me, the business of getting such massive dinosaurs into the air, defied comprehension; how on earth did they do it? The fact that flying against any sort of headwind, the old HP 42 s, with their gleaming silver sides, could be overtaken by a nippy delivery boy on a bicycle, seemed totally irrelevant.

No, more than anything, it was the seductive ambience of aircraft, aerodromes, and air travel that intrigued me – plus the flat-chested ladies with the diamonds and mink, needless to say. Clearly, as aviation was associated with wealth, excitement and an element of danger and daring, flying was the thing of the future; this was the business to be in, right enough. Thereafter, steam engines, about which I was an acknowledged expert, slipped down my list of priorities.

Back home in Lancashire, alas, there was only the occasional aeroplane to be seen in the air and even less frequently on the ground; moreover, in the north, we had nothing even half as grand as the elephantine Handley-Pages.

In Southport, to which resort I would occasionally cycle when I could summon up the energy – 36 miles return, and always against the wind – several D.H. Fox Moths operated from the sands providing five-shilling flights. Their comings and goings I would watch for hours – but only from a distance, the necessary five bob being totally beyond my financial resources.

There were also two itinerant chaps who operated an Avro 504 from a farmer's field not far from Crosby, a mile or two from where I lived. I remember that Avro very clearly as it had a long sort of skid-thing in front of its nose and a strange engine which went round with the propeller. It also made a very expensive whirring clatter when it revved up, as though something was loose inside and just about to fly off into space.

Occasionally, when there were no customers, the mechanic, whose job it was to squirt fuel into the engine and swing the propeller – very often to the accompaniment of some very religious exhortations – would sit on a fallen tree, suck deeply on fags he had rolled himself, and chat with me rather condescendingly. He explained that the engine was a Mono Rotary – whatever that was – and that the pilot who climbed so dashingly in and out of the cockpit clutching helmet, goggles and gloves, had flown D.H.4s in the Great War. Wow! D.H.4s, for heavens sake! In the Great War! I almost fainted away with the sheer magnitude of the revelation.

Alas, although I spent many fascinating hours of my summer holidays in that field watching the Avro come and go, I seldom encountered the pilot – except when there was money to be made; at all other times, he could be found in the local pub, bending his arm.

Meanwhile, during those halcyon, breathless times, when summers seemed always to be warm and endless, much else was happening in Liverpool. And beyond.

The Wirral peninsula lies 'across the water' from Liverpool, and in the early 30s was to become a place very much associated in my mind with the Royal Air Force.

With three other boys, I was foolish enough to take a camping holiday in the hills around Mold, in Wales, during the Easter holiday, foolish inasmuch as we did not properly take into account the vagaries of the British weather.

We set off on our bicycles and having paid tuppence to cross the Mersey on the paddleboat ferry – one penny for me and a further penny for my bike – we pedalled away with the lightest of hearts, me, I recall, loaded down well below the plimsoll line with an outsize bag of potatoes plus cooking utensils.

When about abreast of Chester, I found myself well behind my companions who had had the foresight to allow me to carry by far the heaviest load. At one point, stopping to recover my breath, I found myself alongside an aerodrome with marching airmen in the road and rows of silver aircraft on the grass off to my right. A large sign at the entrance gate disclosed the fact that it was No. 5 Service Flying Training School, Royal Air Force, Sealand. SEALAND! I had read about that! Wow! I was almost overcome!

I sat there for a time, watching in awe, until I realised that my companions might be missing me and beginning to take action. But I knew I had stop there again, if necessary alone, on my return journey.

The weekend was a disaster with the weather colder than I had ever known it to be over Easter. The streams in the hills froze solid; we had no water, very little food, and at night in our flimsy tent and home-made sleeping bags, we nearly died. By the fourth night I had had as much as I could tolerate, and rising before daylight, packed my meagre belongings and stepping over the recumbent forms of my three companions, pedalled off into the darkness.

When I reached Sealand, it was about 8am and a fine day was dawning. There were squads of airmen marching about with young officers much in evidence. I was fascinated. Finding a vacant spot on a grass verge outside the boundary wire, I parked myself and my bicycle adjacent to what I assumed would be the point of take-off and landing. And there I sat for close on an hour – with a wet behind and freezing to death until the sun rose above the mist and I began to thaw out.

Shortly before nine, the flying started and there followed three of the most glorious hours I had ever spent. The silver and yellow aircraft with their gay markings were mostly Avro Tutors and rather angular biplanes I thought might be Armstrong Whitworth Atlas trainers, their airscrews flicking and whirling as they taxied with burps and snarls to within yards of where I lay, before clearing their engines and taking off, their rudders wagging and tails rising as they gathered speed, the waft of their exhaust fumes, perfume to my senses. Then, on landing, they would float over my head, so close that I felt I could reach out and touch the pink and brown heads of the pilots, as, with wires sighing, their aircraft swished and sideslipped to the ground with popping engines, to touch down and balloon delicately across the grass in front of me. All other than the Avro Tutors, that is, whose undercarriage legs would now and then splay out dramatically as the result of a heavier than normal arrival. I was intoxicated. How I wished I were one of those pilots. This, clearly, was the only thing worth doing. What else could there possibly be in life?

Then, just when I was thinking about leaving, an aircraft I perceived to be different banked out of the sky towards me. As it drew near, I recognised it as a Bristol Bulldog. A Bulldog? Surely not! Bulldogs were fighters, weren't they? Then, as it sailed over my head, stubby and pugnacious, its wires singing, I saw that it was a two-seater, a type I never knew existed. Only years later did I have it confirmed that a few Bulldog trainers were employed at that time and that a number were based at No. 5 SFTS.

When I rose finally to climb stiffly onto my bicycle to resume my journey down to the ferry, not for a single moment did it ever cross my mind that within five years I might be a pilot in a famous fighter squadron and that my commanding officer would be a young officer trained at Sealand in one of the aircraft I was watching with such rapturous attention. That officer, later Marshal of the Royal Air Force Sir John Grandy, was my squadron leader, if only briefly. For more than fifty years thereafter, we were good friends, and kept in touch until his death.

I also associate Avro Tutors especially with Sealand, but for another reason entirely.

In the summer of that same year, I was again in the Wirral playing cricket for my school's first eleven. Having completed my first spell of fast bowling, I had been placed at square leg to recover, from which position I was shunted back and forth with nothing very much happening in my area of play. After a time, the weather soporifically beautiful and my interest in the game waning, I welcomed the arrival of an aircraft which buzzed directly overhead and, at a height of about 3,000 feet, began to perform a series and loops and rolls.

I was captivated. I recognised the aircraft as an Avro Tutor and, with shaded eyes and my head on a swivel, followed it around avidly – until, that is, I heard distant shouts and, glancing down, saw a red missile coming in my direction at the speed of light. In horror, I saw it too late even to move and the cricket ball caught me full on the knee with a crack that could probably have been heard in Liverpool. I collapsed in agony convinced that my leg had been broken and lay there writhing until the rest of my team had gathered round.

They were not at all sympathetic. I heard my captain's irritated, complaining voice. 'For God's sake, Neil, you were asleep! Why didn't you catch the ball, you clot?' No one disagreed. After that, I was carried like a sack into the pavilion and dumped, taking no more part in the game.

More than seventy years on, I still carry a scar on my right knee to remind me of that incident – plus the memory of the Avro Tutor from Sealand fading into the distance, its pilot blissfully unaware of the damage he had caused.

I was almost thirteen years of age when Chancellor Hitler came to power in Germany, and about sixteen when the Spanish Civil War commenced. I well recall seeing many of the left-wing diehards of Liverpool – a large number of whom were unable to bring themselves to fight for their own country three years later – trooping off with clenched fists and cloth caps to form the so-called International Brigade in Spain. Because we in Britain had what I considered to be a super King and Queen, whom I solemnly saluted on Empire Day at school and when alongside my father in his bowler hat and medals on Armistice Day, I wondered why these silly people had to choose the republican side. Had I been old enough, I could probably have been persuaded to fight for their opponents, the National Socialists, or Fascists, as they were later referred to – Fascism did not then bear the stigma it quite properly earned in years to come and was regarded by many worthy and influential people in Britain as the antidote to the disease of Communism.

It was also in 1936 that the new German airship, *Hindenburg*, which crashed so devastatingly in New Jersey a year or so later, killing pretty well everyone on board, flew over Bootle and up the Lancashire coast. I have cause to remember it well.

I was out shopping for my mother at the time and everyone had run into the road to watch the massive dirigible drone slowly overhead, its drifting shadow huge, threatening, sinister.

I had seldom felt such latent menace, my recollection of the event sharpened by the strident chatter of a woman alongside me who was warning all within earshot that it had come to photograph the local Danish Bacon factory in Bedford Road. Astonished, I had felt compelled to ask how she had come to that conclusion, whereupon, she had adopted a fishwife's truculence and declared in the broadest 'scouse', 'So's they can bomb it, that's why. Them Germins are starvin', aren't thee?' hinting that they knew the value of ham rashers, by golly, if no one else did.

Looking back, those brief six years of the early 1930s seem an exciting, long-drawn-out age, during which, subconsciously anyway, many in Britain were at least thinking of, if not preparing for, war against Germany. Only Mr. Churchill, whom my father profoundly distrusted, both then and later, branding him a closet Liberal and political turncoat, spoke out trenchantly on the subject.

Needless to say, I was all agog as crisis heaped upon crisis. Patriotism, such a driving force in my youth when Britain knew she was Great and the world was full of Bengal Lancers, outposts of Empire and thin red lines, seems now at a discount. The heroes of my childhood – Nelson, Wolfe, Clive, Scott, Mannock, MacCudden, Ball, and a hundred others – have faded into obscurity, to be replaced as role-models by Superman and the plastic druggies of today's pop industry, most of them wallowing in unmerited riches and drowning in self-indulgence and conscience-stricken radicalism.

As a young pilot officer during the Battle of Britain and after, I earned the princely sum of eleven shillings and tenpence a day (about 55 pence in our present currency) for flying in combat four times daily, seven days a week, fifty-two weeks a year. I doubt that at any point in the process of bestowing their imperishable gifts on bemused humanity, my fellow Liverpudlians, the Beatles, would have bothered to unsheathe their mouth-organs for that sort of 'loot'.

Shortly after my visit to London and my encounter with the monster Handley-Pages at Croydon, I went with my parents to Southport to visit friends. It was to be a fateful meeting because it was there – absolutely –

that I first determined to join the Royal Air Force.

During the afternoon, I had suddenly been confronted by a young man, something under twenty, wearing RAF uniform. It was explained to me that he was an Apprentice who would shortly be passing out of Halton. I had sat open-mouthed as this sun-tanned vision of virility had stood before me, resplendent in blue uniform, his buttons agleam, the coloured band on his stiffened and immaculate hat adding an almost regal touch. It mattered to me not a jot that he might, or might not, fly; I knew nothing of rank, badges, duties or trades, whether even the young man was an officer or someone less exalted. It was the uniform and the overwhelming aura of well-being that influenced me most. To me, he personified a golden future, a personal Holy Grail. From that moment, my path was charted. Irrevocably.

My parents were less than enthusiastic. A mere fourteen years had elapsed since the end of the Great War in which they had each played a minor if gallant role, my father, as a pre-war Territorial, serving first in the Liverpool Scottish Regiment and later in the Royal Artillery, and my mother – a prominent concert-hall contralto in the north – whose passion for good works was realised as a white-coated supervisor in a munitions factory.

For years, the constant companion of scores of young officers back from the front, mutilated in mind and body, my mother especially had a deep but unspoken dread of war. The carnage of the Somme battlefield and the horrors of the trenches remained vividly etched on the mind of each of my parents and, in common with the greater part of the British nation at the time, would not allow themselves even to contemplate another major conflagration, far less consider their only son offering himself up as cannon fodder. Neither had even a rudimentary knowledge of anything remotely connected with flying, my father's awareness of aeroplanes extending no further than to one unfortunate German aircraft which had crashed alongside his siege-gun in 1918, killing its pilot. From that poor man, whose last act of consideration was to remain more or less in one piece, he had lifted a pair of very elegant fur- lined flying boots. These, together with uniforms, gaiters, medals and other war souvenirs and impedimenta were lodged in a vast tin trunk in one of our spare bedrooms throughout my formative years in Liverpool, treasures to be inspected proudly and in awe by myself and selected friends on wet afternoons in the school holidays when there was nothing much else to do. But, the Germans were to have the last word. Blast and an incendiary bomb removed the roof of my parents' home during an air-raid on London in 1942 and the tin box with its treasures was lost. And quite right, too! I have always suspected it was some ghostly Fritz very properly reclaiming his footwear, although my father took every opportunity to complain that he needn't have knocked the house about so much in the process.

Meanwhile, my bedroom, first to the amusement then to the despair of my mother, who watched her wallpaper and furniture systematically mutilated, became a cross between a museum and a junk shop. The walls from floor to ceiling were covered in pictures of aircraft and pilots of the Great War, the majority of the latter, strangely enough and as my father was quick to point out, being German. Magazines and books were stacked in untidy, tottering columns and cardboard models – later balsa and tissue – rich with accumulations of urban dust, hung from the ceiling. My mother was forbidden absolutely to touch these manifestations of aeronautical fervour, an instruction she reluctantly agreed to observe until, when exasperation and hygiene got the better of her, she would attack the place like a whirlwind, removing, cleaning, and replacing everything with such precision and order that it would take me at least a week to restore the original happy state of chaos.

As already mentioned, at about the age of thirteen, I was introduced to *Popular Flying*, edited then by Captain W.E. Johns of Biggles fame, and spent many happy hours rummaging about in Woolworths and similar establishments in search of the American pulp magazines, Flying Aces and Air Trails. Later, when my cash resources were rather more substantial, I progressed to The Aeroplane, Flight, and finally Air Stories, the last-named a fiction magazine introduced about 1935 at 7d a copy or nine bob for a whole year. I once wrote to C.G. Grey, the controversial editor of The Aeroplane – he came under grave suspicion during the war for his pro-German views – on a subject that escapes me now, and received a long and chatty letter in reply which I still possess. I also remember Captain Johns as an agreeable, plumpish man, with a thatch of dark hair parted in the middle and a large pipe from which he manufactured a smoke screen of noxious fumes. He was at the time autographing books in Lewis's in Manchester (as I recall), and I had stood alongside him in worshipping silence.

For three shillings and sixpence, I bought a book on how to join the Royal Air Force, written by a gentleman called T. Stanhope Sprigg – very upmarket! – and read it from cover to cover until I could recite whole passages of the text. I learned that I could join the Regular force as a cadet and go through Cranwell, or take a short-service commission of four (later six) years – I had raised my sights since my earlier encounter with the Halton Apprentice. The education and medical requirements did not worry me in the least and I had complete, if unwarranted, confidence that I would be acceptable to the various interviewing boards. However, in those days there was a parental contribution towards the upkeep of a Cranwell cadet amounting to about £300 a year – a considerable sum in the '30s – which was something I recognised immediately as a formidable hurdle and one which would take some fast talking for me to negotiate.

And I was dead right. I introduced the subject to my parents one evening and there was a frozen silence, after which I fought a losing battle in an atmosphere charged with disapproval. Their response was clear and to the point; patriotism was a fine thing but being obliged to pay for the privilege of serving one's country amounted to nothing less than an insult. In any case, where was the annual £300 to come from? PLUS incidentals, I should understand; that sort of money didn't grow on trees! After which, my father dragged in the weekly wage of the average working man – about £3.10/- at the time – at which point I lost my temper and was obliged to take a long bicycle ride to work off a tidal wave of adrenalin.

Later, when the air had cleared sufficiently, the short-service commission option had been debated, although debate is hardly an apt description of the exchange. On that occasion, as I had expected, the opposition regarded itself as having a cut-and-dried case. Four years only and out of a job at twenty-two? With no qualification either, other than being able to fly an aeroplane and drop a bomb on some wretched Wog on the North-West frontier? Whoever heard of such nonsense! Furthermore, the type of people who took up short-service commissions were… well! The sentence was left unfinished, the implied imperfections too horrible even to mention. When I hotly demanded to know what 'that type of person' did to his discredit, my parents exchanged pious glances before my mother darkly revealed that 'they' usually… *drank*!

Drinking was, indeed, a human frailty – in the opinion of my mother, anyway – only slightly less reprehensible than murder or rape. Had she not seen enough of it during the war? Those poor fellows back from the front? On such occasions, her grey eyes as large as fabled millwheels, she would invariably put a hand to her throat in painful recollection of the unspeakable goings-on and the human tragedies she had encountered.

After that, all friendly forces in retreat, I was obliged to take another bicycle ride to work off the flood of rising passion. God! Why did otherwise quite normal parents have to be so ... so *hopeless*?

At a much later date, carefully and in my most persuasive manner, I introduced the proposal that I might join the Auxiliary Air Force. Greatly to my surprise, whilst not giving it their unqualified support, they indicated some small measure of approval. The term 'Auxiliary' bestowed an element of respectability on the arrangement: one had a real job, then played about with soldiering in one's spare time. That was altogether more sensible. Moreover, it meant that their treasured offspring would not be in continuous association with those... those, well, those dreadful DRINKING people.   The possibility that Auxiliary Air Force officers might have both the time and the means to indulge their vices to a far greater extent than their less affluent Regular counterparts, fortunately never occurred to them.

Thus, it was agreed that at the appropriate time, I would apply to join the local Auxiliary unit – No. 611 (West Lancashire) Squadron, stationed at Speke, on the southern outskirts of Liverpool. Super! I was well content. At night, lying in my bed beneath the gaze of Albert Ball, 'Mick' Mannock and the redoubtable von Richthofen and going through the routine of the medical, I would take my pulse and, closing one eye at a time, attempt to read the bottom line on the calendar across the room. My heartbeat, I discovered to my alarm, was ridiculously slow – down to forty-eight on occasions. God! Wasn't it supposed to be seventy-something? I recall going through the long list of my relations in order to identify the incidence of cardiac-arrest. Fortunately, no one to my knowledge had dropped dead in the street, so the chances were I was fairly normal.

No sooner had the agreement involving the Auxiliary Air Force been struck with my parents, however, that an event of cosmic significance occurred in my young life.

My father, arriving home one evening with the smug and contented look of a man whose ego had just been inflated to explosion point, announced to his wide-eyed wife and son that he had been elevated to some undreamed of status and that the family would shortly be moving to Manchester. Manchester! Aghast, I argued vehemently against any proposal that we should leave Liverpool, but my protests cut no ice and move we did, to the village of Roe Green, some six miles west of Manchester.

Roe Green, near Worsley, was a beautiful place then and, when the sun shines, still is, although somewhat marred now by the elevated M62 motorway which bisects the village and towers over the Green where I used to play cricket and soccer in the appropriate seasons. Few then would believe that the long tentacles of the vast Walkden coal pit, several miles distant, moled their way beneath the trim lawns and flowerbeds of Roe Green.

The steam trains from Bolton to Manchester then ran in a cutting alongside Greenleach Lane, Roe Green, a pleasant sounding name utterly in keeping with the beauty of the road itself, lined as it was with rows of silver birches. Worsley station, too – a sad relic now – was among the most attractive in the land, surrounded by a profusion of beech, elm, and oak, and with gardens which regularly won the 'Best Station Garden' contest. In the months to come, I was obliged to sprint the three-quarters of a mile down Greenleach Lane six mornings out of seven in order to catch the five-to-eight train into Manchester, the enforced exercise – taken with scant enthusiasm, I might add – serving to hone my leg muscles and wind-section to new and undreamed of peaks of condition.

The railway and the trains, in fact, formed a very significant part of my family's day-to-day existence. My father refused to have a car, arguing, not unreasonably, that with the whole of the British and European rail networks available to him and his family at no cost, it seemed pointless harbouring a motor vehicle. Even so, I always knew he would change his mind when his son was old enough to drive. And pass the newly introduced driving test, of course, which I have never done to this day. When I did take my test in 1937, a smart-alec examiner led me into the back alleys of Salford, where I ran into the back of a lorry, almost frightening the life out of my examiner and, not unexpectedly, failing the test. After which, in a fit of pique, I refused to submit myself to an another examination and used a provisional licence – plus a licence belonging to someone else – until the war came and tests and 'L' plates were discontinued.

All of which is probably as boring to read as it is to relate. However, it was later to be of some significance.

2

A German Visit and
First Thoughts of War

Historians may well decide that 1938 marked a watershed in the affairs of Britain and her large and splendid Empire. Certainly, it was during that year that the bulk of the population of the United Kingdom admitted to itself that war was both inevitable and imminent. Herr Hitler's star was in the ascendance. His raucous, ranting speeches were listened to with bated breath the length and breadth of Europe and the sight and sound of his henchmen and goose-stepping soldiers in Nuremburg and elsewhere, struck cold chills into the hearts of many of my companions on the five-to-eight train as they sat with their bowler hats, umbrellas and Daily Mails, grey with concern but rooted in apathy.

Austria succumbed in the spring of that year and there were pictures in the press and on the cinema newsreels of German troops pushing back frontier barriers and surging forward with their tanks, cars, motorcycles, and lorry loads of grinning, helmeted infantry. And strangely, all the Austrians seemed to be cheering and waving – loving it, in fact. There was no doubt about it, whatever else they did, the Germans were highly skilled at propaganda and heavy-handed persuasion.

Attention was then turned to Czechoslovakia, the methods all too familiar, the outcome equally predictable. The crisis rose to a crescendo during the summer months of 1938, culminating in the austere Neville Chamberlain scuttling with undignified haste between London and Germany. On the last day of September, he stood on the steps of his returning aircraft and fluttered a piece of paper in his hand, proclaiming to the small crowd there to greet him that there would be 'peace in our time'. The British people, limp with foreboding and funk, gobbled with relief and, after hailing the Prime Minister as their saviour/hero, gave one-and-a-half rather hysterical and shame-faced cheers. The German army, meanwhile, occupied parts of

Czechoslovakia, with Herr Hitler declaring that it was positively his last territorial claim, whilst the remaining nations of Europe uttered silent prayers for the temporary reprieve and cast speculative eyes upon their neighbours, wondering which of them would be next for the chop.

But, exhilarated as I was with all the excitement as the crises heaped one upon the other and praying that the war would not start until I was eighteen, much else was happening to me personally during those fateful months.

In 1938, I had what I can only describe as an ambivalent attitude towards Germany and the Germans. For the past several years there had been harrowing tales of atrocities against the Jews and the press had reported unspeakable happenings in some of the larger cities of the Third Reich. In spite of all that I read, however, I found it difficult to reconcile the reports with what I knew of the country and some of its people.

I had visited Germany in the summer of 1937 with a party of twelve from school. We had gone there as part of a so-called International Camp which was held that year in Wiesbaden and for part of our visit were entertained by boys of a similar school to our own in Koblenz, where we spent the first week.

After taking the ferry from Dover to Ostend, we went by train through Belgium and crossed into Germany at Aachen. The transformation was breathtaking; whereas Belgium had seemed seedy and disorganised – particularly Ostend, where all our reserved seats on the train were taken up by local residents who refused absolutely to budge – the German scene was altogether different. The station at Aachen was full of tall-hatted, strutting officials, wearing long, grey-green military coats, all looking and sounding dauntingly efficient, and, in marked contrast to what we had seen thus far, the place was as clean as a new pin. And of particular interest to us seventeen-year-olds, were the smiling, chattering, flaxen-haired girls in white blouses and peasant skirts who fairly littered the platform. Wide-eyed, we all sat in wonderment and scarcely concealed lust. Gosh! Everywhere seemed to pulsate with an indescribable electricity. It was all most impressive.

Our week in Koblenz remains one of the most pleasant memories of my youth. My constant companion was Karl-Heinz Mohr, a young man of about my own age. He was smallish and good-looking, with short mouse-fair hair, long colt's legs and the ivory skin that seems peculiar to central

Europeans. Gravely formal, disciplined and courteous, he was one of the most agreeable boys I had ever met. Together, we explored Koblenz on foot and using the multi-coached clanking trams, paddled down the Rhine in a canoe – no one in his right mind ever attempted to paddle up the Rhine! – drank ice-cold beer in the sidewalk cafes (the first beer I had ever tasted, let it be said), and toiled breathlessly up the vine-clad hills beyond the town, with the unripe grapes still in fascinating clusters of small green marbles, to turn, panting, on the ridge and gaze down through the heat haze on the merging of the two rivers, Rhine and Mosel, one blue-grey in colour and the other a mud-brown.

And there were the trains, which interested me almost as much as the flaxen-haired frauleins. The main railway line to and from Koblenz ran adjacent to our riverside camp site, so that we had trains – by the dozen – all day long and most of the night, long, never-ending trails of coaches and trucks, far longer than those I was used to at home, hauled by black, panting monsters in front which barked and strained, with masses of clanking wheels and spurting steam. How I loved those engines, covered in lumps and bumps and with pipes running in every direction, an indelible memory that, as, four and more years later, it was often my duty to shoot at them in France and Belgium and to watch gleefully as my shells and bullets found their mark so that they disappeared in huge spurts of steam and vast rising splodges of white vapour. Poor things! For me, it was like shooting one's dog! A most satisfying memory, even so.

Later, Karl-Heinz, who was member of the Hitler Youth, took me to one of their evening sports meetings and I was persuaded to run in their equivalent of a 200 yards sprint. Coming in a diplomatic second, I felt quietly smug that I had upheld the honour of England but declined to take part in any of the following events, opting instead to retire gracefully with my reputation intact.

After the meeting had been concluded, I was taken to a camp-fire on the fringes of a nearby wood and, with the pungent aroma of woodsmoke in my nostrils, was offered fat, red sausages forked steaming from a pot, hunks of damp grey bread, and mugs of beer that was sharp to the tongue. With hardly a word of German in my vocabulary, my new companions, frowningly grave and with total lack of self-consciousness, practised their

English on me, their conversational efforts ranging from the tolerably fluent to the totally incomprehensible.

Later still, there was singing, mostly thumping martial tunes – in German, of course, and so much gibberish to me – but with lots of catchy hol-lar-hee-ing and ho-ing in which I was all too willing to join. Altogether, it was a most memorable evening marred only by some very stern words from the master-in-charge of our party when I arrived back at 12.30 a.m., by which time he was in the act of contacting the police and no doubt practising his excuses to my parents in explanation of my untimely end.

Then, the day before we left Koblenz, in a final act of courtesy, Karl-Heinz took me to meet his family.

The Mohrs lived in a vast tenement block, so beloved of many German families in the same social stratum. To me, with its mass of uniformly rectangular windows, it looked like an army barracks and had singularly little appeal. Inside, however, there was great warmth, albeit of the silent variety, the family's English being about as good as my German. Karl-Heinz translated, however, and everyone formed up in a line to be introduced. First, were the two grandparents, gnarled, peasant-looking people, who bobbed their heads and grinned a welcome; then, Frau Mohr, a buxom, friendly woman in her mid-forties, I imagine, nodding to the beat of the band. Alongside her was elder sister – the one who did all the donkey-work, I soon deduced – and next in line, younger brother Gerhardt, about twelve, who shook hands gravely, looking over my shoulder in frowning shyness and clicking his heels in military fashion. Finally, came two small girls about five – twins – who stood hand-in-hand, stunned into silence by the occasion, their wide blue eyes almost falling out onto their cheeks. I could not resist laughing. They had flaxen hair in plaits, two cupid-bow mouths, and looked exactly like pieces of Dresden china. An hour or so later, by which time they had uttered not a word and done little but stare at me, I suddenly wiggled my fingers behind my ears and put on a face. After a moment's incredulous hesitation, they flew into each other's arms shrieking in alarm and amusement and, the ice broken, released a flood of chatter which had everyone grinning happily.

Our meal that afternoon was simple indeed, hunks of dark, damp bread with ersatz butter – like axle-grease – and some anonymous yellow jam, washed down with a liquid purporting to be coffee. The beverage, brewed before my eyes, intrigued me greatly. It appeared to be made of barley grains coated with some dark substance which was washed off with boiling water. Then, hey presto, coffee – or something! As I ate, grinning, I recalled pictures in my Children's Encyclopaedia at home of white-smocked European peasants, staring into the camera as they wolfed down their primitive fare off rough, wooden benches. The Mohr household seemed very little different; I felt myself part of an almost feudal event, everyone organised, drilled, courteous and bowingly subservient. Yet Karl-Heinz was as educated as myself. More so, probably. He could at least speak English!

After the meal, I was led into a parlour, not unlike a million Edwardian rooms in England, and Karl-Heinz, after inviting me to play the piano – an invitation I declined, deciding that my party-piece, 'I Dreamt I Dwelt in Marble Halls', was hardly suited to the occasion – settled himself in the seat and launched into his repertoire.

In all my life, I have never heard anything like it. The boy attacked the keyboard with the tooth-grinding application of an Irish navvy pick-axing a hole in concrete. As the notes crashed out and the glassware and pictures shook with the passion of his playing, I watched Karl-Heinz's face become almost livid with excitement. Amid the ear-splitting, thunderous cacophony, during which I half expected the piano to collapse beneath him, I recognised several notes that were vaguely familiar, my suspicions confirmed when the boy turned to me and screamed, 'Polly-Wolly-Doodle! English, no?'

It seemed pointless to observe that 'Polly-Wolly-Doodle' was not an English song, even had I been given the opportunity to do so as the terrible din continued, one crashing melody merging with another until, with a final thunderous chord, the bedlam ceased and Karl-Heinz fell back exhausted. After which, suddenly and magically serene, he turned and asked politely whether or not I wished to sing.

Limp with emotion, I said faintly that I would rather not, whereupon he pressed me so earnestly that I finally agreed, deciding quickly on 'Rabbie' Burns and 'Oh, My Love is like a Red, Red, Rose', and suggesting hopefully that he might not know the tune. Thank God, after frowning and cudgelling his mind, he agreed that he didn't, so that I was able to launch into it unaccompanied, nervously at first, gathering confidence as I arrived at 'As fair art thou, my bonnie lass' and becoming positively emotional as I finally squeezed out 'Tho' t'were ten thousand mile'. At about verse three, when the sea was 'ganging dry, my dear', Frau Mohr slowly appeared around the door followed by the twins, still hand-in-hand and staring as though bewitched. Then, when I had finished, there was a moment's silence before Karl- Heinz's mother reached forward and planted a wet kiss on my cheek before turning in embarrassment and disappearing amid a rustle of skirts and a confusion of squeaks and small girls' legs. It was all very moving – and memorable.

The following day, Karl-Heinz was one of a dozen or so who came to see us off on our railway journey to Weisbaden. As he shook hands with me, bowing and clicking his heels, he said that our train would not stop at Koblenz on our return journey to Aachen but that, as it always slowed down sufficiently, he would be able to wave us a final farewell from the platform. And, a week later, sure enough, there he was, a solitary figure, grave, nodding, his hand raised in a half-Hitler salute as we passed, remaining there until we were a full half- mile down the track and he was little more than a dot in the distance.

We exchanged several letters over the next twelve months but we never saw each other again and I often wonder what became of him. And his family. Especially the Dresden-china twins with their wide, cornflower-blue eyes. Did they cower and die in some flattened cellar or lie crushed beneath a million tons of masonry? It is upsetting even now to think of it – and them.

My German experience impressed me deeply. The area I had visited was an aimed camp with uniforms everywhere in the streets – small groups of armed, marching soldiers, laughing and singing, their steel-tipped boots clashing on the cobble-stones, tall-hatted and jack- booted young officers swaggering about with ceremonial dirks dancing at their sides, the cloudless summer skies above full of fighters and bombers. Over Koblenz, I had repeatedly seen small formations of Heinkel 51s, smart little biplanes not unlike our own Hawker Furys, and I had recognised some big Junker 86 bombers in the distance and a few biplanes that looked like Henschel dive-bombers. The people, too, had excited me greatly; blondely handsome and suntanned, yes, but with an obvious sense of purpose. Of course, there had been a lot of comic-opera stuff, the slightly ridiculous Heil-Hitlering and stiff-armed Roman saluting, together with the wealth of uniforms and colourful badges of the many branches of Army, Air Force, and other organisations. Clearly, these were people who welcomed discipline and loved playing soldiers. At the same time, there was an obvious toughness, about them and an almost tangible atmosphere of dedication that was frightening to behold – quite unlike my pathetic five-to-eight crowd at home. What is more, I had seen no overt Jew-baiting, no racist notices, no books being burned in the streets, nothing untoward, in fact. Could I really believe that Karl-Heinz and his grave and courteous friends in the Hitler Youth could really do such things? It was all very confusing.

In retrospect, it would appear that I was naive and superficial in my judgements, particularly in view of what has since been revealed. But, in that bright summer of 1937, the sun shone from a clear blue sky, the air was warm and scented and I was seventeen years old and full of the joys of spring. I make no apologies; this was pre-war Germany as I saw it.

In the spring of 1938, I became seventeen-and-three-quarters and eligible to apply for a commission in No. 611 Auxiliary Squadron at Speke. I wrote off for the appropriate forms, filled them in carefully, and sent them away. The response was immediate; I was invited to an interview at the Territorial and Auxiliary Air Force Association Headquarters in Liverpool.

On the day selected – a Sunday – I caught an early train from Manchester and imposed on some handily placed relatives to give myself a final polish before catching a bus into the city centre. I found the building without difficulty and did an exploratory circuit to calm my nerves before taking a deep breath and approaching the entrance. I tried the door and, to my surprise and eventually my concern, found it bolted and barred.

Perplexed, I looked at the number and re-read my letter of invitation. I was at the right address, that was clear enough but, equally clear, there was no one around. Oh God! What now? I read the letter once more. Then a third time. After which, a terrible thought. Ought I to be at Speke? It didn't say so but, *of course!*, that was where they would be! I nearly sank to the pavement in dismay. It was less than ten minutes to my interview and the airfield was miles away.

Five minutes later, I was in a public telephone box and through to squadron headquarters. A languid voice answered and, not too coherently, I explained who and where I was – and why.

The voice the other end was not at all friendly.

'You're at the Town Centre? What possessed you to go there?'

I replied faintly that that was where I had been asked to go – I read from the letter in my shaking hand.

The voice, barely civil, disagreed – flatly – and as my hackles rose, there was a brief silence followed by a very holy word being breathed in my ear. Then: 'All right, get out here as quickly as you can; we'll hang on until you arrive.' After which, there was another muttered reference to the Almighty – and the 'phone went dead. No hint of a 'Goodbye', I noticed.

It took me all of an hour to find my way to Speke, wriggling in anxiety on the top deck of a bus. I asked at the aerodrome gate for the offices of 611 Squadron and was wandering aimlessly between some First World War wooden huts, when someone hailed me.

'Mr. Neil?' It was the voice again and the 'Mister' sounded very unconvincing.

A figure in RAF officer's uniform was leaning from a window. The man was dark and in his late twenties, I guessed, with pilot's wings and the two stripes of a Flight Lieutenant. 'Go round the front and use the door there,' I was instructed. The tone was bored, authoritative, and verging on the hostile.

Inside, I was met in the corridor by the same Flight Lieutenant who, with one hand in a pocket, offered me the bleakest of superior smiles. I eyed him nervously, half expecting him to stifle a yawn. He gave a little jerk of his head. 'Go on in.'

The room into which I was ushered was fairly large with a centrally disposed desk, wall maps and charts, some filing cabinets and silver ornaments and the usual paraphernalia of the executive administrator. It was light and airy and there was the faint, rich aroma of something indefinably 'clubby'.

A man sat at the desk. He was in a Squadron Leader's uniform and had a bald head. He half rose in a gesture of greeting and seemed to me terribly old – forty at least!

He said affably, 'Put your coat over there, do, and sit down.'

I did as I was bidden whilst the Flight Lieutenant, still with his hands in his pockets, perched his backside on the corner of a nearby table and eyed me coolly. Quite irrationally, my dislike for the man blossomed like a hot-house plant and I felt an invisible barrier rise between us.

Then the Squadron Leader was speaking again. He had a 'plummy' voice and smiled a lot.

'Well now! You live in the Manchester area, I see. Did you drive across this morning?'

I faltered, 'No, sir. I came by train.' I had to clear the hoarseness from my voice.

'Train!' The man's eyebrows rose like smoke signals. Then he frowned and said slowly, 'I see!' in much the same tone of voice he might have employed had he learned that his wife and three teenage daughters had just been ravished in the woodshed. After which, he looked meaningfully at the Flight Lieutenant who tilted his head fractionally indicating the hopelessness of everything in general.

Sensing the presence of a yawning gap opening up beneath my feet, I swallowed and watched anxiously as the Squadron Leader studied my application documents.

'Yes. I see. You're still at school, I take it?'

'Yes, sir.'

'And you've never flown before?'

'No, sir.'

'As a passenger?'

I bit down a fib. 'Er... no, sir.'

'And... er, you live in Manchester. Or... er, thereabouts.'

I nodded, wearying of saying 'Yes, sir' and 'No, sir.'

'I see.'

Silence. A long, ghastly silence.

Finally, the man leaned back. 'Yes... well. This... er, could well lead to difficulties. I think so. Couldn't it?' He turned towards the Flight Lieutenant, still on the point of yawning, who replied in his irritatingly languid voice, 'Yes, sir, I think so, too.'

'I take it you haven't a car?' The Squadron Leader again.

I had to swallow once more. 'No, sir.'

'And you'll have to come all the way from... er, wherever it is you live...

er, Manchester, or thereabouts. By train… and so on.'

'But only for a time, sir. I should be able to get a car later on.' I was disgusted by the fawning note of explanation in my voice, at the same time marvelling at my own recklessness. A car! My father would have something to say about that!

The bald-headed gentleman was smiling now, but not with his eyes. 'But, it's more than thirty miles away, Mr. Neil. More or less. Yes… ' He paused. 'You see, Mr. Neil, we are a squadron not a flying training school. We train a number of our officers to fly, of course, but only in our spare time, so to speak. When the opportunities arise, you understand? So there's a limit, you see, to the number of chaps we can cope with and, as you can imagine, it helps if those who join us can fly already, even if they are only at the *ab initio* stage. You see that. I'm sure. It also means that those who require flying training as distinct from squadron training, have to be on hand when the opportunities arise. And coming from so far afield as… as, er, Manchester and without a car, would… would, er, present difficulties… I imagine. Wouldn't it?'

Panicking, I was on the edge of my seat. Pleading. 'I could manage it, I know I could, sir. It wouldn't be a problem.'

The man smiled, like a shark eyeing its lunch, and looked to the Flight Lieutenant for support.

'He's very keen, you know, but–'

The smarmy brute with the two stripes stood up straightening his tunic and I sensed that, as far as he was concerned, the interview was over.

'You're absolutely right, sir, it would be very difficult. Why doesn't Mr. Neil try the new Auxiliary squadron likely to be formed in Manchester in a year or two's time?'

The Squadron Leader clutched at the life-line thrown in his direction. 'Wouldn't that suit you better, Mr. Neil? It would certainly cut out all the travelling.'

I went stiff. In a year or two's time! I'd never heard of any such new squadron and didn't want to be told of one, anyway. If there was going to be a war, I wanted to be in it, not watching from the touchline.

'I'd rather be here, sir. Really I would.' I was pleading like a condemned man but didn't care.

But the bald-headed gentleman had clearly seen the exit sign. 'I think that really would be the best solution, you know. Or, have a shot at the Volunteer Reserve in your area.' He turned to the Flight Lieutenant. 'Where's that new list? There's a school somewhere around Manchester, I believe.'

The smarmy brute reached up to pick out a document from a shelf and ran his finger down a list.

'Yes, here we are. Barton, Manchester. No.17 Elementary and Reserve Flying Training School.' He laid down the thin volume and looked up, satisfaction oozing from every squalid pore. 'That's the best solution, I think.'

The bald-headed man was smiling. 'I think so, too. Don't you agree, Mr. Neil?'

Agree! Mr. Neil, who certainly did not agree, was struck dumb and scarcely able to breathe. After that, we were all standing up and, stunned and speechless, I was collecting my coat. Would I be going back this afternoon? I found myself nodding. It was over, all over! Five years of waiting, and hoping, and longing, and it was all over in five miserable minutes. Rejected! But why? Because I used the train and didn't have a wretched car. It couldn't be! But, it was! Quite unthinkable! They just didn't *know*; didn't *care*! What was that they were saying? Nice weather? Who gave a bugger about the weather. Then I heard them thanking me for coming. And leading me to the door. Mind the step, they were saying. Goodbye. And I was nodding, Goodbye. After which I was outside and moments later at the 'bus stop. Standing there. On my own. With my coat over my arm. Fighting back the tears. Crushed. Demolished. Absolutely flattened!

If destiny does indeed shape our ends, it was hard at work during that late summer of 1938.

My father, walking down Market Street in Manchester one day, ran into an old acquaintance whom he had not seen since they had shared the mud and squalor of the trenches in 1918. Having retired for coffee and to reminisce, conversation very naturally turned to the subject of children. My own future being discussed, my father's companion, who happened to the General Manager of District Bank Ltd., Manchester, suggested that I might wish to consider banking as a career and, if so, that I should call on him.

This proposal was put to me and, not taking it too seriously but wishing to humour my parents, I visited the gentleman several days later at the bank's Head Office in Spring Gardens and, in a state of bewilderment and shock, found myself out on the pavement twenty minutes after – with a job! Banking! Until five minutes before, I had never given it a moment's thought.

So, on Monday 29 August, 1938, with the Munich crisis approaching boiling point, I presented myself to Head Office in a stiff white collar and highly polished shoes and was promptly despatched to the Urmston branch, presumably to get me out of the way and have someone show me the ropes – it is a measure of my unpreparedness, that I had to borrow sixpence from the slightly startled head man to get me there by bus.

An utter passenger, they were very civil to me there and I made the acquaintance of a young man named Rimmer, who was the so-called junior – a junior in those days was positively the lowest form of human life in a bank and only one step removed from the chap who stoked the boilers.

Rimmer was a very silent and industrious soul but I managed to corner him halfway through the first morning to discuss the terms of my new job, about which I knew next to nothing – in those days banks did not discuss with their staff such trifling issues as remuneration.

Whilst sorting out a mass of cheques, I asked in a whisper, 'I say Rimmer, what do we get for all this?'

Rimmer, as busy as a bee, hissed a reply out of the side of his mouth, 'Fifty!'

I brightened. 'Fifty! Fifty what? Shillings a week?'

Rimmer stopped dead in his tracks and regarded me with wide-eyed pity. 'Pounds, dear boy! A year! Less deductions. It works out about eighteen bob a week.'

'Eighteen bob! But I pay almost that much to get here! When can I expect a rise?'

'A rise!' His voice was a cracked falsetto. 'Not until you've passed your exams.'

'What exams?' My morale was plunging.

'Well, there's your Cert. A.I.B., Parts 1 and 2, which should take you a couple of years, then there's your B. Comm, degree which you are expected to complete in four – I've enrolled at Manchester University to do mine in the evenings. They – the bank, that is – pay you 50 quid for your B. Comm, and £15 for each of your certificates. After you get them!'

'After I get them! Gosh! So I have to work like a black for five years for eighteen bob a week, plus £80 – perhaps? They're not about to sink into debt because of us, are they?'

Rimmer, pulled a face, winked, then turned away, whispering, 'How d'you think they make those big, fat profits?'

So, in the months to come, although nominally a member of Head Office staff, I was shunted about unmercifully from branch to branch all over Greater Manchester and beyond, all at my own expense – which rankled deeply – besides being obliged to return each late afternoon to the Correspondence Department at Head Office to lick stamps and act as postman. Postman! Me! With my stiff, white collar, sports honours, and educational distinctions in heaven-knows what! I positively seethed.

But, having committed myself, for the next twelve months I dutifully trooped around Manchester and spent three evenings each week attending course lecture on which occasions I seldom arrived home before 10 p.m.., my parents being obliged to pay for all the additional travelling involved and the extra-mural instruction, a point often succinctly and venomously put to them when I pointed out maliciously that it would have been a darn sight cheaper had they allowed me to go to Cranwell!

In retrospect, the hierarchy of the bank should have gone to gaol for the manner in which they exploited their junior employees in those days and I reciprocated by hating every moment of my service with them and making no secret of my feelings in or beyond the bank's premises. Understandably, I was not at all popular with my seniors and reprimands became so much a matter of routine that I soon ceased to pay any attention to them. I had no intention of staying – I knew that even if the bank did not!

3

The Royal Air Force Volunteer Reserve

By July, 1938 – my eighteenth birthday – I had recovered sufficiently from my ignominious rebuff by No. 611 Squadron, to be capable of taking the advice I had been offered and applying to join the RAF Volunteer Reserve. My application went in promptly but it was not until September that I was invited to meet an interviewing board.

The interview to be at 11 a.m., I obtained leave of absence from Head Office and took the No.10 bus to Barton aerodrome, about six miles west of the City. The Bank, aware that war was a probability, whilst not actively encouraging its staff to join the Reserve forces, had a policy of offering no objection.

My first time at the aerodrome, I found the RAFVR accommodation behind the Airport Hotel, a long, low, wooden hut in front of which the grass airfield rolled away into the distance. There were a couple of aircraft parked alongside, a tiny monoplane of indeterminate ancestry and a very senior Gypsy Moth biplane with RAF roundels on wings and fuselage. At the sight of the so-familiar markings, my heart leapt and I suddenly felt quite sick.

Entering the hut, I was greeted by a tall, smooth-looking civilian in a dark undertaker's suit and wearing thick, horn-rimmed spectacles. Three other candidates – I assumed they were candidates – were sitting about, looking apprehensively bored.

'Mr. Neil? My name is Jones.' (Not his real name but it will suffice.) 'Hang your coat over here, will you?'

'Right, the procedure is this; first, you will have your interview. If you are successful, the President of the Board will hand you a chit which you will bring to me. I will then take you to the doctors and you will have your medical examination. If everything there goes well, sometime later – a week or two normally – you will be invited to join the Reserve officially, by letter. Should you decide to accept, you will then be sworn-in at the Town Centre in Manchester. At the moment, you are number four in line, so you may have to wait a bit. When you have finished, whatever the result, come and see me and I will explain the procedure about expenses. Now, if you will kindly sit down, I will call you when your time comes.' The spiel came out with practised ease and Mr. Jones, concluding, gave a nod and turned on his heel.

I sat down, outwardly calm but with my heart going like a steam hammer. I picked up a paper – the Daily Express – with banner headlines: 'THERE WILL BE NO WAR!'

I remember thinking crossly, 'Silly blighters! How the heck do they know?'

There were three members on the Selection Board, two in civilian clothes and a third in the uniform of a Flight Lieutenant. The President was a burly figure in an RAF blazer with a drooping pocket handkerchief, a handsome man of about thirty-eight with a fresh, decisive-looking face. Later, I learned that he was the Chief Flying Instructor and that his name was Corke – Flying Officer E.C. Corke. All three looked friendly enough and eyed me, I thought, with approval. The interview proceeded along familiar lines. What were my academic qualifications, sports honours, hobbies and interests, reasons for joining the RAF Reserve, and so on. Then a dozen other questions a little more searching. Finally, if I was so keen to fly, why had I not applied for a permanent or short-service commission? I provided a flow of well-practised responses, carefully omitting my mother's absolute conviction that all RAF officers were drunks. All three were nodding. Things appeared to going smoothly.

Then the President was leaning back in his chair.

'You have never flown, I take it?'

The lie that flew to my lips was quickly checked as I recalled my last interview with a shudder.

'No, sir.'

'Then what makes you think you would make a competent pilot? One capable of going to war? Because that's what it would mean, you know.'

For a moment, I was stumped; I hadn't practised that one!

I found myself struggling. 'Well, I'm … I'm just naturally capable, sir.' I saw three pairs of eyebrows rise as one and went on hurriedly. 'I've always had the confidence to do things … most things, anyway.' A quick cough and my mouth suddenly full of tongue. 'I've never really thought about it much; I've just assumed I would be able to carry it off.' I wanted to stop but some inner compulsion drove me on. 'No… I can't say that there's been anything… anything so far… well, that I haven't been able to do. Reasonably well, that is.' I swallowed hard, my voice trailing away.

All three were staring at me blankly. Then they exchanged glances and I was relieved to see a flicker of a smile around the President's mouth.

'Would you be willing to die, Mr. Neil?'

'Die!' I stared. No one had ever asked me that before. 'No, I don't think I'd be willing, exactly. But, again… well, it's not something I've really thought about.'

Silence. Oh, God! Had I said the wrong thing?

Then, as I watched, petrified, notes were exchanged on the table and the President was looking in my direction.

'We're clearly very fortunate you've decided to offer your services, Mr. Neil. We can now go to war with complete confidence.' He handed over a piece of folded paper. 'Give that to Mr. Jones outside and he will attend to you. Good day'

There were five people conducting the medical examination, two doctors in white coats, two medical orderlies, and a rather superior-looking gentleman in civilian clothes. For the next thirty minutes, I was passed around like a communal piece of soap.

After squeezing out the inevitable specimen – with difficulty – and being measured, weighed, felt, listened-to, generally poked about and made to stand up and down on a chair, a U-tube of mercury was produced. Monitoring my blood pressure and pulse, one of the doctors instructed me to 'keep the mercury steady on the forty mark for as long as possible'.

After two practice breaths – I'd read about this, by George – I sucked in a mountain of air and had kept the mercury more or less constant for a full minute when the man beside me muttered, 'That'll do. Don't kill yourself.' But, determined to impress, I had reached seventy-five seconds when I was told a little sharply, 'That's enough. You're wearing me out!'

The eye tests were comprehensive and all went well until the Japanese plates for colour blindness were introduced. I had heard of them, of course, but had never seen or used them before. The bewildering splodges of coloured dots I found confusing at first but soon picked up the knack of looking at each plate in turn then looking away briefly before having a second glance. There was just one which presented a problem but even this I saw clearly the second time around. After which the doctor said, 'Fine!' and that was that.

The examination proceeded for a further ten minutes until the point was reached when I was conducted to the civilian gentleman sitting at the table. Without comment or even looking in my direction, the man shuffled through the wad of papers and, after selecting one and making a few brief entries, wrote down, 'Fit for full flying duties', before signing his name with a flourish. Then, looking up at me, he smiled for the first time and gave a wink. 'Well done! You're quite a chap.'

Minutes later, I was outside and Mr. Jones was also smiling and talking to me about expenses and future arrangements. He was wasting his time though, I just couldn't take it in – wasn't even interested, in fact. I was IN! Through! Selected! I was in the RAF! What was that? Coat? What about my coat? Yes, of course. I took my raincoat and half put it on before taking it off again. Two weeks? Yes, I could arrange to visit the Town Centre in two weeks time – in two weeks' time I could arrange to be at the South Pole if necessary! After which, I was outside. In the air. On the road, walking. Then running. And skipping. A No. 10 'bus went hissing past, faces staring down at me as though I were soft in the head. But, to heck with the bus; I'd miss it, there'd always be another. I'd even walk. The whole six miles if necessary. God, life was good! Simply, absolutely wonderful.

On Wednesday 12 October 1938, I was attested as a member of the Royal Air Force Volunteer Reserve. There had been some feeble jokes at the bank; attested had dairy connotations, hadn't it? Wasn't it something to do with milking cows?

Summoned by letter to the Town Centre, I had stood before the Commandant, an elderly gentleman – elderly to me, anyway – in Squadron

Leader's uniform, complete with First World War medal ribbons. The man had slowly and solemnly put on his hat then his glasses and asked me to hold a bible and repeat after him.

We were alone and the room was spaciously gloomy, like the library in an old ancestral home. Outside, the traffic of Manchester was a muted hum so that the Commandant never needed to raise his voice above a murmur. After the swearing-in, he had waved me to a chair before slowly seating himself at his desk and, with great deliberation, examining his papers. Finally, when he had arranged everything to his satisfaction, he had cocked an eye in my direction.

'I, er… I am very glad to welcome you into the Royal Air Force Volunteer Reserve.' A short frowning silence. Then: 'I hope, er… I hope that you have a long and fruitful career. And a safe one. Of course.' Another pause. 'We live in dangerous times and I'm very much afraid that… that, er, that there is very little time left for us to prepare.' The old gentleman was speaking quietly and almost to himself. 'It is especially sad, you understand, for those of us who fought in the last war. We… we had, er, we had hoped for something better. Yes. However…' He bent forward and arranged a further group of papers before readjusting his glasses slowly and precisely to read.

'Now, a few details about your rank… er, and so on. Yes. You are now a Leading Aircraftman. For one day! Now, isn't that fun? Yes. So that, on Friday, you become a Sergeant. Sergeant… er, and, er, paid accordingly. For the occasions you are on duty, that is. Later, and I can't be precise, of course, I have no doubt that, er… that there will be opportunities for… er, advancement. Promotion, you understand?' The old eyes looked sharply up at me above the glasses. 'Meanwhile, you will be expected to fly most weekends and attend instructional classes on two, sometimes three evenings a week.' (I thought wildly, my God, I've only two evenings left as it is!) The voice was going on: 'Again… for which you will be paid. Naturally. All details of which can be had from my Corporal. In the Orderly Room. Which is next door… if, er, you are interested, that is. Furthermore, you will be required to spend a continuous period of fifteen days' training in the summer. Fifteen days! Which… er, shouldn't be too much of a chore, I imagine. Is that so?'

I shook my head and, fascinated by the whole business, watched the

Squadron Leader sit back, frown heavily, blow his nose, then square his shoulders. Silence. I waited. Cleared my throat. Then, rearranging my backside more comfortably on my chair, wondered what was next on the agenda.

With consummate delicacy and deliberation, the old man proceeded to move several articles needlessly around his desk before continuing almost dreamily.

'At first, you will be flying aircraft pleasant and easy to control. Yes. Straightforward and simple, most of 'em. Later, though, the aircraft will get bigger! More wayward! More difficult to handle.' I was fixed by an eagle eye and a raised finger. 'Never forget, though, you are in control! Always. Aircraft are like horses. And some ladies. You have to master 'em! Show 'em who's boss!' He nodded sagely. 'Unless you do that, you know, you'll have trouble. You will. Difficulties.' He nodded again as though in unhappy recollection of some appalling incidents of the past.

'I know! Only too well.' He glanced up sharply. 'So, take my advice and be prepared.' Then, as though suddenly revitalised, he sat up straight.

'Right! Any questions? No? Then report to the Chief Flying Instructor at Barton on Saturday next. And be prepared to fly! Your flying career has begun.' Then, standing up almost youthfully and with a brave, drawn smile, he proffered a gnarled hand. 'And good luck, my boy. Good luck, and may God go with you.'

As I left the room walking on air, I remember thinking: how on earth was I going to cram six evenings learning into a five evening week – and fly for two whole days in addition?

Clearly, life was not going to be easy. But, who cared? I forgot about the Corporal, the Orderly Room – even the expenses.

I flew for the first time on Saturday 22 October 1938. I was not impressed.

Arriving at Barton aerodrome in the early afternoon, after a breathless series of bus journeys from somewhere beyond Stockport, I found I was one of four who had passed between the Scylla and Charybdis of interview and medical the previous month. One of the four was Alan Buck, with whom I became quite friendly; so friendly, indeed, that I borrowed his driving licence, causing him endless trouble in the weeks ahead and obliging him a year later to make the long journey northwards to Montrose, where I was based. Poor chap! It didn't really do him much good as, having joined 43 Squadron, in the spring of 1940, he was one of the first to be killed during the Battle of Britain.

Apart from the flight, it was a memorable day. As shy as any new schoolboy and, with my three companions, on my best behaviour, I was given a locker, after which I moved about in my new, squeaky-clean Sidcot suit, absorbing the atmosphere and waiting from someone to notice me. Tiring of that, I watched the flying, played table-tennis, read every word, dot, and comma on the notice board and also a book entitled A.P. 129, signed all sorts of documents, observed – with covert respect – the dozen or so very nonchalant pupil-pilots who were already part of the establishment, and went to the lavatory – frequently!

Initially, my guide and mentor was the sombre Mr. Jones, still in his undertaker's suit. He it was who stood over me as my first parachute was fitted – why, I have no idea, as it was no part of his job to do so.

That first parachute impressed me enormously, as did the bulky brown leather helmet and goggles, the former having huge earpieces which made me look like Dumbo but which did not, unhappily, enable me to hear other than indifferently. Indeed, one of the more painful memories of those first six months is the recollection that I always had great difficulty in hearing what my instructor was telling me in the air; there being no radio communication in trainer aircraft in those days, information was passed by primitive speaking tube and vital messages very often seemed to get lost somewhere between the front and rear cockpits.

The afternoon passed agreeably enough but by five o'clock, I had given up all hope of flying and not having eaten since breakfast, my stomach gauge was registering empty. The weather, too, was miserable with complete cloud cover and a mild form of industrial fog which reduced visibility almost to the aerodrome's length.

Just when I was thinking about going home, there were heavy footsteps in the corridor and a large man appeared, dressed like Scott of the Antarctic. He looked enormous, as indeed he was, about as tall as myself but with the build of a bison. His name, I learned later, was Sears – Mister Sears. Late of the Fleet Air Arm.

Observing me, he enquired, 'Is your name Neil?'

I replied that it was.

'Right. I'll take you for your Air Experience. Shall we go?' The question was purely rhetorical – we went!

Our training aircraft were Gypsy 1 Moths (D.H. 60s), the type used by Amy Johnson on her record-breaking trip to Australia in 1930. The one we approached had the number K1900 and the unkind thought flashed through my mind that this could well be its year of origin. It looked very senior.

We arrived alongside and Mr. Sears sorted out the straps for me in the rear cockpit.

'Right, in you get. All you have to do on this occasion is sit and watch. Left foot there! Careful, not through the wing! That's better. Now wriggle your bum into the bucket seat. That's it. Straps; left shoulder, right leg; then right shoulder, left leg. Now the pin. Comfortable? Now plug in your speaking tube. Right? And remember to keep your hands and feet away from the controls.'

Safely installed and cold with apprehension, I watched my instructor climb in. His enormous bulk reared up and insinuated itself between the centre-section struts before he let himself down into the front cockpit like a pot-holer going to earth. The aircraft groaned and seemed to sag in the middle.

After that, there was something of a chat between him and a man in front – 'switches off, suck in', that sort of thing – before the airscrew flicked over once or twice and the magic word 'Contact' was exchanged. The expert ahead then gave a deft twist to the propeller and the engine started with a rush of wind – very little noise, which surprised me rather, but a lot of wind.

We taxied out, bouncing and swaying, with bursts of engine and the tail wagging furiously. We seemed to be going jolly fast, with much scraping at the back end and our wingtip almost touching the ground. Gosh, was this normal?

At the far side of the airfield, we turned into wind and without preliminaries, embarked on our take-off run. This was it! My very first flight!

I don't know exactly what I expected but it was all something of an anti-climax. After a few mild kangaroo hops, we took to the air with very little noise from the engine but with a gale of wind howling round my ears. And around my mouth, and into my eyes, and down my neck, and up my nose – everywhere, in fact. After a time, I ducked down behind the cockpit coaming in search of refuge and watched everything vibrate and the control-column move about fractionally – I thought it should be doing rather more than just that.

Then the man in front was blowing down the speaking tube and shouting something I could not understand. After more shouting, he turned around – insofar as that was possible for a man of his bulk – to mouth something else in my direction, then point. Alas, I could interpret neither his words nor his gestures and responded by shrugging my shoulders. After that, we flew around in silence, my instructor no doubt deciding that it was waste of time trying to communicate with the half-wit he had in the back seat.

I sat there miserably, my nose streaming copiously, and being trussed up like a turkey and unable to reach my handkerchief, was obliged to wipe it on my sleeve. Everywhere was a dark grey mist. After a time, a canal slid obliquely underneath – we were jolly low, my goodness! – and, rather to my surprise, some tall chimneys, pluming smoke, drifted slowly past my right ear. I had no idea where we were or which way we were pointing; I could have been in China. On and on. Everywhere a blank expanse of nothing. Mr. Sears, eight feet from shoulder to shoulder – or so it seemed – blocked out my forward view entirely. Also, I was chilled to the marrow. Flying was rather a dreary business, I concluded; not at all the dare-devil, breathtaking affair it was cracked up to be. Fancy anyone flying all the way to Australia in this – a clock in front of me registered about 80 mph – Amy Johnson must have been out of her mind!

After twenty minutes or so, some buildings appeared below and to my left, the engine died away, there were a few minor pops up front, and we were drifting towards the ground, banking quite steeply meanwhile. More interested now, I watched a distant fence slowly approach then flip past, the grass surging up to meet us. Dropping further to earth, the nose of the Moth rose skywards. More. More. Until suddenly the aircraft decided to stop flying and sank to earth with a lurch, the tail jogging and rasping on the rough turf behind me. In front, the engine gave a few strangled pops and the airscrew tried its best to stop but promptly disappeared into oblivion in response to a quick burst of throttle. We slowed down, stopped, then began to taxi in. It was all over.

Mr. Sears, still in his parachute, was out first, rising in front of me like some primeval monster out of slime, the aircraft once more groaning in protest.

'All right?'

'Yes. sir.'

'Good.'

There was no other comment and having unbuckled and shouldered his parachute, he left with the final admonition, 'Don't put your foot through the wing.'

I climbed out. Cautiously. Clutching parts of the aircraft where I could and taking care not to put my feet on, or through, anything vital.

I walked back alone, with no feeling other than that of relief. Wiping my nose. And my face. And my eyes, which were still streaming. Goggles! Of course! Fool that I was, I had forgotten to pull down my goggles.

Later that night, I informed my parents that I had flown for the very first time! They both said politely, 'Fancy!', in much the same tone of voice they might have employed discussing next door's cat. Complete ignorance, it seemed, did that to parents – my parents, anyway.

Some time after, my father enquired, 'Did you go solo, by the way?'

England, unhappily, is not the place in which to learn to fly in winter, particularly if instruction is limited to the occasional weekend. The winter of 1938 was a brute; there were savage gales in November and the bitterest and whitest of Christmases for years. In the four months to the end of January, 1939, I managed to take to the air on twelve occasions only, amassing the grand total of eight hours and fifty minutes flying, precisely.

My instructor was a kindly, elderly gentleman named Lowe – Flying Officer Lowe. He was small, gentle-voiced, and infinitely patient. He had to be! With gaps, sometimes, of four weeks between flights, he seemed fated to keep reminding me of errors I had made the month before – and forgotten! It was not easy for either of us.

After my first rather dismal trip when I had seen nothing other than mist, a clutch of chimneys and my instructor's massive shoulders, I grew to enjoy the business of learning. Nor did I have any problems; not, that is, until I came to landing the aircraft when I can best describe my performance as erratic. For two consecutive flights I would touch down with the feather-like delicacy of an angel alighting on a cloud, encouraging my instructor to believe I was ready for my first solo. Then, when we were both intoxicated with self-satisfaction, the weather would intervene and there would be a gap of several weeks, after which I would bounce him around the airfield as though on a pogo stick, producing holy words and grunts of dismay from the front seat.

And so it went on. February and March crept past, the weather unrelentingly miserable.

My morale began to droop, as did that of Flying Officer Lowe. One of the three others with whom I had joined, gave up the struggle and settled for a career as a navigator. I was less than happy myself.

Then, however, everything clicked into place. By this time we had converted onto Tiger Moths – a momentous happening – but mostly it was because the sun had begun to shine, the ground, meanwhile, deciding to remain more or less where I expected it to be. Yet again, my landings became mirror-smooth so that I was able to go solo on 20 April 1939, exuding self-confidence.

At which point, alas, the instructional staff took little further interest in me and for the four months thereafter, I received little or no further instruction, the faculty preferring to concentrate their attention on the forty or more new arrivals who kept appearing in groups of four or five, so that by the late summer of 1939, there were more than sixty of us pupil pilots at Barton aerodrome.

Meanwhile, life on the ground was not without interest.

No.17 Elementary and Reserve Flying Training School was one of many organised and operated by 'Airwork Ltd.', who were responsible and under contract to the Air Ministry. The instructors – air and ground – were mostly retired Air Force officers assisted by other 'specialists' and administrative staff. Needless to say, they varied in character and quality; most were more than adequate, several less than excellent, and one or two, downright unique.

As explained to me by the Commandant, I was obliged to spend at least two evenings each week being introduced to ground subjects – Airmanship, Navigation, Meteorology, Principles of Flight, etc. These classes, because they mostly involved desk work, were usually held at the Town Centre in Manchester; others, however, such as Engines, Airframes, Drill, etc., were held at Barton airfield, where there were aircraft to be examined and space in which to move around. It was individual tuition, almost – we remained in our original group of four – and for me, quite fascinating; knowing next to nothing about anything, as a pupil-pilot I could only improve And often, it was more than fascinating, it was positively hilarious.

Our engine lectures frequently included demonstration work, in which case we would all troop off to the hangars. The instructor was a young civilian engineer with a university background and an impressive string of letters after his name. As far as I was concerned, he was grossly overqualified as my knowledge of aero engines – indeed reciprocating engines in general – could have aptly been described as the cube root of nil. I recall one memorable exchange.

Instructor, addressing the four of us: 'Tell me. What would be the likely cause if you saw black smoke coming from the exhaust of the engine in your Gypsy Moth.' (Required answer – mixture too rich.)

Stunned silence. Then, someone, hopefully: 'The aircraft's on fire?'

'On fire!' A sigh. 'I see. And if it's blue smoke?' (Required response – burning too much oil.)

'Er... I'd be skywriting.'

This time, a deep and resigned sigh. 'Jesus!'

These answers, typical of many, would have the student body rolling about with laughter and our engineer on the brink of tears. We were very ignorant.

But the engine lectures were models of propriety as compared with our drill sessions.

Our instructor was 'the Sarge'. A large ex-Salford policeman, he looked like Victor MacLaglen – only meaner – and not even his most ardent admirer could have described him as being anything other than thick – nicely thick, mind you, but thick! He and the bespectacled Mr Jones shared an office and disliked each other with an almost visible loathing.

The Sarge's drill sessions in that winter of 1938 were held in the dimly lit and confined space between half-a-dozen Gypsy Moths in the hangar, amid the smell of petrol and on a concrete floor littered with chocks, drip trays, and the impedimenta of engineering and maintenance. If a marching squad were not 'about-turned' in the nick of time, the front man ran the grave risk of having his eye poked out with a pitot-head or being decapitated by the edge of an airscrew blade. All in all, they were hours fraught with hazard. Moreover, bare-headed and in our city suits and hard collars, we hardly gave the appearance of a disciplined force. Added to which there were never more than four of us and, occasionally, fewer even than that. But whether two, three, or four in number, there was always the powerful tendency to giggle.

For example:

Sarge, in a broad Lancashire accent: '*Right*! Now pay attention! When we form-fours, hits one step to the rear with the left foot, one step to the right with the right foot, and we bring the other foot up. Y'all got it? Right then: Squ-a-a-a-a-d, Fo-o-o-o-r-m, fours!' No one moved.

The Sarge, puzzled. 'Cum on! Wot the 'ell's up wi' you lot?

Someone: 'How can we form-fours, Sarge, when there are only three of us?

From the Sarge, a succession of holy words, mimed but perfectly well understood, which had us all in tears, laughing.

On another occasion, arriving at the hangar one dark winter's evening, we found the Sarge sitting on a box and in a pensive mood. Frowning, he revealed his problem.

'Listen. This bluddy 'angar's sneeing wi' bluddy rats.' (With a fair vocabulary myself, I had never encountered the word 'snee' before.) 'Big as cats sum o' the buggers,' he went on. "Ave bin sat 'ere watching 'em. Cheeky sods, runnin' all over the bluddy plaice.' He bent down and picked up something resembling a shillelagh. "Ere! You lot chase 'em out from behind them packing' cases, an' I'll 'it the buggers.'

There followed thirty minutes of the wildest hilarity as the rats were flushed from their lairs amid yelps from us having skinned our shins, shrieks for the benefit of the rats, and howls of laughter. Punctuated also by 'thwacks' from the Sarge's cudgel and hoarse exclamations of triumph. It was positively the best drill session I have ever been obliged to attend. And be paid for!

Again, as already explained, there was a constant feud between the Sarge and Mr. Jones;

Mr. Jones considered the Sarge coarse and the Sarge's opinion of Mr. Jones was, and remains, unprintable.

One day, the Sarge called me into the office the two of them shared. After glancing furtively over each shoulder he adopted a stage whisper which reverberated like shock waves around all four walls of the room.

'You're a munney expert, aren't yer?'

My mouth fell open. With a personal weekly cash flow of about £1, my experience of money verged on the negative.

I faltered, 'Well...'

'You're in a bank, aren't yer?'

'Yes, but–'

'Well then...' He cocked an eye at Mr. Jones, apparently hard at work, and gave me a wink loaded with intrigue. 'I want sum expert advice, like. Know wot I mean? Tax problems.' He winked again, knowingly. 'Next time you cum. Aw right?'

That Friday, the only evening in the week I had to myself, I spent an hour with my father going through the Income Tax form discussing Income, Unearned Income, Personal Allowances, Schedule 'A', and the rest. Some time later, I sat alongside the Sarge in his office, my confidence at rock-bottom, and began to explain what little I knew of the subject. One sideways glance at his glazed expression, however, convinced me that the Sarge was not even listening.

Suddenly, he interjected: 'An' wot about me *'oldin's*!

I looked up blankly, 'Your what?'

'Me *'oldin's*! Me stocks and shares an' things. Property an' all that.' He dug into an inside pocket and produced a folded sheet of foolscap. "Ere, luk't this.'

The old rascal then began to reel off his possessions, running his finger down the page. We both kept our eyes to the desk – studying a blank sheet of paper!

I am proud to report that I kept a straight face and carried on with the charade like a true thespian. Across the room, Mr. Jones's ears were pricked and positively swivelling. Like some Grand National winner!

Towards the end of March, the flying school was re-equipped with Tiger Moths. News of the change preceded their arrival and we had all been agog with expectation.

The Chief Flying Instructor flew the first one to be delivered and declared himself overwhelmed; on opening the throttle, he reported, the kick in the back was fantastic – after our Gypsy Moths, which were only marginally younger than God, a kick anywhere would have been fantastic! Thereafter, we flew our new aircraft very circumspectly and with that special reverence appropriate to all new toys. Yes, Tiger Moths were something special. And it was on a Tiger Moth that I made my first solo flight.

Having taken to the air on my own and the international situation already working up to its frenzied summertime routine of speech-making, goose-stepping, rallies and crises, I decided to put in my fifteen days of continuous training – wouldn't do to be unprepared! – and with several others, started during the weekend of 29 April.

Despite some uncooperative weather – there was a near-gale for days on end which stiffened the windsock so that it trembled rigidly at ninety degrees to its masthead – I flew on average five times daily until a total of forty-five hours flying positively bulged at the foot of the appropriate page in my log book. Sad to say, however, it comprised little or no worthwhile instruction; apart from a circuit-and-bump each morning to ensure that I was not in the mood either to kill myself or, more importantly, damage the aircraft, my tutors seemed content to let me go my own way. Which I was happy to do at first, finally growing weary of taking-off, climbing up to 5,000 feet, which took an age, and executing either stall-turns or spins, which were the only out-of-the-ordinary manoeuvres I had ever been taught. No one having instructed me on even the rudiments of aerobatics, I was obliged to take a deep breath and haul my aircraft around in some extraordinary swoops and tumbles, all purporting to be loops and rolls. My loops, after some heart-stopping silent pauses in the upside-down position when, dry-mouthed, I would sit there waiting for the world to reappear, gradually improved in quality until I was able to get all the way round with a reasonable expectation of finding myself pointing in roughly the right direction when the aircraft had sorted itself out. My rolls, however, were at best dramatic and at worst a disaster – they were never very easy in a Tiger Moth. I always failed to push sufficiently when upside down, the nose would fall away like a dropped anchor and, as I scooped it up in a frenzied endeavour to get back on an even keel, the earth would appear, approaching at an unseemly rate, the Tiger Moth, meanwhile, protesting with every strut and wire at its disposal. No, spins were definitely my speciality; positively my one and only piece-de-resistance.

Later that summer, I took to flying over the bowling greens and tennis courts of the Worsley Sports Club, where my parents were members. My stall-turns and loops were fairly well received but my spins had some faint-hearted members on the bowling greens running for cover, with the result that a complaint was lodged with the club secretary and I received a message, sent via my parents, asking me to give my demonstrations somewhere else and to people more appreciative of my skills.

And there were other more disturbing incidents – well, disturbing then, amusing now.

Still at the stage when I was a virtual passenger in any aircraft I flew, had a serious fault developed in the air, I would certainly have not known what to do. The engine at that stage of my career was merely something that made a noise up front; I knew what to pull, push, and switch on in order to start it, thereafter, it was on its own – the propeller dissolved into a blur, there would be a lot of wind, and that was that.

One afternoon, I was quietly flying along when I happened to observe that the oil pressure gauge, instead of registering a healthy 40 lbs of pressure, was indicating nothing at all. In fact, the pointer had disappeared!

Aghast, for a full minute I sat there gaping at it, my mind in turmoil. What on earth did I do now? Although my knowledge of engines was verging on the negative, I knew very well that without oil, the brute would stop – and soon!

My brain kept screaming, emergency! Do *something*! But what? I had no idea. I was miles away from the airfield, over fields and roads, houses and power cables, the Manchester Ship Canal somewhere to my left and a scattering of isolated trees and woods everywhere else.

After a minute or so, during which time all my thought processes lurched to a halt, suddenly, like a light being switched on, I came to a decision. I would land the aircraft before the engine stopped. In a field! Anywhere! Then, an agonizing thought. Where, though? And what if I broke it? What if I hit some wires or power cables, or turned the thing over? Or killed someone, even? Oh God! They would *shoot* me! Get rid of me at the very least.

My stomach having shrunk to the size of a walnut, I closed the throttle and, half gliding down, began to search for a suitable field in a minor panic. But there wasn't one, or none that I could see. And the wind! Which way was it blowing? – land downwind and I would float for ever and be through the far hedge like a charging rhino. Smoke? Chimneys? Not a sign! Why weren't there some chimneys around here? Or smoke? Oh, Lord!

By this time, having convinced myself that the engine was just about to seize, I was down to less that 500 feet when, by Divine intervention, I caught sight of a field which was green, flatish and fairly big – long, anyway, and narrow. Thank heaven! But, was it spring wheat? A crop of something? What if my wheels dug in and – ? But, no matter, I would just have to chance it. What a thing to have to cope with; less than thirty-odd hours of flying, and *this* should happen! Why me?

By this time I was concentrating grimly on making my approach and, as I grew closer to the ground, was dismayed to observe that the flat field was far less flat than I had imagined and that obstacles were springing up everywhere – telephone wires, poles, trees, even a double-decker bus driving down a lane.

Now totally committed, I gripped the control column as though I were trying to strangle it and pressed ahead. Everything lifting towards me obliquely. Side-slipping. Then a hedge. *Careful!* I was over the top. Holding off, with the ground streaming underneath. At which point – my nerve failed. I opened the throttle with a bang and sailed into the air again, the engine sounding as sweet as a nut.

I was back again at 500 feet before I regained my composure and, still shaking, circled the field and scrutinized it once more – minutely. It looked all right, but what if it wasn't? The possibility that I might break the aircraft worried me almost to death, but the certainty of engine failure worried me even more; with a precautionary landing, I would have the engine to help me down, the other way, I wouldn't! Thus persuaded, I curved in on my second approach.

My second pass at the field was rather more confident as I floated over the hedge and, with my heart in my mouth, forced the aircraft down within fifty yards of the boundary. The ground hard but lumpy, the Tiger Moth rumbled and lurched like a derailed train, the tailskid jogging and digging in to such an extent that my landing run was probably one of the shortest ever. Down though! Thank God for that! Keeping the brute straight and praying that it would not tip up, the Tiger lurched to an untidy stop. Where it stood, leaning heavily, apparently as glad as I to be down. Wow!

With the two of us sitting there forlornly in the middle of the field, I felt rather silly. And limp! Phew! Now what did I do? Get out, or what?

Some sixth sense told me not to stop the engine – if I did, my goose really would be cooked because the propeller would then have to be swung – and I was the only person around. So, I sat there, thinking. Feeling utterly spent.

Then, another brainwave. Of course! I threw off my straps and stood up, lifting myself high enough to look at the instruments in the front cockpit. I closed my eyes. Oh, *no*! The oil pressure indicator there was registering a very normal 30 lbs. What *had* I done?

At this point, it registered that there were at least two small figures in the distance heading towards me – running. It also registered even more firmly that I would have to get off the ground before they arrived, otherwise, all sorts of questions would be asked and there would be articles in the local rag. I could see the headlines: 'RAF pupil-pilot lands in field! Farmer s crop destroyed!' 'Compensation likely to be demanded.' All the usual nonsense.

So, hastily, all fingers and thumbs, I did up my Sutton harness and, calculating swiftly that I had just enough room to take off straight ahead, opened up firmly and began to waddle, then accelerate slowly to take-off speed. As I limped into the air and climbed away, my heart still pounding, two small boys stopped, then waved. I hoped to God they couldn't read!

Back at 2,000 feet, I headed for home, my mind in a whirl. What did I tell them? That I had landed in someone's field and taken off again? The Chief Instructor would go spare! – I could just see his face! On the other hand, if I kept quiet and he heard, or read about it from another source later on, my number really would be up. No, I would have to admit something – anything. Or… would I?

Twenty minutes later, I landed back at Barton and, with a straight face, a thumping heart and having carefully ascertained that there was no straw or wheat in the wheels or tailskid, reported that the oil pressure gauge in the back cockpit was unserviceable – and left it at that.

For the next hour, I hid myself in the lavatory before creeping off early, and for several weeks thereafter slunk about the place like a jackal, avoiding the Chief Instructor and everyone else in authority. But, by the grace of God, I heard no more of the incident and if anyone else knew of what had happened to me, they had the courtesy to keep quiet about it.

And as accidents – or incidents – never seem to come singly, within a day or two I was to have another heart-stopping brush with the Grim Reaper.

Standard instructions in the event of an aerobatic sortie were simple and straight-forward climb to at least 3,000 feet, turn left, turn right, observe that there were no other aircraft in the area, then carry out the manoeuvre. Dead easy. On this occasion, however, it was not I who was doing the aerobatics.

Flying straight and level in my Tiger Moth in a totally relaxed manner, I was suddenly confronted by another aircraft, in plan view and going straight up, about twenty feet in front of my nose, so close in fact, that I heard the sound of its engine.

As my own Tiger jolted viciously through the turbulence of its slipstream and my heart came within a split second of stopping for all time, I saw that one of my colleagues had done a loop around me; without observing that I was directly overhead, he had pulled up and, in the vertical position, had come within a hair's breadth of catching me plumb amidships. And, as anyone who has flown aircraft will know, for one pilot to hear the engine of a second aircraft in the air, the two must be very close indeed.

Strangely, after the initial shock of seeing – and hearing! – the other Tiger Moth, I gathered my wits sufficiently to carry on with my practice sortie and land. It was only later that the full significance of what had happened dawned on me; I had been as close to a catastrophic mid-air collision as it was possible to get and there was no doubt that, had we hit, there would not have been much of either of us left to give details of the accident.

The culprit on that occasion was a young man named Collinge, who had joined the Volunteer Reserve the same day as me. What was almost as upsetting as the incident itself, was the fact that he had no idea of what he had done and was remarkably light-hearted about it when told. To Collinge, it was all a bit of a joke.

As reaction set in, I had the shakes about that near miss and, for some time thereafter, gave any aircraft I saw in the sky a very wide berth indeed. It was the first time I had come within an ace of having a mid-air collision; the next time, a year or so later, I would not be so lucky.

It was also in the summer of 1939 that the Civil Air Guard began to make its presence felt on our airfield at Barton.

The Civil Air Guard was regarded as a 'bit of a hoot', by us, if no one else. Sponsored by the Government to make some contribution towards a possible war effort, the CAG attracted a number of over-age ladies and gentlemen plus a younger element who were not considered immediately suitable for the Air Force proper. They were all issued with a light-blue flying overall and wandered about the airfield smiling sheepishly and looking frightfully aeronautical.

Most, if not all of them unable to fly, the so-called Guard was equipped with Hillson Pragas, a light trainer aircraft which, in some respects were just about the worst possible type on which to learn as it was basically a glider powered by a tiny motor-cycle engine. Being a glider, it showed a marked reluctance to stop flying; it floated... and floated... and floated, so much so that we VRs used to line up and cheer as the Pragas would skate across the entire airfield at a height of about six feet, usually to disappear into the cemetery just beyond the eastern boundary. To us, it was the greatest fun and bets were taken on which one would charge through the far hedge to rattle around among the gravestones. It was seldom that anyone was badly hurt but it did not do the Hillson Pragas much good – nor the gravestones! We insular VRs were all very young – and very unfeeling.

It was whilst I was engaged on my fifteen days of continuous training that a Hawker Hind flew round the circuit one day and landed. From 611 Squadron! At Speke! I regarded it with powerful emotions of interest, envy, and naked hate. It disgorged a sergeant pilot who disappeared into the airport hotel for lunch before climbing back into his aircraft.

I stood alongside, watching. It was camouflaged earth-brown and green, their Airships having decided, apparently, that they should at least paint Auxiliary Air Force aircraft in a manner fit for war. However, the new livery did not prevent me from reflecting that the Hawker Hind was not exactly the sort of aeroplane in which I would like to take on the Germans – or anyone else for that matter.

Presently, the aircraft started up, the big 'plank' propeller whacking away in front and the engine making a pleasant, dark-brown humming noise from somewhere inside. It then taxied 100 yards or so, before turning into wind and stopping. Then, as I watched, the engine noise rose to an angry whirr – no more than that – the geared-down two-bladed propeller began to whack away a little more purposefully, and off it went, surging and hopping across the spring-green turf until it rose into the air and swept magnificently around the circuit.

I was fascinated. Obsolete they might be, the Hawker Hart variants, with their sharp noses, humming engines and great flicking airscrews, were the most beautiful aircraft I had ever beheld. I followed the Hind around with shaded eyes and watched it turn, dive, then sweep overhead – at all of 200 mph! I recall feeling elated but strangely sad. Splendid though it looked, it was no more suited to modern warfare than my Tiger Moth. And this was May 1939! Perhaps the Lord had indeed pulled the right string the previous year when that bald-headed old bathbun at Speke had turned me down!

Another incident, too, occurring a day or so later, remains in my mind. I was playing table-tennis in the afternoon when an Air Marshal appeared in the doorway. My partner and I having frozen to attention, he asked us how we were progressing and whether or not we were happy with our lot. (I have never understood why Air Marshals ask that particular question as the response is fairly predictable. I know of only one person not happy with his lot who was silly enough to say so, after which his career took a distinct turn for the worse.) Brimful of tact, we chorused – naturally – that we were positively ecstatic, and it was at that point that I became aware of the young officer standing beside the great man. He was a pilot officer, presumably an A.D.C. or Personal Assistant, who, impeccable in his neat blue uniform, was one of the most handsome youths I had ever seen. Not normally given to admiring other young men either then or since, he was sufficiently outstanding to make a lasting impression. A year or so later, we were to be colleagues in the same fighter squadron and I was to witness his tragic end. His name was Denis Parnall, a family member of George Parnall and Company, the aircraft manufacturers, who, from their factory in Gloucestershire, produced the Parnall Plover, Elf and other aircraft of the 1920s and '30s.

As the spring of 1939 moved into summer – the traditional campaigning season – and whilst I was feverishly accumulating forty-five hours of flying in my Tiger Moth, diplomatic activity was gathering momentum and war noises were sounding throughout Europe.

The Spanish Civil War all but over, Britain recognised General Franco's fascist government and, within days, the Germans had annexed what remained of Czechoslovakia and commenced their ritual press campaign against the next-in-line for subjugation, Poland. Not to be outdone, Il Ducce, Mussolini, and his comic-opera soldiers marched into Albania and later began a war with the Greeks which was to embarrass them greatly in the months to come. Recalling the Abyssinian fiasco, the British public were of the lofty opinion that the Italians could not fight their way out of a wet paper bag. Had not one of their admirals boasted that their cruisers were so fast that no Royal Navy ship could catch them. Catch them, indeed! Even so, the British Government introduced conscription in the form of the Military Training Act, which plodded through Parliament for months, many Labour members doggedly resisting its passage, declaring it to be 'the first step towards fascism in Britain. Then, in August, the world was shocked to learn of a German-Soviet pact. German-Soviet pact! Between sworn enemies? It was unthinkable. But, it had happened, proving once again the perfidious nature of world politics and politicians.

On the five-to-eight train each morning and during my evening homecomings, the conversations and prognostications were mostly of war. But there was much more talk than action. I found myself arguing vehemently with my friends and acquaintances on our perambulations up and down Greenleach Lane.

'Look, why aren't you chaps joining up? Show that Britain means business.

'Us?' Shock initially, then tolerant smiles. 'You're getting too excited, young Tom. We'll come when we're needed. Won't we?' Knowing nods all round. 'No, they'll tell us when they're ready and we'll all muck in when the time comes. Won't we?' More nods. 'Anyhow, there may not be a war. Then you'll look pretty silly, young Tom. Probably all blow over in a matter of weeks.'

I would raise my head to heaven. What, in God's name, did one have to do to get these *sheep* moving?

There was a girl I knew called 'Tommy' Tomlinson, who had a very lovely elder sister. The sister and I were walking home from the train one evening when I noticed she was wearing a Peace Pledge Union badge.

I was not at all tactful. 'What on earth's that you're wearing?'

The young woman returned a serene smile and told me. 'We're in favour of peace, you see. We disapprove of fighting. Nothing is gained by going to war. Ever.'

'You mean you have religious scruples?'

'Of course. Jesus said we should turn the other cheek. We should lay down our arms.'

'In spite of what Germany is doing?'

'Of course.'

Despite the girl's obvious charms, I found my good nature waning. 'I think your attitude's ridiculous. The bible is full of stories of the Jews knocking seven bells out of anyone who got in their way. The sort of clap-trap you're preaching is for people who don't want war not for those who do. Can't you understand that you and your friends are just encouraging the Germans? They honestly think we won't fight.'

'Nor should we. We should set a good example to the world.'

'Example! To Hitler? You're out of your mind!'

'We must agree to differ then.'

We walked on in silence. In fact, it was the last time we ever spoke.

And in the late evenings, the searchlights were out, feeling about the clouds with tentative, untrained fingers for the single light aircraft whose pilot was being paid handsomely – thirty shillings an hour, it was said – for his contribution in training the nation's anti-aircraft defences.

It was sufficiently novel to bring our neighbours out into their gardens with the usual gratuitous advice.

'To the left, you half-wits. *Left*! I can see the aircraft from here, for heaven's sake! Why don't they shine their lights to the left?' A female voice. 'They're trying their best, dear. And they can't hear you, anyway.'

'They're absolutely hopeless. I could do better myself.'

'I'm sure you couldn't'.

'Couldn't I just! What's so difficult about shining a light on an aeroplane you can hear?'

And so on. Interminably. Not only were the bulk of the British nation sheep, they were pathetic, simple-minded sheep. All baa and no bite. All the time, arguing, procrastinating, or giving advice. I thanked God for giving me a mind uncluttered by even reasonable doubts, one that saw everything in black and white. To consider everything was to do nothing, that was the trouble in Britain. No, there was nothing half-cock about me in 1939. By golly there wasn't!

The Air Ministry discontinued the traditional Hendon Air Pageants after the event of 1938, replacing it a year later with Empire Air Displays at seventy-eight venues around the country. One such airfield was Ringway, Manchester, newly opened and little more than a 240 acre field.

The aircraft to be exhibited on Saturday, 20 May, formed an exciting array, everything from Whitley and Harrow bombers to the brand new Spitfire, only a handful of which were in service, Moreover, as pupil pilots of the Volunteer Reserve, a group of us was invited to act as aircraft marshallers.

With the weather bright, warm, and clear, I donned my uniform for the first time ever. It fitted where it touched; even so, I rather fancied my chance and was childishly excited by the carnival atmosphere and the sight of a gathering holiday crowd of thousands. By mid morning, aircraft began to arrive in a stream from all parts of the country – a Battle, Lysander, Wellesley, several Blenheims, then a Wellington, Hampden and finally a Spitfire. All touched down on the grass and came tripping and swaying across the turf towards us with roars and pops of engine and heady puffs of blue exhaust smoke. I was excited almost to the point of dizziness. Finally a Whitley appeared in the circuit and I was instructed to 'see it in'.

The Whitley was on the far side of the airfield as I set off towards it and I must have run half a mile in my enthusiasm to lend assistance. Having reached it, I found its wingtip far too high for me to hang on to, as I had seen happen with other aircraft, so that I had to run like a stag all the way back as it taxied in, with the crew gawping at me from the cockpit, wondering no doubt if I were soft in the head. When I had finally tottered to a standstill, exhausted, I decided that I had done enough marshalling for the day, and, having recovered my breath, wandered along the long line of aircraft inspecting the panels and rivets, inhaling the delicious odours of petrol, dope and oil, and nodding to the pilots and crews.

The young man flying the Spitfire, I recall, was a tall youth with frizzy auburn hair, but it was the pilot of the Lysander, a dark-haired boy in a white flying suit and service dress hat who nodded to me pleasantly and seemed willing to chat. I remember him distinctly as very handsome and smiling.

After we had exchanged a few words about the Lysander and No. 26 Squadron, to which it and he belonged, he explained that he was to be first on the programme and intended to give a brief demonstration of the aircraft's quite remarkable take-off and climb, then its steep descent with slats and flaps extended. That would be followed by a few general manoeuvres after which he would be flying on to Squires Gate – Blackpool's municipal aerodrome – where he was to give a similar demonstration.

Greatly daring, as I assumed him to be landing back at Ringway before moving on, I asked if I might fly with him in the rear cockpit. After a moment's hesitation, he explained that his airman-observer would have to vacate the back position but that he was prepared to agree provided I could find myself an observers's chest parachute and harness. If I went across to the Watch Office, I would no doubt find the necessary equipment there.

All agog, I rushed off in search of the vital items but with no immediate success. I was still agitatedly hunting around when I heard the Lysander start up and saw it taxi out with both pilot and observer in position. As it passed me, the helmeted figure in front made a gesture I took to be of regret, indicating that he could not wait. Desperately disappointed, I could have wept.

As I stood there, bitterly reproaching myself and everyone around me, the Lysander turned into wind and took off, the engine thrumming a deep and sonorous note. It climbed away steeply and was at 1,000 feet or so by the time it had reached the far boundary of the airfield. Then, it turned, the engine note died to a whisper, and with its nose well up and flaps and slats extended, commenced its slow, descending flypast.

I watched it approach, then when I judged it to be about 400 feet, it suddenly tipped its wing and, at a very low speed, attempted a steep turn to the right. In a moment, the engine began to bellow, but it was too late. The Lysander's right side fell away completely and it began to spiral down, not exactly a spin but something very similar and almost vertical. It was very brief – not more than one-and-a-half turns – with the engine roaring desperately and the pilot obviously in difficulties.

With my mouth agape, I thought to myself incredulously, 'He's going to crash!' At the same time, someone beside me added shrilly, 'Christ, he's going!'

Then, helplessly, I and 10,000 other spectators watched the Lysander plunge into the ground just beyond the airfield's edge in an eruption of dirt which hung in the air like a pale, brown cloud before slowly drifting away. All amid a silence that was almost tangible. Mercifully, there was no fire.

After an age, it seemed, a fire engine and ambulance began to weave their way across the airfield, bouncing and lurching. Then others. One vehicle in its eagerness, ploughed through a distant hedge – and turned over!

Dry-mouthed and impotent, we watched it all happen. Shocked. Stricken. The Lysander, which seconds before had been a living, vibrant thing with two warm, smiling humans aboard, was now a small spread-eagled heap of silent, smoking wreckage. The crew just had to be dead. No one could possibly have lived in such a crash. It being the first time I had witnessed catastrophe in such a stark and instant form, I experienced a totally unfamiliar feeling of fluttering, weak-kneed anguish. It was so unreal. So sudden. And the pilot had been such a fine-looking boy.

I read in the paper that evening that the victim was a Flying Officer H.G. Malcolm, who, mutilated and barely breathing, had been borne away to hospital in a critical condition. His observer, an airman of seventeen, was equally badly damaged. There was sombre talk of them both being likely to die.

But, the pessimists were confounded. The pilot was to survive – at least for a time. Three years later, Wing Commander Hugh Gordon Malcolm was killed in North Africa, leading a formation of Blenheims against the enemy. For his outstanding gallantry on that occasion, he was awarded the Victoria Cross.

I remember him still, a handsome, smiling Flying Officer in a white overall. Alongside his Lysander. At Ringway. And so nearly an end to MY Air Force career!

On Thursday 30 August, I was working in the Gorton sub-branch of District Bank Ltd., Head Office. Several miles out of the city, Gorton, if not exactly a slum area, was not the sort of place one selected for a holiday!

In the batch of Head Office mail that morning was a white sealed envelope which contained the instruction to transfer Mr. T. F. Neil to another branch – its name unimportant – a further three miles distant. Moreover, I was to be there the following day.

The next morning at ten minutes to nine, I knocked on the side door of my new office to be greeted by the manager with rolled-up sleeves. The man looked as though he had been there all night – and indeed had!

He greeted me pleasantly enough. 'Hello! Are you the new chap?'

I said that I was and followed him into the bank. There was not much in the way of security on those days, everyone being taken on trust. The manager had never set eyes on me before so that I could have been Dracula's father.

Over his shoulder he added, 'Thank God you've turned up. The place is in a mess. I've had two juniors leave this week. Both called up.'

I had difficulty in not laughing out loud and said cheerfully, 'I think I ought to tell you right away, I'm likely to be the third.'

The man's face fell like a guilty urchin's discarded brick, and I enjoyed every moment of it.

'When, for God's sake?'

I responded smugly, 'It all depends. Tomorrow, probably.'

The office was in no less of a mess than he had described. There were tilting columns of uncompleted pass-books, trays of unprocessed cheques, letters and papers everywhere and a small heap of unfilled ledgers. My senior waved a weary arm in their direction.

'Well… there you have it. We'll just have to do the best we can.'

I opened the front door at half-past nine and was nearly knocked over by the first customer. As I retreated behind my screen I heard a conversation which sounded like an Al Read comic dialogue.

Customer – in broad Lancashire: 'What d'you think o' that then?'

Manager: 'What do I think of what?'

'The news!'

'I've been here since God knows when. I haven't heard any news.'

'Well, they've gone an' dun it.'

'Who's gone and done what?'

'Invaded Poland. Quarter-to-five this morning. Warsaw's bin bombed and they're at it, good'n proper. Them Germans 'n Poles.'

There was a pause followed by a deep sigh from the manager. 'Well, that's that, I suppose.'

And I'm sure he wasn't thinking only about the war.

With the prospect in view of leaving the bank forever, I worked light-heartedly and more diligently that I had ever done throughout the previous year. At 3 p.m. we closed the front door and worked on, achieving a balance and restoring the place to some semblance of order. But, by five o'clock I had more or less lost interest and showed signs of wanting to go home. The manager took the hint.

'So I shan't expect to see you back, I take it?'

Grinning, I unhooked my keys which unlocked the inner doors of the safe. 'I really can't say, but I think you had better have these, all the same.'

Five minutes later, I left. The bank had already explained that, were I to go on active service, they would make up my Air Force pay to that of my bank salary. Eighteen bob! Banks, I decided, took only calculated risks!

Later that evening I telephoned the Town Centre. Was I called up, or not? Someone told me that I was. And should I go into work tomorrow, Saturday? Certainly not, was the stern reply. I was to report on Sunday at 9 a.m., booted and spurred. The urgency of tone gave me the distinct impression that I was likely to be hurled into the breech immediately.

The following day, my parents and I gathered my kit and polished my buttons to a mirror brightness, as much as anything to take our minds off the future. Before packing my kitbag, I checked over my logbook. My total flying time amounted to sixty hours and fifteen minutes. On Gypsy 1 and Tiger Moths. And no one had thought fit to give me more than a check circuit-and-bump for five months – since April, in fact. I couldn't even do a slow roll properly. But spins! By golly, I could spin! If I couldn't shoot down a Hun, it was more than likely I could *spin* the blighter to death!

4

The War Starts

There were no early trains on the morning of Sunday 3 September, so I had to use the No. 12 bus into Manchester. My father insisted on accompanying me, promising to come no further than the bus station in the city centre. As we climbed aboard and dumped my kitbag under the stairs, I saw we had the lower deck to ourselves.

The conductor, with a black-tipped fag-end stuck behind his ear and index fingers so yellow that they looked as though they had been dipped in paint, eyed me and my uniform and gave me a heavy wink.

'Off't war then are we lad?'

I smiled thinly in reply. Bus conductors were not my favourite people; I saw too much of them during the week.

I was given a sixpenny ticket and my father and I sat in silence, not exchanging a word throughout the half-hour trip.

The No. 12 'bus terminus in those days was beneath the arches of the now defunct Exchange railway station. There, my father and I parted. He behaved very well; no emotion, just a pat on the arm with the injunction to look after myself. After which, I walked through the deserted streets to the Town Centre, balancing my kitbag on my shoulder. There was hardly a person about.

Everyone there was in uniform stiff with newness, most of us diffident and uncertain in our unaccustomed finery. The majority of us were sergeants but several of my friends and acquaintances, who had joined via the University Air Squadrons, were pilot officers, which I had quite forgotten. For the first time we were conscious of rank, an invisible dividing line.

There was the faintest tinge of embarrassment. Did one really have to say 'sir' and salute?

Surely not! Not with one's chums.

We lined up and stood at ease. No one seemed to know what was going on. Several officers I had not seen before, who looked as though they might be in charge, kept appearing and talking urgently, before disappearing again with equal urgency. This mild state of confusion continued before some unfamiliar junior officer, rather self-consciously stood before us and cleared his throat.

'Er... look here, we understand that the Prime Minister is due to say something on the wireless at 11.15. I think the best thing we can do is to have you chaps buzz off for a bit and come back a quarter-of-an-hour beforehand. Meanwhile, we'll try to rig up a loudspeaker so that everyone can hear what he has to say. Perhaps by then, we shall also know where some of you are to go. All right? Back here at eleven o'clock, then.'

We all drifted off in groups. But to where? Manchester city centre on a pre-war Sunday morning was about as busy as the Kalahari Desert at high noon. Added to which everyone was likely to be indoors anticipating an official announcement of some sort. I found myself with several others, one of whom was Harry Davidson – he of the bright blue eyes, the merry machine-gun laugh, and the gleaming false teeth. We mooched around the deserted streets for a time, finally coming across a Kardomah Tea Room which bore the information: 'Sunday – Open 10 a.m.'. Heartened by the prospect of a 'cuppa', we walked around in circles, eventually surprising the waitresses in the act of donning their frilly caps and aprons, by lining up at the door prior to opening time with our noses pressed against the glass.

We sat there for half-an-hour or more, drinking tea and munching jam tarts. (Jam tarts on a Sunday morning!) Conversation was brittle and there was much glancing at watches. Finally, at a quarter-to-eleven, we wandered back to the Town Centre and formed up into lines.

The Prime Minister came on at 11.15. He sounded a sad and weary old man but his speech was dignified. His hopes and efforts for peace had been shattered, he said. Britain had delivered an ultimatum but he had to tell us that the Germans had ignored it so that we now were at war.

There was a lot more but two sentences stuck in my mind:

'There is no chance of ever expecting this man to give up his practice of using force to gain his will. He can only be stopped by force.'

Force! I thought of 'Tommy' Tomlinson's elder sister. Silly damn woman! – how did she feel now?

To all of this, we listened in silence, a few heads bowed, an occasional cough and ripple of movement here and there. Otherwise – nothing. The war had started and nothing had happened. The whole nation, it seemed, was holding its breath. Poised for some cataclysmic happening, all around was merely stillness. It was difficult to comprehend. But, for how long? A matter of months? Years? No one knew.

When the Prime Minister had finished and still in our ranks, a few voices started hushed conversations which gradually rose to a crescendo until we were all speculating, wondering, and finally laughing. Then, a flurry of excitement. An officer appeared with a slip of paper in his hand: the following would proceed forthwith to No. 5 F.T.S., Sealand. Sealand, for heaven's sake! Four names were read out, including those of Alan Buck and Robert Shaw, two fellows who had been in my group and whom I knew well. But four! Out of sixty! What about the rest of us?

But of us, there was no information and after a time, a further announcement was made. We were all to go home and word of our future would be passed on to us. Meanwhile, we were to keep in touch with Town Centre and report fortnightly for our pay. Pay! I had forgotten about pay. That and the prospects of an unlimited holiday cheered me up no end.

After that, we were dismissed but hung about gossiping before gradually drifting away. There was a brief flicker of interest as the word went around that there had already been an air raid on London. London! But, the general view was that it was a hoax; that sort of thing happened in war, didn't it? Sobered by the anti-climax, I made my farewells and walked in the direction of the No.12 bus.

By sheer coincidence, it was the same 'bus in which I had arrived, with the same nicotine- stained conductor, stinking of stale tobacco and with another black-tipped fag-end lodged behind his ear. When it was time for us to depart, he leapt aboard, rang the bell, then gave a start as he saw me sitting in a corner.

His observation was entirely predictable. 'Ullo lad! War over then, is it?'

Which was exactly my father's remark when I arrived home and my parents had recovered from their shock.

I was to be at home for almost eight weeks, which suited me admirably. From Town Centre in Manchester, there was not a word. All I was required to do, it seemed, was to present myself each fortnight and collect £12. For someone mentally attuned to less than £1 a week, it was THE most splendid arrangement.

Meanwhile, the war proceeded quietly and only in places. Within days of the outbreak of hostilities, the RAF sent unescorted formations of Blenheims, Hampdens and Wellingtons to bomb naval targets by day in the Wilhemshaven and Heligoland areas and suffered the inevitable heavy casualties. The Germans made a similar raid on the Forth Bridge in Scotland with more or less the same result. Smarting from its losses, the RAF refused to commit further aircraft on unescorted daylight attacks and, for some months, the Luftwaffe sent only lone reconnaissance aircraft and single bombers up the east coast of Britain, these being picked off regularly by Spitfires and Hurricanes of Fighter Command with only trifling loss to themselves. Altogether, a very gentlemanly state of affairs.

At sea, action was much more violent and desperate. German U boats began to sink all types of shipping, not excluding passenger liners with child evacuees on their way to America and Canada, and the magnetic mine became a formidable threat until its secrets were revealed before the end of the year and a solution found.

The Army, on the other hand, had little to do and was full of smiles. The daily papers and cinema newsreels carried endless scenes of grinning troops on the march, both at home and on the Continent, chanting the ridiculous ditty, 'We're going to hang out our washing on the Siegfried Line', and, inevitably, there were pictures by the dozen of mealtime orgies with lines of Tommies, displaying toothless gaps in wide-open mouths, stuffing their faces with food.

The British public derived almost pathological satisfaction from watching their soldiers devour mountains of 'grub' and 'suet-duff', flopped in heaps onto plates and washed down with outsize mugs of steaming 'char', all accompanied by stomach-slapping and yo-ho-hoing.

For the nation, it was a form of conscience-salving – by God, we're doing our gallant lads proud, aren't we! And the soldiers? 'Bluddy great!' The war was 'bluddy smashin!' Away from the wife and kids, the factory, the office, the mill or other place of employment, away from the tedium of everyday life, in fact. Wot's that? Are we downhearted? Noooooo! Not bluddy likely!

What did it matter that, apart from the few regular battalions, British infantry was mainly a rifle-and-bayonet force; that some of the yeomanry regiments were still riding horses and actually looking forward to going to war on them; that its armoured vehicles were outdated, most of them incapable of fighting anything more lethal than an armoured car, or that the guns in their tanks were little more than First World War pea shooters? So what? The Germans were short of petrol weren't they? And lots of their tanks were made of wood, so it was said. 'Roll out the barrel, we'll have a barrel of fun', the troops chortled. A Norfolk paper displayed a picture of four yokels staring woodenly into the camera alongside a handcart in which there was a single stirrup-pump, the caption reading: 'East Anglia prepares for the Air Onslaught'. Meanwhile, the national dailies reported that, on the Western Front, British and French armies had made limited gains against German forward positions. All this nonsense about a Maginot Line! Absolute rot! Who needed a Maginot Line?

Even though, some 400 miles to the east, the Germans had overrun Poland in a matter of days, in the west, it was mainly a 'phoney war'. There were next to no casualties, other than a few in the air and rather more at sea. A total blackout had been imposed throughout the nation with everyone bumping into each other in the dark and apologising, but there was no food rationing and petrol was still one shilling and fourpence-ha'penny a gallon – and that was the good stuff!

In the evenings, everyone listened to reports on the wireless of what little war action there was and more than a few tuned their sets to 'Lord Haw-Haw', the renegade Englishman, with his 'Jarmony calling, Jarmony calling', whilst outside in the darkness, the searchlights rippled probing fingers along the undersides of the clouds in pursuit of a handful of single aircraft flying for their benefit, the pilots of which shivered with cold in their open cockpits and wished to God they were back in the aerodrome bars. Everyone watched the night skies – and waited. For the air raids that had been promised, but did not come.

Meanwhile, rejoicing in my newly-bestowed affluence and freedom, I drove around in my recently acquired 1937 Morris 10 – sunshine roof, built-in hydraulic jacks and purchased for £47-10/- – visiting all my relations in Lancashire and beyond, my headlights dimmed by the new slitted hoods which reduced the beams to the palest of glimmers. All this with Alan Buck's driving licence warm and snug in my inside pocket.

The days passed. I watched my parents suffer, a little unfeelingly, I regret to say. And waited. But, there was only silence. No summons. Nothing. For almost eight weeks.

Word came in the form of a telegram. Report on Sunday 29 October at 4 p.m., it read. For posting. Which, after another bout of polishing and preparing, I did.

We left on the Sunday evening, about half the remaining members of No.17 E&RFTS, by train for Bexhill-on-Sea and something referred to as an Initial Training Wing.

The scene at the London Road rail terminus in Manchester – now known as Piccadilly station – reminded me of Noel Coward's 'Cavalcade', which I had seen as a small boy of twelve, parents, families and friends in earlier wars saying brave farewells with stiff upper lips and forced smiles. A painful business for me, I was glad when it was all over and we were on our way.

After travelling overnight, we arrived at Bexhill in bright sunshine around noon. It was beautiful on the south coast, the sea calm and blue, the golf courses a brilliant, sparkling green and the temperature mild. An Indian summer, if ever there was one. And no sign of war.

Our billet was the Sackville Hotel on the sea front, then a superior and splendid establishment recently taken over by the military and specially gutted so that we might live in the greatest possible discomfort. With every last stick of furniture removed, it was singularly lacking in charm. By some administrative blunder, the lifts were still working when we arrived but that oversight was soon rectified, with the result that we were obliged to use the stairs almost immediately. For those of us unlucky enough to be on the fourth floor, this represented a considerable hardship as there were 108 steps to negotiate up to ten times each day. At the end of the first week, my calf muscles looked – and felt – like Spanish onions and were so stiff I could barely stand far less walk.

Room 418, I shared with three others, one of whom was Harry Davidson. We slept on the floor on straw palliasses of our own making. There was, however, a wash basin in each room, a luxury grudgingly provided, their removal posing too great a problem, no doubt.

On Monday evening, by which time we had all been fed and watered, we settled down in the knowledge that there were 250 of us from all over Britain, that we were the first contingent to arrive but that others were expected, and that we were to be divided up into squadrons. The list showed me as being in No. 1 Squadron, this bogus seniority a minor consolation, the presumption being that first in would almost certainly be first out. The object of the exercise, apparently, was to introduce us to Service life. Moreover, it was expected that we would be there for about a month. But, no one was sure. As in Manchester, no one was sure of anything. That first night, I happened to walk past the former dining-room and found a number of my companions seated at a long wooden table drinking vast mugs of thick, dark cocoa and pushing down monstrous jam-butties, food I would never have considered eating at home. However, ravenously hungry, I joined in and, finding the atmosphere wonderfully congenial, was one of a number who jawed on until well after midnight.

Later, climbing the 108 stairs into the blackness of the upper corridors and to my prickly, crackling palliasse, I reflected that this was my first night of full-time military service. I experienced a warm glow. It was nice to belong. Yes, the war was all right. So far, anyway.

Even the most daunting of programmes becomes acceptable and enjoyable with the establishment of a routine. After a bewildering period of orientation, kitting up, sorting out, and identifying our seniors and instructors, we settled down to a regular cycle of rising, eating, drilling, marching, physical training and lectures. We started at 7.15 a.m. and finished at 4 p.m., after which we were allowed out on the town until 10.15 during the week and, as a special treat, 10.30 on Saturdays and Sundays. The local populace, elderly in the main, regarded us with smiling interest and we responded with cheerful courtesy.

Within a week, the townsfolk had become accustomed to squads of airmen swinging along the sea-front road and through the town or exercising, half-naked, on the sands and marine parade. If it rained or blew, it made not the slightest difference; we did our physical jerks with the water streaming down our half-naked bodies or marched with our heavy uniforms and greatcoats soaking up the moisture to such good effect that we steamed and stank of wet wool as we dozed in the De La Warr Pavilion, half listening, for example, to Mr. Harold Nicholson giving a mind-numbing dissertation on British Foreign Policy.

And all the time, we were on our best behaviour – more or less! There was no rowdyism, as I recall; in fact, we were so exhausted by all the physical activity that I doubt that many of us had the energy to be anything other that orderly.

Within two weeks, we were drilling with the precision of guardsmen, our cheeks glowing with health from the effects of sea-air, the vigorous exercise and marching, and – probably – the good, plain food and nocturnal jam-butties! There was an air of disciplined achievement abroad and I, for one, was supremely happy. I have seldom enjoyed myself as much as I did during those first few weeks of the war at Bexhill-on-Sea.

By the second week in November, our numbers on the south coast had increased by a factor of four. Bexhill seemed to be full of Air Force and another ITW had been started up in Hastings. We were amused but certainly not alarmed when Lord Haw-Haw let it be known that the Germans were aware that the RAF was training its embryo pilots at Bexhill-on-Sea. But, how on earth did the wretched man know that? Spies? Surely not! Yet he must have had the gen from someone.

The Northern Irish contingent kept making its presence felt. A wild, unpredictable lot, they were not exactly riotous but always in the thick of anything noisy and turbulent. I found myself viewing them at first with amused tolerance, then with some slight irritation. What a strange, difficult crowd they were.

There was also trouble with the conscripts. Fellows who had joined up since the commencement of war were obliged to wear the letter 'C' on their shoulders, whereas, we, as prewar volunteers, wore the letters 'VR'. Perhaps understandably, the conscripts objected to what they regarded as a slight and also some of the remarks made in their presence. The result – trouble, with broken heads and bloodied noses in the pubs. Later, we heard that Air Ministry had relented and everyone in future would be regarded as volunteers. Most of us seethed. What utter rot! We were volunteers, they weren't! But our objections cut no ice. It was the old, old business of lowering the standard to accommodate the masses. Diluting the cream, in fact.

By this time, I had made a number of firm friends. Apart from members of the Manchester contingent, most of whom I knew well, there was, in particular, David Gorrie, a most pleasant and agreeable young man, a farmer in civilian life, with a fresh face and a fashionable black moustache. In his gentle Scottish accent, he spoke to me of his home in Angus and of his mother and sister, both of whom I was later privileged to meet. Unhappily, David and I were never to meet again after leaving Bexhill as he was killed in an air collision after serving with No.43 Squadron during the Battle of Britain.

And there was Cecil Parkinson, who came from the Midlands. 'Parky' complemented my somewhat volatile and effervescent temperament with his own quiet and rather phlegmatic approach to life. He was some years older than me and smoked a big pipe. One weekend, we walked together along the cliffs at Beachy Head, having made an excursion into Eastbourne. The beauty of the coastline and the sheer contentment of the occasion remains vividly in mind. We strolled for miles in the most glorious sunshine imaginable with the cliffs, the green of the hills and distant Downs together with the sparkling blue-grey of the sea, combining to form an unforgettable picture. I remember both of us being deeply moved; our England was such a joy to behold, so quietly and serenely beautiful. Later, we were photographed together, little knowing, or even thinking, of what the future held in store for us.

And Harry Davidson – 'Appy 'Arry! – with his bright blue eyes, his laugh, his flashing false teeth and his broad Lancashire accent. Later, we were to fly together in some of the most violent air battles of all time. And later still, I was to reproach myself endlessly for being indirectly responsible for his death.

On one occasion at night, as we all lay on our palliasses in Room 418, I sang some song or other. When I had finished, there was a brief silence. Then, out of the darkness, came Harry's quiet voice.

'Tommy. You sing like a bluddy canury!'

I remember being greatly touched but it didn't prevent me shaking with silent laughter for some time afterwards. Bloody canary, indeed!

Another event that remains with me involved a delightful young man called Pendal, who had held a short-service commission in the RAF before being obliged to leave because of some flying misdemeanour. A little older than most of us, he was, even then, very short of hair, which made him look older still. But Pendal, very endearingly, was one of nature's gentlemen, unfailingly courteous and with two of the most innocent blue eyes in Christendom.

One morning, on parade, there was something of a fuss. The word was passed down the ranks: 'All right! Who did it?'

Who did what? We all looked about, dumbfounded.

Then, a finger was raised, and there, on a flagstaff on the topmost pinnacle of the highest dome of the Sackville Hotel – pretty high up in all conscience – was a pair of ladies' knickers. In full flight! Three questions had to be answered immediately: whose were they; how were they obtained; and who had perpetrated the foul deed?

In the event, it turned out to be Pendal, and I was amazed. Not so much by the nature of the garment and how he had managed to get it, but by the sheer cold-blooded courage of anyone even attempting to climb up there at dead of night.

Happily, Pendal was to move on with me to Flying Training School where I was to experience more evidence of his eccentricity.

There were many others, too. All of them faces now – boys still, in my memory.

Meanwhile, we were not without female company.

The De La Warr Pavilion, although used by the Air Force as a venue for major lectures and other events, was also the home of 'The Forsyth Players', a repertory company of some distinction which put on plays each week and generally provided the more enlightened type of entertainment. Some of the young ladies in the company naturally attracted attention and were not slow to welcome the experience. The young men, I am happy to add, interested us not at all.

Two actresses were especially favoured, one a bubbling, blue-eyed young woman, full of histrionic attitudes and overstatements; the other, a dark-haired, rather intense but quietly attractive creature. I rather favoured the latter and sat through each evening performance for four Saturdays on the trot, with my neck and buttons scrubbed and polished to almost indecent degrees of cleanliness.

Later, we invited the whole company to our end-of-course dance and, rather to our surprise, they all turned up.

Off stage and at close quarters, the ladies were less enchanting. My dark-haired beauty had spots, hair like hemp, and was clearly out of her depth among brutal and licentious airmen, whilst her blue-eyed companion talked like a runaway tape-recorder and was vivacious to the point of exhausting everyone with whom she came into contact. To their credit, however, on the dance-floor they did their best with the bravest of smiles; dancing could not have been much fun for them as, obliged to wear our heavy service boots, we handed out some brutal on-the-hoof treatment. An untaught and hesitant novice myself, I felt that I scarcely emerged with credit on that occasion; however, I was comforted to note that my companions appeared to be no more expert that I.

Some years later, I again encountered the blue-eyed chatterbox when I was much more senior and she was part of a touring ENSA party. Clutching my arm and radiating bogus sincerity from every pore, she insisted that *of course* she remembered me from Bexhill. *Of course* she did! How could I *possibly* think otherwise?

All of which, needless to say, was a fib. But, as she was attractive still and I was then more sure of myself, we enjoyed a pleasant evening together. Later still, she achieved considerable success as a radio and television actress but, sadly, something, somewhere, went amiss and I read one morning that she had taken her own life. I. was greatly saddened. So bright a light to be suddenly extinguished. But, in my memory at least, her blue eyes still sparkle with eternal radiance and in my ear there still lingers the surge and lilt of her endless prattle. Her name, I remember, was MacKenzie. Mary MacKenzie.

There were many other liaisons, too, between my companions and ladies of varying reputation. Returning home one night in a mixed group of a dozen or so, one member of Room 418 announced behind shielded lips that he would be staying out the night. Not having had any experience of such goings-on and concerned for the health of my room-mate – it was freezing hard at the time – I remarked upon the danger of his catching pneumonia.

I well remember the pitying glances cast in my direction and someone remarking scornfully: 'Tommy, you may be able to sing like a canary but you're pretty bloody dense when it comes to women'.

Which, at the time, was no more than the truth.

Around mid-November, there were rumours galore. The know-alls in the Wing, of whom there are always a number in any organisation, began to tap their noses and speak darkly of commissioning boards and information of our impending postings.

They were, as it happens, half right. On 15 November, I learned that I was to be sent to No.8 Service Flying Training School, Montrose, in Scotland, the posting to take effect from 2 December. Montrose! My oath! From the south of England to the north of Scotland! The Air Force, it seemed, was as vindictive as the Bank. Why couldn't I be sent to Little Rissington, Kidlington, or Sealand, even? Why on earth Scotland?

However, the more I thought about it, the better I liked the idea. David Gorrie pointed out that I should be able to visit his family, who lived a few miles north of the aerodrome; furthermore, I was very fond of Scotland, having spent many childhood holidays on the west coast.

On 1 December, therefore, we were all packed and ready for off when word came through that our postings had been cancelled. Cancelled! Total, but total dismay! Too few casualties, was the explanation; the training schools and airfields were thigh-deep in pilots, so many in fact that the system was clogged. Not only that, but the postponement was likely to be indefinite. Air Ministry had been anticipating 1,000 casualties a month, the information ran, but the Luftwaffe was upsetting everyone's calculations by neglecting to shoot anyone down.

I gave the matter some thought. A thousand casualties a month! The figures sounded pretty unpleasant to me. It was not one my parents would be happy to know about, either.

On 4 December, however, the news was better. It would still be Montrose but on 10 December.

We were reasonably certain it would all happen when the Wing Commander addressed us and was close to tears. We were the first, he said, and he was sorry to see us go, finishing up by wishing us all good fortune in the future. No doubt wisdom and experience revealed to him in greater detail the stark picture of what was likely to be ahead of us.

So, on a fine Saturday morning, we caught the 10.15 train from Bexhill and were in London by noon. There, we were obliged to kill time for ten hours as it had been arranged that we should travel overnight to Edinburgh and beyond. There were forty of us. Suddenly, it appeared that things were really moving at last.

The journey north was uneventful and surprisingly comfortable. Our seats had been reserved and three of us, with our kit, succeeded in scaring off all civilian passengers until well on our way to Scotland. With the result, I slept like a hibernating bear, with my feet up, waking only briefly when the train stopped at York at 2.30 a.m. and later at Newcastle. In years to come, I became quite an expert on the major rail junctions on all four railway systems in Britain – the LMS, LNER, the Great Western and Southern. The stations at Crewe, York and Rugby, as well as those at Euston, Kings Cross, Waterloo and Paddington, I grew to know like the back of my hand, especially as seen between the hours of midnight and 4 a.m.! I often reflected that, were I to survive and have grandchildren, I should be able to claim, not so much that I had flown aircraft during the war, but that I had travelled to every known inch of Britain by rail – and mostly at dead of night!

It was still dark when we arrived in Edinburgh and barely dawn as we 'clonked' at snail's- pace across the Forth Bridge, so recently the target of enemy bombers. As we crossed to the northern side, we could see below the dark outlines of warships anchored in the waters of the Forth and, for our education no doubt, the slim shape of a destroyer arrowed its way slowly beneath us en route for some desperate rendezvous or patrol in the North Sea.

Shortly after 10 a.m., we 'clack-clacked' at walking pace over the girdered bridge carrying the railway line across the entrance to the Montrose basin, a vast expanse of low water, mud-flats and sea birds, to draw up gently with squealing brakes at the station. We had arrived!

I was impressed immediately by the silence – the utter, frigid silence. It being a Sunday morning and in Scotland, there was a bleak non-conformist stillness about the place. The air was keen, clear and raw, the distant hills to the west sharply outlined like cardboard cut-outs against a turquoise sky. We all stood, surveying the scene and feeling a million miles from home, beating our arms to restore circulation reduced to a torpid crawl by twelve hours of cramped inactivity, our breath steaming in the chill morning air.

Brrrr! What a life!

Presently, several lorries arrived and we all crowded into them with our kit and equipment. There should have been excitement but we were mostly quiet and still coldly sleepy. The lorries jerked and rumbled, turning towards the town centre before proceeding through the main square. There was lots of yawning, I recall.

Montrose! We looked about with only moderate interest. The buildings were dark, granite- grey and very Scottish, but not without some stern appeal. There was hardly a soul about and the one or two who were, gazed at us impassively.

The airfield was a mile or so north of the town, someone said. A further voice added that we had an eighteen week course ahead of us – four months, perhaps more. That would take us into April, possibly May. And what then? A squadron? I doubt that there was even one of us who did not have a mental picture of the future. A squadron? Of what? And where?

Later that day it rained, a slow miserable drizzle, but had cleared sufficiently in the late afternoon for Cecil Parkinson and me to visit one of the hangars nearest the sergeants' mess. Being a Sunday, the buildings and flying areas were deserted. Even so, we had little trouble finding a gap in one hangar door through which we could squeeze, the building being obviously very old and certainly not burglar-proof.

It was like entering the silence of a cathedral, albeit a very shabby, secular and down-at-heel cathedral. A dozen or more aircraft were crammed into a confined area in a chaos of wings, airscrews, flying wires, oil drip-trays, chocks, tarpaulins and pieces of servicing equipment. Water continued to fall through several holes in the roof, to collect in 'plipping' pools, brilliantly iridescent with swirling rings of oil and petrol. And heavy in the air was the heady aroma of fuel, lubricants and rubber, combined with the banana-sweet smell of aircraft dope.

Shabby and archaic as it was, almost a First World War scene, to me it was the most wonderful sight I had ever beheld. Almost all the aircraft were Hawker Audaxes, painted a bright yellow with camouflaged upper surfaces, with one or two Harts and, unbelievably, several Furys, their lean noses and stalky undercarriage legs evocatively eager, even in obsolescence. Most of the aircraft seemed to have guns, too, and Scarff rings in the rear cockpits.

We stood, frozen into ecstatic immobility by the sight.

'Gosh! Are these the aircraft we're likely to fly?' My voice was hushed with reverence.

'I suppose so. If we go onto fighters, that is.' Parkinson seemed equally affected.

'D'you think we'll be given the choice?'

'I expect so. There are masses of Oxfords, too, I believe.'

'I don't think I'd like to fly Oxfords. Or be a bomber.'

'Me neither. These'll suit me fine.'

'Not much like Spitfires, though.'

'Oh, we'd soon get the hang. And just think, we'd probably be the last people to be trained on biplanes.'

'D'you think we'll be able to fly a Fury?'

'I don't see why not. I hope so, anyway.'

5

No. 8 Service Flying Training School – Montrose

I have the happiest recollections of Montrose and of No. 8 SFTS.

The aerodrome, within easy walking distance of the town, was by modern standards ridiculously small, a corner-less oblong of grass bounded on the eastern edge by sand dunes and the North Sea, to the south by a golf course and a tangle of barbed wire – with which I was soon to have a sharp encounter – whilst to the north, the landing area petered out into gorse and a small wilderness of what was aptly described at the time as being an area of 'boggy cock-all'. On the remaining side, there was a group of geriatric hangars and a mass of wooden buildings of First World War vintage. Ancient and decrepit though it was, there was a wonderfully cosy atmosphere about the place and an almost tangible feeling of tradition and learning.

The SFTS normally accommodated two courses at a time, each of around forty pupil-pilots. The Intermediate Course, normally of ten weeks duration, flew from the south side of the airfield and the Advanced Course from the north-west and for a period of eight weeks. The Advanced Course on the so-called fighter side – so-called as there was always a possibility that one would end up target-towing or dropping torpedoes – also included Armament Practice Camp, for which the aircraft would be flown either to Evanton or West Freugh, near Stranraer, to use the bombing and firing ranges there for about a fortnight.

Access everywhere to the airfield was easy – except through the main gate! There, airmen with rifles and bayonets zealously guarded the entrance with the traditional challenges and passwords. As we were quick to learn.

A group of us, after our first excursion into town, made the mistake of doing the reasonable thing and attempted to enter by the front gate at something after 9.30 p.m. On a night of stygian blackness, we approached laughing and chatting, to be brought to a precipitate and stumbling stop.

'*Halt! Who goes there?*'

There was much shuffling of feet and some nervous confusion. Then, directed towards the unseen guardian with the gun, our unelected spokeman called out: 'Come on! Stop mucking about. It's us. Friends.'

Our still invisible interrogator was not impressed. 'Advance friend and be recognised. Give the password.'

Someone on my right muttered, 'God, this is ridiculous.' Then: 'Look, we don't know the password.' Followed by an aside, 'Does anyone know the password?'

No one did.

Someone else called out irritably. 'Come on, stop buggering about. We're new and we want to come in.'

There was a general if hesitant advance and another anxious voice from behind put in nervously, 'Watch out! This lunatic's liable to shoot us!'

The 'lunatic', dressed to kill and armed to the teeth, appeared out of the blackness to inspect us by the thin gleam of a torch. Presently, he gave a reluctant grunt. 'Aw' right. Advance, one and be recognised. ONE, I said!'

One advanced.

Some other voice put in less loudly, 'This is absolute bloody nonsense.'

In the guardroom, a Corporal said to me. 'You'll have to sign in, Sarge.'

'Sign in! But we live here. Do we have to go through this caper every time we put a foot out of camp?'

'You do if you don't know the password.' Then: 'Look, Sarge. Why don't you go up the road and get in by the side of your billet? Save us all a lot o' trouble.'

And he was absolutely right. I don't think any of us ever used the main entrance again.

It was our first day at work and we were all marched to a spot adjacent to the Chief Flying Instructor's office and ordered to fall in alphabetically. An unusual instruction, this had us in an untidy row of differing heights. My name beginning with 'N', I was three-quarters down the line and next to

'Jock' Nichol, a diminutive Scotsman from Ayr.

Nichol, with whom I was later to become very friendly, was an amateur boxer of some repute and had the shape of nose that went with the sport; indeed, it was said that he had sparred with Benny Lynch, the one-time world fly-weight champion. A tiger in the ring, outside the ropes Jock was as gentle as a lamb.

Presently, the Chief Flying Instructor appeared with a retinue of Adjutant and hangers-on. It was to be our 'singles' or 'twins' interview, that much we knew. We all shifted about nervously, waiting for the big decision.

The CFI, Squadron Leader John Loudon, was a tall impressive looking man with a formidable black moustache and a reputation for terseness. He confronted the first person in line.

'Your name?'

The name was given.

'And what is your choice, singles or twins?'

'Singles, sir. I'd like to go on fighters.'

'I see. Then tell me why.'

'... er, well, I think I'm temperamentally more suited to singles. I like aerobatics... that sort of thing.'

'You like aerobatics, that sort of thing. I see.'

A terrible pause.

Then the fatal word. 'Twins!' And the CFI passed on, the fate of the wretched man being decided in an instant and no doubt against every expectation he had cherished for years.

And so on down the line, with me feverishly counting the 'singles' and 'twins' decisions and striving to catch the individual arguments advanced. By the time the CFI reached me, I reckoned there wouldn't be one that had not been heard at least three times. I was almost sick with apprehension. If I were selected for twins I would die! A picture of myself stepping in front of a train loomed large in my imagination. Moreover, I knew that the ratio of 'twins' to 'singles' had to be better than two-to-one. Oxfords and bombers! Dear God!

Then, as though in a nightmare, the black moustache was directly in front of me and I heard the question being put.

I tried to remain calm. 'I think I'd do much better on fighters, sir,' I faltered.

'Really? Why?'

I swallowed down the golf ball that had stuck in my throat. 'I'm... well. I'm just that sort of person. A bit... well, pretty mercurial.'

'Mercurial. I see.'

The terrible pause again and two dark eyes boring holes into my skull. Then: 'Singles!' came the verdict and the black moustache moved on.

Eureka! My relief instant and overwhelming, I could have cried out in happiness. Instead of which, I tried to concentrate on what was happening further down the line and heard Jock Nichol's voice drifting up to me from around waist height.

'I'd prefer te fly singles, sorr.' Jock was frowning and swelling up to his full five-feet-three inches.

'And what makes you think you'd be a successful fighter pilot?'

'It's no' sae much that, sorr. It's just that I'd no' be prepairrred te bomb defencelus wumen and bairns, sorr. It's just no'm' style.'

There followed a raw, jagged silence and the world stopped rotating as we all cringed and waited. Then the CFI bent slowly forward until his face was at the level of Jock's cap. His voice when it came, fairly dripped with menace and was accompanied by a trembling forefinger pointed at Nichol's nose.

'If the occasion arises, young man, you will bomb defenceless women and children – and *like* it!' The finger gave a final poke. '*Twins*!' Then to make sure there had been no mistake, he turned and nodded fiercely towards the Adjutant who confirmed the decision with a vigorous nod of his head.

In front of him, Jock appeared to swell like a frog before collapsing into punctured silence. Later that night, as the story was retold endlessly in our twenty-four-bed, First World War huts, we all rolled about on our three-biscuit mattresses, almost sick with laughter.

There was, moreover, a supplement to this incident when, a week or two later, those of us in the singles group were marching across the concrete parade ground adjoining the airfield, having just attended lectures. It was lunchtime and some aircraft were landing towards us, in particular one Oxford whose pilot was making a monumental hash of things. Overshooting horribly, instead of going round again, he decided to land his aircraft, come what may. Forcing the Oxford onto the ground, he struck once then sailed into the air before making a second lunge at terra firma. And so it went on with us cheering and laughing at the man's obvious discomfiture, the Oxford meanwhile leaping about like a demented gazelle.

Suddenly, however, it all became less of a joke. The aircraft, bounding and weaving, missed a row of parked aircraft by a hair's breadth, before heading ominously in our direction. Our laughter dying into silence, without any order being given we hesitated… halted… then scattered in as many directions as there are spokes in a wheel as the Oxford, still doing a healthy 30 mph, plunged amongst us with brakes squealing, finally performing a massive ground loop and coming to a shivering stop.

A minute later, we reformed, laughing sheepishly, whilst the Oxford, miraculously unscathed, taxied back to its parking spot. Then, as we watched, the door opened and the diminutive figure of Jock Nichol jumped to the ground. Dusting himself off self-consciously he gave a quick glance in our direction, feigned nonchalance, then grinned maliciously before giving us a brief but embarrassed wave.

Puir wee Jock! He was not to last for long. Posted eventually to a bomber squadron, he was among the first to be lost in action.

Designated No.15 Course, there were fifteen of us flying Hawker Harts, the remaining twenty-five being committed, with no obvious enthusiasm, to Oxfords. We spent half of each day flying, the remainder on lectures. We paraded six mornings of the week with prayers and an inspection, occasionally with a pipe-band, and marched everywhere in squads. Altogether, our attitude was light-hearted and boisterously enthusiastic. I had not flown since 11 August and was mad keen to get into the air.

In the early morning, our Harts presented a heart-warming sight, about a dozen of them in a line, their engines warming up, their big two-bladed 'plank' propellers flicking over almost as one against a picture-postcard background of rising mist or winter snow. Oddly enough, we pilots were never taught, nor indeed asked, to start our own engines, so that when I was obliged to do so, having landed away at Lossiemouth on one occasion, I did not know how to prime the system, much to the annoyance of the ground crew there who were cranking my engine by hand to the point of exhaustion and calling on the Almighty to come to their aid in the most unbiblical of language.

All Hart trainers were two-seaters, the pupil sitting in front and the instructor, when present, occupying the rear seat. When flown solo, a large lump of metal was hung on a bar at the rear of the fuselage to compensate for the instructor's weight.

An expert on Harts from way back, I could give details of the performance of the operational aircraft and every other statistic, right down to the tyre pressures. Alas, the Harts we flew, besides being at the end of their Service careers and therefore rather tired, incorporated the de-rated Rolls Royce Kestrel X engines, so that no amount of throttle and pushing would persuade them to fly at anything like the speed of those formerly in squadron service. Roaming around the sky, we seldom saw more than 125 mph 'on the clock' except when working up a head of steam for aerobatics or dive-bombing. All the same, fast or slow, there was something very special about the Hart variants which made them everyone's favourite aircraft.

My first impression was that, quite unlike a Tiger Moth into which one stepped, the aircraft was *big*, with the pilot climbing into the cockpit using sundry hand and foot holds. Once inside and in the bucket seat, there was a feeling of being suspended in space with a gloomy hole beneath one's feet, so that later, it was an ingenuous pilot who did not expect some intriguing object such as a screwdriver, a half-eaten 'wad' or even an airman's cap, to come floating out of the depths during a slow roll or other manoeuvre resulting in negative 'g'. Drop a torch, a map, or other essential item into the pit and it was gone for good!

The Kestrel, being a water-cooled engine, required a radiator which was located between the undercarriage legs, the pilot winding it in and out according to the engine temperature. If the engine was allowed to boil – a not infrequent occurrence if kept too long on the ground – a minor geyser of steam would shoot out from behind the propeller so that it was always a problem deciding whether the engine was on fire or merely overheating. At first, and if it happened on take-off, this was apt to frighten the life out of those of us not accustomed to the idiosyncrasies of the aircraft. Moreover, failure to wind in the radiator before embarking on any exercise likely to result in negative 'g' caused it to fall back into the retracted position with a heart-stopping clang, which could be very upsetting if the pilot was not prepared for it.

And, of course, each aircraft had its own particular box of dirty tricks. Several had the wicked habit of squirting a pint or so of fuel from the gravity tank, located in the top wing immediately above the pilot's head, into the wretched man's face during the course of an aerobatic session, a very sick-making problem to contend with as few liquids are more revolting in the mouth and up the nose than a dollop of aviation fuel. Furthermore, in some of the aircraft, the cockpit restraining straps were so old and greasy they were prone to slip under extreme tension, in which case, when upside down, the driver would suddenly find himself out of the cockpit and on his way to eternity, obliging him to clutch wildly at anything clutchable en route. No one, to my knowledge, ever fell out, but I, for one, was a given a nasty turn on several occasions. In fact, after one heart-stopping incident and after examining my straps closely and finding that it was, indeed, possible to have them come adrift, I protested almost hysterically to my instructor, a quietly phlegmatic man called Warrant Officer Macintosh, who added insult to injury by treating my complaint very lightly. It was all in the mind, he shrugged indifferently; anyway, that was what my parachute was for – wasn't it?

But, these and other playful idiosyncrasies were all taken in good part. The aircraft, after all, was a lady and even the most proper of ladies, when past her prime, was permitted the occasional feminine wile.

Even so, there were some quite fundamental deficiencies in the Hart, notably the inadequacy of the instrument display. Engine and flying instruments of that era, besides being fewer in number and far less sophisticated than those later available to us, looked as though they had been thrown at the dashboard in a fit of pique, to stick where they had happened to land. There was no tidy group of six 'blind flying' instruments, a standard feature on all later RAF aircraft, so that cloud flying was very much a seat-of-the-pants affair and an exercise I never at any time relished.

But, all this I was only to learn with experience; in the beginning I knew nothing of any such difficulties. In fact, I was so thrilled to be flying the Hart, I would gladly have taken off without an instrument panel and probably with one of the wings removed as well!

I found the Hart easy, indeed fascinating to fly. The de-rated engine, with its long exhaust pipe, 'thrummed' away pleasantly somewhere inside and was sufficiently reduced in power to rule out any appreciable swing on take-off. On opening the throttle, the big plank propeller would whack away a little more purposefully up front and the aircraft would go tripping across the grass like some ecstatic ballerina, before hopping gracefully into the air. The only minor difficulty occurred during landing when, if the approach speed were even five mph too high and the aircraft injudiciously handled, it would balloon its way across the airfield in the manner of some slow-motion giraffe. On my first flight with the awesome and moustachioed Chief Flying Instructor, I came in a mite too fast, after which he quite civilly pointed out that had I not had his weight in the back, we would have both been picking ourselves out of the far hedge. Which was true enough, as the toe brakes on our Harts were worse than useless – and, of course, had there been a far hedge!

Quite unlike my six months and sixteen-plus hours of dual to go solo in a Tiger Moth, I achieved that golden objective in a Hart in two days and a minute or two over two hours flying. I also found it easy to spin and, more importantly, to recover. All in all, our Harts were a joy to fly so that by 22 December I had completed eleven hours on type and was feeling thoroughly at home in the aircraft. I had even flown it on instruments, which was less of a problem than I had imagined as one could peep through a chink in the fabric hood covering the cockpit – and cheat! Which, of course, I did. As did everyone else.

The following day, the Course broke up for Christmas and I made the eleven-hour journey home to Manchester by train. Overnight, needless to say!

I arrived back at Montrose on 30 December, having sat in the dimly lit corridor of the train throughout nine hours of purgatory, to find the airfield and countryside white and crisp with frost. In our huts, the stoves were cherry-red at night, but that did not prevent the temperature falling well below zero by morning. Our boots froze to the floor and the ablutions and lavatories outside were grottos of ice. Life was very unpleasant, even when the pipes thawed.

There were the usual jollifications over Hogmanay and Arber, a rather sober young man who slept in the next bed to me, having decided to ignore the celebrations and retire at 9.30, was carried, bed and all, and deposited at midnight outside the Sergeants' Mess some 400 yards away. A practical joke which would normally have been laughed off, at minus 10 degrees Centigrade, this one seemed less funny. Sergeant Arber's sense of humour, anyway, did not appear to be very active at that sort of temperature.

Beyond our immediate horizon, the war remained at stalemate. From time to time aircraft would drop in to refuel or catch their breath – Spitfires from Edinburgh, a Blackburn Skua from some aircraft-carrier or other, several Swordfish, the odd Anson and Hudson, not to mention the occasional mine-laying Hampden. Eager for any sight or sound of conflict, we students would crowd around and finger the aircraft reverently. They all seemed fairly weather-stained, the Hampdens especially, whose confined interiors were invariably littered with parachutes, harnesses, maps, flying boots, and a hundred other odds and ends. I fondly imagined that everyone went to war in clean and tidy aeroplanes and in their best uniforms, but apparently this was not so. The crews, too, mostly airmen air-gunners seemed very dismissive of the dangers they faced, an attitude which mystified me. Taking on the enemy in a Hampden did not seem to me a cause for complacency still less a recipe for longevity.

Meanwhile, the Germans continued to send reconnaissance aircraft and single bombers up the east coast of Scotland so that 603 Squadron from Edinburgh were obliged to keep detachments of several Spits at Montrose and also at Dyce, near Aberdeen. They were often airborne and it was as the result of their activity that there occurred a nasty accident at Montrose which nearly put an end to my career.

On that particular occasion, I was one of about a dozen aircraft in a long line, working my way around the airfield's edge towards the caravan at the point of take-off. Alone in a Hart, I sat there impatiently, one eye on the radiator temperature and increasingly concerned that my engine might boil before I was given permission to turn into wind and depart.

When I was next-but-one in line for take-off and preceded by a single Oxford, a red Very light soared into the air and I noticed several Spitfires in the circuit. After breathing a holy word, I sat watching as the leader curved in on his final approach and, undershooting slightly, dragged in on his engine, the nose of his aircraft high in the air.

For a time quite unconcerned, I followed the Spitfire's progress until it dawned on me that it appeared to be heading very much in my direction. After that, in the matter of seconds, I knew that the pilot had not seen at least some of us and that there was going to be a collision.

Before I could react and with a horrible fascination, I watched the Spit fly full tilt into the Oxford a mere ten paces ahead of me. In an instant, there was a catastrophic bang and an explosion of pieces. The Oxford, being a wooden aircraft, disintegrated almost completely and the Merlin engine and airscrew, torn from their moorings in the Spitfire, described a graceful arc against the sky before gouging jagged scars in the earth some twenty yards distant, the fuselage and wings, meanwhile, rearing up in a posture of agony before skidding sideways to a standstill.

After a minute or so of chilling silence there was activity – fire engines, ambulances and figures. The Spitfire pilot – I remember him as dark-haired and in tunic and black flying boots was led away limping and bleeding and after a time the two occupants of the Oxford were recovered from the wreckage and taken off on stretchers. As the small, tragic column passed beneath my aircraft, I looked down from the cockpit on the silent, inert figures and two uncovered faces the colour of grey-green wax.

Strangely, whilst the whole unhappy aftermath was being enacted, I had neglected to switch off my engine, as indeed had everyone behind me, so that when a green Aldis lamp blinked at me from the caravan, I reacted automatically and, taxiing forward, took off, my stomach churning. I have no recollection of what I subsequently did, but I must have done something.

Later that day, I learned that one of the two victims was a chap called Scase who slept in the bed opposite me. Poor old Scase! What a terrible way to go.

And as accidents never seemed to come singly, Sergeant Watkins, a short, roly-poly figure of a boy and also an occupant of my hut, was killed in an Oxford. For some reason, I was not around at the time so that the impact of his loss was somehow less. Much later, however, I saw a picture of his mutilated aircraft which made me thankful I was flying Harts. As someone said at the time with the macabre humour that always seemed to accompany fatal accidents, the wooden Oxford did not seem to bounce very well!

The memory of those accidents remained with me for years. Never at any time in the future was I keen to wait in the approximate path of an aircraft landing – or taking off, for that matter! But, despite my precautions, I was involved in several equally unpleasant incidents later in my career, when, on each occasion, I came near to hearing the swish of the Grim Reaper's scythe!

But, not all incidents were quite so desperate.

Sergeant Pether, a member of the Course, was small, precise, agreeable and obliging. He was the contemplative smoker of a much treasured Dunhill pipe which he polished lovingly and endlessly on the side of his nose. A most likeable young man, we remained on pleasant if distant terms throughout our time at Montrose.

One day, we were all seated in the dining room of the Sergeants' Mess at lunchtime, awaiting our midday meal. The room filled to overflowing, there was a lively hum of conversation and, the morning's flying having encouraged a hearty appetite, we were all eager to be fed. I happened to be sitting within a yard or two of Pether.

As we waited for the first course to appear, the door to the kitchen was thrown back and one of the civilian waiters, a tall, raw-boned man with the most prodigious Scottish accent and referred to – how else? – as Jock, entered almost at a run, expertly balancing four or five plates of steaming soup in his hands and up his forearms. As he advanced in our direction, he tripped and fell forward, a glazed look of horror on his face.

From where I sat, and powerless to intevene, I witnessed the whole incident as though watching a film in slow motion. A plate of scalding Scotch broth took off and after describing a graceful arc in the air, landed squarely on Pether's neck.

Instantly, like some outraged Phoenix, Pether rose to his feet, clawing at the near-boiling liquid whilst the waiter grovelled on the floor amid a quagmire of soup, steam, and broken plates.

In a moment, the whole dining-room was on its feet. It was the funniest thing we had ever seen and the roof shook with unfeeling laughter which continued for quite some time.

Eventually, when Pether had been sponged down and pacified, the waiter helped to his feet and led apologising into the kitchen, and other waiters had gathered to collect the broken crockery and clean up the mess, our mirth decently subsided.

After a time, the kitchen door was again pushed open and a further array of brimming plates appeared. We all watched expectantly, our sides still aching. Then the impossible, positively the unimaginable, happened. The leading waiter – the same one! – finding a trace of Scotch broth somewhere underfoot, slipped, lost his balance like some inebriated ice-skater and an arm-load of brimming plates once more became airborne. Homing in on Pether, they ALL crashed into him from behind so that the wretched man was deluged with boiling soup for the second time in five minutes.

Chaos! Bedlam! We all rose as one. It was *positively* the funniest thing we had ever seen. Charlie Chaplin times ten! There had never been such slap-stick comedy as this. Lunch was entirely forgotten. We rolled about almost sick with laughter. Everyone other than Pether, that is.

Poor Pether. I do not know what happened to him later in the war – he may have won the Victoria Cross several times over. But I shall remember him always as the victim of the Scotch broth, most particularly the agony on his face as the scalding liquid went down his neck. And Pether will remember it too, I have not the slightest doubt.

The snow came in mid-January and the whole of eastern Scotland became a silent wonderland of white, the hills and mountains touched with the most delicate shades of yellow, pink and pastel blue as the sun rose, travelled its southerly arc in frigid, cloudless skies, and set in the west a blood-red ball. It was winter at its loveliest, an endless scene of unadulterated white. And it remained so for weeks; so long, in fact, that we almost forgot what a green countryside looked like. On one of our more formal morning parades, the pipe-band disappeared in sudden flurries of driving snow and from where my own flight stood shivering at attention, could only be located by the faintest of wails as the kilted pipers leaned into the blizzard attempting to play with fingers rigid with cold, their naked knees the colour of celery sticks. It was bitterly cold, cold enough to remain indelibly etched in my memory.

In the air, for the first few days, we felt tentatively for the glistening hard-packed snow and either landed our Harts six feet up – or two feet under! After which everything clicked into place, until we were faced with a similar problem when the fresh colours of spring made their first welcome appearance. On one occasion, I flew with a Flying Officer Porteous, ostensibly to practise flying under the hood. After a statutory fifteen minutes on instruments, the sheer beauty of the scene got the better of us and, the hood pushed back, we wandered well into the Grampian mountains, drifting between towering snow-covered peaks, diving down into glistening valleys with their crystallized streams, then skimming joyously over the lips of hills and precipices. It was an unforgettable hour, the whole of Scotland a barren wasteland of frozen, searing white. More than once, I contemplated our fate were the Kestrel engine in our Hart to decide to spring a leak or stutter to a standstill. Below us, there was no conceivable spot on which to carry out a landing and I was all too aware that on some of the more inaccessible mountain peaks there still languished the wreckage of aircraft which had crashed during the First War and later. But, they were only passing apprehensions and my lasting recollection of the occasion is one of almost intoxicating pleasure.

It was during this lengthy period of heavy snow that, having nothing much else to do one Sunday, I persuaded Jock Nichol and another Mancunian, Noel Parry, to accompany me in a search for David Gorrie's farm which I knew to be some miles to the north of the airfield. We set off on foot in high spirits and in the brightest of weather, wearing our flying boots and well wrapped up against the sub-zero temperature, our breath smoking in the frigid air.

We walked for miles. And miles. On and on, three solitary figures in a silent wilderness as bleak and as deserted as Siberia.

With dusk gathering, we were still in the middle of nowhere and hopelessly lost. I knew the name of the farm, but there was not a single person to consult. We felt like Scott and his sad companions on the last stage of their final walk to the South Pole.,

We came eventually to what was obviously a crossroad half buried beneath feet of snow, its signpost removed in anticipation of an invading German army. Which way? Total indecision. We discussed our predicament, then took a gamble and, turning left, slogged on, praying for some sign of life before darkness set in.

Presently, a long way off and with our morale at rock bottom, a single dark huddle of buildings appeared. We laboured on, our feet sopping and numb with cold. If nothing else, someone to ask!

I knocked at a solitary door, feeling like Good King Wencleslas, and after a time it was opened cautiously by an attractive girl of my own age with dark hair and eyes wide with surprise. Could she possibly direct us to… ? Suddenly, white teeth and a warm and welcoming smile. No need for directions. This was it. She introduced herself as Ina, David's sister.

Almost gibbering with relief, we shook off the snow and removed our outer clothing and boots before being ushered into a cosy sitting-room with a bright coal fire and to three additional pairs of enquiring eyes. Some of David's friends from Bexhill, Ina explained. We were introduced. Two of the other three were pilot officers from Montrose. A moment's embarrassment – the remaining members of the last peacetime course, apparently. But, the ice broken, conversation was soon in full flood.

I found myself talking at length to one of the officers, a tall boy with a shock of dark hair and rather remarkable staring eyes. Later, I spoke privately to Ina about his appearance. She was mildly astonished. Did I not know?

That was Lenahan, 'Scotty' Lenahan. The one who had crashed his Audax on the top of 'Cairn o' Mount', a few miles to the north. The aircraft had turned upside down on the mountain top, pinning him in the cockpit with his head hard against the earth, in mortal fear of fire initially, then hanging and unable to extricate himself for fifteen hours until the mountain rescue team had finally found him more dead than alive. He was somewhat better now but still not fully recovered.

Fifteen hours! No wonder his eyes were sticking out! And what a nightmare, tied down helplessly and waiting for the aircraft to explode. Many years later, I saw a photograph of his crashed aircraft and marvelled that anyone could have survived. But, little good did it do him as, within several months of our meeting, he was dead. Having joined 607 Squadron, he was shot down and killed on almost his first operational flight from Tangmere during the Battle of Britain.

It was a memorable evening, full of warmth and good fellowship. Much later, we drove back to the aerodrome in Ina's Riley Nine, all five of us huddled around her, smelling powerfully of damp wool and laughing and cheering as the little car skidded and lurched its perilous way through the snow and icy lanes.

We arrived back very late. In the blackness, we located our beds by touch, creeping about in the gloom to the accompaniment of a cacophony of farmyard noises and unmusical snores.

And Ina? We remained good friends for more than sixty years.

In both the Intermediate and Advanced Training Squadrons, our instructors, needless to say, varied in rank, quality and temperament. Half were officers and the remainder senior N.C.Os., most of the latter, long-serving regulars. I had a great deal of sympathy for the N.C.Os., as it must have been galling for them to have had their Mess taken over by crowds of noisy adolescents who had few notions of Service rules and traditions and who had achieved similar status to their own without either effort or experience. Not unexpectedly, they resented our presence and not all of them had the grace to hide their feelings. Later, when a few of us were commissioned, it must have been especially irritating.

Of the dozen or so instructors with whom I came in contact, several remain vividly in mind. The Intermediate Squadron in my time was under the command of Flight Lieutenant David Torrens, a languid, laid-back gentleman of generous proportions and impeccable manners. Although he seldom felt it his duty to fly with me, I remember him well. Solo in a Hart, I had disobeyed instructions and flown over the mountains to Dalwhinnie, where I had spent some time as a child. Completely miscalculating time and distance, I found myself returning to Montrose more than half-an-hour late. Realising I had put up a black because of the tightness of the flying programme, the closer I got to home, the more worried I became. And I had good reason to be as, joining the circuit, I saw that everyone had gone to lunch leaving the airfield deserted.

I landed – no air traffic control in those days – and slunk in to join the end of a line of parked aircraft. Not a soul in sight! Utter stillness! I stopped the engine, climbed down unaided, shouldered my parachute, then began to tip-toe into the distance. Then, when I thought I was about to get away with it, the formidable figure of my august senior appeared like Frankenstein in the doorway to his office before wandering ominously in my direction, hands in pockets. When about twenty yards away, he beckoned with a sinister crooked finger. Oh God! Now for it!

We both stopped, with me swallowing anxiously, prepared to be charged with some heinous crime which would result in my being thrown off the course at the very least. But, not a bit of it. The admirable Torrens produced a tired martyr's smile. 'I say, DO try to get down on time, there's a good chap. Otherwise, I miss my lunch, which is really rather tiresome. All right?' Another worn and rather apologetic smile for being so cross with me, and that was that. Humbled by his forbearance and feeling an inch high, I felt much worse than if he had attacked me physically. Twenty years later, we became good friends when serving together in America. A quiet, delightful and amusing gentleman, he never changed, despite nearly being killed in a nasty car accident when in the United States.

Positively the happiest of our instructors was Pilot Officer Wood. Mr. Wood, a dashing blade of about twenty-one, was cast in the mould of a youthful Kenneth More, the actor. Irrepressibly jaunty, nothing seemed to dampen his good spirits and he would whistle and sing his way through the swoopiest of rolls and the crookedest of loops. Mr. Wood never climbed into the rear cockpit of a Hart, like Superman he always arrived, with much conversation with the duty airman as he was being helped with his straps, plus the occasional ditty. My first exercise with him was less than reassuring.

Having joined me in the aircraft with an acrobatic leap he cried, 'What-ho, old boy! Get me airborne, there's a good chap,' before bursting into, 'Three little maids from school are we...' at the top of his voice.

Wishing to impress, I set off carefully but immediately ran into difficulties. A fine clear day, there was a gusting wind from the north into which the aircraft kept weather-cocking so powerfully that nothing I did had any effect, the toe brakes being almost useless. After three or four abortive attempts by me to keep her straight, the singing stopped and my instructor took over the controls with a loud, 'I've got her, old boy!' After which, the situation deteriorated rapidly.

On the southern side of Montrose aerodrome was (and still is) the local golf course, along the edge of which was a barrier of coiled barbed wire about six feet high. Happily, it presented no problem initially as it was on our right and we were weather-cocking to the left. But, not for long!

Having himself had no success in keeping the Hart on course, there were a few gay laughs from the back after which the engine went on with a roar and with full rudder the aircraft broke into a gallop, tail in air. When even that failed to get it back on course, my instructor decided to go round the other way and set off on a left hand turn, still with the engine roaring and the tail in the flying position, clearly intending to take the wind by surprise. But the wind was not about to be fooled.

All this I was watching with interest tinged with concern. However, when we had reached about 30 mph and with the Hart crabbing around like a dirt-track motor-bike, its starboard wing scraping the ground, it seemed to me that things were getting out of hand, an impression fostered by what I interpreted as manic laughter coming from the rear cockpit. Then, when I was seriously thinking about climbing over the side, the Hart headed straight for the barbed wire and charged into it like a maddened rhino. Within seconds, we had hooked up about thirty yards of barrier, which we trailed along in our wake for some seconds, until it eventually wrapped itself round our wheels, wings, and finally our airscrew and we had all jerked to an undignified and juddering halt.

Silence! Then, from the back, a resigned sigh, 'Oh, dear!' After which: 'Hop out, there's a good chap, and see what's happened.'

I climbed down, knowing exactly what had happened; the aircraft was all trussed up like an oven-ready turkey. From down below I reported in a sentence, so we retrieved our parachutes and set off on foot across the airfield with Mr Wood chatting away amiably as though nothing untoward had occurred.

It would be indelicate of me to mention the name of one senior flight sergeant instructor in the Intermediate Squadron who, though thoroughly able as an instructor, had developed profanity into an art form. He had little time for us Volunteer Reservists (or Auxiliaries, for that matter) and his feelings, by and large, were reciprocated. I only flew with him three times and the first occasion was not without its moments.

It did not start well. On our way out to the aircraft, I asked, reasonably enough, what exercise he had in mind. His response was a terse: 'Wait 'n bloody see!' After that, conversation flagged. Then, when we had halted at the windsock whilst an Oxford landed in front of us with a wince-producing crunch, there came an explosive expostulation from the rear, 'God's teeth! See that? Like a sack o' bloody tripe!'

On instruction, I took off and, climbing northwards in the direction of Stonehaven, learned for the first time that we were going to do some cloud flying, which came as an unpleasant surprise as 'actual' in a Hart was not my favourite exercise having completely lost control on one previous dire occasion. Moreover, most of the clouds, including a few meaty Cu. Nims., were out to sea where we were strictly forbidden to fly, having no Mae Wests or other items of life-saving equipment.

By this time my instructor had started his patter explaining how, in a properly trimmed aircraft, I could use my airspeed indicator as a poor man's artificial horizon, etc., etc.

Meanwhile, as though arranged to annoy us, half of Montrose's aircraft seemed to be in our vicinity, producing a rich flow of invective from my tutor. Finally, to avoid them and to find some decent clouds, I was ordered out to sea.

We were about six miles out before I found several clouds large enough to enable me to concentrate on my instruments for more than a minute; however, with my instructor clearly losing patience, I was ordered further afield towards a brute of a Cu. Nim., presenting a solid cliff-like face. My heart sank.

When eventually we shot into its precipitous side, there followed for me nothing less than ninety seconds of sheer terror with the Hart being thrown about like a leaf in a storm. In no time, with all the pointers on my dashboard waving about like semaphore signals, I had lost control, to be steadied throughout with firm pressure on the control column from behind and calm reassuring instructions. Until, after about an hour – or so it seemed – we burst into clear air again and the brightest of blue sky.

Thanking God, I looked about. We were at 7,000 feet, there were isolated dumplings of cumulus all around us, and to our right and about 1,000 yards away, a largish aircraft was flying parallel with us at the same level. Not recognising it immediately, I was looking casually in its direction with no particular interest – at which point the world exploded.

The Hart suddenly disappeared from under me and I found myself shot out of my seat and over the top wing, clutching wildly at the cockpit coaming en route as my harness slipped to the full extent of its travel, after which I was first on my side before being thrown back again all askew, my parachute missing the bucket seat entirely so that I was jammed at a 45-degree angle. After that, the grey sea was in my windscreen and the rising scream of wind in the wires.

Meanwhile, there were howls from behind, very biblical and almost incoherent. 'Did you see it? Did you see that bugger? It was a *Hun*! A bloody *Hun*! A Heinkel! He could catch us with his wheels and flaps down!'

By this time a little more composed but still out of my seat and hanging on like a clam, I thought, not now it couldn't, as we were doing rather more than 200 miles per hour and diving steeply towards cliffs somewhere south of Stonehaven. Still trying to decipher the excited monologue from the rear, I felt the aircraft being pulled out, at which point three Spitfires of 603 squadron, based at Montrose, went past us like darts going north. As they shot by, there came Alf Garnett howls of derision from my companion. 'Whoah-ho-ho! There they go, the dozy sods! Typical bloody Auxiliaries! Sitting on their arses all day reading 'Health and Efficiency' instead of... !' My instructor was clearly not amused.

Nothing much happened after that. Hurrying back to Montrose and having landed and taxied in, my companion leapt out of the cockpit like a jack-in-the-box and disappeared, presumably to register a complaint. For me, it had been something of a non-event. I had not even recognised the strange aircraft as German and even if I had, I honestly believe I would have been more interested than frightened. That it might have shot us down, had never even entered my head.

There is, alas, an unhappy sequel to this tale. By constantly flying up the east coast of Britain in those early months of the war, single enemy bombers and reconnaissance aircraft became a real threat. In October, 1940, some months after I had left Montrose, the airfield was attacked by three Heinkels coming in across the coast in broad daylight and my profane instructor was caught on the ground and one of fifteen who were killed.

We were required to fly at night in our Harts and I completed a total of five hours, dual and solo, between the end of February and May 1940.

I regarded night flying as merely something that had to be done and was neither anxious nor enthusiastic about the prospect. Single-engined fighters in those days were regarded as having a dual role – day and night interception – although I doubt that any fighter squadron regarded its responsibilities at night as being other than secondary. Had it been otherwise, I would not have left FTS with less than two hours solo to my credit.

Night flying at Montrose at that time, and presumably elsewhere in Flying Training Command, was something of a hit-and-miss affair. Aerodrome equipment normally consisted of eight goose-neck flares set out at 100-yard intervals, the flare itself being a kind of Aladdin's lamp in which a paraffin wick gave off a smoky flame; a taxi-post, consisting of a triangle of red, green, and white lights set on the end of a pole; a caravan, accommodating someone equipped with red and green Aldis lamps; and, as often as not, a Chance floodlight powered by a generator – when it could be made to work! There was no permanent electric flare path on a concrete runway, no lead-in, exit, or other marker lights, no radios in our aircraft and therefore no communication or homing information with, or from, the ground. Furthermore, with the whole of Britain, from Land's End to John o'Groats, blacked out completely as an air raid precaution since September, 1939, a pilot, having left the flare path, was very much on his own. If he lost himself on a dark night, even within a few miles of his own airfield, unless he later discovered his whereabouts, that was likely to be the end of him. Indeed, it was an unhappy statistic that, in the five years from 1935 to 1939, the RAF lost on average only slightly less than 100 aircraft and 200 aircrew, each year, mostly resulting from faulty navigation and the effects of bad weather. Even in daylight, without radio aids the Air Force had problems; at night, the difficulties trebled. Even so, the risks, such as they were, were regarded as normal.

Learning that the Oxfords of the previous course were to carry out their final stint of night flying, several of us on Harts, who were not in any way involved, went out to the flare path to see how it was done. And it did not start too happily, either.

The night on that occasion was particularly dark and cold and, as we stood alongside the Chance light in the blackness, the flickering, smoking goose-neck flares, the huddled airmen around us beating their arms and stamping their feet, the sound of engines invisible in the darkness, the slow perambulation of green and red navigation lights and the whirling airscrews of the Oxfords' occasional pale discs of reflected light, all combined to produce an unreal and somewhat chilling Dante's inferno aspect, coupled with more than a dash of high drama.

One by one, each Oxford would move like a live animal onto the grass runway in front of us and into the guttering glow of the first flare, after which the engines would rise to a roaring crescendo, the aircraft straining against the brakes. Then, off it would go to disappear into the blackness, the rudder with its single light wagging defiantly as the pilot strove to keep the aircraft straight, then hover uncertainly before rising into the distance and finally disappearing.

For an hour we watched them come and go, sweeping into the glare of the floodlight when landing, to crunch into the ground with heart-stopping thumps. After which, they would melt into the blackness once more, their presence revealed only by the swaying white light on the tail.

After a time, rigid with cold, we left and returned to the warmth of the Mess, only to be informed just before midnight that one of the Oxfords had failed to return.

Missing! We were shaken. Stunned almost.

The hours passed. The flare path remained lit but silent, everyone quiet – anxious – waiting.

But the aircraft did not come back. God, we thought! What a thing to happen!

The following morning was bright and clear. All available Oxfords and Harts were despatched to search for the missing 'plane. I flew with Flying Officer Porteous up and down the coast, most of the way to Aberdeen and back. At less than 300 feet. But all we saw was the sea beating mightily against the rocks. And the cliffs. Not a scrap of yellow wreckage, anywhere. Nothing. Only masses of cold grey waves and silent, wheeling birds.

It was shortly after that I made my own first flight at night.

We were all hoping for moonlight but the night chosen was spitefully black. Not without some misgivings, I read on the list that my instructor was to be the irrepressible Mr. Wood.

As tuneful as ever, no doubt. But, recalling that he had been singing his head off when we had run full tilt into the barbed wire barrier, I could not entirely subdue flutterings of apprehension.

I climbed into the Hart's front cockpit, clutching my electric torch. The inside of the aircraft was like a dimly lit sepulchre and I knew that if I dropped my torch, I would be sunk.

It was an eerie sensation, taxiing forward into complete blackness. The routine was to proceed towards the three lights of the taxi-post, wait there, then move on again having received a green Aldis signal. I followed instructions to the letter, my companion in the back whistling meanwhile before launching vigorously into snatches of: 'a policeman's lot is not a happy one... *happy one*!'

We lined up on the flare path, the row of eight flickering lights to my left and only blackness ahead. In front, the Kestrel engine hummed away evenly and the big wooden propeller fanned a current of cold air around my head.

'Right. You've got her. Open up slowly, keep her straight, and take off as normal.' Mr. Wood's cheerful voice came from the rear, with me marvelling at his sang-froid. After all, he too would be very much a goner if I made a nonsense of it!

I did so, gingerly, accelerating into the darkness, the exhausts pink spears of fury as the engine note increased to an angry hum. I bounced slightly, then lifted off as the last flare disappeared. Up then into the blackness. Oh, God! What now? I just kept her there. Praying that the engine wouldn't stop. A terrible urge, too, to turn my head and look back for the flares. Then, surprisingly, in the darkness, the faintest of lines. The horizon! Who'd have thought it?

I could actually pick out the horizon, even on a dark night! I turned to the left, slowly and carefully, then throttled back. Phew! Things were not so bad after all. Pretty easy, in fact. I continued to do a wide circuit, my instructor in the rear mutilating some unidentified aria.

Receiving several green winks from the ground, I closed the throttle and the engine note died to a whisper, the wings tilting in the darkness. Ahead, the line of flares gradually moved into place then flattened out. I was suspended in blackness. Then I was coming in straight, my actions instinctive. Watching my airspeed like a hawk. Above all else, mustn't stall the blighter!

The first flare rushed past, with small black figures alongside it, and I held the Hart more or less level, and waited. And waited. More flares slid by.

Then, from the back, 'That's fine, just hold her there.'
I did so, and a moment later the wheels touched. We bounced slightly. Then settled. And were down, the wheels rumbling, the remaining flares approaching, then whipping past.

'Keep her straight!'

I needed no telling. We slowed. Almost to a stop. Then turned. Beyond the remaining flare and into the darkness again.

Phew! What a business. I felt spent but full of enthusiasm for night flying. Dead easy, really. Well, not as bad as I had expected, anyway. Must remember to hang on to my torch, though.

Later that night, I had a second dual trip of thirty minutes, followed by my first solo flight in the same Hart, K6475. A mere fifteen minutes, but it was enough. I was competent to fly in the dark! Who'd have thought it? Now, where were those German bombers?

I did not fly again at night until six weeks later and the event did not go quite so smoothly.

On that occasion, we flew from Edzell, the satellite airfield to Montrose, in those days little more than a farmer's pasture 7 or 8 miles inland and at the foot of the Grampian uplands. I had never flown from the place before, indeed, I had never even noticed it in daylight.

The routine was to be much the same as before; a brief period of dual followed by a forty-five minute solo flight. My instructor would be Flight Sergeant Betty, a delightful older man of a quiet, avuncular and forgiving nature. Very forgiving, as it turned out to be! I had flown with him before when he had taken me for my navigation test, this consisting of a triangular cross country 'under the hood', during which, after an hour or so on instruments, the pupil was asked to come out into the open and identify exactly his whereabouts.

After take-off, I had pulled over the hood, making sure there was a sizeable chink through which I could peep. Then, for a good hour, we flew round the course, my instrument flying immaculate and with me knowing to a blade of grass where we were. Finally, when asked to dispose of the hood and give my position, I had been able to do so immediately, although

I made a show of looking around uncertainly for a minute or two, just for effect. Betty, in his gentle way, had been full of praise for my performance but I later wondered how much he and other instructors were misled by such unerring navigation and instrument flying.

Arriving at Edzell by car with Sergeant Osmand, a small, pale-faced undergraduate of London University, we were instructed to lay out the flare path with goose-necks and generally sort out the other equipment and arrangements – there was a considerable element of do-it-yourself involved in our training at No. 8 FTS! We then hung about until it became dark – which it did, very determinedly. In fact, it was as black as ever I had known it.

When Flight Sergeant Betty and I finally became airborne, we were one of several aircraft in the air. We took off into the night and having made several successful landings, I turned off the end of the flare path intending to return to the taxi-post and thence, with the sanctioning green wink of the Aldis, to the point of take off at the first flare. As I bumped slowly across the uneven grass in absolute darkness, I was quietly pleased with myself and much comforted by the silence of my instructor in the back.

Having reached the taxi-post, I halted briefly before the green blink of the Aldis flashed in my direction. I then opened up and, the whine of the engine rising, the Hart started to trundle ahead. But only for a second or two before the aircraft came to an untidy halt.

Perplexed, I tried to edge forward again but the aircraft wouldn't respond. Furthermore, there was the most unpleasant 'thwacking' noise from somewhere ahead.

I sat and thought. Funny! Something wrong with the propeller? The engine? Or the aircraft, even? I couldn't have taxied into anything as there was only one building on the airfield and that was miles away. I strained my eyes into the blackness but could see nothing.

I was about to make some comment when I heard a flow of quietly eloquent but very unbiblical language from behind me. Good heavens! Swearing! From Flight Sergeant Betty?

Surely not! What on earth had come over the man?

The 'thwacking' continuing, I suggested that I might switch off and investigate.

Betty agreed with a sigh, clearly crushed by the enormity of what he suspected to be our misfortune.

I climbed out and, dropping to the ground, felt my way round to the front by touch, soon to find myself treading on bits of my own propeller – and walking into the chewed-up wing of another Hart. Another Hart!

I looked up into the darkness and all I could distinguish was a pale smudge which, on closer scrutiny, turned out to be the very anxious face of Sergeant Osmand. Thereafter, there followed one of the silliest conversations I have ever had with anyone.

I heard myself saying, 'Hello! What are you doing here?'

'Doing here! I'm sitting in my cockpit, that's what! You've just taxied into me!'

'Me? But how did you get here?'

'Get here! I've been here for ages.'

'You can't have!'

'Well, I jolly well have! Anyhow, I've just been given a green.'

'But that was for me.'

'No it wasn't!'

'Yes it was!'

Suddenly, the circumstances and the absurdity of our exchange was such that I had to suppress a powerful urge to giggle. On reflection, it was a mercy that I did.

That, needless to say, was the end of our dual instruction. With two Harts badly damaged, our flying was sadly curtailed. Later, however, I was sent off solo in another aircraft and, with a disconsolate Betty watching from the end of the flare path, made several circuits in the darkness before coming in to land.

Everything going swimmingly, I was on my final approach and observing the line of goose-necks flatten out quickly and obligingly when there came an almighty '*whump*' from underneath as the county of Angus rose up and dealt me a staggering blow which sent the aircraft fifty or more feet into the air. Stupefied with surprise and shock, I hung onto the control column like a drunk to a lamppost as the aircraft, through no skill of mine, floated into the glare of the Chance light to touch down with the gentle stroke of an artist's brush. As I raced on into the night, I managed to keep the aircraft straight – but only just!

Ten minutes later, still shaking, I was in the flight hut signing up when Betty appeared at my side.

'That was a very nice landing, ' he observed quietly. 'I lost you for a moment, just before you touched down.'

Lost me! He nearly had, and for good! My first landing had been in the next field!

A week later, I was suddenly called to the Station Adjutant's office. In my best blue, if I pleased! Wonderingly, I obeyed and soon found myself outside the Station Commander's room in company with an unsmiling Station Warrant Officer. There was to be a Court of Inquiry I was told sternly and I was there to give evidence. Knowing little about such matters, I took it all very lightly.

When I was marched in, Group Captain Sadler, the Station Commander, was in his golden hat and the office was littered with other officers, all looking very serious. Flight Sergeant Betty was to one side looking thoroughly miserable.

I was asked to describe the events leading up to the collision and did so completely without nerves. After all, I had nothing to hide, had I?

Then, the Group Captain was asking, 'And you were at the controls?'

'Yes sir.'

'And you didn't see the other aircraft?'

'No, sir.'

'Not even when you had taxied into it?'

'No, sir. In fact, not until I had trodden on my own propeller and saw Sergeant Osmond's white face.'

Someone else, incredulously. 'You mean, you couldn't see the aircraft you had just taxied into? What on earth did you think had happened?'

'I had no idea at first. Then I thought I might have taxied into the side of the hangar. Until I saw Osmand's face, that is.'

'The *side* of the *hangar*! But there isn't a hangar.' Amazed glances were exchanged.

'I know that now, but not then. I had never been to Edzell before and it was pretty dark.'

'And you didn't see the other aircraft's navigation lights?'

'No, sir.'

'But we know they were on.'

'I didn't see them,' I insisted. 'Only Sergeant Osmand's face.'

'Just Sergeant Osmand's face!'

'That's right, sir.'

Silence. I was confronted by blank and puzzled frowns.

Then, did Flight Sergeant Betty wish to question me? Betty, looking miserable, resignedly shook his head.

Silence again. And glances. It had been all too much for my interrogators. I was shown the door, leaving them baffled.

I was not asked to make any further contribution to the Inquiry, nor did I hear the result. Within days, I had forgotten all about it and, indeed, the incident itself. After all, it had had nothing to do with me! Had it, now?

Fifteen years later, I ran into Betty, who was then a Squadron Leader at RAF Abu Sueir in Egypt. After introducing myself to him and his wife one night at the officers' club, we were able to laugh about the occasion although I suspected even then he remained pretty sore about his treatment. Being a long-serving airman and knowing the ropes, after being censured he had apparently demanded an interview with his Air Officer Commanding. He did not get his interview but he was suddenly commissioned, which he regarded as some sort of back-handed apology.

A nice, nice man. Unfortunate, too. Years later, we became good friends and corresponded frequently until his death in December, 1995, at which time he was approaching ninety.

The days passed. We continued to fly hard. The Intermediate phase of our Course drew to a close.

We also became 'experts' in navigation, armament, theory of flight, engines and airframes, and the business of servicing aircraft. And, Morse Code!

Required to send and receive eight words per minute, we struggled away with our 'dits and dahs', flashing messages to each other across the airfield by Aldis lamp. Pendal, who had been so successful with the ladies' knickers at Bexhill, couldn't do Morse Code to save his life.

A good pilot, it was his Achillies heel. Finally, he and a friend on the

Course, named Southern, hit upon a plan which produced the right answers 'an easy way' until Pendal was caught out amid a lot of fuss.

With blue eyes wide with concern, he confided in me, 'It's just no good, old chap. I simply can't cope with the stuff.'

I sympathised, feeling much the same about the Vickers gun.

We were surrounded by Vickers and Lewis guns, both First World War weapons, with never a Browning in sight. If we were to fire Brownings in our Spitfires and Hurricanes, we argued, what was the point in mucking about with the Vickers?

Our protests cut no ice, however. With everyone else, I was obliged to strip and re-assemble the Vickers machine gun until, with hands and uniform liberally besmirched with oil, I could do it blindfolded, my head buzzing with details of muzzle velocities, rates of fire, breech-blocks, sears, retainers, keepers and springs, and much else besides. I recall there were four recognised stoppages on the Vickers, all of which we were taught to indentify and clear.

And, given a set of tools for the purpose! Imagine, I thought, fiddling about in the middle of a dogfight, dismantling the guns! And what happened if they were tucked away in the wings?

From time to time, we had oral and practical examinations on pretty well everything with most of us doing tolerably well. However, I always had the uncomfortable feeling that we were concentrating on information and methods more suited to 1918 and the Sopwith Camel!

But, there were other more relaxing moments.

One weekend, with a group of others, I went by train to Aberdeen. There, I was introduced to hard drink for the first time, and to girls, not quite for the first time!

Unusually, we were obliged to fly on that particular Saturday morning, having fallen behind in our programme, so that we did not set off until late afternoon, arriving in the Granite City in unrelieved darkness. After being bear-led through pitch-black streets for most of what remained of that evening and night, I had only a vague idea of where we were, which way I was pointing, or where even our hotel was situated.

After a comparatively uncomplicated start, confusion in my mind developed as, in a perpetual fog of blue cigarette smoke and whisky fumes, we proceeded from restaurant to cinema to dance-hall, each venue separated by either a ride in a tram or endless traipsing through a labyrinth of dark and unidentifiable streets, arm in arm and in the best of voices. Finally, feeling not very well at all, I found myself in a house on the outskirts of the town in the company of one of my colleagues and two young women.

The young lady who was hanging grimly on to my arm was, I have to admit, very presentable and had the most engaging of Scottish accents. After a time, addle-brained as I was, I became aware of glances being exchanged and to my mild concern, my colleague with his partner disappeared so that only two of us remained. The girl and I exchanged meaningful looks. Now somewhat alarmed, I was not sure what was expected of me, added to which I was feeling profoundly ill. So I sank down on the settee – and waited!

My partner, on the other hand, clearly knew what *she* had in mind. Complaining that it was hot and would I be upset if she removed some of her clothes, I found myself nodding weakly, swallowing rapidly meanwhile to keep down an eruption of bile – at that point, I was almost beyond caring whether the girl lived or died. In a fog of whiskey fumes, I clearly remember half-reclining on the settee, sweating profusely and trying desperately to focus on the swaying ceiling. Oh God! if only the room would keep still!

When next I opened my eyes, I became aware of the lady being close at hand, smiling, and that a pale, plumply dangling object with a pink bullseye in the middle was within a foot of my face. Being an only child and having previously had very little 'hands on' experience of the female form, the sight of this provocative object looming ever closer concentrated my mind most wonderfully. What was I supposed to do now? Would I be expected to take off my clothes, too? If so, what about my clod-hopper boots and my most unglamorous braces? Besides being a non-smoker and unaccustomed to strong drink, I had a powerful sense of the proper!

Dimly, I heard my partner breathe, 'Go on! Kiss it!'

Kiss it! I was thrown into confusion. Something that size, where did I start? Even so, from my semi-recumbent position, I half-rose to bestow a chaste peck on the smooth white flesh.

Immediately, I heard a faint, disgusted snort. 'Not there, silly. Here!' The pink bullseye, now entering into the spirit of things, was pushed in my direction.

The next moment, however, was critical. As my partner leaned closer to make it easier for me, she placed one hand on my stomach and inadvertently *pressed*!

That did it. It was like a small atom bomb being dropped into the seething crater of a grumbling volcano. The human lava from below rose in an unstoppable stream and, galvanised into action, I pushed the lady aside and tottered towards a closed door I hoped was the lavatory. Alas, the first was to the broom cupboard but the second led to the WC. I sank to my knees embracing it and gave it the full contents of five hours of unaccustomed debauchery. Faintly, I heard a female voice outside. 'Are you all right, Joe?' And even in that ghastly moment of distress, I remember being smugly thankful. Thank God she did not know my real name. I hadn't been that silly!

Ten minutes later, when I had recovered sufficiently to make an appearance, the good lady was fully dressed and standing by the mantel-shelf looking very boot-faced. Clearly, she had given me up as useless and within moments had pointed out that it was pretty late. I took the hint and left.

In the street below, it was pitch black and I had no idea where I was or even which way to turn. It was too dark to consult my watch but I guessed it was something after 2 a.m. More by instinct than conviction, I turned left and began to walk. I hoped it was towards the city. There was not a person in sight.

An hour later, and still in a maze of roads and houses, I heard the whistle of a steam engine and headed towards it. I remembered that the railway station was somewhere near my hotel but also the docks and hoped fervently that I would not fall into the water somewhere. When I finally reached the station, I eventually found a solitary chap with a peaked hat who was obviously very surprised to see me and at first gave me the impression that he thought I was a spy – everyone was very spy conscious at the time. I did not know the name of my hotel but after describing it and discussing where it might be, I set off again. It was by this time something after 3 a.m. and I was stone-cold sober.

Having found my abode within minutes, I recall that it was a splendid but ageing structure, full of marble and tall ceilings. My bedroom on the third floor, I shared with another member of the group. It was vast, with an en-suite bathroom of Romanesque proportions and plumbing reminiscent of the kitchen of the 'Queen Mary'. There was one bed, an enormous double, which I was obliged to share with my companion – I was less fussy in those days about sleeping on my own and anything that was an improvement on the three-biscuit mattress and springless steel contraption provided by the Air Force, was all right with me. Moreover, in my nineteen-year-old innocence, I had never heard of the word homosexual.

Pushing my way through the heavy black-out curtains which shielded the entrance, I made my way to the lift which itself was unique. It had two concertina-type doors which clashed shut with the echoing clang of the main entrance being closed at any one of His Majesty's Prisons. After that, the passengers in the lift would rise majestically through the ceiling like caged monkeys and in full view of the hotel foyer, thereafter proceeding heavenwards having themselves a view of the floors as they slowly shuddered past.

There being no one around and the foyer in deep gloom, I entered the lift and pressed a button. Rising once more with ponderous and shivering deliberation towards the roof, I finally let myself out and walked along a corridor, heavily curtained and lit with the usual five-watt blue bulb, until I came to my room, which I remembered as being second from the end. My companion no doubt asleep, I hoped fervently that he had remembered to leave the door unlocked.

By this time, not only sober but very weary, I was considerate enough to let myself in quietly and, not wishing to turn on the light, tip-toed across the carpet and round the bed to what we had decided earlier would be my side.

The room in total darkness, I heard the regular 'zzzz' of someone sleeping and started to undress, removing my tie, then disposing of my boots and dragging off my trousers. At which point I became aware that there was rather more 'zzzz-ing' than there ought to have been.

The deduction I arrived at immediately, came as something of a shock. The dirty dog! Someone in with him! A flash of indignation. Well, if there was, that would make three of us, because after what I had just been through, I jolly well wasn't going to sleep in the bath!

I spread out my hand to feel for my pyjamas under the pillow and FROZE. It came into contact with something round and deliciously squashy, that part of the female form which, though seldom mentioned in polite society, is often fondled, but only by mutual consent. Lord above! Another one! Aberdeen was knee-deep in the things!

There was a strangled gasp in the darkness and after some explosive squeaks and grunts, a light was snapped on.

The lady, on whose breast I had just laid a hand, was sitting up in bed with terrified eyes, clutching the counterpane to her exposed parts, whilst beside her was a man I had never seen before. With a moustache!

Equally astonished and pop-eyed, the man croaked thickly, 'Who the hell are *you?*'

I stood there with bare legs and my trousers in a heap, feeling very exposed and very silly. I was in the wrong room, wasn't I? Well, I had to be! But, what to do about it? Apologise? Laugh it off? Or just run for it?

I said limply, 'I'm very sorry. There seems to be some mistake. Either you are in my bed or I'm in the wrong room.'

The man was not disposed to discuss the matter. 'Why don't you *bugger off*!

'Look, I'm sorry.' I stooped to collect my belongings. 'Really, I am.'

'*Bugger off*! The man threatened to climb out of bed but changed his mind. I suspect he was not wearing his pyjama trousers.

I left them to it – whatever it was.

Outside in the corridor, with screwed up eyes I examined the room number in the blue glimmer of the five-watt bulb. It said it all. Right room, wrong floor!

I leaned weakly against the wall before sinking to the floor. Reaction setting in, I shook with strangled laughter until I felt quite sick again. No one, but *no one*, would ever believe this. Not in a thousand years, they wouldn't.

Back at Montrose the following Monday, there were some sidelong glances and knowing grins. I heard someone say, 'It's the quiet ones you have to keep an eye on, by George!'

Our Intermediate Training Course finished on 8 March and 603 Squadron celebrated the occasion by shooting down a Heinkel 111 a day or so before.

A new course arrived, including some familiar faces from Manchester, and preparations went ahead for their introduction to the new Miles Master trainer aircraft which had been flown in beforehand and on which most ITS instructors had been familiarising themselves. The new aircraft looked terribly smart and had variable-pitch, three-bladed propellers, retractable wheels, boosted engines – I was not too sure what that meant precisely! – flaps, and a mass of other modern gadgets. I talked my way into the cockpit of one of them and was tremendously impressed; after the Hart, it was like sitting at the keyboard of a mighty Wurlitzer organ!

Less exciting was the news that of the forty sergeants on the outgoing course, only one had been awarded a commission, and of the fifteen on Harts, only one had definitely been posted to a fighter squadron. The alternatives to fighters, apparently, were torpedo-bombers – whatever they were – and target-towing aircraft, the latter Hawker Henleys in the main. Target towing! What a way to end up!

I had a brief final flight with the Chief Flying Instructor, which passed off uneventfully, and carried out my 'passenger test' by taking up an Aircraftman Russell for twenty minutes. It was the first time I had ever been airborne with a passenger; those so favoured, besides earning themselves twenty cigarettes, seeming to enjoy the experience, our only demand of them being that they deposited the contents of their stomachs over the side and not into the rear cockpit or down our necks if sickness got the better of them.

The significance of the end of ITS was that we were considered fully trained to fly Service aircraft and could now wear the flying badge. However, we learned that there would be no formal presentation, no certificate, no ceremony of any sort, not even an entry in our logbooks – nothing! If we wished, we could draw two pairs of wings from stores, which few people did, preferring to purchase instead the padded variety from the shop in Montrose which altered our uniforms and sewed creases in our trousers. Each of us on No.15 Course had creases sewn in his trousers!

I gilded the lily by buying some wool and picking out the crown of my wings in red. Laboriously, sitting on my bed, with the aid of a needle and a much protruding tongue.

It was a great if uncelebrated occasion. We all felt terribly proud –

dashing blades in fact. Walking round the town in our new finery; without greatcoats, of course, and positively encouraging pneumonia.

What was more, we had three days off. Acceptable, but not quite long enough for me to get home and back.

6

Montrose – The Final Weeks

During the advanced stage of our training, the objective was to introduce us to the practices employed in the operational squadrons – formation flying, air gunnery and bombing, with additional exercises in navigation and battle-climbing. Introduce us, no more than that. But, our period of pure flying was over; we were now real live pilots!

Having moved across to the north side of the airfield, we began flying the Hawker Audaxes, the Furys, to our regret, having been flown off to Hullavington some weeks before to make way for the new Masters.

The Audax, the Army Cooperation member of the Hart family, was much the same as the trainer Hart except that there was no provision for a second pilot, an observer/navigator being carried instead. It also differed in that each had a forward-firing Vickers gun with its associated ring-and-bead and Aldis sights, racks for four small bombs, and an exhaust pipe which ran along the side of the fuselage and was handily positioned to jerk the pilot into life if he inadvertently put his hand on it whilst the engine was running. There was also a camera-gun situated on one wing and provision for a Williamson camera-gun, which looked like a Lewis gun, on a Scarff mounting in the back cockpit.

Docile, agreeable to fly and reliable, the Audax was a wonderful toy. In terms of performance, there was little to chose between any member of the Hart family so that we still flew around at a sober 125 mph, or thereabouts. Except when dive bombing, that is, which was altogether different.

There was a much more relaxed atmosphere in the Advanced Squadron. We had a new set of instructors, mostly senior N.C.Os., my own flight being commanded by Flight Lieutenant Fenton, whom I was to meet later at RAF Kenley as a Group Captain, and the squadron as a whole by Squadron Leader Verdon-Roe, a renowned name in British aviation.

And it was soon after we had started flying in our Audaxes, that I came as near to being sick in an aircraft as I have ever been.

Each student was obliged to act as observer on one long-range cross-country trip and, it becoming my turn, equipped with all the navigator's paraphernalia – instruments, maps, chartboard, pencils, et al – climbed into the rear cockpit carrying my chest parachute. Unlike the pilot's seat parachute, that of the observer was separate and normally stowed away down one side of the rear cockpit, the chap in the back – if he had any sense – tying himself to the floor using a 'monkey tail' hooked to a 'D' ring on his parachute harness; this enabled him to stand up, operate the gun in the back, if need be, and move round without fear of being pitched out if the pilot indulged in any unheralded manoeuvres. There was also a small seat which, again, could be folded away when not in use.

My pilot on that occasion was my taxiing-accident colleague. Sergeant Osmand who, no doubt wishing to impress me with his expertise, did a split arse take-off, during which I was appalled to see all my instruments and equipment become airborne before disappearing into the gloomy hole below and behind me. After rapping him on the head and giving him a piece of my mind, I removed my monkey-tail, got down on my hands and knees, and attempted to crawl around in the back in an effort to retrieve my possessions.

It was not very nice down there and, with everything vibrating as well as gloomy and dirty, I had no success. Moreover, being so tall, I was hardly able to move far less turn around. Almost unbelievably, the observer, in his capacity as bomb-aimer on low level sorties, was expected to crawl forward and lie, full length, peering through a hole in the fuselage bottom before dropping the bombs at the appropriate time. In this position, he found himself under the pilot's seat, not far removed from the engine which would be howling its heart out above his head, and in full possession of every noisome item of nastiness the engine and airframe could between them produce.

Back again in the rear cockpit, I had no means of assisting my colleague so he was obliged to carry out the 220-mile triangular cross-country as best he could. Meanwhile, I sat on my stool, facing backwards, supremely bored, with nothing to do other than watch the tail wander up and down, left and right.

After a time, not surprisingly, I felt distinctly unwell and was only saved from the ultimate disgrace by turning round, placing my head alongside that of my companion and persuading myself that I was flying the aircraft.

For quite some time we had been looking forward to a brief spell of leave over Easter. It came as a great disappointment, therefore, when I discovered that I would be on duty in the Watch Office over the holiday. All course pupils in turn were obliged to put in a twenty-four hour stint as Duty Pilot and it was sheer bad luck that mine coincided with Easter. As consolation, however, I was promised 'time off in lieu'.

Some days prior to Easter, I went down with a monstrous head-cold. Snuffling, dripping, and miserable beyond belief, I took to my bed one early evening, only to be rudely wakened at midnight with the bellowed instruction to rise, dress immediately, and be prepared to disperse aircraft. There had been an air-raid warning and the whole station was on an alert.

I protested weakly, croaking from my bed of sickness that I was probably dying. But, I received no sympathy at all. If I were determined to die, my tormentor informed me, it was better that I died on the airfield doing something useful, instead of being killed, bleating, in my bed.

Thereafter, until 3 a.m., we taxied our Harts, Audaxes and Oxfords through inky darkness to the far ends of the airfield. Dispersal complete, we returned to our beds exhausted, but strangely, with all the excitement, I felt a good deal better. There was, disappointingly, no air raid!

As Duty Pilot over the Easter weekend, I slept and lived in the Watch Office.

The Watch Office was a hut adjoining the Chief Flying Instructor's sanctum on the edge of the aerodrome. It had grown old gracefully and was comfortable in an ancient and decrepit way with a glowing coal fire, telephones, manuals and publications by the score, pistols that fired coloured Very lights, walls covered with maps and charts, meteorological information by the ton, and a comprehensive display of every cloud formation known to man, with their names. I was advised that the CFI was in the habit of testing each Duty Pilot's knowledge of the various cloud types, a piece of intelligence that had me studying the charts assiduously throughout my period of duty. I learned more about clouds that weekend, mostly through fear of being caught out, than I have ever learned since.

The Watch Office was also the home of the 'Airman of the Watch', a dogsbody-cum-office-boy, whose ability to disappear when urgently needed was positively Machiavellian and whose principal tasks were to keep the fire stoked and make endless cups of sweet and usually undrinkable tea, of bull's blood consistency and made with Nestle's condensed milk – 'conny-onny', so called. Countless airmen spent the entire war as 'Airman of the Watch', maintaining a low profile, making tea, and apparently enjoying the experience.

There was heavy mist and rain over that Easter of 1940 and great activity in the North Sea in the form of naval action and mining in Norwegian waters by the Hampdens of Coastal Command, all of which caused something of a stir on the mainland and particularly at Montrose. The goose-neck flare path was lit (almost solely by me!) for most of the hours of darkness to assist straggling, lost, or damaged aircraft, and it was my misfortune that the red obstruction lights on the hangars and elsewhere obstinately refused to work. Throughout both nights the telephone rang incessantly so that I seemed to spend my entire time hunting for the Duty Electrician whose main aim in life, it appeared, was to avoid being discovered.

It was a wearying time. I never once undressed, seldom had time for even a nap, and was alternately soaked and frozen out on the aerodrome or browbeaten in my office. My temper, sorely tried on many occasions, it was probably the first time I appreciated the need and, indeed, the value of military discipline. But, it was a close run thing! I wrote home to my parents: 'In the Bank, I was never allowed to stamp an envelope without supervision. Here, seven months later, I appear to be running the entire Air Force single-handed!'

Such are the fantasies of youth.

I returned by train from three days post-Easter leave in Manchester – overnight both ways, needless to say – to find my course-mates busy on air gunnery 'quarter attacks'. Shortly to go down to West Freugh to practise firing with live ammunition against airborne targets, it was necessary for us to learn the technique of attacking other aircraft, using camera-guns.

We operated in pairs, curving towards each other in turn, pressing the trigger on the spade grip of our control column but taking only pictures instead of despatching bullets. It was much more difficult than we had imagined and the films were very discouraging. We did it again and again with gradually improving results. The trick lay in gauging the distance, judging accurately the curve of pursuit, and firing within range. I found the old ring-and-bead sight difficult to use and we were forbidden to use the Aldis. The exercise as a whole was not the greatest of successes and left most of us dissatisfied. No wonder the aces of the First World War in their Camels and SE5s fired from dead astern and at ranges from twenty to fifty yards! Even employing their uncomplicated methods, I doubted that I was ever likely to hit anything!

After that, there was air-to-ground firing at targets in Lunan Bay, a pleasant but deserted inlet a few miles south of Montrose. It being the first time we had been allowed to fire our single, forward-facing Vickers machine gun using live ammunition, it was something of an event.

After one instructional sortie, each of us was let loose on the range, diving down to within 250 feet of the ground and, making sure that there was pressure in the Constantinesco system which arranged for the bullets to fire between the propeller blades and not through them, we pressed the trigger on the control column. Instantly, the gun would begin to chatter and vibrate, the belt links would whirl away into space, and the stink of cordite would rise excitingly to the nose. Noise, vibration and smell – no wonder air fighting was such a thrilling business!

However, like everything else to do with marksmanship, it wasn't easy. The target would sway in and out of centre on the old ring-and-bead sight, there would sometimes be quite violent air currents low down which jogged our Audaxes off course, and besides ricocheting bullets, there was always the urgent need to keep a gimlet eye on the ground as it rushed up to meet us – fly too low, and you were sent home like a shot! I was always a bit disappointed, too, with the effect of a single gun; it made such a miserable splash when – and if! – the bullets hit the target. Even at that stage of my career, it seemed to me essential that I should be firing at least eight!

We carried out our dive bombing in the Montrose basin, the targets being sited in the middle of the mud-flats. I flew first on a demonstration flight with a Sergeant Clarkson, a pleasant youngish fellow, and we climbed up in a Hart trainer to 5,000 feet.

Approaching the target, we waited until we were almost directly overhead and it had disappeared beneath the intersection of the bottom wing and the fuselage, before pulling up steeply, turning over, and *diving*!

It was THE most thrilling exercise. With the nose tucked down so that I was standing on the rudder pedals, it seemed that we were going down vertically – at times over the vertical! The speed mounted rapidly, the needle on the airspeed indicator winding quickly around the clock – 200 – 250 – 300 mph. The slipstream screamed in the wires and the wings seemed almost to bend. Faster still – almost 310! Heavens! The ground advancing rapidly, growing magically in the gunsight like the villain in a cartoon film, the target swaying tantalisingly in and out of centre.

Clarkson was screaming: 'Hand on bomb release! Ring-and-bead only; on *no account* use your Aldis! Now... *raise* your nose. Then, as the target disappears... *drop* your bombs!' My left hand snapped the lever through its notched gate, our non-existent bombs fell away and the aircraft groaned and strained as we pulled out, the blood draining from my eyes, leaving my sight grey and indistinct. Then we were racing above the mudflats, our shadow streaking along beside us. And climbing, the ground slowing as we surged skywards. Up! Up! Like a leaping salmon! Marvellous! Magnificent! I was excited and thrilled. Dive-bombing was *super*! Absolutely *wonderful*!

We climbed up and did it again, this time with me at the controls, after which we went home. Yes, I was all in favour of dive-bombing. The next time would be in earnest. In an Audax and with bombs. The real thing!

Later that morning, with eight-pound practice smoke bombs, I had my first dive-bombing trip – solo!

Approaching carefully, I watched the target disappear as briefed... pulled up... turned over... and *dived*!

It was exactly as before. Going down vertically. Faster! Faster! The wires screamed. 300 on the clock. The ground surging towards me. NOW'.

I pulled up slowly. The target disappeared under the nose. My hand tightened on the bomb release. First notch. *Pull*! But, nothing happened! I pulled harder. No good. The damn thing was stuck! *Stuck*! The ground coming up at me like a train. Almost in the cockpit! *Pull out*! I heaved. Oh, God! Was I going to make it? J-u-u-u-u-st! Lord above! Mud and water just feet away but now rocketing skywards. I looked angrily at the bomb release, wanting to beat it to death. Why on earth hadn't it worked?

I climbed up and tried again. Four times! But managed to get off only two of my bombs. Returning to the aerodrome, I complained bitterly that the release was not working properly. We tried it on the ground. It operated perfectly.

However, my face was saved. It was a well-known fault, apparently. At 300 mph, with the wings bending and everything stretching, sometimes the wire from the Heath Robinson bomb-release mechanism tightened to the point when it became impossible to move the lever in its notched quadrant. And all the time with the aircraft hurtling towards the ground. Some system!

Later, with more experience, I did rather better and achieved some good results. Things were not so bad after all.

A Flying Officer had been attached to our Course at the commencement of the Advanced stage. He was from an Auxiliary squadron and among fifteen rather uninhibited VR sergeants, something of a rose among thorns. We did not, I fear, regard him very highly and most of us were not sufficiently mature to hide our feelings.

One day, as we paraded in the morning, we were surprised to find him Orderly Officer and, as such, in charge of the parade.

We formed up, marched on, and waited for the routine of prayers, inspection, march past, then dismissal to proceed.

Our new member stood before us not too confidently. We came to the prayers and to the point when he should have instructed the Roman Catholics and Jews to fall out. To our astonishment, the young man screamed, 'Fall out the Presbyterians and Non-Conformists!'

Stunned silence! Then, titters in the ranks. But, it didn't really matter; the Roman Catholics and Jews fell out anyway.

I am reminded of this incident as our Flying Officer was about as successful at dive-bombing. He never seemed able to release his bombs in the dive and, still struggling manfully with the toggle in its notched quadrant, would invariably let them loose on the pull-out and climb, with the result that his became exercises in toss-bombing. To the consternation of the local populace, I might add. Indeed, it was alleged, apocryphally no doubt, that the farmers bordering the Montrose basin used to telephone the aerodrome and, learning that Flying Officer 'X' was on the programme, would take the day off and melt into the foothills!

Poor man! Most of us are good at something, but being a fighter pilot, to use a modern expression, did not appear to be his scene.

There was also the story of a young man on a previous course who, during his dive-bombing exercises, had neglected on one occasion to ensure that the wooden elevator locks, there to prevent the controls flapping about in a high wind, had been removed. After climbing up and making two almost suicidal dives on the target, he had returned to complain that his aircraft seemed rather heavy on the controls. Heavy on the controls! Thereafter, apparently, he was always referred to as 'Muscles'.

Yes, dive bombing exercises resulted in much laughter from time to time.

The days passed, the weather improved and we flew hard – more air-to-air attacks against a drogue; battle climbs to 15,000 feet (which was as high as we were allowed to go without oxygen; indeed, at this stage of the war I had never even *seen* an oxygen mask!); formation take-offs (very dicey, those, but fun); blind take-offs under the hood (Oh, Lord! Must we?).

And, of course, low-level bombing, which I came to do well, with repeated hits on the target and many near misses.

Having by this time fired our Vickers guns on numerous occasions, we began to grow accustomed to the gun's shortcomings. Located about knee high on the left-hand side of the cockpit, the back of the weapon was within touching distance. I knew then why our masters made the gun so accessible – the pilot spent most of his time keeping it in action!

It was all 1918 stuff. On pressing the trigger on the spade grip of the control column, the gun would clatter away noisily, then almost invariably – *stop*! Oh, Lord! What now? The Constantinesco system working? I would check that there was pressure in the interrupter circuit and that the handle in the cockpit was in the *up* position. Still not working? Was it number one, two, three, or four stoppage? But, who gave a hoot! Just pull back the cocking lever and try again. Then, if it didn't work, to heck with it! Back home we go.

Even so, the guns did work from time to time and I began to hit the drogue repeatedly on astern attacks, on one occasion, with twenty-one bullets out of 100! I was becoming a real Mickey Mannock, no less!

Towards the middle of April, the Germans invaded Denmark and Norway and there were all sorts of goings-on in the North Sea. There were rumours galore and a marked increase in air activity in our area. The three-aircraft section of Spitfires at Montrose was constantly taking off and landing and bombers and mine-laying aircraft – Hampdens in the main – began to appear, sometimes in groups of up to a dozen.

What was happening? We didn't know exactly, not in any way worried, just interested. Then on 16 April, nine Hampdens limped into Montrose from Norway on their way back to Lossiemouth. There was a rumour that things were not going at all well and that there were plans to evacuate us to Aldergrove – Abingdon – Canada – Egypt, even! But it wouldn't involve us, surely? – the end of the course was already in sight. And nothing very much was happening in France, anyway. Even the Army wasn't singing that diabolical song about hanging out their washing on the Siegfried Line!

We also began to see – and hear! – more of the new Harvards from Kinloss – dreadful, screeching, noisy aircraft. With their ungeared engines and the din their propellers created, when they took-off everyone in Montrose went to earth! The American aircraft, Harvards and Hudsons, were killing people, too. A pilot couldn't take liberties with them, by George! Try to glide them in on approach, as we were able to do in our Harts and Audaxes, and they would stop flying immediately, and spin. Nasty brutes!

The first real rumour of commissions spread around. Thirteen of the Course were invited to meet the Chief Ground Instructor, to have their records checked, it was said. But the thirteen knew better and returned, tapping their noses and commiserating with those of us who had not been called forward. I was very glum.

Then, in a matter of days, I and others were also asked to meet the CGI, and this time there were no bones about it, it was a commissioning interview. I had had the answer to every conceivable question well rehearsed for months and everything went well. I liked the CGI anyway – a pleasant schoolmasterish man – so the meeting was in no way an ordeal.

After which, I was instructed to see the Officer Commanding the Advanced Squadron. Squadron Leader Verdon-Roe did not appear to be a very jolly or even a popular figure, although I knew of him only distantly and from the standpoint of a student pilot. But he was very civil to me. We went through all the customary points and I was able to impress him, I thought, with my sports record. I left, quietly confident that he approved.

The next step was more formidable. Thirteen of us were interviewed by a Board consisting of the Commanding Officer, Group Captain Sadler, the CGI, and Verdon-Roe again. The meeting was unremarkable. With me, they were quietly friendly – no reference to my taxiing accident, thank heavens! – and I left, a little nervous but happy that I had not made an ass of myself.

After that, there were several days of silence.

Then, one of six, I was summoned to Sick Quarters for a medical. What, another medical?

I seemed to be having one every six weeks and was beginning to think there was something wrong with me!

The Senior Medical Officer was a very polished and urbane Scottish gentleman called MacGregor, who was a great 'tribal' dancer and went to great lengths to see that everyone else was too. He had organised a series of dancing lessons throughout our time at Montrose but I had never plucked up sufficient courage to attend. As I faced him, I wished I had been more enterprising and sociable.

But, he was affability itself and I sailed through all the tests without a hitch.

More days of silence, then a quiet hint over the bush telegraph that those of us who had been given medicals would shortly be required to go down to Cranwell to meet the Air Officer Commanding. But, it was no more than a hint. I wrote to my parents telling them of my good fortune but impressing upon them not to hang out the flags – yet.

After which, silence. A much longer silence this time.

After my Aberdeen 'experience', I, and others, had fallen into the habit of visiting Dundee. We would set off on the bus, a relaxed voluble crowd after our midday meal on Saturday to stay until Sunday evening, putting up usually at the Royal British Hotel. As we approached Dundee, running down the coastal road, I never failed to be lifted to almost ecstatic heights by the silver gleam of the sea to our left, the crystal clarity of the atmosphere, and the brilliant greens and the rolling fairways of the golf courses.

It was there that I met a sloe-eyed young lady named Janet – Janet Robertson – a farmer's daughter from Wormit, across the River Tay. Besides her undoubted female allure, Janet had that seductively soft and gentle Edinburgh accent I found so captivating.

Having spent one Sunday together on some trivial but pleasant pursuit, in an excess of gallantry I offered to accompany her back to Wormit. If we caught the 10.20 p.m. train from Dundee, I could see her to her home (which she described lightly as being a few yards from the station), before returning to Dundee on the last 'puffing billy'.

Hand-in-hand and almost the only passengers in the local stopping train, we sat in a corner as it curved towards the long Tay railway bridge and, after crossing the river, which took quite a time, we alighted at the first stop on the southern side, Wormit. Two of us. Alone. And in pitch-blackness, which was very cosy.

It took about twenty minutes for us to stroll 'the few yards' to her farmhouse home, invisible in the darkness. Finally, we exchanged a chaste kiss and with a final touch of hands, I left her and began to walk, then jog, back down the country road to the station.

With barely 100 yards to go, I heard a brief, distant whistle in the darkness and the accelerating puff of an engine. I stopped in surprise. My train? It couldn't be. There were five minutes at least before it was due. Horrified, I began to run before fairly racing onto the platform to see the faint glimmer of a red light disappearing into the distance.

A man was hurrying about in the darkness, whistling and carrying a swinging lantern. I shouted to him.

'That wasn't the train for Dundee, was it?'

He confirmed that it was in no very concerned tone of voice.

'Not the *last* one?'

'Ay!'

'But it's not supposed to *arrive* for another three minutes!' I heard the hysterical note in my voice.

'Och, weel. If th's no passengers hereabouts, we let it go, y'know. No sense 'n keep'n it.' The man wagged his head, full of reasonableness.

Aghast, I screamed, 'But I'm supposed to be *on* that train. It shouldn't have left! When's the next one into Dundee?'

'Th's nae one the noo, t'l five-thirty.'

'*Five-thirty*! Tomorrow? But, what am I supposed to do now?'

The man began to move away, attending to his own business. He cried unhelpfully over his shoulder, 'Y'll have te stay hereabouts. Nothin' else for't'.

And I was left. In the blackness. Watching the remaining few glimmers of light disappear one by one.

The enormity of my problem began to dawn. Where was I supposed to stay in Wormit where there appeared to be about three houses? – in fact, never having seen the place in daylight, there could even be less! And even if I did find somewhere, how could I possibly get back to Montrose for early morning parade and perhaps the first flight on the programme?

I sat on the station in the darkness. In despair. And thought. With the commissioning business in full spate, I couldn't afford to put up a black. No, somehow, I would *have* to get back. Then, an idea. Brought up in an environment of railways, I was perfectly at home walking on the permanent way; as a child in Liverpool, my father had often taken me to visit the engine sheds 'across the lines' at Bank Hall, Edge Hill, and even Southport. I could walk! Yes, that's what I would do, I'd walk! Across the Tay Bridge, and, if I couldn't climb off the track somewhere, into Dundee station itself. A heck of a walk, though. Quite a few miles, and dangerous, too, as there seemed to be some sort of junction within yards of Wormit station. Moreover, from there and over the bridge, I would be on the main Dundee to Edinburgh line and there would be no shortage of trains on that! But first, I would have to wait until the porter-cum-station master departed.

Five minutes later, I jumped down onto the track and set off, keeping to the sleepers but stumbling every now and then in the darkness. From time to time, I would have second thoughts. What on earth was I doing? Fancy being killed on a railway line, of all places. My parents wouldn't be at all pleased.

Negotiating some points beyond the station, I set off for the bridge, invisible in the darkness, my confidence growing by the minute. A couple of hours and I'd be there. There might not be any buses immediately, but at least I would be on the right side of the river for the early morning. Conveniently putting aside the problem I would face if a train overtook me on the bridge, I reasoned that I was on my way and one problem at a time was quite enough.

I had gone about 400 yards when, out of the blackness and from a distance of only a few yards, there came a shout.

'*Halt*!'

I nearly died.

The voice again, almost a treble. '*Halt*! Don't ye move now!'

I didn't move. Not a muscle.

I called back uncertainly, 'Friend!' There were shuffling steps in the dark and I sensed that whoever had called was a good deal more scared than I was. And I was not far wrong.

The smallest figure imaginable appeared out of the blackness, shivering with fright. About a yard away and reeking of fag-ends, the man reiterated in a shaky voice, 'Don't ye move now.'

I assured him that I had no intention of moving and the small figure, holding a rifle and seeming uncertain as to what to do next, fumbled about in the dark, presumably hunting for a torch or light.   For an instant, I thought of offering to hold his gun whilst he did so and found myself grinning then wanting to giggle.

Then a match flared and I saw the pinched and alarmed face of a tiny, elderly man in a tin hat and woollen Balaclava helmet. He was shaking so much that I thought his rifle would drop.

The match went out.

'Who are ye?'

I told him.

'Ye're no' supposed to be here, y' know. On the brudge.'

I explained my predicament and there was a silence.

Then: 'Awa' then back! I'll follow ye. And dinna move now! I'm b'hind ye!' Suddenly, he seemed full of courage.

I sighed. What was the use? I turned and headed back.

Alongside the track, just short of the station, we stopped at a hut. I was led inside, the bright light searing my eyes, to what appeared to be a cross between a very old kitchen in total disarray and a Crimean War bivouac. There were several mattresses on the floor with bedclothes heaped in wild confusion, a few wooden chairs, scattered items of Army clothing, unwashed cups and plates, jars and open tins of this and that, a fire-blackened kettle, and a powerful odour of body and feet mingled with the rank stench of some foul-smelling pipe tobacco.

There were two occupants, both elderly, one sitting on the floor in his underwear of khaki shirt without a collar, grey 'combs' and with bare feet. In his face was stuck a broken pipe about two inches long, from which rose a nauseating blue cloud.

"Ello Sarge!' The one sitting on the floor had no teeth and seemed very affable. I deduced that he was the one 'in command' and he appeared not to be a Scotsman. There was a brief explanation of my presence, after which the gnome with the rifle and tin hat departed – presumably to carry on guarding the bridge – and I was left in the hut with my two new companions.

We exchanged information. The unit, I learned, was an offshoot of the Royal Highland Regiment – the Black Watch – elderly soldiers recruited apparently to perform guard duties on bridges and other sensitive installations. The one with the pipe was a Corporal. He was very glad to see me, he said, and there would be no problem about a bed. He waved a hand towards the chaotic jumble of brown blankets and other coverings on the floor. I could kip there for the night and catch the first train in the morning. Meanwhile, what about a nice cup o' char? Their concern for me was touching.

I examined my so-called bed, frowning and dubious. Unmade, it looked as though the whole Highland Division had just slept in it! Revolted, I kept my feelings to myself and sipped the near undrinkable brown stew I had been handed in a thick, cracked mug.

That night was hideous beyond my wildest expectations. After yarning for some time, the light was extinguished and the two guardians of the River Tay and its bridge settled down on their mattresses. With the greatest reluctance, I removed my boots, tunic and trousers. Nothing else was coming off, by God!

It was like going to bed in the lion house of the London Zoo. My two companions rolled and flung themselves about, snored, muttered, belched and made other unspeakable noises throughout the night. But it was not they alone who kept me awake. Within minutes, I felt the nip of a score of blood-starved denizens of the blankets and for hours scratched and tore at myself as I was assaulted by most of the fleas in the Kingdom of Fife. Wild with discomfort, I seriously thought of getting up and rushing into the night. Naked! Anything was better than being eaten alive!

But I didn't and 5 a.m. came round, finally and thankfully. I rose, declined the tea, bread and jam I was offered and left, unwashed and unshaven, as the first train for Dundee limped, yawning, into Wormit station.

Shortly after 6 a.m., I boarded the bus for Montrose and was mildly surprised to see another Air Force sergeant sitting bleary-eyed in a corner. He was a member of the newly arrived pilot course at Montrose and, strangely, was from my old contingent in Manchester.

He woke sufficiently to register surprise and to ask me what I had been up to. On edge and in no mood to be chatty, I made some surly reply to which he responded with a lewd wink which hinted, not for the first time, that it was the quiet ones you had to keep an eye on!

I arrived back at the airfield as No.15 Course was forming up to march onto the parade ground. Very much aware that I was unshaven and that my buttons were far from sparkling,

I slipped into the ranks unseen. Minutes later, when the Station Adjutant was making his inspection, I prayed that he would not cast too critical an eye in my direction. When our eyes met for the briefest of seconds as he passed down the line, perhaps it was my imagination but I thought I detected the faintest gleam of amusement in his glance.

It had been a close run thing; by George it had!

It was about this time that, on arriving at the Sergeant's Mess for lunch one day, I was greeted by loud laughter and an advancing figure whose face I recognised as one of the three companions with whom I had started my flying career at Barton airfield in 1938.

Dressed very casually in well-worn tunic, roll-neck pullover and flying boots, Sergeant Alan Buck looked as though he had just stepped down from an aircraft after an operational sortie. We greeted each other uproariously, with me just a trifle sheepish as I knew all too well that, having neglected to give it back for more than a year, his driving licence still sat snugly in my breast pocket.

'You old bugger!', was his cheerful shout. 'I've found you at last. D'you realise that I ve just had to fly 500 miles to reclaim my driving licence. I've got the police breathing down my neck and without it, I'm due for the high jump.' Prophetic words indeed, as they proved to be.

A few years older than me, I had formed an easy but close relationship with Alan whilst we had trained together in Manchester. He, with Robert Shaw, a solemn, rather slow-moving young man with the inevitable student pipe, were two of the four posted to No.5 FTS at Sealand when we had gathered so memorably at the Town Centre on that first day of the war, 3rd September, 1939 – I recalled how I had envied them both at the time. And now here he was, with 43 Squadron at Tangmere, a fully fledged fighter pilot on Hurricanes and looking every inch the experienced warrior. I felt positively humble as I introduced him to my course colleagues.

We discussed, almost riotously, old flying incidents and what had happened to us over the months we had been separated. No, he had not seen Robert Shaw since FTS but Shaw had been commissioned he believed and gone to join No.1 Squadron somewhere. I was greatly heartened. Here were two of my erstwhile mates and they had managed to get themselves into fighter squadrons. Who knew, if God was good, I might be able to emulate their success, the future suddenly looked brighter.

We parted that afternoon in the highest of spirits – but sadly I never saw Alan Buck again. In the late afternoon of Friday, 19 July, a few weeks after I had returned his so important driving licence, he was dead. Shot down by a German fighter in the area of Selsey Bill, he baled out and, seriously wounded, fell into the Channel. The following day, his mutilated body was recovered from the sea.

The mild-mannered Robert Shaw, too, was not to last for long. On 3 September, flying a Hurricane of No.1 Squadron from Northolt, he was posted missing in circumstances never fully explained. Reports suggested that he was shot down somewhere around Maidstone in Kent, the crash being so violent that his remains could not be identified. Such a quiet and pleasant boy, too; I recalled a delightful trip to the Lake District we had made together with two rather special girl friends of mine. Ah, me!

All this was sad, sad news which filtered through to me later. Thereafter, my training days at Barton and even my memories of No.5 FTS, Sealand, seemed somehow less pleasant to dwell upon.

Friday, 26 April. We were due to take off for West Freugh at 9 a.m. – ten Harts and Audaxes – but the weather was vile and we had to hang about kicking our heels until 2.30 that afternoon.

It had been arranged that I should take an Aircraftman Hamilton in the back so I spent some of the time briefing him on how and in what direction he should be sick should that crisis arise, the young man nodding as though I were passing on information vital to his future.

We took off, finally, and formed up.

It was the first time I had flown as part of a sizeable formation and the experience was exhilarating – a wonderful feeling of companionship and freedom coupled with power. I felt that we could have taken on the whole German Air Force there and then.

We flew south-west, cutting obliquely across the River Tay and heading towards distant Glasgow. The clouds were raggedly fierce but broken and the afternoon sun streamed through in great slanting shafts creating vast, irregular pools of light which glistened in endless shades of green, purple, and brown, the mountains to our right rising fearsomely into mist and cloud. A wild, wonderful picture, thrilling even to us, used though we were to the shadowed, endless beauty of the Grampians.

We skirted Loch Lomond and tilted to our left over the Clyde estuary and Greenock before turning south along the Ayrshire coast, the frowning hump of Arran within touching distance. Finally, the promontory and inlet that sheltered Stranraer took shape whilst in the distance, the mountains of the Lake District were painted on the horizon in the palest of pastel shades.

Then West Freugh, the name, strangely, not on any map. From the air, a smooth, irregular oval of rolling meadowland, green and inviting, with a windsock, coloured a bright yellow with black rings, like a wasp. We approached individually to touch down gently on the grass but somewhere in the centre there was a hidden rise which floated our aircraft into the air when we all thought we had made perfect landings. All around, the atmosphere was damp yet crystal clear, visibility a million miles, the air as scented and as intoxicating as the headiest of wines. It was Scotland, positively at its loveliest.

Moments later, we had taxied in – ten blurred then flicking propellers – before dismounting, laughing and discussing, then looking about in wonderment. It was like being on the fabled lost plateau; all around were Handley-Page Heyfords, Westland Wallaces, Hawker Henleys, Fairey Battles, and other types I had seldom seen in the flesh. I found myself searching for a Bristol Bulldog, a Bristol Fighter or even a Sopwith Snipe. But, that was asking too much, perhaps. Even so, the week ahead suddenly seemed full of promise. The sun shone brilliantly and I felt part of the old, peace-time Air Force, with war a distant planet away.

We were at West Freugh for two weeks and apart from a day or two of rain and mist, the weather cooperated fully. We flew hard and according to a rigid programme, so that we knew exactly when we were needed and had more than sufficient time off to take the occasional walk into the silence and solitude of the local coastline and countryside, or to play tennis. I was on friendly terms with most of my colleagues but Cecil Parkinson was my constant companion, so easy to get on with, so even-tempered, accommodating and uncomplicated. It was good to have such people around.

Our air firing sorties against the towed drogues, with Hawker Henleys as the tugs, were both demanding and exciting, the more so as the Henley, an offshoot of the Hurricane fighter, was much more modern and faster than our own aircraft and the tug pilots, if they were feeling 'a bit off', could so arrange matters that we had difficulty in catching the drogue far less shooting at it. Even so, most of us soon grew accustomed to the vagaries of the sturdy Vickers and the idiosyncrasies of the towing crews, with the result that our scores improved slowly but regularly. With my one clattering gun I achieved eighteen per cent several times in water attacks and was so smug when, on a later trip, I shot off the drogue – a sheer accident, let it be said – that I was able to preen myself and claim that I had got to the stage of drawing a bead on the wire!

Considering that there were many other aircraft using the ranges and targets, it was a miracle that the overall programme went as smoothly as it did. With no radio communications, we took off at specified intervals, interpreted the ground signals laid out on the mud flats below, then went on our way. With just the occasional hiccup, it must be said.

One morning, I climbed up to take part in the first dive-bombing sortie of the day. Arriving over the target allotted to me, I noted the signal to proceed, made a preliminary pass, before steadying myself for the live run-in.

The target moved towards me and having passed underneath, I reared up, turned over, and *dived*.

Down! Down! The usual thrilling descent, dropping like a stone, wires screaming, the small triangle below wandering about in my sight. Then, with my hand clutching the release and at the point when I was about to drop the first of my bombs, two blossoming eruptions occurred in the sand-flats directly beneath. Two!

Startled, then wonderingly, I pulled away and tried to work things out. I had had my hand on the bomb release, I knew, but I had not actually 'sprung the trap'. And *two* bombs it seemed had fallen off! I had never heard of such a thing. Strange! Very strange!

I climbed up, ran in a second time and started another dive. On this occasions, however, I had not even placed my hand on the release knob when three brown flowers exploded silently but magically beneath me. *Three*! But three were more bombs than I was carrying!

I pulled away immediately, swerving to one side, and looked up. Three Fairey Battles in formation, about 2,000 feet above me, were laying eggs on *my* target and very nearly on *me*! Or... perhaps I was laying eggs on theirs!

I slunk away, collected my wits… then found my own target! Oh, Lord! What had I done? Completing my exercise, I returned to base, signed up, then disappeared into the lavatory – for the rest of the morning! But, no one had complained, it seemed, and nothing was said. Phew!

On 1 May, I was called into the flight office and told that I was required to go down to Cranwell for an interview with the Air Officer Commanding, Training Command. I left immediately in company with Osmand, with whom I had had the taxiing accident some weeks before, and we spent a pleasant if unadventurous day drifting across Scotland then England by train.

We stayed the night at the Trust House Hotel in Grantham and the following morning, with our buttons agleam and our answers prepared, took a bus to the College at Cranwell.

I have little recollection of where exactly we went except, rather to my surprise, we were interviewed not in the College proper but in a wooden hut tucked away behind one of the hangars. Six of us sat in a waiting-room, feeling as though we had dental appointments, after which we were called in individually.

Of all my interviews, this proved to be the easiest. The AOC was a pleasant, smiling man with grey-white hair, and there was just one officer, a Wing Commander, beside him.

I removed my hat, cleared my throat and sat, remembering not to cross my legs.

The AOC continued to smile. Did I have a good trip?

I said that I had … thank you.

It was a long way to come, the AOC observed.

I agreed that it was.

They studied some papers.

And how was the course going?

The Course was fine. Great fun. No complaints at all.

Then a few questions about sports and did I speak French. The AOC was smiling again. Looking. Weighing me up.

And what about my navigation?

Navigation! My face must have registered surprise. What had navigation to do with a commission? Then, before I could prevent myself, a 'silly' dropped from my lips like a discarded pip. 'All right, I think, sir. After all... I got here!'

A moment of pregnant silence. Then, they both laughed. Of course, they seemed to say. Stupid of them to ask!

After which, 'Thank you. That will be all.'

Nothing else? I collected my hat, saluted, and left. I had been with them less that two minutes.

Osmand and I returned on a train that left before midnight and arrived at Stranraer at 4.30 in the morning. It was a brilliantly clear day with everything bright and cool. We wondered how we were to remove ourselves the eight miles to the aerodrome but, there being no one to consult and walking appearing to be the only solution, we set off on foot.

It took us rather more than two hours but we still had time to kill before the first of the instructors arrived at flights at 8 a.m.

The first to appear was Flight Sergeant Munns, a tall, thin, saturnine figure, who, much surprised to see us there, blew down his nose disgustedly.

'You mean you walked the 8 eight miles? You *clowns*! Why didn't you ring for transport?'

Clowns! We could see exactly what *he* thought of the potential officer material in front of him!

Five days later, Osmand and I were again summoned to the flight office. Flight Lieutenant Fenton sat at the one and only desk with Munns and several other N.C.O. instructors gathered informally in the background.

Fenton was studying a paper before him and said with his head down and without preamble: 'You two have got commissions.' He looked up briefly. 'It's just come through.'

Osmand and I exchanged slightly surprised glances and paused before saying, 'Thank you.' And left. There had been no smiles, no congratulations, no roll of drums or heavenly shaft of light, nothing.

Outside the room, we looked at each other.

'Does that mean we're officers now?' I sounded very uncertain.

'I dunno. I suppose so.'

'So, what do we do?'

'Just carry on as before, I suppose. Until we get back to Montrose.'

As we walked off together, I had a mental picture of the faces of most of those in the office, other than Fenton, all senior men with years of service and experience. They were being left behind and it wasn't their fault. Sadly, it showed in their eyes and I felt sorry for them – and embarrassed.

On 9 May, my logbook records that I flew back to Montrose as one of a formation of ten with an LAC Fraser in the back. With other more weighty matters on my mind, I have no recollection of the flight. In Audax K5591, it was my final flight on No. 15 Course; indeed, I never saw another Hawker Hart or Audax again – except in the pages of books!

I had just arrived in my billet in Montrose and, one of several in the hut, was thinking about packing. The Course was over and most members were dispersed around the camp, going through the motions of clearing or investigating their future. Five of us, apparently, had been commissioned – five out of forty! Suddenly, we were five people apart from the rest.

An airman arrived: I was to see the Station Adjutant immediately.

The Adjutant, a burly, pleasant man, was very much a father-figure and seemed anxious to take me in hand. He greeted me with a joke: why wasn't I dressed as a pilot officer?

I remember shrugging. Was I an officer or not? There had been no formal announcement, no signal or letter, nothing but a verbal message some days before. It had been about as momentous as the award of my flying badge. What, in fact, did I do now?

The Adjutant put a friendly arm around my shoulders. I was to come to the officers' mess with him immediately. The Moss Bros, representative was arriving at lunchtime; he almost certainly would have something to fit me.

The Moss Bros rep did, indeed, have most of my immediate requirements but not everything. The Adjutant, standing over me and clucking like a mother hen, supervised my fitting out and decided finally that I should return with the man in his car to Edinburgh, pick up some outstanding articles of clothing, then return by train. After that, he would see that I was sent home, suitably rigged out, if only for a day or two. Suddenly, I was centre stage, everything seeming to be urgent and most important. Clearly, time was of the essence!

It was early evening when we arrived in Edinburgh and, after several drinks in celebration of my new status – courtesy of Mr. Moss and his brothers! – I left two hours later to catch the train for Montrose. Less my hat! Somewhere, somehow, the rep. and I had mislaid – dropped – lost – my forage cap. We searched for it high and low but without success. What did I do now? I was wearing sergeant's uniform and carrying an officer's service dress hat and other bits and pieces in a carrier bag. I couldn't wear both, not at the same time!

Minutes later, I was walking quickly and furtively down Prince's Street in the direction of Waverley station, when two service policemen loomed up out of the night and I was stopped.

'Good evening Sarge!' The spokesman sounded affable but there was more than a trace of steel in his voice. 'We don't seem to be properly dressed tonight, do we?'

I explained that I had lost my hat and was on my way to the station.

The man replied with firm politeness that it was not in order to 'proceed' anywhere without a hat.

I replied that I saw his point but what did he suggest I do about it? I didn't have a hat to wear. I also had to get back to Montrose by train and that it was very urgent. Furthermore, I felt obliged to tell them, I was really... well, I was really an officer! In sergeant's uniform!

The two policemen exchanged glances, then stared. In all their experience, they had never heard *that* one before!

Finally, one of them said, 'We'll have to report this, Sarge. You know that, don't you?'

'Report it to whom?'

'Well... to Montrose. Where you're going.'

'Then, you'll be wasting your time,' I responded smugly. 'I shall have left there by tomorrow.'

A brief silence. 'Left! For where, Sarge?'

'I wish I knew.'

'You don't know?'

'That's right,' I replied. 'I haven't a clue,'

Silence. They were defeated and knew it. Then, one of them grinned. 'All right, Sarge. Best get out of sight as soon as possible. Good night!'

On 10 May, the Germans launched their offensive against Holland, Belgium and France.

The following day, I wrote to my parents:

'Today, I received the last bits of my uniform and am transferring to the officers' mess. Everything is mucked up completely by events on the Continent. Apparently, I was posted to a place called Sutton Bridge in Lincolnshire but owing to the proximity of Belgium and Holland and the war news, it has been cancelled. Now, I don't know what is happening, except that I shall probably be home in a day or so.'

Later that day, the Adjutant drove me to the railway station. No.15 Course had dispersed, only one or two being left on the camp. Travelling to and from Edinburgh and engrossed in the business of clearing and moving to the officers' quarters, I had missed the departure of Cecil Parkinson, Osmand, Jock Nichol and many others who had been my close friends and companions since November and earlier. Within weeks, Parkinson, Pidd, and Plant would be dead, killed in the first weeks of the Battle of Britain, and others would fall in the course of the months to come, until a year later there would only be a handful of us left.

Deciding to try the east coast route for a change, I took the LNER train which, after a more comfortable night than was usually my fate – I travelled first class now that I was an officer – delivered me to York in the small hours of the morning. So, 4 a.m., found me sitting on a chilly platform seat in the half light with my raincoat gathered round my legs, the station buffets and other minor sanctuaries being filled to overflowing by a battalion of infantry with their tin hats, kit bags, reeking fag-ends and odours of body and damply pungent khaki. Above my head, a dimly lit notice-board disclosed that it would be several hours before my connection would leave for Manchester, across the Pennines. There was ample time in which to think but, strangely, my thoughts were less about the war, fighting, and my prospects of survival, but rather of my parents, my friends and my late companions. Suddenly, I felt coldly miserable and quite alone. A page was in process of being turned but what would a new one reveal?

I arrived at Manchester Victoria shortly after 7 a.m., jaded physically but, with the arrival of the morning sun, somehow lifted in spirit and still looking tolerably smart in my new uniform. It was a Sunday, I recall.

I bought a paper. The war had apparently started in earnest. Rotterdam had been heavily bombed and the Huns had broken through at Sedan in France. So much for the much vaunted Maginot Line!

So, what now – and where? I had no idea. But, who cared? I was almost home.

7

249 Squadron: May 1940

I had barely been on leave for twenty-four hours when a telegram arrived. It read: 'Post 79168 P/O T.F. Neil to 249(H) Squadron, Church Fenton, w.e.f. 15 May 40.'

Three interesting facts were thus disclosed: first, my number, which no one had thought fit to tell me; second, that the Air Force was no more considerate than the Bank when it came to giving notice of a move; and third, that Church Fenton was in Yorkshire, although I learned this only after leafing through my old school atlas. The 'H', I deduced, signified Hurricane. Or at least, I hoped so.

I travelled back to Yorkshire by train the following day, arriving at Church Fenton station in the early afternoon. It was brilliantly fine with a few scattered clouds and the countryside breathtakingly beautiful. I stepped down from the carriage with my luggage amid a balmy silence that was almost tangible; all I could hear was the song of a single blackbird and the muted hiss of steam from the engine at the far end of the train. It was warm. Heaven, in fact. Like going away on holiday.

I was one of only several on the platform, two others being Sergeants Arber and Pether, until recently companions of mine at Montrose. Arber, a strange boy, was totally indifferent to the fitness of things. He shouted 'Hello, Tommy!' at the top of his voice and for one anxious moment I thought he would embrace me on the spot. Pether was more restrained.

We compared notes. Pether was joining 249 with me but Arber was to go to another squadron. Seconds afterwards, we had parted and both went out of my life for ever. For some reason, Pether moved on a few weeks later and I did not see him again before his departure. Much, much later, I learned that Arber had died, how and why, I never learned.

I took a taxi to the officers' mess after cautiously enquiring how far away it was – I was still mentally attuned to 18s a week! As we ran alongside the aerodrome, with its limp windsock and ordered symmetry of sun-bathed hangars, painted railings and clipped green verges, I experienced a quite unforgettable thrill. My first Air Force station! There was a quiet Sunday-afternoon atmosphere abroad with no aircraft to be heard or seen other than a single Whitley standing beside one of the hangars. A Whitley! How odd. On a fighter station.

The mess was quiet and cool, as befitted a gentleman's club. In the tall, glazed entrance hall, I was met by a mess servant who took my luggage and led me to a room on the first floor overlooking the gardens. It was large and airy, with two beds, a wash-basin, carpets and chairs, all spotlessly clean, the counterpanes crisply white, the light-brown lino polished to mirror brightness. As the elderly batman disposed of my clothes and equipment, I gazed out over the quiet lawns to the airfield. Then, when a discreet cough attracted my attention, I was informed that tea would be served in the ante-room at 4 p.m.

Minutes later, not too confidently, I ventured downstairs. There were about six officers spread about the ante-room, reading. All were flying officers or pilot officers and several wore black flying boots. A clock ticked. No one spoke. Nothing happened. Being unsure as to what was expected of me, I sat and tried to look inconspicuous. I was astonished to see flying boots in the mess. In the mess! I had already been warned about that, my goodness. Were these chaps 249? They looked so much older.

After a long time, I summoned up sufficient courage to consult a young man spread-eagled in the next chair, reading the *Tatler*. He was a Canadian of 242 Squadron. Two-four-nine? He frowned and looked perplexed. No, he didn't know it. Was it due to arrive?

Arrive! My heart sinking, I replied that it should already be there. My neighbour nodded. Yeah, well, probably a new one forming. Then, having imparted this pearl of intelligence, he rose to his feet and left.

I sat, beginning to worry. Had I come to the right place? But Pether was here, too. Both of us couldn't be wrong! Then, salvation. An older man walked in, a flying officer with an observer's brevet, a DFC, and Mutt-and-Jeff ribbons of the last war. Noticing me, he came in my direction.

'Hello, old son. Are you 249?' He smiled with crinkling brown eyes, the most welcoming and engaging of smiles. 'My name's Lohmeyer and I'm the squadron adjutant. You're one of the first to turn up.' It was like a lifebelt being thrown to a drowning swimmer and I was to be devoted to the man for the next twelve months.

No. 249 Squadron was, indeed, in the process of forming and I was one of the first pilots to arrive. Others appeared in ones and twos the same day, or immediately after – Pilot Officers Lowther, Meaker and Beazley and Sergeants Beard, Smithson and Fletcher. New faces all of them, it was difficult to identify one's own squadron colleagues, the NCO pilots in particular – living apart, it was weeks before I met several of their number. Some, such as Pether, came and left almost unnoticed; others, more senior, were posted in from existing units to provide a nucleus of experience – Kellett, older and an Auxiliary from 616 Squadron, Barton from 41 at Catterick, Nicolson from 72 at Acklington, and 'Dobbin' Young. Soon after came Pilot Officer 'Wotcher' Bayles and Sergeants Main and Boddington, the last named an old Manchester companion. And later still, to my great surprise, the rather striking pilot officer I had seen briefly at Barton before the war, Denis Parnall, now a senior flying officer. And, of course, there was the Commanding Officer, John Grandy, twenty-six at the time, a handsome, slightly portly young man with sleek fair hair, very white teeth and an engaging chuckle.

It was a time of rumour and uncertainty. In every doorway there seemed to be an enquiring face. One thing though was plain and undeniable: the squadron had no aircraft.

Then, there were two surprising developments: we were to move immediately to Leconfield, some thirty miles to the east, and be equipped with Spitfires, *not* Hurricanes. Moreover, the first of our aircraft were to be collected at once.

I went by road to Leconfield, sitting in the cab of one of the larger squadron vehicles, part of a long convoy and driven by a corporal who ground the gears unmercifully en route. I said not a word for the whole journey but at least it enabled me to see, if not to become acquainted with, the bulk of the squadron's NCOs and airmen. It was all new, slightly frightening, but fascinating. I was still a very young nineteen-year-old. With eyes on his cheeks.

No. 249 shared RAF Leconfield with No. 616 Auxiliary Squadron, who flew Spitfires. The airfield then was a large, rolling area of grass, with its inevitable damp patches, set in pleasant but flat countryside, the station itself very new; in fact, several buildings were still incomplete and some of our NCOs were obliged to make do with tents on the airfield. The officers' mess, however, was immaculate and we lived in great style and comfort.

Being the South Yorkshire squadron, 616 were on their home ground. Again, the officers seemed an older, more sophisticated set although their number included one or two noisy extroverts, notably a Pilot Officer Dundas – a tall, ginger-haired youth known as 'Cocky'.

Our number gradually increased as the days and weeks progressed, Pilot Officers King and Crossey arriving with Sergeants Killingback and Davidson – the latter NCO the redoubtable ''Appy 'Arry', with the shark's false teeth and the machine-gun laugh, who had been with me at Bexhill and earlier at Barton. Finally, in mid June, to bring us up to strength, there was a group from the University Air Squadrons who arrived via an Operational Training Unit – Pilot Officers Wells, Barclay, Burton and Fleming, plus several other NCO pilots. In addition to Crossey, Wells and Burton were South Africans, and Barton, who was the flight commander of 'B' Flight, a diminutive Canadian. The other flight commander was Kellett – Ronald Gustave Kellett – a unique individual, of whom more later.

A Fairey Battle had appeared in our midst early on and was used to ferry those familiar with the Spitfire to fetch some of our new aircraft. In twos and threes they were brought back until we had a sufficient number with which to start serious flying.

But first, those of us who had been trained on Harts had to be introduced to low-wing monoplanes and, to this end, two Masters were temporarily attached to the squadron.

I first flew in a Master on 20 May and my instructor was Kellett. Then referred to as 'Boozy' – but not by me, I hasten to add – Kellett, soon to be promoted to squadron leader, was half French and then in his thirties. A rather stout little man with thinning fair hair, prominent pale blue eyes and some of the more obvious manifestations of shyness, Boozy, in contradiction of his nickname, always seemed to me the soul of sobriety. Though physically active, he gave the impression of being totally non-athletic and he was in turn patient, irascible, charming, abominably rude, courteously understanding and disconcertingly dismissive.

A wealthy man by my standards, Boozy was also absurdly generous. A little short of transport in the squadron, he at once produced an ancient Rolls-Royce which he drove everywhere – including the rough grass of the airfield – with cheerful abandon, allowing any of us to do the same. Until, one day, there was a series of sepulchral 'clonks' which were diagnosed as a big-end. Repairs being inevitable, they were undertaken by our own NCOs and airmen – naturally. At that time, such practices were accepted by all as the 'done thing'; an RAF fighter squadron in 1940 was very much a close-knit family affair.

My first efforts in the Master were not impressive. Surrounded by a mass of new-fangled systems, gadgets and instruments, I was almost overcome with the novelty of it all. After take-off, which was shatteringly impressive after a biplane, I would be fiddling with the airscrew pitch when I should have been raising the wheels and, in the excitement of pulling up or lowering the flaps, would ignore every known speed limitation. And so on, if not these, then other elementary errors. Time after time.

In the back, my instructor's patience was sorely tried, particularly when it came to operating the engine. Kellett had no feeling for any engine; the supercharged Rolls-Royce Kestrel was there simply to be used and he did so with a heavy hand, repeatedly banging the throttle through the gate so that the Master kept springing about like a demented gazelle with the engine howling in agonized protest. Finally, limp with emotion, I mastered the procedures and after three short trips, was declared safe if not expert in a modern aircraft. After that, it was the Spitfire. But only on trestles. And in the hangar.

For half a day, I sat in a Spit with a blindfold round my eyes, feeling about in the cockpit for the controls and switches and going through my newly-learned cockpit drill. For several hours, I mentally took off and landed a hundred times, the hydraulics groaning and squealing as I lifted and lowered the wheels, the flaps – which were operated by compressed air – hissing in and out like some large but extremely bored python. Finally, I reported myself fully confident and in the late afternoon of 21 May, went solo.

As I waited a little apprehensively for my first Spitfire to be refuelled and made ready, I was treated to a catalogue of helpful hints by Flying Officer J.B. Nicolson. A tall, rather dishevelled young man with bushy dark hair often resembling a brush, Nick was about four years older than me, and although we had been together less than a week, I had come to know him quite well. In fact, it was difficult not to know Nick quite well. The most congenial character, Nicolson, in the nicest possible way, was a self-confessed expert on pretty well everything. An amusing talker and mimic, he could be wound up and once provided with a drink, was guaranteed to produce good, clean entertainment for an entire evening.

He was speaking to me seriously.

I was not, repeat *not,* to let the engine boil. Understood? Which meant taxying quickly both ways – it was the offset radiator, that was the problem. But not too quickly, mind! The small wheels on the Spit tended to dig in on soft ground and a little too much brake and – *kerpow!* – over she'd go. And even if I didn't go completely arse-over-tit – a rather inelegant phrase, that, to be used only in the proper company – at the very least I would damage the airscrew and probably ruin the reduction gear. So I wasn't to do it! Okay? And I wasn't to forget to jink, either; the view forward was hopeless in a Spit so the nose had to be moved about constantly. Always paid to be careful because anyone who wasn't would be for the chop, double quick! Okay?

On take-off, there'd be a bit of a swing to the left but nothing really nasty. The important thing was not, repeat not, to push the nose forward in order to see what was going on in front. If I did – *kerpow!* – a new propeller, if nothing worse.

But once in the air, she was a dream. No problem. Light on the controls, especially the elevator. Sensitive as hell, that elevator. A chap could bend a Spit with one finger. *One finger!* Oh, and another thing, coming in to land, the hood was not likely to open above 180. Bad design, if the truth were admitted. And, it was no use trying, so I wasn't to frighten myself into thinking the damn thing had jammed. And I was always to take off and land with the hood open, by the way. *Always!*

Otherwise, everything was dead easy. Wheels down below 180, and a curved approach – it had to be curved or I wouldn't be able to see where I was going. (I knew all about that, by gum!) Flaps down at 140 or less. Not above, mind, or they wouldn't come out properly and might even be damaged. About 100 on final approach and 85 over the hedge. Dead easy. Okay? But, careful with the brakes. And, remember, Don't boil the bloody engine! Nick went on and on until there wasn't a hazard that was not explained in every gory detail. My morale began to droop. Flying Spitfires couldn't possibly be this difficult.

I sat in the cockpit, tied down and everything in place, the nose stretching ahead the length of a cricket pitch. Now what did I do? Start the engine. Oh, God! How? I'd never been shown! A senior NCO, name unknown to me then, together with two members of my crew, was standing at the end of the wing and by the chocks, looking bored and waiting for something to happen. Totally abashed and thankful that my pink cheeks were hidden beneath my face mask, I beckoned to the sergeant and explained my predicament, after which, like a couple of conspirators, we went over the priming and starting procedures.

I did as instructed and pressed the appropriate buttons. Ahead, the reduction gear gave a clank as the airscrew began to rotate against compression and almost immediately the engine burst into life with a roar producing a minor hurricane of wind. Momentarily unnerved by what I had just achieved, I gradually regained my composure and made some adjustments in the cockpit. After which it was all plain sailing – comparatively!

I taxied out across the grass, cautiously, with half an eye on the radiator temperature, kicking the nose left and right, as advised, and being especially careful with the brakes to avoid standing the aircraft on its nose. A mile away in front, the big engine growled and spat at me through its exhaust stubs, but seemingly without malice. All right so far!

At the far end of the airfield, I turned cross-wind, braked to a standstill, and experienced a stomach-clenching moment of black apprehension. The Spitfire, meanwhile, stood there, a restless, trembling stallion at the end of a none-too-certain rein.

I opened the engine to 0 lbs boost and checked the two ignition switches in turn, after which I ran hands and eyes quickly around the cockpit. Trim – elevator one notch down; rudder bias – full right; mixture – rich; airscrew fully fine; fuel – both levers up and content full; instruments – checked, compass and D.I. set and uncaged; oxygen – on and flowing; harness – locked; hood – open and secure. I took a nervous breath and gave a last quick look round. Anything else? Then, I turned and opened the throttle slowly but firmly.

There were no half measures about that aircraft. With the howl of a Dervish, the Spitfire set off across the grass like an electric hare, the acceleration alarming. As it raced ahead, the curved wings dipping and rocking, I suppressed a burning desire to look over the nose and only gently lifted the tail, feeling the controls grow lighter, the elevator as sensitive as a balanced needle. The racing wheels tipped a rise... again... once more, and then I was up and away, shooting skywards, the engine raging away in front at almost 7lbs boost and 3,000 revs. Crikey! My first solo in a Spit! Electrifying! Wonderful!

Once airborne, I changed hands on the control-column and raised the undercarriage, hearing first the rumble of racing wheels then the 'clunk' as they locked into the 'UP' position, after which I gently reduced power and, putting the airscrew into coarse pitch, heard the engine note die to a more sober level. The wind howled around my ears – the hood was still open but I was reluctant to commit myself to becoming totally enclosed in so small a space. So, I straightened out, throttled back, and watched the speed settle at around 230 mph. Then, like an apprentice skater on wafer-thin ice, I cautiously turned to the left and looked around.

I was at 1,400 feet with the airfield below me and somewhere behind. I lifted the nose to climb away and saw the needle on the altimeter wind around the dial. What if the engine stopped now? What would I do? Oh, Lord! But, why should it, for heaven's sake? It was roaring away throatily in front and, to my relief, continued to do so as I opened the throttle again, the speed falling back to 180 in the climb. After which, I felt for the hood catch behind my head, pulling it forward so that the perspex bubble slid on its rails and locked shut with a minute thud. Silence! Well... not quite silence perhaps but far, far less noise. And no gale of wind either, thank God! A mite cramped around the shoulders for a chap my size, but otherwise quite comfortable. And, strangely, not anything like as claustrophobic as I had feared. Everything roaring and vibrating minutely. I settled into my seat and felt my breathing return to normal.

I flew around, my confidence growing by the minute. What a wonderful aircraft! Such a sense of power, agility and strength. The nose stretched ahead a full furlong, it seemed, the engine hurled its raucous challenge to the world, and the two elliptical wings with their brave, colourful roundels rocked at my slightest touch. I pushed forward and, momentarily, the engine hesitated, the exhausts gave out a smudge of dark smoke and my backside rose majestically from its seat. I pulled and the universe dragged at me with long, clawing fingers, reducing my sight to a mottled grey as gravity took its toll. Heavens! The elevators were feather-light and devastatingly effective.

I climbed again until I was above a thin layer of broken cloud and at 8,000 feet. After that, I dived then flattened out, brushing the racing white fluff with my tilting wings and flicking joyously through a flimsy patch here and there before pulling back and soaring upwards, the white carpet falling away like a discarded mantle. Oh, the sheer joy of it! The aircraft was alive! The sky was my playground. My God, I could do anything! I forced down the nose and watched the speed rise rapidly – 300, then 350, finally 400. Everything tight and the starboard wing dropping. Hard left aileron now – it must be the radiator under one wing. I trimmed forward... more, then more, working the rudder bias at the same time. God, I had never been so fast! 430! The needle steady with everything trembling and as vibrant as a bow-string. The Spitfire was alive, exulting in it, pulling hard like a wayward horse. I reined her in, picking the nose up gently, gradually, feeling the blood begin to drain again. My sight, greying at first, faded into almost complete darkness, though all the time I was fully aware and faintly amused by this odd, new phenomenon. Strange, most strange. Then, with returning vision I was rocketing up... up... up, a flash of cloud and a brief violent shudder as my aircraft rode a few corrugated strands of turbulence. After which I was curving skywards like a leaping salmon into a void of endless blue... and stillness... with the hard white line of the horizon, tilting... and falling away... then tilting again... before rotating and levelling out magically until it was exactly and soberly in its rightful place. Wonderful, sensible things, horizons.

Intoxicated by the sheer joy of it all, I suddenly became aware of time. Fifteen minutes was all I had been allowed and I had already been up almost twenty. I dropped the nose and began to search for the aerodrome.

I approached the circuit quietly, tried first to open the hood at too high a speed and, not succeeding, dropped down to 180 and tried again. This time, I forced it back along its slide, the slipstream buffeting my elbow and shoulder. Then, down with the wheels; I moved the lever in its quadrant precisely and unhurriedly so that I should not risk jamming the rotating pins. The undercarriage fell away cleanly and, after a few seconds, locked down, a single green light showing left of centre on the dashboard.

The airfield ahead and to port, I curved towards it looking alongside the lifting nose. An Aldis light winked a green signal in my direction. All clear! Down to 140. Then the flaps; I flicked down the flat disc and felt the flaps extend, the aircraft wallowing a little in protest, then steadying. Airscrew in fine pitch, the engine raised its voice, and I was trundling in nicely with 100 showing on the ASI and the tail settling. The hedge slid towards me then flashed underneath. I held off, the grass approached with deceptive stealth then raced past, a green blur. No, not yet! I porpoised slightly, holding the control-column firmly to the rear. The nose way up now. Floating! Floating! Gosh, I ought to be down by now! I should – !

The port wheel struck and the aircraft bounced. Not much, just a trifle. A second touch, stick hard back, the smallest ballooning jolt and everything was rumbling and bouncing and jigging, the wings rocking, the exhausts crackling and spitting out minute puffs of blue smoke. Straight! Keep her straight! *Straight*! I kicked hard and corrected, the nose wandering as though the aircraft was wilfully testing my skill. I was down! Safe! Whoah! Keep still, you brute! *Still*! The mettlesome Spit, tamed at last, slowed to walking pace. I turned. And stopped. My first solo. I was down. In one piece. Thank God!

I began to taxi in, relieved, a little breathless, and feeling like a king. The radiator! Crikey, I'd forgotten the radiator! I operated the lever which dropped the flap; at all costs I mustn't let her boil. Temperature a little over 90. Yes, I'd just about make it.

My crew were waiting for me, climbing onto the wing-roots with polite smiles.

'Everything all right, sir?'

I feigned nonchalance. 'Fine. No problems. Everything went beautifully.' I threw off my straps, climbed out, and dropped to the ground.

An hour or so later, I was airborne again. On a sector reconnaissance, which was the official term for a joy-ride. The next day, I started in earnest.

In the remaining ten days of May, I flew thirty-six times and put in over thirty-two hours of flying. Which, considering the occasional period of duff weather, orderly officer duties and other tasks I was obliged to perform, was some going.

8

Spitfire Interlude: 1–11 June 1940

While those of us in 249 were first preparing then beginning to fly from Leconfield, the German Army was delivering a succession of massive blows against Allied forces in the west, ably assisted by the Luftwaffe, its dive-bombers spearheading a series of decisive armoured thrusts. A new word was coined – Blitzkrieg!

Within ten days of their initial assault, the Germans were at the gates of Paris, and, further north, a steel ring was closing around the retreating British Army falling back in desperation to the Belgian coast. By the last day of May, it occupied a small enclave centred on Dunkirk and the now famous (or infamous) evacuation had commenced, the beaches and armada of ships being covered – as far as was possible – by Fighter Command Spitfires and Hurricanes operating from airfields in East Anglia and Kent.

Sadly, the embattled Army saw little of the RAF and bitterly resented its apparent inactivity. The Air Force, on the other hand, whose squadrons were fighting as hard as they knew how, at the limit of their range and in the most unfavourable circumstances, had little more than contempt for the 'brown jobs'. Among other more wounding epithets, they scathingly referred to them as the 'Dunkirk Harriers', such remarks and attitudes creating a legacy of suspicion and distrust that was to linger for many months to come, resulting occasionally in spilt blood and broken heads when tempers were lost in the pubs.

Even so, listening to the sombre news on the wireless and reading of events in the newspapers, I was never more than mildly concerned at the time. Yet to achieve operational status, we were not in any way involved and I doubt that even one of us felt for a moment that Britain was on the brink of defeat. Indeed, very much the reverse. Our morale positively soared. The Hurricanes based in France had apparently achieved overwhelming success against the

German Air Force and we were confident that in Spitfires we could do even better. Moreover, brought up with the traditional and unquestioned belief that an Englishman was worth three of any other nationality, for the RAF to lose or even draw was far less than a remote possibility, it was positively unthinkable. Defeat? What utter rot! We had not even begun to fight!

So, whatever else it did not achieve, the Dunkirk debacle underlined the need for 249 to become operational as soon as possible. It had been rumoured that we would be allowed four to six weeks from the date of forming which set us the approximate target of early July.

We bent to our task with a will, achieving – amazingly – the all-time record of 1,010 hours of flying in a single month, of which my personal contribution was just short of 100. Those were the most arduous but happiest of days. In my mind's eye there remains a score of incidents, trivial in themselves but sufficiently outstanding to provide a lifetime of memories.

I had been allocated a recently-arrived Spitfire; all my own, brand new, with pump-driven hydraulics and a wonderfully virginal aroma. It had 'D' on its side – GN-D. I was beside myself with pleasure.

One day, having landed immediately before lunch, I had not even climbed down from the cockpit when I was asked if I would fly across to Church Fenton to pick up some radio crystals waiting to be collected. I readily agreed; in my nice, tight, bright new aircraft, I would happily have flown to Timbuctoo and back. Moreover, the sun was shining, I could 'Bradshaw' along the railway line between Market Weighton and Selby and wouldn't even need a map.

When I arrived at Church Fenton, everyone had gone to lunch, the place was as quiet as a tomb and I had to wait for the man with the crystals to be found and the small parcel delivered into my care. Having parked my aircraft beside the watch office, I passed the time of day with the duty pilot.

He was a pilot officer, a rather disconsolate young man who had been trained on Lysanders and who looked about sixteen years of age. Resting between jobs, so to speak, he desperately wanted a posting to a fighter squadron.

Alone, we lay on our backs in the warm grass, yarning and chewing straws. I felt very superior. It was a brilliant day and I belonged to a wonderful squadron. I told him loftily that I would see what I could do to help.

Half-an-hour later, the parcel of crystals safely tucked away in my radio compartment, I started up for my return journey to Leconfield. Wishing to impress my companion, who was watching sadly and enviously from the wing-tip, I decided to take off directly into wind and across the grass from where I stood. Opening the throttle with a flourish, I roared away, realizing when totally committed that I had chosen the shortest possible take-off run and that, with a line of trees ahead of me, was going to be very lucky indeed if I made it. With my heart in my mouth, I dragged the Spitfire off the ground and staggered across the clutching branches with an explosion of leaves and twigs. Wow!

My concern was short-lived, however, as, with a perfect summer's day and unlimited visibility all around, boyish exuberance took over. At 1,000 feet and flying again along the Selby-Market Weighton railway line, I opened the hood, took off my helmet and face-mask and, in my shirt sleeves, with the big Merlin snarling and beating in front and a 240 mph slipstream howling around my head and ears, I sang, and shouted, and screamed with sheer uninhibited joy. Of all things, what could possibly be better than this? My life's ambition. Everything was wonderful! Just... just... *perfect*! I had never been so happy.

John Grandy invited the commanding officer of 74 Squadron to visit us and speak of his squadron's involvement during Dunkirk. He arrived with a very handsome flight lieutenant who did all the talking in a quiet, unemotional voice. We all listened intently. It seemed clear that the Spit was more than a match for anything the Germans could produce but, with a mere 85 gallons of fuel, it had been operating a little too far away from home for comfort and had at most fifteen minutes' patrol and fighting time over and around Dunkirk. The flight lieutenant continued with his graphic description of the event, speaking in the most sober of tones.

I was most impressed. He was a very good-looking man, well-built and of middle size, with fairish hair and sun-tanned features. I learned afterwards that he was a South African called Malan. Then about thirty, he had been in the Merchant Navy, apparently, before joining the RAF and went by the name of 'Sailor'. A year or two later, I was to serve on his station.

In the same crew room in which we had listened to the account of the

Dunkirk fighting, one of the station medical officers, Flight Lieutenant John Anstee, gave us a talk on how to use the first-aid kit provided in each of our aeroplanes. In the course of his demonstration, a standard pack of equipment was opened up so that the table was littered with bandages, needles and small phials of this and that.

John Anstee was possibly 249 Squadron's most fervent admirer. An engaging young man of about twenty-eight, he spoke very rapidly and amusingly and, something of a thespian, could quote yards of Gilbert and Sullivan and much other doggerel and poetry, all with the appropriate gestures. He was quite one of the most gifted and entertaining people I had ever encountered and he certainly enjoyed chilling our blood with his droll description of the actions we were to take if wounded, demonstrating how the morphia needles were to be inserted and the manner in which we should tackle a wound and staunch a massive flow of blood.

Halfway through his dissertation, I became aware of an unusual silence. A number in our group, Denis Parnall and George Barclay in particular, looked unnaturally wan and when the lecture was over, they rather shakily admitted to feeling very queasy. How odd, I thought.

I grew to know John Anstee very well and we were to part very sadly and for good some weeks later, at which time he presented me with a pair of inscribed gold cuff-links, which I wear as I write. One piece of his advice remained firmly in my mind: that sleep and rest were all important in times of stress and that in the event of an accident, the most desirable and immediate course of action was to take a nap. I remember frowning. A nap, for heaven's sake! How could anyone possibly take a nap having just crashed or been shot down? Even so, it was something that took root – to my considerable advantage.

We were to go up to Acklington to the ranges there for air-firing practice against drogue targets – the whole squadron. Nicolson was delighted. He was returning to his old home base. We were to put up a good show, by gum! He spent some time impressing upon us what we were to do and how to do it.

The trip up was uneventful; we flew in an orderly but fairly loose formation, pulling ourselves together as we approached Acklington and tucking ourselves in tightly to impress the natives as we swept over the airfield. After which, we spread out slightly and came in, intending to land on the grass in a series of threes in close formation. It was going to look splendid, by George! A real 249 extravaganza!

As we did not normally use the radio to pass vital actions during landing, I found myself flying tightly on Nick's right hand, watching him make the signs for throttling back and reducing speed, turning left, lowering the undercarriage and finally the flaps. With my wing within inches of his own, we trundled in, me working hard to keep absolutely in position, watching his every movement, glance and sign. Over the hedge now, nose coming up, beginning to hold off, the grass streaming past. I concentrated like mad. *I must not overshoot my leader*!

Suddenly, not only was I overshooting my leader, I was positively racing past. What the – ? I jerked my head. Nick had disappeared. Astern.

Concentrating still, I brought my Spitfire to a stop and turned. Nick's aircraft was sitting forlornly on its belly in the middle of the aerodrome. Busy signalling to everyone around him, he had forgotten to lower his own wheels! Poor Nick! He had a terrible time in the mess that evening. A few days later, he went away on a week's course. To learn how to put down his wheels, some of us archly suggested.

For two whole days, we fired against the drogue – astern attacks, quarter attacks, *et al*. I made six sorties and must have fired something approaching 20,000 rounds. I did not hit the target once! Not with one, single, solitary bullet.

In a Hart with one clattering, hesitating old Vickers, I could achieve eighteen per cent several times. But with eight Brownings going like the clappers – *nothing*! I returned to Leconfield a very pensive young man.

Then, on 10 June, we heard that our Spitfires were to be withdrawn and replaced by Hurricanes. I was to lose N9332, my beloved 'D'. We had mixed feelings but were in no way depressed. The Hurricane had a wonderful reputation and was supposed to be a much better gun platform. With my standard of shooting, it jolly well had to be!

I flew a Spitfire for the last time on 11 June. The following day, the first of our Hurricanes arrived.

9

Operational in a Hurricane: 12 June–14 August 1940

My first Hurricane was brand new, its number P3616 and shortly to bear the letter 'F'. It had a constant-speed Rotol propeller with wooden blades, which was quite new to me. Also, it was tight and bouncy, like a new car, with the intriguing smell of fresh paint. Very impressive. I was delighted.

The Hurricane was little more than an updated version of the old Hawker Hart and Fury, with only one wing, of course. The family likeness was immediately evident, the cockpit being much the same with the pilot sitting in space and lots of darkness below and behind him. There were many more instruments, naturally, but after the Spitfire the layout seemed bitty and the cockpit generally less well finished. The throttle I especially disliked; after the Spit, a flimsy little lever – very insignificant!

The pilot sat a good deal higher in a Hurricane and, through a hood that could be opened in stages, saw rather more of what was going on. Also, there was a feeling of solidity about the aeroplane, the wings especially being much thicker and the wheels widely spaced so that it sat on the ground very firmly and in a no-nonsense way. Happily, too, the radiator was centrally placed so it caught the slipstream when taxiing and there was not the eternal business of counting the seconds before the engine boiled.

In the air, the pilot immediately detected a feeling of steadiness. The ailerons were lighter than those of a Spit, markedly so at speed, but the elevator much less sensitive. The Hurricane couldn't be bent with one finger – with two hands, even – but having said that, there was no feeling of heaviness, the controls, if anything, being better balanced that those of the Spitfire.

If I was expecting the aircraft to be noticeably slower, I was to be pleasantly surprised. There was not much in it at the lower end of the speed range so that we still flew around at about 230. However, the Hurricane just did not have the legs of a Spit or its sprightly acceleration in a dive; moreover, at its best climbing speed of 140 mph, though it went up more steeply, it did so at a much slower speed. *And* – very disappointingly – there was no rudder bias, which meant that on a full-throttle climb, the aircraft required a heavy right boot on the rudder and an even heavier left one when descending quickly. A thoughtless and irritating omission, I always thought.

On the whole though, we were not disappointed. While it may not have had the refinements of a Spit, our recent acquisition was rock-solid and possessed an obvious ruggedness and strength. No shrinking violet, this! Furthermore, its reputation as a fighter was as impressive as its unbending toughness.

There was no question of 'converting'; we flew our Hurricanes four times each day from the outset. With ease and comfort and feeling perfectly at home. The remaining days of June fled by. Almost unnoticed. A mixture of sunshine and rain and in a fever of flying and preparation.

Night flying! During the night of 17 June, I carried out my first non-operational night flight in a Hurricane – for about an hour and in almost total ignorance of where I was. Arriving back at the airfield, I found myself in the midst of a considerable commotion. There were aircraft streaming around the circuit and I learned that several Huns were at that very moment over Hull. I landed, profoundly thankful that the guns, which were banging away like mad, had shown such restraint.

For the next several nights there were other sporadic raids around Leconfield. On 19 June, I was languishing in the watch office as duty pilot when a Hun droned overhead and dropped a stick of bombs. Several exploded just beyond the aerodrome boundary but one fell with a terrible crack rather less than 100 yards away. After picking myself off the floor, where I had instantly taken refuge, and in a high state of excitement, I ran to investigate. To my surprise, I found it had been a small one which had landed on a concrete path beside the sergeants' mess but had made little more than a shallow crater. No one was injured and the general reaction was one of interest and amusement rather than concern.

The following night, several Huns again came over to the accompaniment of much scissoring of searchlights and banging of guns. One of the bombers was caught by the lights and intercepted as I and others watched with excited expectancy, but, although it was later reported to have been shot down, I did not see it crash. Nor, unhappily, did a number of the local sheep which were killed by bomb blast and splinters.

Throughout the several nights of Hun activity and bombing, I was pleasantly surprised to find myself much more interested than scared. I never expected for a moment that anything would happen to me.

Shortly after, six of us of 'A' Flight, with Boozy Kellett in the lead, flew up to Prestwick in order to put in a spell of night flying away from the threat of bombing and intruder Huns. Prestwick then was just a grass field set in the beautiful, crystal-clear surroundings of lowland Scotland. It had a flying club atmosphere and it was said that Amy Johnson – Mrs Jim Mollison by then – was there, although we did not see her.

We were billeted on someone-or-other, which caused rather a fuss, Boozy becoming involved in an embarrassing contretemps with a woman who objected strongly to the arrangement, particularly the business of providing clean sheets. Clean sheets! It was the same dreary business, everyone vehemently patriotic until it became necessary to make some tangible, personal contribution to the war effort, at which time there was resentment.

I flew several times without incident, but one of our number undershot in the dark and came to rest about half-a-mile short of the airfield with about four bushels of grain up his air-intake. He explained in hurt tones that although he had opened the throttle to trundle in, nothing had happened. Small wonder with enough corn in the works to feed a herd of Guernseys.

It was a pleasant change. We flew back to Yorkshire in brilliant weather, the Lake District and Pennines shadowed entrancingly with drifting puffs of white cloud, an endless heart-stirring landscape of muted greens, browns and greys, presenting an unforgettable picture. How beautiful England was. Worth all the anguish of fighting.

Saturday 29 June. A great day. We became operational. We flew across to Church Fenton, fifteen aircraft, positively on our best behaviour, our formation-keeping immaculate. It had been arranged that some air officer from 13 Group would inspect us and that we would carry out simulated scrambles, interceptions, and refuelling and re-arming exercises. Three Blenheim target aircraft had been organized from somewhere up north. It was like sitting for Matric again; we felt just about as nervous.

We scrambled in fine style, roaring away in considerably less than the prescribed three minutes. After that, it went slightly less well. I had expected the Blenheims to be conveniently on hand to be intercepted without any fuss or bother, instead of which those of us in 'A' Flight were vectored all over Yorkshire before finally tracking them down. They were trundling along in a wide vic and we went through our standard fighter attack routine – 'No. 3 attack, No. 3 attack – *go!*'

Like guardsmen, we sorted ourselves out and slid into echelon port, surging into the rear of the Blenheims in tidy, line-abreast threes, *(careful!* – *musn't overshoot my leader, or else!)* and waiting until the range-bars of the gunsight were filled completely by the full wingspan of the target aircraft. Then, wallowing and bucking in the slipstream of the six engines ahead, on command, we went through the motions of firing. After which: 'Breaking starboard, breaking starboard, *go!*' And off we went, pushing and dropping away like stones, my head thumping against the roof of the Hurricane's perspex hood, our straining engines pausing to eject smudges of dark smoke as the negative 'g' caused the floats to rise in the carburettors and produce brief rich-mixture splutters. Then, diving, racing, turning hard and climbing, we formed up again and set course for home. Dead easy!

Having watched us land and refuel in a very operational manner, the very senior gentleman expressed satisfaction, after which we all flew back home to Leconfield. Very pleased with ourselves. Real, live fighter pilots.

The squadron went into Hull to celebrate its 'coming of age'. John Anstee, the doctor, accompanied us as a special guest and was in sparkling form. We dined at a well-known restaurant and John insisted on putting all his cutlery in the hat of a rather prim young lady sitting behind him, who was only faintly amused.

Later, we did the round of the pubs and unused to drinking beer in large amounts, I was waterlogged within an hour. Desperately wondering how I was going to last out the evening, I suddenly felt a hand on my arm. It was Lohmeyer, the adjutant, who had been taking a particular interest in my welfare over the past several weeks. With smiling eyes he indicated quietly that he would dispose of the several pints already lined up for my attention. Then, later still, when I decided imprudently that I would drink whisky, I again felt the hand on my elbow and was faced with a faintly disapproving shake of the head. The whisky disappeared as well – to my great relief.

In spite of Loh's intervention, however, I was feeling very odd indeed by the time we returned to Leconfield that night so that the outrageously bawdy songs we bellowed at the top of our voices, went right over my head. I didn't know many of the words, anyway. A nice, nice man, the Adj. It was the first of many times he was to come to my rescue.

My first opportunity to defend the nation came rather sooner than I expected. The morning of 4 July was brilliantly fine and there were several scrambles throughout the day starting shortly after dawn. Then, towards 4.30 p.m., 'Dobbin' Young, Sergeant Smithson and I were ordered off. Our first occasion ever.

Rushing into the air in a lather of excitement, we climbed up in the direction of Flamborough Head and were told that a 'bogey' was approaching from the south-east. Crossing out just south of Bridlington, we continued to fly north-east until we were ten or fifteen miles off the coast and at 13,000 feet. There was a fair amount of broken cloud starting at about 7,000 and towering in isolated columns up to something much higher. I was excited but not the tiniest bit apprehensive.

We had just been given a further report from control, when I saw the bogey immediately, about three miles away, a slim, dark shape cruising as calm as you like between scattered white dumplings of cloud. On a converging course, too, and several thousand feet beneath. I could scarcely believe my eyes. A German! A Dornier Flying Pencil, in fact, the distinctive outline obvious.

Discipline and commonsense flew out of the window. I forgot all about my radio and screamed and beat on my canopy to attract Dobbin's attention. He remained stoically indifferent. I pulled level with him and waggled my wings furiously, pointing. Dobbin looked at me as though I were cracked. Finally, although I cannot even now say by what means, I got through to him.

I suspect Dobbin saw the Hun and the Hun saw the three of us at about the same time. And had the German turned and run, we would have had him. But he didn't. He made a very brave and calculated move; he turned in our direction and towards the coast, diving.

Going through the nonsensical No. 1 attack routine, we reared up like startled pheasant chicks, dropped into line astern, then plummeted down on the Dornier which was now making to fly between our legs. I found myself behind Dobbin, almost over the vertical, jumping around with excitement and willing him to get out of the way. The Hun was at that point about 2,000 yards ahead, going hard for a cloud. Overtaking him rapidly and almost screaming with frustration, I saw that he would just beat us to it. And he did. He was in, then out. Then in again. A dark shape, twisting and turning in slow motion.

We shot into the cloud after him and out the other side. The three of us. Then, like terriers around a rat-infested haystack we raced up – down – in and out – over the top – underneath – and round the other side yet again. He must be somewhere. Where, for heaven's sake? *Where?* But nothing! Absolutely nothing! The Hun had disappeared. Vanished! Quite unbelievable!

Control came on giving advice and we rushed about for some minutes before swarming up to 20,000 feet in order to get a better view of things. But to no avail. Only masses of sea and cloud. We hung around for fifteen minutes or so, gradually losing heart. Then, reluctantly, we turned for home. On the way back, I was still wildly elated but terribly disappointed. Our first Hun. And we'd let the blighter get away. If only – !

I was scrambled twice the following day, being recalled on each occasion when the 'enemy' radar plots disappeared. Then, getting on for midnight, I made my first operational trip at night – I was now an 'ace' operator, with ten whole hours' experience of flying in the dark! Patrol a line from Gilberdyke to Pickering, the man said, and off I roared, full of enthusiasm.

But to little effect. Wandering about in the blackness, my night vision ruined by only partially obscured engine exhausts, I had no idea of where I was other than approximately in Yorkshire. There was supposed to be at least one Hun about and, eager to shoot at something – anything! – I religiously obeyed the instructions, straining my eyes into the darkness and following the occasional searchlight beam in the hope that something might be revealed. But, after a time, control seemed to lose interest and I was left to wander around for more than an hour. My spirits began to droop. What was the point? Chilled to the marrow and my nose streaming mucus into my oxygen-mask, I stared blindly into the black void beyond.

Eventually, I was given the order to 'pancake' and, turning thankfully towards base, landed after an unproductive seventy minutes.

It was on the morning of the following day that a section of 'B' Flight shot down a Ju 88 in about the same area we had encountered the Dornier.

Having scored some juicy hits on it, the Hun had apparently flown inland before crash-landing in a field near Aldeburgh, three of the crew baling out. Cock-a-hoop, the boys flew home, delighted with themselves. The squadron's first victory!

The following day it was in all the papers. It appeared that the pilot had been killed and the three who had taken to their parachutes, feeling pretty miserable no doubt, had staggered towards a farmhouse to surrender, whereupon the farmer's wife had set about them with a pitchfork.

Of course, the press, slavering for a human-interest story, was full of the lady's alleged heroism, giving her a good deal more credit than our three chaps who had disposed of the Hun in the first place. Then, insult to injury, we learned that someone of 41 Squadron, stationed up at Catterick, had apparently also put in a claim and had been given credit for at least a shared victory. Our fellows were astonished; they had never even seen a Spitfire!

Some days later, several of us went to a cinema in Leeds to see a report of the event on British Movietone News. Their commentator, too, credited the Spit with shooting down the German aircraft, producing whoops of disbelief and annoyance from our seats in the stalls. Such, we decided, was the folk-lore surrounding the Spitfire. People believed only what they wanted to believe!

It was also during the weekend of 6–7 July that we learned that 249 was to move back to Church Fenton – there was little significance in it being a weekend; on duty almost continuously, all days and nights were the same to us.

We left on 9 July amid moving scenes of concern and regret, a fairly general view being that 249 was the best squadron the station had ever encountered. John Anstee, especially, was very blue. His nickname for me was 'Copper' and he was unusually solemn as we parted. (John was later killed in the Middle East.) With other things on my mind, however, I took it all a good deal less gloomily, although I thought I should miss my very excellent quarters in the mess. Also, our trips down to Beverley to watch the cricket. John and I had been there once or twice as Maurice Leyland, the famous England middle-order batsman, played for the club occasionally. We met him one gloriously sunny afternoon in the pavilion, a short thick-set man with a broad Yorkshire accent. I found myself towering above him.

Church Fenton was much the same as we had left it. 73 Squadron, which had just returned from France in a pretty depleted state, was reforming and gathering strength. With many new faces.

I spent the next few days doing little other than night-flying tests and sitting about at all hours of the night at Readiness. Until the night of 15 July, which turned out to be rather special. I had been 'loaned' to 'B' Flight, who were short of night operational pilots, and at 9 p.m. was in their crew room, all kitted-up and ready to go. We had been warned of a possible night attack on targets in Yorkshire. Midnight approached; we were in a relaxed mood and there was a lot of light-hearted banter around the card table, particularly from a pleasant-faced young man I had never really met before, Sergeant Main. Outside, several aircraft of 73 Squadron were doing night circuits-and-bumps.

Then, the telephone rang. Unidentified aircraft flying up the east coast. A raid on Leeds was suspected; we were to make preparations. Chairs were pushed back and conversation ceased. I examined the 'state board a little nervously and saw that I was fifth in line for take-off.

Shortly after, several of our aircraft were ordered off. Pilot Officer Meaker – Bryan Meaker – was the third to go. As he hurried out into the night, we moved outside to watch. It was very dark indeed with a sprinkling of stars and we heard Bryan's engine start up behind us and dimly saw his aircraft taxi out quickly in the direction of the flare-path. After which, there was a misunderstanding.

As 73 Squadron began to remove themselves, someone switched off every light on the aerodrome. Bryan was in the act of opening up. In total darkness, he roared off unseen into the night. We stood around shivering. Waiting. Watching the searchlights flitting silently across the clouds away to the left and in the direction of Leeds.

In the silence that followed and high above, the thin unsynchronized drone of bomber engines. A Hun. Probably several. Going where, we wondered?

Then, a rising and unusual wail. Different. An invisible aircraft came slowly into the circuit. A shouted message from the crew-room: Meaker had hit the taxi-post taking off and had lost part of his airscrew and possibly a piece of his undercarriage as well. His wheels would not extend. He would be making a belly landing.

The lights on. Then off. Raised, irritated voices. Who the hell was buggering about with the lights again? Then the Chance floodlight. Bryan's aircraft, still only an invisible noise, appeared from out of the darkness and into the glare. Held off briefly, then flew into the ground. A faint bang and a grinding, rearing skid. Silence. He was down. Probably all right. We all exhaled.

Tension. Then another Hurricane was taxiing out quickly behind us. Who was it? Sergeant Main, somebody thought. Main's Hurricane took off into the darkness and as the sound of his engine died away, we heard the drone of the bombers overhead. And saw the searchlights a long way off. Crossing like scissor blades. Moving. Crossing again. Then doused. All in silence.

Suddenly, a mile or two away, a sudden blossoming of light. Bright and violent at first, dying to a fading splutter. Incendiaries, someone said. The blighter was bombing us! Well, if he had been, he'd missed. We waited, ears pricked, for the whistle of high explosive. But none came.

Once more in the dispersal hut, I waited for the command to take off. It was not long in coming. 'Scramble: Gilberdyke-Pickering patrol-line, Angels 15.' God! Not again! I ran out into the darkness feeling faintly sick. Thereafter, it was a nightmare.

My beloved GN-F unserviceable with a coolant leak, I had to change to a spare aircraft. Cold, damp and with a farmyard smell, not only had it not been flown that day but it must have been one of the first Hurricanes ever built! And, as I was soon to find out, with the original system of raising the wheels, an arrangement quite new to me.

Having taken off in complete darkness – the airfield's lights *again* being switched off at the critical moment – it took me five minutes of frantic feeling about and experimenting to sort out the undercarriage. After which, I climbed up to 15,000 feet before wandering all over southern Yorkshire. Then, by degrees and first to my consternation then to my horror, my radio died away into complete silence. By which time I was totally and absolutely lost!

The enemy now entirely forgotten, I drifted around in the darkness for almost an hour – high and low, in and out of cloud, with the hood open most of the time and shivering with cold and misery, my mind in a turmoil. I was lost, utterly lost! Without a radio I would never be able to get back and would be forced to bale out. The trouble was, was I over land or sea?

Then, a moment of divine inspiration. The generator! I felt around in the dark. It was 'off'! Permanently wired 'on' in my own aircraft, I had never given it a thought. Bloody old cow! But, relief! Glorious, overwhelming relief!

With the battery recharging, my radio slowly came to life and, re-establishing contact with the ground, I was given a vector for base. From the area of the Wash! The Wash, for God's sake! I was miles away to the south! Thanking the Lord, I turned northwards and after skirting the balloons over Hull, flew west and eventually caught sight of the searchlights in the area of Leeds.

Later, I was back in the crew-room feeling utterly spent when John Grandy appeared, his face solemn with concern. The splash of light we had seen earlier had not been incendiaries but Sergeant Main, crashing to his death. Then he turned and, noticing me, brightened.

'Ginger!' – my newly acquired nickname and a foul slur, in my opinion! – 'Glad to see you back. In the Ops room, you disappeared off the table altogether and we thought you'd gone for good.'

Gone for good! I made some off-hand remark, trying to look and sound imperturbable. If he only knew! The night dragged on. Poor, poor 'Masher' Main. Our first war casualty.

Boozy Kellett left in the latter half of July to command No. 303 Polish Squadron and the handsome Denis Parnall became flight commander.

I flew up to Acklington again for more air-firing, this time with marginally better results. On the whole, though, life was fairly dull. Despite growing activity in the south, at Church Fenton we seemed out of it all.

We established a routine of flying across to Sherburn-in-Elmet on each of the evenings we were on night duty, returning in the morning to Church Fenton. I became rather bored with flying operationally only in the dark; day-and-night fighters we might be but the balance seemed to be tilted very firmly in one direction. Anyway, we were so useless at night.

There was a power station at Selby whose gun-crews occasionally asked for a Hurricane to act as target, and I and others were only too keen to oblige. Possibly as a reaction from all the night-flying tests and periods of Readiness at Sherburn, when cooperating with the guns, the urge to provide something a bit special was overwhelming. On one occasion, I flew down the barrels of the guns to such good effect that the nerve of gun-crews failed and they all scattered and ran. Very satisfying!

Unhappily, a day or two later, I made the mistake of doing more or less the same to the gun-crews at Church Fenton, whose sense of humour was sadly lacking. After landing, very pleased with myself and while still in the cockpit, I saw Nicolson marching towards my aircraft very determinedly, his hands in his pockets.

From a distance, he called out, 'Ginger, you're in the Ess, Aitch, One-dot, Tee!' And I was! I collected several days' duty pilot for displaying poor airmanship and behaving in an unseemly manner.

In spite of his lording it over me occasionally, Nick and I became firm friends and we flew together a great deal. However, although my senior and section-leader, he was not above behaving irresponsibly at times.

A married man, Nick's wife Muriel lived in the Tadcaster area. One bright morning, he and I were engaged in a little specialized formation flying. Directly over the house in which his wife was living, Nick had me on the inside of a tight formation of three. In a slow climbing turn almost from ground level, and watching me maliciously, he reduced speed until I felt my aircraft begin to stall. I shook my head at him vigorously but he persisted. Then, when my Hurricane fell away at less than 800 feet into the first twitch of a spin, I left him and flew home on my own, screaming my opinion of Nicolson and his peculiar brand of fun. Back on the ground, we had words and I lost my temper with him. But our relations were soon mended; Nick was not one for feuds which was very fortunate – for me!

The days fled by. There were several additions to the squadron, notably a rather elderly squadron leader (about thirty!) named King, a Pilot Officer Richard Wynn, and a Sergeant Davis. For some obscure reason, the squadron leader, who was supernumerary and waiting to take over another squadron, was immediately christened 'Whizzy', while the other two soon established themselves as being charming and capable companions – no question of diluting the cream!

It was at the end of July, too, that I learned that several of my former friends on No. 15 Course at Montrose had already been shot down and killed in the battle over the Channel. Killed! It was difficult to comprehend. Fellows I had known so well only weeks before. The Huns were really concentrating on big raids in the south; unlike us, the chaps down there were really getting it.

August came. Lots of pleasant weather and hours and hours of sitting about at Readiness. Church Fenton was transferred from 13 to 12 Group and we had visits from two air vice marshals on successive days – Saul, our former commander, and Leigh-Mallory, our new master. Each was introduced and made friendly noises.

It was around that time, too, that an armourer in 73 Squadron let off two guns in a Hurricane, which was standing on trestles, and shot one of our corporals the other side of the airfield. The man was standing in line to receive his pay and the speed at which the twenty or so other airmen melted into the distance was almost comical. No one moved faster that a British airman under fire!

We continued to train. To carry out 'standard fighter attacks' like guardsmen on parade. And to sit around all day and night – waiting. Why didn't the Huns come up to *our* sector?

14 August and early morning at Sherburn-in-Elmet. Asleep in our hut, our Hurricanes were standing outside, hub-deep and silent in wet summer grass, rivers of dew streaming from wings and hoods.

Dimly, I heard the telephone ringing and John Grandy's voice answering. A brief exchange of words, then, excitedly: 'We're going down south. Boscombe Down!'

I came-to. Slowly at first. Then, almost violently, the adrenalin pumping. Off? To the real fighting? But, Boscombe Down! I'd never heard of the place. Moreover, it suddenly occurred to me that I had never flown further south than the border of Yorkshire – except by mistake and at night! I threw on my clothes. That I might not be up to the new challenge never crossed my mind.

By late morning, after feverish activity, we were ready, and around lunch-time, twenty of us took off – as many Hurricanes as were flyable – our troops and baggage going by 'Bombay' and 'Hannibal', two monster aircraft which had arrived in slow-motion an hour or two earlier. We were going for a week, it was said.

Somewhere up front, I just followed my leader. We flew at a few thousand feet. Down through the haze and shadows of the East Midlands, always beneath cloud but emerging now and then into vast pools of light and the slanting rays of the August sun. We were flying south to war! To war, for heaven's sake! This was *it*! But, it was all just too difficult to take in.

10

Into Battle from Boscombe Down: 15–31 August 1940

Having arrived at Boscombe Down at about 1.30 p.m., we found ourselves parked in the south-western corner of the airfield, a cluster of Hurricanes roughly dispersed and refuelling, heaps of baggage and equipment lying about on the grass and no one knowing quite which way to turn or what to do. Gone for the moment was the ordered routine of life at Church Fenton and Leconfield. There was nowhere even to sit.

The aerodrome mainly tenanted by the Aircraft and Armament Experimental Establishment, I saw many aeroplanes that were new to me. Of special interest were some old bombers, long since obsolete, which had been dispersed around the airfield boundary and presumably left to rot. Close by, was an ancient Vickers Virginia, its cavernous fuselage lying in the tall grass, later to become a wonderful plaything for the more juvenile among us steeped in Service folk-lore.

Boscombe Down was totally unlike Yorkshire. There was a vibrant feeling of tension in the air. But it didn't affect our appetites. Within minutes, we were trooping off to the mess for lunch. Back again at dispersal, we sorted ourselves out. Tents were erected for the men and we established communication with Middle Wallop Sector Operation Centre, drawing up a roster so that we junior officers might take it in turn to be Operations Officer.

Several times we heard the dull roar of massed aero engines above the clouds and occasionally, small groups of aircraft could be seen heading urgently in varying directions, below cloud but too far away to identify.

Shortly after our arrival, John Grandy flew across to Middle Wallop, some eight miles away, to make his mark with the Operations Centre there, returning to report that he had found the place in a mess, with smoking craters between the buildings and one of the hangars a skeleton and still smouldering. Several Ju 88s had just carried out a dive-bombing attack

– while we had been watching, in fact – three unfortunate airmen being killed when a huge hangar door had fallen on them and a further dozen or so injured in Station Headquarters. It was incredible. Just across the hill. Within sight of us, almost.

The day drew to a close with 249 still preparing itself for action. Everything was new, uncertain and a bit confusing. But thrilling. A delicious undercurrent of excitement. There was *bound* to be action tomorrow.

The officers' mess at Boscombe Down, one of the older type, was very comfortable in a staid and traditional way, the ante-room quietly welcoming with a mass of newspapers and magazines amid black leather armchairs and settees. It was wonderfully snug with many old watercolours in the passages and an atmosphere of serenity totally unruffled by war.

I slept in the mess that night and going down to dispersal early the following morning, found Pat Wells and one or two others climbing out of their camp-kits and padding around through the wet grass in their bare feet, having spent the night on the airfield by their aircraft. Pat said it was wonderfully fresh sleeping in the open but the sight of rivulets of dew on the canvas of his bed and everything running and dripping, rather put me off. In any case, I didn't possess a camp-kit – thank the Lord!

There were signs of it being a very hot day and most of us were in shirt-sleeves. Again, there was the noise of many invisible aircraft high above and I found my eyes straying to the horizon, constantly on the look-out for aeroplanes, friend *and* foe, in the light of what had happened at Middle Wallop the day before. Extraordinary! Hun aircraft wandering about the English countryside below cloud and thirty miles inland. As cool as you like!

Having up to twenty Hurricanes and around twenty-four pilots, even allowing for leave and sickness, not all of us could fly in the twelve aircraft that formed the squadron. Those not on the 'state' were expected to carry out some duty or other, stay in the mess, or go off into town. If they were anything like me, however, they mooned about in dispersal with long faces and made pests of themselves. In the days to follow, the adjutant became very good at circulating quietly, oozing tact and exercising a much-needed calming influence on all of us. Especially on me!

From the information we received, there seemed to be lots doing in the late morning but we were not called upon until after tea. Around 5 p.m., the whole squadron was scrambled but in two separate flights. I found myself with John Grandy, Nicolson and three others and we climbed hard to 15,000 feet into the bluest of skies towards Warmwell in Dorset, and beyond. We were vectored hither and thither but saw nothing. And yet there were obviously Huns about, I could sense it from what little information we were given. If so, why on earth weren't we seeing them? With unlimited visibility and south-west England spread out before us like a map, it seemed incredible that even a single aircraft could escape our notice. But, after further wanderings and long periods of silence from control, we returned with nothing to show for our trouble other than eyes bloodshot from the glare and necks positively aching from swivelling about looking for 'Huns in the sun'.

Landing back, we learned immediately that 'B' Flight had run into a dozen or so Ju 88s accompanied by around fifty Me 110s. Having returned a little before us, they were discussing their engagement and, green with envy, I joined the circle to listen to their excited chatter. 'Butch' Barton, Bryan Meaker and Denis Parnall were each claiming a 110 and there were vivid tales of combat and other Huns being shot at and damaged. John Beazley, normally so pedantically calm, was explaining animatedly how he was right behind a 110 which was burning and creating a terrible smell. Not only did he have to avoid pieces falling off, he complained with feigned concern, but he also had to put up with the pong! The new de Wilde ammunition, with which some of our guns had been partially loaded, was spectacularly effective, it seemed; it gave out sparks and a good smoking trace and positively twinkled whenever strikes were obtained. There was also a rumour that anyone found carrying it was likely to be shot by the Germans. What utter nonsense! In any case, I'd be happy to take the chance.

Amid all the excitement three Huns were claimed as 'destroyed'. Most of 'B' Flight being involved, it was not easy to decide who had done what. But for 'A' Flight, there was no ambiguity; we had achieved nothing!

I was off again later, patrolling base at 20,000 feet, positively aching to see something. But nothing materialized and we returned after fifty minutes. Control didn't seem to help very much. Again, there had been long periods of silence, then, out of the blue – 'pancake!' Were there Huns about, or weren't there?

It being such a problem getting through on the telephone, I wrote to my parents at length telling them in detail of what was happening and instructing them not to worry. Poor things! I felt deeply for them. Listening to the wireless up north and not knowing. Just waiting. Hoping. And praying.

I was on duty at dispersal all that night, until 8 a.m. the following day, which was Friday 16 August. I was not on the 'state' early on and stood around, restless with frustration. I had been obliged to hand over my aircraft, GN-F, to Pilot Officer King for the morning, which I greatly resented. I hated anyone else flying P3616 and always inspected it carefully after every such occasion.

Word had also come through that there had been mass raids the day before on targets in Yorkshire and the north. Wasn't it killing? As soon as we come south, the Huns attack our former parish.

The morning passed without incident and I returned to the mess for an early lunch. No sooner had I arrived than I heard the squadron taking off. I rushed back to dispersal and awaited their return, pacing about, with others, like a caged bear.

Then, word from Ops. Another section required to patrol base at 20,000 feet. More aircraft? It *must* be serious!

I took off with three others – John Grandy, Pat Wells and George Barclay – at about 2 p.m., and climbed away determined to sell my life dearly. Up and up, until we were four miles high, looking down on the line of the south coast and an enormous pool of grey-green haze littered with white dumplings of cloud. After which, true to form – nothing! More and more it was a case of receiving the initial scramble instruction, followed by silence. It was my fourth major sortie since arriving at Boscombe Down and the various formations I had been in had not even made a sighting far less an interception, despite there being some sizable raids in our area. What on earth was going on?

When we landed forty minutes later, most of the original twelve were already down. Immediately, I sensed tension in the air. Something had happened.

What news?

News? There'd been an engagement. Of sorts. We'd lost some aircraft.

Some! How many?

Not sure yet. Two of Red section, possibly more.

God! Two lost!

Then, Squadron Leader Whizzy King was among us. Excited. Garrulous. Hurrying about. His face creased by sweat and the lines of his oxygen mask. Yes, he'd been hit and damaged. No, he wasn't wounded, but the others had gone.

Gone! Who? Where?

Nick and the other boy – what's 'is name? King, was it? Both shot down. In flames. The blighters had come down and caught them unawares. Down from behind. Me 110s. Whizzy was in a highly emotional state and kept talking about tactics. We'd have to do things differently. Talking quickly and gesticulating.

Pilots moving around in a circle. Wiping their faces. Hot and excited. Most were in shirt-sleeves. Gradually the facts emerged.

The squadron, with Butch in the lead, had been ordered to patrol a line from Ringwood to Poole. At height, they had seen aircraft in the distance and Nick's section had been sent to investigate. Rejoining the main formation after observing that the Huns had been dealt with by a squadron of Spitfires, they had been jumped by 110s in the act of climbing up. A little north of Southampton. All three hit in seconds. The whole of Red section clobbered.

Poor Nick. And young King. But, in a way it was almost funny. Nick, who had been telling us for weeks how to do pretty well everything, shot down on his very first operational engagement! Not so funny was the loss of my aeroplane. Dear old GN-F. Still, I was jolly glad not to have been in it. I could well have been, by gum! But, they might turn up, although it didn't sound too hopeful. We'd know in a few hours. Or a day or two.

Everyone was still talking about the incident. Our first real battle casualties. Later, someone remarked upon the AOC, a Sir Quentin Brand, visiting us. Who? Had he? I hadn't noticed. Where had I been? Somewhere important, no doubt.

I did not write to my parents that night. When I did, two days later, I did not mention our losses. Or even the engagement. No sense in worrying them.

Saturday 17 August. I did not fly at all during the day, but hung about and did a spell as Ops officer, having several long conversations with a pleasant-sounding WAAF on the other end of the line. There were no Huns about. The enemy was licking his wounds, it seemed. It was nice to know that even they had to recuperate.

We were all delighted to receive news of Nick who was in hospital in Southampton. Badly burned, apparently. Certainly unable to write because he dictated a letter to one of the nurses which arrived the next day. It appeared he had shot at the Hun who had set him on fire. Stout fellow. The account which John Grandy received was very factual and not at all in the manner of Nick, who could be quite imaginative at times. We were all especially amused when we learned that an LDV (Local Defence Volunteer – forerunner of Home Guard) had shot him in the backside just before he had landed in his parachute. In the bum, for heaven's sake! Everything happened to Nick!

Loh, the adjutant, drove down to Southampton to visit him in hospital and later reported that he was cheerful but had been wounded by cannon-shells as well as being badly burned. He looked terrible, apparently – his hands and face. We were rather more sympathetic when we learned about the burns *and* the wounds. The Hurricane seemed to catch fire all too easily when hit and we wondered why.

King, apparently, had also come down by parachute in more or less the same area but his brolly had collapsed when still 1,000 or so feet in the air. It was rumoured that a Hun had shot at him on the way down but we did not believe that; no self-respecting airman, friend or foe, would do such a thing. It was difficult to imagine GN-F as nothing more than a few twisted pieces of incinerated metal. I was very fond of that aircraft.

Whizzy King had disappeared and was believed to be heavily involved in writing a treatise on tactics. After one fight! The brush with the Hun had certainly focused his mind on the subject.

Nothing much happened on the morning of 18 August, which was a Sunday. The weather glorious, we were again in shirt-sleeves basking in the sun, the rolling hills of Boscombe Down and beyond a fairy-tale English summer scene despite the shimmering haze.

I was on the 'state' in the afternoon and in yet another unfamiliar Hurricane, an 'L' series aircraft, as old as God! How I hated going to war in aircraft I didn't know. A little after lunch we were scrambled with the usual instruction: 'Patrol Middle Wallop: Angels 20.' I wished to heaven they could think of something else to tell us. After a day of rest, the Huns were bound to be in a warlike mood.

We climbed up, wondering what to expect, eventually swarming up to 25,000 feet in pursuit of some high flying aircraft, presumably 109s. But, as usual, either we missed them, they weren't there, or it was just an insurance exercise. Whatever the reason, we stayed up only for a short time and pancaked after thirty-five minutes.

As we refuelled and hung about, word came through that there were more Huns off the coast than ever before. It looked as though there would be plenty of action *this* time. We began to talk excitedly about the prospect of a fight and I found myself very much on edge but more keyed-up than worried. At least I could then say I had seen some Huns! I was beginning to feel guilty!

Shortly after, about 3 p.m., we were sent off, this time in squadron strength, being vectored south towards the Isle of Wight. We crossed out over Southampton – where Nick and the others had been knocked down two days earlier – flew over the Solent, then turned east along the south coast, the whole of which was spread out before us in a glorious if hazy panoramic view. There was obviously something going on as, far below, there were columns of black smoke rising from Thorney Island and from somewhere beyond Tangmere. As usual, however, we seemed to be arriving on the scene too late.

Even so, I caught sight of a number of aircraft beneath us, dark minnows barely distinguishable against the background of sea and haze, but hurrying about with the urgency that suggested action. Most seemed to be heading out into the Channel which meant that we were witnessing the tail-end of an engagement in which there had been quite a few Hurricanes and Spits and some other aircraft that might have been Ju 87s.

By this time, I was fairly hopping about with excitement and expecting to be jumped from above at any moment. But, no such luck!

We then flew out into the Channel ourselves until the coast of France seemed almost within gliding distance before turning round and coming back. Very much trailing our coat, it seemed. I again saw other aircraft below me, going like mad. But all friendly. Well, they seemed friendly!

Where on earth did all the big Hun raids get to? Extraordinary how fifty or more aircraft could fly past only yards away, apparently, yet not be noticed. Interesting, too, the almost overwhelming urge to follow something that was diving. Lesson No. 1, I decided; to attract attention, start diving; to remain inconspicuous, stay put!

We began to return, empty-handed as usual. Either Ops was making a howling nonsense of controlling us or we were as blind as bats. I was beginning to feel it must be the controlling; there was nothing wrong with my eyesight. And why did we always have to be late?

We landed after one hour twenty-five minutes in the air. Later, we heard that ten Ju 87s and eleven Me 110s had been accounted for in our area. Twenty-one Huns! Incredible! But, wouldn't it make you sick?

I wrote a long and impassioned letter to my parents that evening, vehemently and petulantly displeased, and at 10 p.m. went on duty again down at dispersal.

Nothing much happened for a day or two thereafter. The weather changed somewhat with cloud and fits of rain and for several days there was near-gale which made taxying very difficult. On several occasions, my aircraft kept weathercocking into wind so that, in a fury with the useless hissing brakes, I had to pick up my tail and make several complete turns in the middle of the airfield in order to get back on course. I kept complaining about the brakes but it did no good.

In fact, I did not fly operationally on 19 or 20 August, partly because I was not asked to, but also because I, with others, had a day off on 20 August, which was a Tuesday. An Air Marshal Ludlow-Hewitt visited us on the Monday, a tall, pale, rather lugubrious-looking man who had a high voice and was not very jolly at all.

On the day following, I went into Salisbury. It was Market Day and the centre of the town was full of animals and Australians, the latter in their slouch hats and rather antiquated-looking uniforms which buttoned up to the neck. They were noisy but quite impressive looking chaps with leathery skins and a complete disregard for rank; that we were officers did not impress them in the least. In fact, I was not sure that they knew! Even so, they were nice enough in a rumbustious, back-slapping way. After crossing town and ending up at pub called the Rose and Crown, several of them pushed into our car – a four-seater which was already holding four – and begged a lift. I had a huge earthy creature on my knee who, when he dismounted full of beery thanks, pressed a two-shilling piece into my hand with the instruction to get myself 'a pot'. As at least one other of us received two bob, it was a profitable ride.

Arriving back, we learned that Squadron Leader King had been posted to command 151 Squadron. We had hardly seen him since Nick and his namesake's disappearance.

On 21 August, the weather was still miserable with low cloud and wind, but mid-morning I was sent off with John Grandy and Sergeant Beard on a quick scramble. Low flying aircraft approaching base, was the terse report. We rushed about like scalded cats but, not making contact, landed after twenty-five minutes. I was greeted with urgent faces and waving arms.

'Didn't you see them?'

'See who?'

'Two Huns, you clot! Came out of the cloud over there. They were on one side of the airfield and you the other. We were shouting like mad and pointing.'

'You're joking!'

'No we're not! You're blind, that's the trouble!'

'Well how the hell was I supposed to hear you shouting?'

'You're blind, Ginger! Let's just leave it at that.'

Nothing much happened until the afternoon, when, shortly before tea, there was another scramble and yet another abortive interception. As I signed the authorization book at the end of the flight, I saw that I had flown four different Hurricanes on the previous four trips. I was fed up with not having an aircraft of my own. Almost as much as not seeing Huns.

Our week at Boscombe Down having elapsed, there were expectations that we would return to Church Fenton. But, no news. And no desire to go. We were quite happy to be where we were; the south was where the action was likely to be.

The feverish activity of scrambles and full-throttle climbs having abated for the moment, we were able to indulge ourselves with a protracted sector reconnaissance on 22 August which took us over Bristol – to look at the recent damage inflicted there – down the Severn to Weston-super-Mare, along the south coast to Southampton, then back to base. A comparatively relaxed flight of one hour twenty minutes, a lot of attention was given to our backsides, even so; no one flew anywhere in August 1940 without his head being on a swivel.

We continued to hear that the north was getting visits in strength from the Hun; it appeared that we had actually come south *out* of trouble!

Meanwhile, there were single raids over our area at night with the constant discordant droning of aircraft overhead and isolated bumps and thumps. I took little notice of them and I doubt that anyone else did either. I still didn't have my own aircraft, damn it.

We were not required on the morning of 24 August and, the weather being fine, it was arranged that we should cooperate with a group of Lysanders from Old Sarum. I had another Hurricane, P3902, which was rather newer and better than some of the others I had recently flown, and was moderately happy with it.

We intercepted about a dozen Lysanders over Salisbury Plain and they acquitted themselves well, whirling about in fine style. Rather sniffy about the Lizzie, I was surprised by the manner in which they dog-fought, although I would have hated to have had to fly them. They were reputed to be very heavy on the controls. They looked odd, anyway. I couldn't help remembering the poor chap in the white overall at Ringway the previous year.

Later in the day, about tea-time, I was scrambled with Pat Wells and Sergeant Killingback, after which we embarked on the usual fruitless full-throttle climb and aimless wander around Hampshire and Dorset, not knowing really what was happening or what we were required to do. Meanwhile, 'B' Flight were sent off over Bristol to intercept some high flying Hun, or Huns, at 30,000 feet. Which rather proved a point. Control obviously didn't know what they were doing as Hurricanes were just about useless at that height. Still, they probably had to make a gesture.

Later still, the whole squadron, without me on that occasion, was despatched towards the Isle of Wight. 'B' Flight spotted some 109s and in a very quick encounter, apparently – the Huns were high above them and only came down for a quick swoop – claimed at least one of them, Butch Barton and Dicky Wynn doing the damage. 'B' Flight was certainly getting all the opportunities, lucky beggars!

The following day, Sunday 25 August, we did nothing in the morning but were scrambled at about 2.15 p.m. and sent off south-west towards Warmwell at 15,000 feet. As per usual there was a dearth of information and we encountered nothing. Much later – some time after 7 p.m. – we were again sent off to the same area, only to wander round at anything from 10,000 feet downwards until it was time to come home at 8.15 p.m. By then the light was beginning to fade and being very uncertain of the geography of the area, I was very glad to be led home safely by Pat Wells. If he, too, was lost, he kept quiet about it and put on a most convincing performance.

Later, and almost incredibly, we learned that Warmwell had taken some heavy punishment when more than 200 aircraft, mostly fighters but with a nucleus of bombers, had attacked the airfield and other targets in the area. Which had us spitting. What on earth was going on? With no controlling at all, by the law of averages, we could reasonably expect to intercept enemy forces of that size simply by running into them! As it was, I had been 'controlled' on ten scrambles and completed more than ten hours of full-throttle climbing and flying against some of the biggest raids ever experienced, and had not seen a thing. We were wasting our time at Boscombe Down, that was crystal clear. I wrote home to my parents in the most indignant of terms.

The following day, it was more of the same. Very little happened in the morning and it was not until tea-time that we were sent off and ordered to climb to 25,000 feet over the Isle of Wight. Having arrived there, fairly hopping about in anticipation of a fight, we were told that the enemy had turned back when within twenty miles of the coast. Turned back! Did major raids come all that way across the Channel just to turn back? It was hard to believe.

John Grandy disappeared on that occasion, being forced to land at Tangmere when he lost oil pressure in his engine. It was explained to me by the experts that there was a tendency occasionally for the oil to stop circulating through the radiator in very cold air conditions, causing it to by-pass and overheat with considerable loss of pressure. Well, it hadn't happened to me, but I felt sure it would. And I could well understand it freezing, by gum! Although not directly related to the CO's oil problem, the

Hurricane was a terribly cold aircraft in which to fly at altitude, with holes and draughts everywhere around the cockpit. And no heating, either. No creature comforts in a Hurricane – that wouldn't have been British! Mustn't make it too difficult for the Hun, by God!

Back on the ground we learned that there had been another thumping great raid on Portsmouth and a major fight in that area. And 249, yet again, had missed it. But, what did it matter? I would be going on leave shortly. I might just as well be sitting at home as thrashing about at Boscombe Down!

There were Huns over again that night and more bumps and bangs in the distance. But nothing close enough to keep me awake for long.

It had been arranged that I should take a Hurricane due for inspection back to Church Fenton and, the weather being reasonable, I left for the north shortly before noon the following day. Happy, but with reservations. I would be glad to be home again, yet the prospect of missing something exciting had me looking over my shoulder.

I collected my car at Church Fenton and set off across the Pennines. It rained miserably as I travelled and my one memory of the journey is letting down from the hills into the mill streets of Rochdale and across cobblestones slick with running water and glinting in what little remained of the daylight.

11

September 1940 at North Weald

Although due back at Boscombe Down at noon on Monday 2 September, in the event I had only four days at home, deciding meanwhile to return by car, bringing my parents as far as London, whence they could return by train.

We arrived on Friday evening and stayed at the Regent Palace Hotel which was 10s a night, including a monster breakfast, and much frequented then by junior officers and hordes of small, fat, gentlemen with black, crinkly hair who never somehow managed to get into the war. In the months to come, we could always gauge the level of bombing in London by our room numbers; the greater the intensity, the closer the small, fat gentlemen were to the cellars and the higher up the Air Force's accommodation became. Even at the height of the Blitz, there was never any question as to the importance of people and their contribution to the war effort; the small, fat crinkly-haired chaps were obviously doing something vital I didn't know about!

The following morning I met 'Ozzie' Crossey in the foyer of the hotel. One of the South African members of 249 – 'Ozzie', because he invariably wore a black roll-necked jersey in the manner of Sir Oswald Mosley, the Fascist leader – it was he who passed on the information that the squadron was in process of moving to North Weald.

North Weald! Where was that? Somewhere around Epping Forest, he thought. North of London, anyway. He was on his way there. And, yes, he would be glad to join me in my car, if there was room.

We set off the following morning and wended our way slowly through the northern suburbs of London, then totally new to me. Eventually, we found ourselves in Epping and drove in the direction of the aerodrome, a mile or two north of the town. We were all in good spirits, even my parents. On the surface anyway.

Coming in sight of the airfield beyond the edges of the Forest, we were stopped at a sentry post on the road which ran parallel with the southern perimeter track. The airman who stuck his head in the car seemed agitated.

'You ought to get out of here as soon as possible, sir. It looks as though there'll be another air-raid.'

'*Another* air-raid!'

'Yes, sir.' The man was looking anxiously over his shoulder. 'We've had one already plus a couple of scares. And the siren's gone.' He clearly wanted to get away and shouted as he left. 'Get into the forest somewhere.'

Undecided, I drove up to the main gate where there were signs of real concern, people hurrying about in tin-hats and airmen and WAAFs going down into air raid shelters. Crossey and I dismounted. There was a roar of aero engines and I saw Hurricanes with US on their sides, hurtling off the ground and climbing away towards the east in an untidy formation of a dozen or so. God! Look at those masts! Scores of them! People were running. There was noise and tension in the air. An officer with a tin-hat came up to the car. The station adjutant. He was courteous but terse. Get off the camp immediately, was the gist of his message. I drove off hurriedly the way I had come.

We stood on the edge of the forest and waited. Looking into the sky. Silence. Minutes passed. More waiting.

'D'you see anything?' My mother.

'No. It's probably a false alarm.'

'Are you sure?'

After a time, the steady note of the 'all clear' sounded and I drove back to the main gate. WAAFs were filing out of a shelter by the building which looked like Station Headquarters. Twenty-odd girls and one man – the station adjutant!

I said jocularly, 'The best possible way to die!' But my parents did not respond to my humour. Later still, I took them back into Epping, where they said they would take a train back to London, and we parted, I with brittle gaiety, they with sombre faces.

'Take good care, won't you?'

We held hands.

'Of course I will.' Then: 'Look, I'll have to go now.'

An hour or so later, I was in the officers' mess at lunch when a mess servant called me to the telephone. To my great surprise it was my mother's voice, tremulous and worried.

'Are you all right?'

'Of course! Did you see the Hurricanes come back? They were ours, apparently.'

'No.'

Silence.

'You're sure you're all right?'

'Yes. Of course I'm all right. The mess is super. Everything's fine. Is Dad there?'

'Yes. Well... he's walked off for a moment.'

'I see. Look, I'll write as soon as I can. Tonight, in fact. Promise. Come on, cheer up, I'll be all right. You catch your train. Goodbye, then.'

'Goodbye. And do take care, won't you?'

'Of course. Don't you fret.'

Many years later, I learned that my father had been so affected by the Hurricanes taking off that he had completely disintegrated with grief and, in a state of collapse, could not be consoled. For a long time they had both been in tears, convinced that they would never see their only child again. It was more than an hour before they felt presentable enough to take the train back to London.

I found 249 in dispersal in the north-west corner of the aerodrome, a collection of wooden huts, hard-standings and blast pens. There was also a group of strange Hurricanes with US on their sides. Apparently, 249 had exchanged aircraft with 56 Squadron who, sadly reduced by casualties, had taken ours and flown off to Boscombe Down. There was also another reason: theirs had VHF radios whereas ours were still equipped with TR9ds, which were HF and therefore unusable in 11 Group. Rather than change the radios, it was considered expedient to change the aircraft. Moreover, Lohmeyer, the adjutant, the intelligence officer and our servicing crews had also been left in Wiltshire, requiring us to use those of 56 Squadron.

After a week away, I felt lost. Everything seemed disorganized, confused and rather strange, not least the aerodrome itself. *And*, I didn't like those masts at all! Dozens of them in the circuit, more or less. How on earth were we supposed to operate in bad weather with 350-foot masts within touching distance?

I learned that the squadron had arrived in the early afternoon of the previous day and had been pitched in at the deep end. Earlier, some four hours before Crossey and I had arrived, they had been vectored onto a raid of about 100 plus in the Rochester area – Dornier 17s, Me 109s and 110s – and had claimed one bomber and several fighters 'destroyed' and 'damaged'. But not without loss. John Beazley had been forced to bale out, Percy Burton had crash-landed at Meopham and Dicky Wynn had also been shot down, being nastily wounded in the neck by a bullet which had come in through one of the semi-armoured side-windows of his windscreen. Poor old Dicky! Having had an engine-failure two days earlier, the fates seemed to be against him.

There were several other scrambles during the day. An afternoon sortie resulted in the squadron intercepting some 110s in the Southend-Gravesend area and claiming three 'destroyed'. Butch Barton had a grisly story to tell. Earlier, in hot pursuit of a burning, disintegrating aircraft close to the ground near Rochford aerodrome, one member of the Hun crew, rather than be incinerated, had clambered out and had appeared to run along the wing before tumbling to his death a hundred or so feet beneath, bouncing like a half-filled sack as he hit the earth. A horrible way to go and very upsetting.

So, the day's total: four 'destroyed', three 'probable', and four 'damaged'. Not a bad start.

It seemed that the station had been heavily bombed only a week before, with considerable damage and loss of life, and that everything since had been in a state of flux. 151 Squadron, who had shared North Weald with 56, had left the day before I arrived with only about a dozen pilots remaining and rather fewer aeroplanes. They had also lost their commanding officer, our late companion, Squadron Leader Whizzy King. I was greatly saddened. Poor Whizzy hadn't lasted long for all his new ideas on tactics. Such earnest enthusiasm.

In their place, or partially so, a flight of 25 squadron had just arrived from Martlesham Heath to occupy the dispersal area on the north side of the aerodrome. 25 Squadron flew fighter Blenheims, and mostly at night. They had my deepest sympathy. I regularly thanked God that I didn't have to fly Lysanders, Battles, Defiants or Blenheims! Moreover, the Blenheim looked so much like a Ju 88, they were constantly being attacked by friendly fighters, sometimes with fatal results.

All this Crossey and I gleaned as we familiarized ourselves with our new surroundings including the hut which constituted the crew room, half occupied by beds. There, most of us officers lived, ate, and for much of the time, slept during our eighteen-hour (occasionally twenty-four hour) working day, the NCO pilots having separate sleeping accommodation. When not required for immediate duty, we had rooms adjacent to the officers' mess. Always a slight irritant, this, the junior pilots' quarters were in huts, each room, with a tiny coal-stove, snug-looking at first sight but fairly primitive. And desperately cold in winter-time. Needless to say, the more important people, such as intelligence, equipment and administrative officers, lived in the comparative luxury of the mess proper. In the weeks to come, I asked for a room in the main building on a number of occasions but, although on the station for nine months, never succeeded in obtaining one. Later still, the several Polish pilots who were posted to 249 – archetypal survivors they and much more worldly-wise than us simple-minded British – were accommodated in the main building of the mess within days of their arrival. How they managed it, I never learned.

Appearing for duty in the afternoon of 2 September and not being on the 'state', I was asked to take a Hurricane across to Henlow, one of the principal maintenance units. A 56 Squadron aircraft, I assumed it to be for a major inspection and gave it no more than a cursory glance. I collected a map, drew a line on it, arranged for Sergeant Smithson to bring me back in the Miles Magister, one of which was held on the establishment of most fighter squadrons, and took off.

Having landed on the grass at Henlow and taxied in, I climbed out and took a sheaf of documents into a hut which was pointed out to me.

After a short time and while I was waiting for the 'Maggie' to appear, a sergeant approached.

'Did you fly this one in, sir?'

When I said that I had, his eyebrows disappeared almost into his hair-line. Surprised by his expression, I asked him why.

The man shrugged. 'It's an absolute wreck, that's why. One of the main fuselage members had been shot clean through. We expected it to come by road.'

I was on the 'state' when we all came to Readiness in the early morning of 3 September. The weather was brilliant with little more than an early morning mist and I had a new aircraft, V7313. I thanked God that it wasn't an 'L' or 'N' series – I was fed up with them. 56 Squadron's aircraft were newer than ours, probably because they lost them a good deal more quickly! I had no particular feelings of excitement or concern, just the proper degree of eagerness.

We stood or sat around a large unlit stove in the crew-room. Waiting. An airman occupied the tiny office by the entrance and manned the telephones. From time to time, a bell would ring and we would all hold our breath as it was answered. As the weeks passed, we grew to hate that telephone.

But other less urgent messages were passed as well, particularly before a major raid when Sector Ops would inform us that plots were building up over France, providing us with a picture of the general situation. The difference between operating in the Middle Wallop and North Weald Sectors was most noticeable; at North Weald, we were invariably kept informed before the event and controlled with understanding and helpful information throughout the interception. At Middle Wallop, we were frequently given just the scramble instruction, after which – silence! There were probably perfectly good reasons for this, but they cut no ice with us; we were concerned only with the quality of service.

At 9 a.m., the whole squadron was scrambled. I was in the leading section of three on John Grandy's right with Percy Burton on his left. We took off in a wild rush towards the east and I found the masts floating past my left shoulder while climbing up. Not so bad after all.

Patrol Chelmsford, we were instructed. Enemy plots were building up – twenty, then forty, then fifty plus! We were being positioned as a precaution.

As we laboured up, I switched on my gunsight, adjusted the intensity of the red graticules, set the wingspan adjuster to sixty feet and turned my gun button to 'Fire'. I then leaned forward and 'pulled the plug' – the device which over-rode the boost governor mechanism. Nothing much happened to the boost but at least I knew I was having all there was. My engine at 2,600 revs was quite smooth. I always flew at 2,600 revs except in combat when conventional wisdom had it that 2,850 produced a better performance.

We climbed hard, turning slowly, the whole squadron lifting, falling and leaning in slow motion. Everyone together. In position. There was no cloud worth mentioning but I was too busy keeping station to be scanning the horizon or be much concerned about the enemy.

The plots were still building up, it seemed. An unspoken thought: were we too early? And in the right place? Time would tell.

We wandered about, lances levelled. Ready. Waiting. Essex spread out beneath us – the Blackwater, the east coast, and to the south, the line of the Thames. Visibility at height, a million miles. The Huns seemed to be taking a long time, though. Round once more. And again.

We had been airborne almost an hour when the order to pancake was given. What a sell! We dropped down quickly towards base. Well, at least we would have been in position if they had decided to come. Better that than being too late.

We landed, taxied in quickly and the bowsers lumbered forward to hook up and begin refuelling. My airscrew tottered to a standstill. Crew members on the wing-roots.

'Everything all right, sir?' New faces, but eager and smiling.

'Fine!'

Turn round quickly was the urgent instruction. We needed no persuading.

My own aircraft was full but some of the others weren't when the air-raid siren began its banshee wail and our second scramble order came. Patrol base, this time. Crikey! That didn't sound so good.

I raced across the grass to my position on John Grandy's right. Then, full throttle, 3,000 revs, and off again. Wheels up – I didn't even look. The masts drifting past. Climbing like hell. The squadron strung out. Cutting corners and catching up. Climb! Climb! Hell's bells! We couldn't climb any faster. My throttle lever at full stretch. Being up-front, I was all right, but think of the poor blighters behind!

From Sector: 'Fifty plus bandits approaching from the south-east. Angels 17.'

We clawed our way up, my engine raging. Through 7,000 feet; 10,000. Up to 12,000. Flying roughly east.

Then, above and at eleven o'clock, ack-ack fire. Faint brown smudges. Pecking. More ack-ack. Blossoming. A growing cluster of it. Everything in slow motion. Then, *aircraft*! In the middle of all the puffs, Huns! Oh, God! Masses of them! '*Tallyho*!' My eyes glued to them. Fascinated. Growing closer. Clearer now. Large ones in front and in the middle. Others like flies, stepped up and behind. Thousands, it seemed. And there were only twelve of us!

We were below them and to the south. The Blackwater was in the background and they were heading due west. We turned slowly to the left, climbing hard still. I could see them properly now; the bombers were Dornier 17s, the fighters Me 110s. Forging steadily ahead. Through the flowering puffs of ack-ack. Taking no notice. Oblivious.

The CO said in a tense voice: 'Steady GANER squadron', and I was aware that I was the outside aircraft on the right of the formation, looking up and to my left towards the bombers and above and to my right for the 110s.

The 110s close now. Very close. I could see them clearly. Some sort of coloured markings on the nearest aircraft. I was going to pass right underneath! If they chose to come down now we were finished. Closer. Turning to the left still and going hard. But I couldn't hit any of the bombers from here! *They* were the important ones, to heck with the fighters! Right underneath now; I could reach up and touch them. Why on earth weren't they coming down? My head bent right back. One 110 suspended above me – I could see its airscrews rotating.

Then, wings flashing. My leader turning on his back. Other aircraft diving. A moment of utter surprise and panic. Mustn't be left! I tumbled after them in pursuit. What was happening? Were we being attacked? I kept screwing my head around but could see nothing. My Hurricane dropping like a stone, dust rising from around my feet, my head pressed against the roof of the cockpit. Other aircraft to my left. Diving like hell, then pulling out. Hurricanes! I joined them. John Grandy's aircraft. But, I hadn't fired! I hadn't had time to fire!

The RT and a voice from below. High pitched with excitement but controlled. 'We've been hit GANER squadron, but we're all right.'

I looked over the side. To my surprise, we were directly over North Weald and far below, the whole aerodrome was hidden beneath a huge, spreading grey-brown pall of smoke and dust. They'd bombed us! The airfield! The blighters had bombed our airfield! It never occurred to me for a moment that we might not be able to land on it.

I looked up. Far above, aircraft were turning away northwards. Were they the bombers? I couldn't see. Join up! I looked about. I was in a formation of sorts. More Hurricanes were surging into position. Urgently. Rocking, bouncing, and with tilting wings. We flew around. The sky suddenly clear. Magically. Then the 'pancake' instruction. We began to let down. But I hadn't fired! Not a single bullet. I turned my gun button to 'Safe'.

By the time we were back in the circuit, much of the smoke and dust had disappeared. All that remained were scores of large molehills on the grass. There had been other damage, too, and lives lost, but I was aware only of the need to get down and the business of finding space on which to land.

We flew in from the direction of the masts, in rough sections of three, and touched down across the concrete and on the grass, weaving gently between the bomb-holes. As they raced past, mostly to my left, I watched them quite dispassionately. There was no problem, no one was the least bit concerned and we all landed safely and without incident.

Within twenty minutes, all twelve Hurricanes had been refuelled and were ready for off. On the airfield itself, there was activity. The shock passing, life was returning to normal. Jolly good job the bombing had not occurred the day before; my poor parents could well have been killed! The bombs seemed all on that side of the aerodrome. Two hangars had been hit, we were told. We could see smoke from a distance but had not the time to go over to the far side of the airfield for a closer inspection. Nor, indeed, did I particularly want to.

We collected. Excited. Discussing. The Tannoy system was out of action, apparently. The water mains, too. No washing! Someone laughed. The small boy's dream!

Things quietened down. Gradually.

Nothing much happened until the afternoon. News began filtering through. The Ops room on the airfield and other buildings had been badly damaged, one of the hangars, massively. Someone said that some of 25 Squadron's Blenheims had been burned out but we were too far away to see. We all felt fine and not the least bit upset, although some of the chaps who had not been flying and who had been forced to take shelter when the bombs had come down, hadn't liked it very much. The noise and blast, more than anything. A terrible din.

I found it all vastly interesting, as though witnessing some epic film performance. But, I hadn't been killed, had I? Or injured?

Later, the sun still shining, dispersal was a hive of industry and some of the holes were being filled in. Some bombs had not gone off.

We had lunch. Talking like mad but not finding it difficult to eat.

There was another scramble in the early afternoon – Maidstone-Canterbury patrol line, was the shouted instruction. I had only a rough idea where Maidstone and Canterbury were so I just followed my leader.

We climbed up steeply over the Thames and to the left of the huge pall of smoke-haze that was London. It was my first time over London and Kent. The river had more kinks in it than I had expected and was silver in colour, the estuary stretching away to the east into mist and oblivion. Below to our right, were masses of balloons. More than I had ever seen in my life.

We went south, the air electric with tension, my head turning constantly, the sky vast, and blue, and empty, the sun a golden ball. Down towards the south coast.

We were warned of bogeys high up but did not see them. Then we did. A few. Me 109s, probably. They were very small and fast so couldn't be anything else. I had never seen a 109 before. I was not in the least apprehensive, just enormously interested.

Very far south now. Over Dover. Away below, the ring of the harbour mole and balloons. News of more aircraft and ack-ack smudges. Pretty close, too. Were they shooting at us, I wondered? Silly blighters! I didn't see any more aircraft, probably because I was too busy keeping station. Fairly buzzing about, rocking this way and that and on tenterhooks for fear of being jumped. This Hurricane of mine wasn't too bad. Quite good, in fact. I would see if I could hang on to it.

We turned and retraced our path. Back over Kent. Round again in wide circles then up and down before finally heading north towards the river and losing height over Essex. Home! We'd been up a long time – one hour and forty minutes. Bit of an anti-climax, though. Still –

Back in dispersal, my crew told me that one of our chaps had just crashed on touch-down and that his aircraft had caught fire. What, one of ours? Now? I hadn't seen it. Sergeant Rowell, a voice said. Damaged by ack-ack, it appeared. By ack-ack? Probably those clowns at Dover!

For the first time I noticed that one of the hangars was in a terrible mess

with the remains of a Blenheim looking like a fish's skeleton the cat had left.
I was not on the 'state' on 4 September and did not fly. Instead, I went
into Epping to bathe and change at the Thatched House hotel, there being
no water on the station. Later, I returned and fell asleep in my room. The
weather was beautiful but I was much more interested in sleep.

Meanwhile, the squadron was scrambled twice but despite there being
sizeable raids to the south, they saw nothing. It was quite extraordinary
how twelve pairs of very acute eyes, their owners positively aching to make
an interception, could fail to see literally hundreds of enemy aircraft. But it
happened. All the time!

I came to slowly, feeling deliciously warm and quiet and rested. I had the
ability to sleep almost at will, a characteristic which stood me in good stead
in the weeks to come and one, indeed, which has never left me.

Earlier, I had met the station commander, Wing Commander Victor
Beamish, a smiling, affable man of about thirty-eight with a distinct northern
Irish accent. I immediately sensed that if you flew and pulled your weight
– fine! If you didn't – as Nick would have said – curtains! He flew one of our
Hurricanes wearing the letter 'B', the squadron holding one aircraft above
establishment for the purpose.

Relaxing to the point of indulgence, I went to the cinema in Epping that
evening.

There was lots of activity in the night and during the course of the
following morning we learned that one of 25 Squadron, a Pilot Officer
Herrick, had shot down two Huns, one after the other. In a Blenheim! In
my opinion, anyone brave enough to *take off* in a fighter Blenheim deserved
a gong! And here he was shooting down *two* Huns within minutes! And
at night! I met him in the mess later in the day, drinking his coffee. A pale-
faced chap with dark hair. Everyone thought him a whale of a hero.

I was on the 'state' early on in V7313, which rather looked as though it
might be mine in future. After a quiet start, we were scrambled at about ten
o'clock and ordered south, climbing away over London and the balloons
towards Northolt and Brooklands. However, whatever action there may have
been was over by the time we arrived as we saw nothing of interest. I suspect
ours was just a precautionary exercise as we were only up for forty minutes.

Our next scramble, however, was anything but precautionary. At about 2.30

p.m., we were off again and vectored towards the estuary to counter a raid said to be at 20,000 feet. Which presented a problem, as taking off from North Weald and flying approximately in a straight line, we could not make 20,000 feet by the time we had reached the river immediately to the east of London.

However, we clambered up very hard indeed and once more it was the ack-ack we saw first, smudging away on the horizon. After which, about a dozen Hun bombers materialized in a thin wedge, Heinkel 111s only I thought, although others reported Dornier 17s – perhaps there were both – and, infinitely more worrying, a cloud of midges above and behind which were 109s.

Again, in a beam attack and still climbing, I was in an unfavourable position to get in a shot at the bombers. Moreover, with more than half an eye on a group of Hun fighters on which I was turning my back, I found my attention diverted up to the moment when the squadron broke away. Anxious not to be left behind, I followed hot-foot!

And it was just as well that I did as, far from *not* taking part, the 109s fell upon us in a swarm, after which I had my hands full, for hours it seemed, but which could not have been for more than two minutes.

The 109s, being several thousand feet above us, had the advantage. Never having seen one close-to, I suddenly had several within yards of me. One, in fact, overtook me almost within touching distance to my right so that I could plainly see all the details of the fuselage with its coloured nose and black cross, and the spinner on the propeller, which had some sort of spiral emblem on it, rotating.

I was fascinated. It looked so pretty, slim and waspish. And fast, my goodness! It fairly scooted past me and, no doubt thinking I might be intending to turn on it, put its nose down with a jerk and dropped away like a stone.

Immediately there were others, all around me and passing above and below, diagonally, and in a variety of attitudes, so that for a few panic-stricken seconds I did not know which way to turn. But for no longer than that. Aware that I had been 'ball watching', I was suddenly galvanized into action, pulling and pushing like a madman and watching the horizon whirl and dip and soar and fall away, my engine screaming. Aircraft, friend and foe, flashed around my head like flies but I was intent only on escaping, expecting any moment the bang and pungent reek of exploding cannon shells. Round and round, desperately, my vision greying.

Then, in a magical second – nothing! I was on my own. Or, almost. The enemy had disappeared and there were several single Hurricanes only in the near distance, all flying in different directions. I formed up on one and together we joined a third. Soon there were several more. Finally, about five of us in an untidy group began to circle, as though dazed by the sudden and violent activity, before turning north. We were over the Thames still. In the region of Gravesend. Far below, pillars of black smoke were rising from the northern side of the river. The Huns had hit something and again, I had not fired a shot. I felt almost ashamed.

I landed back, limp with emotion and irritated by my inept performance.

In the crew-room there was the usual excitement and both jubilation and concern. One or two were missing; Butch Barton had been caught by one of the 109s and had baled out with his engine damaged and his aircraft on fire. Several Huns were being claimed as 'destroyed and 'probably destroyed' but, feeling something of an outsider, I did not pay much attention as to who had done what. 56 Squadron's intelligence officer, a thick-set man in glasses who always wore his service dress hat even in the crew-room, asked me what I had achieved and I replied glumly, 'Nothing!'

That night, on my bed in dispersal, I gave the matter a lot of thought. I was not very good, was I? I just couldn't go on *reacting*; I had to do something *positive*. To concentrate on one Hun aircraft at a time. Although, God knew, that was easier said than done. Those 109s had been dangerous and had darted about like minnows. Moreover, as they always hunted in twos, it would be jolly difficult, foolhardly even, to keep track of just one of them. If only they'd keep still for a moment! It had been the first time, too, that the blighters had come down; normally, Hun fighters just stood off and made faces. Someone back home must have been having a word with them.

As usual, bombers were over again that night. Lying there in the darkness, I listened to the noise of their engines, a thin, constant drone in the heavens. And at times, there would be the rapid tonk-tonk-tonk of the guns and, after an interval, the crump-crump-crump of bursting shells high above. Until I fell asleep. Unhappy. Exhausted.

6 September. A Friday, although it could have been any other day. And the

dawn chorus. In fact, it was a pre-dawn chorus and not of bird-song!

Our working day in a fighter squadron was from half-an-hour before dawn to half-an-hour after dusk; in early September, a mere eighteen hours.

In my bed in dispersal, one ear took in the sound of a Merlin starting up. Oh, God! So soon? I turned over restlessly, as did everyone else in the hut. What was it? Four a.m.? Something like that. Another engine burst into life. Then another. Finally, they were all going – twelve or more. Sleep was impossible.

Still with eyes closed, I waited, my mind dwelling on the familiar routine: warm the engine until the coolant temperature reached 60 degrees Centigrade, then open up to Olbs boost to test the mag. switches. After that, sometimes but not always, an enthusiastic 'erk' would apply full throttle. Oh, *no*! Not at this time in the morning. But no silent entreaty stopped them.

Finally, after twenty minutes or so, the clamour died away. Slowly and by degrees. To a deafening silence. Thank God!

If the squadron was at Readiness immediately, it also meant getting out of bed, dressing and donning flying clothing, or putting a Sidcot suit or Irving jacket – the ubiquitous 'goon-skin' – over pyjamas. After which, back *on* the bed, if not *in* it, to die once more.

Breakfast normally came around 8 a.m. in insulated boxes. Always bacon, hard-yoked yellow eggs and squares of fried bread as hard as rock. Like sleep-walkers, we would line up and take our share. And eat.

But, usually, not without interruption. The Huns, we decided later, had our meals timed to the second. As soon as the first forkful was lifted to the lips, the telephone would ring and the whole room would freeze. At worst, it would be 'Scramble!' At best, some preliminary warning of 50 plus, or 100 plus forming up over Calais. Just to whet the appetite!

Each officer had his own routine in the morning. My bed was next to Denis Parnall's, who was in a corner. Opposite and to my right, was Crossey; John Beazley was ahead at ten o'clock, Pat Wells on my left hand, and George Barclay, the other side and further down. Others, Percy Burton, 'Boost' Fleming, Butch Barton and more, remain faces – somewhere.

The tall, organized Denis Parnall was always up before me in his underclothes, shaving. Methodically lathering his face and applying the razor. Crossey, with a small black moustache, sitting up in bed holding a gold cigarette case with the outline of a map on it; and John Beazley, the Common Sergeant's son, with a big pipe, and a pretty revolting one at that. Pat Wells had one, too, his with a piece of sticking plaster wrapped around the stem. And George Barclay: tall, dark, good-looking George, also with his pipe, the undergraduate model with a long stem and small bowl, which he puffed like a novice. George, the son of a clergyman, had been at Cambridge when the war had started, but no one needed to be told; it was all there in his speech, his conversation and attitude to life.

Despite a pilot's camouflage of helmet, goggles and mask, individuals were easy to pick out in the air. Barclay, although six feet tall, always flew with his hood open and sat so low in the cockpit that only the top half of his face appeared above the coaming. John Beazley had a small head and once had us in stitches describing how his helmet had fallen over his eyes when in a tight and desperate turn avoiding a Hun. Then there was Crossey's impassive stare and Butch's minuteness. And Pat Wells always leaned and crouched in his seat. Each one different and recognizable.

I was not on the 'state' early on and missed the first engagement of the day. With breakfast in full swing, the whole squadron was scrambled about 8.30 a.m. and, after climbing up over Kent, ran into a large force of Dornier 17s and Ju88s accompanied by a sizeable fighter escort.

It was the situation as before, except that on this occasion the Hurricanes were properly at height. As on the previous day, a beam attack was carried out on the bombers but with no noticeable result, the 109s dropping down immediately and preventing a more deliberate and sustained assault. And, as before, the squadron was split up and after a time returned to base in several smaller groups.

They arrived back a little after 9.30 a.m., less John Grandy and Crossey. Each had been attacked by 109s, apparently, the latter force-landing safely but the CO being somewhat less fortunate. In process of reforming the squadron, he had been hit, wounded slightly, and forced to bale out when his aircraft had caught fire, catching a leg in his parachute lines and damaging it sufficiently to remove him from flying for some months thereafter.

I was on the second scramble, though. During the lunch hour – naturally!

Climbing up hard in the direction of the estuary, we were vectored over Southend but either missed our quarry or were positioned merely as insurance. I suspected it was the latter as we were up for slightly less than an hour, which was some twenty or thirty minutes less than the flying time of our average operational sortie.

Even so, I fell asleep immediately on my return. The weather was beautiful, which was a mixed blessing as the business of staring into the sun was very hard on the eyes. And the nerves!

I was awake – just – but still in a dream when we were scrambled again around 5 p.m. Running hard for my aircraft, I decided that the first thirty seconds after any scramble order was probably the most unattractive period of any operational trip, including being shot at! One's whole body and system jerked from torpor into violent activity in a matter of seconds. Barely twenty though I was, I felt like a corpse rising from a grave and being forced immediately into some horrendously strenuous ball-game. Every day it was the same. I *hated* it!

With Butch Barton leading, we were instructed to climb quickly to 20,000 feet and vectored towards the estuary yet again – Thameshaven, in fact – where, far below, there still rose a column of smoke from the attack of the previous day. As 'Lumba' – North Weald Sector Control – insisted that there were aircraft in our vicinity, we were all agog and poised to do battle in spite of there being nothing visible in an unending wilderness of cold, clear blue.

Anxious and a little perplexed that we were somehow missing something important, we paraded up and down the estuary and into Kent for quite some time until the inevitable 'pancake' order came and we dropped down westward over Essex. What on earth had gone wrong *this* time?

We were soon to learn. The station commander, Victor Beamish, having arrived at dispersal too late to accompany us, had taken off on his own in pursuit and in the act of climbing up to make a rendezvous, had run into a gaggle of Ju 87s which were dive-bombing Thameshaven from about 6,000 feet. Scarcely able to believe his luck, he had attacked them immediately and shot down two.

It transpired that we had been in exactly the right place, but 15,000 feet too high! Ju 87s! Ye gods! We positively drooled. We had never seen an 87, except from a distance. Why should it always happen to us?

Meanwhile, Thameshaven burned with renewed intensity, columns of black smoke towering to the heavens and providing a landmark and a beacon for days and nights to come.

Nothing much happened during the hours of darkness. One or two Huns came over high up but there were no thumps or bangs. Even the guns were silent. No sirens, even.

We had been discussing the fire problem in Hurricanes and what we should do to minimize the risk of being burned. Also, the open-or-shut-cockpit argument was resurrected.

A known fact was that a fire in a Hurricane caused by blazing fuel presented the pilot with a desperate and fearful crisis. In a matter of two or three seconds, the aircraft became untenable and the act of opening the cockpit hood for the purpose of baling out, had the effect of drawing the flames into the pilot's face. There were lurid tales of dashboards melting and running like treacle and the more imaginative and childish of us found heartless amusement visualizing scenes in which all the instruments dropped like stones into the bottom of the cockpit.

At first it was thought that the reserve fuel tank, located in front of the dashboard and containing about thirty gallons, was the source of most such fires but it soon became obvious that this was not so. The two wing tanks were the culprits. Not only were they easier to hit and puncture – the reserve tank was largely shielded by the engine, the pilot, and armour-plate – but there being no blanking-plates between wings and fuselage, the blazing fuel was drawn into the cockpit by the natural draught pattern, particularly if the guns had been fired and the linen patches which covered the gun ports blown off. Clearly, while the use of self-sealing tanks would obviously be of benefit, nothing short of redesigning the Hurricane would make much of an improvement. All fighters were susceptible to the fire hazard; the Hurricane was perhaps worse than some.

Meanwhile, the problem being insoluble, we would have to minimize the risk of being horribly burned by covering our arms, wearing gloves, goggles and flying boots at all times, and remembering that to open the hood was to encourage a rush of flames into the cockpit. Gone were the shirt-sleeve days. Moreover, the George Barclays of the many Hurricane squadrons would in future have to fly with closed hoods and suffer the disadvantage of sighting their enemy through a piece of perspex, a small price to pay in the circumstances. Personally, I was always in favour of flying with my hood closed; not only was it much more comfortable but, in my view, it increased the speed of the aircraft appreciably when flying above 250 mph.

By the end of the first week in September, therefore, we were all very fire-conscious and went into battle properly dressed for the occasion. And were we tempted to forget, the horrifying sight of dozens of pilots with faces and hands charred and livid beyond description, was a salutary reminder. None of us had seen Nick. But we had heard. By gum, we had!

The morning of 7 September dawned brilliant if misty; yet another example of the most perfect of Indian summers.

I was on the 'state' throughout the day and we were airborne twice before noon, the first flight around 9 a.m., but for a mere fifteen minutes; the second for almost an hour-and-a-half, during which we patrolled the estuary, the Isle of Sheppey, and as far east as Canterbury. There was an air of expectancy abroad. Something was most definitely *up*, the feeling almost tangible. There had been talk of invasion for some time. Was this the overture? The prelude?

Far below, the endless, unsullied grey-green map of the Thames estuary stretching to North Foreland, south-east England, and the line of the coast as far south as Dover and beyond, all suggested otherwise. We cruised about, backwards and forwards, in a sky of brilliant blue, while, at eye level and in every direction, there ran the straight, firm line of the horizon. We alone were alive, it seemed. My engine roared endlessly in an otherwise silent world. Nothing moved. No aircraft. Nothing. All quiet on the eastern front! Behind us, Thameshaven still burned, its smoke, a solid, motionless pillar of grey, rising thousands of feet.

Finally, we were brought back. Another fruitless sortie. Letting down yet again over the villages and flatlands of Essex: Basildon, Brentwood, Chipping Ongar and, at last, North Weald, the tapering woodland of Epping Forest curving away towards London.

With almost everyone else, I slept in the afternoon. On my bed and in my flying kit and Mae West, the enemy making no call on us until almost 4.30 p.m..

Then, we were scrambled again. 'Rochester-Maidstone patrol line,' was the shouted order. We raced into the air for the third time since breakfast, climbing up steeply towards the south and into the sun. I was Yellow 2, in the third section of three. What would it be this time?

We were in the area of Maidstone and at 18,000 feet when we sighted the tell-tale ack-ack bursts and immediately after, an armada of Huns: a thin wedge of Heinkel 111s, then Dornier 17s, all beneath a veritable cloud of fighters, 109s and 110s.

The cry went up, '*Tallyho*!' After which we slanted towards them purposefully. Twelve of us against 100, at least. Dear God! Where did we start?

We came in from the beam again – must we *always* attack from here? – but this time I had a clear sight of my quarry. Heinkels! Big, fat Heinkels. Like slugs. Huddled together as though for warmth. This time we couldn't miss.

Almost dispassionately, I watched them grow in my windscreen. I would hardly need my sight. Heavens! Were my guns on 'Fire'? A hasty glance down to confirm that they were then back again to the pink graticules, moving my head in order to centre it exactly. Hurricanes bunching and rocking furiously to the left of me. Keep *away*! I banked even more sharply to get a clear run. Curving hard. Pulling. Only moments now. Close enough to distinguish separate aircraft. Surging towards me. *Watch out*! I began to fire.

The Hurricane's eight Brownings did not chatter, the noise was of a thick, coarse fabric being ripped, a concentrated tearing noise which shook the aircraft with a vibration that was indescribably pleasant. Ahead, smoking tentacles reached out in clutching traces and felt about the leading vic of Heinkels with blind, exploring fingers. The briefest ripple of twinkling lights. Like a child's sparkler. I was hitting them! I couldn't miss!

Then, in a moment they were enormous and I was upon them. I thrust forwards, rising violently against my straps and, conscious of my engine pausing breathlessly for one – two – seconds, with several other Hurricanes, I flashed beneath a trio of pale, curved bellies before turning on my back and pulling hard so that my aircraft fell away like a stone, the slipstream rising to a scream, the distant earth plumb in my windscreen and dust whirling around my face. Then, I was pulling out. Hard. And searching upwards. There were other aircraft. Everywhere. Going like hell. In every direction. I pulled harder. Turning. Then climbing. Searching for 109s. Where were the bombers? Gone! I couldn't see them.

But the 109s were there. One was off to my right, coming towards me. Slightly above but flying in the opposite direction. I instinctively turned towards it and, pulling hard, fired. The Hun ignored me, curving away in a slight dive. Emboldened and wildly excited, I shot after him, urging my aircraft on. Faster! Faster! Had he seen me? Surely he must have! Everything straining and shaking, but catching up. I fired again. And again. A few bright strikes. A brief puff of dark smoke. A thin plume of white, then a slightly thicker tail of darkening grey.

The 109 suddenly looked tired. It leaned slowly to its right and slid downwards gently. I fired again. And again. It sat there, tilting. In a way, pathetic. Then, momentarily, a small puff of debris exploded into the air. It was dying. The aircraft was dying. Like an animal, mortally wounded. Not the pilot or a man, but an aircraft. It fell away. Sadly. The angle steepening, the trail thickening. I let it go. To its death. Watching.

I came to with a jerk. I was committing the cardinal error of being alone. I looked about hastily. The squadron had vanished. I was down at something less than 10,000 feet. Turning towards the north, I began to climb, my neck on a swivel.

There was a group of aircraft ahead of me and higher. Crossing left to right. About a dozen and they looked like Hurricanes. I climbed towards them going flat out.

They were, indeed, Hurricanes and I attached myself to the rear of the formation. A fellow, noticing me, turned and stared then looked away. The letters on his side were J–something, N or Z perhaps. (In fact, they were probably JX, I learned later). Not being on the same radio frequency, I found myself a silent observer. But, they were friends and meant security. That was enough for me.

Climbing slightly, we flew north-east. For almost five minutes. Then, I saw why.

Roughly parallel to us and going in an easterly direction, was another armada of Huns. Dornier 17s and 109s. The bombers about 1,500 feet lower, the fighters at our own level. It was about the first time I had ever looked down on the enemy from above.

As we were flying on a slightly converging course, we seemed to be looking at each other for hours. They had obviously seen us, too, and were bracing themselves. Then, as we grew closer and I sensed that we were about to attack, half-a-dozen yellow-nosed 109s – my Hun had been a very ordinary grey-green colour – peeled off to the right and came round to our rear. My rear! But, in an instant, my fears were forgotten. My leader began to dive and I tumbled down after him.

It was to be a madly exciting twenty seconds, a cavalry charge of the wildest kind with all weapons bared. I found myself going down in a thirty degree dive towards the starboard front quarter of the bomber formation. One of a solid wedge of Hurricanes. *Firing*!

In a fever of enthusiasm, I watched the Dorniers grow in my sight until they were fairly rushing towards me. Thin streamers of white were curling in our direction but they were ignored. Then, when a collision seemed inevitable, we were through – a chaos of wings, engines, and fuselages with black crosses. A series of violent bumps after which, in an instant, they were gone and I was somewhere below, diving like a gannet, the wind screaming around my head and my controls tight and vibrating. My guns had stopped. Down! Down! Faster! Faster! The Thames somewhere around my right ear. Pillars of smoke rising crookedly and spreading. Thameshaven? I didn't know. I began to pull out. Everything straining... and going grey. Then quietening down. Gradually. I straightened out. And recovered my breath.

With my guns empty, there was no use hanging about. Time to go home.

As I was down to less than 3,000 feet, I had to fly eastwards initially to avoid some balloons I saw in the distance so that I crossed the river to the east of Gravesend. On my right, the smoke was still thick over Thameshaven and there seemed to be more smoke and the red flicker of flames in the direction of the City. The last batch of Huns had obviously been going home having done their worst.

I landed, alone, and taxied in. There seemed to be very few Hurricanes around and my crew looked concerned, explaining that only several had returned. I climbed down wearily and walked off as they clustered round attending to the refuelling and rearming. However, I had not even reached the dispersal hut when the air-raid siren went. I looked up hastily. Not another bombing attack!

I ran back to my aircraft but it was still crawling with airmen. I hung about, fuming and impatient, while several of the squadron took off. Then, far above and directly overhead, a large enemy formation drifted across, their engines a dull throbbing roar. Crikey! Were we just about to be deluged? Well, we'd soon see!

My aircraft ready, I leaped in, started up, and roared away towards the masts, mad keen to get off the ground. The enemy formation was still in sight but miles above me.

I climbed away as fast as I was able and, at about 8,000 feet, was surprised to see a parachute above and ahead, drifting down in my direction. I watched it sail by my wing as I laboured upwards. Whose, I wondered? One of ours? It couldn't be. There was not time for them to have reached the raid.

The enemy force in the far distance and marked by a moving barrage of ack-ack, I toiled on in pursuit as steeply as I dared but with a feeling of utter hopelessness. I was alone. What could I hope to achieve?

I was back over London at almost 15,000 feet and in the middle of a heavy barrage of ack-ack myself when I came within shooting distance of one of the Dornier 17s. Straggling and to one side of the main formation, it was still a little too high and far away for me to get in a really damaging shot. However, I was weary and becoming increasingly alarmed by the manner in which the ack-ack was bursting all around me. Bloody guns! They didn't give a hoot about *me*!

As a final, forlorn gesture, I lifted my nose, drew a bead, and fired. Several long bursts, until all my ammunition was expended. That was *it*, I'd had a go! As I fell away downwards and turned towards base, my last glance was in the direction of the Dornier, still forging ahead. Unmoved and as though nothing had happened.

I flew back. My guard down. Totally spent. Since breakfast, I had been in the air for more than four hours.

The dispersal hut was a scene of restrained anxiety. The squadron had been decimated. George Barclay had force-landed in a field somewhere close to North Weald, Pat Wells was missing, Boost Fleming had been shot down in flames and seen to bale out, and both Sergeants Smithson and Killingback had gone, the former badly wounded, apparently, someone having seen him in the air holding up an arm covered in blood. And the parachute I had encountered on my last trip had been Sergeant Beard's. But how? No one was sure. Ack-ack, probably, someone said. Our own!

Our interrogation by the intelligence officer that evening was a subdued affair. All told, five Huns were being claimed as 'destroyed' and 'damaged', my own included. But somehow, they didn't seem that important. We were down to a few aircraft – about five or six. God, what a day!

Bryan Meaker and 'Stooge' Loweth, who had been down to collect John Grandy from the hospital in Maidstone, appeared in due course with a lurid tale about being bombed in the region of the Blackwall Tunnel and having been obliged to abandon their car and run for it. Which cheered us up considerably.

But by dusk there had been no news of Pat Wells and we learned that Boost Fleming had died. Poor, poor Boost. Someone said that he had landed in a field by parachute and had been seen rushing about beating out flames in his trousers, which sounded very much like a Laurel and Hardy comedy and caused some hilarity. But, alas, it had been no laughing matter; he had died later of burns and shock. The quiet, charming, courteous Boost. So gentle and unwarrior-like in nature and appearance.

Smithson and Killingback were safe, it seemed, which was a blessing, Killingback having baled out in the Maidstone area. Even so, both wounded, they would be lost to us for some time. Good men, the pair of them; we would miss them greatly.

The dispersal hut seemed empty that night and there were Huns over London until dawn, the searchlights and guns active throughout the hours of darkness. The glare from the blazing oil tanks on the river could be seen in the sky for miles around. What a wonderful beacon for the bombers!

For the next two days, the Huns sulked in their tents and the squadron was not called upon to fly other than to carry out two half-hearted patrols, one over the Isle of Sheppey in the late afternoon of 9 September when some 109s flew high overhead. But who cared about 109s on their own?

Down to five serviceable aircraft for at least part of the period, there was not much we could have done anyway. And as my aircraft insisted on showering oil over the windscreen from the rear of the airscrew, I was none too pleased with that either, serviceable though it was listed.

There was more news of an invasion, barges and other small craft being seen congregating in some of the Channel ports. Victor Beamish, a frequent and very welcome visitor to our dispersal hut, kept mentioning it gleefully and rubbing his hands at the prospect. Invasion? I was not too concerned one way or the other. On balance, however, I preferred it *not* to happen. Opinion was that we would cope all right in the air but that the Army was an unknown quantity. Quite apart from the professionalism of the non-regular element – something questionable, it had to be said – they didn't seem to have enough of anything. Sombre memories of Dunkirk still lingered in our minds.

No. 46 Squadron, which operated from North Weald's satellite airfield, Stapleford Tawney, had run into trouble over Sheppey on 8 September and had lost several chaps at the hands of some 109s. Concentrating as they did on the bombers, Hurricanes were often sitting ducks for escorting fighters, and even when stooging about on patrol, we often felt at a great disadvantage in our inflexible formations, especially above 18,000 feet where the 109s were so much more nimble. The old Hurricane, as strong as a carthorse and thoroughly capable lower down and among the bombers, was somewhat lacking when it came to fighter versus fighter combat. We were not in any way concerned, just irritated when our aircraft did not have the performance to catch the Hun fighters or give us the initiative other than when we held a clear tactical advantage, which was so seldom as to be unique. There was constant talk of a Hurricane Mark II with a bigger engine, a better performance at altitude, and cannons. Why weren't we getting them, then? How much better employed they would be in 249 at North Weald than sitting in some field in Scotland, or wherever.

There was talk, too, of us flying in pairs rather than in sections of three, and also of operating in larger formations, 249 and 46 being lumped together. No. 12 Group, which commenced at Duxford to the north of us, favoured the larger formations of up to sixty aircraft known as Balbos, after the Italian General Balbo who used them during the Abyssinian Campaign and after. This produced some bitter comments from North Weald from time to time. What was the point of flying about in hordes if you never arrived at the scene of the battle in time?

On both nights, there was heavy bombing over London. The nocturnal droning continued unabated and the mess was so shaken by gun-fire that we assumed that mobile artillery was being shunted up and down the railway which ran alongside the aerodrome.

Even so, none of us seemed in the least upset by all the bombing, noise and fuss. In wartime you became used to anything.

11 September Wednesday. A misty start with promise of fine weather to come. More invasion talk, which was shrugged off.

We were at '30 minutes available' until the afternoon. New Hurricanes had been flown in and we were back to full strength. No one knew, or cared, where they had come from; they just arrived. Shortage of aircraft? Not as far as we knew. Our squadron code letters, GN, were also reappearing in place of 56's US, making us feel whole again, my own aircraft once more bearing the letter F.

Several new pilots were posted in to fill the gaps in our ranks. Things were looking up. The wounds were healing.

At about 3.30 p.m., we were sent off in a hurry to patrol east of London at 17,000 feet; the routine climb, my engine raging away at almost full throttle and 2,650 revs. I was Blue two, in front and fairly comfortable. But, God help those behind!

London, down on the right, as ever. The balloons – they must be holding the place up! – and the Thames below; I was beginning to know every twist and turn of it. We shuddered and flicked through a little cloud but it was nothing to worry about.

At around 15,000 feet, crossing Gravesend, we were suddenly turned south. There was urgency in 'Lumba's' tones and, within minutes, we knew why.

'Tallyho!'

Ack-ack bursts – distant, silent brown flowers. The instant wave of surging excitement mingled with apprehension. A thick line of bombers, almost at our own level, and the inevitable cloud of fighters behind. The whole force like a cloaked villain stepping out of the blackness in some horror film. Advancing towards us. Slowly. Inexorably. Aiming directly for the City. Thirty? Forty? Fifty? Who knew? Too many, anyway.

No beam attack, this. Straight for them. A head-on attack, by God! Perhaps not quite. Guns? Sight? My revs rose to 2,850 with a minor scream, my Hurricane hesitating fractionally as the airscrew fined and bit. Then, everyone jostling, leaning, squeezing together, my eyes flicking left and right for station-keeping, then ahead, focusing on the Huns. Growing now. More jostling. This was going to be difficult. Everyone pushing. Squeezing. Then *firing*!

The line of Heinkels growing magically in my windscreen. My guns *ripping* and shuddering. Lines of sparks and smoke streaking ahead. Curving. But only briefly. The wing of another Hurricane wobbling crazily by my left ear. *Watch out*! I was forced to pull away, shrieking expletives.

Then, it was all over. I was falling away earthwards, my engine and the wind a high-pitched scream. Were we being followed? I didn't know and couldn't turn to find out. I pulled back, everything straining and going grey then black. Other Hurricanes about. I climbed. Looking about urgently. The sky still stained with drifting ack-ack smoke and the bombers away to my left and mere dots in the distance. Had we hit them? Impossible to say. What a disaster! Full throttle. I raced in their direction. Climbing. Keeping a watchful eye above and on my tail.

I was going north again and aware that there were many isolated aircraft flying in that direction seemingly with lemming-like compulsion. Then, suddenly, others flying south, a large formation. This time with ack-ack blossoming around them. Huns again! Bombers, but apparently no fighters. No fighters? Warily, I searched about. None obvious. Had they been drawn off or scattered?

The bombers, once more, were Heinkels. In a loose and irregular formation, as though they had already been attacked. Returning, no doubt. Were they the ones we had shot at? They couldn't be!

I turned sharply across the rear of the formation, about 1,000 feet above. What a luxury. Above the bombers and no fighters! I selected the one on the right hand side of the formation and dived down, noting with satisfaction several Hurricanes turning with me to my left.

Deciding to attack from underneath, I was dipping below the tail when the rear gunner shot at me. The tracer came out, a twisting streamer of white which curled lazily towards me then flicked by so close that I instinctively ducked. It so put me off my stroke that I veered away for a second or two before turning back and, pulling up slightly, fired to discourage the man doing the shooting.

Whatever it did to the enemy, my own tracer was an immense morale-booster for me as it clawed and rippled all around and over the aircraft in front, twinkling briefly as some of the bullets struck. No sense in breaking away. I dropped back a little and fired again, carried away by an incredible blood-lust and feeling of exultation. I was *hitting* it! I *must* be. Smoke! Was that smoke?

A greasy trail began to stream from the starboard engine, not smoke exactly but a darkening stain which, after about twenty seconds, ceased. But, damage had been done. I saw that the Heinkel was losing ground and falling away from the formation. Encouraged, I fired again. And again. I couldn't have much ammunition left. I willed it to go down. It *must* go down. Other Hurricanes were still away to my left, plus a Spitfire. I had no thought of 109s.

I followed the Heinkel down as it gradually lost height. A long way, through patches of thin cloud until, eventually and still under control, it crash-landed in a field alongside a railway line some long way south of London. I circled it several times at about 500 feet and saw one – two – figures emerge from the wreckage. They didn't wave. But then, I could hardly have expected them to.

I was so elated that I thought of landing somewhere nearby. In a field. Anywhere. Except that I didn't know where I was. So, I climbed up again and flew north at only several thousand feet. Shouting and screaming my head off and feeling like a king.

Back at dispersal I learned that Sergeant Davis had been shot down; baling out after being set on fire, he had landed somewhere in Kent. Poor chap! A nice boy, Davis. Bit of a P.G. Wodehouse character, I had always thought.

I hardly had time to draw breath before we were off once more, this time being vectored due south until we were in the Dover area yet again. Far below, the harbour and the balloons.

Lower than usual, we were at 13,000 feet when several separate formations of 109s flew across the top and followed us about. They did not attack but came close enough for us to see quite clearly their brightly-coloured noses. Were the yellow-nosed fellows a special breed? Or just a Hun squadron or two wishing to look different? Either way, we were not impressed; all 109s were the same to us.

Even so, those chaps made a nuisance of themselves, keeping our necks swivelling around for almost twenty minutes. Someone said later that bombs had fallen in Dover Harbour but I did not see any.

We flew back home wishing we had an aircraft with the performance to meet the Huns on even terms. That was the trouble with the Hurricane; once underneath, always underneath. One day, though – !

Enemy bombers were over throughout the night and the guns were going like mad, 'tonk-tonk-tonking' and 'crumping' away in fine style. Able to sleep through anything, I was not unduly disturbed but several of the others were kept awake. Two Hun bombers were brought down fairly close to us, we were told, but no one was very interested.

I wondered how many ack-ack rounds were needed to bring down one Hun bomber. About a million, I imagined. Jolly expensive way of doing things.

The following day dawned cloudy and windy and soon rain added to its quota of unpleasantness. For us, it was welcome relief. Even so, I was off on my own shortly after 10 a.m., after a single Hun, wandering around southern Essex for almost an hour and at one time finding myself well to the south into Kent. But, no Hun.

I found I did not mind prowling about in such weather. Even at its most miserable, cloud invariable comes in layers so that it was possible to find oneself in the clear but in endless galleries of the most sombre and daunting grey, unable to see in any direction other than straight ahead and to the sides. Such conditions being ideal for the single, marauding Hun bomber, it was *the* most thrilling and satisfying experience to come across a Dornier 17 or Ju 88 skulking between the layers or drifting from cloud to cloud, dark silhouettes of menace. There to be shot at! A most exciting game of hunter and hunted.

Now and then, those of us so engaged would find all the London balloons sticking out of the cloud-tops, providing a perfect guide for any Hun wishing to dispose of his load of high explosive. On such occasions, it would be our duty to inform 'Lumba' so that the balloons could be hauled down to a lower altitude. A thousand balloons! It always gave me a unique sense of power to pass on such information.

The weather becoming steadily worse, nothing more was asked of us and we were brought to 'one hour available' and allowed to go to the mess. We all passed a quiet afternoon and evening reading and sleeping. Dennis Wheatley was a very popular author at the time with his Gregory Sallust stories and there was a well-thumbed 'naughty' called *No Orchids for Miss Blandish*, by James Hadley Chase. Then and later, I played endless games of snooker in the mess with Crossey but hardly ever won. I was too impatient for the game.

There was good news about Pat Wells who had been traced to Shorncliffe Hospital, having been missing a week. But, how did anyone go missing for that length of time in England? Disgraceful!

The telephone had been hopeless since the station was bombed earlier in the month and I had given up ringing home. Instead, I wrote every day, missing out the gory bits and anything that might upset my parents.

There was hardly anything over that night and the guns were silent. I slept undisturbed in my room alongside the mess and felt positively pampered when my batman brought me morning tea.

The weather was much the same the following day and I did not fly at all. Another officer and two more NCO pilots were posted in, one of whom was 'Dusty' Mills, who had been with me at Montrose. I did not know him that well but it was nice to see a familiar face. ''Appy 'Arry' Davidson, meanwhile, was very much a popular and well-established member of the squadron and had done excellently in a not too flamboyant way. Some fellows were 'always there', he being one of them and Ozzie Crossey another. Someone remarked that Davidson's laugh was better than a box of Beecham's Pills. It was, too. A tremendous morale-raiser. Yes, I was in a jolly good squadron all right.

The weather was better on 14 September although there was plenty of cloud around 9,000 feet. We were not very well organized as a squadron going up through thick cloud. Climbing in sections of four usually, those at the rear sometimes emerged at the top either ahead, above, or to the side of those in front, indicating that they had either passed or crossed over in the murk. Not very comforting! On the whole though, we managed tolerably well and did not worry about it too much.

I flew three times during the day and my letter home, written the same evening, gave emphasis to one of the misconceptions of the moment.

I wrote: 'Much more action today with bags of flying but no shooting. The yellow-nosed 109s and the newer Heinkel 113 fighters were about in force. We didn't actually come to grips but nearly did so several times.

'The Heinkel 113 is almost identical to the Spitfire with a curved wing and, as the Hun has taken the precaution of camouflaging them similarly to the Spit and painting on red-white-and-blue rings, they are a bit difficult to distinguish.'

The dastardly Hun! There never were any Heinkel 113s, although there wasn't a pilot in 249 who would not have sworn on his grandmother's bones that he had seen them. Such were the fantasies of war; the so-called facts vehemently asserted with the deepest of sincerity.

Several new chaps joined the squadron that day, one an impressive looking South African named Lewis, who stood about 6ft 3in and had flaxen-blond hair, together with a baby-faced sergeant called Palliser. Lewis came from 85 Squadron and, already decorated, was very experienced. Palliser, too, had come from another squadron though I did not know which.

15 September. A momentous day and more talk of invasion. The weather misty initially then fine with much broken cloud at around 10,000 feet. A wonderful backcloth for fighting, the Hun bombers we were later to encounter, starkly revealed against a carpet of white interspersed with towering pyramids of billowing cumulus.

After an undisturbed breakfast and in line with the new policy of concentrating forces, we were sent off around 11.30 a.m., climbing up on the well-worn path to the east of London in company with 46 Squadron. There being a fair amount of cloud, we charged in and out of it for a time before bursting through like salmon at around 12,000 feet, condensation streaming from our hoods.

I always had mixed feelings about coming out on top and into the sun, mostly of sheer exhilaration tinged with just a little concern. As we emerged, shadows of our aircraft would race alongside us surrounded by the most brilliant of rainbow rings. On the other hand, we could be seen from above for miles around and were easy targets initially, blinking in the sunlight and, for perhaps half-a-minute, a little disorientated.

We were vectored south over Kent and were at 17,000 feet when we saw the first ack-ack puffs. What *would* we do without them!

Then, in the middle, the enemy. Dorniers, this time, their shoulder-wing silhouettes easily identified. We had been discussing whether the Dorniers we had been meeting were 17s or 215s. Something to do with the engines, apparently. But, what difference did it make? They were all Dorniers!

Again, the hunter's primitive surge of exultation mixed with unashamed fear. Another attack. Would I survive?

They were above us, but only just, and flying in the opposite direction. We turned, climbing hard, crossed their path then turned again, coming in from their left. The squadron seemed jumpy on that occasion and more spread out than usual. I found myself approaching quickly from the quarter and, inexplicably, neither comfortable nor happy. A Dornier swam into my windscreen, growing in the gun-sight. There were Hurricanes all around and some other aircraft overhead. Where were the 109s? My back felt naked.

My attention riveted on the target, I closed and fired, my guns jarring, the tracer, flecked with sparks, curving away. The flash of wings as one – two – Hurricanes peeled off. More aircraft. Banking. Whose? The Dorniers right above me now, passing almost within touching distance – pale wings, engines, and black crosses. Smears of oil on the undersides, even. God, I was close! I fell away, not so much because I had to, but to take stock. There were aircraft everywhere, some of them Spitfires. The bombers now in the distance and to my left. Forging ahead. One of them trailing and falling behind, surrounded by Hurricanes – wolves worrying a flagging deer. After the others! I climbed flat out and closed, handling the controls violently, my aircraft for some reason vibrating. And fired again. Then fell away. Above, 109s. Crossing, quickly. Three or four. An aircraft attacked me from behind and I whirled about. A Spitfire! *Bloody Spitfires*! Why couldn't they attend to their own business? More aircraft and ack-ack in the distance. After which... nothing! Serenity. Just masses of cloud, the faintest stains of ack-ack smoke and several Hurricanes. I flew towards them, limp with emotion, and joined up.

My crew were excited when I returned, the charred gun ports a sure sign of action. Running towards me, their enthusiasm waned when my face told the story. Nothing? Hard luck, sir, they sympathized.

They hooked up the bowser and tore off the wing panels to rearm my guns with endless yards of bullets. Guns OK? I thought so; they didn't stop, anyway. A man dragging oxygen in my direction. Engine all right, sir? I said that it was but thought fit to complain of oil from the airscrew. Couldn't see to hit anything if the windscreen was covered with goo, could I? They agreed and set about cleaning it and inspecting the front where yellow smears feet long trailed back along the front cowlings. Also for bullet holes. Had I been hit? I didn't think so, but you never could tell. They searched – hopefully.

In the dispersal hut I learned that several aircraft were missing. Both the new chaps Lewis and Palliser and another fellow called Lofts, who had lately come from one of the Auxiliary squadrons. Too soon to worry, though. They could have lobbed down anywhere, or simply lost themselves.

A lot of chatter. A few Huns were being claimed as 'probable' and 'damaged' by unidentified voices. Not a great squadron success, though. Odd that, because it should have been.

Lunch arrived with combat reports, plates and food sharing the same table. I sat on my bed, eating. Not too happy with life. Finally, I lay back and, still in my Mae West, slept like a log.

I was dragged from the deepest pit of unconsciousness by the telephone and the bellowed cry of 'Scramble!' Rolling off my bed, I followed in the wake of the thumping boots like a zombie. Two o'clock, for God's sake! What were the Huns doing to us?

I was awake sufficiently to strap on my parachute which was draped over the tailplane – I hated it being in the cockpit seat – and scrambled aboard. Yellow 2! Fairly far back this time as Butch, Blue 1, was leading. I raced into position, turned, and took off.

We were not far removed from the scene of our fight in the morning when some 109s flew across our heads several thousand feet higher. The harbingers of trouble! Then, the familiar ack-ack and line of bombers. Dorniers again. We were about the same height and not badly positioned. We curved towards them, climbing slightly.

The Dorniers – I counted seven or eight of them in the nearest group – were in a broad vic and I mentally resolved not to fly into the middle of the formation and risk being shot to pieces by rear-gunner crossfire. Instead, I concentrated on an aircraft out on the right and, everything clicking into place, found myself dead astern, just below it and pitching about in its slipstream.

Closing, I fired immediately and the whole of the port side of the German aircraft was engulfed by my tracer. The effect was instantaneous; there was a splash of something, like water being struck with the back of a spoon. Beside myself with excitement, I fired again, a longish burst, and finding that I was too close, fell back a little but kept my position.

Then, astonishingly, before I was ready to renew my assault, two large objects detached themselves from the fuselage and came in my direction, so quickly, in fact, that I had no time to evade. Comprehension barely keeping pace with events, I suddenly recognized spreadeagled arms and legs as two bodies flew past my head, heavy with the bulges that were undeveloped parachutes. The crew! Baling out! I veered away, shocked by what I had just achieved.

But I had little time in which to dwell on the matter as I was immediately engulfed by 109s which swept over my head and turned towards me venomously, clearly intent on murder.

I have no recollection of what precisely I did except that, in a frenzy of self-preservation, I pulled and pushed and savagely yanked my aircraft about, firing whenever I caught sight of a wing or a fuselage in my windscreen. They were not sighted bursts, just panic hosings designed to scare rather than kill and directed against aircraft that were often within yards of me. For all of, what? – twenty seconds? A murderous, desperate interlude.

Then, as so often happened, they were gone and I was alone. Not alone, exactly, but not immediately threatened. There were perhaps half a dozen aircraft visible in that vast arena of clouds and space in which I was a single moving dot. Including one Dornier, slightly higher, heading purposefully across my bows for a massive cloud on my right. Aware that I could see vestiges of the Thames ahead and far below, I began to cut the corner and chase after it.

It took me perhaps half a minute of hard flying to catch up, by which time I saw that I had another aircraft on my left, a Spitfire. We flew line abreast, some 200 yards apart, following the Hun who was then about 800 yards ahead.

I doubt that either of us achieved a worthwhile shot before it disappeared into the first large cumulus. However, racing round to the far side, I – and I am sure the pilot of the Spitfire, too – was enormously relieved to observe it reappear. After which, dismayed no doubt by the limited size of his temporary sanctuary, the Hun began to dive, not steeply but in a ten degree nose-down attitude.

Thereafter, it was easy. Without interference, we took turns in carrying out astern attacks and were gratified to see a translucent stain of dark smoke emerge from one, then both of the engines. Meanwhile the Dornier continued to descend, flying eastwards down the estuary and out towards the sea, gradually losing height and speed.

Realizing that I could not have much ammunition left, I carried out one careful attack from dead astern during which all my guns, other than one, fell silent. I pressed again. A faint shrill chatter continued for a second, after which – nothing. The rear gunner long since inactive, I pulled aside to starboard and watched. The Spitfire approached, fired, then did much the same to port. The Dornier laboured on, down – down – barely clearing the masts of a convoy of ships some five miles beyond Shoeburyness, then continued into the open wastes of the North Sea.

I watched, impotent and fairly jumping about with frustration, formating a mere thirty yards to one side. Were we going to lose him? I *willed* that aircraft into the water.

Now about twenty feet above the waves, I was beginning to think that the Hun would finally escape when I noticed the Dornier's tail dropping and the nose rising. Up, up, up, it came... slowly... the aircraft struggling valiantly to maintain height. Then, all at once, the tail touched, the fuselage lurched forward and the Dornier crashed down in an enormous flurry of white spray. Disappearing, initially, it came to the surface and lay there for a short time, waterlogged. Then, slowly, gradually, it sank.

No one – nothing – remained. Only a smudge of slightly paler green. The Spitfire and I flew round once – twice – then turned back for the shore. As we crossed the convoy for the second time, steam spouted from a row of ship's whistles. Someone was pleased, anyway.

We flew inland together. The Spit had EB on its side and, with a wave from the cockpit, pulled away shortly after crossing the coast. I had no idea to which squadron it belonged.

Back at dispersal, I found a queue of pilots leading to the intelligence officer, everyone in a high state of excitement. It had been a fantastic fight, no one missing and a mounting tally of Huns: seven, eight, nine 'destroyed' and about a similar number 'probable' and 'damaged'. What a to-do! Crashed Huns burning on the ground everywhere; someone said that he had seen at least two. Plus mine in the sea, of course!

The station commander, Victor Beamish, was grinning to beat the band and congratulating everyone. Calling me 'Ginger'. Marvellous, he kept saying, broad smiles all over his Irish face until I thought it would crack. This was the day, apparently; if the Huns had pulled it off today, the invasion was on.

The invasion! I'd forgotten about the invasion. Well, the Hun hadn't pulled it off, had he? We, plus the chaps in the Hampdens, Wellingtons, Battles and Blenheims, who'd been bombing the Channel ports every night for a week or more, had been successful. Had it ever been in doubt? Those poor blokes in the Battles, though!

We were still deep in discussion when we were scrambled once more, a little after 5 p.m.

Not Thameshaven again! We climbed up and up until we were more than 20,000 feet over the estuary where we stayed for well over an hour, getting colder by the minute. Backwards and forwards, up and down, round and round. My oath, it was freezing! If I lowered my seat and bent right down, I could just touch the warm pipe which ran from the engine to the radiator with the tips of the fingers of my right hand. Why, in God's name, couldn't they put some heat into these *bloody* aircraft?

But there were no Huns about in the clearest if darkening of blue skies and we finally turned for home. Frozen, but on top of the world.

I wrote to my parents, almost breathlessly, in the short interval before dinner. We had heard on the wireless that 180-odd Huns had been shot down. One-hundred-and-eighty! It sounded an incredible number, but I supposed they knew what they were talking about. If all the squadrons had done as well as ours, it could add up to that. We were a splendid bunch of chaps, all right!

There was a party in the mess that night and I drank whisky and ginger ale, which was the only grog I could stomach, until the room started to move around and I began to hear myself talking nonsense. After which, I felt sick and was obliged to retire. If there were any Huns about that night, I didn't hear them!

It was arranged the following morning that Crossey and I should have the day off but, in spite of that, I was on an early show which took off a little after 7 a.m. The weather was miserable – low, medium and high cloud up to 20,000 feet – and we jogged and buffeted our way up through the murk before being vectored south.

En route to the Channel, we watched groups of 109s contrailing above our heads and way beyond our reach, our only consolation being that they were probably a good deal colder than we were at that moment. It was a minor relief to realize that if they did decide to come down, we would see them as we too were trailing, off and on.

It was a messy trip; with 46 Squadron close to us, there were lots of Hurricanes about and we kept getting in each other's way. Then, when we finally headed for home and began to descend through cloud, the squadron was split up and half our number disappeared. At which point I began to lose interest, wanting to get back to North Weald. Mostly, because I was cold and hungry, but also because I did not want to miss my day off.

In the afternoon, 'Ozzie' Crossey and I went into London and after spending a relaxing hour with the hairdresser in Austin Reed's – always a must for Crossey – we had tea and shopped around for model aircraft.

The evening proved to be a disappointment. London had been heavily damaged in places and was so obviously on edge that we found the theatres and cinemas planning to close at 9 p.m. The Regent Palace, as usual, was full of small, fat, crinkly-haired gentlemen – where did they all come from, for heaven's sake? – and the guns made a terrible din all night, being trundled through the streets (we assumed) to where the action was fiercest. The only good thing about guns, we opined, was that with every bang regarded as a shell being fired, with a bit of imagination, there were no bombs being dropped at all!

We arrived back at North Weald the following afternoon and I went back on the 'state' immediately. Within an hour, the squadron was up on patrol again, south of London, listening to 'Lumba' telling us that there were Huns in our vicinity. There were certainly a lot of aircraft high up, contrailing, but they could have been anything. It was jolly cold again.

Increasingly, there seemed to be masses of Hurricanes about. I decided that there was such a thing as having *too* many friends; it was a curious fact that with twelve Hurricanes and twelve 109s in the same piece of sky, one tended to see eighteen Hurricanes and six 109s. Paradoxically, I was beginning to believe that it was better to be one of a minority group than the other way round. Then, one could more easily pick out the Hun and had something to shoot at.

It was on that trip that my air speed indicator seized up, or almost so, worrying the life out of me. Fool that I was, I had forgotten to switch on my pitot-head heater. Nothing was worse than to have one's ASI stop working. Particularly in cloud.

Wednesday 18 September. The weather good but blustery with blue sky and masses of cumulus.

We were off at 9.15 a.m., climbing up towards the south, enormous white icebergs on all sides of us, dwarfing the squadron with their size and majesty as we sailed between them. Without the worries of station-keeping and impending combat, such magnificence would probably have aroused a greater passion in my breast than it did, although I never failed to be stirred by the sheer grandeur of the heavens, particularly in autumn and spring. A vast, fascinating and, at times, frightening place, the sky.

Climbing to 20,000 feet, we roamed around between Southend and North Foreland but, despite warnings of high-flying Huns, saw nothing of interest.

Around lunch-time, we were scrambled again – an unusual liberty, in our opinion. The unwritten rule was, one or two trips in the morning then up to two in the middle and late afternoon. But, not over lunch, for heaven's sake!

We climbed up towards the estuary and were about 16,000 feet flying eastwards when we were warned of a big raid approaching from the Deal area. Immediately dry-mouthed, I sensed another major engagement and checked around my cockpit.

Then, straight ahead and emerging out of nothing, the ack-ack and a mass of aircraft high up. 109s! After which, the familiar slow-moving wedge of larger aircraft. Heinkels again! Coming straight for us and at the same height. No climbing up on this occasion. A classic head-on attack. Classic? Head-on attacks didn't suit me at all! Or the squadron either, from past experience.

The familiar stomach-clenching tension and surging wave of excitement. Another check around. Gun-sight on? Gun button to 'Fire'? Plug pulled and 2,850 revs? Everyone jostling and hopping about like mad and squashing together to position themselves for a decent shot. On the right of the formation, I was acutely aware of Hurricanes massing and swaying to my left. Bursting ack-ack, larger puffs now, marching in silent strides toward us. The Heinkels growing in size like characters in a cartoon film. Any moment! Some Hun fighters wheeling away to the north, getting round behind us. Watch those blighters, for God's sake! Everyone bunching. *Careful*!

Now... *fire*! Tracer, a mass of it, reaching out. Streaking. Smoking. But, only the briefest of bursts before the Huns were upon us. *Jesus*! We would collide! A moment of terrible suspense as I was hurled violently against my straps. Followed by relief. Down underneath. A fleeting glimpse of round perspex noses. Then, something horrifying. Unnerving! Open bomb doors! And in that fraction of a second required to convey a visual message to the brain, bombs began to tumble out as the Huns dropped, or jettisoned, their loads.

I had a micro-second's glimpse of something flipping out then cartwheeling onto my head. But, before I had time even to cringe, we were away, veering and dropping and skidding earthwards, engines screaming, aircraft missing each other by feet or possibly inches. A frenzied glance about. Anyone hit? I didn't know. If not, it had been a miracle!

I pulled up, with others, my wings almost bending in protest, and turned. Where was the enemy? A mass of aircraft everywhere, mostly Hurricanes. But, of course, 46 were with us. The 109s? I couldn't see any but they'd be around – bound to be. Confusion. Where was everyone and which aircraft were which? The bombers and ack-ack some way off now. I climbed hard in their direction, keeping a close watch on my tail. They seemed to be turning – going home. Several stragglers among a cluster of ack-ack. Some violent goings-on high above. The bombers hadn't penetrated as far as London this time. Nowhere near. Yes, they were going home. Definitely! Hurricanes racing in pursuit. I joined several of them and charged towards the coast, my throttle wide open, my engine howling and vibrating. Chasing, but at the back of a queue. Finally, giving up and turning back. Lots of friendly fighters ahead. They didn't need me.

Respite! Everything dying down now. I was still alive. Thank heaven for that. Phew! I hadn't liked those bombs. A lot of chatter on the RT. Had 46 been jumped? Sounded like it. Someone had, anyway.

I turned north, my heart-beat returning approximately to normal, and flew across the estuary with several others. Southend far below and to my left. Looking for 109s and keeping a beady eye on my tail.

Back in dispersal, there were confused reports. Everyone agreed that the Heinkels had been hit. We couldn't have missed them, for heaven's sake! However, nothing had been seen to go down and no one claimed anything other than 'damaged'. Head-on attacks were hopeless. And dangerous, too, by God! Why did we go on doing them? And what about those bombs coming out! No more of *that*, thank you very much!

The 109s had attacked 46 apparently, and we had one chap unaccounted for. Who? Faces were examined. It looked like being Denis Parnall. Anyone seen him? He'd come back shortly after take-off for another aircraft, we were told, his own being unserviceable. Then flown off again. Not to worry though, he'd probably turn up later.

Someone was talking about a 109. A 109! There hadn't been a 109 within a mile of me. Not to my knowledge, anyway.

Lunch had been hanging about for ages and we ate, still excitedly discussing the events of the day, all tied up in our Mae Wests. It took some time to wind down.

We were off again around 4 p.m., climbing up over the estuary. Far below, the remains of several of the oil tanks at Thameshaven still sent up an almost stationary pillar of dark smoke. Extraordinary how something like that could go on burning for days on end. It had been more than a week now. And, clearly, more attacks were expected.

And, of course, there was the invasion. Was that on or off now? There had been talk of fitting Tiger Moths with bomb racks. Tiger Moths! I wouldn't be volunteering for that job! Worse than Battles, and that was saying something!

We didn't fly around for very long, just about thirty minutes. But that didn't stop me being sharply vigilant. 46 Squadron had lost two or three chaps on that last trip, we had heard. Same old story. Concentrating on the bombers, they were jumped by fighters. I decided I would never be able to fly over Kent at any time in the future without having eyes in the back of my head.

We landed. There was no news of Denis Parnall, though there was still plenty of time.

We had barely been refuelled when the fourth scramble order came. Not again, for heaven's sake! Maidstone, this time. What now, I wondered?

Climbing up, it soon became obvious that we had been sent off as an insurance measure. Approaching the estuary, we could see ack-ack high above the Isle of Sheppey and, much higher, some bombers flying north-west and outlined against a pearl-grey background of high cloud. There were quite a few friendly fighters about and several traces of aircraft disabled and trailing – Huns, I hoped. One bomber came down like a falling comet, a vivid red tongue flaring from one wing and emitting a pencil-line parabola of dark smoke, while above, several parachutes were stationary flecks of white against the sky. Then, something else, straight ahead, unrecognizable at first and falling like a stone. Oh, no! A man! With an unopened, trailing canopy. As the figure passed by my aircraft, close enough for me to recognize it as human, I breathed a silent prayer. What a way to go!

Back on the ground, Sergeant Beard reported shooting down an Me 110. A 110! I had not so much as seen an Me 110, and I was in the forefront of the squadron. But there was no doubting the veracity of any statement from Sergeant Beard, who was an excellent chap with a splendid record.

Again almost four hours of action during the course of the day. And Denis Parnall still missing. No one appeared to know what had happened to him either, which was distressing. Which demonstrated the folly of taking off and climbing up alone, we decided. Another lesson learned the hard way.

Messages of congratulation arrived from the Air Minister, Sir Archibald Sinclair, and Sir Cyril Newall, the Chief of Air Staff, for our work over the previous several days, in particular Sunday 15 September. Gave us all a warm feeling. Although the squadron jolly well deserved them, by gum!

London suffered again that night, the hours of darkness a constant drone of Hun aircraft accompanied by the bark and crump of guns. There were reports of someone shining a light from the woods beyond the airfield boundary. A fifth-columnist? What sort of malicious half-wit would do a thing like that? All he could expect was a bomb dropped on his head. And serve him right!

19 September. A miserable day with the sky full of leaden clouds and the wind increasing. I led one of a number of sections which took off throughout the day.

John Beazley and George Barclay shot at a Ju 88 which later crashed in the area of Deal. A good day for hunting Huns in the clouds, in fact. But not for me, unfortunately. I saw nothing.

John Grandy was back among us, hobbling about on a stick. However, it appeared that it would be some time before he would be able to fly up-front again.

A Pilot Officer Millington joined the squadron, a small fair chap with a tiny moustache. An Australian, apparently, though he did not look or sound like one. Pretty experienced, too, with a DFC. Seemed very nice.

In spite of the day's happenings, my letter home that evening contained no mention of combat or flying, concentrating instead on a different subject.

Two intelligence officers had arrived at dispersal during the afternoon, one a squadron leader. After consulting John Grandy, they called me across. Was I the fellow who had shot down the Dornier over the convoy on 15 September? I said that I was and there were nods all round.

A Pilot Officer Eric Lock, flying a Spitfire of 41 Squadron from Hornchurch, had been full of the encounter, it seemed, reporting that a Hurricane pilot had not only joined him in the destruction of a Dornier 17 out to sea but, immediately prior to that, had knocked down *two* Me 109s before his surprised and admiring eyes. Could they have my account of the whole affair? I was happy to oblige.

They spent more than an hour writing copious notes then informed me that the event had enormous publicity value and was a subject suitable for a world-wide broadcast. If I agreed, they would arrange a meeting between Lock and myself and produce a script.

I was quite stunned by all the fuss but also gratified and flattered by the attention I was receiving. Of course I would take part! I would await developments.

The intelligence officers departed and my parental letter was written only after I had tried unsuccessfully to telephone. If the Huns only knew what a mess they were making of our telephone system!

For the next several days, the weather was marginal and the Huns soporific – except at night. I flew two or three times, through and between massive cloud banks and towering pyramids of cumulus, but intercepted nothing.

A bevy of press photographers arrived, to roam about with their cameras asking us to pose and making everyone feel self-conscious. Not all of us were in dispersal at the time but those present were rounded up like sheep and made to walk from our aircraft in groups. These photographs were later to achieve world-wide circulation even among our opponents, the German fighter squadrons. Our smiles were probably more of derision than good humour. Not permitted to take photographs ourselves, supposedly for security reasons, here were all these civilian nonentities snapping everything in sight! A silly arrangement, in my opinion.

Down at dispersal, where we seemed to spend most of our life, besides eating, sleeping, sitting around and talking, the games of L'Attaque and Totopoly were very popular. As with snooker, Crossey seemed always to beat me at L'Attaque but I did rather better at Totopoly, winning as much as five shillings – almost half-a-day's pay – on several occasions. There were many raised voices in the course of the games, Butch, in particular, becoming positively animated.

Such periods of comparative inactivity also allowed us to give more attention to the intelligence summaries which appeared at regular intervals. Those produced by 11 Group, gave details of each squadron's achievements over the preceding several days and always included a list of the more successful pilots and their tally of Huns. There were also comments, sometimes in the plainest of language, on the situation in general and the manner in which 12 Group had repeatedly failed to provide reinforcements in time.

The 12 Group summaries were largely similar, except that the virtues of the large formation were constantly being extolled and accounts of what had recently occurred given in terms scarcely flattering to 11 Group.

As the weeks passed, this peevish tiff – because it was nothing more dignified than that – became so childishly acrimonious that even I, who had no interest in the politics of command, began to feel that the group commanders, Air Vice Marshals Park and Leigh-Mallory, were demeaning themselves. Did high-ranking officers really speak to each other in such a way? To us, as might be expected, Park was the hero and Leigh-Mallory the villain, although never once did we even approach the point of being openly critical of either.

Squadron Leader Douglas Bader, of 242 Squadron, the protégé of Leigh-Mallory and a person of considerable influence in 12 Group, was generally regarded as being the main advocate of the Balbo and usually led the huge formations we encountered from time to time. Acknowledged everywhere as being a tremendously gutsy character, flying as he did with artificial legs, he also had the less enviable reputation of being somewhat over-devoted to his own interests, a characteristic which did not endear him to everyone, particularly those of us who suffered as the result of his personal enthusiasms. All too frequently, when returning to North Weald in a semi-exhausted condition, all we saw of 12 Group's contribution to the engagement, was a vast formation of Hurricanes in neat vics of three, steaming comfortably over our heads in pursuit of an enemy who had long since disappeared in the direction of France. Our reactions on such occasions, though mostly of resigned amusement at first, grew to be more harshly critical later on.

But of far greater interest and importance to me, it was during that brief interlude that John Grandy, after an encouraging chat, appointed me as section leader, which pleased me enormously. I felt I was going up in the world. Also I much preferred to lead then be led; a volatile and rather uncomfortable person to live with, I disliked being organized or tied down.

Then, in the evening of 24 September, I drove down to Hornchurch and met the two intelligence officers who had interviewed me a week or so earlier, and also Pilot Officer Lock.

'Sawn-off' Lock was a bouncy, dark-haired little chap who hailed from Shropshire, an area well known to me. Full of quips and high spirits, he had a tremendous reputation in 41 Squadron and quite embarrassed me with his version of our combat on 15 September, describing my contribution in terms I could scarcely have improved on myself. I warmed to him immediately; a couple more trips with him and I was destined for stardom!

Suitably fortified with grog, we retold our story at length and a script emerged. Finally, when all was completed, Eric Lock and I hung on each other's necks – insofar as that was possible, he being all of 5ft 4in – and over innumerable whiskies and ginger-ales, continued to fight the war to our complete satisfaction, becoming positively lyrical by the time I left towards midnight.

I drove back to North Weald in a haze of good spirits, convinced that next to 249, 41 was absolutely *the* greatest squadron ever created.

The Huns were active that night and bombs fell all around my driver and me on our way home, apparently. But, feeling no pain, I neither saw nor heard them!

25 September. A memorable day. The adjutant, Lohmeyer, and the rest of 249's airmen having returned from Boscombe Down the previous day, there were many old faces around dispersal and wide, welcoming smiles. It was good to have the 'family' together again, in particular the old Adj. I had missed him more than anyone, although 56's representatives had given good service and were firm friends of all of us.

Because of renewed talk of the invasion, we were on the top line from dawn onwards and at breakfast time – when else! – there was a patrol in squadron strength over Southend.

Rested from the arduous happenings of the previous week, we were fairly bouncing about with fervour but the enemy did not oblige by putting in an appearance so that, after about an hour, we dropped down again through cloud and landed.

In the afternoon, I was accosted by a grinning Victor Beamish and informed that Bryan Meaker and I had each been awarded the DFC. 'Good show, Ginger,' he was saying, nodding away and obviously delighted. 'Well done!'

I was stunned. Breathless. And absurdly happy. The first decorations in the squadron. And that it should have happened to me! Everyone was congratulating us. In my view, Bryan Meaker especially deserved recognition; a quiet, unobtrusive boy several years older than myself, he had been one of the first to arrive on the squadron and, with seven or eight Huns to his credit, had been involved in every major engagement from the start.

As if to celebrate the occasion, I took George Barclay up in the afternoon and intercepted a Hun over the estuary, a Dornier 17, its dark distinctive silhouette flitting in and out of the cloud fringes. But, unhappily, with no positive result, the blighter seeing us in time and ducking back into oblivion before we could get close enough to shoot. Hot on the scent, we flew around for a time but, not catching sight of it again, returned after forty minutes.

I found I was becoming quite adept at these bad weather jaunts and thoroughly enjoyed the excitement of the stalk and the leaping thrill that came with sighting the enemy. The engagement itself was almost an anti-climax, possibly because there were so few occasions when we managed to approach unseen to within firing range.

For me, it was one of the greatest of days, even if nothing of operational significance was accomplished. I walked on air and tried to telephone my parents but without success. What on earth had got into the telephone system in Britain?

We awoke the following morning to find dispersal in an autumn fog and to hear someone observing that there seemed to be a land-mine hanging by its parachute from a nearby tree which brought us round pretty smartly.

It being decided that we should not fly until the mine was made safe, we mooched about with our hands in our pockets, eyeing it from a respectable distance. While we were enjoying this masterly inactivity, a Lysander – of all things! – approached from out of the mist and, without warning, landed with a terrible crunch within yards of it. As it did so, we all turned away and bent down with our fingers in our ears; laughing, I should add, as we were not expecting it to go off, although there were no obvious grounds for such optimism.

The Navy having defused the brute – what heroes those chaps were – we started our patrolling by sections around mid-day. John Beazley, Percy Burton and Sergeant Palliser caught a Dornier 17 somewhere over Kent and managed to damage it before it dropped back into cloud and escaped over the south coast.

Later, Keith Lofts and I took off hoping to emulate their performance but my companion had to return almost immediately with engine trouble. Continuing without him, I ran into another Hun close to the aerodrome and, being encouraged by the occasional glimpse, chased it all the way to the coast where it, too, disappeared without my getting in a shot.

Later, I sat on my bed and removed my wings, placing them a little higher on my tunic to accommodate the ribbon of my DFC. Lots of tongue work as the needle and cotton dipped and rose, with the Adj looking on smilingly and remarking that he could do better with a knife and fork!

Marshal of The Royal Air Force Lord Trenchard paid us a visit that day and chatted with a number of us. Father of the RAF and with a great reputation, he was a tremendously impressive figure, about 6ft 5in tall and with features and hands as though chiselled from granite. Most people being smaller than myself, I was seldom impressed by the appearance of others. But with him it was different. Moreover, he smelt powerfully of pipe tobacco, which for some strange reason stuck in my memory. An outstanding personality and a great morale booster.

The Huns were over again that night with all the usual thumps and dronings. But they always were and no one took much notice any more. London was catching it again, it seemed.

The following morning, 27 September, was cloudy in our area with more than a hint of rain. The squadron was at Readiness at dawn and there was the usual hanging about wondering whether we were going to be allowed to have our breakfast in peace.

At around 8 a.m., Sector Ops warned us that plots were building up around Boulogne and we began to fear the worst, so that when the scramble order came a little before nine o'clock, it was not exactly a surprise and most of us had already eaten. For me, to go to war without a cooked brekker was nothing less than calamitous and Victor Beamish was of the same mind, later confiding in me that, as far as he was concerned, breakfast and tea were the only meals worth eating. Perhaps it was because we both came from the north.

We climbed up through some light cloud initially, being joined by 46 Squadron who had taken off simultaneously from Stapleford. Thereafter, we were vectored due south, a departure from routine as we usually patrolled a line from the estuary through Canterbury to Dover. It looked as though we were reinforcing squadrons in the Tangmere, Biggin Hill and Kenley Sectors, which normally dealt with attacks from a more southerly direction.

We toiled up, my right leg, as ever, firmly extended to counteract the tendency of the aircraft to pull to the left at anything like full throttle. God bless the designer of the Hurricane who decided not to incorporate a rudder bias, thought I. If this business went on indefinitely, they would have to breed pilots with one leg longer than the other, an added complication being that, at any speed greater than 300, it was the *left* leg that had to cope with the not inconsiderable foot-load

I checked my cockpit for the umpteenth time: oil pressure 70lbs, radiator temperature 85 degrees, oil temperature coming up to 60 degrees, oxygen on and flowing, gunsight on but a little bright – I turned it down a fraction – gun button to 'Fire', everything else in order. With tension mounting, I wriggled in my seat, heightened it a notch to allow me to see just that little bit more, then flicked up the unlocking device on my straps in order to lean forward. Satisfied, I pushed my shoulders firmly to the rear so that the lock clicked into position. I didn't want the gunsight thumping me between the eyes, did I? Rock-hard that brutal device, fitted as it was with a sorbo pad – the humane killer, Nick used to call it. Poor old Nick! What was he doing now, I wondered? It seemed an age since he was giving us all advice.

Down below on my right, the grey huddle of London slid slowly by beneath scattered fragments of cloud, the balloons, a thousand silent sentinels, dully motionless at the extremities of a thousand invisible cables. A quick glance at my instruments again. Rising now through 12,000 feet with slightly more than 140 on the airspeed indicator. The horizon a firm line in every direction in a clear sky. The whole squadron, twelve of us, rocking, lifting and swaying slightly, like the undulating wings of a giant flat fish. In position. Prepared. Ascending quickly. And steeply.

Heading in the direction of Dungeness as instructed, we were suddenly vectored to our right and were approaching 18,000 feet in the area of Redhill when we saw the first ack-ack. After which, a little to our surprise, a mass of aircraft higher up, small insects that were 109s, then a trail of larger aircraft at about our own level and flying in a circle. A defensive circle! Instant recognition. Me 110s! A tactic of theirs I had heard about but never encountered.

It was a fight into which we were pitchforked rather than embarked upon; there was no time for thought, a considered attack, or even for apprehension. The Huns were there, in front of us, wheeling around; large aircraft, predominantly grey-green in colour and leanly sinister. But not attacking, this time. Defending.

Instinctively, and in a flurry of haste, I fired into the tilting silhouette of one rushing straight at me. A brief burst of a second only and the Hun was gone. Followed by another, which loomed overhead and swept by only yards away but, fortunately, not with its nose pointing in my direction. 110s had 20mm cannons which were lethal at close range.

The squadron scattering, I broke away to the right then reversed direction, watching for 109s. There was no point in flying against the stream of traffic for the rest of the morning!

The sky seemed full of Hurricanes, climbing and diving, wings whirling, a mass of aircraft racing in all directions. More 110s below me and still turning. I dropped down behind one of them then remembered my tail; there'd be another behind! I reared up and, wildly anxious, screwed my head about before tearing after the same Hun. Now some 400 yards ahead, it was still turning quite steeply which made easier my task of cutting the corner. Then, as I sought to drop into line astern again, the rear-gunner fired, his tracer flicking past above and to the right of my head. I fired in response, which seemed to galvanize the aircraft in front into turning even more violently, causing – I was relieved to note – the gunfire from the rear to cease. The result of 'g' forces on the gunner, I thought grimly, in which case, keep the blighter turning! I fired again, this time from much closer range. The 110 dropped its nose and began to level out. Immediately, more fire from the rear cockpit, twisting and flicking in my direction so close that I flinched, expecting the metallic thud of bullets. Wow!

Even closer now, less than fifty yards and all fear erased by a flood of surging adrenalin. The gunner ignored and forgotten. I fired again, tracer, sparks and twinkling flashes everywhere. Right up its backside with a clear sight of the twin rudders, wobbling. Then, the Hun was dropping away, turning slowly with no response from the rear cockpit. A puff of something dark on the right and a haze of smoke, nothing more. The 110 diving still and going down with level wings. I had the blighter! Watch your tail, an inner voice screamed. A quick and anxious glance in my mirror. No sign. I would take a chance. I fired again. Without apparent effect at first. Then, a brief bubble of red which produced a developing stream of the blackest of black smoke. I'd got him! He was going! Diving hard. Straight. Now steepening. Fairly tumbling down in pursuit, my aircraft bobbing in and out of the dark flood. That terrible smell again. Of burning aircraft. Oh God! Surely not! I looked around, panic in my glance. No sign. My altimeter unwinding like a clock gone mad. Faster. Steeper. The whole aircraft stiff and trembling. Pull out! *Pull out!* Down to 5,000 feet and going like hell. The 110 disappearing into haze and still diving steeply. Streaming. A goner! It must be! Finished!

I pulled away, turning left, then began to climb. With no feeling other than of relief mingled with satisfaction. No bubbling jubilation – not this time. But no feeling of compassion, either. It was just another aircraft.

I climbed up towards the north. Steeply and almost at full throttle. With about half my ammunition left, I had to fight on. There were some aircraft ahead but higher. The usual confusion, the air thick with RT. I laboured upwards, as steeply as I dared, finally passing into clearer air at about 14,000 feet.

Then, in front, an aircraft moving quickly from left to right, a mile away and slightly above. Followed by another, rather smaller. I curved towards the larger one instinctively and began to follow. It was another 110 and the aircraft chasing it a Hurricane. As I closed from the rear quarter, the Hun began to dive and another chase developed. I sensed that we were going almost due east, which was surprising.

I cannot recall which of us in the two Hurricanes fired first, but the result was immediate; the Hun tucked its nose down hard and made for the ground, two thin trails of dark smoke visible evidence of the power being demanded of its engines. My excitement heightened by the thrill of the dive, I tumbled down after it, aware of the rising scream of the wind around my cockpit hood, my controls stiffening again and more than 380 showing on my ASI. By George, this chap was moving – for a twin!

Then, when I was more or less in position and preparing to fire, the rear gunner opened up and sent a curling ribbon of white which streaked over my port wing. I fired in response and the tracer stopped. After which, I was conscious of the other Hurricane abreast of me and also firing.

The 110, which by this time was approaching the ground, levelled out and racing still, clung tenaciously to the contours of the countryside, lifting itself over hills and other obstructions so that woods and fields streamed past at little more than fifty feet. This presented a problem as I could not take up the comparatively safe position below its tail.

As I pulled up slightly to take another shot, the rear gunner fired a further burst, but this time not at me. Immediately, the Hurricane to my left reared into the air and peeled away to port, leaving me in sole possession.

It was at that point that I realized that all was not as it should have been. Accustomed to my windscreen becoming soiled by the faintly yellow stain of oil from the leaking seal behind the airscrew, I saw with dismay that there was now much more oil about than usual and most of it dark in colour. Not only was it on the rectangle of armoured glass in front of my face but also on the side panels as well as the top of the fuselage, which was glistening with a film of black goo. Either I'd been hit or there was a nasty leak from somewhere. Whatever the cause, I couldn't go racing out to sea if my Hun managed to cross the coast. It was now and or never.

No more than 200 yards behind and being twisted about by the invisible hand of the 110's slipstream, I fired again, as carefully as my restricted vision would allow, a long burst this time which produced a sudden flurry of heartening flashes. I then lifted myself briefly to repeat the performance whereupon the rear gunner responded with another burst which whipped into my face and over my head. A brave chap, by George! Would I be doing that in his position? I had a mental picture of the man sheltering behind his piece of armour plate then jumping up and firing whenever the opportunity presented itself.

But it proved to be the last act of desperation as the 110 began to turn slowly to the right and slacken speed. Greatly encouraged and finding myself closing quickly, I fired once more and was rewarded by more twinkling strikes. As I did so, the clamour of my eight Brownings fell to the shrill chatter of two guns... the thin rattle of one... followed by silence. All gone! I was finished.

I drew to one side, opened my hood in order to see more clearly, and watched a growing trail of smoke streaming from the starboard engine. Flames? I couldn't decide, there being a miniature smoke screen around the wing of the German aircraft. Also a new development, a pencil line of white – coolant, obviously. In front was a very sad and desperate Hun.

As a line of sand swept beneath my wings the thought passed quickly through my mind, not another one in the sea! But, this time I couldn't risk following it out across the water to confirm my victory. I had to get down somewhere quickly in order to investigate the cause of all the oil. With mixed feelings, I turned round and flew inland.

I carried on for a time, during which my imagination began to conjure up pictures of disaster, persuading me finally to land at Detling, near Maidstone.

Dropping down onto the grass, I found the aerodrome deserted and everyone taking shelter because of an air-raid warning which was more than understandable. I learned later that not only had enemy aircraft been overhead for most of the morning but, unlike North Weald, the aerodrome was on the direct line of approach to London and such warnings and goings-on were an unpleasant everyday occurrence.

I taxied to one side and shut down. An ominous silence. Someone waved to me from a distance but no one came in my direction. For an uncomfortable moment or two, I thought a bombing attack was imminent and scrambled out hastily with the intention of taking shelter myself. But, my feet back on the ground, immediate feelings of panic subsided and, deciding that everything seemed peaceful enough, I became sufficiently emboldened to hang about until the 'all clear' had sounded, after which an airman came up and promised to find me a bowser and have me refuelled. No one else seemed very interested and the atmosphere remained thick with tension.

As I waited, I examined the front of my Hurricane, expecting to find bullet holes galore. To my surprise there were none and, faintly disappointed, I saw that all I had was a good old-fashioned oil leak. Black goo ran out in a steady stream from the small drain hole between the undercarriage legs and there were huge smears stretching backwards from the rear edges of the engine cowlings. Something was leaking with a vengeance!

In the five minutes that elapsed before the bowser appeared, I stood around, noting with interest the dummy wooden Blenheims parked around the perimeter of the airfield, conclusive evidence that Detling took air attacks very seriously indeed. Meanwhile, I cleaned off my own windscreen and was sitting in the cockpit wondering if I should risk the journey back to North Weald without refuelling, when a Hurricane came into the circuit and landed. As it taxied towards me, I recognized it as one of 249's and was even more surprised and delighted to find ''Appy 'Arry' Davidson in the cockpit.

Davidson was without fuel but in the highest of spirits. He'd also run out of ammunition and told me that at one stage he had been a mere twenty-five yards behind a badly damaged Hun but without the wherewithal to administer the coup de grace.

'Could've knocked the bugger down with me 'at,' he shouted cheerfully in his broad Lancashire accent, his laugh echoing like a machine-gun burst.

An hour later, refuelled, my leak inspected and the oil tank replenished with *three* gallons of oil instead of the usual one, Davidson and I took off together and flew northwards for twenty uneventful minutes before landing at North Weald to find our corner of the aerodrome deserted.

Lohmeyer, the adjutant, came hurrying out to meet me even before my airscrew had stopped rotating, his face a picture of relief.

'Thank God you're back, old son.' I climbed down and fell into step beside him as he continued. 'Four missing and one wounded until you two arrived, that is. Butch and Percy Burton are down somewhere and John Beazley's been taken off to hospital. The rest – what's left – have gone off again and we've just been told they're in another fight. Good news about the Huns though. A lot have been shot down.'

The remnants of the squadron eventually returning singly and in small groups, the dispersal hut was soon an excited mass of bodies, lined faces and unbuttoned Mae Wests. Combat reports were being sorted out amid fragments of lunch, with plates and cutlery littering the tables. On the last trip, apparently, they had become involved with two groups of 109s and, almost unheard of, a genuine dogfight had developed with aircraft trying to out-turn each other. It had been in the Canterbury-Ashford area and the Hurricanes fighting on more even terms, several 109s were being claimed as 'destroyed' and 'probable'. With no casualties either, which was comforting to hear. While on the previous flight, it looked as though most if not all of the 110s had been shot down, 46 Squadron also taking their toll. Marvellous! Quite stupendous! Butch had been hit by a 110 and forced to land at Gatwick but there was no news of Percy Burton, which did not sound too good. And, of particular interest to me, John Beazley had been in the other Hurricane which had partnered me during our combined attack on the 110. He had been struck by one of the rear gunner's last bursts, a bullet piercing his foot and lodging in his instep. His boot full of blood and his foot immobilized, he had courageously returned all the way to North Weald before being removed to Epping Hospital. Poor old John! So, he had been the one!

To cool off, I walked out to inspect my Hurricane. The engine cowlings were on the floor, the fitters hard at work, and I was heartened to hear that the leak, though considerable, was less dangerous than it had at first appeared. They would have it right in a jiff, they said. Were they quite sure? Be all right in the air, sir, was the reply. That, and a swift rub with an oily rag, was the airman's immediate response to any sign of oil emerging from within. Even so, I was greatly relieved; I hated going to war in strange aircraft.

As I walked back, I thought about the chaps working like beavers on my aeroplane. Since joining the squadron, I had never failed to be impressed by the enthusiasm and devotion of our riggers, fitters and other tradesmen. In particular the senior NCOs, who provided the expertise and the disciplined organization which helped so much to keep our Hurricanes in the air. Theirs was not an exciting or highly rewarding war; just one of graft and dogged hard work at all hours of the day and night. The salt of the earth, without a doubt. But more than that, supportive friends, who took as much interest in my welfare as I did myself and were as proud of my success as if it were their own.

There was little time for sleep that afternoon, which was just as well. At 2.50 p.m., we were ordered off to patrol Hornchurch and streamed into the sky, a full squadron again, to rendezvous with 46 and go climbing off to the south-east. Another try by 110s? We'd soon see.

We were at 18,000 feet, a long way south and in the Guildford area again, when we spied the inevitable ack-ack and turned towards it.

It was the mixture as before but with something of a difference. The cloud of 109s well above our heads was the same but instead of 110s, Ju 88s formed the core of the armada. I counted about ten in several boxes, all forming what appeared to be a large vic. We were properly at height and curved towards them immediately in yet another beam attack. Beam attack! To relieve the tension, I screamed my disapproval. Why did we fritter away time and ammunition doing things the hard way?

Despite being at the head of the squadron, I hardly managed a shot on the first headlong charge and, without observing the result of our attack, swept overhead and turned sharply to find the 88s immediately below me. Without thinking, I dropped down on them before realizing with a start that I was about to fly into the centre and rear of the whole Hun formation. There were two Hurricanes slightly ahead of me, one to the left and one almost parallel with me to the right. The 88s seemed to be going unusually fast and scissoring streaks of tracer began to flow from the rear gunners. If I continued, I saw that I would collect everything on the way forward and probably not even reach the Hun directly ahead of me. Reacting instinctively, I veered off to starboard, determined to tackle one or other on the right of the group.

It was almost a carbon copy of the attack I had made on the Dorniers some ten days before when the Hun crew had baled out. Except that this time, they didn't!

Wallowing in the slipstream of an 88, I fired a long burst from slightly underneath, manhandling my aircraft violently as it strove to rise above the level of the tail and into full view of the rear gunner, and had the satisfaction of seeing a succession of vivid strikes on the rudder and starboard wing. Some inner voice shrieked at me to break away and look to my rear but, carried away with the fervour of battle, I remained in place and was about to fire again when there was a minor explosion on the right-hand side of the 88 and a shower of debris which produced a thin blade of flame and a developing stream of smoke. As if mortally wounded by whatever had occurred, the aircraft immediately began to fall away to its right and, utterly intrigued, I watched it slowly drop its nose and drift over onto its side and beyond as though totally uncontrolled. The sight was almost unnerving. What on earth had happened? Had I done that? I found myself following it, then spiralling down in pursuit, but not for long! Suddenly there were aircraft all round me – friends, as it happened – triggering a violent and aggressive response from me, with the result that I lost sight of my former target and was obliged to look anew for the bomber formation.

Curving in pursuit of a group of Hurricanes ahead of me, I caught up and recognized some of 249, one in particular being flown by our new Australian, 'Bill' Millington. As I surged alongside, he looked up with a start then waved, after which we flew together towards a cluster of ack-ack bursts, in the centre of which were some other 88s, now widely spaced and going at high speed in a southerly direction. The ones we had already attacked, or others? I had no idea. But, who cared?

In turn, we fired at one slightly apart from the rest and yet again, the starboard engine was quickly set alight. But this time with a difference. The fire was a raging, violent, bubbling red, as angry a conflagration as ever I had seen in the air, almost frightening in its intensity and spewing out a rolling cloud of greasy black smoke in its wake. It was the Thameshaven blaze in miniature, and presumably of the same combustibles.

Amazingly, the 88 flew on at almost the same speed so that we had our work cut out just to keep up with it. But, the fire still going like a blow-torch, it gradually lost height and was obviously desperate to get home. Would the wing fall off? It seemed inevitable. But it didn't.

My ammunition expended, I followed it down with Millington alongside me and together we shepherded it over the south coast and out to sea where it finally splashed down a mile or so off Shoreham in a Niagara of pluming spray and steam. Like the Dornier of ten days earlier, it remained on the surface, a waterlogged hulk, long enough for a small inflatable dinghy to appear with at least two members of the crew. But, after a short time and as we circled, both aircraft and boat disappeared. As did the occupants, as far as I could see. Leaving nothing.

We arrived back at North Weald like marathon runners, singly and in twos, exhausted, yet with eyes still bright from the passion of battle. My crew proudly reported that I had been hit in the tail by a cannon-shell. A cannon-shell? I went back, frowning, to finger the damage and express surprise. The blighters! Who on earth had done that?

In the hut we counted heads. George Barclay had gone – force-landed, we heard – also Bryan Meaker. Someone was saying that Bryan had been hit by return fire when attacking the first group of 88s, which set me wondering if it had been he in front of me and to my left at the outset. Later still, we learned that he had baled but, his parachute not opening, had been killed on reaching the ground. Bryan! The imperishable, imperturbable Bryan! It seemed impossible that he should have gone.

The statistics of the day were frightening; Burton and Meaker killed, Beazley wounded, Barton and Barclay shot down, all of us in one form or another deeply affected by events. And five, six, seven Hurricanes, lost or damaged. On the other hand, around twenty Huns had been claimed 'destroyed', 'probable', and 'damaged', an almost unheard of number. Our rejoicing was thus tempered by sorrow. But not shock, strange to say, or none that was discernible. I was unhappy about our losses, of course, but, if the truth were told, not really distressed. How impervious we were becoming to injury and death. Was it because we did not actually see the crashed aircraft, the terrible burns, or the gory remains? Probably be different if we did. No, it was the parents I felt sorry for, imagining its effect on my own if I had bought it. Who'd be a parent?

Passions subsided. Several of us went to the cinema that night. It was just an ordinary evening.

Later on, there were empty beds in dispersal and the Huns droned on well into the small hours with the guns tonk-tonk-tonking away in the distance. The invasion threat seemed to have faded, but who gave a hoot about the invasion anyway?

A violent, traumatic day. But there were lots of us left. I slept that night as though drugged.

We were half prepared for another series of bombing attacks the following day and were surprised and relieved when nothing much happened.

Off at 10 a.m., we were despatched in the direction of the estuary at 25,000 feet, which was something of a pointer as the Dorniers, 88s and Heinkels never operated at that height. Nor, for that matter, did we – very efficiently, that is. The Hurricane performed indifferently at anything much above 20,000 besides being wretchedly cold. Even with three pairs of gloves – cape leather, silk inners and gauntlets – my hands invariably turned to stone, as did my feet. Moreover, fool that I was, on that particular morning I was wearing only a uniform tunic under my Mae West and in the ninety minutes we were airborne, being reduced to a semi-crystalline state, had ample time to regret my stupidity.

When a little north of Maidstone, some 109s flew directly overhead several thousand feet higher, a clutch of curving white lines against the blue. I sat and watched them, small coloured insects silently extruding gossamer threads in their wake, not in the least concerned or even impressed, except by their agility. They were so much more nimble than we were at height that I never regarded our chances of catching them as anything better than slim. Irritating rather than frightening, when they did stay to fight I always felt confident of more than holding my own. But it seldom happened; they would swoop and climb, or occasionally dive right through us, on almost every occasion leaving us standing.

We were off again an hour or so later, this time flying between Maidstone and Canterbury. Again, a group of 109s sat over our heads and had us all on the *qui vive* for more than an hour as we ploughed back and forth, simmering with frustration. Then, when we thought they had gone and were heading for home, a couple of the rascals dropped down like hawks out of nowhere and picked off Gerald Lewis, our seasoned South African. Set on fire immediately, he was obliged to bale out. Later we learned that he had been taken to Faversham hospital with some nasty burns.

It had been a curious coincidence. Over dinner the night before, Lewis and I had talked long and hard about the best means of combating the fleeting surprise attack, the formation we habitually employed being one which achieved the objective of combining mutual support and concentration of force but was much more suited to attacking bombers than dealing with fighters. One possible solution was the employment of weavers – two aircraft given a free rein to wander above and below the main formation for the purpose of spotting a diving attack, a method we did, in fact, start to use a day or two later. In our hearts, however, I believe that Lewis and I felt that our experience and know-how put us in the league of untouchables; only the negligent and half-witted fell victim to such attacks. But, how wrong we were! Within twelve hours, he was shot down in just such a manner and I did not even see his attackers, although several others did and gave chase, Sergeant Beard claiming a 109 'destroyed' somewhere out to sea.

The circumstances of Lewis's misfortune caused me to think. At that stage, I was beginning to be regarded as the Hawkeye of the squadron, always among the first to see any enemy aircraft that were about. Yet, I had known nothing of the attack until I had noticed, with considerable surprise, Gerald's parachute hanging in the sky. How could I possibly have missed two Huns attacking a formation of which I was often a part? Incredible! But more than that, worrying. Clearly, I was neither as smart nor as observant as I believed myself to be.

The day was also remarkable in several other respects. John Grandy had come into dispersal and announced that Denis Parnall's crashed aircraft had been identified by the numbers on its Browning guns, several of which had been unearthed, unbelievably, in a field a mere five or six miles from North Weald. Having gone in at high speed, the aircraft was unrecognizable, as, unfortunately, was the pilot. But how had it and he finished up there? All the action that day had been very much further south. Clearly another of the inexplicable mysteries of air combat.

Though not unexpected, it was sad, sad, news to have confirmation of Denis's death, so handsome a young man, so able, and so splendid in every way. His bed alongside my own had remained poignantly empty. Now it could be used again. But, could we, the squadron, or the nation even, really go on losing such fellows?

The Vice Chief of Air Staff, Air Vice Marshal Sholto Douglas, also called on us between our first and second flights – we were becoming a little blasé about meeting celebrities of one sort and another. Someone was heard to remark, unkindly perhaps, that it was probably because they regarded North Weald to be rather less dangerous than Biggin Hill, for example.

Knowing little about the man and unaware of his record as an airman in the Great War, I was not impressed. Supposedly coming to congratulate us on our performance over the previous several days, he had very little to say for himself and seemed rather wooden and bored. Then, when talking to me separately for a moment or two, he asked me if I liked flying Spitfires. Spitfires! I could hardly believe my ears.

Discussing his visit afterwards, some put it down to pressure of work but not everyone was as charitably-minded.

We were off again, twice, the following day, wandering about at 25,000 feet over Kent and freezing to death. Some 109s, contrailing prettily, flew overhead on each occasion and we sat and watched each other, they not wishing to fight and we unable to. A silly business. At this rate, the war could go on for ever! It didn't worry us though, except for the cold. I was even beginning to think morbidly of how pleasant it would be to be shot down in flames!

On both occasions 46 Squadron were with us and, not for the first time, there was a marked lack of flexibility and cohesion in our combined effort, more time being spent avoiding collisions than searching for the Hun. It had been arranged that they should come across to North Weald that night to discuss tactics. Not before time, some of us felt.

They arrived after dinner and we found them a good crowd, though in a strange way quite unlike 249. 'Rags' Rabagliati, the senior flight commander, was a delightful man, thoroughly Anglo-Saxon in looks, slow and deliberate in speech and with a wonderful sense of humour. Not at all the excitable Latin his name suggested.

Several new chaps were posted in that day including our first Polish officer, whose name was Solak. Older than every other pilot in the squadron, he was an engaging fellow who had escaped through Europe and North Africa after the fall of Poland. Speaking good English, he held strong opinions on the way the war was being conducted, his thesis being that although the RAF was doing tolerably well, the British – civil and military – were not war-minded enough and were not fighting with sufficient venom and dedication. As examples, he instanced the constant industrial strikes and the ridiculous clamour for leaflet raids voiced, as he put it, by mischief-makers and the naïvely innocent, who still held the mistaken belief that the German population was somehow anti-war. The Germans were '*bleddy bastards*', all of them, their villainy exceeded only by that of the Russians who were even bigger 'bleddy bastards'. Britain should take its head out of the sand and fight with all its resources not just some of them.

Unaccustomed and a little shocked to hear such sensitive issues discussed by a group of serving officers, I was, nevertheless, much in sympathy with his views. To me, half the population of England appeared to be onlookers on the war, some even using it to their own advantage, and despite the tub-thumping and patriotic fervour coming from some sections of the press and public life, one had to go no further than the Regent Palace to see evidence of the fact. On the other hand, had Poland performed all that brilliantly? With the experience and wisdom of just twenty years, it was hard to judge.

We also received telegrams that day from the Air Minister, Sir Archibald Sinclair, and the Chief of Air Staff, Sir Cyril Newall. More congratulation? It was becoming almost monotonous! We really must be as good as we thought ourselves to be!

More sobering was the news that Percy Burton had definitely been killed. It was said that, badly wounded, he had deliberately rammed a 110 in a final act of retaliation and sacrifice. What outstanding, almost frightening devotion to duty. It was difficult to associate such bravery with the pleasant mild-mannered boy with whom I had lived, cheek by jowl, for the past several months. A hero, no less. And not only him but Nicolson, Meaker, Parnall, Main and all the others who had been shot down, killed, burned or wounded. Was I cast in the same mould? I was not at all sure.

The following day, we were up in squadron strength shortly after breakfast, climbing through several layers of cloud until we came out on top at around 12,000 feet. Beneath, was a brilliant, rainbow-studded carpet of white as far as the eye could see – a dazzling background against which to be spotted from above. Acutely aware of my naked and sensitive behind, I was much happier when we had put some distance between it and ourselves, even though we were still a little north of the river.

We had climbed up in our usual close formation of twelve, each of us wondering how thick the murk was going to be, Butch, in front, keeping down to a modest 3lbs boost in order to give the rest of the formation plenty of throttle to play with. Paradoxically, the closer aircraft were to each other in cloud, the easier and safer it was to ascend. It was when one's neighbour, either in front or alongside, suddenly disappeared, that the trouble usually arose. On such occasions, imagination ran riot and it was always a problem to decide whether or not to climb straight ahead, continue on a diverging course, hope that the ghostly shape which had just vanished would reappear, or pretend that nothing untoward had happened. There were simple rules to be followed at such times but none of them ever seemed to make a long ascent (or descent) through cloud any the easier. We were always relieved to emerge on top, or underneath, in approximately the same formation in which we had entered. However, the dangers, as on so many other occasions, invariably proved to be more imaginary than real. To my knowledge, there never was a collision in cloud during the many months of vile weather through which we operated – frights galore, but no collisions.

In company with 46 Squadron, we toiled up to more than 20,000 feet and settled down on our hidden patrol-line between the estuary and Canterbury. More than 1,500 feet above, and as arranged the previous evening, 46 weaved across our heads protectively, two flights in line astern. As I watched them veering and streaming this way and that for a full hour, I had visions of those at the rear of each line of six blessing the arrangement through very tight lips indeed; in order to maintain position, they would be devoting their attention entirely to station-keeping, at the same time using considerably more power and fuel than even their own leaders. Victor Beamish, possessed of a thousand virtues, had a fixation about 'snakes', constantly suggesting that each squadron should fly twelve aircraft line-astern, even on patrols. Dearly though I loved and admired the man, on this particular issue I always felt that he was talking nonsense. Later still, when we experimented with his idea, I *knew* it to be nonsense. Towards the rear of the 'snake' myself and at only a little less than full throttle throughout an eighty-minute trip, I almost ran out of fuel, muttering savagely into my beard meanwhile that if the Huns were looking down, they would consider us absolutely barmy. Such were the occasional delusions of even the gifted and famous.

After a time, we were warned of bandits in our area and, sure enough, about a score of 109s streamed silently overhead, too high to reach but close enough for us to pick out a yellow nose at the head of each white pencil-line. Such pretty little chaps. If only they weren't so vindictive!

We sat and eyed each other for five minutes, after which they all fled away towards the south, honour satisfied, no doubt. We were happy to let them go. They had our permission to play that silly game all day long.

Back on the ground, I had barely been refuelled when there was news of a reconnaissance aircraft heading towards London and George Barclay and I were scrambled to head it off. Once again we climbed up over the eastern outskirts of London, this time hard and steeply, until we were more than 26,000 feet, at which height we could see the Hun contrailing majestically a good 4,000 feet above us and drifting away to the south.

Pursuing the still visible tadpole as far as Dungeness but resigned to being engaged on a fruitless exercise, we etched our own progress across the sky with two elegant curving traces of white, admiring meanwhile the long stretch of coast-line spread out below us from North Foreland to Dover thence to Beachy Head and beyond. The south coast and Channel, now totally clear of cloud, France, from Cap Gris Nez to the Somme, seemed almost within touching distance. Thousands of Huns with their 109s, 88s, Dorniers and Heinkels, were presumably sitting there, some of them no doubt looking up in our direction. But, not a single aircraft, ship, building or moving object could we see, the whole world still, as though frozen into immobility, the war obliterated by distance. Only the constant vibrating roar of my own engine and the drifting nose of my Hurricane gave evidence of life. I looked down into France. What would they be saying about us? I wondered.

After a time, our blood congealing and our fingers and feet leaden with cold, we turned northwards, empty-handed but with hearts lifted and quickened by the majestic beauty of the scene. Moreover, we couldn't be jumped, could we? Not without seeing the varmints trailing towards us.

There were two more flights that day, both between 17,000 and 25,000 feet, on each occasion with 109s spinning endless, delicate webs of white across the sky. Always overhead. Looking down. Waiting. Calculating. Smiling, no doubt. We returned their stares from below. Eyes narrowed against the sun. One of these days, you blighters! One of these days!

On the first of the patrols, several of them had dropped down like sparrow-hawks and attacked 46 Squadron who were weaving indefatigably above us. We saw the flurry of activity against the blue followed by a thin trail of smoke as an aircraft curved away downwards to its death. Then, a parachute. Whose? No one knew. Not one of ours, we hoped.

On the final trip, there were many 109s but no attacks. We patrolled for eighty-five interminable minutes. Freezing. Dear God! It really was becoming cold.

The stove was alight when we returned to dispersal, the flames roaring in the chimney pipe. And not before time! We thawed out, all agreeing that it was greatcoat weather. And barely October, too.

When darkness fell, there came the first faint droning of the nightly parade of bombers. London again, we guessed. Still, they didn't worry us. Not a scrap. There were the usual thumps and bangs in the far distance.

After dinner, we went into Epping. To the Thatched House first, then to the cinema. Another day completed. Four hours and thirty minutes in the air and not a thing to show for it.

At midnight, sitting on my bed, I wrote my daily letter telling my parents I was still alive and that there was no need to worry.

12

An October of 109s

The first day of October was uneventful. I flew twice, once high up over Kent, with 109s in the far distance, the second time being obliged to return when my engine developed an oil leak and began to spray black stuff all around my windscreen.

I didn't miss much, however; there was no action, everyone wondering where the bombers had gone to these days.

Two Frenchmen were posted in, Perrin and Bouquillard, of indeterminate rank – something akin to that of sergeant pilot. They seemed nice enough, although I only saw them from a distance. Unlike the Poles, whose uniform was largely similar to our own but with different wings and cap badges, they wore a dark-blue-and-gold rigout with strange hats that could only be French.

With winter approaching, we were spending more time in the mess where life was ordered and pleasant. Lunch and dinner were still substantial five-course meals, although there were mild complaints about the unvarying appearance of beef on the menu; what had happened to the thirty million sheep in Britain? Bars as yet unauthorized, soft-footed mess servants still brought drinks into the ante-room at the touch of a bell and there were the large black settees and armchairs around the fire in which to while away the hours with books from the library. The snooker tables, too, were in constant demand, Crossey continuing to beat me with depressing regularity.

I wrote up my log-book for September. During my twenty-eight days at North Weald, I had been airborne forty-seven times against the wily Hun, involving fifty-three hours of flying. It had not been an especially difficult period; demanding, exciting and often frightening, yes, but nothing more. In fact, surrounded by a score of agreeable and competent companions, I was quietly content, thoroughly happy, and utterly at home. But then, I hadn't been clobbered, had I?

The following morning, rather against my wishes, as I didn't want to miss any of the action, I flew Lohmeyer, the adjutant, down to Boscombe Down via Tangmere in the 'Maggie'. Apart from other more weighty considerations, I disliked flying the Maggie as in any sort of a wind, it spent much of its time going sideways.

In the event, I quite enjoyed the relaxation of the journey. We flew over Northolt and the Staines reservoir, carefully avoiding the balloons, and in good clear weather, buzzed slowly southwards across the green and pleasant hills of Sussex.

We arrived at Tangmere in time for lunch. The sun was shining and the mess was an oasis of decorum and quiet comfort. There were two Hurricane squadrons in residence, one of them Auxiliary and, drinking my coffee reflectively in the ante-room, I found it fascinating to study the young, unconcerned faces of fellows who were fighting just as hard as we had been and with as much success. It was interesting, too, to recall that only six weeks earlier, from the safe height of 15,000 feet, I had watched the hangars and buildings vomiting flames, with dark smoke rising in solid, leaning pillars.

We took off again immediately after lunch and flew westward along the valleys in the direction of Boscombe Down, not only for the pleasure of low flying but also with the thought in mind that, in the flimsy and defenceless Maggie, I wouldn't find it too pleasant running into a marauding Hun.

The broad sweep of Boscombe Down was exactly as we had left it, with 56 Squadron in residence.

Of all the squadrons in the Air Force apart from 249, 56 was nearest to my heart. I knew every detail of its history and accomplishments in the last war – Ball, McCudden, Rhys-Davids and the rest – and here they were, a new generation admittedly, but all of them seemingly aware of the mantle of fame they had inherited and basking in the rich traditions of the past.

Over tea, I found myself talking to an engaging youth about my own age, whose hair stuck up at the back like a cockatoo's and whose uniform looked as though he had slept in it. He introduced himself as Michael Constable-Maxwell and I immediately recalled that a Maxwell had been a prominent member of 56 in 1918, with a most impressive tally of Huns to his credit. His father, I wondered? Surprisingly, the gallant gentleman turned out to be an older brother.

We fell to discussing recent events and it soon became clear that Michael had about one Hun and no less than five or six Hurricanes to his credit – crashed, dented or bent, a record which surprised and amused me rather. Six months later he was to join 249 at North Weald, when I found him to be a most agreeable and pleasant companion, and later still to distinguish himself as a most successful night-fighter pilot.

Finding myself at a loose end while the adjutant went about his business, I was taken by car into Salisbury by Brooker, Wicks and one or two others of 56. Before going on to the cinema, I suddenly came face to face with a Dornier 17, which was on display in the market place, and stood alongside studying it with interest. It felt strange seeing at close quarters an aircraft type I had shot at on so many occasions. Who had knocked this one down, I wondered? And where? Poor thing, it didn't look half so menacing on the ground, holed and dented as it was. Rather pathetic, in fact, with a sad, defeated look.

The weather was filthy the following day and we were unable to continue our journey by air. After hanging about until mid-afternoon, the adjutant borrowed a Service car and, with three others of us aboard and our knees in our chins, we had an excruciatingly uncomfortable five-hour journey back to North Weald in pouring rain.

Back in the mess, I found a small bundle of letters in my pigeon-hole, including one of congratulation from the Chief of Air Staff for my recent decoration and another from the General Manager of the District Bank. I had mixed feelings about the one from the Bank; I would have been more impressed had they been a little more solicitous of my welfare when I was a junior member of staff.

I learned, too, that C-in-C, Fighter Command, Air Marshal Sir Hugh Dowding had visited the squadron in my absence, also Captain Harold Balfour, the Under Secretary of State for Air. Mention had been made of the Mark II Hurricane but no hint had been given as to when we might be re-equipped. Some of the Spit squadrons had already been given the Mark II Spitfire, apparently. Why them, for heaven's sake? Even the Mark I could run rings around a Hurricane high up!

Pat Wells, recovering from his wounds and burns, had also visited the mess but had since departed on sick leave. He reported that when he had landed unconscious in his parachute, some Army types had thieved all his personal belongings, including even his Mae West and parachute. What sort of people would do a thing like that? To a member of their own side? Shooting was too good for such louts.

Friday 4 October. A brute of a day. George Barclay and I took off late in the afternoon after several Huns but the weather was so vile, we were recalled after little more than ten minutes in the air. I didn't mind flying in bad weather when there was hope of an interception, but the chances on that particular sortie were clearly nil.

With GN-F (V7313) on inspection, I had inherited another Hurricane, V6854, which was just as pleasant to fly and without the former's almost perpetual oil leak. Even so, my affection remained with 7313. I felt about aircraft much as I had done about my old dog, who had recently died and with whom I had grown up, a combination of loyalty and love. Silly, really, but it was a genuine and deep-seated emotion.

News also came through that several more of the squadron had been decorated, Butch Barton and Keith Lofts each receiving the DFC, Gerald Lewis a Bar to the DFC, and Sergeant Beard, a well-earned DFM. Butch, a not very impressive chap in appearance, following in the tradition of Canadians in the last war, was proving to be a splendid leader and a first-class fighter pilot. Beard, too, one of the longest-serving members of the squadron, had done wonderfully well. A quiet and retiring fellow, he was given to occasional outbursts of wild eccentricity which included shooting out the electric light bulb in his tent with a revolver – so his slightly wary NCO colleagues reported, anyway.

There was a binge in the mess that night with lots of noise and revelry and not a few thick heads. I managed to get through the evening without being sick and was much encouraged by my growing powers of endurance. However, whisky and ginger ale being the only drink I could keep down, parties in celebration of decorations were apt to become a bit expensive.

We were all very pleased for Butch, especially. So very well deserved. And such a harmlessly pleasant chap when well and truly honking drunk.

The Huns chose to ignore our thick heads and came over in droves the following day, causing us to fly twice, immediately before and after lunch.

With 46 Squadron leading, we swarmed up to more than 20,000 feet on the first occasion and wandered about in a triangle between Canterbury, Dover and Dungeness, with 109s coming and going. There were supposed to be 109 bombers about but the only Huns we encountered were escort fighters, the first group of which showed signs of being warlike but had second thoughts when they saw we were prepared for them.

On our second flight in the same area and well above 20,000 feet, we piled into a strange formation only to find they were Spitfires. Great disappointment! Too many friendly aircraft around, that was the trouble. There being a lot of high cloud about, the wear and tear on the eyes was reduced enormously, the cirrus making aircraft spotting very easy. A gentlemanly day altogether. I didn't mind this sort of war at all.

The following day, 6 October, was vile. However, Crossey and I took off shortly before noon in pursuit of a lone Hun.

As 'Lumba' reported it to be in our immediate vicinity, I instructed Crossey to stay below cloud, then at little more than 1,000 feet, while I climbed up through the first layer. Emerging at about 4,500 feet into the most dismal of dark grey galleries, to my utter astonishment, I found a Dornier 17 doing precisely the same less than 400 yards ahead of me.

I doubt that the Hun crew were more surprised than I was. For two or three seconds, we looked at each other, stunned by each other's presence, after which action exploded. I saw the Dornier's nose dip violently in the direction of the cloud some 100 feet beneath, at the same time I slammed open the throttle in order to close the gap between us.

I had managed to get to within 200 yards when the Dornier began to sink back into the fringes of mist. I followed it into the murk, firing at the disappearing silhouette and between the stains of dark exhaust smoke, shouting meanwhile to Crossey to catch it should it appear below.

Dropping quickly through the cloud myself, I rejoined my partner and we raced about in the drizzle and fog until it became obvious that the Hun had disappeared for good. After which, like two tongue-lolling hounds returning from a faded scent, we landed after thirty-five minutes, excited but a little disgruntled.

I had barely been refuelled when the whole squadron was scrambled, an instruction which, in view of the weather, I regarded as quite incredible. But climb up we did and promptly ran into difficulties, the various sections losing each other almost immediately in the thickest and most miserable of murk.

After wandering about with my section for some fifteen minutes, totally blind and growing thoroughly bolshie, I decided to return and spent the next fifteen minutes trying to find the airfield. Eventually, everyone landed safely but in no friendly frame of mind. What an extraordinary, almost criminal thing for 'Lumba' to do. But my problems were not to end there.

An hour or so later, George Barclay confronted me with a stern face. 'Ginger, you've just shot down a Hampden!' He was palely incensed and trembling with outrage. I was stunned. What on earth was he talking about? I asked him to explain and out it came with a rush.

A Hampden had been shot down in our area apparently, the rear gunner either wounded or killed, and as I was up at the time, I was the obvious culprit. George, exploding with righteous indignation, had it all worked out.

I replied succinctly and with rising anger. I had shot at Dornier 17s often enough to know what they damn well looked like. Moreover, I had one important advantage over him; I was there, he wasn't! And he should bear that in mind. We parted, stiff-legged, and there the matter rested.

Later in the afternoon, John Grandy appeared and reported that Ops had confirmed that my damaged Dornier had been finished off by a section of 17 Squadron and had crashed somewhere beyond Chelmsford. I would be credited with one third of a Hun destroyed.

It took me some time to cool down. Eventually, I was persuaded to write out a combat report. One third of a Hun, indeed!

I did not receive an apology from George and our relationship cooled for a time. But not for long. In the turmoil of events, such incidents were soon forgotten.

I had been planning to take leave for weeks – my last trip to Manchester in August had only been for four days – and the poor weather sharpened my appetite for a brief rest. Even so, as a founder member of the squadron and one of the few originals left, I felt an obligation to remain. The adjutant, however, in his own quiet and persuasive way, talked me into it and I made arrangements to go north by car on 8 October, my mother's birthday. However, there was 7 October to contend with.

In the event, I flew on four occasions, twice in the morning and twice in the afternoon.

The weather changing completely, there was a blue sky and the widest of wide horizons. There were also 109s about in shoals. We saw them from a distance on the first sortie, which occurred around 8 a.m., and almost bumped into them on the second flight when, in the area of Ashford, we came across a streaming melee of Huns, Spitfires and Hurricanes. With 46 above us, we waded in but the result was inconclusive. Bill Millington claimed a 109 as 'probable' but, for some reason, I did not get within shooting distance of anything.

At one stage, disconcertingly, I found myself flying about quite aimlessly, aircraft watching, my attention completely divorced from what was happening around me, being obliged suddenly to pull myself round with a jerk.

It all arose from observing several 109s sitting above a group of Hurricanes and one of the Huns dropping down quietly and neatly, taking up a position some fifty yards to the rear of one of our aircraft, then shooting it down with the clinical deftness of a surgeon wielding a scalpel. And all the time the Hurricane pilot sat there as though hypnotized, clearly oblivious of the 109's presence. Horrified and at the same time fascinated, I heard myself screaming a warning over the RT. But to no avail; the Hurricane was from another station and on a different radio frequency. Wide-eyed and helpless, I watched a man being killed. Methodically. Like a bullock being pole-axed.

Whether in anticipation of leave or for some other reason, I was not in a warlike mood that day. Was I tired? I didn't know. I was just not interested in fighting.

I set off for Manchester the following morning with a passenger – Harry Davidson. By sheer coincidence, I discovered he was also taking leave and returning home. I returned to London by train on 14 October.

It was a miserable and frustrating journey. As we progressed southwards, the stops became more frequent until finally the train came to halt at Wembley, where it stayed for two hours. Although we had been unable to hear them, the air-raid sirens had sounded, there were Huns overhead and bombs were dropping like rain on the West End.

Heading in the direction of the Regent Palace, I found Piccadilly Circus ringed with fires and quite unapproachable. All streets to the west of that point appearing to be blocked, I dropped back into the nearest tube station with the intention of moving east.

There were thousands gathered there below ground, lying on the platforms in their blankets and makeshift beds, whole families who had settled down for the night with flasks and bottles and food. There were even crude bunk arrangements with children, nursing mothers and grandparents – resigned, calm, cheerful, boisterous even – powerful odours of humanity rising in waves. No hint of despair or of fear; just another burden to bear. There being barely space to walk along the edge of the platform, I boarded the first train with considerable relief.

Coming to the surface again, I walked into the flame-flickering blackness and eventually found myself at the darkened entrance of the Strand Palace Hotel. Inside, there were more crinkly-haired citizens, scores of them, all with pillows and blankets and heading for the basement. I had an overwhelming urge to rush forward and kick their fat, useless backsides.

The staff at the reception desk were civil, but only just. Single room? For how long? A girl with a Veronica Lake hair-do scanned her list and selected a cubicle right at the top of the building!

It being midnight and having already been travelling for twelve hours, I was tired, hungry and testily on edge. I turned away in disgust. Parnall, Meaker, Burton, Main and the rest! For what? To make the world safe for this contemptible crew?

I arrived at North Weald a little after lunch the following day and went immediately to dispersal. There were welcoming shouts and I was told that during my absence there had been a fair amount of action and one or two casualties. One of the sergeants, Bayley by name, had killed himself by diving into the ground – oxygen failure probably – and (rather more gleefully this), Perrin, the Frenchman, had been shot down, baling out over the estuary. From GN-F! *What?* My aircraft? They were pulling my leg!

Sadly, they weren't. My Hurricane, for the second time, was in fragments somewhere. Unbelievable! It just didn't pay to turn one's back for a second!

Noticing with surprise some other Hurricanes parked on the north side of the airfield, I learned that the Blenheims had been replaced by 257 Squadron. I met some of their officers in the mess a little later and they seemed a nice enough bunch, their commander a handsome, rather smooth-looking chap with a scar on his face and a small black moustache. A Squadron Leader Tuck, somebody said.

My batman had built a roaring fire in my room, which smelt warm and welcoming; it was nice to get back to the familiar routine of the mess and the companionship. North Weald was very much home to me then, in spite of all the noise and the bombing. A shame about GN-F, though. Who would have thought it?

As if to celebrate my return, the Huns were overhead for most of the night, dropping six bombs on the airfield, two of them within yards of dispersal.

Keith Lofts was shot down the following day. In the Ashford area, he tackled a Dornier 17, which was flitting between the clouds, and after being hit in the engine by return fire, crash-landed his Hurricane, writing it off completely. We were faintly amused; it never paid to take even the humble Dornier too lightly!

I did not fly that day, receiving a message from Air Ministry to report to the BBC for my broadcast. However, the order being cancelled at the last moment, I was still in my best-blue and down at dispersal when another Hun popped out of cloud during the afternoon and dropped a stick of bombs, all of which went off with terrible cracks. As we were obliged to take to the floor, rapidly and ignominiously, I was not amused. Not in my best-blue, for God's sake!

There was a bleak, autumn fog on the morning of 17 October, which silenced the telephones and allowed us all an uninterrupted breakfast. Dispersal seemed full of new faces that day: those of two pilot officers, McConnell and Thompson, and of two not-so-new sergeants who were returning having recovered from wounds and accident damage. And John Grandy, hoping to fly operationally again.

We were ordered off shortly before noon and climbed away to the south through heavy mist and a thickish layer of cloud, to emerge, blinking, into bright sunshine at around 5,000 feet. 'Lumba' vectored us east then south-west so that we patrolled a line roughly from Hornchurch to Biggin Hill. High above an endless carpet of gleaming white, we saw nothing of the ground and nothing of the enemy.

At 17,000 feet, we cruised back and forth. Endlessly. And by degrees, froze. Everyone watchful at first we then, with difficulty, maintained a diminishing degree of alertness as the minutes dragged by and boredom set in. Throughout, the two weavers crossed overhead with metronomic persistence while, in my own cockpit, my eyes flicked regularly over my instruments, surveying amounts, temperatures and pressures. From time to time, too, I would pinch my oxygen-tube to check the flow of that vital commodity to my face. At 17,000 feet, there wasn't much of a risk but it was necessary to continue the routine just in case. Anoxia was a deadly and insidious enemy, encroaching silently and without warning, one's critical faculties the first to be affected.

Eventually, and by this time bolshie as well as bored, we were brought back northwards to drop down through cloud and mist into the sombre murk above Essex.

Later in the afternoon, we were sent off again in search of some mythical bombers; mythical, as in a clear sky, several squadrons of us chased all over Kent but totally without success. By which time the thickening mist and a dipping, brassy sun had combined malevolently to reduce visibility to the point where it was almost impossible to see the ground from below 2,000 feet.

Returning north of the river, we crept about in sections for some time before locating the airfield. Then, with wheels and flaps down, I was in the act of landing when a Hurricane swerved in front of me about twenty yards ahead, causing me to climb back into the mist, shrieking imprecations. Later, I learned that it was Victor Beamish, which reduced my annoyance, but only marginally. A scourge to the enemy, my admirable station commander was also a perfect pest to those with whom he flew, obeying no circuit rules nor any others for that matter. But, as ever, once more in the dispersal hut, the Irish grin and the abject apology were immediately and generously offered. So who could be cross with the man?

Later, we all went down to the Thatch in Epping and, for the umpteenth time, the old Adj took over my gathering collection of brimming pint pots. I just couldn't cope with beer in quantity.

It was during the evening, too, that I learned that my broadcast with Pilot Officer Eric Lock was to be on 22 October, the following Tuesday.

The weather the next day was much the same, a little worse if anything. Grounded for the entire morning, we were sent off shortly after lunch to wander about over Kent at 15,000 feet in anticipation of attacks by 109s, some of which, it was confirmed, had been modified to carry a single 500lb bomb.

It was one of those days. After hanging about above Hornchurch then wearing a groove between Maidstone and Canterbury, we were vectored hither and thither and kept up for so long that we all began to complain about lack of fuel. Possibly because the controller miscalculated or maybe for other reasons, after being airborne for a little under two hours and seeing not a sign of enemy aircraft, we let down into a thick mist and spent valuable time trying to find the airfield. As we did so, the second of our new Frenchmen, Bouquillard, ran out of 'essence' and crash-landed a few miles short of North Weald.

Back in dispersal, voices were raised. What the hell was going on? Couldn't Ops grasp that the fuel used by those at the back of a formation was far greater than that of the leader or those at the front, with the weavers worst off of all. By way of explanation it was pointed out that there had been quite a few Huns high up above Essex and that it had been necessary to keep us airborne. But, we were not in the mood to be convinced. Necessary! After two hours in the air? Absolute rot! Anyway, were we the *only* squadron in 11 Group? No, they'd just made a howling cock-up of things, that was the truth of the matter.

Later that evening, Crossey and I visited the sick and spent some time at the hospital in Epping, knowing full well that if we played our cards right, supper with the nursing staff would be our just reward.

Life was becoming boring again. Wretched weather, no Huns to shoot at, and hours of freezing to death at altitude. It was getting to be like Church Fenton. And still no news of our Hurricane IIs.

The night was very quiet; no thumps, crumps or dronings. The Huns must be taking a holiday.

The weather unrelenting, there was no flying in the morning of the following day because of fog. Down at dispersal, we lazed over breakfast and sat around a cherry-red stove, jawing. Butch was explaining that after the war he was going into business running Chinks between somewhere and somewhere. He had a fixation about Chinks; apparently they were a valuable commodity and in short supply in certain areas of America and presumably Canada. We heard about Butch's Chinks almost as often as Crossey, Burton, Lewis and Pat Wells had regaled us over the weeks with stories of South Africa and of life bare-footed among the natives, their accounts liberally garnished with coarse anecdotes and rude words in Afrikaans.

We also attended to our pets, which included several kittens, Wilfred the duck and Pipsqueak, a little black-and-white terrier of indeterminate ancestry, both introduced by Millington, our Australian.

Also, by this time, some 12-bore sporting guns had found their way into dispersal and were used to shoot rabbits and rooks in the nearby wood. For the rooks, this was a one-day event only; thereafter, they gave us a wide berth, being able to spot a 12-bore at 1,000 yards range. Not to be outdone, one of our newer officers, Pilot Officer Worrall, turned up with a fowling piece the size of a howitzer and normally carried on the prow of a boat. This he loaded and fired with great ceremony, nearly breaking his shoulder in the process after which he was led off limping to sick-quarters.

In the early afternoon, the fog had lifted sufficiently for McConnell and me to be sent off after a lone Hun. After wandering around Kent in and above mist and cloud for almost an hour-and-a-half, we returned without success but having enjoyed the flight. It was nice to do some flying without perpetually having to look over one's shoulder.

Then later, we took it in turns to fly beyond Harwich to shepherd a convoy on its slow progress northwards up the east coast. Our parish in this respect stretched from the Thames estuary to as far north as Southwold, where squadrons from 12 Group usually took over. Convoy patrols were *the* supreme bore – backwards and forwards along a line of ships anything from two to ten miles long, usually some five or six miles out to sea, often beneath low cloud and in the most miserable of weather conditions. For more than an hour we would sit huddled in our cockpits, as often as not trying desperately to keep warm and, more importantly, to stay awake. Perhaps on one trip out of ten, a Hun bomber would appear out of cloud and drop a stick of bombs, invariably behind the backs of the escorting fighters or at the other end of the convoy, after which there would be much scurrying about at full throttle and charging in and out of the murk. Even so, there was the occasional success and a Hun, trailing smoke, would go limping back into obscurity or crash into the sea. In the main, however, our presence was intended more as a deterrent than a means of destroying any attacker.

It was well past 6 p.m. and growing dark when I landed from my last convoy sortie. After the excitement of August and September, October was proving to be a mournful, miserable month. But what did we want, for heaven's sake? To fight? Or to relax? It was difficult to say. A bit of both, probably. It was hard being twenty, and idle more or less.

Sunday 20 October. A 'nothing' day with masses of morning fog allowing us to breakfast luxuriously in the mess. We heard that two Huns had been shot down in the Harwich area overnight, but no one was very interested.

I flew for one hour and twenty-five minutes that afternoon, high above Kent and along the south coast, without result and after climbing up with the squadron through a mass of mist and cloud. We were all getting fed up with cloud. And mist. And seeing nothing.

My aircraft due for inspection and the date of my broadcast having arrived, Crossey and I resolved to spend a night in London. We drove in on the morning of the great day using an ancient Austin 16 (with vast spoked wheels and bald tires) which the adjutant, generous fellow that he was, had bought for us junior pilots.

I found 'Sawn-off' Lock already at the BBC and a mass of nerves; a tiger in the air and the life and soul of any party, he could barely speak.

Due to go on the air in the early evening, we spent the afternoon rehearsing but by tea-time our producer was in despair. Couldn't we ham it up a bit? Inject a little life, a little sparkle into our voices and conversation? He knew how we fighter types felt about such things but forty million people, at a conservative estimate, would expect to hear something rather more than two chaps reading the fat-stock prices. At the mention of 'forty million', Lock nearly fainted away and even I felt a bit queasy in the stomach.
In the event, the broadcast went off quite well, so well in fact that we were invited to stay on and perform a second time for the Overseas Service.

Much later, totally relaxed and with several whiskies from the BBC canteen lapping around inside, I sallied forth into the night. To find that someone had stolen the car!

Some time after, standing humbly in an office in Scotland Yard, we learned that it had been towed away by the police. Needless to say we were vastly relieved but uncertain as to why *we* had been so discriminated against. What made our car so different from the hundreds of others? We never really learned, although we recovered our car – without a fine!

The following day, Wednesday, we motored back to North Weald and were back on the 'state' in the afternoon. Expecting flattery and congratulation, I asked how I had sounded but could find no one in the squadron who had even bothered to listen. Such was my fame and reputation!

Back at Readiness in the afternoon of Thursday 24 October, and finding my own still on inspection, I used GN-J, John Grandy's aircraft. As I arranged my parachute on the tail in the manner which suited me best, some painful gurgling down below caused me to retire to that most private of places. Too much grog, I decided, or the aftermath of broadcastingitis!

I had barely begun communing with nature when the scramble order was given and I heard voices and pounding feet in the background and the sound of engines bursting into life. As quickly as I could, I pulled myself together and, clutching my trousers, ran towards my own Hurricane, by which time most of the others were at the far side of the aerodrome and in the act of taking off. By the time I was airborne, they had departed, racing towards the south and into the first fringes of cloud.

Climbing up in pursuit, I broke out into clear air at 7,000 feet and headed towards the estuary, hoping to catch sight of the rest of the formation above and ahead. At 12,000 feet and a little south of Gravesend, I was still on my own, listening to 'Lumba' reporting bogeys in the area, when I decided that it would be foolhardy to continue alone; to a score of marauding 109s, I would be a tempting morsel indeed. Discretion overcoming enthusiasm with scarcely a struggle, I turned towards the north and began to let down again.

The river underneath, I was just entering the tops of some broken cumulus off Southend pier when, to my utter astonishment, a Ju 88 came into view some 500 yards away, slightly below and flying in the opposite direction.

Surprise being instant and mutual, we passed within thirty yards of each other without firing, after which I whirled about and raced in pursuit; hastily, all fingers and thumbs: pulling the plug, switching on my gunsight and turning my gun button to 'Fire'. Meanwhile, the Hun aircraft, just as keen to escape as I was to catch it, was heading purposefully for the nearest cloud.

I was well in position and within 250 yards before I had properly sorted out my cockpit. Even so, I had time to get in a reasonable burst before the 88 bolted into obscurity like a rabbit down a hole. In a lather of excitement, I raced around to the other side, climbing up meanwhile to get a better view, then, with drawn sword, waited for it to emerge. It did so, twice, but only briefly, disappearing on each occasion before I had time to get into position. The blighter! Now where? I climbed up again and flew down the estuary still bubbling with expectation. But no Hun. Where had the beggar got to now? How could an aircraft as big as that just disappear?

But it could, and did. And for good. I persevered as far as North Foreland and out to sea off Manston, but saw nothing more of it. Finally, when it was obvious that I was wasting my time, I flew back to North Weald on my own and landed. Damn it! If I had been better prepared with my sight, buttons and plug attended to, I would have had that Hun. Another lesson learned the hard way. Had I hit it? Possibly, but it was hardly worth bothering about other than just reporting. What a wretched thing to happen! I was still cross with myself long after landing.

My batman had built a welcoming fire in my room that night and with the blackout screen in place and the flames flickering cosily on the darkened walls, I wrote the routine letter to my parents in the half-light, reporting that life was pretty comfortable and that I could not hope for anything better.

There were Huns over London again that night but, with only a few crumps and bumps in the distance, the disturbance was nothing to speak of. It didn't bother me, anyway.

Despite the prospect of early morning Readiness the following day, I did not return to dispersal and after about ten minutes of sleep in my own bed, or so it seemed, my batman brought me hot, sweet tea in the usual white mug. Very civilized, although I did not enjoy the early rise. Waking up never came easily to me; I was just not that sort of person.

It was quite dark still when the Commer aircrew transport came to collect us at the mess around 5 a.m. and we sat in the back, silent, yawning and barely awake, listening to the muted roar of the 'dawn chorus' across the airfield. The weather had changed, the mist had gone and there was a new freshness in the air. The Huns would be up and about today.

And indeed they were. In the dispersal hut, we had barely raised the first forkful of breakfast to our lips when we were scrambled. Patrol Chelmsford at Angels 15, was the instruction, but we knew that that could mean anything.

As we climbed away, we were informed of bogeys approaching from the south and were vectored immediately towards the estuary, levelling off at 15,000 feet and remaining there and in the north Kent area for quite some time.

What now, we wondered? The pattern of recent Hun activity more or less established, we knew that we would probably be encountering high flying 109s with bombs, accompanied by others acting as fighter escort. Except for individual bombers operating independently in weather conditions favourable to themselves, the Dorniers, Ju 88s and Heinkels were relics of the past, especially the Heinkels, none of which had been seen for weeks. They and the Ju 87 dive-bomber, together with the Me 110, were clearly regarded by the Hun as having poor survival prospects and were obviously being held back, if not withdrawn. Precision bombing was out, the Huns no doubt seeking to create panic and dismay by using 109s to throw bombs almost indiscriminately at widely-spread targets.

Our eyes skinned, we remained airborne for almost an hour-and-a-half before dropping back over Essex and landing. Disappointing, after all that build-up.

At 11.30 a.m., we were off again with instructions to patrol base, an order I never much liked, being unpleasantly reminiscent of events in September. However, we were almost immediately ordered south and taken across the river and on a course, roughly, for Dungeness. Levelling out somewhere to the south of Biggin Hill, we were flying in a south-easterly direction at about 18,000 feet when, suddenly, and greatly to our surprise, about a dozen 109s flew across our bows a little lower than ourselves and without observing us.

Lower, by George! It had never happened to us before and my own astonishment was matched only by that of the Germans. With no recent warning from 'Lumba' and flying in a comparatively relaxed manner, our two formations were within 1,000 yards of each other when we saw the Huns and, a second or two later, they saw us. The effect was electric.

Finding several 109s crossing underneath me in perfect position to be attacked – pretty, colourful, spiteful little aircraft in plan view – I was so dumbfounded by my good fortune that I did not take full advantage of the tactical bonus. Spoilt for choice, I hesitated in picking my target, at which point the 109s, suddenly aware of us, scattered like minnows before pike.

Selecting one, not the nearest, unfortunately, I whirled in pursuit and still in a turn, fired a burst which streaked away, my tracer clearly missing the fuselage of the 109 but a brief flash indicating at least one hit on the starboard wing, regrettably much closer to the wingtip than the cockpit. The damage trivial, my attack had the effect of making the German react as though a hatpin had been jabbed in his rump. In an instant, he had jammed the nose of his aircraft forward so violently that for a moment I actually sympathized with the man, visualizing him being pitched out bodily through the roof, straps included.

My concern, however, was short-lived. Hurling my aircraft in his wake, I was checked momentarily when my Hurricane hesitated and a smear of dark smoke streamed from my engine exhausts – negative 'g' and the inevitable flooded carburettor – but I remained sufficiently in touch to fire again. However, as my tracer curved and weaved around the 109's diminishing silhouette, all I seemed to succeed in doing was make him go faster.

The chase really on, I tumbled down after him, manhandling my controls violently. Now almost vertical and the speed and scream of the dive rising rapidly, I saw that I had lost ground and was about 800 yards behind. He was getting away from me, nothing was more obvious. But could I catch him? Almost dispassionately, I weighed up my chances. There was a layer of cloud below and, with a micro-second's glance, I saw that my ASI was already indicating around 380 mph with the needle moving steadily around the dial. Down... down... down... like a plummeting stone, my controls stiff and trembling, my left leg rigidly outstretched, dust from the cockpit depths whirling disconcertingly around my eyes and face. Then, cloud! Surging up like a train. Racing towards me until suddenly I was *in*! A white 'whupp!' and a series of violent, rapid, jarring bumps as though I were riding crazily over cobble-stones. I eased out gingerly. Holding firmly then gripping hard and pulling determinedly. Up, you blighter! *Up*! Everything straining... protesting... and going grey, the ASI unwinding and the toppled artificial horizon cannoning wildly from edge to edge in its circle of glass. My heart pounding. Then, the noise dying away. Out of cloud in a flash, then in again. More bumps, some of them violent. God! Then, clear air and... *nothing*! No Hun. Not a sign anywhere. *Gone*!

Not exactly surprised, I was disappointed, even so. But in my heart I knew I could never have caught him; with a Spit it might have been different but not with a Hurricane and the carburettor problem we always had. Even so, I should have had him, damn it, given the element of surprise I had enjoyed. Once again, I had fluffed it; ought to have been better prepared. In thirty minutes time, he'd probably be home, guzzling schnapps and crowing about his escape to all his pals.

Turning towards the north, I kept below cloud and watched my tail like a hawk all the way back to the river. On my own again, I didn't want to be picked off.

After landing and as my ground crew rearmed and refuelled my aircraft, I saw that it was 1 p.m. and we had been up almost an hour-and-a-half – three hours all told for the morning. I also learned that Harry Davidson and I had been the only ones to fire our guns. In spite of our tactical advantage, too. Astonishing!

And even more surprising, I learned that Sergeant Beard had been shot down and that, Bouquillard, the Frenchman, had been wounded and obliged to force-land at Rochester. Poor old Beard! He was spending more time in his parachute than he was in his aircraft! It was all very strange. Had we in turn been attacked? Obviously so. But by whom, and when? Nothing was more confusing than air combat!

We were hardly given time to draw breath before we were sent off again, climbing hard across the river and towards the south. We had 46 Squadron somewhere behind and above us and I was leading Yellow Section consisting of Crossey to my left, the new boy Thompson on my right, and the ever-reliable Davidson behind.

We were approaching the south coast in the area of Bexhill when we ran into another formation of 109s. There were about fifteen of them going fast at around the same height as ourselves – 17,000 feet. In a wild curving chase, we pursued them across the coast and out to sea, in the process of which both 46 and ourselves were attacked from above. A melee ensuing, there were aircraft everywhere and the squadron broke up.

My section remaining more or less intact, I eventually found myself separated from the main body of aircraft a little north of Hastings. The Huns seemed to have departed but there was a good deal of uncertainty and chatter on the RT. What now?

We were flying east some ten miles inland, on guard but not immediately threatened. My section was tucked in nicely and everything was fine. I looked at Crossey some ten yards away on my left and he returned my gaze impassively. Things had quietened down and we were all in one piece.

It was at that point that I became aware of bright white flecks passing very close to my left shoulder. After which, I had a fleeting worm's-eye-view of Crossey's starboard wing as he upended his aircraft and vanished.

While I was struggling to interpret these strange goings-on, an aircraft rose up in front of me some twenty yards ahead like Excalibur out of the mere. It was small, grey, single-engined, with struts on its tail, which I saw quite clearly, and obviously extremely unhappy at finding itself where it was. In short, a 109 which had just attacked me from behind and had overshot.

As comprehension dawned, the Hun, in a repeat performance of his colleague's behaviour several hours earlier, thrust down his nose with a jerk and fell away vertically. And, yet again, in an attempt to follow, my engine faltered, my exhausts vomiting a stream of black smoke.

For the second time, tumbling down in pursuit, I fired, this time from a distance of around 200 yards, watching the Hun wriggle frenziedly as the sparks and tracer reached out in his direction to clutch him briefly. With the scream of my descent heightening, I fired again, aware that Thompson, unseen, was still somewhere off to my right, and was encouraged to observe a twinkling flash and a puff together with some unidentified fragment which whirled away from the 109's starboard side.

But, as before, my engine's hesitation had allowed the enemy to increase the gap between us and, as it dropped like a stone, try as I did, the 109 kept pulling away. As it grew smaller, I fired again, this time almost as a gesture of despair. I was losing it and there was little I could do about it. But was it streaming? Smoking? It was hard to say. Possibly just the dark exhaust smoke of an engine being flogged to death. On the other hand – !

Meanwhile, as the speed mounted rapidly and as cloud and earth as well as the small silhouette of the Hun sat squarely in my windscreen, some inner voice shrieked out to me: 'Beware!' This would be the first of *two* Huns, no doubt. Where was the second? Behind me? For a moment my spine crawled. Continue or pull out? The big decision! At which point, above all the vibration and din there was a deafening 'WHAP!' accompanied by the roar and rush of air and dust. *Jesus*! What was that?

It proved to be the emergency-release panel situated in the left-hand side of the hood, a piece of perspex less than a foot square, which had been sucked out by the speed of my descent. It had happened to me before – once – at something over 400 mph, which was about the rate I was then travelling. Of no great significance, it was, even so, a heart-stopping shock and a momentary distraction at a moment of high drama. I looked up. The Hun, still diving vertically, was disappearing into cloud. Not too far from the ground now, could it possibly pull out? A victory? I didn't know. After which, in a flash, it vanished, still heading like a dart for the earth.

I pulled away, everything draining, and turned towards the north. After a time, Thompson and some others appeared, surging and bucking, and settling down we all went home.

Back in dispersal, it was immediately obvious that there had been a fair amount of action. Heads were counted and stories exchanged. Millington was claiming a 'probable' and Worrall a 'destroyed'.

Later we learned that 46 Squadron had had some success but that on the previous trip, one of their aircraft had crashed into a house in Romford when returning. The pilot, a young officer named Patullo, had been posted briefly to 249 some weeks before but had left to join 46. A nice fellow, we heard subsequently that having first been wounded in combat, he had died from these and other injuries arising from the crash.

I remained awake for a long time that night, unsettled and thinking some very dark thoughts. I had been caught out absolutely on that final flight and if the Hun had not been so erratic, my number would have been up. Moreover, the whole of my section had been put at risk. Never before had I been surprised like that. Never! Other chaps, yes. But not I. It was very worrying indeed.

We were up on three occasions the following day, in all, almost five hours of flying. With 46 Squadron, we patrolled between Maidstone and Canterbury until we were rigid with boredom and cold. 'Lumba' reported the presence of Huns from time to time but not a single one did we see. The weavers wove until they were dizzy.

On the second trip, the oil in my radiator froze and, for the first time, I experienced the symptoms I had only heard about from others. Glancing down, I noticed the oil temperature needle marching around the dial and the pressure dropping towards the 30 lb mark – much less than the emergency minimum. Greatly concerned, as we were out of sight of the ground, I gave a duff engine report and dropped away, intending to land at the first place I could find, provided the engine was still running at that point!

With my eyes glued to my instruments and the oil temperature approaching 100 degrees instead of the usual 50–60, I was down to about 5,000 feet when, in the space of little more than a minute, the temperature needle fell back to its normal position and the pressure rose comfortingly. Whatever had frozen had unfrozen itself, to my great relief. Back on the ground, I reported the incident and a little later all Hurricanes were modified, part of the oil radiator being blanked off in an attempt to prevent the oil congealing. Which it did for me although others were again to be troubled in the weeks to come.

During October and November, patrolling as we did for anything up to ninety minutes at a time and regularly losing some of our most experienced pilots, we had plenty of time to consider our methods and how we might improve them. We were still highly vulnerable to attacks by darting 109s; not only did we not see them coming occasionally but even when we did, there was not much we could do to catch them as they swooped and zoomed away or dived right through us. With the Hurricane's lack of performance at altitude and because they held the initiative, they did pretty much as they pleased; we simply acted as targets, flying about in our inflexible formations and trudging around the sky with little more than 220 mph showing on the ASI. Something had to be done but no one knew what exactly. We were still bomber orientated; destroying bombers was the Hurricane's primary role and fighting 109s a fringe exercise, so to speak. Moreover, every trip since August had been an operational sortie; there had been neither the time nor the opportunity for training or to experiment, be it in tactics or gunnery.

Yet, strangely, I doubt that there was even one among us who did not feel absolutely confident that he could successfully take on a 109. If only the blighters would stay-put long enough for us to catch them. In a dog-fight, the Hurricane was acknowledged as being the more versatile aircraft although it was learned later, using a captured 109, that as the latter had slats, if the Hun pilots had chosen to do so they could actually have out-turned us at very low speeds. Happily for us, however, they were too much married to the tactic of hit-and-run to prove the point.

It was at about this time too, that we tried out Victor Beamish's snake formation for one trip only! It was a disaster. Strung out across the sky, no one bar the leader had a chance of looking for anything other than the aircraft in front; moreover, after an hour in the air, all those towards the rear of the snake were fast running out of fuel.

Finally, it was suggested that a Defiant be co-opted to fly at the back of our formation; with a turret of four Browning guns and a backward facing observer, any Hun making a surprise attack on our rear would himself be unpleasantly surprised. In the event, it, too, was something of a disaster as the Defiant had not the performance to keep in position so that we all had to reduce speed to allow it to do so. That experiment also, to our relief, lasted for one frustrating sortie only.

No, the only solution, in 249's opinion, was re-equipment with Hurricane IIs. Why then were we having to wait? The aircraft were available, apparently, some of them with the new 20mm cannons. What was the problem, for heaven's sake?

No one bothering to explain, we continued as before, in no way disheartened or lacking in confidence, simply irritated by Air Ministry's apparent lack of understanding.

We were off at 7.30 a.m. on the morning of 27 October, in conditions of mist and low cloud. We had barely become airborne and were joining up in a stream around the circuit when a Dornier 17 popped out of cloud at not more than 1,000 feet and dropped some bombs, one of which fell on the aerodrome.

The Hun, no doubt horrified by the sight of a dozen or more Hurricanes within a mile of him, turned for home but not before several of us had caught up and harried him as he climbed away, twisting and turning in slow motion in and out of layers of stratus and banks of cumulus.

It was a fascinating game, for us, less so for the Dornier. Surprisingly, the Hun made less use of cloud cover than he might have done and offered himself to be shot at several times when he might quite easily have escaped.

After some minutes of persistent stalking, I found myself alone but still in pursuit, getting in bursts from astern whenever I could but at longish range. Finally, when approaching the estuary and having registered a number of hits, I was surprised to see it carry out a spiralling turn into cloud somewhere in the vicinity of Sheerness, after which I lost it completely. Landing back at North Weald, I found the others still airborne and was happy to kill time in dispersal toasting my feet before the stove until they returned.

Two more longish trips followed, in the late morning and afternoon, involving dreary patrols over the estuary and Kent. Constantly above an endless carpet of white studded with towering mushrooms of cumulus, it was often difficult to know exactly where we were, the legs of our patrol-lines being estimated by time. Butch was very good at this and was showing himself to be a quiet but splendid leader in whom we all had the greatest confidence.

I found that I had landed after the morning show with my gun button still on 'Fire', hastily changing it to 'Safe' before taxiing in. And not for the first time, either! It was a wonder that more accidents did not occur on the ground with our loaded guns, especially as there were occasional instances of a quick burst being let off while landing, usually when the control column was being held back and the aircraft in the touch-down position with its nose in the air. It was Sergeant Davis (I believe) who startled everyone one day by letting off a brief 'burp' at the point of touch-down. Everyone pulled a face because they felt it was required of them but we all regarded it as something of a joke. Anyway, what was a short burst between friends? I had been sorely tempted to loose off a few shots at Victor Beamish out of sheer irritation on the several occasions he had baulked me when landing in bad weather. Moreover, millions of rounds had been fired over Kent since August but I had never heard of anyone being struck by a live or even a spent bullet. On the other hand, perhaps they had and were not in a condition to complain!

Altogether, a not very satisfactory day although some of us had at least fired our guns. Cloud was becoming more of a problem when operating as a squadron but we were beginning to cope with it quite adequately.

A noisier night, too, than of late with a few bombs and guns going off from time to time. But, who would have thought a year before that we would be able to live quite serenely under an almost unending succession of nocturnal air-raids? And hardly give them a thought?

I was sent off after a lone Hun in the early morning of the following day, just when breakfast was being served. With 'Tommy' Thompson as my companion, we roamed through rain and cloud above Essex and Kent for almost an hour and fifty minutes before returning empty-handed. Such bad weather jaunts were not to everyone's taste. Tommy just sat alongside and watched, saying not a word.

I had barely been refuelled and was picking over what remained of some congealed food when the whole squadron was scrambled at 9.50 a.m. and vectored south.

We were at about 16,000 feet somewhere north of Hastings, in bright sunshine and looking down on a brilliant carpet of small white dumplings, when Millington, who was Blue 1, gave a 'Tallyho'. Directly beneath, crawling in a southerly direction on top of the cloud layer, was a Dornier, its small, dark, distinctive shape triggering the usual surge of excitement and the primitive urge to hunt it down.

My own section, Yellow, being instructed to intercept together with Blue, we tumbled down in the grand manner, praying that the Hun would not catch sight of us before we arrived within firing distance. As we careered towards the clouds at an angle of perhaps 60 degrees – which in a Hurricane seemed almost over the vertical – I experienced yet again the unforgettable thrill of combat. This, by God, was *the* greatest feeling in the world; no one who had not experienced it had *lived*!

I had about 8,000 feet to lose, with tension and excitement rising to fever pitch, my engine howling, the slipstream a wild, roaring scream, the controls tight and vibrating and my left leg rigidly extended and trembling. Stay *still*, you blighter! Just for ten, brief, golden seconds!

The Dornier, still creeping ahead, seemed willing to oblige, apparently unaware of our headlong approach and of its likely fate. With more than 400 showing on the ASI, we swept to within 500 yards at which point, the German aircraft nodded its head in an almost dignified manner... and sank into cloud.

Screaming my frustration and annoyance and carried ahead by the momentum of my dive, I shot into cloud like an arrow and thereafter had something of a problem interpreting my instruments and recovering from my dramatic entry. After some seconds and back in a climb, I leapt out into sunshine like a game-fish and, looking around, saw only one Hurricane somewhere above me and off to my left. Instinctively turning towards it, I noted that we were at 9,000 feet and slightly above a sea of white cumulus icebergs.

As we banked and curved on collision courses, I recognized the other aircraft as Bill Millington's. Straightening up at the last moment, we drifted together and looked about. At which moment, unbelievably, another Hun, a Ju 88, emerged from the cloud ahead like a train from a tunnel.

The German aircraft being 1,000 yards in front and for a second or two forgetting about my partner, I just had time to shape up to a head-on attack when the 88, presumably not relishing the prospect, turned to my right and spoiled the manoeuvre. I pulled away, everything thrust to the maximum, and whirled about, considering how best to attack. Dorniers I adored; 88s I liked much less; in my experience they were fast, prickly brutes and able to absorb almost unlimited punishment.

First to the Hun and racing in uncompromisingly from dead astern, I opened fire with a sustained burst and had the immediate satisfaction of observing a series of brilliant flashes from the area of the rear cockpit. Then, either by accident or design, the 88 began to climb quite steeply into the eye of the sun so that, below and behind, I was dazzled by the glare. Pulling away, I approached again and attacked once more from dead astern, this time from above, risking the likelihood of a response from the gunner. To my relief, none was forthcoming and I settled in position and fired several times more, my shuddering, spark-flecked tracer enveloping the port wing and engine, which obligingly began to trail a thin line of white then a thicker and perceptibly darkening grey stream. As I maintained position, wallowing and bucking in the German aircraft's slipstream, a haze of dark oil spotted my windscreen and I detected the hot reek of burning paint and rubber. Knowing full well it was from the aircraft ahead, I could not, even so, resist a quick and anxious glance towards my own instruments. Fire, the greatest enemy of all, I was never able to steel myself to take the terrifying scent of it for granted.

Pulling yet again to the side, I watched Millington carry out his own attack after which we each made one more assault from behind before our ammunition was expended. But, the Ju 88 flew on. Looking decidedly unwell but there. Like a sick animal, reeling, exhausted, but on its feet, I formated on its starboard side a mere twenty yards away. The rear of the crew compartment was a shambles and the starboard airscrew – surprising this, as it was the port engine which had streamed smoke – motionless. I felt almost sorry for it even though it showed every sign of escaping. Another fight, if not lost, inconclusive. But, we could do no more.

We crossed the coast, an unlikely formation of three until, with a final forlorn glance and by mutual consent, Millington and I turned back towards the north, failure and disappointment weighing heavily on my mind and, I daresay, on his.

But any such self-recrimination was premature. We had barely left when the remaining members of Blue and Yellow sections, whom we had not seen throughout, came across the 88 as suddenly and as accidentally as we had done and, attacking immediately, tipped it over into the waves beneath. It fell like a weary, crippled bird and the gently heaving Channel claimed one more victim. In the space of seconds, every trace had been obliterated.

Back in dispersal, I found there were no combat report forms available and was obliged to write my account of the action on a spare sheet of paper. The result was the same, however; I was officially credited with one-quarter of a Hun destroyed. A whole quarter!

We were off again later in the afternoon on the inevitable Maidstone-Canterbury patrol-line and, landing well after 5 p.m., I missed my tea. Again, almost five hours of flying during the day and all in the most hostile of environments. Would it ever be safe to fly over Kent without one's neck being on ball-bearings?

Tuesday 29 October. A 'nothing' day early on: mist, low cloud, dull and miserable.

Fretting with the inactivity, I was happy to be sent off shortly after 9 a.m. in company with Tommy Thompson and for more than an hour we were taken through, between, and above layers of cloud over the Blackwater, the estuary and across in Kent. 'Lumba' seemed lethargic – a little early for them possibly – and did not appear too clear as to the nature or the position of our target, so that the trip, like the weather, proved to be a disappointment.

The morning passed uneventfully and by lunch-time it was decided that 'A' Flight would be released. Much cheered by this decision, those of us concerned departed in the direction of our respective messes. After which, the weather improved, the cloud broke up and the sun appeared, which made our good fortune all the more to be savoured.

It was about tea-time and I was sitting in my bedroom in the hut alongside the mess, busily constructing a model aeroplane. Crossey, Pat Wells and several others were in adjoining rooms and with voices and laughter in the distance, there was a quiet, holiday atmosphere about the place.

After a time I heard the far-away noise of engines and concluded that the squadron, entirely or in part, was being sent off on patrol. I was barely interested. Nothing of note about that; utterly normal, in fact. I glued two pieces of balsa together and held them between my fingers, looking up at the sky reflectively as the cement dried.

Then with rapidly growing intensity, the noise of more engines and every hair on my neck stood on end. Familiar, absolutely, with the sound of Merlins, singly or together, this noise was different. Quite, quite different! Rising quickly to my feet, I crossed to the window, just in time to see the first of a stream of 109s flash across the top of my head, low enough even for me to pick out the black crosses on the wings.

Thereafter, it was bedlam. As the bombs began to drop, the air was thick with the sound and fury of explosions, the ripping burp of machine-guns, and the roar of engines. The hut wilting in the blast of detonations far and near, I flung myself to the floor still clutching my model and expecting every moment to hear and feel the roof collapsing about my ears. On and on it went for an eternity – of probably no more than twenty seconds! Then, after the briefest of intervals, a monster bang made the floor lift as though we were all about to become airborne. After that, a period of comparative silence in which the despairing clump-clump-clump of a distant Bofors gun and the diminishing buzz of fast retreating aero-engines seemed almost intrusive.

Scrambling to my feet, I ran out of my room to find Crossey, Pat Wells and others in the corridor. Excitement and confusion everywhere. Anyone hit? Where did that last one go? We clattered outside, falling over each other. Had the boys been able to take off? Would they catch the blighters?

Outside, everywhere was smoke, hovering dust and smell, all amid the stultifying atmosphere of tension and breathless uncertainty. Fifty paces away, a huge thick-lipped crater in the rosebush-encircled lawn in front of the mess. The *lawn*, for God's sake! That must have been the last bang. And an old man, a gardener, shocked into petrified silence, was shaking uncontrollably and standing as though transfixed.

We collected the poor creature, who must have been seventy, and sat him on the steps of the hut breathing words of sympathy and encouragement in his ear. I had never before seen a person utterly broken by an event beyond his experience and comprehension and was mutely horrified by what I beheld. Here was no dignity, not even a flicker of retaliation or resistance. Just silent, shivering defeat, so greatly in contrast with the man's thick frame and brawny, veined arms. A cup of tea? Not even a nod. The eyes blankly vacant, the spirit crushed. An urgent nod towards my batman. Tea! Sweet tea! Quickly!

Within minutes we were in a car heading for dispersal. A number of buildings had been destroyed, there were dust, smoke and fires everywhere, a scattering of bomb craters across the airfield, and fire-engines and other vehicles and people moving about either urgently or as though in shock. A greasy, black column rose from our dispersal area. Something had happened down there, by God!

A Hurricane, pointing west, sat outside our dispersal hut. On its belly and on fire. I hurried towards it to find Crossey and others standing beyond the circle of intense heat with their hands in their pockets. I peered through the smoke and flames. Not our code letters. Must be one of 257's. I turned to Crossey. Where was the pilot? A nod. Inside!

It was like a funeral pyre. As the flames took hold, we watched a blackened and unrecognizable ball that was a human head sink lower and lower into the well of the cockpit until, mercifully, it disappeared. Then the fuel tanks gaped with whoofs of flame the ammunition began to explode, causing us all to step back a pace, and the fuselage and wings began to bend and crumble in glowing agony. Finally, there was only heat and crackling silence and ashes.

And all the time, we watched. And talked quietly. And wondered how the rest of the chaps were faring.

Butch and the others, with elements of 257, were not long in returning and we were able to piece together a picture of what had happened. Most of 249, having been ordered to patrol base at 15,000 feet, had just become airborne when the first of the twenty or more 109 bombers and escorts had appeared. One section, consisting of Lofts, Thompson and McConnell, were in the act of leaving the ground when a bomb had fallen very close to them, badly damaging Keith Lofts' machine but, fortunately for him, not sufficiently to require an immediate landing. Thereafter, it had been a running fight as far as the coast with Butch and Sergeants Davidson and Stroud claiming one

109 'destroyed' and four others 'probable' and 'damaged'.

No. 257 Squadron had also been caught taking off but had fared rather worse with Sergeant Girdwood's Hurricane, whose demise we had just witnessed, being hit by bomb splinters before crashing in flames dangerously close to our dispersal hut. A number of 257's ground-staff had also been killed and others wounded and a Polish officer of theirs had been forced to bale out. For them, a messy and unpleasant business.

By nightfall, the full extent of the action was becoming known. A considerable amount of fairly superficial damage had been done all over the camp but not sufficient to halt or even suspend operations. Casualties though had been heavy with between fifteen and twenty people killed and a further forty wounded, including one of 249's ground crew, an airman who had been caught in the lavatory at dispersal. Always a situation likely to raise a snigger, this was less funny as the man was to die the following day. Also, the station guardroom, which I had seen damaged on the day following my arrival at North Weald and which had just been rebuilt at great expense, had been flattened for the second time. Some buildings seemed fated to suffer.

The news also leaked through that three or four of the attacking force had come down somewhere south of Colchester; several 109s crashed to destruction and one, Butch's, which had been hit in the radiator, landed wheels-up in a field. As it was said to be in one piece, we decided to visit the scene to inspect it when the first opportunity presented itself. I had never seen a 109 close-to; except in the air, of course.

The excitement died away. Nobody liked the crater in the mess lawn very much. Silly blighters! Fancy doing a thing like that.

I retired that night more than a little concerned that I had treated the cremation of 257's chap so lightly. What on earth was coming over me? I had watched a colleague burnt to a cinder and had felt... well... almost nothing. Not like me at all. Downright worrying, in fact.

Expecting a photographic aircraft, I took off at dawn the following morning with the hope that I might catch it. The weather was vile and at 6.30 a.m., black as well as miserable. A long way out into the North Sea, off Barrow Deep, the waves looked miserably cold and inhospitable in the pale grey light. Definitely not the day for a duff engine!

It all came to nothing, however; the Huns obviously had more sense than to be abroad on such a morning.

The weather unrelenting, it was something of a surprise when we were sent off shortly before noon, climbing through some dense cloud before coming out on top over Kent. Immediately after take-off, oil began to accumulate on my windscreen and, after fifteen minutes or so, the leak became so bad that I was unable to see ahead and was obliged to pull out and return home. The rest disappeared towards the south without me and, it transpired, into a long drawn-out and rather unhappy engagement.

Over the south coast and at 28,000 feet, which was well beyond the Hurricane's best fighting height, they ran into a dozen or so 109s and a chase and melee ensued with the Huns apparently enticing our aircraft out across the Channel. When the Hurricanes returned towards the coast, the Huns followed and there was some sporadic swooping and fighting which, at that altitude, was as difficult to observe as it was to take part in. The result: Thompson was able to claim a victory and a further 109 as 'damaged', Bill Millington disappeared, and one of our formidable Polish NCOs, Sergeant Maciejowski, managed to lose himself for about the third time, force-landing, wheels and flaps down, in a field a little to the north of Bexhill. And for him worse was to follow. Unable to make himself understood in English, the police marched him off to durance-vile as a suspected fifth-columnist with the result that someone had to trail all the way down to Sussex to bail him out. Amusing at first, 'Micky' Maciejowski's unscheduled landings in the southern counties had begun to wear a bit thin and he was warned that they had to stop, or else!

I was off again before tea and after almost an hour-and-a-half in the air, became separated from the rest of the squadron, landing finally at Martlesham Heath short of fuel. Taxying across the grass towards the hangars, it became obvious that an air-raid warning was in progress and knowing full well of a heavy attack on Martlesham by a force of 109s only days before, I made myself scarce, retreating quickly to a far corner of the aerodrome. Parking my aircraft, I dismounted and for the next twenty minutes, with eyes wide and ears cocked, was quite prepared to run for it had the need arisen. Happily, it did not and having refuelled, I returned to North Weald later in the afternoon.

It had been a miserable, bitty and perfectly bloody day, with the loss of Bill Millington especially upsetting. He might turn up, of course, but the fact that he had been over the Channel seemed to reduce that possibility.

In dispersal the little dog, Pipsqueak, and Wilfred the duck wandered about, mournful reminders of their absent master. If only they knew! But, perhaps they did.

The weather excelled itself in beastliness on the last day of October. We mooned about in the morning looking dejectedly at the low cloud and drizzle and, there seeming little likelihood of an improvement, several of us provisionally arranged to go in search of Butch's 109. By lunch-time our stand-down had been confirmed and we set off in the squadron Humber, Butch driving, with me sitting in front map-reading and two others in the back.

There being at least three 109s which were known to have crashed in the area at about the same time, we had some difficulty initially in identifying Butch's victim. We located it, finally, in a field a few miles south of Colchester, sitting forlornly on its belly in an area of flatland not far from the coast. It was guarded by a soldier with a rifle who approached us, if not truculently, with a rather irritating air of proprietorship. He had orders not to let anyone go near it, we were told, to which I responded by saying that if the chap who had shot it down was not entitled to do so, I didn't know who was. That seemed to satisfy the man who, a bit daunted no doubt by the sight of four officers from another Service, backed away with a slightly embarrassed smile.

It was the first time I had been within touching distance of a 109 and I was not too impressed. There were no obvious signs of battle damage and we assumed that it had been struck underneath in the waterworks, resulting in a loss of coolant and the engine seizing. The pilot, an NCO, was said to have been wounded but that might have been as a result of the landing.

It seemed a good deal smaller and slimmer than a Hurricane and, with an engine of approximately the same power as the Merlin, it was obvious why the 109's performance was so much greater than that of our own aircraft, particularly at altitude. The cockpit seemed tiny by comparison and the instrument layout and controls, simple to the point of being primitive. The hood, too, had bars everywhere and we were all agreed that visibility could not have been anything special. In fact, it seemed a wan, pallid little thing, not at all the venomous, waspy creature we had so often encountered zipping around the sky. Even so, this was the type that was running rings round us at 20,000 feet and picking off our best chaps whenever it felt inclined to do so.

We walked around it examining the guns, the cannons, the wing slats, riveting and finish. The metal blades of the airscrew had been bent forward by the impact on landing but otherwise the aircraft was in quite good condition. Given a little attention, it could probably be made to fly again.

We left it sitting there, on the whole encouraged by what we had seen. The next time I ran into one over Kent, I would think of this little chap sitting dejectedly in an Essex pasture, looking like the family dog left in a kennel.

It was dark when we arrived home. The last day of October. Winter was setting in.

13

Winter Sets In: November 1940

November!

The turn of the month passed entirely unnoticed. Our activities as a squadron remained the same; only the change of temperature, the shorter days and poorer weather marked the onset of winter and reduced the tempo of our flying. With the continuation of British Summer Time – by Government edict – even dawn Readiness was now at a civilized hour.

I had been with 249 almost six months, six turbulent months which had seemed a lifetime. Montrose and No. 8 FTS were an age away and civilian life entirely forgotten. One of the few survivors of the squadron of May 1940, I had watched my friends and colleagues killed, wounded or disappear, either permanently or temporarily, with an indifference that almost frightened me. My sensibilities seemed at times to be anaesthetized. Never at any point did I expect to become a casualty myself and as the pattern and intensity of fighting showed signs of changing and abating, I saw no reason at all why I should not continue to survive in spite of all the so-called statistical evidence to the contrary. Even so, my constant and greatest fear was of the shattering blow it would be to my parents were some evil stroke of luck to result in my death. Although I cannot ever recall being inhibited in the heat of combat by the thought of them, hardly a day passed in which they did not form part of my more reflective moments.

With the shorter days and winter weather, we officers returned to the mess to sleep although dispersal remained the centre of our day-time activities. Evenings were spent in the mess itself or, after dinner, at the cinema and the two pubs in Epping, the Thatched House and the Cock. By mutual but undiscussed agreement, we tended to use the Thatch and the NCO pilots, the Cock. There were no rules about this, however, and not the slightest embarrassment if we all finished up in the same place. The squadron was still very much a family affair.

In fact, about half of the established sergeant pilots in 249 were eventually commissioned into the squadron, the newer ones –officers too – tending to move on to other units as part of the constant interchange of aircrew which took place as battle casualties occurred. Overall, 249 did very well in this respect; in what we now know as the Battle of Britain – an unfamiliar appellation at the time – we lost only eight killed. However, almost everyone else either crashed or was shot down or wounded at one time or another, returning to the squadron as and when they recovered.

John Grandy, although remaining in command, was still incapacitated by his injury of September and unable to fly operationally. His role as leader fell to Butch Barton, 'B' Flight Commander, with Keith Lofts, a comparative newcomer, taking command of 'A' Flight on the death of Denis Parnall. Meanwhile, I had become an established section leader and was quietly pleased with my advancement and the freedom of action the appointment afforded.

Inevitably, as the weeks progressed, friendships were formed and cliques established although it was rare that we did not take our pleasures in a body, be they in the local pub or the less wholesome haunts of the West End.

While certainly not a drunken group, alcohol, principally beer, was always considered an essential part of any evening's entertainment and there were the occasional wild parties both in and beyond the mess. Such events were a unique blend of genteel formality and irresponsible chaos, it being mandatory to indulge in the more hearty type of horse-play, some of which amounted to nothing less than grievous bodily harm. I well recall, for example, putting my foot on Butch Barton's face and breaking his front teeth and I have not the slightest doubt that he will remember the incident too! It was also considered de rigueur to smash everything in sight – a strange but time-honoured habit of the British junior officer – bring back road signs and other trophies from the outside world, rip up or otherwise mutilate perfectly good uniforms and shirts, sing songs positively diabolical in their crudeness, and generally behave like mentally-retarded members of a third-rate rugger club. Much being traditional, one felt duty-bound to join in and, in this respect, such goings-on posed a problem for me as I always succumbed to sickness long before the joys of intoxication were experienced, the subtle charms of debauchery utterly at odds with the act, odours and after-glow of throwing up.

But such outbursts of outlandish behaviour were only the occasional foible of an otherwise normal, controlled and courteous group of young men whose average age was twenty-two and who had very little opportunity for physical expression. A keen sportsman in every way, I did not play a single game or take any strenuous exercise for the ten months commencing June 1940; our working day of twelve to eighteen hours entirely taken up with flying, fighting, eating and sleeping, there seemed little time left for anything else.

This, however, was not true of our station commander, Victor Beamish. A man of thirty-eight and having left the Royal Air Force for several years to recover from tuberculosis, he could often be seen in singlet and running shorts, padding around the perimeter track in all sorts of weather and at hours of the day when most of us were barely conscious. A man, too, of formidable physique and flaring temper, he was not above confronting and physically assaulting some of the so-called workmen from Southern Ireland who were employed on labouring duties around the station and who, at the first notes of the air-raid siren, would disappear down the nearest shelter and remain there for the rest of the day playing cards. Either that, or stream out through the main gate, an act of provocation which would so infuriate Victor that he had been known to rush out of his office in station headquarters, collar some offender with his bare hands and scream insults at the man for his cowardice. As if *they* cared!

Though never driven to such excesses, there were times when we felt almost as strongly about the several civilian bricklayers employed during the late autumn of 1940 to build blast walls around our wooden dispersal hut. Admittedly beyond the age when they could reasonably have been expected to fight, our good nature was sorely tried when we learned that their 'danger-money' alone exceeded our salaries as fighter pilots and commissioned officers.

Such is the way the British arrange their affairs in wartime and the pathetic manner in which the patriotic element turns a blind eye to such blatantly offensive treatment.

November 1940 was also a time when the Americans were much in the press headlines and, indeed, our thoughts. Though more than a year was to pass before they were forced into the war and a further two before they appeared in Britain in any numbers, British purchasing missions had been in the United States for some time buying aircraft, some of which looked promising enough on paper. Moreover, the presidential election was reaching its noisy climax, the contenders being Franklin D. Roosevelt and a Mr Wendell Willkie.

As likely recipients, we were naturally interested in some of the aircraft on offer and of two in particular, one later to be called a Tomahawk and another, said to be built to British specifications, a Mustang. They looked nice enough, the Mustang especially, but we had our doubts. Americans seemed to go in for streamlined bricks; we were looking for something which climbed like a rocket, turned on a sixpence, performed well at altitude and had a decent battery of something with rather more punch than .303 Brownings. Did these aircraft measure up? We had to be convinced.

And the presidency? Insofar as we had a favourite it was Mr Roosevelt. But only because Mr Churchill – our man of the century – continued to speak well of him and he seemed to be on our side. And anyway, who was Wendell Willkie? But we all so wished Roosevelt wouldn't go around in that ridiculous trilby hat of his, all turned up at the front, making him look like that half-witted adolescent in the Andy Hardy films.

In 1940, we insular British took a far less exalted view of the United States, its people and its armed forces than we do now. We were a beleaguered nation fighting for freedom, or so we were told, while they were obviously coining money hand over fist, talking a great deal, but doing no fighting. Why not? We wanted something more than advice. It was the Great War all over again, wasn't it?

As the days passed, we found ourselves taking-off into the winter gloom, patrolling for hours, then landing. Endlessly. Now fairly proficient in cloud flying, we clambered up in formation through thick layers of damp, grey murk and wandered about in vast canyons of towering cumulus, their awesome, frowning menace positively frightening. But despite all our toil and vigilance, we saw next to no Huns; there was very little happening at height and lower down, the clouds offered too much easy cover for the lone Dorniers and 88s. It was early November, too, when John Grandy appeared, heavily encumbered with pheasants. Deciding that the squadron should have a social evening in celebration of his prowess with the gun, they were presented to the kitchen and in the evening of 4 November, twelve officers of 249 sat down to dinner to do justice to birds whose rich and odoriferous ripeness was seeping through the corridors of the mess.

It was a grand occasion; there was sherry, champagne and other wines with port and cigars to follow. A gay but semi-formal gathering, in peace-time we would have gilded the lily with mess-kits, but that attire not being a requirement in war, we made-do with best-blues. Having by this time acquired two uniforms, and still not paid Messrs Moss Bros. of Covent Garden for either, I was at least able to look the part. The wine loosened my tongue until I became magnificently garrulous but, being a non-smoker, I drew the line at cigars.

Fortified by a Niagara of drink, for me the evening passed in a roseate haze, one in which the walls and ceiling were constantly on the move. Later, there were games, violent and bloody. Heads were broken, glasses smashed and all the usual songs sung, everyone roaring in unison.

As the night progressed, we grew friendlier and friendlier, our jokes became funnier and funnier, and the war developed into the hugest of larks. Remember old Gerald Lewis who sat there looking at lights flashing between his legs before he realized there was a Hun right behind him? Killing! And Butch – good ol' Butch. Our baling-out expert! Butch, who was so small and light that when his parachute opened he went up not down. And John, in September. Remember? 'Reform, GANER squadron, reform,' he was saying. Followed by a ruddy great bang! True! Absolutely true! Great chaps, all of 'em. In fact, we were *all* splendid fellows, weren't we? Every damn one of us. Especially dear ol' John who provided the grouse. Pheasants? Well, grouse – pheasants, same difference. No, seriously, it was the poor Huns we were worried about. Really. I mean, who'd be a Hun these days? How they ever hoped to win the war we would never know. And 109s? Need one ask? Kid's stuff! Absolutely!

The hours slipped by. More songs. And stories. And tired laughter. Wonnerful evening, by God! Marvellous! Wassat? Gone midnight? It couldn't be! Never mind, we'd just have to have another. When John managed to run over some more pheasants. And when we got our Hurricane IIs. What was happening about those Hurricane IIs, incidentally? Probably mislaid them, that's what. In a field somewhere and their Airships couldn't remember where they'd put the bloody things.

I went to bed sweating like a horse and with grog running out of every pore. Later, I was sick. Many times. All night long, in fact. Oh, God!

Guy Fawkes evening! It was decided that in order to minimize the possibility of a bomb writing off the entire complement of squadron officers, some of us should be lodged temporarily on the outskirts of Epping. With commendable patriotism, an elderly lady had offered the use of her very considerable home and John Grandy, several others and I arrived to spend our first night there. Very much on our best behaviour.

The house, redolent of Dickensian melodrama, was cavernous with enormous gloomy rooms and creaking Victorian furniture. It also came equipped with a family spinster, a bleak-looking female in her early thirties with a lace collar to her dress, who looked like a character from *Wuthering Heights*. Silently awed and my eyes wide with interest, as we were led up the groaning staircase, I felt that at any moment I would encounter a stuffed owl, a jangling skeleton, or a chained parrot squawking some fiendish challenge. It took a great deal of restraint to suppress an outburst of giggling. I also remember climbing into a vast bed that night and lying awake for ages listening to the house grinding its teeth.

A more inappropriate home for the youthful and earthy members of a fighter squadron could hardly be imagined. What would the daughter's response be, I wondered, were we all to turn up one night amorously pixilated? But perhaps that was a hoped-for part of the arrangement!

One night was enough. To the best of my knowledge, none of us ever returned.

The Commander-in-Chief, 'Stuffy' Dowding visited us again on 6 November and once more I missed him, though I cannot recall why. We also heard that we were to be known in future as the 'Gold Coast' Squadron. Really? What fun! Perhaps they would send us an elephant. Or a couple of coconuts! Sadly, the honour, though much appreciated, did not improve the performance of our Hurricanes.

Thursday 7 November: a welcome change of weather, with traces of sun and a damp green freshness everywhere. A good day for flying, in fact. My early morning zest for life, however, was soon overwhelmed by misfortune.

The squadron being scrambled shortly before the arrival of breakfast at 8 a.m., I was racing across the grass to the south side of the airfield when my aircraft stumbled violently, then tipped forward, digging its nose into the ground and throwing me up in the air. For one frightening moment, I thought I was going over onto my back but the Hurricane gave a brisk quarter-turn as though screwing itself into the ground, the engine and propeller stopped with a metallic jerk, and I was left like a monkey up a stick looking straight down and wondering what on earth had happened.

As the rest of the squadron roared into the air, I climbed out and slithered gingerly to the ground to inspect the damage and the cause of my downfall. There was no need for lengthy deduction. A gaping hole had opened up beneath my wheels and there was a crater – an undermined bomb-hole – some four feet deep and six feet across. My Rotol airscrew, which was mainly wood, had been chopped off at the roots, the spinner dented and the wheel-fairings bent and distorted. There was no telling, either, what other damage had been done. Damn and blast! My aircraft would be out for days.

John Grandy came roaring up in his car, his expression and voice a mixture of irritation and sympathy. 'Ginger, what the hell's happened?'

No explanation being necessary, we stood ruefully inspecting the crater and were soon joined by 'Tommy' Tucker, the engineer officer, who put on his martyr's face and supervised the aircraft being brought down to earth and towed away. Nothing vital, in his view. A new airscrew and a few other bits and pieces together with a shock-load test for the engine. A couple of days work at the outside.

I rode back with the CO who said that I could use his own Hurricane, GN-J, and a little later I killed time by transferring my parachute and equipment into its cockpit, noticing as I did so an oval St Christopher medallion attached to the coaming next to the gunsight.

We were ordered off at noon and climbed up through a fair amount of haze and broken cloud towards the estuary and, we assumed, the Maidstone patrol line. There were clearly Huns about and 'Lumba's' instructions were passed with a note of urgency. Higher up, we emerged into bright sunshine and there was the odd contrail of high-flying aircraft away to the south.

When high over the river, we were turned east and at around 15,000 feet, were warned of 'bogeys' in our vicinity. In our vicinity! That was promising, but where? Hopping about with excitement, we strained our eyes into the glare. 109s? We were ready for them; all we had to do was *see* the blighters.

The voice of the controller was coming up to us with an edge of exasperation. 'Bogeys' should be in sight now, our plots were overlapping. We turned, rocking and jumping in anticipation. Where? for God's sake.

Then: 'Bandits are bombing the convoy! The *convoy*!' The voice high with urgency.

Bombing the convoy! From 15,000 feet? No wonder we couldn't see them; they were miles below, probably at mast height. Butch began to tilt his nose and we all tumbled down after him. Bloody fools! This was the second time at least that we had been far too high. Would they never learn?

By the time we had descended to 5,000 feet in a wild, scattered dive, I doubt that any of us were doing less than 380 mph. At around that height there was broken cloud and a thick glare-reflecting mist which merged with the brown-green water of the estuary.

As I burst through a fragment of cloud, an aircraft appeared directly in front of me, indistinct in the haze and of a strange outline. A moment of perplexed scrutiny. Then recognition. An 87, for God's sake! A Ju 87! As large as life! The first I had ever seen, close-to. It was turning and climbing slightly, an upright aircraft with cranked wings and, in actuality, rather bigger than I had imagined.

The sun shining brilliantly on the haze, the picture directly below me was blurred and indistinct; even so, my eye recorded it in every detail. There were faint dark arrowing outlines of ships in a line and, in the water, the pale circle of a bomb-burst, or something, with silent, blossoming flowers of ack-ack smoke all around. But it was the aircraft that interested me most and I was going too fast! The one roughly ahead, though flying in the same direction, was surging towards me at an unseemly rate – backwards! Unable to bring my nose to bear on it, I grabbed at my throttle and worked my wheels brakes furiously in an instinctive effort to slow down. But to no avail; the 87 swept alongside and, for two ridiculous seconds, its occupants and I looked at each other in tense, impotent suspense.

In moments it had disappeared behind but, hauling my aircraft around and up again, I was suddenly confronted with a second 87, again turning and climbing. As I swept in behind it, the Hun suddenly cocked up his wing and began a rate-four turn to the right. I followed, quickly reducing the gap until our two aircraft were no more than 150 yards apart. But I couldn't hold him, damn it! The blighter was out-turning me! An 87 was actually out-turning me! I pulled like a madman then, finding myself slipping to one side and too close, fell away and came in again.

This time the 87 was on an even keel and looking very self-assured. I bored in and was greeted by a curl of tracer which whipped in my direction and flicked past before I could decide whether it had gone above, below, or to one side of me. This chap knew what he was doing, by gum! Another twisting streak from the Hun and a mass of my own as I fired, watching the spark-flecked de Wilde curve ahead in smoking fingers to touch first one wing then the fuselage. I found myself pumping the control-column violently in order to keep the German aircraft in my sight. Keep still, you blighter! Turning again, harder still, desperate to keep the 87 in place. And firing. The familiar, exciting, shuddering, ripping noise. A series of brief flickers. Hits! Close now. *very* close! Woah! Anchors! I was suddenly aware of every detail of the tail and the glass canopy of the Hun aircraft glinting. Then it was dropping away, downwards and to my left. I followed, wild with excitement, kicking hard and skidding furiously but firing still. But I couldn't hold it. The 87 toppled over in slow motion and passed beneath my port wing.

I climbed steeply looking back over my left shoulder. Where was the blighter? Yes, there he was. Going down – straight down, almost. Into the haze and towards the sea. Too low for that sort of thing.

Hypnotized by the spectacle and determined to watch the Hun crash into the water, I banked hard with the intention of spiralling down in pursuit but had barely completed half-a-turn when three or more aircraft appeared slightly above and to my right. Catching sight of me in the reduced visibility, they turned abruptly and ominously in my direction and began to converge. 109s! And I seemed to be alone.

I recall no feeling of panic or fear, just being possessed by a desperate urge to defend myself by attacking. I flew directly at them, firing meanwhile, and was vastly relieved when they broke suddenly and turned away, no doubt momentarily discouraged by the antics of the lunatic Hurricane they were just about to despatch. In a second, we had passed from each other's view and, thereafter, either they lost sight of me completely or were preoccupied with some other instruction or objective as, in and out of the fringes of the cloud, they paid me no more attention, allowing me to catch up and fire at close range, first at one of two that were together, then at a third which appeared from nowhere and flew obligingly across my path.

Obtaining several bright strikes on both aircraft, it was with a strange feeling of unreality that I watched them veer this way and that, seemingly without purpose. Having apparently lost interest in me, they were not even in formation and intent only in flying approximately out to sea. Encouraged, I raced in pursuit and fired again, producing a pencil-trail of white coolant from one and noting with savage pleasure one of the others further ahead losing height and leaving a thin dark stain in its wake. They'd had it, by God! Two of them! Quite, quite, unbelievable! This couldn't be happening to me. At which point, with a single Browning maintaining a shrill chatter for a second or two, I ran out of ammunition. The whole affair from start to finish had taken about three minutes – or even less.

The realization that I was unarmed, over pretty inhospitable-looking water and heading for Denmark, brought me to my senses. I was entirely alone and I didn't know where. Dropping down a little, I turned westwards and, taking stock, saw through the haze what I took to be North Foreland some way off to my left. I was wildly excited still. Incredible! What luck! But, where was everyone? The squadron? The Huns? How could a mass of aircraft just disappear?

I flew back on a westerly heading until I came across the convoy again praying that they wouldn't take me for a Hun. Would there be a pale circle in the water still where the 87 had gone in? Usually it lasted for quite a time. I did a complete turn searching hopefully but without success. Perhaps I wasn't looking in the right place. Anyway, the chaps in the convoy would be able to confirm what had happened.

Barely able to contain myself on the way home, I flew back at tree-top height and landed. Most of the others had returned and were standing about in groups around dispersal. No one missing, apparently, we compared notes excitedly. There had been some action but less than I had expected.

Someone was saying he had seen a whole formation of a dozen or more 87s going eastwards in close array and groups of 109s. A dozen 87s? How odd! I had seen two only and three, perhaps four, 109s. Even allowing for poor visibility low down, how could twelve members of a single squadron be engaged in the same fight and come away with such widely differing reports? Everyone was agreed though that 'Lumba' had made a complete nonsense of the height. And not for the first time! A strange thing, combat. I would believe anything in future. Anything!

It took me some time to wind down so that I was not particularly pleased when we were ordered off in squadron strength shortly after 3 p.m. Hell! Not the Maidstone-Canterbury patrol-line again!

We climbed away to the south in three sections of four, line astern. With Butch leading as usual, I led Yellow section, the second four, and there were four other aircraft behind us. Directly in front of me was Victor Beamish, flying as No. 4 of Butch's section – in the box – and using GN-B, his own aircraft maintained by 249. It was a routine exercise. A bit of a bore, in fact. There might be 109s high up but we were unlikely to be able to reach them. Anyway, who wanted to go to war at tea-time?

There was a layer of cloud at 5,000 feet and we ploughed up through it coming out on top at 6,000. Thereafter, apart from some high cirrus, there was nothing.

Reaching Maidstone and at 15,000 feet, we turned east and commenced our parading back and forth, listening to 'Lumba', meanwhile, passing reports of the enemy situation – such as it was. There were Huns away to the south, it appeared, and I remember thinking idly that that was the best possible place for them to be. Time passed. Back and forth. More reports of Huns but a long way off. I sat there in a semi-somnolent state, watching Victor's aircraft some ten yards ahead of me and slightly higher, rising and falling in slow-motion as he maintained his own position in Blue section.

Then, suddenly, he was away. Lifting up and to the right. In a second, he had gone, obviously bored to tears by the inactivity.

As Victor Beamish did this regularly, his departure came as no surprise; where the Germans were, Victor wanted to be. He had clearly gone south to investigate. We, however, had no such freedom of choice. Continuing our patrol, I moved my section into the gap – purely for aesthetic reasons – and in a matter of seconds had dismissed him from my mind. We flew on. Back and forth. Endlessly.

At about 4 p.m. and with the sun dipping in the sky, I was just calculating that another fifteen minutes would probably produce the welcome order to 'pancake', when there was a cataclysmic, grinding bang from somewhere behind. My aircraft, shunted monstrously from the rear, immediately pointed its nose vertically to the heavens and I found myself looking quite stupidly at cirrus cloud sitting squarely in my windscreen.

My immediate response was to try righting the Hurricane, at the same time thinking furiously as to what might be happening. My first thought was that we had been jumped and that I had been hit. But by whom? There were no Huns about. And why me, in the middle of the formation? But, if not that, what else?

I was not allowed the luxury of further contemplation as my aircraft tottered to a standstill in the straight-up position, flopped over onto its back and began to spin.

My mind icily cool, I went through all the recovery actions I knew of but to no avail. The controls were useless; nothing I did made the slightest difference. The world beginning to swirl around me crazily, I sat there and thought, being thrown about meanwhile like a ricocheting squash ball and undecided as to whether I was in an inverted spin or just an ordinary one.

Astonishingly, for almost 10,000 feet, I sat in that aircraft trying to recover some semblance of control, with never a thought of abandoning it. In common with most pilots, I had an in-built reluctance to leave while my Hurricane was apparently whole, the engine still working, and there was no fire. In fact, it was only when a voice from far above said dolefully, 'I think Ginger's had it!' that the seriousness of my plight began to dawn. Furthermore, it was at that moment that I fell into cloud which I remembered all too well as being at 5,000 feet, going up, or 6,000 feet, going down. Clearly, there was no time to lose.

The decision to bale out was not an easy one to make. Thereafter, much relieved in mind, my actions were surprisingly methodical. I opened the hood and, deciding to keep on my helmet, undid my straps, rose to my feet, with difficulty, and pushed myself over one side. Immediately I was catapulted forward by the lurching of the aircraft and out over the windscreen, for several horrifying seconds being restrained by my long oxygen tube which, still connected, was stretching like a piece of elastic, and also by my toes which were hooked over the edges of the windscreen frame. Lying along the top of the reserve fuel tank, I was aware of the very unsettling presence of the propeller whirling like a circular saw within several feet of my head.

I cannot account for the following two or three seconds except to say that the next incident of moment was when my head struck the top of the starboard wing with a very solid thump and I felt myself slithering into space. Expecting to find my stomach leaving me, I was relieved to find that it didn't, after which everything was peace and quiet. Falling feet first and in a most gentlemanly fashion, I watched some woods moving in my direction rather more rapidly than seemed appropriate. Which suggested that my parachute was not open. Which it wasn't.

Once again, a snippet of advice flashed across my mind. Moving my right hand from a known position – my tie – and thereafter from button to button down my Mae West, I located the rip-cord still in its housing. And pulled, taking care to hang on to the D-ring, which I had heard was the 'done thing'. Immediately, there was a flurry of activity behind my back followed by a formidable tug between my legs. After that, sighing stillness – gentle, blissful stillness. *And* undreamed of relief. I'd made it! I looked down. Trees were floated up in my direction. Then with the terrible thought that I might somehow fall out of my harness, I raised my arms and clung for dear life to the straps above my head.

I was in my parachute for so short a time, I later calculated that I could not have been much above 1,000 feet when it had opened. Which was a sufficient interval, even so, for me to view with growing apprehension the wood into which I was falling and the likelihood that I was about to be hurt.

And I was. I had a fleeting vision of large branches thrusting up at me and recall closing my eyes. After which – nothing.

When I came to, my face was against cold earth, my parachute strung out somewhere behind me and I was feeling desperately tired. Then, recalling John Anstee's helpful hint about sleeping when shot down or shocked, I closed my eyes again and lay still, for how long I shall never know.

After a spell, I became aware of distant voices and the sound of feet. A man and woman were discussing in agitated tones whether I were alive or dead and one of 'ours' or 'theirs'. Still in a mildly euphoric state of shock but now quite comfortable and relaxed, I offered no assistance and allowed them to work it out for themselves. Then, more voices and feet. And lots of panting and awed excitement.

Eventually, I was lifted to my feet. However, my right leg, having been bent backwards was now quite dead and collapsed beneath me. After hopping about like a stork, solicitous arms took hold of me again and laid me back on the ground like a salmon on a slab, where I remained until a small crowd had gathered including two Army officers who arrived by car. After being carried for fifty yards and shoe-horned painfully into the back of their vehicle, I was taken to a house which was the officers' mess of the local ack-ack gun-site. There, I was given tea and offered a hot bath.

By this time a little more composed and while I was struggling to undress, I was asked if I would like to be taken to see my aircraft which had crashed about half-a-mile away. It took only a moment for me to decline. I was utterly indifferent to the condition of the Hurricane and, a little to my own surprise, had not the slightest desire to see it, whole or in pieces. My only concern was for the St Christopher medallion. Ought I to make an effort to rescue it? – after all, it wasn't mine. Quite ridiculously, that and hanging on to the D-ring of my parachute, were my only worries.

I had the greatest difficulty in getting through to North Weald by telephone and did not succeed until early evening. After asking for John Grandy, I was mildly gratified when he seemed surprised but delighted to hear from me; as I had disappeared into cloud still spinning, the rest of the squadron had given me up.

Having come down a mile or two from Maidstone, I was obliged to endure a long and dreary trip through drizzle and blackness in an Army 15cwt van before arriving at North Weald in the late evening, still clutching the D-ring and with my parachute a white heap in the back.

Back in the mess, Victor Beamish greeted me, apologizing profusely for his part in the accident, abject penitence written all over his broad Irish face. He explained that, having left the squadron and after a fruitless excursion further south, he had returned and attempted to take up his former position in our formation with disastrous results. Minus his airscrew and damaging his engine, he had crash-landed in the Detling area, happily and very luckily escaping unscathed.

Later, when cheerfully noisy accounts of the afternoon had been exchanged, I was led into the billiard room by John Grandy and the station medical officer, who inspected my injury while I was stretched out on one of the covered tables. My leg clearly below par, it was decided that I should be sent home immediately to rest and recover. Home! I had mixed feelings about that arrangement; what on earth was I going to tell my parents? I had no intention of announcing that I had just baled out. None at all.

The next day, after visiting the parachute section to pay the statutory 10s to the parachute packer for his contribution to my escape, I took the train north to Manchester. Practising hard en route to conceal a very pronounced and painful limp.

After four days at home, I returned to London by train. Arriving at North Weald, I was told of exciting and unusual goings-on a day or so before. A strong force of Italian aircraft had flown up the east coast and all three North Weald and Martlesham Heath squadrons had been scrambled in pursuit. 257 and 46, being vectored further north, had run into formations of BR20 bombers and CR42 fighters around Harwich, while 249, finding themselves as usual over the estuary, had intercepted a small back-up force consisting of an old Ju 86 and a Heinkel 59 air sea rescue seaplane.

Murder had followed, the Italians being decimated apparently, and 249 accounting for both the Ju 86 and the He 59, each being shot down burning into the sea, the latter with some reluctance.

In the warm comfort of the ante-room and our backs to a roaring fire, I found myself in conversation with Victor Beamish who was telling me about the event. With his nose for action, he had chosen to fly up north rather than remain with 249 and had been with 257 and 46 when they had intercepted. Launching himself at some CR42s, he had found himself completely outflown and out-turned by the slower but remarkably nippy Italian biplanes.

He was wagging his head and smiling ruefully. 'They got behind me before I could blink, Ginger. I thought I was a goner, I swear to God, I did. They were good, y'know, Ginger. Really good.'

I found myself hopping from foot to foot. What a fight to miss! Bombers without armour and *biplane* fighters! Why did it have to be me?

But there was one compensation at least. Victor had also informed me that I had been awarded a Bar to my DFC. Not a bad homecoming, by gum!

I did not take part in the first flight of the following day, the squadron running into some 109s high up so that a ragged engagement resulted at about 20,000 feet over Kent. Some of the 109s carried bombs, which they dropped, and others attacked Worrall, who was acting as weaver; both he and Victor Beamish were hit – though not at the same time – the latter very badly. Victor's aircraft looked a mess when it returned. He did ask for it at times and usually got it, though it seldom seemed to worry him.

My aircraft still unserviceable and having already disposed of John Grandy's, I found myself down to fly GN-G, a Hurricane I had never used before. The weather miserable, I went out to inspect it, walking around it carefully, fingering all the cowlings, buttons and studs and looking for oil leaks. It looked all right but I was not well pleased. If I were to be pitched in with the Italians, I would be happier fighting in an aircraft I knew something about.

But nothing much happened. Low cloud sat overhead like a shroud and we toasted our toes by the stove in dispersal, reading, playing L'Attaque, and yarning. The trouble with hanging about, the more one did the easier it became. I found myself yawning massively and had to walk about outside again to waken myself up.

We were ordered off at 3 p.m., climbing away towards the south through fairly dense layers of stratus until we came out on top at 8,000 feet. Throughout, I was strangely on edge, shying away from other aircraft close to me. The collision had certainly done me no good, by gum! And it *had* to be on that day that the new and inexperienced Sergeant Smythe, flying directly in front of me as Red 4, kept dropping back on top of my head, causing me to lose my cool and shout at him in no uncertain terms.

Later, I was to admonish myself privately for being so short-tempered. Most odd that the accident should have affected me so. But, it would soon wear off. I hoped!

There being nothing about other than one or two friendly aircraft, we returned to base after ninety minutes. GN-G hadn't been so bad. Strange how individual Hurricanes varied.

We were off shortly before noon the following day and, somewhat to my surprise, I found myself leading the squadron. My first time in front of twelve aircraft, I felt immensely proud and much less overawed than

I had imagined. Full of concern for those at the back, I climbed up very circumspectly at never more than 2lbs boost and carried out a long but uneventful patrol in the Canterbury area without comment from my eleven companions. Even the Huns considerately kept their distance. On our way home, I smugly decided that I couldn't have been *that* bad as a leader. Moreover, having been totally preoccupied leading my flock and peering into space, I had no time to be concerned about colliding.

We had barely eaten lunch when we were ordered off again, this time being vectored towards the estuary. For the past several days there had been many more ships than usual in the mouth of the Thames and their presence was obviously attracting the attention of the Huns. 'Lumba' reported hostile plots in the area and, as there had been talk of further raids by the Italians, our mouths watered. But, if BR20s and CR42s seemed too much to hope for, Ju 87s would do. Anything.

In the event, the enemy turned out to be 109s. We ran into a group of them in the North Foreland area and a running engagement took place culminating in half-a-dozen of us concentrating on two aircraft which dived away to the east. One escaped by soaring upwards in a most impressive climb, but we hung on to the other and managed to get close enough to fire.

With everyone shooting at it in turn and down to about 1,500 feet, the 109 suddenly began to trail a white line of coolant. Although I had not registered any really damaging hits of my own, I experienced the familiar wave of raw satisfaction as the tell-tale sign of defeat appeared, mingled, even so, with a stab of sympathy for the poor wretched man in the stricken aircraft. Several miles out to sea, he could never get home now. What would he do? Splash down in the water, or turn back towards land?

He chose to turn, somewhat to my surprise and greatly to my excitement. Manston! He would probably try to make a wheels-down landing on Manston aerodrome. In which case, we would have a 109 absolutely whole and *flyable*! What a tremendous prize!

Now resigned to landing in enemy territory, the 109 reduced speed and, continuing its turn to the left, re-crossed the coast over Margate and, still with a faint white trail in its wake, settled onto its final approach, about five of us in close shepherding array. We'd got it, by George! A perfectly whole 109! What a triumph!

By this time, in formation about thirty yards away to the left and close enough to see every detail of the Hun aircraft, even the pilot's head, I was absolutely on the German's side. He was trying hard and I *wanted* him to survive. I *wanted* him to land safely. I *willed* that engine not to seize. I found myself jumping about in the cockpit, urging him on. Hang on! Hang on! He could make it if he tried.

The 109 was at 150 feet and within a mile of the airfield boundary when, out of the corner of my eye, I saw a Hurricane surge into the line-astern position. At less than seventy-five yards range, it steadied itself then poured a long burst into the rear of the German aircraft which staggered like someone struck with a club before tipping forward and nose-diving into a wood just short of the aerodrome's edge. Immediately, there was an eruption of flame and a column of black smoke. The pilot was killed – instantly.

I had seldom been as shocked by any incident involving an aircraft. Shocked, and enraged; enraged beyond words. In five seconds some bloody fool had undone all our good work besides wantonly murdering a man and destroying what was patently a helpless and surrendering enemy aircraft. I whirled about. Who was it? I would kill the bastard! Even one of my own side. I would *kill* him!

It was an act of providence that I turned to the left and in so doing lost sight of the Hurricane which had fired the fatal burst, so that when I had straightened out, blind with rage and intent on murder, I could not identify the culprit from among the six or seven members of 249 flying in a group around the crashed 109. But for a full minute, I flew about almost demented with anger until gradually my passion subsided into grief. After which, deeply disturbed still, I continued to circle the smoking wreck until eventually, recognizing the futility of what I was doing, I joined up with several other Hurricanes and flew back across the estuary and in the direction of North Weald.

The villain was later identified, a new, fresh-faced and inexperienced NCO pilot of 249 who, carried away by combat fervour during his first engagement with the enemy, honestly believed that he was acting correctly. Formally reprimanded by Butch and roundly abused by the rest of us, he left the squadron within days. Even so, I doubt that he ever knew how lucky he was to get away with his life.

The incident so upset me that I wrote of it in passionate terms to my

Right: 1. Aged 18, the author with his Tiger Moth – April 1939 at Barton Airfield, Manchester.

Below: 2. An early de Havilland Moth, the author's first aircraft, in 1938.

3. The hangar at Barton (right), where the drill sessions were held and the rats massacred.

4. The CFI's hut and the Watch Office, Montrose, in 1939.

5. Montrose, 1939. Sergeants Parkinson, the author, Newton, Arber and Pidd. Parkinson and Pidd were killed in the Battle of Britain and Newton shot down and wounded. Arber died later in the war. The aircraft is a Hawker Hart (trainer).

6. Single-engine pilots, No. 15 Course - the author extreme right.

7. Leconfield – airfield dispersal hut. Left to right: Sergeants Killingback, Beard, Smithson, with doctor Flight Lieutenant John Anstee – June 1940.

Above: 8. Portrait of the author by David Pritchard.

Below left: 9. The front cover of the author's log book covering the Battle of Britain.

Below right: 10. Sergeant Parkinson and the author at Beachy Head in 1939. Parkinson was to join 238 Squadron and be one of the first killed in the Battle of Britain.

11. Having just landed at Boscombe Down – 14 August 1940. Seated left to right: the author, Wells, Nicholson (probably), Barclay. Standing: Sergeant Smithson.

12. A Hawker Audax (8 SFTS).

13. Discussion at Boscombe Down – 14 August 1940. Left to right: Wynn, Barton, the author, Nicholson (behind), Grandy, Beard, Burton and Wells.

Above: 14. A night-flying casualty, Montrose.

Below left: 15. Some 249 pipe-smokers at Boscombe Down: Barclay, Burton, Wells and Meaker, August 1940.

Below right: 16. The author flew K 5012 many times, but was not responsible for this.

17. The author, taken in October 1940.

18. The author's wife, Flight Officer Eileen Hampton – when she was Operations 'B' Officer at RAF Biggin Hill.

Above: 19. The author in cockpit of Hurricane – GN-F, V7313.

Left: 20. The author sleeping in between sorties, 1940.

Below right: 21. Flight Lieutenant J. B. Nicholson, 249 Squadron, was the only VC in Fighter Command during the Second World War.

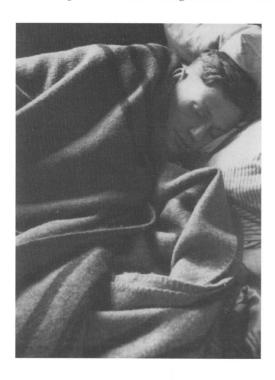 

22. June 1940 – one of 249's first Hurricanes, with metal wings and a Rotol airscrew.

Right: 23. P9506 – the author's first Spitfire, in which he went solo on 22 May 1940.

Below: 24. One of the hangars at Middle Wallop after it had been bombed on 14 August 1940. Three airmen were killed when the hangar door shown here fell on them.

25. Ground NCO with Swastika of JU 88, outside dispersal hut July 1940.

Below left: 26. Early September 1940. Back row: Sergeant Davis, Pilot Officer Meaker, Pilot Officer Crossey, Sergeant Rowell. Front row: Flight Lieutenant Parnall, Flight Lieutenant Barton, Pilot Officer Wynn.

Below: *Below right:* 27. Barton, having just bailed out, returning by car.

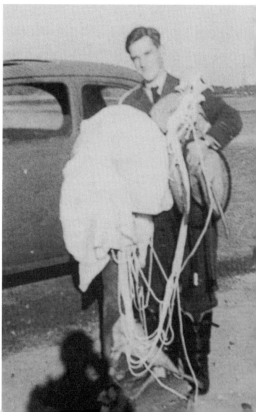

28. 'Butch' Barton, the author and John Grandy.

29. A Cecil Beaton photograph of the author, September 1940.

30. The author with crew: Aircraftmen Jones and Steadman, both about 20, who kept in touch with the author for many years thereafter.

Above: 31. Winter 1940. From left to right: Mills, unknown Australian, Palliser, Davidson, Lewis, Barton, Lohmeyer, Crossey, Wells, Wynn, Thompson, Cassidy, Woolmer (IO), the author, unknown. Note the change of spinner colour and the rim behind the airscrew to prevent leaking oil soiling the windscreen.

Below left: 32. Wing Commander F. V. Beamish, North Weald Station Commander.

Below right: 33. Crossey, Palliser and the author, outside the newly erected pilots' dispersal building. This building survived the war despite being badly damaged on several occasions.

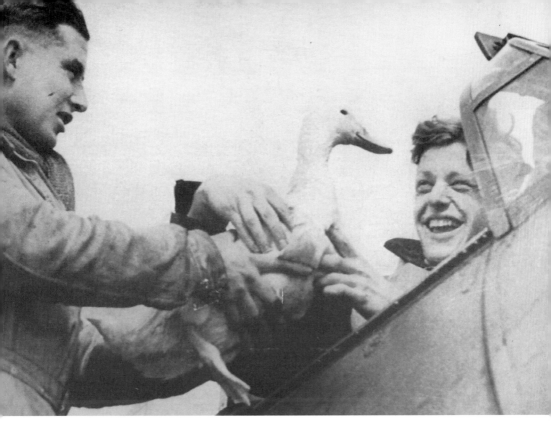

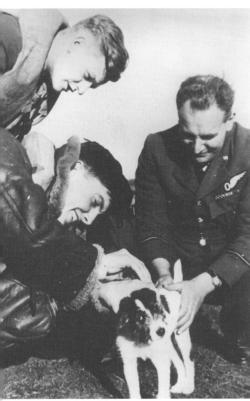

Previous page, above: 34. Pilot Officer P. H. V. (Pat) Wells and the author, with Wilfred the duck between.

Previous page, bottom left: 35. The author, Barclay and Lohmeyer, the adjutant, de-fleaing Pipsqueak, whose eye says everything.

Previous page, bottom right: 36. The author, standing, with Tommy Thompson – in dispersal hut at North Weald.

Top: 37. A vanquished Me 109. Identical in almost every respect to one of three shot down by 249 Squadron on 29 October, after the raid on North Weald.

Bottom: 38. Heinkel 111 bomber brought down over Kent, September 1940.

Top: 39. Junkers 87 dive-bomber as encountered by 249 Squadron on 7 November 1940.

Middle: 40. Pilot Officer E. S. ('Sawn-off') Lock of 41 Squadron in his Spitfire. Lock partnered the author in the events of 15 September and the BBC broadcast of 22 October. Terrible line-shooters, 41!

Above and previous page, bottom: 41, 42. Perhaps the most widely circulated of all Battle of Britain photographs. Taken by the press on 21 September 1940 and used in the 1941 Ministry of Information publication on the Battle of Britain. Also widely distributed among the Luftwaffe as representing the type of RAF pilot they were up against. From left to right: Percy Burton, 'Butch' Barton, Gerald Lewis, 'Ozzie' Crossey, the author, John Beazley, John Grandy, George Barclay and Keith Lofts. Note the black spinners on the airscrews.

Left: 43. Keith Lofts in front of Hurricane – September 1940.

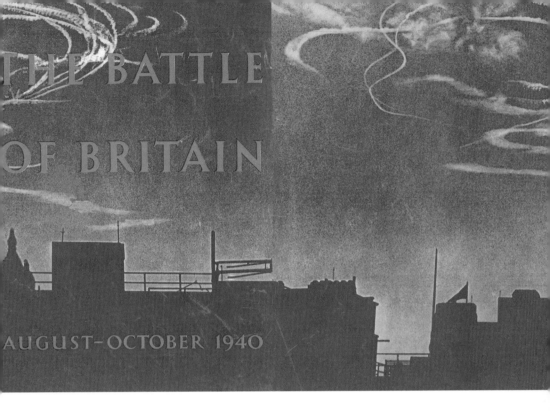

THE BATTLE
OF BRITAIN

AUGUST–OCTOBER 1940

44. Cover of the 1941 Ministry of Information publication on the Battle of Britain in which the author was featured.

45. Junkers 88 bombers. Probably the toughest aircraft 249 Squadron came across.

Above: 46. Dornier 17Z. The most frequently encountered bomber during the Battle of Britain and the first aircraft the author and companions did not shoot down on 4 July 1940!

Below: 47. Rearming Wells's Hurricane with Sergeant Palliser on wing. Behind, GJ-N, from which the author later bailed out.

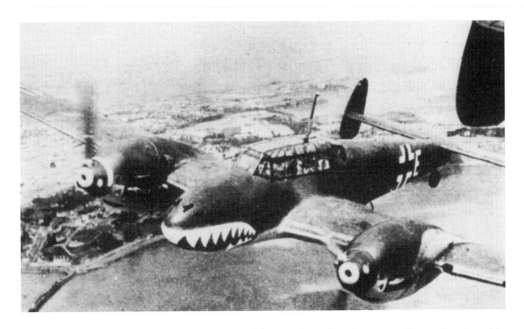

Above: 48. An Me 110 fighter, as encountered by 249 Squadron in August, September (notably on the 3rd) and October 1940.

Below: 49. Pilot Officers Bryan Meaker and Percy Burton, both of whom were killed within hours of each other on 27 September.

Above: 50. The author looking amused in Hurricane V7313.

Below: 51. North Weald airfield (looking north) as it was during 249's tenure in 1940–41. 'A' is 249 Squadron's dispersal area; 'B' was occupied in turn by 25, 257, 46 and 56 Squadrons; and 'C' was the officers' mess and junior officers' sleeping quarters. No. 2 hangar (missing) was virtually destroyed by the bombing attack on 3 September 1940.

Above: 52. No. 2 hangar North Weald after the raid of 3 September 1940, with one of 25 Squadron's Blenheims 'looking like a fish's skeleton the cat had left'.

Below: 53. A dispersal scene and a game of L'Attaque. From left to right: Lewis, Crossey (behind), Beazley (an eye), Lofts, Burton, Barclay. Burton is wearing the old type black flying boot – much treasured – and Lewis its cheaper replacement.

Above: 54. The Officers' Mess at RAF North Weald, September 1940, with the author's Morris 10 in front.

Above: 55. The author talking in the dispersal hut. From left to right: Wynn, Barton, Lewis, Crossey, Cassidy, author, Fayolle, Woolmer, Palliser. Seated right, Wells, Thompson.

Above: 56. Typical scene in the dispersal hut 1940. Left to right: Lewis, Cassidy, author, Wells (seated), Fayolle (French), Palliser, Woolmer, Thompson (seated).

Left: 57. Seated: just-commissioned Pilot Officer Beard with the author. Behind: Sergeant Popec and Flying Officer Skalski. In the background, Wells, Thompson and Mills. Dispersal hut late 1940.

58. Group of pilots. Pilots left to right: Lewis, Crossey, Wynn, Barton, Garvin (supernumerary), Skalski with two members of the American Senate (America was not yet in war).

59. American Senator with Lewis and Crossey at North Weald.

Above: 60. Pilot Officer Crossey, Pilot Officer Davis and Pilot Officer H. J. J. Beazley. All three would fly with the author later in the war in Malta. Davis was killed in the Western desert flying Kittyhawks.

Below: 61. Pilot Officer Munro, Pilot Officer Thompson and Pilot Officer Wells. Wells was wounded in the foot on virtually our first day. Munro was the first to be shot down and killed in Malta.

Above left: 62. 'Butch' Barton with Wilfred the duck.

Above right: 63. Davidson and Palliser in front of a Hurricane at North Weald.

Below: 64.The author and George Barclay by the dispersal hut blast-wall which caused some hard feelings.

65. Barton sailing paper ships in the ditch behind dispersal at North Weald.

Above left: 66. Part of a prop of downed Ju 88 – July 1940.

Above right: 67. 'Butch' Barton shooting at North Weald.

Above left: 68. Millington and the author, with livestock.

Left and above right: 69, 70. The author being debriefed by Intelligence Officer, 'Shirley' Woolmer.

COMBAT REPORT

Sector Serial No.	(A)	——
Serial No. of Order detailing Flight or Squadron to Patrol	(B)	——
Date	(C)	7 Sept. 1940
Flight, Squadron	(D)	Flight: A Sqdn. 249
Number of Enemy Aircraft	(E)	30 Bombers 100 plus fighters
Type of Enemy Aircraft	(F)	He111s Do17 or 215s Me109s Me110
Time Attack was delivered	(G)	1715 approx.
Place Attack was delivered	(H)	Vicinity of Maidstone
Height of Enemy	(J)	18000 feet
Enemy Casualties	(K)	1 Me109 destroyed
Our Casualties Aircraft	(L)	4
Personnel	(M)	1 killed, 1 missing, 2 wounded
GENERAL REPORT	(R)	

P/O T. F. NEIL   Yellow 2

Attacked formation of about 30 enemy bombers, from beam & fired a 4 sec burst into foremost vic of Heinkels. Broke away sharply & did not observe effect. Range was very close & E.A. were so packed that fire was bound to have effect. Encountered Me109 flying in opposite direction. I pulled up sharply and gave him short burst full deflection. Turned sharply & got on tail of E.A. firing short bursts. Large pieces flew off E.A. which turned over slowly & went down smoking. Fired at other E.A. with no effect. Later joined another Squadron (either JN or JZ) & attacked formation of bombers from above & in front. Fired 2 second burst & continued my dive with others of the Squadron to 2000 feet. E.A. were firing at us from rear. No result was observed.

I claim 1 Me109 destroyed & ~~1 bomber damaged.~~

Signature	Thos Neil
	Section Yellow
O.C.	Flight A
	Squadron 249 Squadron No.

Above: 71. My first combat report. The Heinkel was deleted by an over-zealous intelligence officer.

1 Ju 88 destroyed
(I claim ¼ share).

P/O T. F Neil DFC   Yellow 1

Whilst on patrol with Gamer Squadron. Blue 1
sighted a Dornier 215. I was Yellow 1. & led
Yellow Section into attack. The Dornier disappeared
into cloud before any effective attack could be
made. I later joined up with Blue 1. &
encountered a Ju 88, at 9000 just in the higher
cloud layer. I did a head-on attack but
E.A. turned right & spoiled the manoeuvre
I attacked again from astern & blew
the rear gunner & his cockpit to pieces.
No fire was experienced after this.
      Attacking from astern again.
I fired at the port engine. A cloud
of white vapour came out & oil spattered
the windscreen. I further attacked the
starboard engine. After running out
of ammunition I formated on the
bomber, & saw the right engine had been
stopped, & there was a large gap in the
rear of the cockpit — where the gunner had
been. The port engine was still running
& the white smoke had ceased.
      This EA was further attacked later
(I having left it at 4000 feet.) & finally
forced into sea.
                    T. Neil P/o

72. There being no combat reports available, the author scribbled this account of the
engagement of 28 October on a spare sheet of paper, his spelling suffering as a result.

73. Map showing the 249 Squadron operational area during the Battle of Britain.

Previous page, bottom and top left:
74, 75. British gun-camera images of German aircraft being shot down.

Left: 76. Some of the Dornier 17s the author encountered on 7 September, taken by the observer of another German aircraft. This formation is over Canning Town and West Ham football stadium – Upton Park – is towards the centre of the picture.

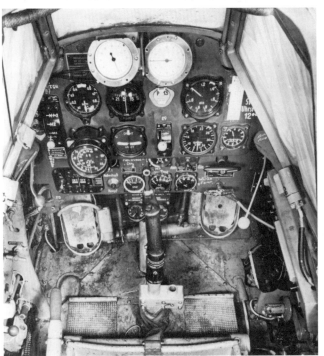

Bottom: 77. The cockpit of one of the first Me 109s to be captured. The instrumentation has been altered slightly to assist the RAF pilots who evaluated the aircraft.

78. Left to right: Robinson (Intelligence Officer), Grandy, Lohmeyer.

79. Looking up towards a German reconnaissance aircraft over London. Beamish (with pipe), the author, Millington, Worrall, Lofts. All, other than the author, were later killed.

Below: 80. Keith Lofts's Hurricane, damaged by a bomb on take-off during the raid on North Weald by 109s, 29 October 1940.

Above: 81. One of the many bomb-carrying Me 109s encountered by 249 Squadron in October 1940.

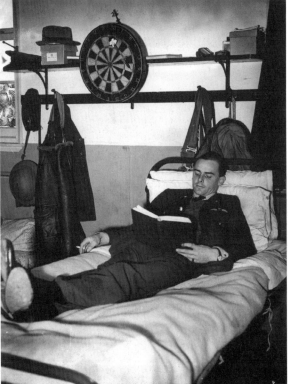

Below: 82. John Beazley – at ease – showing the foot in which he collected a bullet on 27 September 1940.

Above: 83. Barton, Wynn, Cassidy (behind), the author in a balaclava helmet and Palliser.

Below: 84. Four 249 stalwarts. Sergeants Stroud, Palliser, Mills and Davidson.

Above: 85. Late 1940. From left to right: Palliser, Cassidy, Wynn, Fayolle, Mills.

Left: 86. The rascal who did it! Oberleutnant Joachim Müncheberg, who, with several of his mates, wiped out more than half of 249 before they had made even their first flight from Malta. Müncheberg, a much decorated officer, was later credited with more than 100 victories in the air before being killed in Africa in 1943.

Above: 87. A Fulmar, similar to those which led 249 to Malta, preparing to take off. HMS *London* follows behind, 'trotting alongside like an Old English Sheepdog'.

Above: 88. The Hurricanes of Flying Officers Wells and Harrington after the German attack of 25 May 1941. The pilots' tent 'with the rolled up sides' can be seen between the two aircraftwith the first-line servicing crew's tent to the right.

Above: 89. The immediate aftermath of the attack on 25 May.

Above: 90. This type of tropicalised Me 109, E-4, flown by Mücheberg, was much in evidence over Malta and in the Western Desert throughout 1941. This aircraft of JG27 is seen over the North African coast in September of that year.

Left: 91. HMS *Furious*, in full war paint. 'Cripes! Are we going to war in THAT?'

Below: 92. Pilot Officers Graham Leggett and Robert Matthews in December 1941. Matthews was to be killed within days of this photograph being taken.

93. HMS *Ark Royal*, in life.

94. Air Vice-Marshal 'Hugh Pughe' Lloyd, A. O. C. Malta, and Vice-Admiral Leatham, C-in-C Malta.

95. Torre Cumbo – the author's bedroom (behind the tree to the left), and the stone balcony from which he and others watched the attack on Grand Harbour in the early morning of 26 July 1941. Rabat (M'dina) is in the background, behind the trees to the right.

Above: 96. The Macchi 200. This Italian fighter was the one most frequently encountered over Malta in 1941. Most flew with an open cockpit but some had wind-deflectors incorporated, as seen here.

Left: 97. A Hurricane Mark 2c starting up, with one airman about to remove the battery-cart plug. Note the Vokes filter and the rim behind the airscrew, there to cope with Git's seal oil leaks – perhaps!

Below left: 98. Untropicalized Hurricanes taking off from HMS *Furious*.

99. The Macchi 202, which made its first appearance over Malta in October 1941. With a performance comparable to that of an Me 109E, it could outstrip the Hurricane and, with its .5-inch machine guns, carried a formidable punch.

100. The Grumman Martlett (Wildcat), one of which came to the rescue of the author on 28 December 1941 and was promptly shot down for its trouble!

101. Two Hurricane Mark IIs carrying long-range fuel tanks, which overshot at Ta Kali when landing from the reinforcing flight of 9 September 1941.

Above: 102. The author in Hurricane LF363 – taken in 1951 when flying from Bovingdon, Herts.

Left: 103. A captured Savoia 79. This was the most numerous and effective Italian bomber/torpedo-carrying aircraft operating over and around Malta in 1941.

Below: 104. The author in 1942.

105. The SS *Sydney Star,* which transported the author to the Middle East and which weathered the torpedo attack of 28 December.

106. The 5.75 inch-gun cruiser, HMS *Dido*, which, with 6/8 destroyers, escorted the convoy of four merchant ships from Malta to Egypt, 26 to 30 December 1941.

Above: 107. The author visiting a cotton mill to see how various articles of airmans' clothing are made. The author said at the time to the mill girls 'When this war is finished the men in the services will have fought the war but you will have won it.'

Below: 108. The author's future wife (on extreme right), Eileen Hampton. They first met at Biggin Hill when she worked in Fighter Command as an Ops 'B' Officer. They married June 1945.

FLT/LT. T.F. NEIL. D.F.C.   249 (GOLD COAST) SQUADRON.

109. Sketch portrait of the author made in December 1940 by Cuthbert Orde. This is now held at the RAF Museum at Hendon.

Next page: 110. Author in 1953.

Above: 111. A recent photograph of the author.

Above: 112. Author talking to the Duke of Kent during a recent meeting of Capel Le Ferne Memorial Trust.

Left: 113. Author talking to 249 Squadron colleague John Beazley, outside RAF North Weald entrance.

Above: 114. Author recently talking to John Beazley, a colleague of 1940.

Right: 115. Author recently with John Beazley and Mary, his wife, with Terry Gill the Secretary of the 249 Squadron Association, outside RAF North Weald.

Above: 116. Author and wife outside Westminster Abbey following a recent Battle of Britain Memorial Service.

Below: 117. The author's Hurricane V7313 as gate guardian at North Weald – he flew this aircraft 61 times against the enemy between 3 September and 14 October 1940.

Above: 118. Author talking to young relatives of Air Chief Marshal Keith Park.

Below: 119. Author is back row, fourth from right. Others: Christopher Foxley-Norris, front row left (in chair); John Grandy, front row third from right.

parents before lying awake for a long time that night. What a tragic and unnecessary waste. Then, as calmer thoughts prevailed, was it any worse than a hundred other tragedies taking place daily in a war that Germany had so manifestly provoked? And what about the nightly air-raid victims? Were they any less deserving of my sympathy? Furthermore, the 109 pilot himself had probably just dropped a bomb on some unsuspecting civilian or non-military ship. Dear God! Things were so difficult. Blame! Blame! Blame! Who was to blame? Where did it start and where would it end? It was a long time before sleep brought relief.

I did not fly on 15 and 16 November, although the squadron carried out several uneventful and dreary flights along the Maidstone-Canterbury patrol-line. Everyone was becoming bored with the sight and sound of Maidstone and Canterbury. Moreover, it was now so wretchedly cold at altitude that we were all returning stiff and immobile and with hands and feet almost at the point when they ceased to function.

As the squadron was overmanned as the result of several old members returning from convalescence, about half-a-dozen pilots, mostly sergeants, moved on to other units and there was an air of uncertainty and disorder which lasted for several days. The weather somewhat brighter, there were still some showers around, reducing the airfield and dispersal to a quagmire, the mud plastering the wheels and undercarriages of our Hurricanes and making them look very part-worn. Our flying boots, too, were thickly encrusted with the stuff as were the metal footrests in the cockpits and the cushions of our parachutes. I hated having a dirty aircraft and particularly a filthy cockpit, not only from the appearance standpoint but also because I objected to having mud and filth in my face every time the Hurricane was upended or flown at speed.

A further cause of irritation, for me, anyway, was that GN-F was still unserviceable. In a childishly bolshie mood, my attitude was: to hell with them; if they couldn't provide me with an aircraft, someone else could do the dirty work. After which, for most of the time huddled in my Irvin jacket and toasting my feet by the stove in dispersal, I either sat looking miserable or moped about the place. Thank God for the ubiquitous 'goon-skin'. That and my flying boots, which were the old-style black ones and much treasured.

But other more important events were afoot. The morning papers and news broadcasts of 15 November were full of a bombing attack the previous night on Coventry. The place had been razed, it seemed, and the cathedral destroyed. Horror, indignation and outrage were being expressed, but although the destruction of the cathedral came almost as a personal loss, the volume and vehemence of the protests puzzled me more than a little. Was it any worse than the bombing that London, and we, had endured over the past three months? And what were the Huns supposed to do? Make only raids that met with our approval? Either we were at war or we weren't. The only sensible response was not to keep crying foul but to bomb Germany into oblivion. Perhaps if we had shown the capacity to do so at the outset, or, better still, before the war, the Huns wouldn't have tried it on. I made some remarks to this effect but no one seemed to agree.

15 November being a Friday, another social evening had been arranged in the mess with a dance and cabaret show. Our guests having arrived, the party was in full swing when the Huns began to drone overhead in large numbers and scatter bombs in all directions, the guns meanwhile going berserk. Finally, when there was an enormous explosion in the near distance which made everything jump, Victor Beamish intervened and called the party to a halt. It would be running a risk to continue, he felt. Everyone disappointed but appreciating the good sense of his decision, most of the visitors had just departed when a Hun bomber received a direct hit from an ack-ack shell and fell in flames, exploding with a tremendous commotion on the far side of the airfield. Having been outside at the time, I had witnessed its fiery descent and disintegration from close quarters. But there was no point in going across; it was too dark and there would only be a hole full of bits. Such incidents, if not common-place, were accepted casually. It was war, after all.

And there had been another surprise, too. Earlier in the evening, when walking into the Ladies' Room, I had run into Crossey and one other – both wide-eyed.

'Have you heard about Nick?' Crossey asked.

'No. What about him?'

'He's been awarded the VC.'

I was stunned. As indeed they had been, and were.

'You mean *our* Nick?'

'Yes, *our* Nick. The Victoria Cross! It's just been announced.'

I doubt that I was more astonished than others of the squadron who had know him three months earlier. Dear old Nick! Just one of the chaps whom we had treated so casually. Well, he must really have done something to have merited that sort of award. I had no idea! I recall experiencing a tremendous feeling of pride – pride that we shared the same squadron and that I was a colleague and friend. Mingled, too, with just a trace of shame for my lack of appreciation of what he had accomplished. Well, it just went to show how wrong one could be. Good old Nick! Damn good show! His wife, Muriel, would be speechless. And his family. Who'd have thought it? We talked about it all evening.

A few went over to see the crashed bomber the following day. It was a Dornier 17, apparently, although there was very little left by which to identify it. Or of the crew, of whom only a few gory fragments remained. Not being that much interested, I didn't go. Later that night, a curious piece of news. At the Chase Hotel in Ingatestone, I ran into Eric Lock of 41 Squadron, with whom I had made my broadcast a month earlier. Having arrived some time before me, he was with a group of pilots and WAAF officers from Hornchurch and obviously feeling no pain.

During a long-winded, slightly inebriated conversation with me, it came to light that he had been in one of the Spitfires which had been involved with the Hun bombers over the estuary during the late afternoon of 18 September, when I had witnessed the unpleasant spectacle of one member of a Hun crew falling past me with an unopened parachute. Horrible, was my comment. I wouldn't wish it ever to happen to me.

Lock gave a gay laugh. I needn't feel too depressed about it. The bloke in question had fallen into the Thames off Southend pier and had been fished out with nothing more than minor injuries and a couple of black eyes; his undeveloped parachute having kept him vertical, all he had done was made a very high dive. From 18,000 feet, a *very* high dive! After which, he had been taken across to 41 Squadron on Rochford aerodrome to be entertained briefly before being sent off for interrogation and to pokey.

I was astonished and quite ridiculously relieved. Was he absolutely sure? Sure? Of course he was sure. As sure as he was riding this bicycle! Pilot Officer Eric Stanley 'Sawn-off' Lock was not one to be missed!

I flew during the afternoon of 17 November, the usual patrol of almost an hour-and-a-half over Kent but starting from 15,000 feet above Hornchurch and the estuary. In yet another Hurricane, my own still being unserviceable. What on earth were they doing to it?

Later, I walked up to the maintenance hangar to investigate. GN-F was more or less back to normal, I was told. If I hung about for fifteen minutes, I could taxi it back. Which I did, sitting bare-headed and high in the cockpit, the slipstream tearing my hair to pieces. God, we were pleased with each other! The engine sounded healthily raucous, the brakes splendidly squeaky and the controls light and tight – just right. Even the sharp smell of the exhaust smoke was... well, different.

We parked on our usual hard-standing and I walked away, happy and light-hearted. Things were back to normal. The war could start again in earnest.

The weather clamping completely, we did not fly the following day but sat about in dispersal toasting our toes by the stove, reading, playing Totopoly and L'Attaque and jawing. Butch was going on again about his Chinks and the shove-ha'penny board was working overtime.

Towards noon, Victor Beamish arrived with the Duke of Kent, whom I had never seen before. We all lined up alongside our chairs and beds and were introduced.

The Duke was smaller and slighter than I had imagined and, in the uniform of a group captain, wore a very rakish hat. He was very brown – I couldn't imagine why or how – and embarrassingly shy. Shaking hands with each of us in turn he asked everyone the same question – how long had he been with the squadron? After which, he stood at the entrance of the hut and listened almost without comment to an account of our role and what we had achieved over the past few months. Then, a rather shy 'goodbye', and that was that.

Poor chap! What a job. Meeting hordes of very blasé young men who were in the thick of it and being critically inspected like a Christmas ham. He might have had more to say for himself, though.

My first flight in the restored GN-F – and almost my last!

The following day, the whole squadron having been sent off shortly after breakfast in miserable weather conditions, we climbed up through a mass of mist and cloud before coming out on top and commencing our usual parade up and down north-eastern Kent. Was our journey really necessary?

It didn't seem so judging from the enemy response and the formidable mess of fog and murk spread out thickly below us.

An hour later, we turned north and let down again to find cloud right down to 200 feet over Essex and our approach to North Weald barred by fog. Up again then, through a mass of cloud and into a grey and gloomy space between layers. What now?

Trying once more to find the ground, the various sections of the squadron became separated and it was only after an hour-and-a-half and becoming worryingly low on fuel that, leading six other aircraft, I managed to locate Martlesham Heath, all of us mightily relieved and not a little resentful. What the hell was 'Lumba' playing at?

The whole of southern East Anglia being submerged in murk, there was no prospect of our returning to North Weald so we settled down and spent the night at Martlesham, returning at noon the following day in weather conditions only marginally better.

But we had not been the only ones caught out, it seemed; quite a few of 615 and 229 and also been stranded and obliged to make emergency landings at North Weald a little before we, ourselves, had made our own attempt to return.

What an annoying and ridiculous business! Three months of hard fighting, only to have one's neck put at risk flying in impossible weather conditions against a non-existent enemy. How easy it was to fight the war down a hole! I found myself becoming more and more critical of the decisions of some in control of our affairs. Were they as thoughtless as they occasionally appeared to be? Or was I becoming over-sensitive?

Around breakfast-time the following morning, a Dornier 17 flew directly over the top of the airfield and dropped several bombs. As we stood outside dispersal looking up towards a cloud-base that was little more than 500 feet, we heard the Hun drone across just in the fringes of the murk, the noise of its engines strangely foreign to our ears. The poor Bofors gun crews around the perimeter didn't know whether to fire or just look pretty but finally took the plunge and sent strings of red balls curving away into the cloud, a morale booster for themselves as much as anything as they normally only engaged on visual contact.

On the whole, however, everyone was well satisfied. The bombs had caused no damage; it had brightened up our own morning in dispersal; and the aerodrome defence wallahs, who led unutterably dull lives, had plonked away with their guns, giving them something to talk about until Christmas.

Later, I spent forty-five minutes wandering around the estuary in search of a lone Hun – quite unsuccessfully – and Tommy Thompson and Sergeant Palliser shot at a single bomber – equally unsuccessfully – which had appeared over the convoy they had been protecting.

Otherwise the day was just cloud and occasional drizzle overhead and mud and misery underfoot. And cold, with it. November, in fact.

For almost a week, life was monotonous beyond belief. Rain and low cloud were relieved only by endless clammy mists which developed almost sadistically into water-dripping fog, reducing visibility to yards and transforming our aircraft to silent ghosts as they stood chocked and tarpaulined on their hard-standings.

I flew twice in five days, roaming endlessly through thick grey banks of murk and over coastal and estuary waters so dark and sullenly hostile that I thanked God for GN-F and its endlessly roaring Merlin. Never once had it let me down despite the punishment I had inflicted upon it over the weeks. My dear old Hurricane might not be the fastest, the sleekest, the warmest, or the most beautiful fighter in Christendom, but it was strong, it was willing, and it worked. We were more than companions in battle, we were comrades – staunch and inseparable friends, in fact.

In the cosy silence of my stove-warmed, blacked-out bedroom, I listened each night to the dull drone of Hun bombers passing overhead. Bound for somewhere, but where? There were fewer bombs being dropped in our vicinity these days, the Huns appearing to have lost interest in our part of the home counties. On the night of 24 November in particular, there was a constant throbbing din for four interminable hours; after which, promptly at 11 p.m., it stopped. And throughout, not a bomb was dropped. What were the Huns seeing up there from their Dorniers, Heinkels and 88s, I wondered? Nothing probably. Not a single searchlight, torch-beam, headlight or candle, even. Just an endless wilderness of dark grey cloud and fog. Underneath which, was England. Waiting!

But, on 26 November, which was a Tuesday, the weather cleared sufficiently by lunchtime for the whole squadron to be sent off to give cover to a convoy in the estuary. There were Huns about, apparently.

And there were! Off Southend, fairly low down and in misty conditions, we ran into a group of 109s, one of which dropped a bomb. After that, in a confused melee, two others attacked my own section but not in any determined way so that we were able to avoid their curving assault quite easily and give chase ourselves.

The running engagement at high speed and the poor visibility and ragged cloud combining to break up our various sections, I eventually found myself on my own somewhere south-east of Foulness. By which time, having lost sight of the enemy and everybody else, I thought it prudent to turn back and head up-river. I had barely reached the tip of Shoeburyness when a 109 appeared out of the mist and cloud, flying in the opposite direction and a mere twenty feet beneath me.

For one fleeting moment, I thought we would collide. As, I imagine, did the Hun, for his aircraft visibly hopped in flight and immediately ducked away downwards as I reared about and set off in pursuit.

Being so close initially, I was still less than 500 yards away when I had him again in my windscreen. He was fast going away into cloud but it was worth a shot. Lining up quickly on him, I gave a long burst and had the satisfaction of hearing and feeling the noise and tremor of my own guns and seeing the red-flecked tracer reach out exploringly.

I doubt, however, that I did more than speed the German on his way. Within seconds, and still full of zip, he had melted into the mist and had gone for ever. Even so, I felt enormously elated. It was nice to have shot at *someone*. Even if I had missed. Moreover, it was a joy having 109s down at a height we could deal with them.

Back at North Weald there were neither claims nor casualties and everyone was in good spirits; everyone other than George Barclay, that is, who was complaining that someone had wrongly warned him of a Hun on his tail at the point when he was about to open fire. Poor old George! A very earnest and enthusiastic officer was George.

27 November: the convoy, in and beyond the estuary now and as far north as Clacton, was clearly exciting the interest of the Huns although the weather kept us on the ground for most of the morning. By lunch-time, however, it had improved and we were advised to gird our loins.

Scrambled a little after 3 p.m., we climbed away in the direction of

Southend through a mass of mist and cloud, coming out into brilliant sunshine around 8,000 feet. It was going to be another of those days, I sensed; the sun viciously hard on the eyes and everything around us obscured by a gleaming haze. Low down, conditions were such that a whole armada of Huns could have steamed past unnoticed as little as a mile away, while for aircraft sitting up at 20,000 feet, the glistening murk provided a wonderful backcloth of white against which we could readily be picked out.

The 109s were about in strength, mostly in sections of two and four but occasionally in larger formations of up to eight. Several small groups passed overhead and, climbing up beneath them, we were nakedly aware of their presence in the sun, expecting any moment to have one or more aircraft darting among us. One of these 109s was damaged by Spitfires and forced to land at Manston. It is now on view at the RAF Museum at Hendon.

From the estuary, we were vectored up the coast towards Harwich and, rather surprisingly, saw a formation of about a dozen beyond Clacton, surprising as it was unusual for 109s to venture north of the Thames because of their limited radius of action. At the time at 16,000 feet, we chased after them at full throttle but they pulled away to the east, climbing meanwhile and no doubt making faces in our direction. It was very clearly a non-fighting day. In which case, why the hell didn't they stay at home?

Returning towards the estuary, we were kept up for more than an hour, by which time I had the familiar tight and aching band above my eyes which came from squinting continuously into the glaring mist and sun.

Back on the ground, no one was very pleased. Always the same; lots of fruitless haring about, with the Huns having the initiative all the time. Who would voluntarily go to war during an English winter?

Conditions showing signs of perking up and having had the 109s suspended dangerously above our heads the previous day, we were discussing yet again the best way of combating the menace of a swooping attack from behind.

Supporting the accepted view that weavers were necessary, with the supreme arrogance of one who had never been clobbered, I felt convinced that if I were weaver, surprise would be out of the question. What about the more experienced members of the squadron taking turns at the back? We jawed around the subject for a time and it was decided that Pat Wells should be top weaver for the next flight at least.

We were sent off shortly before 2 p.m. and climbed away to the south until we were over our familiar stamping grounds in Kent at heights varying between 18 and 25,000 feet. It was blindingly bright, devastatingly cold, and a day made for Huns. Masses of them around, they chalked their presence above us in wide, icy curves while we sat impotently beneath and noted their every suspicious move. While they were contrailing, everything was fine. It was when the trails stopped, which could be anywhere and at any height, that was when our problems were likely to arise.

The 109s coming and going, we ploughed around for more than an hour. 'Lumba' kept us informed but, to whatever height we rose, it seemed we were never in a position to do more than defend ourselves. And, as ever, the winter sun sat tantalizingly and obliquely in the southern sky, shining brilliantly in our direction and providing constant and impenetrable cover for the enemy.

And it was on one of the northbound legs of our patrol that it happened. A confused jabber on the RT and a swift and urgent look to the rear. A thin trail of whitish smoke wriggled its way towards the earth and far below, the tiny white blob of a parachute hung motionless in the air. Oh, no! We had been done again! Everyone immediately poised to retaliate and kill, it was too late. The Huns had come and gone and I – indeed the whole of our formation – had not even seen them. How did they do it? How on earth could it happen?

We were up for almost an hour-and-three-quarters on that occasion and the victim was our experienced weaver, Pat Wells. Poor, poor Pat! The third time he had been shot down. Or was it his second? I couldn't keep track.

Later, and to our relief, we heard that he had been taken to Leeds Castle Military Hospital, having been nastily burned. The old Hurricane hazard again. Not only that, but he had come down in almost exactly the same place as on 7 September. What a coincidence! So many of the squadron had come to grief around the Maidstone-Leeds Castle area, myself included, that we were almost beginning to have an affection for the place. Maidstone! The name would live in my memory for ever. That and Canterbury!

That night, I found a thick bundle of mail in my pigeon-hole in the mess, news of my recent decoration having filtered through to the north. Apart from a number from friends and the 1940 equivalent of teenage fans – none of whom I knew – there were several letters from the headmasters and staff of my old schools plus two others which caused me to blink. One was from the manager of the Gorton Branch of the District Bank in Manchester, whose customers had apparently subscribed generously to present me with a gift of my own choosing, and the other was from a fellow passenger on the 'five-to-eight' train into Manchester, a confirmed Peace Pledge Unionist and an arch, silver-tongued procrastinator. His message was meant to be generous. I had been right and he had been wrong in the months before the war, he admitted. But, of course, if he and others had *then* been aware of what was likely to happen and had since taken place, they would naturally have acted differently.

I pitched the letter immediately into the fire. Self-righteous bugger! It was because of him and thousands like him that things were as they were. Still prating from the sidelines, too, I noticed. How comfortably convenient to have a conscience that functioned only at other people's expense! I could not bring myself to reply.

George Barclay was shot down the following day, in circumstances not unlike those leading to the downfall of Pat Wells.

On fine days, it was the habit of the Huns to send high flying reconnaissance aircraft over London and for those of us enthusiastic enough to go after them, it became something of a game to try to catch them before they retreated over the Channel. Mostly, it was a fruitless exercise as the German aircraft were usually at 25,000 feet before we even left the ground. But, it was a challenge – what German aircraft wasn't? – and it disposed of a lot of frustration and adrenalin. A few were caught but not many.

Having been sent off shortly after 11 a.m. with Keith Lofts leading, the squadron had climbed up on a southerly heading and, in the course of our ascent, had observed several such reconnaissance aircraft contrailing high above our heads.

It being George's day for glory, when we were well south of London and at more than 20,000 feet, he and Harry Davidson were detached to chase a single Hun, then a mere dot in the distance. Leaving the main formation, they set off in pursuit but, after a while and having given up, the two of them were brought back northwards in order to rejoin the rest of us, at that point a little to the west of Maidstone.

En route, the inevitable happened. Although warned of a Hun in their immediate vicinity, they saw nothing until a shower of cannon shells struck George's Hurricane, hitting him in the legs and setting his aircraft on fire. Baling out successfully, he fell for a long time before opening his parachute and landing safely in an orchard near Pembury, after which he was taken to the local hospital, apparently in the highest of spirits.

Unaware of George's despatch, other than by what we had gleaned over the RT, we landed back frozen to the tripes, my own Hurricane with a thick rind of frost on the interior members of the hood. Davidson, who had escaped injury, was in full voice, his staccato laughter echoing around dispersal. It had been a close run thing, apparently. He had been weaving over George's rear when the Huns had dropped down on them, but had been powerless to intervene. 'Like bluddy stones', was his description. 'Couldn't get near the buggers!'

Later that evening and back in the mess, it was rumoured that John Grandy would be leaving, that Butch Barton would assume command and that I might become flight commander. I held my breath as I heard the new arrangements being discussed. How fortunate I was. George Barclay and several others were older and senior to me; George especially was the more obvious choice – until the events of the afternoon, that was! But, if this was how the cards were to fall, who was I to object? I found Lohmeyer winking at me from a distance, and smiling. Good old Loh! A friend and ally if ever there was one.

We flew twice the following day, the last day of November, once in the morning and again in the afternoon. Over Kent as usual. Backwards and forwards at 15,000 feet with eyes well and truly skinned. High above an endless carpet of cloud and, by degrees, freezing into rigidity and silence. But there were no Huns in our area, or none that we saw, which was not quite the same thing.

The nights drawing in, we were usually released from the 'state' at 5.30 p.m. and back in the mess by six. After which, a steaming hot bath, followed by a drink, dinner, then civilized conversation around a heaped and glowing fire in the ante-room. Either that or, relaxed and physically tired, a quiet game of snooker. And a book. No, life wasn't at all bad. Not bad at all. In fact, I was absurdly, and ridiculously happy. And twenty years and four months old.

14

The Last of the Year: December 1940

The first day of December 1940 was a Sunday. The weather worse than abominable, the squadron was released before noon and a discussion took place as to what we might do. After a few suggestions, someone mentioned the Officers' Sunday Club. Ears pricked and immediate interest! What could be more appropriate?

The Officers' Sunday Club, a very superior tea-party, was held each week at Grosvenor House, Park Lane. The brain-child of an eminent Lady of the Realm, it was something in the nature of war-work for the nobility, a gathering of young ladies who would otherwise have been debutantes and who, properly though discreetly chaperoned, entertained at tea junior officers of the three services. It lasted from 4 p.m. until 7, after which 'other arrangements' might be made – and usually were! Having often read of it in the *Tatler* and *Sketch* but never having myself attended, I was intrigued by the possibilities and, at 2 p.m., was one of a well-scrubbed and suitably pomaded group of eight waiting for transport at the entrance to the mess.

We arrived. It was a glittering affair, almost Ruritanian in its splendour, the chandeliers brilliant, the ball-room packed to overflowing with elegantly attired officers and their ladies, a score of circular tables for twelve or more, gleaming with crisp white linen and silver, and a solid mass of dancers in the centre, swaying like breeze-caressed corn to the music of Sidney Lipton and his band. Wow! We all swallowed, put on our Sunday smiles and straightened our tunics and cuffs. In the middle distance, our hostesses approached. Like white swans!

It would hardly be fitting to give a blow-by-blow description of the events of the next several hours. Sufficient is it to say that my partner was so stunningly attractive that by early evening, I was deeply in love and feverishly considering how I might further our relationship. A quiet dinner perhaps? Somewhere... special? But then, a ghastly thought. What with? I had two £1 notes in my back pocket, which would hardly get me past the first head-waiter. But-a rush of blood to the head – I'd take a chance. With luck, I would be able to borrow a fiver from Crossey or the others. Well... I could try, couldn't I?

In a voice I barely recognized as my own, I put the question. Two sparkling brown eyes lit up. Dinner? How perfectly *lovely!* And a nightclub? She knew of a place I would simply *adore.* And as she and Mummy lived at the Dorchester, dining there would suit her *splendidly.* The Dorchester! I nearly died.

Carried away by something akin to a death wish, I went on to explain that I had already arranged to join my Commanding Officer and friends at the RAF Club, but that I could meet her at 8 p.m. At the Dorchester. Would that be all right?

Of course! She held my hands to seal the contract and we parted.

Alone again, my knees turned to jelly. Dear God! What had I let myself in for?

I had never been to the RAF Club before and, as a guest of John Grandy, was tremendously impressed. There were terribly senior officers everywhere, all gloriously and informally chummy. How could these elderly pinnacles of authority and wisdom be so human?

Time passed. The conversation became friendlier and marginally louder. I found myself giving my opinions on Hurricanes, Spitfires, the Huns, and the iniquity of paying bricklayers more than pilot officers – or flight lieutenants, for that matter. I kept glancing at my watch. Coming up to eight o'clock. But I couldn't just leave, could I? Not just walk out. And what about the five quid? I hadn't been able to ask any of the others. Lord! And she'd be waiting, even now?

With my seven colleagues, I finally managed to get away just before nine. In a muck sweat, I took a taxi to the Dorchester and groped my way inside, through the blackout arrangements.

After some moments, a liveried servant, looking as though he had just stepped down from the back of the State Coach, moved in my direction. Was my name Pilot Officer Neil? I nodded. He bent forward a little, tilting his head confidentially. He had a message for me.

The message was courteous but to the point. Her Ladyship had waited forty-five minutes but had now retired. She *very* much regretted having to do so but trusted I would understand.

Deflation! But more than a little relief. Even so, the evening was by no means spoiled. We were suddenly confronted by John Grandy, who was also in the Dorchester and in the company of a Wing Commander Geoffrey Aste. Perhaps we would care to join them for dinner? We exchanged glances. We certainly would!

The evening proceeded. We dined sumptuously with waiters hovering in the background. Wine flowed and tongues were loosened. Occasionally, my mind strayed to 'her Ladyship'. Sitting upstairs like Cinderella, no doubt. In tears, too, I shouldn't wonder. And to the two £1 notes in my back pocket. Which raised a point; who was going to pay for all this?

We had reached the port and cigars stage and Geoffrey Aste – I felt I could call him Geoffrey by this time – was telling a long-winded story, his face suffused with an alcoholic glow. As he meandered endlessly ahead, we all sat with patient courtesy waiting for the punch-line.

Meanwhile, behind him but in front of me, a waiter gravely approached with a monster cigar box. He bent obsequiously in the Wing Commander's direction. Would the –

He got no further. Interrupted at the moment of dénouement, Aste flung out an irritated hand which caught the box of cigars a resounding crack; the contents went sailing into the air and an old gentleman to my left, busy with his angel-on-horseback, found King-size Havanas pattering around his ears like summer rain. As the waiter backed away, we all froze. Everyone, that is, but Geoffrey Aste, who carried on as though nothing had happened.

Later, the bill arrived and I chanced to see it. £5 10s 11d for nine of us! I nearly swooned. Almost a fortnight's pay for one meal! As our gallant commander made to foot the bill, he grinned in our direction. All the *best* people came earlier, he informed us. We had missed them, unfortunately.

A memorable evening. A memorable day, in fact. I wrote of it in detail to my parents.

The weather during the first week of the month was unusually bad even for December. After being ordered off in the late morning of 2 December, we were recalled within minutes when the cloud came down and nearly caught us out. After which there were strong winds and rain for days on end so that flying was ruled out completely. In total, I flew for twenty-five minutes during the first four days and most others did less. The fifth day, however, was different.

With Butch back in the lead, we set off shortly after breakfast-time and carried out a patrol which had us trailing over much of southern Kent. Around Dungeness the weather was comparatively clear and we marched up and down at slightly less than 20,000 feet, being informed from time to time of incoming raids across the Channel. Finally, after ninety minutes in the air and with less than 25 gallons in my reserve tank, twenty 109s came streaming in from the south and sat over our heads, less than 1,000 feet above and obviously spoiling for mischief. Not content with that, they feinted, lunged and swooped, each time veering away as we turned towards them like stags at bay. We were caught, damn it! We couldn't enter into a full-blooded chase. Or fight. Or run, even. We hardly had the fuel to return to North Weald. I had seldom felt so helpless.

Butch led us into a defensive circle, a manoeuvre I disliked as it not only smacked of defeat, it also recalled unpleasant memories of the Hun 110s in September and their ultimate fate. Moreover, it was an unpleasant and tiring business turning hard and screwing one's neck around at the same time, knowing full well that there was a score of 109s above, behind, and within shooting distance. And all of them quite obviously as fresh as paint.

It was while I was turning in a gradually descending spiral and looking anxiously towards my tail that several 109s came down, one shooting past on my starboard side a mere thirty yards away before swooping up again out of range. Almost simultaneously, I caught sight of a brilliant ball of flame and a Hurricane tumbled down beside me trailing a dense column of black smoke. The sight positively unnerving, I wondered whom it might be. More to the point, if the rest of us didn't find some means of escaping, we would all suffer the same fate. We had to make a break and hope they wouldn't follow.

In some semblance of order, we twisted and turned towards the ground before diving away and flying towards the north. After following us down for several thousand feet, for whatever reason, the 109s suddenly disappeared and we were left alone. Thank God for that! I throttled right back, coarsened the pitch of my airscrew and crept back towards Essex. Twenty minutes later, with a bare 5 gallons of fuel remaining, I landed at North Weald. One of only six! I looked at my watch. I had been airborne for two hours and five minutes.

It took some time to obtain a clear picture of what had happened to the rest of the squadron. It was Sergeant Stroud's aircraft I had seen falling in flames, its owner, to his own and everyone else's relief, taking to his parachute. Sergeant 'Titch' Palliser – he of the baby face – had crashed his aircraft just north of the Thames and four others had force-landed at Redhill, Rochester and Hornchurch. Only our non-speaking Pole, 'Micky' Maciejowski, had claimed a Hun – a 109 'destroyed'.

Altogether, a sad affair but one which could have been worse. But why? The simple truth was, we had been totally over-extended. Our fault? Or 'Lumba's'? My views on the incident I thought best to keep to myself. More and more, we were becoming Hun bait.

A gale had developed by 6 December which kept everyone on the ground. After the debacle of the previous day, I was not too unhappy about that. Nor were there any Huns about, or none that we knew of.

Two Frenchmen were posted in, officers this time, one a devastatingly handsome chap called Labouchère, the other, Fayolle, whose father, we learned, was a French Admiral. Two more Poles also arrived, an officer, Skalski, and a sergeant, Popec by name. Skalski seemed much older than the rest of us and had a mouthful of gold teeth; when Skalski smiled, dispersal fairly glittered. All seemed nice enough chaps, if quiet – as I imagined I would be if posted to a Polish or French Squadron. We appeared to be becoming a very cosmopolitan squadron although, in fact, there were only seven foreigners among twenty-six of us, Perrin and Bouquillard having moved on meanwhile.

It now appeared certain that John Grandy would be leaving us. Although able to move around reasonably well on foot, he could not sit down for any length of time, which ruled out operational flying. Hearing that he was to be sent to Headquarters, Fighter Command, he took the day off in order to contest the arrangement.

With Christmas approaching, I was keen to get away over the holiday period but could only arrange for ten days starting 28 December. What a terrible thing for my parents if I were shot down in the meantime! On Christmas Day, for example. Some people would be. The thought depressed me. Like getting killed on 11 November 1918.

We had a long trip over the Channel the following morning, at 28,000 feet and freezing to death. I had seldom felt so cold, not so much my body as my hands and feet which, after thirty minutes or so, ceased absolutely to function. Several of the formation fell away with oil-freezing difficulties until, after a time, there were only nine of us left. Fortunately, there were no Huns about, although we seemed to be getting progressively closer to France each day.

Back on the ground someone said that, due to the adiabatic lapse, the temperature at 30,000 feet was about minus 50 degrees Centigrade, someone else adding that that was outside the cockpit; inside it was a damn-sight colder. Why must *our* aircraft be so wretchedly cold? We bet the Huns' weren't!

Sunday 8 December. A not-quite normal day. The weather tolerable, almost reasonable in fact, with large banks of cumulus and sun. Sun!

A Wing Commander Hamblain, of Headquarters, Fighter Command, had been visiting us for several weeks in order to make at least one operational flight. We thought it was something to do with his job. On every occasion, however, he had been thwarted by bad weather. Arriving on 8 December, he was once more included on the 'state' and briefed to fly as my No. 2 where, I decided, he would be least vulnerable and least likely to get in the way.

I was not at all sure about the wing commander who, in my view, was far too old for operational flying. Without knowing the man and sufficiently young to regard everyone over thirty as having one foot in the grave, I felt that he was taking an enormous risk. Still – if this was the way he wanted to die.

We were scrambled about 3 p.m. and, climbing in the direction of Maidstone, it soon became clear that the sun had brought out the Huns; a number of formations were at large over Kent and, if we made sufficient height in time, we could expect action.

Clawing ourselves upwards, there followed the usual rapid and sometimes conflicting reports of hostile plots together with warnings of bandits in our area. Turning this way and that amid solid banks of cumulus, at around 17,000 feet a clutch of 109s suddenly went streaming across our heads. Then, observing us underneath, they circled in our direction and prepared for trouble.

Never too concerned about Huns I could see, I watched them carefully as they approached, noting that the squadron was spread out nicely around me and that my No. 2 was at least somewhere adjacent. Then, several 109s detached themselves and came down on us.

It was not a very determined attack and I followed them around almost casually as they curved towards me firing as they came, rods of white tracer shooting out but falling away behind me. Tightening my turn, I saw that they were not very serious and that I was quite safe. On the other hand, it might be less amusing for those further back. Then, alarmed suddenly by the thought of the wing commander, I reared around but could not see him.

Meanwhile, the rapid RT chatter continuing in shrill, urgent tones and with the Huns still wheeling about overhead, for the best part of several minutes we pulled and climbed and turned and generally behaved with the urgency of a squadron on the fringe of combat and being threatened with murder. After which, in a moment, it was all over and the sky clear.

Still racing about, we collected ourselves and within moments, my No. 2 came surging alongside, bouncing and rearing like a frolicking buffalo. Relief! *There* he was, for heaven's sake! Twenty minutes later and back on the ground, we discussed the incident in the usual way. Sorry not to have had a couple of Huns for the wing commander to take back, we sympathized, but how did he enjoy his first bout of combat?

Frowning silence. Combat? A blank stare. Huns? So *that's* what all the turning was about!

We had the rest of the afternoon to ourselves but were warned that a Hun attack was likely to be launched in the early evening. Three of our aircraft being required to stand-by for night-flying, as flight commander designate, it fell to me to prepare and take part.

I was sent off at 5.30 p.m., by which time it was already dusk, and as I climbed away on my own, I was struck by the sheer, stark beauty of the winter scene. The earth below now fading into misty blackness, the sky was a clear, cold, silent void of cerise and indigo. It seemed that I was the only living organism in the universe; one solitary Hurricane, engine roaring and with pinkly-flaring exhausts. A single dot climbing endlessly into space.

I was vectored towards the estuary and out to sea, soon to be turned and brought back to land. Far below, the faint outline of the coast was visible, but only just. 'Lumba' was silent. There was no information of Huns. All was quiet. At 15,000 feet and chilled to the marrow, I drifted back and forth between Southend and Clacton. For a long time. Nothing much doing tonight. The intelligence people had got it wrong this time.

Then, suddenly, news of a bogey. I was turned north. And told to climb to 18,000 feet. Then, vector 095 degrees. North then east? Funny! 'Bogey' directly ahead, I was informed. I strained my eyes into a starlit darkness still tinged with areas of fading blue. A bogey flying east at 18,000 feet? What Hun would be doing that at this time of night? Sounded pretty rum to me.

And then I saw it. About 600 yards away, suddenly and fleetingly silhouetted against a patch of lighter sky. A lone aircraft, heading east.

I opened up, switched on my gunsight, turning the rheostat until the pink lines and dot faded to a comfortable brightness, then rotated my gun button to 'Fire'. Another minute and I would be in position. Careful, though. Mustn't frighten the blighter into retaliation.

Barely visible, it was a large twin-engined aircraft with a single tail. I sat directly behind it and slightly lower, the dot and lines of my sight moving gently around the faint, blurred outline of the fuselage and wings. But a Heinkel or 88, which were the only single-ruddered Huns I knew of, flying east? I checked with 'Lumba'. I had the bogey in my sight. Could they confirm it was a bandit? It certainly didn't look to me like one.

'Stand-by!'

Silence. With my sight dead on target but wandering a little, I wallowed like a whale in the turbulence of the two engines ahead. Range, 150 yards. Dead easy!

But 'Lumba' had no information of friendly aircraft in the area and said so. Could I not identify it?

Identify it! What, at night and from where I was?

I pulled aside and gently eased myself forward. Slowly. On edge. Stealthily. If whatever-it-was chose to fire, I was a goner. Larger, now. Bigger. Until I was within yards of it. Tall single rudder. Of course! A Wellington! A *bloody Wimpy*!

Tension draining, I turned and fell away downwards in disgust. God! If anyone asked to be shot down it was *that* character.

But there was more to come. Letting down into the blackness of eastern Essex, I was given several headings which brought me eventually into the area of Chelmsford. At which point, I was immediately illuminated by one, then several, and finally a clutch of searchlights, all of which turned their dazzling blue-white beams on me. At 3,000 feet, I was blinded absolutely, ducking back into the cockpit to avoid the direct glare of the lights. The *fools*! Couldn't they see I was a Hurricane? But still they persisted, following me about until I was flashing my navigation and downward identification lights at them and screaming at 'Lumba' to call them off. These people just didn't have enough to do!

It was on that day, too, that I learned that my appointment to command 'B' Flight was confirmed; I could go ahead and change my rank badges. There was only one small snag: the code letters for 'B' Flight aircraft being from N to Z, I would be losing GN-F. How very sad!

December continued miserably. There was fog, drizzle and frost with cloud so threateningly low that it sat on the hangar roofs like a shroud. Everything dripped. Constantly. Or froze.

We flew when we could; the occasional patrol, high up; the odd abortive interception, low down; and long and tedious convoy patrols in the estuary at less than 1,000 feet with Victor Beamish flying behind me as No. 4 in my section. All the time, we waited interminably, both in the air and on the ground, for the lone Huns we were told of but never encountered.

At night there was the usual drone of aircraft overhead, mostly en route for the north but now and then deluging our area with bombs in an apparent frenzy of spitefulness. And always the guns, tonk-tonk-tonking away, followed by the crumps. I could never hear the bark of a 3.7 without counting the seconds and waiting for the shell to disintegrate in the high, far distance. On the night of 8 December, another Dornier received a direct hit and came down in our direction with a terrible wail, so close and unnerving that we thought for a moment it would land on the mess. But it didn't. It fell instead into the woods nearby. No one bothered to investigate.

It was on 8 December, too, that I cycled all the way into Epping and back – a whole five miles! – to buy rank-braid for my tunic. After which I sat on my bed in dispersal for hours, sewing laboriously with needle, thread and tongue, only to start all over again when the stripes were crooked and spaced too far apart.

On 13 December, 46 Squadron departed for Digby and 56 Squadron joined us from Boscombe Down. Though I had enjoyed my association with 46, I was especially pleased to have 56 back again – a splendid crowd. One of their first acts was to place a small display case in the dining-room of the mess containing Captain Albert Ball's flying helmet and gloves – sad, brown, wasted things. Several times, long after dinner, when the room was deserted and in shadow, I found myself examining them. Alone. Thoughtful. Nostalgic. Always with the same odd feeling of tragedy. He had been twenty too, at the time of his death.

I took two days off around 14 December for the purpose of flying the Maggie up to Manchester and landing triumphantly at Barton, my pre-war training airfield. But, what a hope! I had barely reached Cambridge when cloud and rain forced me down to 200 feet so that I had to return. What a perfectly blood-stained country England was to fly in during the winter; the Huns didn't know the half of it!

The following day, a spot of excitement. One of the huts down at dispersal caught fire and a mass of documents, records, equipment and tools was destroyed. Everyone ran about like headless chickens and there was great consternation. But, why? If the Huns had dropped a bomb on it, no one would have been in the least put out – had a good laugh, in fact. Instead, it became a terrible to-do. Exactly the same with aircraft clocks. An 'attractive item', so called, the equipment wallahs valued time-pieces above gold. Lose a Hurricane – *with* the pilot – and no one gave a damn. But lose a clock worth £2 and people began fainting in heaps.

Meanwhile, a flurry of comings and goings. There were several new faces and Sergeant Smithson, one of our gallant originals who had been badly wounded in September, appeared briefly among us to say farewell; he and Sergeant McNair had been posted to 96, one of the newly-forming Hurricane night-fighter squadrons up north. Boozy Kellett, who had done so well with 303 Squadron at Northolt, had been placed in command. 249 had certainly spawned some heroes.

And Gerald Lewis was back, his wounds and burns healed. It was nice to have his tall, fair-haired and familiar figure at the dinner table again, talking endlessly of the glories of South Africa. According to him and Butch, the only two places worth living in after the war would be the Drakensburg mountains in Natal and British Columbia – among Butch's Chinks, of course! After the war! A million years hence! What *were* we talking about?

It was around that time, too, that Air Vice Marshal Trafford Leigh-Mallory came to see us, having recently, and rather surprisingly, taken over No. 11 Group from Keith Park, who had moved on with a promotion of sorts.

Unfamiliar with the politics of high office, we were nevertheless aware of the constant dissension and mutterings among our seniors. The acrimonious debate and mud-slinging between Leigh-Mallory and Park on tactical issues had been a feature of the intelligence summaries over the past four months. To us, it had all appeared rather childish – but then, who were we to judge? Leigh-Mallory I had seen before; Park I felt I knew. Indeed it was Park who had landed briefly at North Weald in his unmarked Hurricane in September and had stopped his aircraft most inconveniently outside our dispersal hut at a time when we were expecting any moment to be attacked. I had run outside and ordered him away peremptorily, only later learning of his identity. But he had taken it very well, apologizing to me afterwards for his thoughtlessness. Somehow, I couldn't see Leigh-Mallory doing that.

I had been on an abortive interception with Tommy Thompson shortly before the great man arrived and was sitting on my bed when he came in to be introduced. He was very civil and friendly in a rather unbending fashion and, after a time, perched on one of the beds himself as we talked. What did we think of this and that? – the usual questions. But always questions, never answers or statements of intent. Addressing me by name, which pleased me rather, he asked my opinion of a proposal to change the colour of the spinners on our aircraft. I replied forthrightly that I much preferred them to remain black; as the Huns went in for gaudy colours, if I looked round and saw a black nose behind me, I was much less concerned than if it were coloured. Most important, I insisted, vital, in fact. He kept nodding and giving the impression he agreed. Shortly after, all our airscrew spinners were repainted duck-egg blue – which just went to show! In fact, in the weeks ahead, our Hurricanes were painted and repainted in so many different colour schemes, we began to joke about their being able to get off the ground with all the extra weight. 249 was not a gaudy squadron. Some of the leading lights in other units had black crosses and swastikas daubed all over their cockpit-sides, but not 249. I once painted the name of a girlfriend on mine, in small letters, but became so embarrassed about it that I had it removed within days.

When the AOC had gone, we compared impressions. Stiff-looking, immaculate, and with a very un-airmanlike appearance, he conveyed to us all an aura of pomposity. Privately, and although our conversation had been very easy and conducted in the most friendly of terms, he had not impressed me as a leader. A brain-picker, yes. But not a standard-bearer. Victor Beamish I would have followed to the ends of the earth; Keith Park even, whom I barely knew. But, about our new AOC, I had reservations.

In the several days before Christmas it became desperately cold. The aerodrome was white with frost, the water-pipes choked with ice and life in our uninsulated wooden huts quite intolerable. My minute stove, cherry-red at night, was always a cold grey mass of ashes in the morning. The temperature well below freezing *inside* the room and as I lay pale and rigid between the sheets, it was glorious relief when my batman brought me morning tea and a jug of steaming water for shaving. I reflected savagely that the Romans had central heating in AD 200, since when domestic heating arrangements in Britain had gone to the dogs. Rising at dawn was sheer, undiluted purgatory. Even the cockpit of a Hurricane was warm by comparison.

Word was also received that all squadron and flight commanders were to gather on Christmas Day at RAF Hornchurch to hear the AOC's plans for the future. What was this about, we wondered? And why choose Christmas Day, for heaven's sake?

With 'Hopalong' Cassidy, late of 25 Squadron, I took off on 23 December and roamed about over Essex in filthy weather and below a solid layer of cloud that was seldom above 1,000 feet. Vectored this way and that, I finally caught sight of a Hun aircraft far away to my left, which faded into mist as soon as we turned towards it. We did not see it again and, after chasing about for a while, landed. To heck with it, it was far too close to Christmas. The following day it snowed.

We set off for Hornchurch on Christmas Day morning on roads slick with ice and between fields stiff and white with frost and snow. In the back of the Humber staff car, my breath rose like steam from a kettle. It was to be ten years at least before British car manufacturers were forced reluctantly to install heaters in their vehicles, they and the makers of the Hurricane clearly believing it to be their professional duty to ensure that the users of their wretched products should never be beguiled by anything so insidiously decadent as warmth and comfort. Meanwhile, our teeth chattering and the roads deserted, we seemed to have Essex entirely to ourselves.

The officers' mess at RAF Hornchurch was similar to that at North Weald; the same quiet and dignified club atmosphere, the black leather armchairs and settees, the roaring ante-room fire and the discreet pictures, crests and silver. Arriving just before lunch, we found the place jammed with staff cars and their occupants.

A flight lieutenant of barely two weeks seniority, I was awed into silence by my companions – Leigh-Mallory, Embry, Broadhurst, Beamish, Bader, Malan, and scores of others whose names had been on the nation's lips for months, representatives of every fighter station in 11 Group and twenty or more Spitfire, Hurricane and Blenheim squadrons. The cream! The élite! And all comrades. Handshakes, laughter, back-slapping, reminiscences and jokes. I felt like a peasant at the court of King Arthur.

We dined, the room a hubbub of conversation and good spirits. A Christmas lunch, too. A splendid meal which I ate in silence, my eyes restless. After which, moving in a stream into the ante-room, we looked for chairs in which to sit to drink our coffee and in preparation for the AOC's address.

All the seats being occupied. I was obliged to squat on the floor by the fire. Leigh-Mallory reclined in front of me, cosily, informally, a benign father-figure and, as he commenced, I was reminded immediately of a bedtime story.

The Battle of Britain had been won, he informed us with quiet but obvious satisfaction. We had clobbered the Hun. The invasion threat had been averted. It was time now for 11 Group squadrons to take the offensive.

Offensive! Absolute silence. Everyone attentive. God, I thought, what next? And as though in response, I heard him continuing.

We would do so in a number of ways. By means of fighter sweeps, which would draw the enemy into the air where his aircraft would be destroyed. By carrying out fighter-escorted bombing attacks on continental targets within range of our Blenheims and Bostons. And by 'mosquito' raids, in which pairs of fighters operating at low level and in suitable weather conditions would attack every legitimate enemy target within fifty miles of the Channel coast and by so doing keep the enemy constantly on the alert. In short, our aim was to wrest the initiative from the Hun. We would put into effect one of the fundamental principles of war – offensive action! In the months to come we would defeat the Luftwaffe over its own territory. And we would start... *tomorrow*! Boxing Day!

Once more – silence! And immediately and ridiculously, there flashed into my mind the fable of the mice and the pussy-cat: 'A splendid arrangement but which of us mice is to tie the bell around the cat's neck?' I was soon to learn!

A raid would be made on an ammunition dump in the Forêt de Guines on 26 December by six Blenheims, led by Group Captain Basil Embry, escorted by nine squadrons of fighters. Various details followed, concluding with the momentous announcement: 'and 242, 56 and 249 Squadrons will act as close escort to the bombers... at 7,000 feet!'

My stomach shrivelled. 7,000 feet! Oh, *no*!

Much more was to follow – discussion, details, queries, observations. I sat and listened to it all, very much aware that I was going to be in the bottom squadron – the one nearest the ground and closest to the enemy! – flying an aircraft which was all but useless against 109s even over my own country. Well might the Spitfire boys slap their thighs and begin to crack jokes. At 15,000 feet and more, they could jolly well afford to!

I sat in the car on the way back to North Weald with mixed feelings. Everyone else so obviously in favour of offensive action, I almost felt obliged to share their enthusiasm. Indeed, in a way, I did. At least we would have the initiative. The Huns would be climbing up to attack *us;* they would be underneath and with any luck I would be diving down on *them.* But, at 7,000 feet! And flying at the speed of the Blenheims! Weren't we about to repeat exactly the mistake the Huns had made in the so-called Battle of Britain? You couldn't defend bombers by flying alongside them. And Boxing Day! Who in God's name had dreamed up Boxing Day? How could we be expected to do justice to drumsticks and Christmas pud tonight, with death staring us in the face tomorrow morning?

At North Weald, a big dinner had been planned for Christmas night with oysters, champagne, plus all the usual seasonal fare. Followed by fun and games, no doubt. With my thoughts on a quiet family Christmas at home, I felt that, for once, I could do without the rough-stuff.

In the late afternoon, I went into the room that served as a bar to watch Andy, the drinks steward, open the oysters. There were masses of them, piled high in every direction, every officer receiving six. The mess was agog with preparation. Very exciting. Pity about the show tomorrow morning, though. What a thing to do to us!

Dinner was a grand affair. The dining-room crowded to overflowing, we ate as I had seldom done before. After the sherry, the oysters slid down deliciously, the champagne fizzed gloriously and warmly in my stomach and soon I was at peace with the world. Then there was the turkey, the Christmas pudding, dark and rich, and all the rest of the fare. On and on. Endlessly.

Long before the port was passed, the flight of the following day had been pushed to the back of my mind. What the heck? If I was shot down, I was shot down, and that was the end of it. Bring on the 109s! The flak! Anything!

After the royal toast, the party began to get noisy and the PMC valiantly but unavailingly tried to keep order. Some of the roughs at the far end of the room were in no mood to be silenced, however, and events came to a head when, after a fusillade of bread rolls, a large orange sailed the whole length of the dining-room and struck one of the top table in the eye. In very considerable pain, it was all the victim could do to keep his temper under control and, soon after that, the PMC thought it prudent to rise and by so doing allow the more unruly ones to leave.

Everyone collecting in the ante-room, the games started and there was the usual inter-squadron mayhem, a conflict long drawn out and bloody which came to a swift conclusion for me when, engaged in a titanic tussle with several members of 56 Squadron, I ran foul of their intelligence officer, a thick-set and immensely powerful man of Hebrew ancestry. Gripping me in a bear-hug round the middle he lifted me off my feet and *squeezed*.

To this day I can feel the oysters, champagne, turkey, Christmas pudding – everything – being slowly forced upwards like toothpaste out of a tube. Not being able to breathe I couldn't even squeak, the only course of action open to me being to kick. Which I did. Like a mule. With the result that I was dropped – hastily.

But the damage had been done. I staggered out into the night, managing only to totter as far as the rose-garden.

It is not often that rose bushes are treated to a complete Christmas dinner – champagne included.

I awoke the following morning, Boxing Day 1940, to find the weather gloriously and wonderfully vile. Even so, we were made to hang around on tenterhooks until 3 p.m., when the show was finally called off. Thank God for that, I thought. On leave on 28 December, the bad weather had only to persist for another day and I was, literally, home and dry. Moreover, the portents looked pretty good.

Considerably cheered, in the late afternoon I went into London with several others. To a film – Charlie Chaplin in *The Great Dictator*. Not expecting to fly again in December, I made up my log-book for the month. Not much flying in the last four weeks but a fair amount since July – almost 200 operational hours in fact, comprising 153 flights against the enemy. Who'd have thought it a year ago? Five months ago, even?

The following day, 28 December, I returned by train to Manchester and was joyfully welcomed into the bosom of family and friends. Not exactly Christmas, but it would do. The war was hardly mentioned.

New Year's Eve. I had planned it to be rather special – the theatre in Manchester followed by dinner at the Midland, the city's largest and most prestigious hotel.

Back on my home ground and among northern voices and familiar places, I felt happy and relaxed. North Weald – the squadron – seemed an age and a continent away, yet were never far from my thoughts. Had the weather changed down there? Had they all been over yet? I listened to the wireless and read the news, but nothing was mentioned. I hadn't wanted to miss it; on the other hand, I was glad to be away from it all. To be home. Just for a while, anyway.

I had a beautiful, dark-haired partner that night. Wide-eyed and her cheeks flushed with happiness. We were very pleased with each other.

First the theatre – not bad – and, later in the evening, the Midland. The huge dining-room brilliantly lit with chandeliers. Not quite the Dorchester but in its way equally impressive. And for me – us – more homely.

We sat and read the menu and wine list. And ordered. Read, too, with amused appreciation, the inoffensive stares in our direction. Look over there, they were saying. So very young.

What should we drink? Champagne? Why not! *Of course* I could afford it! A special occasion wasn't it? New Year's Eve!

Time passed. Endless, urgent conversation followed by moments of reflection. Both of us quiet. How long in the squadron now? Eight months. Eight whole months – and still in one piece! Would things be easier in future? I heard myself lying – reassuring. Yes, the worst was over. For a time, anyway. And then? Difficult to say. I turned away to avoid answering. I couldn't tell her; not even a word. The orchestra, a muted rhythm in the distance and couples on the floor. We listened, far away. Dance? Not just now. Let's watch. We watched. Not speaking. Occasionally smiling. For a long, long time.

The meal was served and we ate, laughing often and touching hands, occasionally in silence. Savouring the wine, feeling our cheeks grow pink and warm. Gosh, it was hot in here, wasn't it? I glanced surreptitiously at my watch. Soon be midnight.

Now eleven o'clock. The evening performance of a well-advertised pantomime over, the distinguished cast and their friends were celebrating. A crush of them crowding in the entrance to the ball-room, laughing and calling to each other. Not objectionably so. Just good spirits.

My eyes suddenly wide. 'Look who's here!'

'Who?'

'Stanley Holloway, for heaven's sake. And look who else.'

'The big man, you mean? I've seen his face.'

'You certainly have. It's Wendell Willkie.'

'You mean – ?'

'Exactly.'

They were led in our direction and seated in groups within yards of us. In an otherwise crowded room, we had wondered why six tables had been left vacant. Willkie, who had lost the election for the United States Presidency only weeks before, was within feet of me, sitting awkwardly on his chair, a big man with his backside hanging over the edge. But pleasant, withal. Like an amiable buffalo. An agreeable face, too, with dark hair in waves over his forehead. Talking apparently to no one in particular, all the time his eyes wandering. Our glances met several times and once, he winked, solemnly. Then, astonishingly, he put a monster cigar into his mouth and, selecting a match, struck it on his pants with a sweep of his arm. Real Abraham Lincoln stuff. We stared, open-mouthed, then exchanged surprised and amused stares. What an incredible thing to do.

Midnight almost. Everyone preparing for the New Year. Glasses being charged. More champagne? Her eyes sparkling. Phew! Did I think she ought? Why not? Life's too sh – ! Silence. Not exactly tactful. An apologetic glance. Yes, let's, should we?

Then the band was crashing out a chord with everyone on their feet and in a circle, hands joined. 'Should auld acquaintance' – and so on. Backwards and forwards, bumping happily. The touch of her body beside me. Several times. Everyone laughing and kissing. Positively the best part. Happy 1941! *Happy new year*!

We returned to our seats, flushed and excited. Then everyone calling for Stanley. Up! Up! Up! An insistent chorus.

Stanley Holloway, on his feet. Smiling. Nodding. Up! Up! Up! We were still shouting as he climbed onto his chair. Then the table. He feigned bashfulness, raised his hands, then out they all came: 'Sam, Sam pick up th' musket'; 'Albert and t' Lion', and half-a-dozen others. Deafening cheers then more cheers and clapping. More! More!

Poor man. We wouldn't let him go. On and on. Well into the small hours, until the bottles on our table were empty and the chandeliers began to wobble and sway out of focus. And still Wendell Willkie was striking matches on his pants, and puffing his cigars, and clapping and shouting with the rest of us. Gosh, it was hot! Massive applause and cheering. Lord, what a night!

We left, finally. Out into the blackness and frost to find my Morris 10.

'I bet the radiator's frozen!'

'Oh, *don't* say that!'

Stumbling. Giggles. Then, a gasp and the warmth of her body and clinging arm.

'Can you *see*?' Me being very masculine.

'*Of course* I can see. It's just these... these pygmalion heels!' More giggling. 'There! I knew it! I've lost my shoe!'

The car was as cold as a sepulchre and wouldn't start. It had to be cranked endlessly and the journey home took an age. Hours in fact.

But, who cared? It was 1941. A brave new year. And a brave new leaf to be turned.

15

Offensive Action

Friday, 10 January 1941 — bitterly cold but bright, south-east England frozen into petrified silence and enrobed in a mantle of white. In the distance, yellow smoke rising from a tall chimney leaned towards the heavens as though congealed into a drunken pillar.

We had climbed into our cockpits to buckle on parachutes and straps with fingers clumsy with cold, our breath steaming in the frigid air, our minds soothed by the calming ritual of preparation. After which we had taken off from North Weald a few minutes before noon, curving away to the south in an untidy gaggle, to climb up shallowly over Essex in the direction of Southend. There were thirty-six of us, all Hurricanes — 56 Squadron ahead, then 242, with Douglas Bader in front, and finally 249. As flight commander of 'B' Flight, 249, I was leading the final section of four at the rear with Victor Beamish directly ahead of me — in the box, to use the accepted term. Victor, restless warrior that he was, always followed, never led, being able then to come and go as he pleased, which only he as Station Commander and a lesser God was entitled to do.

As we flew south, the routine of piloting and station-keeping loosened the fetters of tension; there was little hurry, no frantic climb. We had barely 7,000 feet to make as we were to act as escort to the first bomber formation to attempt a daylight raid on a target in France since the so-called Battle of Britain. So-called, as that then-familiar phrase related to a national crisis which for us had been merely part of a sustained period of activity against the Luftwaffe, a tidy but emotive expression for a tidy sixteen-week event, conveniently terminating on 31 October 1940. As though the war for us had started in July and ended in October, which it most definitely had not! And now, here we were, on the offensive. For the first time. Six Bristol Blenheim bombers and nine squadrons of fighters — 108 Spitfires and

Hurricanes. About to commence a campaign to achieve what the Germans had manifestly failed to accomplish four months earlier — air supremacy. Today, the six Blenheims were the bait and I, and 107 others, were there to knock down the 109s like ninepins; I, in a Hurricane Mark I, whose hope of catching a 109, other than by accident or freak of circumstance, was unlikely, to put expectation at its highest. Whatever next? Were we not about to repeat exactly the policy and tactical errors the Hun had made the previous summer?

We were over the Thames and in the area of Gravesend when the Blenheims appeared; one moment nothing, then, suddenly, there they were, six camouflaged twin-engined shapes, huddled together, tilting, turning. We curved in their direction, 56 forming up alongside, 242 and 249 in a slow meander left, right, and behind. Then, all together, we slanted ponderously towards the Channel, knowing that aloft, six more squadrons, Spits from Hornchurch and Hurricanes from Northolt and elsewhere, would eventually be stepped up behind us to more than 20,000 feet.

As we flew in the direction of Deal, I looked down on the silent white undulations of Kent with a new affection. For more than four months, I had fought over the area almost daily, so that Canterbury, Maidstone, Gravesend and Dover were names indelibly etched on my heart and mind. But, would this be the last time? Would I ever again surge over its hills and woodlands in pursuit of some crippled and streaming enemy? Because nothing was more certain than that our future battlefield would be the broad acres of France, deceptively docile to the eye yet bristling with flak, whose malicious threat already loomed larger than life in our imaginations. Hun fighters were one thing, impersonal, faceless flak, which thrust upwards at us with sly, lethal digs, was definitely another. And, of course, in between France and Kent — or Sussex — there were from 20 to 90 miles of cold, inhospitable water. Despite being brought up in a major port, as an airman the sea had very little charm for me; just one stray bullet in my Hurricane's coolant system or any other of its vital parts, and in I would be, floundering about in its freezing embrace. To survive in winter for what — twenty minutes? Our adversaries, the Hun fighter pilots, were reported as having personal dinghies, but no such luxuries for us! In fact, even my old and familiar Mae West was suspect; one of the original type without an inflating CO_2 bottle, if the time came, would I have the puff to blow it up?

All these and other thoughts passed morbidly through my mind. Then, with Dover off to my right with its attendant halo of balloons, I was out over the water and heading for France. After which, speculation was firmly put aside and reality advanced with a grim face . . .

Our target that day was an ammunition dump in the Forêt de Guines, some 10 miles inland from Cap Grisnez. The bombers would go in at around 7,000 feet and 242 and 249 were there to protect the Blenheims from Huns climbing into them from below. For this reason, our twenty-four aircraft were to fly at around 5,000 feet. Five thousand feet! Over a part of enemy territory bristling with guns — an unpleasant enough prospect in all conscience.

We had discussed tactics at the AOC's conference at Hornchurch on Christmas Day, when, to my dry-mouthed concern, I had heard an expert affirm that 7,000 feet was the best height at which to fly over enemy territory, being too high for the low flak and too low for the high stuff. Seven thousand feet! Was he absolutely sure? If the Huns had done that in September, we would have thought them mad. I would have liked to have questioned the man, a penguin (a derisory term for non-flying ground officer) needless to say, but juniority had shackled my tongue. So, here we were, at 5,000 feet. Simply asking for trouble.

As we approached the enemy coast, I scanned my cockpit with a professional eye. Seat the right height; straps tight and locked; oil pressure 70 lbs; oil temperature 50-plus degrees; coolant 85 degrees, or thereabouts; gun sight 'ON', brightness just right and the range-bar set at 40 feet (for a 109, naturally); gun-button to 'FIRE'. Everything set. I then leaned forward to 'pull the plug', which cut out the governor controlling the engine boost, increased my revs to 2,850, and wriggled my bum firmly into my parachute cushion. All set and ready to go.

The Blenheims crossed in over Gravellines, as briefed — less flak there, we had been told — at which point I found myself well to the right of the formation and gazing down almost dispassionately on the Hun fighter airfield at Calais Marck. From slightly less than 5,000 feet too! My whole body tense and expectant. Waiting.

But nothing came; no red balls, no tracer, no angry crimson- centred puffs of black, nothing. Northern France, a wilderness of snow lined with thin tracings of hedgerow, rail and road, was as still as a tomb. Nothing stirred. The old Hun was asleep, by George! Surely he must have known we were coming. Didn't he have RDF (Radio Direction Finding – early name for Radar) too, or something similar?

Then the Blenheims were tilting to starboard and the Hurricanes in front accelerating. Weaving about. And going lower. Lower, for God's sake! Were there 109s about? On edge but full of resolve, I cast anxiously around but could see nothing. The Blenheims level now and running in — huddled, determined, unflinching, splendidly brave. Aiming straight for the dark mass that was the Forêt de Guines. At which point the first ack-ack appeared.

It was quite innocuous at first, dark puffs, pecking away in front, not far from the bombers and moving with them so that it was behind and below them but slightly above my own height. Then closer, until I was flying through residual traces of smoke that flicked disconcertingly past my cockpit hood. Nothing really nasty though, nor dangerous. And no tracer or clusters of those glowing things either. Yet!

The Blenheims dropped their bombs. Watching with half an eye, I did not see them fall but picked out pin-pricks of red at the centre of several explosions whose violent circles of blast flattened the trees. Then the bombers were turning and I, with others, was on the far side of them. Racing. Dropping down further and turning. Following the others. What in heaven's name was Douglas Bader doing? We shouldn't be down at this height, damn it! More brown flak-bursts but above me now and some way off. Hurricanes everywhere and the Blenheims high and in the distance. Huns? I couldn't see any. Down to 2,000 feet now and going north like mad. Bouncing about in someone's slipstream with 280 on the clock. Fields, roads and isolated buildings streaming beneath. A water-tower. Lower still and following others in a shallow dive. What the hell were we supposed to be doing now? Then, in the distance, the coastline. And water.

I was at about 800 feet when I crossed the coast and had a fleeting glimpse of yellow and white sand-dunes and marram grass. And flak!

It started coming in the shape of white streaks and red balls, the latter rising obliquely in clutches of five or six, curving quickly towards me then whipping past. On my right mostly, where there were other Hurricanes in an untidy gaggle. In a moment of naked fear, I pulled back and climbed steeply — then wished I hadn't. As my speed fell away, I had the sensation of being suspended in space, hanging! Meanwhile, the balls kept coming, overtaking me with vicious intent and curving away into oblivion. Steeper still now with my speed right down to 140. An aircraft just ahead of me and to my right, the fiery projectiles flashing between us. Then, in a brief moment of shock and horror, the chap in front was hit. Amidships. The aircraft staggered as though struck by a club and fell away downwards, turning over and dropping like a crippled bird. To disappear from what? — little more than 1,000 feet? A goner for sure! More fluorescent things streaming past. Me, cringing, waiting for the lethal bang and jolt. Pulling, turning, but climbing still, my engine raging with all the boost I could muster. Then . . . my nose dropping . . . levelling out. Sea, in every direction, with its cold, grey sneer. But safety, thank God! Safety . . . more or less!

Some three miles out, I turned and took stock. There were Hurricanes everywhere, flying northwards close to the sea and forming up. No bombers, though, nor any sign of 56 Squadron. Several small boats were lying like matchsticks a little to the north of Calais and the flak had stopped. There were one or two other aircraft, moving urgently but not in my direction, which may have been Huns but were too far away to identify. Completing my turn, I flew towards far-off Dover and the welcoming white cliffs, crossing eventually into snowbound Kent. Immediately, my engine sounded much more cheerful; no damage there it seemed. I formed up on several other Hurricanes and set course for North Weald with a light heart. Thank God! What a glorious relief to be flying over dear old Kent again. Terribly sad about the chap who had just been hit, though. One of 249 almost certainly, but who?

I landed, with others, a little before half past one, having been airborne one hour and thirty-five minutes.

In the dispersal hut there was relieved laughter and excitement mingled with annoyance. What had possessed Douglas Bader to go down like that? Vulnerable enough at 5,000 feet, at less than 2,000, we were sitting ducks. 'Hopalong' Cassidy was in full voice, having been hit in the tail by flak, and 'Tommy' Thompson had lost a piece of his airscrew. Bloody silly business! Had I been hit? No, I didn't think so, just frightened. But, as it turned out, I had. Only a minor hole, though. Straight through my elevator, which, because it was fabric, could be repaired in minutes. Trivial, hardly worth mentioning or worrying about. All the same, I tried hard to persuade myself that the damage had been caused by a stone. But a stone wouldn't go through top *and* bottom surfaces, would it?

Victor Beamish had fired at the boats, apparently, and had also shot down a 109 that was attacking a Hurricane over the Channel. And there was the chap I had seen hit amidships, by flak, wasn't there? Who was he? Concerned, we all looked round, counting. Two – McConnell and Maciejowski – were missing. Anyone seen them? 'Shirley' Woolmer, the Intelligence Officer, was looking from face to face, being ignored by everyone and appearing totally bewildered by all the chatter. I repeated my story of the Hurricane being hit by flak and he wrote something down, his brows gathered, his pencil tripping over the words in his excitement. Was I sure it was one of ours? Of course it was! – me, tersely abrupt; it couldn't have been a Hun, could it? Not within thirty yards of me! He agreed, grudgingly, then pushed his way through the crowd, eager for other reports.

Gradually, a picture emerged. McConnell had been shot up by a 109, which, in turn, had been attacked and shot down by Victor Beamish. Wounded, and his aircraft streaming glycol, Mac had limped back across the Channel and had baled out when crossing the Kent coast, his Hurricane crashing into the cliffs at Dover. But it was only some time later that Sergeant 'Micky' Maciejowski landed and clumped into dispersal. His story, delivered in fractured English and accompanied by a wealth of Polish hand-signals, was different – it always was! He had shot at half-a-dozen Henschel 126s on the small airfield at Guines and had then run into two 109s at low level. Following a brief fight, one of the German fighters had apparently crashed into a wood but, in the course of the engagement, Micky's throttle had jammed in the fully-open position so that he was obliged to roar around France at full bore before high-tailing it for England, finally putting down at Hornchurch, short of fuel. We all shook our heads in amused despair. Everything happened to Micky!

I retold my story about the flak and its victim, adding hotly that it was nonsense to suggest that it hadn't happened. Woolmer kept saying he was sorry but McConnell was our only casualty and there it was. Perplexed and not a little irritated, I had occasion to telephone Group some time later and brought up the subject. There had to be at least one more casualty, I persisted. One of the other squadrons, perhaps? But there wasn't, it seemed, the voice at the other end snidely hinting that I must have been seeing things, which did nothing to soothe my ire. Silly blighters! I knew exactly what I had seen, I wasn't blind! On the other hand, I hadn't seen the 109s, had I? Or the Henschels. Or very much else, apart from those loathsome red balls coming at me from all directions.

Everyone was agreeing that although useful in terms of experience, it had been a pretty pointless exercise. Six bombers, 108 fighters. McConnell's aircraft lost and the poor chap wounded and in hospital, all for what? A few twigs off some trees in the Forêt de Guines and very little else, unless one counted the 109s, of course. And I had not even seen a Hun! Strange, that. Nothing was more confusing than air combat.

The following day, a little to our surprise, we received a signal from Commander-in-Chief Fighter Command, passing on a message of congratulation from the Prime Minister, Mr Churchill, and adding that, he, too, thought we were all splendid fellows. Splendid? Nothing I had done was particularly splendid. In fact, the whole show, in our view, was a bit of a non-event. We were quite willing to go over to France and fight, but no more of those low-level escort dos, thank-you very much!

16

The Start of the Year

I had returned from leave on Tuesday, 7 January. By train, and at night, needless to say!

The journey from Manchester to London normally took four hours. However, with Britain blacked out completely and being bombed almost incessantly, anything less than six was a bonus and an interminable journey of seven or eight not unknown. Those periods of hanging about in trains, usually at such unstimulating places as Watford Junction or Willesden, were sheer purgatory, the compartments and corridors jam-packed with reeking humanity, the glimmering five-watt bulbs – even in the first-class sections – making reading impossible, and the windows, plastered with curtaining material to reduce the effect of bomb blast, running with smoke-rich condensation which collected maliciously in pools on the mahogany surrounds before seeping into elbows and thighs. Sleep, if it came, was never more than fitful.

On that occasion, however, I was lucky as the train was only an hour late into Euston. Even so, it was approaching midnight, bitterly cold outside and the pavements ankle-deep in slush, when I found a taxi and began my nocturnal hunt for accommodation. An hour later I was back at Euston having tried no less than six hotels and found them full. So, the railway hotel it had to be.

The night was hideous, full of clanks and thumps as I shivered in a bedroom that was seedily damp, ghoulishly Victorian, and almost the size of an aircraft hangar. The following morning, I sat down to a breakfast curling at the edges and served by a minion wearing an undertaker's outfit of black tie and tails, after which I left, having been charged an extortionate sixteen shillings and sixpence for a night of memorable discomfort.

But my misfortune was not to end there. Deciding to take the Green Line bus to Epping and having enquired of a passing inspector where it started from, I stood in Portman Square for more than an hour, stamping my feet and freezing to death, learning only then that the route had been changed and that I should have been standing in Cavendish Square. Two hours later, I arrived at North Weald, miserable, my nose streaming with a head-cold, and in a savage frame of mind, to find my hutted room like an ice-box, my stove unlit, and my batman missing. Outside, the fog was thickening to a pea-souper. Bloody hell! What a war! What a country! And what a homecoming!

And it was whilst I was indulging in this bitter soliloquy, that a Hun bomber droned across the top of the mess, very low indeed but invisible in the murk. I went out, hunched and shivering, to listen to the unfamiliar beat of its engines, and to observe. But nothing happened. Silly blighter! Probably lost, and serve him right!

During the night it snowed again and I awoke the following morning to a silent wonderland of white. Driving down to dispersal, I learned that things had been very quiet since my departure ten days earlier. The most excellent Sergeant Beard had been commissioned and 'Butch' Barton and Dicky Wynn had carried out a low-level 'mosquito' (original term for low-level attacks on enemy targets by a pair of fighters) raid in France some days before, running into flak south of Boulogne and attacking a petrol-bowser on St Anglevert airfield. A whole petrol-bowser! That would shorten the war!

Later, just to reacquaint myself with flying, I took off in GN-V and acted as target for someone doing cine-gun. Nice and simple, nothing strenuous. Despite the weather, it was good to get into the air again and, landing comfortably on the snow a little later, I was reminded of Flying Training School (FTS) at Montrose a year earlier. However, the weather clamped completely in the afternoon enabling a number of us to be given a Cook's tour of the Bofors-gun emplacements around the airfield. What a life! Who'd be a gunner, standing about all day in a woolly Balaclava hat, bored to death and being called into action once every Preston Guild?

The following day, 9 January, being much better with a clear sky, I took my flight for a formation exercise, our first since the previous August, in fact. Very morale-raising, though not in my own aircraft unfortunately, GN-W being on inspection. I had a hollow feeling that if the fine weather continued, the bombing attack we had planned on Christmas Day would almost certainly take place. And how right I was! Later on, I was told that 'Der Tag' was to be 10 January. The next day. Wow!

With a few others that evening, I went to the cinema in Epping, outwardly unconcerned but with an unpleasant niggle in my mind that it might be my last visit to this or any cinema!

After which, to bed. My hutted room temporarily warm and cosy in the cherry-red glow of the stove, I knew that in the morning there would only be dead ashes in the grate, my breath a fog of condensation and the windows opaque with ice. Brrr! What a life! I snuggled down. But, expecting to have the drone of bombers and the thump of guns in my ears all night, I was pleasantly surprised. Nothing at all. The Huns must be having the day off!

249 Squadron had been at North Weald since 1 September 1940 and now shared the airfield with 56. We flew Mark I Hurricanes, as did the various squadrons operating in turn from Stapleford Tawney, our satellite aerodrome situated a few miles to the south. Apart from 249, which was to remain at North Weald for almost a year, a number of other squadrons had come and gone as casualties occurred 151, 25, 46, 257 and of course 56 – all of them joining us for a few weeks, or months, at a time. In terms of losses, having suffered eight fatalities and around twenty pilots wounded and injured during the Battle of Britain and after, 249 had fared better than most, and as many of the lesser damaged pilots had since returned, the squadron retained much of its early identity and character.

At the commencement of 1941, Squadron Leader R. A. Barton - 'Butch' to us all – commanded 249, John Grandy, the original CO, having moved on after an injury sustained in September when he had baled out. Keith Lofts, late of 615 Squadron, was now the flight commander of 'A' Flight and I commanded 'B' Flight, longevity, good fortune and a modicum of success resulting in my promotion in December to Flight Lieutenant – acting, needless to say! During our six months of fighting, we believed we had become the second-highest-scoring squadron in 11 Group and with one Victoria Cross and eight or nine DFCs and a DFM to our credit, among the most highly decorated. All in all, we were pretty pleased with ourselves, justifiably so in our view, and smugly aware of our prowess as fighter pilots.

One fly only was there in our ointment; we were equipped with an aircraft which, whilst it had been adequate during the Battle of Britain, could not now engage enemy fighters on even terms. Not surprisingly, therefore, we constantly, and often belligerently, discussed the late delivery of our Mark II Hurricanes which we had been promised for months past. Most of the Spit squadrons had been re-equipped with the Mark II Spitfire the previous autumn and there was even talk of them getting something called a Mark V, with cannons and all sorts of things! What about us? What was going on, for heaven's sake?

After a summer and autumn of frenzied activity, December's winter weather had brought with it period of relaxation which showed every sign of continuing throughout January and beyond. For the first time since June, 1940, we had time to examine tactics, polish up our formation flying, and check up on our marksmanship using our cine-guns in mock combat and our eight Brownings against ground targets at Dengie Flats, a firing range off the Essex coast. At the same time, we still had our operational duties to perform, principally the protection of convoys in the Thames estuary and up the east coast, the interception of lone raiders by day and night, and the occasional foray into France both in strength and in harassing sections of two. These last named excursions were left to volunteers and were not exactly popular; considered in terms of profit and loss, the odds were heavily weighted in favour of loss, as, at low level, the chances of being damaged by flak were considerable and the likelihood of inflicting any worthwhile hurt to the enemy, pretty remote. However, these 'mosquitoes', so called, were encouraged by both Command and Group as a means of fostering the offensive spirit. Offensive spirit! Although only twenty years of age, I had already made more than 150 flights against the enemy, so that I did not consider it necessary to demonstrate my offensive spirit by taking part in any such unprofitable exercises; with eight machine guns we could not inflict much lasting damage on a water-tower or even a railway engine and the French farmers were not likely to thank us for killing their livestock, destroying their farm vehicles and buildings and generally putting the fear of God into their workers. In fact, the only enemy installations worth attacking were airfields, gun positions, military transport and trains, together with shipping, and it was a very short-sighted Hurricane pilot indeed who took on any of those targets without a good deal of careful thought and planning. Germans, in the main, shot back and could not be relied on to miss; moreover, we were flying an aircraft which was at least 30 mph slower than the Me 109 (now referred to as the Bf 109; We never knew it as such during the entire period of the war) in level flight, so that, if intercepted, we had a fight on our hands whether we liked it or not.

It was against this background and because it was 249's allotted day, that I prepared for my first 'mosquito' on the morning of 12 January, having selected Sergeant Davidson to accompany me.

'Appy 'Arry Davidson was one of 249's stalwarts and had been in the squadron almost from the outset. A long-time acquaintance of mine, having been with me at No. 17 Elementary and Reserve Flying Training School in Manchester before the war, Harry Davidson and I knew each other well and I had the greatest respect for his courage and ability. Moreover, besides having a northern accent that would shatter glass, he had a grand sense of humour and his laughter – positively infectious – was one of the squadron's greatest assets. Together we pored over a map and made our plan.

We would go in over Gravellines, I proposed; they hadn't shot at us there last time and there was at least a chance that they would not do so again. Davidson nodded – all right so far! After which, we would go round the back of Calais, cross the main railway line running from Calais to St Omer and Arras, then continue round the rear of Boulogne to come out a little north of Le Touquet. With luck we might catch some military vehicles on the roads or an unsuspecting train; on the other hand, if luck was against us, we could well run into some of the 109s based at St Omer. How did he feel? Davidson approved, but not with any enthusiasm. What did we do if we bumped into any of those little yellow buggers? – Davidsons frequently used term for 109s. My reply was succinct: nip into cloud as quick as a flash and head for home; two Hurricanes taking on the whole German Air Force over one of its own bases was simply asking for trouble. My partner agreed – none of this hero stuff for him, if I didn't mind. Then, after discussing emergencies and other tactics, we separated for lunch, a meal I ate with far less than my usual relish.

We took off at 2.45pm. There was complete cloud cover at little more than 1,000 feet and a good deal of thick mist. Splendid! Just the conditions we needed. Maintaining RT silence, we flew south over Essex and Kent, feeling our way forward in the fringes of the cloud, and eventually crossed the coast north of Deal. At which point, the mist thinned out, the clouds broke up and the sun shone through. Still heading south and now about twenty feet above the waves, my heart sank. However, as arranged, I maintained a tight-lipped silence and pressed on.

By the time we were approaching the French coast, there was hardly a cloud in sight. Davidson, on my right, was looking at me stoically but with a mute and pleading stare that suggested he was willing me to turn back. I couldn't, though, could I? Not until we had had a proper look.

With the flat coastline at Gravellines racing towards us, my mind was in a whirl. Did I press on as a hero, or make the common-sense decision and turn round; 'mosquitos' were never intended to be carried out in clear weather, the essential ingredient was cloud cover, and of that we had none. Were we not inviting trouble? But, too late; the water's edge slid obliquely beneath us and France lay ahead, white with snow, blue sky above, and visibility more than tolerable. Perfect, in fact – for the Huns!

Feeling a responsibility for Davidson's skin as well as my own, I broke RT silence. 'Red two. How d'you feel? Do you want to go on?'

My partner's response was prompt and to the point. 'No!'

Without another syllable being uttered, we flung our aircraft into rate-four turns and beat a hasty retreat. No heroes, we!

As a postscript to this incident, shortly after, two others of 249 were engaged on a similar exercise. Following roughly the same course, they let down from the fringes of the cloud, expecting to find the French coast immediately ahead. It was. But so was a flock of 109s. Horrified, they barged their way through the enemy before turning to escape. Which they succeeded in doing, but not with much to spare.

Landing back at North Weald limp with emotion, they immediately contacted Sector and Group demanding to know the reason for the quite unusual Hun activity, soon to be informed that aircraft of 242 Squadron had apparently been abroad since early morning, stirring up the enemy on what was *not* their allotted day.

The solemn prayer that rose from our dispersal hut on that occasion invited God to *bless* Douglas Bader and 242 Squadron – and to reward them, richly!

January dragged on with fog, and snow, and cold. Our Hurricanes, silent mist-draped spectres, stood chocked and tarpaulined on their hard standings – dripping. In fact, everything dripped. Then froze. Then dripped again.

Several times, we attempted to clear snow from the main runway using garden shovels, becoming painfully aware of its vast dimensions. Victor Beamish joined us, exhorting us to greater efforts in his Irish brogue – 'Come on, Ginger! You can do better than that!' And Ginger, exhausted and with his feet and fingers frozen to stone, grinned back and wished he were miles away; in a desert somewhere, anywhere but North Weald at that particular moment. Someone observed that not only did we have to fight for our lives, we were 'Works and Bricks' as well; we'd be painting the ruddy aircraft next! But our grinning protests were made in the best of spirit; anything we did, Victor did. A fine man, whose watchword was example; *the* fundamental of successful leadership.

No sooner had we dug the runway clear, however, than the snow came in a blizzard and nullified all our effort and sweat. And with it on the 15th, the unsmiling Air Marshal Sir William Sholto Douglas (appointed Commander-in-Chief, Fighter Command, November 1940) with heartening news of our Hurricane IIs and an outline of plans for the better spring weather ahead. Our new aircraft were on the way, he assured us – within two months, anyway – some with twelve guns and others with four 20mm cannons. As for the future, we were going to have a busy time; lots more bombers to escort, many more fighter-sweeps to take part in, masses of everything, in fact. We listened in silence, on the whole uplifted but with reservations. Seeing was believing as far as our new aircraft were concerned; we had heard those promises before. Moreover, no one at North Weald had yet flown a Mark II so that we knew nothing of its capabilities; we just hoped it had the performance, particularly above 20,000 feet, that would enable us to fight with some expectation of success. The sweeps over France, two and three squadrons strong, seemed promising enough but playing nurse-maid to bombers raised doubts in our minds. The Blenheims always insisted on staying low and didn't go fast enough for our liking, moreover, we in Hurricanes seemed always to be stuck with the unenviable task of providing close-escort. Why didn't the Spits take their turn? Instead of waltzing about at height, away from all the flak and having that cushy speed advantage that height always afforded?

The following day, Air-Vice-Marshal Trafford Leigh-Mallory (AOC No. 11 Group since November 1940) turned up and repeated Sholto Douglas's message, more or less. However, I was not there to hear him, Victor Beamish and four others of us in 249 being summoned to Duxford that day. To an investiture. To meet the King.

I travelled up to Duxford muffled to the ears and exhaling a fog of vapour in the back of Victor's ice-box of a staff car. The countryside crisply white and in the iron grip of winter, we hardly saw either a vehicle or another living person during the twenty-five-mile journey. Strangely, I had never been to Duxford despite it being so near; Duxford to me was 12 Group, up north, and as foreign and remote as Tibet. At North Weald, we always looked south towards the enemy and flew in that direction.

We arrived a little before lunch and assembled in the ante-room of the officers' mess. Shortly after, the King and Queen joined us and were introduced to a number of the more senior among us. Victor Beamish was called forward and immediately went into shock, remaining frozen at attention and almost speechless as the royal couple attempted, not with much success, to converse with him. I was surprised and amused, secretly that is; Victor, a lion in the air, totally abashed in the presence of his monarch.

The occasion was stiffly formal at first but within minutes the ice was broken when the royal couple was invited to play shove- ha'penny. An inexpert game followed in which the King used his left hand and he and his spouse exchanged a flow of light-hearted banter, the Queen making loud and uncomplimentary asides about her husband's lack of expertise. And all the time, he responded without a trace of the stammer we knew so well, a profound relief to all of us who, over the years, had listened to him labouring through his Christmas Day broadcasts to homeland and Empire. As honoured guests of the mess and in the presence of their loyal officers, Their Majesties were relaxed, charming, and utterly normal, personifying for me in a quite remarkable and emotional way, the spirit and steadfastness of the nation. The King's moving broadcast message that first Christmas of the war remained fresh in my mind: 'And I said to the man who stood at the gate of the year, Give me a light that I may tread safely into the unknown–' and so on. An inspiring expression of faith from a sensitive man who so genuinely and obviously cared.

After lunching together, we walked across to one of the hangars where, because of the weather, the investiture had been arranged. As we were being marshalled and briefed, one of the resident squadrons circled the airfield as a precaution against attack.

There were about twenty-five of us to be decorated. When my name was called, with a degree of composure that surprised even me, I made my approach, saluted, then stepped forward. I was conscious of the King very much below me, quite a small man really, very brown with blue eyes, his face drawn and finely chiselled. The Queen alongside, her head cocked and a half-smile on her lips. The decoration was attached, His Majesty frowning in concentration. Then a few murmured words of congratulation, and a hand-shake – merely a touch of the fingers. After which I was turning and marching away, wondering what on earth I did next. Not to worry, though, my medal was spirited away and boxed, after which I was led off, all very quietly, smoothly and expertly done. No fuss. I hadn't tripped or bumped into the furniture! The investiture was over.

Minutes later I was with Victor Beamish and part of a small group around which members of the press were circling like vultures.

Victor, embarrassed, was protesting and waving them away. The men with the cameras were insistent, though, following us about at a run. Victor had his way, however, and they gradually fell back. We didn't want all this publicity, did we Ginger? Ginger, not sharing his reticence, lacked the courage to say so. With the result, I was led away like a lamb, looking sorrowfully over my shoulder at our pursuers who were trailing behind and losing ground.

Back at North Weald the following day, I was one of only two who took to the air a little after dark. Bogeys expected off the east coast, was the urgent message. As I climbed away eastwards and into the blackness to wander about miles out to sea off Clacton at 12,000 feet, the ritual and ceremony of the previous day seemed as remote and as distant as a dream. Would the royal couple – sitting down to meat and two veg, no doubt – be aware that their 'trusty and well-beloved' Flight Lieutenant Neil, was protecting the nation pretty well single-handed? Freezing to death, too, by George, and trying hard not to think about what would happen if the Merlin engine, roaring and flaring in front of him, suddenly conked out.

Days later, in all the daily papers, there were photographs of the Monarch decorating some of his gallant 'Few'. But none of Victor Beamish nor of me. My parents were surprised and disappointed. I did go to the investiture, didn't I? In which case, what had happened to the pictures of their son?

For the last ten days of the month it was English weather at its most vile – snow, low cloud, and fog. Most of the squadron went into hibernation, yarned and read around the huge coal-fire in the anteroom, played endless games of shove-ha'penny and snooker, or went to the cinema and the pubs in Epping. Even toiled all the way into the seamier corners of London.

One morning, in order to ginger ourselves up, a football game was arranged between 56 Squadron and 249 and held at 56's dispersal. Victor Beamish took part and trotted onto the pitch all togged out as though for Twickenham.

It was a game notable for its enthusiasm rather than its expertise, although there were several among us who were more than competent. After an hour of racing about, shouting and kicking, fatigue took its toll and it was clear that 56, who were winning, were rather the better side. Victor, who was playing with 249 and had very little skill at soccer, even to the point of trying to stand on the ball, kept roaring us on, his face set with determination, calling us a 'clapped out set of bloody ducks'. Alas, his insults and exhortations had very little effect, as, bent double with laughter as much as tiredness, we were quite unable to respond, which, of course, infuriated him even more. No, Victor Beamish was not one of nature's losers, not even in a game he knew so little about.

And it was on 17 January that I learned I was to be sent north on an unusual duty. A telephone message from Air Ministry explained that I had been selected to take part in a month-long Cotton Industry War Exhibition in Lancashire and that I would be expected to give a number of speeches to various official bodies and tour a group of mills in the area. Meanwhile, as a preliminary, I was to call upon Wing Commander Lord Willoughby de

Broke at Air Ministry, to be briefed.

The briefing was harmless enough. I was taken to lunch by the Wing Commander – a charming man who had commanded one of the Auxiliary Squadrons before the war – who explained that as I came from Lancashire and knew all about mills and cotton and that sort of thing, I was the natural choice. I replied that although I came from Lancashire I knew absolutely nothing about mills and cotton, except that the raw material – very smelly – came into Liverpool and Manchester in big ships. Not to worry, said the Wing Commander comfortably, any speeches I would be required to make would be produced for me by experts. And, of course, I could expect to be warmly entertained by officials of the Cotton Board, if I saw what he meant – he gave a conspirator's wink. He would be sending details of who I was and what I had accomplished over the past six months, so that there was no question of my not having a good time. Which he did, causing me endless embarrassment, as his letter was sent to my home where it was opened in my absence by my parents, who, among other incidents I had never thought fit to mention, learned for the first time that I had recently had a mid-air collision and been forced to bale out. But, unaware of the frowns and rod-in-pickle that awaited me, I was happy to be given the opportunity of spending an unscheduled week at home and travelled north to Manchester by train.

The crowded week that followed, during which I was given a fascinating insight into the life-style of the Lancashire cotton-worker, broadened my education no end. Although I had grown up within a few miles of some of the largest mills in the county, I had only occasionally rubbed shoulders with the male element of the cotton-mill community when watching Rugby League football at Swinton or soccer at Old Trafford. And, as I was soon to learn, they were astonishingly different – and not just the men!

The exhibition opened in Oldham, where, in company with a Flight Lieutenant Stanton of Bomber Command, I was called upon to address an impressive gathering of local MPs, Mayors, mill managers, cotton VIPs and union officials, all of them sombrely and noddingly attentive in dark, shiny suits and gold chains of office. And my speeches, mostly high-flown compliments and mild exaggerations, were formulated without a single word of guidance from the so-called 'experts'. After which there was the first of an endless series of pub lunches, the menu unvarying – wafer-thin slices of almost inedible topside beef, rubber circles of Yorkshire pudding, and mounds of wet cabbage, followed by trifle or sticky pudding topped with inches of custard the consistency of yellow glue. All of which, I shudder to admit, I fell upon with the zest and appetite of youth.

But it was the visits to the mills that really opened my eyes.

The Lancashire cotton-mills played a vital part in the war effort making the basic fabrics for a wide variety of articles, including the parachute harness I strapped to my behind and the Sidcot flying suit I seldom wore. The spinning and weaving mills themselves were enormous, vast five- and six-storey buildings crammed with clattering machinery producing a cacophony of sound that beggared description. The mill workers – thousands of them – were mostly lip-reading women, old and young and of all shapes and sizes, most of them wearing clogs and all with a peasant earthiness about them in matters of dress, manner and speech. Even the most spectral of Lowry's paintings of the industrial north fail to convey to me now the starkly primitive atmosphere of the cotton industry in war-time Lancashire. And these were the people of my audiences!

Problem number one was to make myself heard. As the machinery could never be switched off, I was usually obliged to make up to twelve speeches in each mill, one at each end of the six floors and all at the top of my voice. After which there was always one extra performance for management, followed by a 'jug o' summat roun' t' corner'. Twelve speeches each mill! Five mills each day! And two or three 'bevvys' to follow. My week was anything but tame.

Most off-putting, however, were the female operatives. To them, I was fair game. Twenty years old, clad in my best blue uniform with wings, decorations and gloves, pinkly naive and having a posh accent, I must have seemed like someone from outer space. Throughout, I was referred to as 'luv' or 'chuck', invited to sign everything from autograph books to pieces of lavatory paper, given buns and 'toffees'as though I were a Belle Vue chimpanzee, and touched, pinched, kissed, generally explored and made the recipient of some pretty earthy proposals. All of which I bore with manful aplomb, my cheeks a permanent scarlet. In fact, a remark made before one of my earlier addresses will long be remembered. I was standing on a box, looking down rather uncertainly on a crowd of about thirty girls, all of whom were eyeing me with every emotion from amusement to downright lust. As I opened my mouth to utter my first sentence, a voice cut through with crystal clarity:

'Ayee! Wot about one night o' luv in bed wi' 'im?'

That was the sense of the remark anyway; the words employed were more colourfully farmyard!

I drove back to North Weald on 7 February to find that little had happened in my absence. There was still a lot of snow about and the threat of more to come. The squadron had made two uneventful sweeps over France in conjunction with 56 and 611, the latter flying Spits from Hornchurch, and there had been sporadic activity by individual Hun bombers in our area, resulting in one or two interceptions. 'Butch' Barton, with Palliser and Thompson, had caught an Me 110 off Clacton and forced it into the sea and had then shot up a second which was later seen to crash off the Kentish Knock lightship. C-in-C Nore had been greatly bucked and had sent fulsome congratulations to the squadron; the average matelot, poor chap, was always tremendously uplifted by the sight of Huns crashing into the sea. On the debit side, however, the newly-promoted John Beard, who had been detached temporarily to ferry some aircraft around the country, had crashed a Spitfire and was back again in hospital at Melksham. Poor old Beard; misfortune really dogged his steps.

On the 8th, I took up GN-T and did a few loops to get my hand in, being pleased and not a little surprised when one of them turned out to be straight so that I thumped through my own slipstream. It struck me at the time that I had never really done any aerobatics since leaving FTS, flying in combat not requiring any such artistic irrelevancies. 56 Squadron was terribly good at the showbiz stuff, someone always seeming to be turning his aircraft inside-out over our dispersal. Strangely, 249 was not an 'aerobatic' squadron; I never saw any of our fellows put on a show, although we appeared to be the more successful operationally. 56 was full of good chaps, even so – Gracie, Wicks, Brooker, Higginson, Constable-Maxwell and others, and a little later their new commanding officer, Norman Ryder, whom I had met when he was with 41 Squadron. In all, a grand crowd.

February the tenth, and action – action I was to remember mainly for its consequences.

We had been instructed to escort six Blenheims of 114 Squadron, who were to bomb the docks at Dunkirk. Clinging to the old formula, the Blenheims had decided to attack from 7,000 to 8,000 feet, and 56 were to act as close escort. 17 Squadron, with whom we had not worked before, were to fly on the right flank at 14,000 feet, with 249 to the rear, acting as top cover, 1,000 feet higher. I was fairly light-hearted about the whole event. I would be well above the low flak, which had frightened me half to death in January, and, high up, we would have complete freedom of action to move around as we pleased.

Making up the state board, I decided to lead the rearmost section and chose Crossey, Lewis and Davis to make up my four. In my opinion, I could not have had a more worthy bunch; Lewis, who had about eighteen Huns to his credit, Crossey, who had fought alongside me since August, and the charming Sergeant Davis, who reminded me so much of P. G. Wodehouse's Bertie Wooster. For Davis it was a red-letter occasion. He had heard only the day before that he had been commissioned, but being unable to provide himself with a pilot officer's uniform, had turned up at dispersal in the only uniform he possessed, that of an NCO. We all congratulated him, laughing meanwhile and speculating as to what would happen if he were shot down; he would never be able to convince the Huns that he was an officer and would probably spend the rest of the war digging lavatories.

We took off at 11.50, with the weather fine and clear. I was feeling bright and alert, eager to see something and to have a go.

After meeting the bombers over Kent, we climbed up in the direction of Calais, having decided to cross into France at Gravellines and to fly inland before turning left towards Dunkirk. Around Calais, the first ack-ack began to pockmark the sky with its silent puff-balls of venom, not too accurate though and no threat to me or my section. At around 15,000 feet, I led my three companions in a wide meander at the rear of the main formation, the bombers a long way below, the rest of 249 and other Hurricanes, dots of varying size, moving en masse to the south and east. This was it! If we were going to be jumped, this was the place it would happen.

Just short of Dunkirk, there was an urgent jabber of RT; the enemy somewhere, but where? Eyes darting, I tucked down my nose to work up a little speed, my cockpit already prepared for an emergency. Thereafter, events moved quickly before degenerating into confusion.

At about 14,000 feet, I was tidily leading my section of four in a streaming turn. On the qui-vive for 109s, I saw a twin-engined aircraft far below – plainly not a Blenheim and therefore a Hun –and deciding that there was nothing much doing at height, tumbled down in pursuit, the thrill of the chase an ecstatic, bubbling surge.

A little inland now and going very fast. Far below, the Hun was flying parallel to the coast but veering south, no doubt alarmed by all the commotion above. Then, more ack-ack to my left, rather high this time, and something distinctly red, a signal flare, possibly. For the 109s? I had no idea. My Hurricane now tight and shivering with speed. Where were the others? I looked about but could see no one. Damn it, why had they left me? Very fast now, at about 40 degrees, fairly racing down and absolutely committed. Some aircraft away to my left but not identifiable. Bomb bursts in the water off a town I assumed to be Dunkirk. And smoke, rising – they'd hit something, anyway. But, having taken my eye off the Hun bomber, it had disappeared, as had everyone else! Where was everybody, for God's sake? I pulled out, everything bending and draining, and turned left. Then, climbing hard, crossed the coast without interference. Feeling very naked, I looked urgently for 109s; but there weren't any, or none that I could see. Masses of flak, though, and Hurricanes in the distance, turning away. What was happening? I flew towards them. More urgent chatter on the RT. I was not at much more than 5,000 feet, on edge and unhappy, clearly missing something, but what? Then, in the distance and at about the same height, the Blenheims, going home, with more aircraft which I hoped were Hurricanes. I climbed in their direction and found myself flying north-west. Masses of cold looking sea. Lord, what a mess! Still, I was in one piece, wasn't I? Feeling more secure, I maintained a careful watch on my tail even so, until, after a long time, the coast of Kent approached to within gliding distance. At which point there were Hurricanes everywhere. All going home. Unconcerned.

When later I taxied onto my hard standing to stop, I saw Gerald Lewis's

Hurricane just ahead of me. He was still in the cockpit as I dropped to the ground and I saw him waving his arms in my direction. When I walked towards him, I could see why. There was massive damage to the left-hand side of his cockpit, as though some demon axe-man had been hard at work. No wonder he was upset; it was a miracle he had not been killed or wounded badly. His voice, when I approached, was shrill with outrage.

'Look at this bloody lot, for God's sake!'

As I looked up, surveying the damage, Crossey approached. We had been heavily attacked, it appeared.

Attacked! By whom? I had seen nothing.

They were 109s apparently, Hun fighters seen by both of them, but not by me.

We discussed and commiserated together excitedly, the aftermath of battle quickening our speech. Where was Davis? We looked about counting. No Davis! We looked again. No sign of Davis or of his aircraft. Not a goner, surely? Poor old chap! So cheerful and happy a mere ninety minutes ago.

Full of suppressed annoyance, more from my own lack of involvement than anything else, I walked off in the direction of dispersal, fell into step with Victor Beamish, who was also returning, and let fly. What on earth was the use of trying to take on the Huns in Mark Is? We couldn't catch anything, we couldn't even run. And now Davis looked as if he had been shot down, with Lewis, as near as dammit, another casualty. I would rather be anywhere than this, I lamented, the Western Desert, anywhere. At least in the desert the weather was decent and, if clobbered, a chap could always force-lob and walk home. If only we had some decent aircraft!

Victor listened sympathetically, more than mildly interested, I sensed. Was I really serious about going abroad? The adrenalin surging, I rashly confirmed that nothing would suit me better. The squadron, too, for that matter.

In the dispersal hut, things were being sorted out: the Blenheims, with 56 and 17, had returned unharmed, only 249 had been engaged. Our two Polish NCOs, Maciejowski and Bjeski, were each claiming a 109 destroyed and the little man Palliser was describing how the pilot of the 109 he had shot at had apparently been killed, his aircraft continuing to fly dead straight and level. He thought, too, that he had seen Lewis being attacked by a 109 and that Davis had most certainly gone, shot down into the sea, probably.

Talk and more talk, queries, laughter, explanations. The emotion ebbed away. Slowly. Poor old Davis. Such a nice chap, who had fought so gallantly for months on end. To be lost on the day he was commissioned, too. Most strange that I had not seen those 109s, though. How could it possibly have happened? No, on the whole not a good day, in spite of the several Huns to our credit. And so confusing.

Nothing happened the following morning, but in the afternoon we were back on the treadmill of scramble, climb and patrol. Ten of us swarmed up above North Foreland then turned south to beat a path between Manston and Dungeness for more than an hour, a wilderness of cloud beneath us with glimpses of Kent still white from the ravages of winter. We froze, our hands and feet leaden with cold, and were monumentally bored. As there didn't seem to be any Huns around, why all this patrolling, we wondered? The enemy knew perfectly well we were now on the offensive, and as their invasion plans had plainly been shelved and with their own fighter attacks on England only of nuisance value, surely their best course of action was to sit tight and wait for us to turn up over France, escorting our slow- motion bombers and doing all the damn silly things they had done six months earlier. So what were we doing up here, freezing to death?

Then, a day or so after, there started an endless series of convoy patrols in the estuary and up the east coast, a chore which was happily denied me as Air Ministry telephoned and instructed me to go north again to make more speeches and visit more cotton mills.

In the event, it was the mixture as before, except that this time I was better prepared to cope with the more tiresome and embarrassing aspects of the visit. And the pub lunches with the wet cabbage!

My penance completed, I returned to North Weald on 16 February. It was good to be home again.

17

A Time of Change

The early months of 1941 saw 249 Squadron in the midst of change. Those of us who had been with the squadron since the previous summer had each completed around 200 hours of operational flying, many being shot down, burned, wounded or having suffered some other traumatic experience. Inevitably, therefore, the first weeks of the year saw a gradual drifting away of some of our longer-serving members, a period of sadness and nostalgia for those who remained, despite there being a lively flicker of rejuvenation as new faces began to appear.

At the outset, 249 was largely made up of Volunteer Reservists, stiffened by a nucleus of regular officers who provided Service if not combat experience, our average age being twenty-two. The vast majority of squadron members in Fighter Command were from the United Kingdom, although in 249 there was a significant overseas element, principally from South Africa. There were, in fact, quite a few South Africans in the Royal Air Force at the outbreak of war, as were there New Zealanders, Canadians, Australians and others from the Dominions, all forming a gallant and highly successful fighting element in our midst, if indistinguishable from the rest of us in terms of language and uniform. But of French, Polish, Belgian, Czechs and others, in 249 there were none – none, that is, until the last few days of September, 1940, when several suddenly appeared on the doorstep of our dispersal hut. Such was their contribution to 249's success and their sometimes unique flair for the unusual, that not to mention them would be to distort history.

When France fell in the summer of 1940, a substantial number of trained airmen from the recently subjugated countries moved across to Britain where plans were made to form them into national squadrons within the RAF. By the spring of 1941, these plans were well advanced but, in the meantime, a number of the more experienced had been farmed out to most fighter units, 249 being host and guardian to five or six over a period of seven months.

Not unexpectedly, there was a language difficulty, which was less of a problem on the ground than in the air, where the exchange of vital information could not only be a trial – and a yawning bore to everyone else who happened to be on the same radio frequency! – but sometimes, too, a wildly hilarious exercise in non-comprehension. Getting our allies to the scene of the action proved easy enough, they simply followed the rest of us and piled in on arrival; getting them home, however, was another matter entirely, particularly in bad weather and at a time when Air Traffic Control, as we now know it, did not exist and the means of identifying and 'fixing' aircraft involved radar and triangulation procedures carried out at Sector, often miles away from the parent airfield.

249's first group of 'foreigners' included a Polish officer, 'George' Solak, who not only spoke good English but was soon to emerge as the squadron philosopher and Job's comforter, and four NCOs, two Polish and two French. The two Polish airmen were delightful – but silent! One in particular, Sergeant Maciejowski, quickly resolved the problem of returning after combat by landing on the first convenient spot he could find, if not an aerodrome, a field – any field! – a solution which occasionally resulted in situations degenerating into pure farce. On one occasion, having landed in a pasture near the south coast and being unable to make himself understood, he was marched off by the police and locked up on suspicion of being a fifth-columnist, only being released when one none-too-pleased member of the squadron had been obliged to travel more than 100 miles in order to identify him.

Operationally, the five more than played their part during the late-autumn battles. Within days of arriving at North Weald, 'Micky', later to be awarded a much deserved DFM, had a spirited encounter with one of our own Hampdens and, at about the same time, Sergeant Bjeski stunned us all one day by announcing that he had engaged a four-engined Focke-Wulf Condor off Cherbourg. Focke- Wulf Condor! Off Cherbourg! We could scarcely believe our ears.

The Frenchmen, too, Perrin and Bouquillard, threw themselves into combat with true Gallic flair and panache. Within days of arriving, Bouquillard had run out of fuel and crashed his aircraft and both managed to sustain battle damage at times when it was difficult to understand why, Perrin, in particular, not exactly endearing himself to me when he bailed out of GN-F (As I write, the remains of this aircraft, V7313, are in process of being dug up in the area of Canterbury), my own beloved Hurricane, when I was away on leave. Even so, they were liked and admired by everyone so that we greatly regretted their departure towards the end of the year, at which time they were replaced by two French officers, Francois de Labouchere and Emile Fayolle. At about the same time, two additional Polish pilots were posted in, Flying Officer Skalski and Sergeant Popec, and later still, another French officer, Captain de Scitevaux.

Having watched their homelands crumble to defeat and been shattered by personal misfortune, it is hardly surprising that the newcomers were, in the main, survivors. Despite being in England only a matter of months, each of them had a knowledge of the less salubrious parts of London that had the rest of us wide-eyed with respect, and to witness the two French officers, in a perfumed fog of talc and pomade, preparing themselves for a night of divertissement in the big city, was something of an education – for me, anyway. Labouchere, who was devastatingly handsome and looked and sounded more like Charles Boyer (with hair) than the man himself, had captured the heart of Cecilia College, the then world ice-skating champion, a ravishing young lady in whose direction I was only too happy to make sheep's eyes myself when the opportunity arose. Even George Solak, who exhibited few signs of being a ladies' man, was in a class of his own when it came to knowing not only the 'dives' but also the more respectable establishments, including one on Euston Road which dispensed a three-course meal to rival that served in Claridges for a mere half-a-crown

Even the more mature Skalski was awash with talents. In one of my letters home during the latter part of January I described how I, and others, had borrowed 'Butch' Barton's venerable Opel in order to spend a night in town – always a risky venture this as 'Butch's' cars seldom had a street value of more than £5! A little beyond Epping on our way in, smoke began to emerge from beneath the dashboard and there was a powerful smell of burning car, eventually diagnosed as no water in the engine. After filling the radiator several times, we eventually arrived in London and separated, agreeing to meet later that night for the return journey.

It was approaching midnight and pitch black when we set off and we were still well within city limits when all the electrics failed – no engine, no lights, nothing! In Stygian darkness we collected around the bonnet, looking miserable. Who knew anything about Opels and their innards? No one, it seemed. At which point Skalski stepped forward, eased us aside, then burying his head in the hot blackness of the engine, by feel alone conjured up a galaxy of sparks and had everything working in minutes. Except that the light switch operated the trafficators and everything else worked through twisted connections that could only be guessed at.

And Skalski possessed other talents, too.

As bad weather had ruled out all but essential flying since December, neither he nor the two new Frenchmen had done much in the way of aviation. To rectify this, Skalski was sent off one afternoon on a low-level sector reconnaissance, disappearing with a wave of his hand and a glittering gold-toothed smile.

An hour or so later, just as it was growing dusk, much of eastern Essex suddenly found itself without electricity; our intrepid Pole had flown through the main power cables near Colchester.

Later that night, he arrived back at North Weald by car with his face looking like a well-wrapped parcel. He explained that, unsure of his position (not lost, mind you), he had been consulting his map, when – pouff! – lights! At which point his Hurricane had hit the ground and his face had connected violently with the gunsight. When we enquired at what height he had been flying, our continental colleague admitted with engaging frankness – twenty feet! As though twenty feet was the only height at which to consult a three-foot-square map in the gathering gloom and in the confined space of a Hurricane cockpit.

Sometime later and mindful of Skalski's potential for disaster, I carefully briefed him and two of the Frenchmen, Labouchere and de Scitevaux, for a simple formation-flying exercise. Various formations were to be attempted and each member was to take a spell at leading on an agreed signal, details of which we then discussed. Everything clear? A trio of heads nodded agreement and all three of them took off and disappeared into the eastern sky.

After a silence of twenty minutes or so, there came a spine-chilling wail. Tumbling out of dispersal to investigate, we observed a Hurricane limp slowly and painfully into the circuit before dropping to the grass like a shot grouse. Tottering to a standstill, it remained there – leaning – smoking – spent. Skalski had returned!

We raced across the airfield to where the aircraft stood and as we approached, the cause of the din became apparent. The Hurricane's Rotol airscrew was less than half its usual diameter of eleven feet, the oil tank in the port wing root had been torn out, and there was considerable damage to the bottom of the fuselage, most of which was coated with a thick layer of black goo.

At first, Skalski was not in a fit state to say anything, after which the horrible truth was revealed. Apparently, the first fifteen minutes of the exercise had gone swimmingly, after which Skalski as leader had made a sign which had been misinterpreted by both Frenchmen, each of whom had decided to take over the lead simultaneously, the whole event culminating in a wild and clamorous explosion of wings, airscrews, and bits of fuselage.

Skalski, the least affected, had been able to toil back home, his engine over-revving almost to melting point. The others, crippled, had fallen away earthwards from a very low altitude, de Scitevaux managing by some French miracle to round out sufficiently to strike the ground at a comparatively shallow angle, after which his Hurricane had made a brisk excursion through several fields, hedges and ditches, shedding pieces as it went, before rearing to a standstill – wrecked. Meanwhile, Labouchere, unable to control his aircraft, had jumped out at around 800 feet and by the greatest of good fortune had hit the ground on the first swing of his parachute. Later, the two of them returned to North Weald grinning like gargoyles and not in the least abashed, having with the aid of Skalski destroyed three perfectly good Hurricanes in the space of twenty minutes, something the Luftwaffe had failed to achieve since Christmas. That night, in our apology for a bar – bars were still officially frowned upon in officers' messes – there was loud laughter and hilarious descriptions of the event, in the course of which someone was heard to mutter in a rueful aside that we might do worse than persuade all three of them to fight on the other side!

Such a draconian solution was unnecessary, however, as within weeks, all our foreigners, Poles and French alike, had departed, to fade anonymously into the mists of distance and time. And little more than a year later, Bouquillard, Fayolle, and the handsome Labouchere were all dead, leaving with us only the memory of their deeds, their laughter, and their comradeship.

For most of 249, the final two weeks of February were remarkable for a single event, our new aircraft were delivered on the 15th. Up north at the time, I returned to find dispersal a mass of Hurricanes, eighteen of our old Mark Is and fifteen Mark IIs, some with eight guns, some with twelve, and several with four cannons. The squadron was delighted. Like children with new toys.

Four days later, I flew the one I had selected – GN-W (Z2638) – and was excitedly impressed. Like my first Hurricane nine months earlier, it was tight and bouncy, the engine silk-smooth, and there was the heady, intoxicating aroma of new paint. Super! I could hardly wait to go to war in it.

In fact, and on reflection, there was very little difference between the two marks of aircraft. The Mark II had a Merlin 20 engine which produced around 250 more horsepower, the principal advantage being that it had a manually controlled two-speed supercharger which, when engaged, came in with a disconcerting thud but increased the performance above 20,000 feet very substantially; whereas in a Mark I, I was never too optimistic when going into combat above 25,000 feet, the Mark II was still pretty active at something over 30,000. Moreover, in addition to allowing us more boost to play with low down, the makers had stuck a rudder-bias control on one of the cross members of the cockpit, the fuel tanks were self-sealing, and there were wing-root blanking plates installed to reduce the powerful draughts from wings to fuselage and therefore the risk of fire in the cockpit. These, plus a few other minor refinements, all added up to an aircraft some 20 mph faster than the original, more spritely at height, and a little more comfortable in which to fly. One thing they had not done, however, was provide us with any creature comforts; we were going to operate at altitudes where the ambient temperature was around minus 60 degrees centigrade, without a vestige of heat. I was in despair. Why, oh, why? Surely they could have done something!

In the days following, Pat Wells, who had just returned to the squadron having been shot down and wounded twice in three months, took his Mark II to 38,500 feet. I took my own to just under 37,000 feet, at which height I was so cold, so lacking in breath and so bored, that I gave up. Our oxygen system in the Hurricane remained fairly primitive as we still wore the old, ill-fitting fabric masks into which oxygen blew in the general direction of nose and mouth in a constant and wasteful stream. Moreover, I had never properly appreciated that towards 40,000 feet, due to the rarefied atmosphere, the voice disappeared almost completely, and that one's sinuses had to be in pretty good condition, too!

The introduction of our new Hurricanes, however, altered our activities not one jot, except that between bouts of sleet, rain and fog, our patrols over Manston, Dungeness, Boulogne and Calais, were at 30,000 instead of 20,000 feet. Patrols! Endless patrols, high and low, and as the days dragged by, increasingly over convoys moving in slow motion up and down the east coast. But ne'er a Hun did we see. Well ... almost none.

On the night of 25 February, I spent well over an hour high over Harwich and succeeded in intercepting one enemy aircraft which melted into the blackness before I could get in more than a fleeting burst. Lots of excitement, though, as my de Wilde ammunition produced a brief firework display in the darkness and as, for one moment, I really thought I might have shot down my first Hun at night. I then intercepted two of our own Wellingtons in quick succession, after which, with the adrenalin surging, I found myself in the midst of an intense ack-ack barrage which had me screaming abuse at the trigger-happy fools below.

It was about that time, too, that we heard that Davis, who had been lost over Dunkirk on the 10th, was a prisoner-of-war. The news bucked me up no end. Some chaps who had gone missing in the past hadn't concerned me particularly, but for Davis, who had been a member of my section at the time, I felt a special responsibility. Good old Davis! And having been identified as an officer, it seemed he wouldn't be digging lavatories after all.

We also had information that most of our Polish colleagues were to join 306 and 317 Squadrons immediately – Solak, Maciejowski, and the quiet and smiling Bjeski. Sad, sad news. And, at about the same time, an Air Commodore turned up to talk about the air-sea-rescue organisation, bringing with him one of the new seat-type dinghies, which he demonstrated. We were all to get them, apparently. Soon, too, enabling those of us who fell into the winter waters of the Channel to die of exposure by degrees instead of freezing to death quickly and painlessly. Yes, things were looking up all right.

Making up my logbook for the month, I saw that I had only flown twelve hours in February. Still I had been away for almost a fortnight, hadn't I?

Being in a fighter squadron just north of London in the early months of 1941, was, however, not all convoy patrols, flak, and sweeps over France. Since Christmas, and because of duff flying weather, we had been blessed with more than enough time off. Also, the publicity merchants were about in strength arranging photographic sessions and visits by foreign potentates – mostly American, coming to see whether or not we were going to lose the war (and their money) as predicted by their toothy Ambassador, Kennedy – and war artists, the latter commissioned to record Battle of Britain scenes and personalities. In December, with a number of my companions, I had sat for two of this small and prestigious group of war artists, Cuthbert Orde and Eric Kennington, on each occasion perched on a chair in the Ladies' Room of the mess, trying to look solemn whilst they sketched my face for posterity. Orde did me in charcoal and was really quite chatty; Kennington drew me in pastel and hardly uttered a syllable. Orde's drawing, in my opinion, was indifferent, Kennington's very good, although I did not think so at the time. He was a very tall, rather lugubrious-looking man who had been a close friend of Lawrence of Arabia and had illustrated Lawrence's famous book, 'Seven Pillars of Wisdom'. Throughout the sitting he produced not even a smile and when he had finished, I asked if I might examine his work (this portrait can now be seen at the RAF Museum, Hendon). When he agreed, with characteristic lack of tact, I damned it with faint praise, remarking that I thought it was 'all right' but that he had drawn my mouth incorrectly. Kennington, of international fame and who clearly had never before had his artistic accomplishments criticised in such a manner, was quite taken aback. That was the way he saw me, was his quietly contemptuous remark, and if I didn't like it, I had only myself to blame. And, of course, he was right, it was an excellent likeness, mirroring all my youthful moodiness and impetuosity.

Sadly, as the man is long since dead, I shall never be able to apologise and tell him how wrong I was.

And with the war artists and other visitors, there were the photographers, chief among whom was Cecil Beaton, who arrived at dispersal looking like an advertisement for Sandeman's Sherry. Most of us, including our Intelligence Officer, Woolmer, who, unbeknown to us, was a friend of his, were in the dispersal hut when he arrived and the several seconds that followed were nothing short of memorable.

Crossing the threshold, his face alight with recognition, Beaton cried out: 'Shirley!'

And Woolmer responded joyously, 'Cecil!'

After that, the rest of the day was never quite the same.

But no one could fault his photography. After taking a score or more photographs of the squadron in groups, I was invited to pose singly, which I did, then with one or two others, plus Wilfred the duck (249 Squadron then had a small menagerie of dog, kittens and ducks plus, from time to time, a broody hen to hatch the duck eggs – produced by 'Wilfred'!), most of the pictures appearing in the glossy magazines a few weeks later and in exhibitions and book-form for the next seventy-five years! One early series was printed in the American periodical Vogue and went around the world, the photographs superb but the accompanying text, quite nauseating – gross exaggerations and untruths which had me, and others, curling up with embarrassment. Were future generations to learn about the war reading this sort of nonsense?

And on our days off, I occasionally went into London, mostly with Crossey and the others, but now and then on my own. One such visit was rather different.

Throughout the winter, the Huns had bombed London constantly, the East End in particular being reduced to a shambles and even the West End shattered and torn in places. Rarely a night passed without our hearing the discordant drone of enemy aircraft, en route to somewhere, if not London, accompanied by the whistle and thump of bombs and the rapid 'tonk-tonk-tonk-tonk' of our own ack-ack. Eventually raids became so commonplace that the citizens of the capital city hardly reacted, continuing to go about their daily affairs with a quite extraordinary attitude of indifference.

I had gone into London to meet an old school acquaintance of mine. Some three or four years older than me, he had been at university reading chemistry when war had broken out and now, in a reserved occupation, had taken up an appointment in London. After spending the afternoon together we had dinner in the West End, after which he insisted on taking me back to his digs, which were in Kensington.

As darkness fell, the bombers began one of their nightly visitations and towards midnight the raid became so heavy, with some pretty violent thumps in our vicinity, that it was deemed prudent to go down into the basement.

Having by this time been persuaded to stay the night, I found myself below ground and in the company of a dozen other people of varying ages who shared the same four-storey house, mostly professional men and women, some dressed, others in night-wear and slippers, all of them with pillows, torches, candles and flasks. There was no fuss or excitement; they had obviously done this many times before and either conversed quietly, read books, or tried to sleep. After all, it was business as usual tomorrow, wasn't it?

I was sitting on the floor, dozing, with my back to a wall and the head of some strange young woman, who was asleep, on my shoulder. It was about 2 a.m. Suddenly there was a single crash which shook the whole building and brought down bits of the ceiling. Everyone awoke with a jerk but after a minute or two of relieved laughter and conversation, peace was restored and nothing more was heard for the rest of the night. An hour or two later, the all-clear sounded, although I did not hear it at the time.

With everyone else, I was up early the next morning and ready to leave shortly after seven. Very much aware that I was in uniform but unshaven – there was neither water nor electricity – I went out into the street intending to get back to North Weald as quickly as possible.

Further down the road, about fifty yards away, there was a mountain of rubble crawling with men of the fire, ambulance and rescue services, obviously the source of the big bang we had heard in the night. As I approached then stopped to watch, stretcher bearers were carrying out bodies, alive and dead. I looked on, silently shocked by the sight of so much tragedy. There was no dignity in some of the sprawling forms, night-clothes filthy, ripped and torn, waxen figures with bloodied and naked limbs splayed out, private parts modestly covered, even on the dead. At one point I stepped forward to lend a hand as two dust-encrusted men in tin hats stumbled and almost fell with one of their lolling, stretchered burdens. One of them looked up and taking in my uniform and rank, motioned me away with a jerk of his head.

'Mind yer back, guv. You'll only get yourself dirty.'

I fell back. Dirty! Get myself dirty! I, who had been fighting almost every day for more than eight months! I felt a sharp pang of rejection, hurt and shame. Dirty, for God's sake!

And my school chum? I never saw him again. His quietly envious glances at my uniform, wings and decorations during our all too brief time together had disclosed feelings of deep unease. Shortly after, he talked his way out of his reserved occupation and volunteered for aircrew. More than a year later, and a trainee navigator in an Anson, his pilot flew him into a Welsh mountain and he was killed. A sad, sad loss. He never saw combat, never even reached a squadron; one of three fine brothers who were to die in action or on active service. Some families seemed fated to suffer so much, and so unfairly.

March. Wind, rain and low cloud. And convoy patrols.

Convoy patrols! The memory of them remains. Two aircraft at a time. Take-off, but keep below the fringes of the cloud. Zero-nine- zero degrees on the compass, set the Direction Indicator. The Blackwater – always the same mirror-smooth inlet with its stationary sailing ship at the top end, probably a wreck but it looked whole enough from the air. Then Clacton, or somewhere, and the sea. The sea! – my Hurricane's single engine suddenly much less smooth. Grey, endless, chilly water and in the distance, ships lying like matchsticks end-to-end in a gutter. Over the mast-tops now, a quick wag of the wings for recognition purposes, then up and down at 1,000 feet; up and down, up and down. Endlessly. Further north now, the balloons at Harwich off to the left, glowering at us from the fringes of the cloud. Balloons! Avoid those blighters at all costs! Backwards and forwards, huddled and bored. Anything doing? 'Lumba's' reply: nothing to report. Counting the minutes, thirty, forty-five, then sixty, occasionally longer. Now and then as far north as Southwold. Southwold! God, we'd be in Scotland next! Eventually turning wearily for home. First the coast and the balloons again, then the familiar, dead-straight railway line from Colchester to Chelmsford, racing a train below pluming a long trail of smoke and steam. At Chelmsford, right-turn onto 270 degrees to fly for three long-drawn-out minutes. Then, if greenhouses suddenly appeared beneath, turn round and go back because we had overshot. Eyes straining for the faint lines of the North Weald masts through all the mist and cloud. Bloody weather! Thank God for the masts!

In our new Mark IIs, we flew on nothing other than convoy patrols for the first twelve days of March, stopping only for bad weather, of which there was plenty. No Huns. Nothing. Only the cold grey sea, and ships, and boredom.

Then, on the 13th, with 56 Squadron and 303 from Northolt, we took six Blenheims to bomb a target near Dunkirk. Poor old 56 were alongside the bombers yet again, with 249 stepped up to 20,000 feet. And above us the Poles of 303, not exactly to our liking as we were well aware that if our gallant allies became fed up – which was more than likely – they were not above dropping down on those beneath and giving a quick squirt, apologising afterwards with the excuse that they thought they were shooting at 109s!

I did not see the bombs explode, nor did I see any Huns. And the flak when it came plopping silently in our direction was pretty feeble. The whole show very uncomplicated, probably because we were much more confident now in our Mark IIs, fairly romping around at 20,000 feet. Back on the ground someone said he had seen a Hun destroyer off Dunkirk, but I hadn't, probably because I was rather too high and looking for 109s.

There was lots of to-ing and fro-ing within the squadron throughout the month; besides the departure of most of our Poles and others, Keith Lofts, who commanded 'A' Flight, had already left and many new faces were beginning to appear – Matthews, Munro, Marshall, Welman, Davis – another Davis! – and Cooper. Every doorway seemed to frame a new officer or NCO pilot. The old order changeth! A great pity, even though there were at least fourteen of us remaining from the previous summer.

And a further surprise: we heard that 'Boozy' Kellett, formerly a flight commander of 249 and more recently the commanding officer of 303, was being posted in to become our newly established Wing Commander Flying – 'Whisper King', so called. The incomparable Boozy! With his old Rolls Royce, I wondered? It would be nice seeing him again.

The month dragged on: more convoy patrols, miserable weather, the occasional sweep high up over the Channel coasts, and night operations.

The Hurricane was an easy aircraft to fly at night, much easier than the Spit, which had a longer nose and an indifferent view from the cockpit, besides being waywardly frisky on the ground. However, because our aircraft were not normally fitted with exhaust-blanking plates, the flare from the engine effectively ruined our night vision. Also, as so few of 249 were regarded as fully night operational, it fell to only several of us to do the night flying.

In the North Weald sector, in the event of a threatened attack at dusk or in the early hours of darkness, the routine, referred to as 'forward layers', was to place single fighters at heights varying from 10,000 to 20,000 feet out to sea off Clacton. Why Clacton, particularly, and why twenty to forty miles out to sea, was a mystery, appearing to be a knee-jerk reaction among controllers: what's that, a possible night attack? – send the Hurricanes forty miles out to sea off Clacton! Dead easy, they didn't have to do it; sitting up there in the blackness, freezing to death with the hood open, and knowing full well that if anything stopped, we were in the water and goners. I never much cared for the 'forward layer' arrangement; we so seldom saw anything and when we did, the bogeys were usually our own Wellingtons. I did several of these in March and on at least two other occasions was kept at 'Readiness' the entire night but not called upon. The working day of a day-and-night fighter pilot at that stage of the war could be of anything up to twenty-four hours duration.

On the 19th, we were patrolling Dungeness at 33,000 feet when we saw a sizeable formation at about our own level. Eureka! Huns! We swung towards them full of venom and expectation and piled in, only to find they were Spitfires. For a full minute thereafter, we circled each other like packs of stiff-legged dogs before separating. I was terribly disappointed; my first sight of a likely target for ages. Ah, well; at least we had shown ourselves capable of fighting at altitude, although during those turns at 33,000 feet, I found it almost impossible to maintain height.

The following day, being called upon to visit Hendon, I took Pat Wells and one other along with me. We landed and I recalled that it was my first visit since sitting in one of the nearby fields as a fifteen- year-old, watching the 1936 Hendon Air Display.

After we had conducted our business, we killed time in the old Auxiliary Squadron mess, an elegant place which had more the air of the Athenaeum or Reform about it than anything connected with the Air Force. We found ourselves sipping our after-lunch coffee and whispering in its hallowed surroundings, fearful lest we should disturb the dozen or so elderly officers who were reading, or, with papers over their heads, sleeping off their midday meal. We darkly discussed the situation; the war against tyranny raging in Britain, Europe, the Middle East and beyond, here were these chaps really roughing it, living in abject squalor and having to put up merely with five-course lunches and all the daily newspapers and glossy magazines to keep in touch; in short, fighting as heroically and as hard as they knew how. They needed a morale-raiser, by George!

Shortly after, we took off and, climbing to several thousand feet, aimed ourselves at the mess. In close formation, the three of us swept to within twenty feet of the roof and blasted across the top at more than 300 mph before climbing away rapidly to make ourselves scarce. Lovely! That had shifted the blighters, we only wished we could have seen their faces. At the time, the feud between old and young in the Air Force, between those we perceived to be the doers and the deadbeats, was sometimes bitter and always more than just a game.

It was in March, too, that several of us sat down and gave some thought to designing a crest for our new squadron, the general view being that as we were associated with the Gold Coast, we should have an elephant, or tusks, or a couple of coconuts even, as the centre-piece. Settling on the elephant, I sketched one which I copied from a picture of the Gold Coast coat-of-arms in my Children's Encyclopaedia. After which came the motto. With much hilarity, we went through a score of possibilities but found all the good, pithy ones, such as 'Seek and Destroy', already used. Finally, we settled on, 'We Shall not Fail', which I thought a bit overly Churchillian, being further put off by some wag who kept muttering, 'Not all the time, anyway'. In due course, this was the version submitted to Air Ministry, and subsequently rejected. Much later, a revised version appeared using the original elephant but having a motto which only Latin scholars could translate (Pugnis Et Calcibus - 'With Fists and Heels').

The month drew to a close. We heard that Percy Burton had been awarded a 'Mention in Dispatches', Percy, who had been killed on 27 September, when, mortally wounded, he had rammed an Me 110, bringing them all crashing to earth. So long ago now but still so vividly in my mind. Just a 'Mention', though; we all thought he deserved something more than that – some people appeared to receive 'Mentions' for just polishing the aircraft!

The following day, we were airborne with 56 and several other squadrons, whom I did not even see, for the purpose of taking six Blenheims to bomb two ships in the Cap Grisnez area. The weather clear and fine, I found myself barely on edge as we flew southwards towards Maidstone to pick up the bombers. Pretty run-of-the-mill stuff these days and so rarely any Huns about. Where did they all get to?

With 56 again acting as close escort, 249 were spread out in sections at around 5,000 feet. As we crossed the English coast and headed for France, I found myself almost eager to witness some really effective precision bombing; the Blenheims were going in at 2,000 feet this time and couldn't possibly miss from that height, surely.

As we approached the French coast, the ships lay dead ahead, silent, motionless victims, defenceless targets in an attack they could do nothing about. I felt almost sorry for them.

Then, flak; a dozen or so bursts from around Calais, not too close to me though and no real threat. The bombers running in. My own section wheeling in a fast curve within a mile or so of the French shore. Anxiously watching for 109s, I kept more than half an eye on the bombers, even so. Any minute now.

The bombs fell, innocuous curving specks. Fascinated, I followed their descent – and was vastly disappointed. Not one of them on target; all instead plummeting harmlessly into the sea, producing slow-motion eruptions of grey-brown water and smoke which collapsed gently into pale green discs. They had missed! All of them! Missed! What a damn silly business. Six Blenheims, twenty-odd bombs, and heaven knows how many fighters, for what? Nothing! I raced on in a wide curve, looking inland into France before turning towards the north. What a dreary waste of effort.

It was around this time, too, that an incident occurred which was an example of the occasional pig-headedness and insensitivity displayed by some in control of our affairs.

With a heavy cold, one of several I was plagued with throughout the winter, I had flown at height for longer than was good for me and on letting down, was so badly afflicted by sinus pains that I had to break formation and climb up again in order to relieve the discomfort. Finally, when running short of fuel, I was forced to land with dagger-thrusts above my eyes and my head about to explode. Still in misery and completely deaf in one ear, I had crept off to sick-quarters to spend an hour there inhaling menthol steam with a towel draped over my head. After which, feeling utterly wretched, I had returned to the mess, missed my dinner, then retired to bed around 7 p.m., intending to sleep the clock around.

But, what a hope! Several hours later, I was dragged from the deepest pit of unconsciousness by my batman who was shaking my shoulder and telling me in a quite unnecessary stage-whisper that a heavy raid was in progress over London and that the squadron had been ordered to put as many aircraft as possible into the air. Without delay! Now, in fact!

It took more than a minute for my sleep-befuddled brain to grasp what was being said to me. What was that? Fly? Now? What on earth was he talking about? What time was it, for God's sake? On being told, I could scarcely believe my ears. The middle of the night! What was going on? Then, clutching at a straw; someone was pulling his leg, one of my dear brother officers telephoning from the Coconut Grove or some such place in London, having a lark. But the youth, who was growing steadily more apprehensive as the bad news brought me to life, assured me that someone wasn't. As many pilots as possible, the man had said, although there seemed to be only several of 249 in the mess. Perhaps he could get me a cup of tea?

I rose as though from a grave and, sleep-walking to the window, removed the blackout frame. Outside it was unrelieved darkness tinged with the grey opaqueness of mist bordering on fog. Fly? Now? Sector must be out of their collective mind! Anyway, the squadron had been released hours ago; most of the chaps were in London and I was ill, wasn't I? No, the whole thing was a ridiculous mistake! I'd have a word with the controller.

But in spite of the word I subsequently had and the flood of savage and mutinous thoughts that cascaded through my mind, within half an hour and feeling like death, I was down at dispersal in company with 'Butch' Barton and Pat Wells, whilst out in the dark beyond, a handful of NCOs and men, hastily mustered from the various messes, were struggling with tarpaulins and making ready a few of our aircraft. Everyone numbed by resignation, we were puzzled and affronted by the injustice of it all. Why us? for God's sake.

Then 'Butch' was on the telephone to the controller, querying the instruction and, in his most forthright Canadian voice, pointing out that the weather was totally unsuitable for flying and that the whole exercise seemed ridiculous. After speaking for several minutes, he finally confronted us with a grim face. We would have to go, it seemed; orders from above, the controller's hands were tied. The weather was a bit better to the north, apparently, and if we could manage to get off, they would probably bring us back to Debden, Duxford, or somewhere even further afield if conditions didn't improve. Probably! I didn't like the sound of that. But, that seeming to be the end of it, we began to make ready.

The three of us grim-faced and silent, I had a private vision of some very senior gentleman sipping his after-dinner port and casually ordering the North Weald Hurricanes into the air with a flip of his hand. What a stupid and pointless business. Outside in the blackness, the thin drone of enemy aircraft filtered down to us through a wilderness of seemingly impenetrable cloud and fog.

'Butch' was the first to leave, his boots clumping out of the dispersal hut and into the darkness, followed by Pat Wells. My head still bursting and feeling utterly miserable, I trailed in their wake, humping my parachute, helmet and other equipment.

My aircraft on its usual hard standing just beyond Victor Beamish's blast-pen, I had about 100 yards to walk, a simple enough chore in normal circumstances but rather more of a problem on a pitch-black night, in a heavy mist, and without a torch. As I moved forward, I heard the muffled noise of 'Butch's' engine as he taxied away into the fog and saw in the far distance a nodding pin-prick of light which I took to be the shaded torch-beam of one of my crew. Stepping cautiously but blindly in that direction, I was about halfway there when I trod on something – which I later discovered to be a wheel- chock – and, staggering sideways, fell heavily into a group of parked starter trollies, the sharp edge of one of them catching me on my right shin just below the knee.

For a few brief seconds, the world stood still. In the most excruciating pain, I found myself draped across the flat top of a heavy battery-cart, having dropped everything I was holding in the mud. And it was then that something snapped. That was *it*! Not one step further would I go! Almost in tears of hurt, anger and frustration, I gathered my equipment and mutinous self together and limped back towards the dispersal hut, mouthing my opinion of those who didn't fly themselves and who didn't give a damn about those of us who had to.

Within seconds I was on to Sector and speaking to the controller in language that can only be described as vehement. Did he *really* understand what he was asking us to do? The weather was unfit for flying; not only did I doubt that we could get ourselves airborne but, thus far, I hadn't even managed to *find* my aircraft, which was true, but not for the reason I was hinting at. And even if we did get into the air, our chances of an interception were nil - *as well he knew*! So, what was the point of all this? Perhaps he could tell me, because the logic of it escaped me! On and on, my bursting head and aching shin spurring me on to new heights of eloquence.

Rather to my surprise, as I was expecting a blast in return, the man listened in silence before responding calmly. I was invited to hang on for a moment, which I did, quaking with anger meanwhile but half- regretting my outburst and wondering if I had already overstepped the mark. Then, the voice again, as nice as pie. All right, if conditions were as bad as I had described, of course we could stand down. Had anyone taken off yet? Trying to find the end of the runway, were they? In that case, perhaps I could stop them (in 1941 there was no Air Traffic Control, as we now know it). Unbelieving but vastly thankful, I jerked my head in the direction of the airman-of- the-watch, who almost fell out of the door into the night before sending a red Very light curving into the darkness. All over! Thank heaven for that! The others would be relieved.

Some ten minutes later, 'Butch' stamped into the dispersal hut having taken an age to taxi back from the far side of the airfield. Looking as white and as angry as ever I had seen him, he snatched up the telephone and demanded to speak to the controller. What the hell was going on? First we had been ordered into the air, against our better judgement, let it be said, then, because his flight commander had had the guts to make a fuss, the whole thing had been called off. Was it essential or wasn't it? Because if it wasn't, what the hell were we doing down at dispersal in the middle of the night? Whoever was issuing these orders should make up his mind! And so on, the exchange was quite lengthy but that was the gist of it.

In the next room, Pat Wells and I listened to the tirade. Guts! It had nothing to do with guts. I was hopping wild because I had been dragged out of bed feeling like death; because I had walked into that damned starter trolley and well-nigh broken my leg; and because the insensitivity, the injustice, and the time-wasting nonsense of the whole affair had rankled. No thought of us! Our lives and aircraft were being jeopardised when everybody knew that nothing, but nothing, would be achieved. Moreover, it seemed that no one cared or understood. Wasn't it simply a case of someone wishing to cover himself in the event of questions being asked later? As we talked about it, Pat confided to me half-seriously that he had even thought of taxiing into a blast-pen and knocking a bit off his propeller – only a little bit, mind! And after a time, we were all able to laugh a little – just a little! All the same, and because we were normally on very good terms with the controllers at Sector, it was an unpleasant incident which ruffled our feathers. Whoever was responsible was being more than just silly, his decision had bordered on the criminal.

It was well after midnight before I was back in bed, still simmering with resentment. Strangely, though, my head seemed much better. Probably the shock of it all!

April: for the first six days of the month, an endless succession of convoy patrols; ten miles out to sea off Clacton, then Barrow Deep, after which Clacton again, followed by Harwich and all the way up to Southwold. On one occasion, huddled in a goonskin (leather, sheepskin-lined coat and trousers) and bored to distraction, I actually fell asleep in the cockpit. My last recollection was of turning at the southern end of the convoy and flying north; then, after a time, looking down to find the convoy not there. Gone! Missing! Good God! I turned about in shocked concern and found it several miles astern. How on earth had I got up here if I hadn't nodded off? Later, when my No.2 remarked rather pointedly that he wondered what I had been up to, I explained, not too convincingly, that I thought I had seen something. Asleep! My oath, what next?

Then, on the 7th – tragedy!

We had started off with more convoy patrols, eight sections of two aircraft throughout the morning, after which there was a wing-show over the same convoy – 56, 249 and 242 squadrons, in all thirty-six aircraft. It was, of course, to boost morale and no doubt the sailors gazing skywards from below were suitably heartened by the sight of us; it was a trying life for them, constantly on the qui vive and being bombed from time to time without the means to defend themselves adequately. But for us, it was merely a diversion; thirty-six aircraft at little more than 1,000 feet, wheeling about uncomfortably for almost an hour. What if a Hun popped out of a cloud now, to come face to face with this armada? Frighten the blighter to death, probably, and serve him right!

Then in the early evening, a further six aircraft of 249 were returning from the same convoy when Dicky Wynn, who was in the middle of the formation, for no apparent reason, broke away at low level and dived straight into the ground. Within several minutes flying time of North Weald, too, and with everyone preparing to land. We were shattered. No warning. Neither sign nor word from him. Just a straightforward plunge into oblivion. What a tragedy! The smiling, level-headed, experienced Dicky, who had been with the squadron almost from the start and who had fought bravely for more than six months, being shot down, wounded nastily in the neck, and crashing more than once through engine failure. To die not as a victim in battle, but as a casualty in an inexplicable and seemingly needless accident. Had he, too, fallen asleep? Surely not, not within two minutes of landing and in the middle of a formation. What a way to go! We were all sobered by the thought of his passing.

The following day, on an air-test, I flew over the crash-site, a field close to the village of Ongar, and circled several times the brown scar in the earth and the few remaining fragments of his Hurricane. A sad and silent trace of a gallant colleague.

That night, I was airborne for almost two hours on a 'forward layer'. Alone in the cold, blue-black solitude of space and a long way out to sea with only the magenta flare from my exhausts to claim my attention, my thoughts were with him more than once. How grossly unfair that someone as talented, as mature and as companionable as Dicky Wynn should have died so casually and to such little effect. A terrible waste. The endless expanse of frigid, starlit blackness was a quiet companion and fitting venue for my poignant musings.

10 April; the day fine, bright and cold.

I led an offensive formation of six – Wells, Crossey, Palliser, Mills and 'Boozy' Kellett – on a high altitude sweep to Le Touquet and beyond, then northwards to Boulogne and Calais. Looking for 109s.

It was the first time that 'Boozy' – 'Whisper King' – had flown with us and I was quietly and smugly amused that only nine months earlier, he had been my flight commander and instructor during my first, very amateurish circuits and bumps in that new-fangled, low-wing monoplane, the Miles Master. Deciding that he would act as weaver, he tagged on to our rear and said not a word throughout.

We took off at noon and full of consideration for my five companions, I climbed up at a very gentlemanly rate towards the south. At 19,000 feet over Kent, I bent forward and pulled the small handle that moved my two-speed supercharger into FS. There was a mild 'clump' up front and the boost needle shot an extra five pounds around the dial as my Hurricane gave a comforting surge. Mmmm! Very nice, too! We climbed on steadily and in mid-Channel were at 33,000 feet and on the alert for Huns.

Some fifteen minutes later, by which time we were well into France and flying north-east, my enthusiasm for combat had died the death. It was *unbelievably* cold! My feet and hands like stone and my body beginning to crystallize, I lowered my seat to the bottom of its travel and, with my right hand, fished about for the hot pipe that ran between engine and radiator. I could touch it – just – but with only the tips of my fingers and to little effect. I sat there, straining – and suffering. Through the frost-caked metal frame of my hood, some 30 yards away I could see only the top of the helmet of my nearest companion, who was no doubt equally cold and doing much the same as myself. Why, oh why, couldn't they put some heat into these bloody aircraft?

Meanwhile, 'Boozy', at least ten years older than any of us and 1,000 feet higher, was fairly zipping around above our heads. I sat there, watching his white-trailed manoeuvres in frozen awe, my mind congealed into a stupor. Wasn't he, too, feeling the cold? And why did his aircraft always appear to be so much faster than my own?

Then, away to the south, four distant, slow-moving pencil-lines of white. Huns! Not in the least concerned by their presence, what did disturb me was that they were a good 1,500 feet higher – 34,000 at least. What did we have to do to get above these blighters?

There was little point in attempting to climb up and fight, even had we possessed the performance to do so; we had already been airborne for more than an hour and were wallowing about as it was. They approached. Then stood off. And looked. Watching them carefully as they kept to a respectable distance, when roughly over Calais we turned away slowly to the north and began to let down. Frozen to the tripes! Thank God for warmer altitudes!

A little to my surprise, 'Boozy' did not turn up at our dispersal to discuss the flight and we later learned that he, too, had been greatly affected by the arctic conditions. Later still, we heard that he had gone to sick-quarters, or was it hospital? Wherever it was and for whatever reason, we did not see him again at North Weald. Ever! Poor old 'Boozy'. What the Huns couldn't do in months, the frost and his Hurricane had achieved in a single flight – unaided.

Dicky Wynn was buried in North Weald churchyard on the 11th and the following day I did some air-to-ground firing on Dengie Flats. Our new 12-gun Hurricanes performed excellently but the four 20 mm cannons in the several aircraft equipped with them gave a lot of trouble. The cannon Hurricanes were noticeably heavier than the machine-gun variety and, when fired, the guns did so at a much slower rate than the Brownings and with violent thumps which shook the wings and airframe unpleasantly. Invariably, one or more cannons would stop after a few rounds, causing the aircraft to slew sideways, depending on where the offending weapons were situated. The 20 mm rounds of ammunition were huge by comparison

with the .303 bullet, the ball and armour-piercing heavy chunks of metal
which pulverised anything they struck. I would have hated to have been hit
by anything fired by our new Hispanos; the Huns mostly used ammunition
which exploded on contact so that only the small armoured nose ploughed
on, a characteristic for which many in 249 had been profoundly thankful
during the autumn battles. I didn't much care for our cannon Hurricanes
and only flew them when I had to; I liked guns that fired all the time and not
just when they felt inclined.

Later in the month, leading most of my flight, I took off for Sutton Bridge
to use the ground targets there, only to be overtaken immediately by bad
weather which forced us all to make an emergency landing at Bassingbourn.

Fretting with the unexpected turn of events and being obliged to kill
time in the officers' mess for the rest of the day, with my back to the fire in
the ante-room, I found myself in conversation with a pleasant-faced little
fellow wearing a DFC and Bar, who told me that he had started off on
fighters but had now moved on to the bigger stuff. I pulled a face and said
he was welcome to heavy boilers, thank you very much; I didn't have the
sort of courage needed just to sit still and be shot at. He shrugged, implying
that it wasn't that bad. I remember him smiling a lot and having twinkling
eyes. Before we parted, he introduced himself as Gibson – Flight Lieutenant
Guy Gibson (later, Wing Commander Guy Gibson, VC, DSO, etc., of 617
Squadron and Dambuster fame).

April drifted by – more convoy patrols, uneventful sweeps over France,
some practice flying now and then, and more than sufficient days off. The
Frenchman, Fayolle, in one of his last flights with the squadron, ran into an
Me 110 over a convoy and claimed it as a 'probable'- otherwise we barely
saw a Hun, except from a distance. Anywhere!

Since the heady and violent days of the previous summer, autumn and
early winter, the war for us had changed dramatically. Here we were, all
ready and willing in our new Hurricane IIs, doing a fair amount of flying
but encountering nothing to shoot at. Where had all the Huns got to?

Things were also changing on the ground, new faces each day in dispersal
and, to our great sorrow, even Victor Beamish was said to be 'on his way'.
Victor! So splendid a man and so gallant a leader; it was like mourning a

parent. Without him, North Weald – the war even – would never be quite the same.

But, a little before his departure, it was he who came into dispersal one morning just before noon and shattered us with a single sentence. I remember every word, where I was in the hut at the time, and its effect on those around me.

'You chaps are going overseas!' I recall the grin on his face. And the silence that followed.

When we all heard of the squadron's posting, I was standing in the middle of the hut, just beyond the stove. Harry Davidson, soon to be commissioned, was on my left and I turned to him, excited by Victor's statement but privately concerned that it might have been my outburst some weeks before that had prompted him to bring up the subject at Air Ministry, where he was a frequent visitor, and somehow start the whole business in train. Whatever the truth of the matter, when I looked at Davidson, his face, normally so cheerful, was condemning.

'I don't bluddy-well want to go overseas.' Then, with a look of frozen hostility I had never seen before: 'That was you, wasn't it?'

His words were like knife-thrusts and, in the event, our posting proved to be a turning point in his life as he was soon to join the newly-forming Merchant Ship Fighter Unit and be killed in tragic circumstances. Poor unfortunate Harry! The most willing of fighter pilots, a great morale-raiser and a good friend whom I had known since we started training together in the summer of '38. Was I really responsible, even remotely, for his untimely end? I like to think not but the doubts have remained.

And it was in line with Air Ministry policy, which decreed that married officers should, whenever possible, remain in the United Kingdom, that Gerald Lewis and others were soon to go their separate ways. But, at that point, we had no idea where we were going, not even that we were off to the Middle East.

With the war at stalemate in Western Europe and the Navy beginning to cope with the magnetic mine and, to a lesser extent, the U-boat, the focal point of conflict had undoubtedly shifted to the Middle East. General Sir Archibald Wavell (G.O.C. Middle East) had captured literally armies of Italians in the Western Desert, compelling the Germans, now less than happy with their lame-duck ally, to reinforce Libya, having for months past been heavily committed in southern Europe and in Greece. For them, one route to victory led through the Suez Canal to the oil-rich deserts beyond and the soft underbelly of Russia.

But although there was something of a lull in and around Britain, the Hun bombers were overhead almost every night, if not to attack London then other major cities of the realm. In fact, nightly bombing raids were so commonplace, we were beginning to regard them much as we did the cloud and the rain – part of the national scene. Bombing, blackout, and the endless, hollow 'tonk-tonk-tonking' of the guns – that was the sound and picture of England. Plus the five-bob meals and food rationing, the fire-watching, ARP, and new Home Guard. And the shattered buildings, the sandbags and tin-hats, the tawdriness, and the general lack of paint. No, I wouldn't mind going overseas, and not only for the better weather. But where? At the outset, none of us knew.

On the 17th, though, we did – almost! The official warning order arrived and, soon after, a small group of officers appeared from somewhere-or-other to answer questions and build upon the bare bones of the initial instruction. All very secret, of course.

We would be going abroad by aircraft carrier and flying off. Flying off! Wow! Precisely where, though, would remain a secret until we were seaborne. Our troops would not be accompanying us, however, but would go separately, to join us at our destination. Frowns, objections, and dismay! The squadron split up? Why, for heaven's sake? The voice was continuing: we would cease operational flying at North Weald on 1 May and would be granted a week's embarkation leave. Meanwhile, additional pilots would be posted in and others would leave. There would be inoculations – groans! – and kitting out, and each of us would be allowed 30 lbs of accompanied luggage, the rest of our baggage to go separately 'by other means'. 'Other means' – what were we to understand by that? And two Hurricanes with long-range tanks would be attached temporarily to the squadron to enable us to familiarise ourselves with our new mounts. They would be the tropicalised version (more than a pointer, that) and would all be brand new. Brand new Mark Is.

We were all struck dumb. Mark Is! Oh, no! Not again! We were back again on the old, out-distanced, out-performed, out-everythinged Mark

I, and this time the tropicalised version, which was even slower and less combat-worthy than those we had flown in the Battle of Britain. Anything, it appeared, was good enough for the overseas units. A remark made to me months before by my father came to mind: 'Take my word for it, when you are in the Services, the further you are from London, the worse off you are likely to be in terms of equipment – and consideration!' If that were correct, we were surely bound for the Far East! Both elated and sobered by the news, we went about our business; another major sweep over France, a long night's vigil at Debden waiting for a scramble that didn't come, and convoy patrols. Endless convoy patrols! My last operational flight from North Weald was on 29 April; a convoy patrol of more than one and a half hour's duration. After almost a year of strenuous combat flying, it seemed that we were to go out with merely a whimper.

Meanwhile, so many new faces were appearing in our midst that I gave up trying to keep track of who was in my flight. As I was the only flight commander at the time, a new officer arrived, a Flight Lieutenant F. V. 'Tony' Morello, who looked very much like his name, dark and Italian, though very English-sounding and pleasant.

And the two tropicalised Hurricanes appeared, each with 44 gallon underwing drop-tanks and a bulky Vokes filter disfiguring the nose. With all the built-in headwinds, I thought they looked dreadful and climbed aboard one of them with a heavy heart. Same old Hurricane I! Then some expert appeared to tell us that, used economically, it would fly 1020 miles, or for six hours and twenty minutes. I remember thinking sourly, not with me in it it wouldn't! Hurricane Is, for heaven's sake!

After which, I went on leave for a week, my left arm stiff with jabs and laden with pith helmets and masses of heavy woollen khaki stockings and unwearable shorts and shirts. Who on earth designed this stuff, and when? I thought of General Gordon's army going down the Nile to Khartoum fifty years before in temperatures of more than 100 degrees, wearing thick, flannel spine pads! Well, we didn't have spine pads, but we seemed to have everything else!

The arrangement was that we should all meet on Euston station on 8 May before journeying up to Liverpool by train. Liverpool! My birthplace and where I had spent much of my childhood. What an odd coincidence.

18

Journey to the Middle East

I arrived at Euston station shortly before 8 a.m. The train was already at the platform and most of the squadron were in our reserved compartments, looking decidedly jaded. Some of the tales I was greeted with were harrowing. The South Africans, Rhodesians and others without an English base had indulged in a final orgy of good-fellowship in the Coconut Grove and other places of doubtful reputation, and were barely able to tell the time. Having returned to North Weald from one of these exhausting forays, one officer had dozed off when low-flying in one of the new long-range Hurricanes and had only come to when his aircraft was in the act of ploughing through the topmost branches of a tree. Surfacing with a jerk and recognising catastrophe a mere second away, by a miracle of reaction he had snatched the aircraft from disaster and was counting himself lucky to be accompanying us. Had the Commander-in-Chief, Middle East been treated to the sight of one of his reinforcing squadrons, he would probably have retired that night in no easy frame of mind.

We arrived at Lime Street, Liverpool, in the early afternoon. There was a heavy overcast and it was foggy. But the air of desolation within the station was only a foretaste of what lay beyond.

The city had endured seven nights of almost continuous bombing, the previous night being the most recent. The main square, onto which the station faced, together with John Brown Street and the area around St George's Hall, was deserted – and this at 1.30 p.m.! The streets were patterned with hoses and blocked with fire-engines and ambulances whilst on all sides, columns of smoke arose from unseen fires before spreading out like a dark stain in every direction. The stench was abominable. This was

Liverpool! My Liverpool! The city I had grown up in! I was stunned into silence.

It is a testimony to the resilience of youth and the rapidity with which one becomes accustomed to catastrophe in war that, after the first shock of being confronted by such chaos, we surveyed the devastation more with interest than concern. Clutching our belongings, we piled into three-tonners and set off for the Gladstone Dock at the Seaforth end of the city. Then, as we proceeded at snail's pace along the dock road – an unhappy choice in all conscience – bumping and wallowing between the craters and the paraphernalia of fire-fighting and rescue work, we were treated to the depressing spectacle of twenty or more ships in the basins and docks, in varying postures of defeat – listing, lying or simply upturned – many smoking and on fire, some upright but twisted and shattered by high explosive.

To our right, huge warehouses which I had explored as a child when bulging with sugar, cotton and the produce of a dozen nations – all redolent with nostalgic aromas – burned and crumbled, cascading showers of sparks into the smoke and mist. And all around, tired men in soiled uniforms hurried about like worker-ants, picking their way across ground criss-crossed and littered with the appliances of rescue. A weird and terrible sight, hell reconstituted!

After a stop-go journey of more than half an hour, we turned to the left and there, much smaller than I had expected, a flat-topped silhouette in the heavy mist – dark, grey, war-stained and silent. HMS *Furious*! Motionless in a green-black cesspool of jetsam-strewn water, with gulls wheeling and crying overhead, her spectral outline suggested a breaker's yard rather than a major ship of war. We halted and dropped stiffly to the ground. A voice, thick with awe and foreboding, breathed in my ear: 'Cripes! Are we going to war in that?'

Preconceived notions are often far from the mark. My *Boys Own* image of the Royal Navy, with which I had enjoyed little contact prior to 1941, was of ships pristine in appearance, of jolly Jack Tars in bare feet, knuckling their forelocks and holystoning the decks until they shone, and of officers with jutting jaws and white- topped hats set at rakish angles, crying 'Close the enemy!' or 'Keelhaul the dogs!' Alas, HMS *Furious* was a great disappointment. As we approached with our bags like a group of itinerant salesmen and gazed up at its steep rusting side, concern was reflected in every face. Was this the right ship? Surely the Navy could do better than this!

Our arrival was greeted with total indifference. Laden with luggage, we stumbled up the gangway and, as carefully briefed at North Weald, solemnly saluted the quarter-deck, although few of us would have recognised that area of the ship had it been introduced with a fanfare of trumpets. Then, we were pushing and shoving our way below through the crowded, clanging, banging, steel-sided corridors towards our quarters. En route, I suddenly became aware of a Royal Marine standing properly-at-ease with rifle and bayonet. As I squeezed past, the man eyed me so sourly that I had the uncomfortable feeling that were I to decide at that late stage that a voyage to the Middle East was not exactly what I had in mind, I would have had trouble convincing him and no doubt a few others on board.

Being a flight commander, I rated a cabin of my own – all of six feet square! There was a high-sided, rock-solid bunk, some heavy mahogany drawers, an electric fire, and tubes, channels, holes and pipes seemingly by the dozen, each of which appeared to hiss, suck, blow, howl, or in some other way contribute to the cacophony of sound that appeared to be part and parcel of every cabin, corridor, corner and area of that ship. The reason for the Navy's unparalleled record of defiance in the face of overwhelming odds was plain to see: the order to surrender never percolated down to the crew through all the din!

Later, in search of a little tranquillity, I found my way to the flight deck. Crossey and several others were already there, still reeling from the news that they would be sleeping in hammocks. Like redundant grave-diggers, we stood around, hands in pockets, and watched as a continuous stream of ant-like figures threaded its way to and from the dockside carrying boxes, bags, crated stores, 20 mm cannons, ammunition, and every shape and size of commodity capable of being transported by hand. Above us, cranes clanked and whirred as netted stores and tarpaulined mysteries came swinging dangerously in our direction. A dozen times, we shifted hastily to the roars of, 'Mind yer backs!' and other instructions more crudely expressed and in no way considerate of our rank and status. Clearly, this was not a naval crew, these were pirates! There was not a uniform in sight, no white hats at rakish angles, no forelocks being knuckled, nothing. Not even an aircraft. This was certainly not the Navy I had read about!

Word then filtered through that the ship had received a direct hit during the night, a 500 lb bomb, apparently, striking the back end. Deciding to examine the damage, we wandered astern but, after poking our noses into several places and nearly being asphyxiated by hot and pungent fumes rising mysteriously through grilles at the rear of the flight deck, we found neither bomb nor hole and concluded facetiously that either it was lying unexploded in the basement or that it had gone right through, in which case the ship was probably not floating at all but sitting on the bottom! Such was our nervous and childish mood and the nature of the remarks we exchanged.

Within the hour, it was announced that we would be moving out of Liverpool with all haste; the Royal Navy at that time – indeed, at all times – had a phobia about air attacks and those in charge were plainly in no mood to face another night in a prime target area. By late afternoon, tugs had appeared, the ship began to tremble and produce froth at one end and, sliding gently astern, we manoeuvred backwards into the Mersey. After which, enveloped still in a thick mist so that no land was visible in any direction, we forged slowly towards the bar and into the Irish Sea, finally working up to twenty knots and heading blindly towards the north. Soon after came dusk then bone-chilling darkness, at which point we all retreated to the warmth and comfort of the wardroom and later to our sleeping quarters.

By no stretch of the imagination could it be said that I had a restful night as my cabin appeared to be the focal point of every sound that was manufactured within the hull. It was patently obvious that I was travelling in an enormous steel-sided sounding box so that every blow and bang reverberated with deafening intensity. Somewhere, I concluded, a sailor had been specially briefed to drop one of the anchors at thirty-minute intervals throughout the night so that a shattering crash resembling the noise from a thousand cymbals would ricochet from a hundred steel walls within the ship until, satisfied no doubt that everything built of flesh and blood had been reduced to a quivering jelly, it would filter out through a hundred nooks and crannies to disappear into the blackness beyond. I woke twenty times, on each occasion to whistles, hisses, suckings and bangs, my only consolation being that a torpedo strike in the next cabin was likely to pass entirely unnoticed.

I was awakened finally by silence and an almost eerie atmosphere of suspense. I sat bolt upright in my high-sided bunk and decided that we had reached wherever it was we were going and, dressing hurriedly, threaded my way aloft. Up on the flight-deck in the pale, clear light of a cool early morning, I saw that we were in a bay surrounded by hills, the whole scene tinted delicately in the palest of yellows, greens, blues and purples – a most moving experience. It was Scotland – Scotland at its loveliest. We were anchored off Greenock.

Around the *Furious*, there seemed to be 1,000 ships, motionless in a wide expanse of water, although, in reality, there were probably no more than forty. Next to us, about 100 yards away, the lip of the funnel and the top of the mast and superstructure of what was obviously a destroyer, peeped almost mischievously out of the water, the ship itself appearing to be firmly planted on the bottom. It turned out to be a destroyer of the French Navy which had decided to join the Allied cause and which, with typical Gallic flair, had apparently sunk itself, the word going around that its crew had somehow contrived to launch one of their own torpedoes which, after careering around the bay like an intoxicated dolphin, had returned most inconveniently to sink its erstwhile owner. I remember laughing and pulling a face at what was so obviously a tall story and one which had clearly been embellished in the telling. But, whatever the truth of the matter, the destroyer was on the bottom right enough and presumably did not get there on its own. In any case, we were prepared to believe almost anything of the French; they were decidedly unpopular at the time, Marshal Petain having recently gone across to the enemy, and it was just the sort of damn silly thing that they were likely to do. Poetic justice, in fact.

Later that day – it was Friday 9 May – we went ashore in order to bid a final farewell to Britain, home and beauty. If we had heard about the air attacks on Clydeside, which presumably we had, I, for one, was not fully aware that Greenock had been heavily bombed on the nights of the 5th and 6th. Nor was I prepared for the melancholy sights I was shortly to witness.

We were first confronted with the results of the Luftwaffe's handiwork when, on stepping off the liberty boat, we encountered a compound in which there were a dozen or more Catalina flying boats piled one upon the other in total chaos – mutilated, crushed, destroyed. Then, in the town proper, we were confronted by a funeral procession half-a-mile long as a score or more hearses proceeded at snail's pace to the place of burial. If our morale was in the doldrums before, it reached an all-time low as we stood and surveyed the lines of grieving faces, standing as we did among the onlookers three-deep on the pavements. Then, as the crowds drifted away, we became aware that the whole town was closed, all, that is, other than one rather seedy-looking bookshop, whose front door had been left furtively ajar. There, I purchased two small books published by the pretentiously named 'Thinkers Library', one being the classic, 'The Life of Jesus' by the renegade priest Ernest Renan, which I carried off probably with the subconscious thought that it might prove a useful crib were I suddenly to turn up unexpectedly at the Pearly Gates. I still have them, as I write.

Back on board, we found the ship had been tidied up and the flight deck cleared. We knew that our aircraft were down below in the hangar but the word was that, as chaos reigned there, it was an area best left alone. Instead, we tried to familiarise ourselves with naval routine, to find the wardroom without doing a tour of the entire ship, and to keep in touch with other members of the squadron in different parts of the vessel.

As the day drew to a close, it was fairly obvious that we were about to move off again and, with most of us squadron pilots lined up on the flight deck, the engines began to tremble and the *Furious* nosed its way towards the sea. Left, right, and in the distance, other ships kept pace with us – six or eight destroyers, a biggish-looking ship later identified as the eight-inch gun cruiser HMS *London*, and a massive but squat creation on the horizon which looked as if it might be a battleship.

I found myself alongside an elderly, weather-beaten naval man who nodded in its direction.

'See that thing over there which looks like the Kay-Gee-Five (the new battleship, HMS *King George V*)? I nodded – cautiously. 'Well, it isn't!' My informant was almost smacking his lips. 'It's the old Centurion, which we've used as a target ship for donkey's years. All the guns and upper works are made of wood and, as it's only carrying a skeleton crew and won't do more than twelve knots, we've got a long trip ahead of us.'

Reduced to silence by this chilling piece of intelligence, my mind grappled with the prospect of our taking on a brace of German pocket-battleships with our principal means of defence a twelve-knot, First World War hulk with wooden guns!

Reading my thoughts, the man gave a twisted smile. 'You needn't worry, old son, the *London* there is capable of taking on anything we're likely to come across.'

I looked at the venerable square lines of the *London* which was trotting beside us like an Old English sheepdog, and was not entirely reassured.

Soon after, when daylight began to fade, we all went below. Later, and alone, I climbed up to the flight deck again and, with a chill night wind plucking fiercely at my hair and clothes, stared blindly into the velvety blackness, uncomfortably aware that we were in the centre of a dozen or so hidden ships. As a tiny precaution, I offered a silent prayer that the chaps doing the steering be given a little Divine guidance so that they wouldn't either run into each other or trip over an island they had somehow overlooked on their charts. When I awoke the following morning, we were well and truly into the Atlantic. The sea heaved and tumbled with a terrible slow intensity and the *Furious* creaked, trembled and groaned like a 16th-century galleon. Up on the flight deck the wind tore us to pieces, but I noted with satisfaction that our escorts, spread out from horizon to horizon, were more or less where I expected them to be, the nearest being the *London* which sat comfortably on our starboard side, some 400 yards away, a formidable moustache of white creaming from the plunging knife of its bow. Above, the clouds were dark and low enough to touch and it was clear that the weather was determined to be as beastly as it possibly could.

In the days that followed, it deteriorated to such an extent that the destroyers were frequently lost to sight in the huge troughs between the mountainous, wind-snatched waves. Heaving, soaring and butting their way forward, they seemed to spend most of their time below water and, magnificent spectacle though it was, my heart went out to their occupants for whom life must have been intolerable. Conditions eventually became so bad that plaintive winks were received from them, asking that the speed be even further reduced so that, for a time, we were forced to proceed at a fast walking pace until the wind and sea had abated.

By the time we had reached mid-Atlantic, we had established something of a routine and could find our way about. With three RAF squadrons on board, the ship was vastly overcrowded and there was a clockwise one-way traffic system. As the Navy seemed to do everything at a thumping double, to attempt to go against the tide invited not only the coarsest of comment but physical abuse as well. The Navy, I decided, was a brutal organisation; the officers berated the crew in the crudest of terms and everyone thumped and banged about amid a constant barrage of piping and incomprehensible chatter over the Tannoy system. Meanwhile, we, the RAF contingent, cowered in our various corners as this strange race of men went about its duties in bludgeoning style, hurrying to and fro and up and down holes in the decks like monkeys on sticks. The only stationary humans, it seemed, were the Marines, with their sour looks and rifles at the ready; there, no doubt, to quell mutinies.

As the Royal Navy ponderously manoeuvred its iron charges around the Atlantic, the focal point of the Air Force's seaborne existence became the wardroom, towards which we all gravitated unsteadily like nervous dogs seeking the solace of a fireside basket. In the dining room there were white cloths on the tables, something seldom seen in an RAF officers' mess, and my first meal was ruined by the sight of a weathered Lieutenant Commander wolfing down his breakfast clad completely in hat and oilskins. My God! First a set of pirates for a crew, then hats and coats in the dining room! Whatever next?

The wardroom, however, had more acceptable customs, one of which was to serve gin at all hours of the day and night. With grog at only several pence a tot, the allure of the bar became irresistible and a hard core of at least a dozen in light-blue uniform hung on to it manfully, determined, no doubt, that it should come to no harm as the ship reared, wallowed and creaked its way across the Atlantic. With glistening eyes and lips, they would start off the day quietly benevolent, becoming confidentially chummy by mid-afternoon, garrulously happy by dinner, before lapsing gradually into silence as the night progressed. Finally, owlish with bonhomie and oblivious to the threat of instant destruction posed by lurking U-boats, they could be found in the early hours of the morning, swaying in harmony with the ship's movements, totally and endearingly waterlogged. If some of them ever slept, they managed to do so without my knowledge, remaining at station throughout the entire voyage, a lasting tribute to the endurance of the RAF and its single-minded devotion to a just cause.

There were, even so, some duties to perform for those of us who were not of the ship's company, one such responsibility being to collaborate with the gun-crews, presumably in the belief that we would be more familiar with aircraft of the Luftwaffe than they. We were all allotted stations around the ship and I, to my dismay, found that I had been appointed to one of the larger guns up front. Clad in my most seaworthy garb – an RAF raincoat designed to ward off showers at royal garden parties! – I struggled forward along the streaming deck until I began to run out of ship. There I found my gun – a whopper!! (two whoppers, in fact; it was a twin turret)– not far removed from the anchor, manned by a huddled group of buccaneers glistening in sea-drenched oilskins. The increase to their number of one officer and high-priced expert from the Royal Air Force left them totally unmoved. I was ignored completely as they went about their various duties with much crashing and banging and harsh, wild cries.

After a time there came a lull and we crouched in a circle like a huddle of gorillas – dripping – as the shuddering prow of the *Furious* battered its way into the Atlantic and vast showers of spray enveloped us in cold, stinging douches. Meanwhile, a crackling voice on the Tannoy directed questions at us, one of them being: what was the speed of the Stuka dive-bomber? My circle of faces was blankly silent; no one, other than myself, had the slightest idea and I, by that time in a totally uncooperative mood, was determined to keep quiet. Then, further questions about other aircraft and, finally: what German aircraft was large, had four engines, and could be expected to attack us even in mid-Atlantic? The pirate in charge, a large, shapeless mound of thuggery straight from the seamier end of Liverpool's Scotland Road, thrust a red-eyed, dripping face in my direction.

'Wassat, whack?'

My spirits rose – my chance at last. 'A Lysander', I replied firmly. Then, seeing a look of total bewilderment on his and five other faces, I added convincingly, 'Long-range, of course! Very good aircraft.'

The days dragged by. Whilst we pilots were making our modest contribution towards ensuring the safety of HMS *Furious*, the hangar below was a hive of industry. Hurricanes by the dozen, lashed to the deck, were being prepared for our journey to the Western Desert; long-range tanks were being fitted and electrics tested. Crossey, who was in the habit of visiting my cabin to escape the congestion and bedlam of his own quarters, reported that when the time came, he doubted that there would be sufficient pilots to fly off our allocation of aircraft; several had already fallen down the suicidal ladders that abounded throughout the ship and there had also been casualties among the hammock-dwellers, who, in their first moments of consciousness, were apt to raise their heads smartly, forgetting the existence of a steel deck immediately above.

In groups, we all visited the vast shifting cavern below the flight deck in which our aircraft were tightly quartered like kennelled animals. It was harshly lit and a maze of wings, wheels, tanks, chocks, ropes, mounds of equipment – and pitot heads! The Hurricane pitot head, face-high to a stooping, unsuspecting person with his mind on other matters, was a gruesome implement. To be poked in the eye with one of those was more than just a painful experience and I was informed that at least several walking wounded had already been led away to the sick-bay.

My own aircraft was plainly brand new, as were all the others, and being a tropicalised version of the mark, had the complicated and ungainly muzzle on the air-intake, designed to limit the amount of sand and dust being sucked into the engine. Besides giving the aircraft a most unstreamlined appearance it, and the two 44-gallon long-range tanks, would, I reckoned, reduce the aircraft's performance to little more than that of a nippy Tiger Moth.

Each of us was responsible for ensuring that the electric pumps in our overload tanks were working properly; however, there were no means of verifying this other than by listening carefully for a subdued hum in each tank – no easy task given the noise level in the hangar. As the system required that the extra fuel was passed from overload to internal tanks before reaching the engine, each pilot would be obliged to use first the fuel in his main tanks before replenishing them constantly by pumping petrol from the overloads. If, in the air, the main tanks showed no sign of being replenished, i.e., the pumps were faulty, the unfortunate pilot then had a problem he could do little about. Happily, my tanks and pumps worked perfectly but Crossey's didn't, so that he spent the next hour or so with his ear glued to his aircraft, like some inquisitive tenement dweller absorbed in a next-door quarrel.

More days and nights of tossing and heaving, the weather unrelentingly miserable.

By this time, the reinforcement plan had been explained to us. We had all gathered in the wardroom to be told that we would be tying up at Gibraltar alongside the carrier, HMS *Ark Royal*. 249 Squadron's Hurricanes would then be man-handled across planks onto the *Ark* where they would remain on the flight deck. Because the Hurricane's wings would not fold and as the *Ark Royal*'s lifts were too small to accommodate our aircraft, all twenty-three would be disposed in such a manner as to enable the carrier's fighters to operate should there be an air attack. Our time of arrival at Gibraltar was also revealed – 9 p.m. on Sunday 18 May.

With a rapidly drying mouth, I listened to the rest of it. After the contents of the *Furious* – men and machines – had been successfully off-loaded onto the *Ark Royal*, it was intended to collect a larger fleet so that the three carriers, the *Ark Royal*, *Furious* and *Argus* could be escorted into the Mediterranean. Arriving within 450 miles of Malta, probably at dawn on 21 May, we would be flown off, after which we would be on our own. Then, after a refuelling stop at Malta, there would be a further 850 miles of sea to negotiate before landing at Mersa Matruh, in Egypt. Mersa Matruh! I had never even heard of the place!

The plan finally explained, I thought of the 1,300 miles of water, pretty well all of it in hostile territory, causing me to speculate sombrely that if anything dropped off my aircraft or stopped, I would be in, with little hope of ever being rescued. On the other hand, each of us had a dinghy. Even so, the more I thought about it, the less I was enthused, and all the time a mental picture kept appearing of dear old North Weald, our brand new Hurricane IIs, a blazing fire in the ante-room, and quiet games of snooker after dinner. Fool that I was, what was I doing here?

Meanwhile, the weather showing little sign of abating, we plunged and hammered our way southwards at a steady twelve knots. The London continued to sit steadfastly abreast of us, and ahead, astern, and on either side, the destroyers put in an occasional appearance above the waves. From time to time, there would be a brief winking session between the ships, otherwise, there seemed to be little communication or fuss.

Regularly, around midday, the Navigation Officer would appear in the wardroom, looking very wise and authoritative, in order to pin up a chart showing our position and those of the U-boats believed to be in our approximate area. The procedure thereafter seemed routine but nonetheless disturbing; wherever the U-boats were, there we made for, presumably in the belief that those were the spots we would be least expected.

As the days elapsed, strange faces in the wardroom became familiar and even friendly and the different rank stripes – straight, wavy and others – together with their colour code, began to make sense. Padres, 'pussers', doctors, engineers and 'real sailors', seemed all on an equal footing. And rightly so; when all was said and done, when the ship went down they all went down, regardless of rank or calling. Not a bit like the Air Force where some warriors I could name were likely to pass the entire war without coming within earshot of even the smallest bang.

It was early on in the voyage, too, that I and others had been invited to assist in censoring the mail, as the result of which a new dimension was added to my education. The lower deck, God bless it, was totally uninhibited when it came to discussing its more personal needs and more than once I found myself wriggling in embarrassment as my fellow countrymen revealed to me the activities that were clearly taking place the length and breadth of Britain. Brought up in the belief that my sceptred isle was the home of knights, gentlemen, honest yeomen and virginal maidens, I was harshly introduced to reality; gentlemen were clearly at a premium and virginal maidens as scarce as hen's teeth.

After an endless ten days at sea, we were somewhere south-west of Gibraltar. By the eighth day, the weather had improved considerably and it was an emotional moment for me when I first glimpsed the faint and distant outline of the Atlas mountains in Morocco. As we edged northwards and to the east, the Rock of Gibraltar eventually appeared and in the gathering dusk, we threaded our way in silence between scores of buoys and ships before gently jostling alongside the quay, back-to-back with the towering *Ark Royal*. I consulted my watch. It was 9 p.m. on the button!

19

Flight to Malta

In the warm and sultry blackness of the Mediterranean night, Gibraltar was a blaze of light, a stirring and nostalgic sight for those of us who had lived in conditions of blackout for almost two years. Gathering our meagre belongings, we bade farewell to the *Furious* and stumbled along the debris-strewn dockside towards the *Ark*. Above us, planks had already gone down and the first of our aircraft were being trundled across

The *Ark Royal* was as different from the *Furious* as chalk is from cheese; it was bigger, cleaner, brighter, more orderly, more civilised and, above all, more comfortable. I was shown to my cabin in which the bunk, though dauntingly hard and with a hump down the middle, seemed positively inviting. Also, thank God, there were no sepulchral noises – no bangs, clatters, howls, anchors being dropped or subterranean gurgles. Only a decent civilised hiss, which no fair-minded chap could possibly object to.

In the wardroom, huge by comparison with that of the *Furious*, we were greeted formally by officers in mess-kit and regaled with drinks before dinner. From our hosts we learned that we would be sailing as soon as the transfer of aircraft had been completed. Later, much later, with pink gins fairly slopping around inside, I returned to my cabin, my morale restored absolutely by the sophistication of my surroundings and the courtesy of my new-found friends. Then, in the wee small hours, tremors and subdued grumblings started up somewhere underfoot and, in a cosy, gin-induced stupor, I concluded that we were once more heading seawards and about to embark on phase two of our death-defying journey to the Western Desert. Good ol' Navy, I thought; Cap'n Bligh, or whoever, would probably know the way. Two points to starboard, if you please, Mister Christian! Dear

God! If only the sides of this cabin would keep still.

The following day was warm and bright and the Navy being resplendent in whites, we donned our tropical kit, most of us I suspect, a little self-consciously. I ascended to the flight deck, a vast aircraft-strewn platform, and sniffed the salt-laden south Atlantic air. Mmmm! Delicious! All around, the sea was blue and calm and, in every direction, there were light-coloured ships, proceeding at a leisurely pace and heading more or less in a westerly direction. A truly magnificent sight.

That, of course, was the trick. Because the German consul sat at Algeciras, a stone's throw from Gibraltar, and spied on all the port's activities, if it were necessary to go into the Mediterranean, the Royal Navy invariably sailed into the Atlantic, only to sneak back through the Straits at dead of night. The Germans, needless to say, were well aware of this simple subterfuge and the game of bluff was apt to become so involved, it became a problem to decide who was fooling whom.

However, after the liquid entertainment of the night before, my mind was in no fit state to dwell upon anything more involved than sunbathing and counting the vessels as they appeared over the horizon. Which they continued to do throughout the day as, in a gentle, swaying meander, we picked up two battleships, the *Rodney* and *Renown*, at least one elegant Sheffield-class cruiser, and a further clutch of white-moustached destroyers which served as a screen as far as the eye could see. There were smaller cruisers, too, of what I always chose to call the *Aurora* class, that ship itself becoming all too familiar in the months ahead. The faithful *London* was also there, together with the carriers *Furious* and *Argus*, the former giving more than a hint of the First World War cruiser from which she had been converted, whilst the angular *Argus*, poor thing, was reminiscent of nothing more exciting than a floating shoe-box. In all, there must have been twenty ships, a mighty display of naval strength, enough to make any Englishman's heart swell with pride. No enemy force in its right mind would dare attack us. Even so, I was glad to be on the *Ark*. Good old *Ark*, almost the largest ship in the fleet – and furthest away from the water!

On the night of 19/20 May, we crept silently through the Straits of Gibraltar heading east. When dawn broke, we were well into the Mediterranean, with the Navy visibly dry-mouthed and nervously on edge.

After twenty months of often bitter strife, Britain's war effort in the Middle East, and especially in the Mediterranean, had not been too successful. There was scarcely a blob of pink left on the map between Gibraltar and Egypt; in the Western Desert, what would be called the 8th Army cantered to and fro on what was sportingly referred to later as the Benghazi Handicap; Greece had fallen only weeks before, and a savage battle for Crete was in progress, soon to be lost.

Throughout this unhappy period, the Royal Navy suffered grievously. Two battleships, *Warspite* and *Valiant*, together with the carrier *Formidable*, were within days of being put out of action around Crete; the cruiser and destroyer force was still reeling from a stunning series of losses; and *Illustrious*, one of Britain's latest carriers, together with its supporting force, had been severely damaged when reinforcing Malta several months earlier. Small wonder, therefore, that the Navy had an almost obsessive horror of bombing attacks. They hated all aircraft and were apt to fire without warning at anything that moved, asking no questions and offering few excuses if the unfortunate target happened to be friendly.

The Fleet Air Arm, too, was beset by problems. Very much a Cinderella service, it was poorly equipped with Fulmars, as fighters, and Swordfish, as torpedo-bombers. The Fulmar was a large two-seater and a direct descendant of the Fairey Battle, a name which struck a chill in the heart of any RAF pilot who had had the misfortune to fly one during the first year of the war. With a performance considerably inferior to that of the Hurricane I, the Fulmar was outclassed by almost everything used by both the Germans and Italians. As for the Swordfish, a biplane which would not have looked out of place even in 1918, it was alleged – apocryphally no doubt – that their comparative immunity during the successful battle of Taranto was due to the enemy not having gunsights capable of accommodating anything that flew quite so slowly.

Fortunately, however, and with outstanding bravery, the pilots of the Fleet Air Arm ignored the unfitness of their mounts and roared into battle with the stoutest of hearts, tolerating their Fulmars and positively doting on their 'Stringbags'. This quite extraordinary loyalty to the Swordfish in particular, came to the fore when, over a large pink gin, I was commiserating with a group of the *Ark*'s naval aviators on the shortcomings of their aircraft. I was rewarded with silence and such icy stares that for a moment I thought I might be given a taste of the lash. On what other aircraft, I was coldly asked, could I carry ashore a fully-laden motor-cycle, strapped between either the undercarriage legs or the interplane struts? To which I was tempted to reply, in what circumstances would I ever wish to? Thankfully, I had the good sense to keep quiet.

Throughout the daylight hours of 20 May and beneath a solid cloud bank, the Mediterranean, anything but blue, streamed by, every ship trembling with apprehension as we ploughed towards the east. Up on the flight deck we ran our engines, tested everything we could lay hands on, and attended briefings.

There were twenty-three Hurricanes of 249 Squadron and about a similar number for each of the squadrons on the two other carriers, *Furious* and *Argus*. Those of us on the *Ark* would be taking off in two batches, one of twelve and the other eleven, the first to be led by 'Butch' Barton and the second by myself. I was happy to afford 'Butch' pride of place; he would be twelve aircraft nearer the sharp end!

We were also faced with the pressing problem of where to store our belongings, including the two ridiculous pith helmets, which, though light, were extremely bulky. Each of us had 30 lbs of clothing and essentials to find a home for but the Hurricane, being a fighter, had room for little more than a couple of maps. In the event, our kit was crammed anywhere and everywhere – in the radio compartment behind the armour plate, tied to the 'floor' in the rear of the fuselage, left and right of the pilot's seat, and in the ammunition boxes in the wings, the 3,000 rounds of .303 being removed for that purpose. This last arrangement had us chuckling; if the enemy were sighted en route, we would be able to give them a quick squirt of McLean's toothpaste from all eight guns, followed by a little of the hard stuff – a few bars of Lifebuoy soap!

In the operations room in the island of the carrier, we drew lines on maps and wrote down courses. For reasons of security, we would be flying just above the water and maintaining RT silence throughout, and each group of Hurricanes would be escorted by a Fulmar; as the naval fighter carried an observer-navigator in the back, this was felt to be a prudent measure.

Which led to a rather odd discovery: besides whatever else the observer carried in his cockpit, the beneficent Navy provided him with a Thompson sub-machine gun, one of the Al Capone variety. We discussed this choice of weapon with incredulous laughter. A Tommy-gun, for heaven's sake! With a range of about twenty yards! What on earth was that for? Then, on second thoughts, we decided it was probably for the observer to shoot the pilot, then himself, if things got out of hand.

The route we were to take was anything but straightforward. After take-off, we would fly for about an hour before sighting Cap Bon on the northern tip of Africa, where, more than likely, we would be intercepted by the Vichy French with their Curtiss Hawk 75s, an aircraft they had recently bought from the Americans. That our ex-allies were hostile, we knew; whether or not they would attack us, remained to be seen.

After Cap Bon, there would be a dog-leg to avoid the island of Pantelleria, inhabited by Hun Me 110s we were told, taking care thereafter to skirt both Lampedusa and Linosa, both enemy-held. Finally, with God's grace, we would hit Malta, whereupon we were to circle Filfla Rock, to the south of the island, in order to identify ourselves, before landing, one-third each, on the airfields of Ta Kali, Luqa and Hal Far. In all, we would be flying about 450 miles over a period of two and a half hours, a journey well within our maximum range and endurance of just over 1,000 miles and six and a half hours, respectively.

The decision that we were to fly off at dawn the following day was greeted with glum disapproval. Dawn! The Air Force seemed obsessed with dawns, whereas I, not being a dawn person, heartily disliked them. Dawn patrol brought to mind Errol Flynn and the old Sopwith Camel, with life at its lowest ebb. Why not mid-morning, or mid-afternoon, even? If I had to risk my neck, I always felt I should be permitted to do so on a full stomach and after a good night's sleep – preferably both! But, dawn it had to be, apparently, on Wednesday, 21 May.

The early morning of the fateful day was anything but welcoming, being damp, chilly, heavily overcast and as black as a boot. Four hours flying-time to the east, the battle for Crete was raging to a desperate and tragic conclusion.

Silent and yawning, we went in single file to one of the deserted dining rooms and were each handed a fried breakfast through a serving hatch by a member of the kitchen staff whose bare and bulging arms were liberally garnished with red-and-blue pictures referring to Love, Mother, and a lady called Doris. The malevolent yellow eye of an egg stared back at me unwinkingly. There was little conversation as we ate and all the time the ship trembled in spasms with the exertion of maintaining twenty knots.

Up on the flight deck, the wind tore at our clothes and hair as we assembled, shivering, in the operations room for a final briefing. Then out into the darkness again, threading our way between a mass of wings and propellers, maps and papers in hand, feeling empty and not at all happy. Lord, it was chilly! And damp! And miserable! Suddenly, another nostalgic vision of dear old North Weald, so far away now but so very, very desirable.

I climbed into my Hurricane and once in the cockpit felt rather better. The one small map-pocket already stuffed tight with some anonymous garment, I wedged my maps and the all-important paper on which were written the courses we were to follow, into the windscreen crevasse to the left of the gunsight. All around me were towels, shirts, my raincoat and service dress hat and some of the essentials of day-to-day living. Between me and my parachute proper, was the new pilot-type dinghy with its rock-hard gas-cylinder already very much in evidence against one bone of my backside. Some judicious wriggling helped a little, but not very much. Safety demanded its price!

For a time, nothing; the carrier slowly swayed in trembling surges, left and right, up and down. Then the twelve aircraft ahead of me were starting up; no appreciable noise, just airscrews dissolving into blurs as the reflected light caught them with a ghostly sheen. After that, a weirdly-attired officer with illuminated wands in his hands, his head nodding and his face mouthing some incomprehensible instruction, was motioning to me. I turned on the fuel, primed the engine, set the throttle and flicked up the mag switches before pressing the button which turned the airscrew. It moved around, jerked once – twice – before the engine caught with a sudden surge, acrid blue smoke spouting from each side. I throttled back to 1,200 revs and let her warm up. Ahead, pink and blue tongues of flame rippled from the exhausts and the Hurricane rocked slightly as a gusting 30 knot wind plucked at its sides. It was quite dark still but with a growing greyness.

Suddenly I was aware of the ship moving ponderously to the left as she turned into wind and the tremors and shaking grew to a minor frenzy as she wound up to thirty knots. A thin pencil-line of white smoke trailed backwards from the prow, soon to come directly down the centre-line of the deck. The *Ark Royal* was ready. Waiting!

With the coolant temperature showing 60 degrees and with encouragement from the man with the wands, I ran up my engine, exercised the constant-speed unit, and tested the switches. Everything sweet and even. I then set my compass and direction indicator, checked my gauges and settings several times over, adjusted the tail trimmer and lowered the flaps fifteen degrees. Finally, with a swift tug at my straps, I nodded to the wandsman beneath me. I was ready for off.

For several minutes I was kept waiting. Ahead, the first of the twelve Hurricanes began to take off. Spotted in groups of three, each aircraft moved first to the centre-line, then, under the influence of full throttle and with each rudder giving a brief but defiant wag, one aircraft after another surged forward, tail raised, and took off, rising like a lift in a climbing turn to the left.

Then the wandsman again, waving urgently and beckoning in exaggerated gestures. My turn! My mouth dry, I opened up and taxied forward, straightening on the centre-line. The wands gyrating, urging me to rev up. *Up! Up* ! Then suddenly, with a sweep of the arm – Down! I was *off*!

With full throttle but only a modest 6.25 lbs showing on the boost-gauge and my tail up almost immediately, I set off down the deck at a smart walking pace, my Hurricane feeling ridiculously light. The island drifted by, faces gawping. At this rate I would be airborne in seconds. This really was a stroll!

A moment later I was in the air, despite the extra 88 gallons of fuel, the deck dropping away beneath. In my left hand, I grasped the throttle and clutched a duplicate of the paper on which were written the various compass headings that would take us all to Malta. Veering immediately to the left and away from the ship's prow with its great curving bow-wave – wouldn't do to drop in front of that charging brute! – I changed hands on the control column in order to retract the wheels, the selector being on the right-hand side of the cockpit.

I had barely slipped the knob into the 'UP' position when there was a loud bang, as though a paper bag had been exploded in my left ear. The aircraft dropped a wing sharply and began to fly sideways in an alarming manner. Horror-stricken, I grabbed at the throttle and as the Hurricane continued to slew wildly to the left, was assailed by a flurry of white missiles. The paper on which my courses had been written and which I had released involuntarily when diving for the throttle, zipped past my head to disappear into the great wide world beyond, and with a disconcerting '*whap*', the maps and other papers I had so deftly tucked into the windscreen crevasse, were sucked out of their hideaway to wrap themselves briefly round my head before being snatched away by the slipstream.

My first and instant diagnosis was that I had lost the port wing-tank. The aircraft, at low speed, was barely controllable even with hard right rudder and full stick and was slipping sideways and downwards disastrously. For one terrible moment, I thought I was bound for the water some fifty feet beneath, but the briefest of glances to my left enabled me to recognise that, although the tank was probably still in place, something almost as unpleasant had occurred. The largest of the gun and ammunition panels on the top surface of the port wing had come adrift and a piece of metal several square feet in area was sticking up at an angle of about forty-five degrees, having jammed in its triumphant moment of escape. Obviously, the McLean's toothpaste and Lifebuoy soap had tried to make a break for it with the result that I now had an unwanted third aileron fully applied, as well as a very effective airbrake on my left side. Rigid with fear, I raised the flaps and climbed away with tight and trembling hands, thinking wildly that I would have to land back on the *Ark* immediately and wondering how on earth I was going to do so without a hook and with two overload tanks bulging with fuel and just aching to catch fire. Moreover, there was the aerodynamic effect of the breakaway panel to consider, which meant that I would have to approach the deck at a much higher speed than would otherwise be necessary. Whichever way I looked at it, the outlook was bleak. Engrossed absolutely with keeping the Hurricane out of the water, I dismissed from my mind completely the maps and other papers. To hell with them, they could swim!

As I laboured around the *Ark* in a wide circle at about 300 feet, the other members of my group of eleven began to catch up and formate on me, silent, gawping and totally unaware of my predicament. Below, the carrier's deck looked no bigger than a handkerchief and, on its far side, suddenly – a Fulmar. Our Fulmar!

The engine now well throttled back to 0 lbs boost and 1,800 revs, my Hurricane behaved a little more reasonably. With the gun-panel resolutely rampant, at the higher speed of 170 mph, surprisingly, a little less opposite stick was required but, without a rudder bias, the load on my right foot was painfully tiring after barely two minutes, so that the prospect of two more hours with it in that position was mind-boggling. But – and it was a big but – the alternative was to land back on, and that was even less attractive. The decision, therefore, was not hard to make: it was Malta for me, with or without a usable limb at the end of the journey. In a loose gaggle around the Fulmar, therefore, and with me in the lead, we turned eastwards and set off; with luck I would not even need my sheaf of maps and courses. Shaking and breathless still, I gazed around; the gently heaving sea was endlessly grey in every direction, glittering like molten lead in the early morning gloom.

After about thirty minutes, when my main tanks had emptied sufficiently, I tried transferring fuel and was gratified to see that everything appeared to be working normally. My right leg, which was awkwardly pushed forward almost to its full extent, had long since begun to tremble and grow numb but as I was able to keep changing hands on the control column, my arms did not tire unduly. Those first thirty minutes, though, seemed endless. I consulted my watch regularly, listening and watching for strange happenings up front, but the big Merlin engine was buzzing away quite happily, obviously determined to be cooperative, so that after a time I forgot about it, the wretched gun-panel, my own acute discomfort, and the possibility of missing Malta altogether, being problems of much more immediate concern.

Shortly before the hour, some rocks appeared far off to my right which I concluded were part of Cap Bon. We could expect to be intercepted here by the French and I considered what we might do if attacked. Minutes passed in watchful expectation but no aircraft were seen. Then, when I was just beginning to relax, quite inexplicably and without warning, the Fulmar suddenly began to accelerate and in the space of a mile or two, having left us all standing, pulled up steeply and disappeared into cloud. One moment it was there, the next, it wasn't! Gone!

It all happened in seconds. In horrified silence I sat and watched, stunned by the awful significance of its departure. After which, I flew in an aimless curve to my left, my mind grappling weakly for an explanation of its precipitate departure and, more to the point, as I had neither maps nor a list of courses to steer, what I was going to do. Meanwhile, ten Hurricanes, uttering not a word, dutifully followed me about like a trail of lemmings looking for a cliff, wondering, no doubt, what on earth I was up to.

With RT silence to be broken only on pain of death, I flew in a circle without uttering a sound, my mind numb with foreboding. Apart from knowing that Africa was somewhere to the south and Malta approximately to the east, I could have been in Tibet. All around were thousands of square miles of very inhospitable looking water and mist, and immediately overhead – at about 500 feet, in fact – unbroken cloud as far as the eye could see. Behind me trailed my ten disciples, observing my every movement and clearly unaware that I was nearly demented with worry and on the point of tears; a modest twenty years of age and my account barely in credit with the bank of experience, there were precious few resources to call upon.

Then, God-given resolution. To heck with RT silence, we were probably too low for our conversation to be picked up, anyway. Thus reassured, I called up Pat Wells, who was deputy leader, and briefly explained my predicament: would he care to take over the lead? His reply was prompt and devastatingly succinct. No, he wouldn't! Then I spoke to the formation at large. Was there anyone capable of leading us to Malta? Silence! Not a word! I can only assume that at that precise moment, all their radios suddenly went unserviceable!

I suppose it was the lack of response from my companions that generated a spark of rebellion somewhere beneath my parachute release-box. Bugger it! We couldn't just keep flying in circles in the middle of the Mediterranean. There were only three possible courses of action: to fly south and make a present of ourselves to someone in Africa; to go east for Malta with the probability of missing the island altogether and finishing up in the water; or to go west and return to Gibraltar, using the coast of Africa as a guide. The first option was out of the question, the second I didn't like very much, but the third was a possibility, provided we had sufficient fuel. Desperately, I totted up the miles in my head: a day and a night's sailing at twenty knots – that would be around 650 miles. Add to that an hour's flying at 170 mph. Total, 820 miles, or thereabouts. We could just about do it. Well, almost! Gun-panels and footloads forgotten, I turned my brood about and set course for Gibraltar. And to my everlasting surprise, they all followed, without so much as a word.

As we headed westwards, to describe my feelings as low is to liken a molehill to Everest. I was devastated almost to the point of being physically sick. But, so resilient is the spirit of youth that, after a few minutes, I actually began to perk up. Right or wrong, we were going back to Gibraltar and, God willing, we would all make it safely. In my mind's eye a picture of our arrival took shape. Stap me, they would say when eleven Hurricanes suddenly appeared out of the mist, where have you chaps come from? And I would ask – all innocence, of course – whether we had landed at Ta Kali, Luqa, or Hal Far. This was Malta, wasn't it? No? Well, I'd be blowed – it would seem I had flown in the wrong direction! A mere 1,500 miles in the wrong direction! I even managed to raise a smile at the thought of it.

My morale rising as I went, I flew for about thirty minutes on a course of 270 degrees; a little later I would veer south and pick up the African coast, after which it would be easy. There was no turning back now, the die was cast. With my engine running smoothly and everything other than my right leg and backside in fairly good order, my confidence grew by the minute. All we needed now was time.

It was about then that I noticed a change of colour in the water beneath, a streak of lighter green, barely perceptible but there. Immediately, I sensed that I had come across the wake of our returning fleet, sailing hot-foot for safer waters no doubt, and like a hound on the track of a particularly odoriferous fox, I flew with my nose to the trail for some minutes until, there, in the distance and scarcely visible in the haze, the British fleet – pounding for home!

As we approached low down, my aircraft radiating goodwill, our presence had what might euphemistically be described as a stimulating effect on His Majesty's ships. Suspicious as ever of a low-flying attack, every vessel assumed action stations and at least a dozen wheels were thrown about, causing destroyers and cruisers alike to heel over crazily and disperse as quickly as their throbbing screws could urge them. Half-expecting a rash of shell-bursts in my immediate area, I thought desperately of how I could indicate friendly intentions, RT communication being most definitely out. I then remembered my downward identification light and my eight- words-per-minute of highly individual Morse Code. What did I say? 'SOS'? 'Don't shoot'? 'Wotcher'? Or just plain 'Friend'? I half- decided that 'Friend' seemed the most appropriate but, in the tension of the moment, couldn't remember 'F' in dahs and dits. Then, it was all too late; we had been recognised.

The *Ark Royal* being somewhere in the middle of all the careering, heeling ships, I climbed up with my silent gaggle of followers and circled it at a respectable height and distance. Far beneath, the carrier's decks were littered with aircraft.

I decided then that we would all have to land-on, hooks or no hooks, and the thought chilled me to the marrow. As the *Ark*'s lifts were too small to take the Hurricanes below, after landing, each one would have to be pushed forward in front of the heavy wire barrier which would then be raised in order to catch the next aircraft should it overshoot – which was more than likely. Not only would it all take time, even assuming there were no accidents, but space on the deck would be severely limited when it became my turn to land-on, the responsibility of leader naturally demanding that I should see everyone safely down and be the last. As I circled and looked down, the more I thought about it, the less attractive the whole business became.

And it was at that point that an aircraft appeared- level with my shoulder before dropping like a hawk towards the *Ark*, landing without ceremony, and clinging on for dear life. It was a Fulmar – our Fulmar. Later, I learned that an oil pipe had burst in front of the pilot, spraying him with hot oil, and anxious to get as far away from the sea as possible and back to the carrier before his engine seized, the unfortunate man had decided to leave us in haste, climbing through the cloud and heading for the fleet. As if we didn't know!

For ten minutes or so, we circled the *Ark* whilst the deck was cleared, an agonisingly slow procedure for all of us looking down. Malta, at that stage, could not have been further from my thoughts as my mind was already attuned to our landing-on.

Then, to my considerable surprise, a Fulmar – another Fulmar – from where I was looking down exactly like a model, crawled to the rear of the ship, turned, then slowly took off. I followed it instinctively and, certainly with no clear idea of what either I or the naval pilot was intending to do, formated on it. The Fulmar then waggled its wings in a friendly fashion, the chap in the back pulled a cheerful face and waved, and ten Hurricanes surged up, left, right and behind me. Looking down at my compass I saw we were heading roughly east again. I then consulted my watch. We had already been airborne for rather more than two hours.

It is sometimes difficult to explain later why one takes a particular course of action. I had no clear idea of what we were about to do or even that the Fulmar was intending to lead us to Malta. But, follow it I did and, thank the Lord, it was. Back again at 300 feet and still maintaining strict RT silence, we clustered around it and with engine settings well reduced and 175 mph on the clock, we settled down on our second attempt to reinforce the Middle East. By the roughest of calculations, there were now about 600 miles between us and Malta, a further three and a half hours of flying for everyone and for me and my right leg, an extended period of pure, undiluted purgatory.

Meanwhile, I had been regularly topping up my main tanks from the overloads and wondering if I might possess a couple of the legendary cornucopias; they seemed bottomless although common sense reasoned that they would soon be empty. And indeed, they were. After two and a half hours of flying, the main-tank contents showed signs of reducing, which meant that I then had less than ninety gallons of fuel remaining.

With the disturbing prospect of landing back on the carrier removed and my Hurricane showing no signs of temperament, I was able to concentrate on my own physical misfortunes. The gun-panel remained stoically obstructive and my right leg ached to the point at which I would have happily agreed to it being sawn off – without an anaesthetic! The metal cylinder in my dinghy-pack, too, was doing its best to cripple me permanently and, to relieve the pressure on the left-hand bone of my backside, I undid my straps and, opening my hood, bounced up and down as far as flying the aircraft and safety would allow. I then rooted about in the bottom of the cockpit and found a towel which I attempted to stuff between my rear and the dinghy-pack. But, to no avail; all my efforts provided only fleeting relief so that I resigned myself to having an insoluble problem for the remainder of the flight. I didn't allow myself even to think of the next leg to Mersa Matruh which would involve a further five hours of flying over 850 miles.

When hope of ever seeing land again began to fade, Cap Bon appeared for the second time on my right and we changed course in order to skirt Pantelleria. Meanwhile, the cloud still sat on our heads in a grey and forbidding layer – so much for Mediterranean sunshine! – and we had been flying for so long, it was difficult to comprehend that it was little more than our normal breakfast time. On and on. On and on. Interminably. The Mediterranean couldn't be this big! Then, off to my right, a low mound that I presumed was Pantelleria, at which point I recalled my own firm instructions that no one was to straggle. I need not have worried; at the first sign of the island, the ten Hurricanes behind me fairly scuttled past so that for a few minutes I actually found myself last in the formation. But of the Hun 110s we saw not a sign, and forty years later I can still raise a rash, speculating on what they might have done to us had they known we were limping past within 15 miles of their airfield. One German aircraft, a twin-engined bomber, did sail over our heads however, but if the pilot saw us, he had the good sense to ignore us, as indeed with empty guns, we were obliged to ignore him.

From then on, my main preoccupation was considering my fuel state. As leader, I would be better off than the rest of my formation so that the bleats, when they came, would undoubtedly be from those at the rear. As I watched, the two main tanks in my aircraft slowly emptied and I switched onto reserve knowing that only about thirty gallons stood between me and a ditching. From horizon to horizon there was nothing but an endless vista of sea and mist, whilst above, the cloud, though lightening somewhat, still completely obscured the sun.

At this stage we had been airborne for about five hours and I began to pray very earnestly that Malta would materialise. Or, had we already missed it? I had no idea what Malta looked like and visions of the island kept appearing like mirages, only to fade just as quickly into vaporous oblivion. The fear that we had already passed it grew like a cancer.

With a bare 15 gallons remaining in my reserve tank and little more than a smell of petrol in the mains, I decided to break RT silence. The Fulmar had to be told that we were almost finished and if the enemy tuned in, good luck to him; all he would find would be eleven patches of oil in the sea. I put it as briefly as I could; if we weren't down in fifteen minutes, I announced sombrely, we were all in the water. To this I added a personal and silent message to the duty angel, something to the effect that we would all appreciate a little assistance – if he had a moment or two to spare! But, for some minutes there was no response, no shaft of light, no heavenly revelation, nothing other than mist and sea in every direction.

Malta, when it came, appeared with magical suddenness and in the form of cliffs adjacent to my left ear. They loomed white and brown out of the mist and sea and were almost within touching distance. At the same time, the sun broke through, warm and brilliant, as though to crown our discovery and arrival. A miracle – *the* miracle – had happened!

Filfla Rock being just ahead, I made a token dart at it before turning north in order to climb up over the cliffs that formed the island's southern boundary.

As I approached the precipitous edge, my aircraft rocking violently in the up-currents, red tongues of flame darted out all around me. How odd, I thought, cliffs don't usually behave like that! Then I was over the top with barely fifty feet to spare and above the island itself – ochre-coloured sandstone, glaringly bright, tiny brown stone-fringed fields the size of pocket handkerchiefs, everything hot and lumpy and harsh to the eye, a searing landscape of brown and white, utterly different from the Malta of my imagination.

Low as I was, I had no difficulty in picking out the airfield of Luqa; it was dead ahead and I could see the hangars, the pale runways and a scattering of light-brown buildings. I flashed a glance at my fuel gauges. Less than ten gallons remaining. I would go straight in, to heck with a circuit!

Down with the wheels – two green lights. Airscrew in fine pitch – the engine-note rose. Everything bouncing, lurching and bumping. Heavens, was Malta *always* like this? Then the flaps. The aircraft slewing sideways and difficult to handle with the jutting gun-panel, I pulled up the port wing firmly but with the greatest of care and found myself going much too fast.

Whoaah! Slow down you brute! About 100 feet up now and the Hurricane fairly jumping about in the convection currents of heat. The runway directly ahead, tilting obliquely. Almost there now, thank God!

Not until I had reached that point did it dawn on me that all was not as it should have been. On the far side of the airfield, the nearest edge of which was about 400 yards away, flame-centred puff-balls exploded into silent flowers of black and brown and a large twin- engined aircraft directly ahead of me disintegrated as if by magic in a violent bubble of flame and oily smoke. And in the several seconds it took for me to interpret these strange goings-on, a stick of bombs came marching towards me with measured strides across the parched brown earth and white streaks of something-or-other flew past my starboard wingtip to curve away into oblivion. I gave a startled glance upwards; so keen was I to get my wheels on the ground, I had never thought of looking in that direction. Immediately above, the sky was filled with white-grey anti-aircraft bursts and pale-bellied aircraft, clearly unfriendly, raced over my head, fortunately in the opposite direction. Great God! I was right in the centre of an air attack! No wonder there had been tongues of flame on the cliffs; they had been anti-aircraft fire, with the gunners obviously not too concerned about my being in their line of sight.

Galvanised into action, I opened up hard and lifting my wheels and flaps in almost frenzied movements, fled away southwards at tree-top height towards Filfla, our planned point of assembly in the event of any such attack.

Within seconds, however, and still hugging the contours of the ground, concern overcame panic. 10 gallons of fuel! What was the point of rushing out to sea if the engine was going to stop as soon as I arrived! If victim I was to be, better by far to be a victim over land rather than in – or under – the water. Without so much as a second thought, I hauled my aircraft about and headed back to the airfield.

Approaching Luqa for the second time, I saw that the raid had passed, although stark evidence of it remained. The twin-engined aircraft I had seen hit was producing a pillar of smoke that could probably be seen in Cairo and there were other fires, too, billowing their filth into the atmosphere, all forming a vast and almost solid pall of drifting dust more than 1,000 feet high. Luqa lay silent, inert and in a way pathetic, like an animal which had just been run over!

All this I noted in a glance but, with surprising and calculated indifference, dismissed it as incidental to my own immediate predicament. My aircraft still bouncing around like a mad thing, I lowered the wheels and flaps yet again and prepared to land on as much of the runway as I could see remained undamaged. Then, with the gun-panel rampant to the end and masses of aileron and right rudder, I shot across the airfield boundary, skidding and slewing and a good 20 mph too fast, and plonked the Hurricane down amid a huge swirl of dust-devils. As the wheels screeched on the hot tarmac, my heart lifted and a prayer of thanks came audibly from my lips. What glorious, wonderful, rock-hard earth! God bless Malta! God bless its drystone walls and tuppenny-ha'penny fields! God bless its bomb-holes! God bless everything about the place! Joyfully, I allowed my Hurricane to race ahead, its tyres singing in tune with my feelings.

Braking to a stop at the end of the runway and with my engine ticking over as though it hadn't a care in the world, I looked about to see which way to taxi. Not a soul in sight! It was breathtakingly hot, blindingly bright, very quiet, and very still. Except for one other Hurricane, in the middle distance and buzzing faintly around the circuit, I had Luqa entirely to myself – fires, burning aircraft, pillars of black smoke, dust, corruption, stench, the lot!

Undecided, I opened up and moved towards some low buildings half a mile away and after some minutes a solitary khaki-clad figure appeared – with a pipe in its mouth. Running towards me with a hand clutching his hat, the man, a Flying Officer, jumped onto my wing and put his face to my ear.

'Over there,' he screamed, hanging on.

Nodding, I opened the throttle, whereupon the slipstream caught the burning embers of his pipe and whipped them straight into my left eye, which clamped tight, like an oyster, as though someone had poked it with a stick.

There followed several moments of exquisite pain during which I sat there half-blind and streaming, exercising all the self-control I could muster. This bloody man! – I even thought of punching him. Then, with bowed head and my remaining good eye, I found myself taking in the clock on my instrument panel and doing some quick mental arithmetic. We had been airborne five hours and twenty-five minutes; probably the longest operational trip ever made by a Hurricane.

I parked my aircraft and, with a trembling sigh of relief, switched off. The airscrew tottered to a clanking standstill and after almost six hours of noise, physical discomfort and tension, the silence and blistering heat were in stark and unforgettable contrast. In the distance the other Hurricane was landing.

And it was then that I found to my embarrassment that I could scarcely move, my right leg being locked in spasm and the left bone of my behind, where the steel carbon dioxide bottle had impinged for more than five hours, painful beyond description. I tried to rise but couldn't and for a moment thought I would need to be lifted out – except that there was no one around to help other than the single officer who, by this time, was looking up at me from below and hopping agitatedly from foot to foot.

After a few moments, he shouted truculently, 'You'd better get out, there's an air-raid on.'

To which I shouted back, equally testily, 'I know there is, chum, I've just landed in the middle of it!' – thinking as I did so, that after almost six hours of what I had been through, what was an air-raid?

All the same, some of his concern transferred itself to me and with a determined effort I managed to haul myself to my feet and clamber down, looking like an advertisement for Sloane's Liniment. Immediately, I was grabbed by the arm and hustled, limping, towards a hole in a wall from which stone steps disappeared downwards into the darkness. My guide gave me an unceremonious shove and down I went, stumbling into the gloom.

At the bottom of the steep steps was a mass of hot, sweating, garlic-flavoured humanity, mostly dust-white, chattering Maltese workmen and khaki-clad airmen. However, among the many faces dimly visible in the half-light were several I recognised, one of them belonging to Crossey, who had flown in 'Butch' Barton's group.

'Hello!' I heard myself saying. 'What a perfectly blood-stained journey.' I then explained briefly what had happened to me, and added, 'I'm not looking forward to the next leg one little bit!'

Crossey replied without a smile, 'You needn't worry, there isn't going to be a next leg. Haven't you heard? We're staying here.' 'Staying? Here?' My voice rose to a cracked falsetto. 'You mean we're staying in Malta?' I had an instant mental picture of millions of square miles of sea in every direction, minuscule brown fields, stone walls everywhere, and nowhere, but nowhere, to put down a Hurricane in the event of engine trouble or battle damage. Malta, for God's sake, when all I wanted was miles of open desert!

Crossey nodded. 'The AOC wants an experienced squadron to stay on the island because they've been getting hell. 261 Squadron will take our aircraft on to Egypt and we'll take theirs, or what's left of 'em. We're to get unloaded as quickly as possible!'

Minutes later the 'all clear' sounded and still in a mild state of shock, I found myself once more in the heat and glare of the Maltese sun; although I seemed to have been flying for a week, it was still not yet noon. With others, I limped back to my aircraft and for the next thirty minutes supervised the removal of my possessions. By degrees they all emerged – parachute bag, towels, shirts, raincoat, rolled-up this and that, everything – including the pith helmets. At that stage the pith helmets were becoming something of a joke.

Finally, it was all stacked in a pathetic little heap on the dusty concrete; everything I possessed, which wasn't very much. I looked around with hands on hips – resigned – crushed – defeated. Malta! Who would believe it? And what about our troops, would we ever see them again? And all my other kit, which was going the 'long way round'? No, it really was too much!

An hour later, the eight of us who had landed at Luqa – one-third of both 'Butch' Barton's group and my own – were on our way to Ta Kali airfield by bus. Ta Kali! I had no idea where Ta Kali was exactly or what it looked like other than it was a landing ground and several miles to the north. By that time, however, I was past caring. Hot, running with dust-caked sweat, tired and ravenously hungry, reaction had set in and I was in a depressed frame of mind. Malta, for God's sake! Of all places, Malta! What would my parents think of this arrangement?

The bus was unique, reminding me of pictures I had seen of those taking the French army to the Battle of the Marne in 1914, although it must have been more modern – just! It roared off, shaking, banging and creaking abominably, being driven by a lunatic Maltese who careered wildly around dusty, unpaved tracks barely wide enough to accommodate the width of the vehicle, the man hooting his horn and shouting at each bare-footed urchin, peasant or herd of goats that cringed into doorways or flattened themselves against stone walls as we hurtled past like a careering collection of tin cans. And it was at that early stage of my stay in Malta that I learned that 'Ar-right!' was the password for everything; 'Ar-right' started the bus and stopped it, it meant yes, no, thank-you, good morning, I want to get off, slow down you half-wit, everything! 'Ar-right!' Wonderfully ubiquitous! In front, the driver demonically cheerful, kept turning round and crying 'Ar-right!' to us in the back, driving meanwhile with one hand and seeming hell-bent on suicide. In the rear, gripped by speechless apprehension, we all hung on like clams.

The events of the next few days remain a kaleidoscope of fleeting memories and impressions. The officers' accommodation, within half a mile of Ta Kali airfield, was a large stone building with a courtyard and spiral steps rising to the section used as an ante-room. There, I found 'Butch' Barton and others who had landed at Hal Far and Ta Kali, everyone looking resignedly dazed by our sudden change of circumstances. My flight had not been the only one to suffer misfortune, apparently; only half the complement of Hurricanes had managed to take off from the *Furious*, and other aircraft from both the *Furious* and *Argus* had turned back, there being a story –untrue as we later learned – that one whole flight had landed in North Africa. Of my own group, all had been critically short of fuel, one pilot having his engine stop when still in the circuit, obliging him to land with a dead stick, whilst another had insufficient fuel even to taxi in. What a scrape! And what a shambles!

Then, an anonymous voice in my ear: 'By the way, why didn't you turn back when the *Ark* came on and said that we couldn't make it?'

I turned, questioning and astonished. 'You mean the *Ark* said that?'

'That's right. Fifteen minutes after we'd set off again, they broke RT silence and said we were all to return and land-on because we wouldn't have the fuel to get here. We thought you pressed on because you didn't think much of the idea.'

I looked blankly at the speaker with an expression of genuine amazement. 'I didn't hear that,' I said limply. 'Honestly I didn't!' And I hadn't, although I doubt that anyone present really believed me.

After a thoroughly indifferent meal, which I hardly ate, I found myself confronted by a number of familiar faces, including those of several ex-members of 56 Squadron, whom I had known at North Weald, and Worrall, who used to be in 249. I formed the impression that most of 261 were mad keen to get off the island, which was not exactly encouraging. Then someone was asking if my aircraft was all right. I replied that it was fine, provided he was looking for a Hurricane with three ailerons – which left my questioner a bit perplexed.

But it was that first night that has always loomed large in my memory. Unable to be granted a room because of temporary overcrowding, I found myself on a camp-bed in a stone corridor down which, it appeared, the whole population of Malta – stark naked – pushed past at two-minute intervals en route to the single lavatory situated within feet of where I lay. Furthermore, as there was high incidence of what was termed 'Malta dog', a particularly nasty form of dysentery, the noises-off were as unpleasant as the other manifestations of the affliction.

All this, however, was but a minor inconvenience when compared with the onslaught of the mosquitoes which, relishing this latest import of sweet, new English flesh, circled me throughout the night, singing like choristers and imbibing voraciously. Driven almost demented by their persistent biting, I struck out blindly in the darkness and awoke to find myself a mass of red bumps which itched abominably. Indeed, in the months to come, I found the mosquitoes much more of a nuisance than the Germans and the Italians combined as, with none of the present-day insecticides available, they proved to be a remorseless and seemingly indestructible enemy.

As I crept miserably towards the bare, stone dining-room on that first morning-after and viewed with distaste the plateful of fatty bacon, fried bread and the rest, all curling at the edges and swimming in congealing grease, my morale was as low as ever I had known it. Malta, for God's sake! What malevolent angel had decided that we should be holed up in this ... this dump?

Having landed on 21 May, for several days thereafter we did little other than settle in and find our way about. Malta, although a great shock to the system initially, gradually began to take on a more favourable aspect despite the oppressive heat and lack of facilities in the mess.

We officers were quartered in a rather sombre castle-like building known as Torre Cumbo, situated less than a mile from Ta Kali airfield. Looking as though it had been erected at the time of the Crusades, it was formidably built of large stone blocks, a method of construction with which we were soon to become all too familiar and which later proved to be a greater threat to life than the enemy bombs themselves, as a collapsed building caused by a near-miss invariably meant death – or at least a braining – for those within, unless they had the good sense to dive beneath the nearest table or bed. During my seven months in Malta, I was to spend a good deal of time under my bed.

Thankfully, I was soon able to vacate my camp-bed adjacent to the musical lavatory, having been offered a room on the other side of the courtyard, which I subsequently shared with 'Ozzie' Crossey. A largish, rather sepulchral place, it was reminiscent of a monk's cell, gloomy but cool and with a single shuttered window. However, as all the bedrooms led off each other, it too was something of a thoroughfare, there always seeming to be a trail of pale, naked forms padding sleepily to yet another lavatory just beyond our door, a scene once picturesquely described to me by a colleague as looking like the production line in a black-pudding factory.

With our new accommodation went a shared batman, a little boy of about twelve called Charlie, whose duties were to keep the place clean, look after our laundry, and fight off the mosquitoes. This last named task he attempted by closing the shutters and laying down a fog of 'Flit', which did considerably more damage to Crossey and to me than ever it did to the mosquitoes, as scarcely a night passed without my being bitten to pieces, the little brutes not only surviving the almost solid veil of insecticide but worming their way through even the most scrupulously-inspected of mosquito nets.

And Charlie had other qualities, too. One of a family of twelve – the Maltese were (and probably still are) practising Catholics! – he had the face of an angel and the voice of a fog-horn, his vocal chords honed, by endless competition at home, no doubt, to produce a sound not unlike a distress signal at sea. Despite his choirboy looks, he could also be a savage little animal at times and, on one occasion, it was only by the grace of God that murder was prevented when Crossey caught him brandishing a knife and about to slit the throat of another of the child batmen who had apparently upset him.

With little that was modern about the place, such as electric bells, the only means of communication was by voice. Requiring assistance, we simply howled 'Charlie', and kept on howling until the little lad appeared, and as everyone else did the same and Charlie's answering voice was more strident than all of ours in total, the volume of sound across the courtyard could, on occasion, be considerable.

It was also on my second full day in Malta that I went into Valletta.

Valletta, the principal town on the island, was the seat of government, the site of the Citadel, the dockyards, the Army, Navy, and Air Force headquarters, our own fighter control centre, everything. About six miles away, it was normally reached by bus – Maltese bus! – and in order to catch the bus, those of us at Ta Kali were obliged to walk into Mosta.

In 1941, the village of Mosta represented perhaps the most blatant example of poverty and wealth in juxtaposition I had ever beheld. The massive Roman Catholic church, its hugely magnificent dome decorated internally with the most breathtaking display of marble and gold, was the focal point of a village that was primitive and deprived almost beyond description. The streets between the unkempt ruins of houses were mere rutted paths streaming with urine and excrement through which dark, bare-footed children shouted and played and goats dragged their bloated, milk-heavy udders as they scavenged among the filth and rubbish, the whole area buzzing with clouds of green-bodied flies all seemingly mesmerised by the summer heat (Mosta has since been transformed).

And the bus, in its way, was scarcely better. At least as ancient as the relic we had travelled in from Luqa to Ta Kali, it was crammed with flat-hatted, black-robed priests and Maltese peasants, all squat, bulky, work-stained, pungently sweating and garlicky – and vociferous! The driver shouted and gesticulated, the passengers shouted back, and all this before the bus had even started! Then with loud 'Ar-rights', we were off, hooting, clattering and roaring through the narrow stone-walled lanes and unkempt villages until eventually, and miraculously, we entered the outskirts of Valletta. By this time I was alive with fleas donated by my earthy, malodorous companion in the next seat and being bitten almost into a solid lump. My oath, what a place! How long could I stand it?

Valletta was a distinct improvement, however, many of the buildings and streets being of grand dimensions and possessing an ordered and noble air. With several others, I inspected the one-street shopping centre, Strada Royalle, looked out over the many harbours and inlets crowded with warships and other craft, examined from a safe distance, the Gut – the naughty place! – and finally entered the Union Club, a cool and pleasant haven cast in the mould of a St James's gentleman's establishment. There, among other civilised services available, I could have my hair cut and washed – an absolute necessity in Malta, as I was soon to learn – and be offered delicate turkey sandwiches with my afternoon tea. An oasis in the midst of a desert of sandstone, smells, mosquitoes and fleas, I signed the appropriate application form immediately and became a prospective member, although I never recall paying my subscription! Later still, I was introduced to Monico's and Maxim's, where a bulky but extremely amiable ex-ship's steward, who was to become a great friend of us all, served cool John Collinses and other multi-coloured concoctions – plus hot pork sandwiches! In the months to follow, and although I never saw a pig on the island – they were alleged to share each farmhouse with the farmer and take precedence over all his family – the hot pork sandwiches remained in constant supply despite the severe food shortage that resulted later in the year when the Axis besiegers tightened the screw.

But if my spirits had been raised by my excursion into Valletta, they were dashed absolutely when 'Butch' and I, with others, gathered on Ta Kali airfield to inspect facilities and consider how best to arrange ourselves.

The facilities were soon inspected – there were next to none! A single 12-foot square tent, with its sides rolled up, constituted the operations room and pilots' accommodation, and there was another to shelter the NCOs and airmen forming the first-line servicing crews. Around both, roughly dispersed, were about six Hurricanes, some tropicalised, others not, all of them patched and grey with accumulated dust, some with metal De Havilland airscrews, others with wooden Rotols. With not a squadron marking in sight, the dejected- looking aircraft sat there with hung heads like hounds exhausted by a fruitless chase. Alongside, several starter-batteries, their chattering chore-horses 'putt-putting' away endlessly, trailed their hoses to a few of the defeated hulks, whilst on the hill several miles to the south and west, the yellow walls and towers of M'dina and Rabat (I never knew which was which, learning later that M'dina was, in fact, the Arab name for Rabat) looked down hotly and impassively in our direction, the afternoon heat rising in breathless, shimmering waves from a jigsaw of intervening drystone boundaries and dusty, postage-stamp fields. And as we formed a lack-lustre group, running with unaccustomed sweat and with our white knees blinking in the near-tropical sun, we all became aware of the subtle but unmistakable aroma of Malta, half-Middle Eastern, half – something.

A group of 261 Squadron pilots, yet to embark on their journey to Egypt, clustered around us and a gharry, hauled by a decrepit- looking nag, its ears protruding through a squashed straw hat and with a young officer at the reins, creaked past on the dusty track which ran across the end of the airfield and adjacent to dispersal. Another of 261, I was informed, as mild cheers and waves were exchanged, a pastoral, totally incongruous scene when contrasted with the violent air attack I had landed in only hours before.

I found myself in conversation with someone. How many of the squadron were airborne? None, I was told. I wondered incredulously if those six, clapped-out Hurricanes were all there were? No, not quite, they could usually muster around eight or nine – one Mark II and the rest Mark Is. Seldom more than nine, though, and they were all pretty tired. Tired! I remember looking at them in dismay – euphemism taken to extreme!

With so few aircraft available and more than twenty-six pilots in the squadron, 'Butch' and I decided to operate as two groups, one led by him and the other by me. We would use the same aircraft, of course, and share the daily task of defending the island which, at that time, was a twenty-four hour job as we were also expected to operate at night, when required. We were encouraged to learn that there were about the same number of Hurricanes in 185 Squadron, stationed at Hal Far, some 10 miles to the south and east, the total available force of fighters on the island being eighteen at best. With 185's Hurricanes about as impressive as our own – as I was soon to find out! – the defenders of Malta towards the end of May 1941 had about them a distinctly jaded air. Who comprised the enemy in Sicily I had no idea, except that they were Germans with Italian assistance, the whole force being pretty effective, having succeeded in making a mess of

261 Squadron in recent months and putting the fear of God into the Royal Navy. But what of it? We had dealt with Huns and Eyeties before and could lick them again, of that we had no doubt. Our only concern was the quality of the rubbish we had to fly and the real fear that our aircraft might not be up to catching the blighters. Why couldn't they give us Spits or some decent Hurricane IIs at the very least?

We also learned that we were to take over 261's duties the following day, 25 May. None of us had flown since arriving on the island, nor would we have the opportunity to do so before being thrown into battle in aircraft totally new to us. Moreover, apart from our brief glimpse of Malta on the day of our arrival, we had not even seen it from the air. Still, what did it matter? All places – all Huns, in fact – were the same to us.

After deciding on how we should organise the squadron, I wandered out to the parked aircraft in order to select one that looked even half-way decent. I was not encouraged. God, what a rag-bag set! Tomorrow? We'd just have to see.

Meanwhile, the sun beat down with tropical intensity and it occurred to me that as the Air Force did not provide us with any sort of flying suit, I would have to go into battle in shorts and shirt or, more precisely, bare arms and knees, unless I wore my own black overall, purchased privately during my training days at Barton in 1938 and made of a heavy and most untropical linen. Still, better that than nothing; only too well were we aware of the Hurricane's proneness to catch fire and its unpleasant habit of barbecuing its pilot in the cockpit. Memories of poor old Nick's (our former colleague, Flight Lieutenant J. B. Nicolson, V.C., shot down on 16 August 1940) hands and face, and those of a hundred other victims, remained a terrible reminder.

Sunday, 25 May: stiflingly hot with most of us bathed in sweat and uncomfortably aware of the brassy sun overhead. Through narrowed eyes I found myself gazing skywards. Talk about Huns in the sun; we were going to have a hard time of it here, I could see.

'Butch's' group had taken the first stint of duty starting at dawn, but nothing much had happened. By noon, the whole island was wilting in a breathless, humid heat. On the white drystone walls, tiny lizards basked unblinking in the midday glare, to dart off at lightning speed when threatened, or lose their tails when pinned down by amused fingers. Away on the hill, the ochre-and-brown walls and castellations of Rabat and M'dina stared down with the serene gaze of two thousand silent years. No birds. No movement. Just stillness, oven heat, and talcum-powder dust. A lone gharry with its drooping straw-hatted horse and somnolent driver, creaked wearily across the end of the airfield as though we, and the war, were a million miles away.

I had arrived with my group shortly before 1 p.m. to begin the ritual of change-over. There were nine aircraft, all hooked up to starter batteries whose chore-horses puttered away endlessly.

The pilots' tent and so-called operations room was merely a cover to keep off the sun, the four sides rolled up to enable even the smallest breeze to fan a dozen lolling forms. A bored airman sat at a table confronting a small battery of telephones connecting the airfield to the control centre in Valletta, six miles away. The equipment was primitive, instruments that had to be held down and wound, with wires everywhere. All day long the airman on duty was obliged to listen in frustrated silence to 'officer' and 'pilot' talk, much less spicy, no doubt, than the conversation to which he was accustomed. There were compensations, however; he at least knew what was going on and could spread the word among his mates later in his own quarters. The airman-of-the-watch that day was a non-smiling, faintly truculent Scotsman with a Glaswegian accent that would have curdled milk.

For ten minutes or so, we sorted ourselves out. I took over V4048 and, leaving my plugged-in helmet hanging on the gunsight, draped my parachute over the tail – I disliked having it in the cockpit seat and being trodden on all the time. Making the brief ritual inspection to satisfy myself that all the main parts were in place, I ran my hand over the tailplane and found the metal almost too hot to touch. Well, we had bleated constantly about too much cloud in England; now we had the sun – and how! I walked back to the tent; our first spell of duty in Malta and about seven hours before we were likely to be 'stood-down'.

For more than half an hour, nothing; no excitement, no tension even. We sat around, fanning ourselves and trying to keep cool. Waiting. Outside the chore-horses chattered on monotonously and the sun continued to bake the acres of glaring white sandstone beyond our canvas cover so that the heat rose in shimmering eddies, making Rabat on the distant hill wobble and shake. And all around was that subtle smell – of Malta.

I had already spoken to control some fifteen minutes earlier and been assured that nothing unusual was happening, so that when a distant air-raid siren began its whooping dirge, it came as a surprise and an unpleasant shock. Air-raid siren! What were we doing sitting here if the Huns were within even fifty miles of us? I jumped to my feet, as did everyone else, and went outside to waken myself up and to observe. Nothing though, or nothing that I could see. Even so, I didn't like it – some sixth sense. We wouldn't be hanging about like this at North Weald, by George!

Anxious to be in the best possible state of preparedness, I ordered everyone to 'Standby', which meant that they sat, strapped up, in their cockpits, after which I spoke again to control.

We could hear air-raid sirens, I observed tersely. What was going on?

Hearing voices in the background and discussion, I sensed uncertainty. Then their reply: nothing as far as they knew. As soon as anything developed they would let us know. Okay?

Still suspicious, I went out into the sun again and, walking back to my aircraft, climbed in and strapped up, leaving off my helmet.

Minutes passed. Nothing. Then another air-raid siren, this time very much closer.

Hell's bells! What was going on? I flung off my straps and, jumping down, ran the fifty yards back to the tent. By God, I'd give them what-for!

Jogging into the tent, I had barely ordered the airman-of-the-watch to 'Get me control!' when it all started.

First, the shrill, deafening scream of racing engines and the ripping, tearing bedlam of machine-guns and cannons. All hell let loose!

I dropped the telephone like a hot plate and threw myself to the ground, only to find the airman-of-the-watch had beaten me to it and, knees to chin, was clutching his head like a hear-no-evil monkey. Lying on my left side, with my face to one open end of the tent, I had the briefest glimpse of a small aircraft, which I immediately recognised as a German 109, about 50 feet up and pointing, it seemed, straight at me. *Firing*! Shocked absolutely into a numbed paralysis, I closed my eyes and cringed, waiting for the impact of bullets and shells, wondering quite stupidly meanwhile whether they were likely to go right through my body or only partly so, and if they would penetrate that of the airman as well. For all of four seconds.

Then, with a final explosion of sound and fury, they were gone, their lightning departure marked by the rapid 'clump-clump-clump' of the several Bofors guns around the airfield and the chatter of defending machine-guns.

Scrambling to my feet, I ran outside to see the rapidly diminishing silhouettes of at least three aircraft, their wings glinting in the sun as they sped away to safety in the direction of the area later known to me as St Paul's Bay. In their wake streamed curving clutches of red balls as the Bofors gunners strove to catch them before they finally disappeared. But, what a hope! Within seconds, the last of them had gone and a breathless, trembling peace had been restored, a terrible, stunned and pregnant silence.

My first impression was that we had lost at least one aircraft and that several people had been either killed or wounded. One Hurricane in the middle of the dispersed group was already on fire, though in a small way, and at least one other had been hit and was shedding smoke.

Then, out of the small group of people moving about urgently but seemingly without purpose, a figure hopped almost comically in my direction. It was Pat Wells and he was calling out to me; he had been hit, it seemed, and was apologising. Apologising! Obviously in shock, he was shouting: 'Ginger? Sorry, Ginge! Sorry about this. I really am sorry. Before we've even flown, too. Always seems to happen to me. Sorry!'

I moved in his direction, still nervously on edge, steadying him with an arm.

'Where've you been hit?'

'Here. In the foot.' He painfully proffered a leg like a puppy with a sore paw. 'Saw them coming but couldn't do anything about it. Didn't feel it happen; didn't even know anything about it until I got out.'

Then Crossey, Harrington, Palliser and others were crowding round. Everyone tense but relieved, talking excitedly, laughing even. Christ! That was a close one; everyone strapped in and unable to move, looking straight down the muzzles of those guns. No more of that, if you don't mind! But why hadn't we been told, for God's sake? Those stupid sods in Valletta. They *must* have known! And if they didn't, why? – all the rest of Malta seemed to. Then more relieved laughter and experiences being recounted. A few yards away, the second Hurricane was beginning to burn, but there was nothing available to put out the flames so we all watched impotently as the fire spread; I even thought of throwing handfuls of sand at it but it seemed a silly thing to do.

In minutes both aircraft were massively alight and black smoke was billowing to the heavens in two almighty pillars. Then other people approaching from everywhere with rising dust and the noise of several vehicles, including an ambulance; everyone urgent, questioning, helpful. MacVean, one of the NCO pilots, was badly damaged apparently; having been in the Hurricane nearest to the Huns when they had opened fire, he had scrambled over the side in double quick time, breaking – or badly damaging – both his legs. Bit of a joke really, as MacVean was a portly youth and not given either to moving or thinking quickly. Not until today, that is!

Anyone else hurt? Several airmen, apparently; no one killed though, which was a miracle. What a thing to happen! Our first stint of 'Readiness', and none of us off the ground yet. The smoke from the aircraft towering columns now that could probably be seen in Sicily! In seconds our whole squadron neutralised – demolished! Well, almost!

Harrington, our tall, scholarly colleague from the Bank of England, was bewailing the loss of a pair of polaroid specs; wearing them when the shooting started, he was explaining querulously. Terribly expensive, old boy, wouldn't want to lose them. His was one of the two burning Hurricanes and he had been hit in his parachute, too. Right under his bum! Pretty close, what?

People swirling about now and, amid the sound of laughter, things being done in some semblance of order. The two aircraft, burning still with a vicious red-and-black intensity, were collapsing and stinking, their ammunition exploding with zipping cracks, which made some of us jump. I suddenly became aware that Crossey and I were standing directly in front of one of them and I pulled him away. Suddenly aware of his vulnerability, he jerked in response before controlling himself almost sheepishly; not really dangerous, said he, until I reminded him of rounds 'up the spout'. We both moved away – just in case.

I had a brief situation report from the senior NCO, whom I did not even know. Two aircraft burnt out and two others badly hit and goners he thought, a total of perhaps five out of commission. Then the ambulance was moving away to hospital, carting off the wounded. The smoke was now billowing densely to at least a thousand feet, the two Hurricanes merely embers, each with engine intact and propeller pointing ridiculously to the heavens. Harrington, still worrying about his polaroid specs, was circling the ashes of his aircraft, trying to get at it to make a search but being forced back by the heat. He was sure he was wearing them when it happened, he was telling us endlessly.

Finally, calmness and order. Everyone back to normal. But, what a thing to happen! And all before we had made even our first takeoff. What had got into those clowns down the hole? They must have known something.

Later that same afternoon, leading the three remaining aircraft, I was scrambled twice, whether in response to genuine Hun activity or as a reflex action by control to show that they were still alive and in charge of our affairs, I do not know. Whatever the reason, we encountered no enemy aircraft, my recollections of the flights being mainly of my Hurricane lurching more violently than I had ever known in the convection currents of heat, and the dust-storm we created when taking off, a grey and ochre pall that rose to 500 feet and hung in the air for minutes like a drifting balloon. With such conditions, no wonder the Hurricanes were falling to bits!

That seemingly endless first day drifted to a limp conclusion. Knocked for six before we had even made a move! Who'd have thought it?

Unable to produce more than four aircraft, we were ordered across to Hal Far the following day to use 185 Squadron's Hurricanes, an arrangement that would continue for about a week. Initially, we made the ten-mile journey by bus.

Hal Far was another dishing patch of worn grass at the southern end of the island. Arriving for the first time with my half of the squadron, I set about organising the 'state'. On an airfield I had never seen before, aircraft we had never flown before, and with ground- crew who were friendly enough but quite foreign to us, our first period of 'Readiness' was endured in an atmosphere that was neither homely nor cheerful.

Selecting one aircraft for myself – about as wearily decrepit as any of those at Ta Kali – I arranged my parachute and equipment, and waited.

After a short time, we were scrambled. I raced out, started up, and fled to the end of the airfield, streaming dust in every direction. My tattered mob following me, I roared off towards the south in a typhoon of rising filth and in a wide turn climbed away towards the north and in the direction of the enemy.

Information began to come up to us. Fifty-plus bandits approaching from the north; climb to Angels 15 – the usual stuff. Fifty-plus! And eight of us! But, what the heck? We had heard it all before.

We were just south of Valletta and at around 6,000 feet when I noticed that the little pointer on my oil pressure gauge was registering about 30 lbs instead of the usual 70. And sinking! Oh, no! A duff gauge? I hoped so.

My eyes glued to the instrument, I continued to climb hard at the head of my swaying formation but by the time we had reached 8,000 feet the pressure was down to about 10 lbs, and as I sat there watching in torment, the pointer dropped to the bottom of the instrument before disappearing altogether. Oh, God! What did I do now? In front, the Merlin engine sounded cheerful enough but, as the book said, if I had a complete oil failure, I had only two or three minutes before the brute seized. I climbed on, submerged in despair. Then, as though to confirm my worst fear, the oil temperature needle began to march around the dial; no doubt about it, it was a failure right enough and it looked as though I was due for a forced-landing. Bloody aircraft! Bloody Malta! What a hell of a place to have come to!

It was at that moment that the voice of an angel rose up from below with news that the fifty-plus plots had now turned away and that we should pancake without delay. Pancake! Thank God for that! My dilemma resolved, I dropped my nose and started back towards Hal Far.

The airfield about twelve miles distant, I began to have doubts that I would make it when there came a powerful smell of hot Hurricane and a haze of blue smoke began to rise around my feet. Throttling right back, I coarsened the airscrew pitch lever down to the full extent of its travel and half glided towards the hangars now well within sight. Praying! Hang on you brute! Hang on! I felt myself urging the aircraft forward against my straps, willing the airscrew to keep turning.

To my great relief it did, and with a glad heart I swished across the top of the hangars and almost threw the aeroplane at the ground. And barely had the wheels touched and with the Hurricane still racing ahead, than the propeller jerked to a halt, the engine stopped with an ominous, juddering click, and lots more blue smoke rose up from below. Wow! Close shave! Thank God for that!

Even before it had rolled to a standstill, I had climbed over the side and dropped off the wing-root. Then, retreating to a safe distance, I stood watching, half-expecting the whole thing to explode. Nothing much happened though, apart from the smoke and lots of hissing and ticking as the vastly overheated engine cooled down. Then, as there seemed little I could do, I walked the half-mile back to dispersal, limp but greatly relieved.

As I trudged on, I ruminated wearily. What else could happen to me? After the longest Hurricane trip in history and nearly being written-off in an air-raid on arrival, I had survived a near-lethal strafing attack before I had made even my first trip. And now, here I was with an engine failure after less than two hours of flying! All this in five days! It only remained for some lunatic Maltese driver to maim me in the aircrew bus and my week would be a sparkling success.

Back in dispersal, I sought out the crew of my machine but managed to locate only one youth who warily described himself as a fitter. Our encounter was unforgettable.

'My engine's just seized,' I announced crossly. 'Where's the Form 700 [the servicing record]?'

The youth – grass-green by the look of him – stared back.

'Well, where's the 700?' I repeated.

'700, sir? There isn't one.'

Me, dumbstruck: 'No 700? But there has to be a 700! Every aircraft in the Air Force has a Form 700. Where's the one for this aircraft?' The boy shifted uncomfortably. 'This one doesn't,' he asserted vehemently. 'We haven't had a 700 for this aircraft for ages.'

I was almost beyond responding. 'But you must have signed the 700 after the Dl [Daily Inspection]! Before you declared it serviceable. You did sign for it, I take it?'

But even as I spoke, the terrible truth dawned on me that in the heat of the change-over and amid our other distractions, none of us pilots had signed for any of our Hurricanes; we had simply taken the few that were lying around – and gladly at that! Nor had we signed any Authorisation Book, a truly terrible omission as, even in war, things had to be 'done proper'; their 'Airships' didn't mind their pilots being killed but they did insist on the paperwork being in order.

Sensing defeat but determined that the youth should accompany me so that we might investigate the cause of the engine trouble together, we tramped out into the sunshine and heat.

Having twisted off the oil-tank cap in the wing-root – no easy task as it was still barely touchable – the lad gave an experimental poke into the depths.

'There's no oil in it,' he announced triumphantly, as though it were all my fault.

I said ominously, 'That doesn't surprise me. The point is, there should be eleven gallons.'

'Well, there's none now. There must be a leak.'

'Leak! When did you last fill her up?'

The other looked vague. 'Can't remember, sir.'

'Well, was it today? Yesterday? Last week? When?'

'Not today, sir – I don't think.' Then with a perplexed but almost engaging frown, 'Can't remember, really. Someone else might have, though.'

I experienced a terrible weariness. No Form 700 and he couldn't remember when he last put oil in the engine. No, it was all too difficult: the hopeless aircraft, the heat, the mosquitoes and revolting food, chaps like this who hardly knew which way was 'up', the lack of almost everything. Malta! What a bloody awful place to come to!

We both turned and left the aircraft standing there. Right in the middle of the airfield.

20

Action Commences

Malta!

The present-day island with its package-tour image, crowded holiday apartments and lobster-coloured tourists bears few similarities to the Malta of 1941. Indeed, little of its former primitive character remains and such places as St Paul's Bay, Mosta, Ghajn Tuffeiha, and even the old airfield at Ta Kali, are hardly recognisable. But then, as now, the Maltese, never a warrior race, were kindly, gentle folk, with a few exceptions darkly Mediterranean in appearance and much given to the Roman church, its priests and trappings, and the business of warding off the evil eye.

On the whole, they were very pro-British, although being so close to Italy and with many of the more educated speaking Italian and having links with that country, during the period of the siege there were naturally some who felt more emotionally if not politically aligned with their next-door neighbours. Even so, there was never a noticeable undercurrent of resentment towards us and, as far as I am aware, never any activities even remotely subversive. At the time, the Anglo-Maltese family of Strickland, who seemed to own almost everything on the island, including the single newspaper, the Times of Malta, were an obvious and powerful influence.

Quite a few Maltese traditionally joined the Navy, many of them being employed in the kitchens and messes, and those who took to soldiering formed the bulk of the Royal Malta Artillery, which manned the ack-ack defences. Those who weren't militarily inclined went about their business as usual in what was primarily an agricultural community, the bare-footed peasant farmers and their families tilling the meagre fields with impassive indifference as the tracer soared and the air battles raged above their heads, the pregnant women among them delivering their squalling infants in the odd moment between hoeing a line or two in the brown earth, bending always with straight legs, so that one of my more vivid memories of Malta is the sight of backsides of all shapes and sizes pointing defiantly towards the enemy. Some of the more affluent members of the populace, who normally lived in the grander suburbs of Valletta, had taken the precaution of evacuating themselves to Rabat and other such places in the centre of the island, so that in the summer of 1941 it was possible to rent a magnificent four-storey furnished house in Sliema for as little as £5 per month.

Even under the greatest stress, the Maltese menfolk, of whatever class, were courteous and helpful to the point of being obsequious and the young and attractive ladies of courting age were as obliging as their religion and hawk-eyed parents would allow. Maltese mothers, in the main, tended to be less favourably disposed towards us, warning their daughters that these handsome RAF officers would not always be around and then who would be willing to seek their favours?

Despite our initial difficulty in locating the island and our not undramatic arrival on 21 May, to say that I had not known where Malta was, would not be strictly correct. Along with Hong Kong, Singapore, Zanzibar and Manila, the precise position of Malta had been the subject of a question on the geography paper of my mock-Matric examination in 1936. Moreover, the more recent exploits of Faith, Hope and Charity, the three Gladiator fighters which had earlier defended the island, had been headline news at home, as indeed had the Mediterranean war in general. No, I knew where Malta was all right and the unpleasant things that were happening there, as did my family and friends, who were horrified when they learned that the squadron had been retained in its defence.

I was also tolerably familiar with its history and was aware that the inhabitants, far from being fifty per cent priests and fifty per cent goats, as was facetiously alleged, were not only heavily involved in the Crusades in medieval times but were descendants of the Phoenicians, who were civilised traders when we Ancient Britons were carrying spears and daubing ourselves with woad. And, of course, there was the Bible and those worthy Saints, Paul and John – wasn't Paul shipwrecked somewhere on the north coast of Malta? So, what if their language was all 'exes and vees upside down' and if, at one time, my mother did harbour the unspoken fear that my new Maltese girlfriend might be black and have crinkly hair?

It was this slightly patronising ignorance of Malta and the Maltese, coupled with their national reverence for dogged resistance, that led the British people in 1940 and later – me included – to believe that the island was totally preoccupied with defending itself, which was far from the truth.

Throughout the period of the Mediterranean war, Malta was a vital base from which offensive action by air and sea caused such crippling losses to the enemy that, in 1942, the Germans seriously considered invading it in order to maintain their supply lines to General Rommel and his forces in North Africa.

The three main centres from which this offensive action was launched were the airfields of Luqa and Hal Far and the port of Valletta. For this reason, all three came constantly under attack by Axis aircraft for more than two years, the airfield at Ta Kali – in my time the home of at least half the fighter force on the island – being merely a secondary target which was bombed and strafed more or less for good measure. In particular, Valletta – its harbour, dockyards and installations – came in for a terrible drubbing, requiring it to be heavily defended by anti-aircraft guns of all types and sizes, whose soaring tracer, fiery balls and formidable, crumping barrage, provided constant and colourful entertainment for those of us at Ta Kali, who often took our after-dinner coffee and sat in the darkness on the flat roof of the mess in order to enjoy the free firework display.

Until the eventual rout of the German and Italian forces in North Africa in the late autumn of 1942, the Royal Navy viewed Malta with scowling trepidation and only lodged its ships there when it had to, although from time to time this became necessary as the naval vessels themselves had to be supported and the island, with few resources, had to be supplied constantly with aviation fuel and oil, ammunition, food, and almost every other type of commodity. At regular intervals, His Majesty's submarines would creep in and out in such sinister silence that we seldom knew of their presence until the familiar, cheerful and bearded faces of their commanders turned up in the hotels and bars in Valletta. Without exception, they were proud and splendid men, whose exploits were to inspire the nation, the names of Wanklyn VC, and others, becoming household words.

The main group of naval surface ships in Malta, known as Force 'K', consisted of one or more six-inch gun cruisers of the Aurora class, of which HMS *Aurora* herself, and occasionally HMS *Penelope*, were the representatives, and around six destroyers, all of which, like the submarines, came and left with great stealth, going about their deadly business with such secrecy that we in Hurricanes were occasionally despatched into the Mediterranean to find them, as often as not being shot at for our pains immediately we ventured within range. To Force 'K', indeed the Royal Navy in general, every aircraft was a German aircraft, which in one respect was a bonus as we knew that whenever ack-ack bursts began to pock-mark the sky around us, we need go no further as they were the chaps we were looking for!

The small Navy air contingent, in the form of Fulmars, Swordfish and Albacores, operated from Hal Far and carried out torpedo attacks and mining operations, mostly at night and over a wide area, the Fulmars specialising in intruder work. The Fulmars and crews who had escorted us to Malta had been incorporated into this hardy group and those of us in 249 were able to renew our happy association with them. And our sympathy, too, as they were obliged to fly their obsolete and barely serviceable aircraft on the most hazardous of sorties, always over the sea and often well into the harbours and airspace of Sicily, seldom returning without some sort of mishap.

Luqa, the airfield on which I had first landed, was the only one with runways and accommodated the reconnaissance and bomber force. 69 Squadron carried out the reconnaissance work and flew Martin Marylands, an American twin-engined aircraft, one of whose better characteristics was a high cruising speed enabling it to outdistance most of the opposition. In the capable hands of Warburton, Devine and others, the Marylands ranged far and wide, providing vital intelligence on enemy shipping and other activity in the greater Mediterranean area. An irrepressible group, some of their antics around Ta Kali did not always meet with our approval.

Also at Luqa were the Wellingtons and Blenheims, the former making nocturnal trips to Axis-held North African ports – principally Benghazi, Tripoli and Tobruk – plus other targets in mainland Europe, whilst the latter carried on a remorseless and bloody war at mast-height against all Axis shipping within a 300-mile radius, in the course of which their casualties were little short of catastrophic. At Luqa, too, the occasional Beaufighter squadron, passing through to or from the Middle East, would be 'hijacked' and obliged to make attacks on one or more of the Axis airfields and ports in Sicily, some 60–100 miles to the north of us. And then, of course, there were the slow-motion Sunderlands, like the submarines, creeping in and out of the island under cover of darkness and using Kalafrana Bay as their alighting area. Although I was well aware of their presence and activities, I never once saw a Sunderland during the many months I spent on the island.

All of this – the sharp end of Malta, so to speak – we in Hurricanes were there to defend, although our role was to develop considerably later in the year. However, it would be many weeks before I became aware of the full extent of the island's offensive activities and even then more through personal contacts in the bars and hotels of Valletta than as the result of formal briefings or intelligence summaries; not only were we ignorant of what the enemy was up to, we knew very little of what our own side was achieving, other than by accident and word of mouth.

Furthermore, despite it being a very small island, I was painfully ignorant of those in control of us early on, and not much wiser by the time I left. Lieutenant General Sir William Dobbie, the Governor and senior military personage, was a distant and venerable gentleman known only to me by photograph and through the medium of the Times of Malta. The Air Officer Commanding, however, an appointment soon to be filled by Air Vice Marshal H. P. Lloyd, was someone I came to know a good deal better and about whom I was to harbour mixed feelings. Air Headquarters, Malta, together with the Sector Operations Centre and the controllers, were, and would remain, anonymous bodies and occasional names, existing somewhere below ground in Valletta in what was darkly referred to as 'the Hole', a place to which I was never invited nor encouraged to visit. And finally, although I sometimes encountered Wing Commander John Warfield, my Station Commander at Ta Kali, who seemed a nice enough man, in no way did I feel that he was actually in charge of my destiny, whether even he would be there the following day when I turned up in the mess for lunch.

However, one notable officer who had arrived on the island about the same time as ourselves, was Wing Commander 'Bull' Halahan, a man who had served with No. 1 Squadron in France in 1939, and who, looking very much like his name, had earned himself an impressive reputation as a man of action. By the end of our first week, I had met him several times without knowing precisely what his responsibilities were, although he appeared to have some sort of authority over us, which seemed a step in the right direction.

Somewhere beneath this shadowy and uncertain command structure, we operated – at first anyway – in an atmosphere of mild bewilderment. Officers and NCO pilots of other units arrived out of nowhere announcing they were now part of 249, all with such lack of warning and explanation that there were times when I did not know who was in my flight much less my squadron. Instructions and information materialised, from where exactly was often a mystery, so that on occasion we felt that we were merely pawns in a game beyond our understanding. With our 'troops' somewhere in Africa, our first- line and maintenance crews at Ta Kali were totally foreign to us; moreover, for a lengthy period we were without an adjutant, intelligence officer, or even an engineer officer, our only shared possessions being the tent with the rolled-up sides and a distinctly part-worn, sit-up-and-beg Austin 16, painted a sand-yellow, which served as squadron transport and which 'Butch' drove mostly and I occasionally. My one and only task as flight commander, it seemed, was to organise as many as I could of the dejected-looking Hurricanes dispersed around the airfield's edge and adjacent walled fields into some sort of dog-eared fighting force, lead them into the battle, and land them back in one piece – if at all possible.

Still mildly resentful about our own 'hijacking' into Malta, the unaccustomed summer heat – then in the high 80s and 90s – our lack of kit, the mosquitoes and other more personal wildlife, and the type of food and insanitary messing conditions which had many of us beating a path to the musical lavatory, all these I found additional, morale-sapping sources of irritation. After the staid and ordered comfort of North Weald, everything was strange, disorganised and uncomfortably new. On the other hand, would we have fared any better in the Western Desert? Perhaps we had had it altogether too easy thus far.

At the end of May 1941, the German star, if not in the ascendant was certainly not on the wane. Crete, only a few hundred miles to the east, had just fallen to their airborne forces with heavy loss to Britain in ships, men and material, and the taciturn but admirable General Wavell was in process of being thwarted in his effort to relieve Tobruk in Libya. In the Atlantic, too, there had recently been setbacks, HMS *Hood* being sunk by the *Bismark* with almost the German battleship's first salvo. The *Hood*, for heaven's sake! –just about the biggest warship we had. All right, the *Bismark* had been sunk, too, but that was to be expected, wasn't it? – the Navy being the Navy and all that. No, things were definitely not right and it seemed that at least in part, our equipment was letting us down. In the Western Desert, British tanks were a joke, being completely outgunned by something called a German Mark 4, and the Air Force there seemed to be fielding all sorts of obsolete or obsolescent aircraft, of which, in my view, the Hurricane Mark I was a prime example. The Huns were running rings around us and must be laughing themselves sick. Even the new American Tomahawk, which had recently been used in the Desert, was said to be a poor climber and generally lacking in performance – another American streamlined brick, it seemed.

Much of this we knew, if only vaguely, the business of flying and fighting tending to concentrate our minds on events of more immediate and personal import, such as scrambles, ropey engines, forced landings, and staying alive! But what we did not know, although others no doubt did, was that Germany's plans to invade Russia were well advanced and that massive forces, including those of the Luftwaffe in Sicily, were being assembled in eastern Europe for that purpose. Soon, the Hun units, which had dealt so harshly with our ships and aircraft in and around Malta, would be departing for the borders of Russia, leaving us only the Italians with whom to wage war. Had we known of this at the time, we might have felt rather better; the Germans we could just about cope with, the Eyeties we regarded as easier meat. After all, were they not the chaps whose tanks were said to have one forward gear and four reverse, and who boasted that nothing could catch their cruisers and destroyers? None of us in 249 had ever encountered an Italian aircraft, despite being involved in the raid off the Essex and Suffolk coasts the previous November. On that occasion, 249 had shot down the accompanying spotter and rescue aircraft – an unpleasant task – after which, from the other North Weald squadrons, we had heard all about the Fiat BR 20 bombers and CR 42 fighters. Biplane fighters! – I wouldn't mind fighting those chaps any day of the week; even the old Hurricane would be good enough for them!

Thus it was during the last week of May 1941; in the glaring, humid heat of Malta. With most of us turning lobster-pink and being bitten to a standstill by plagues of mosquitoes and fleas. For fair-skinned me, they were the main enemy; something had to be done about them!

I was at 22,000 feet, some 15 miles north of the island, my shirt sticking clammily to my body where the sweat had congealed to form a chilling adhesive. Alongside me, well spread out in battle formation and properly alert, were three others of my section, everyone more than aware of a sun so glaringly bright that it was impossible to look in its direction even with our newly-issued sunglasses. Some fifteen minutes earlier we had scrambled in a lather of excitement, but disappointingly, there was little news, the enemy plots having either evaporated or turned away.

Far below and to my left, the island of Malta appeared brightly, almost luminously, sand-coloured. Not a trace of green; just light brown and white, surrounded by the sea, a million square miles of unending, shadowed blue. On every side the dark azure of the heavens paled into the whitish haze of a horizon which encircled us in a straight, unbroken line. Not even a small cloud. Anywhere.

There were three islands, I observed – Malta itself, lying roughly south-east/north-west, Comino, a little north of the main island and hardly more than a rock, then Gozo, about half the size of Malta but sparsely inhabited and used, we had been told, for sheep, goats and prisoners-of-war. A ferry normally ran between the two major islands in peace-time but only occasionally in war. I hardly gave Gozo a thought; we were never expected to go there.

Away beneath, on the northern side of Malta, was the toothy huddle of Valletta, with its rectangular inlets forming Grand Harbour, its bastions, berths and dockside buildings, all of them heavily protected and accommodating naval and other vessels, all details of which were obliterated by distance. In one respect our job as defenders was easy; there was little doubt as to where the enemy was heading, quite unlike in Britain where there were targets galore.

I tilted to my right in a wide sweep, my gaze alternating in disciplined movements between the heavens, the horizon, and the sea below. Emptiness – nothing but emptiness, enough space to conceal a thousand enemy aircraft which could quite easily stream past us, silent and unobserved. In the distance, some 50 miles to the north, the pale mass that was Sicily was plainly visible, merging left and right into the mists of distance. A parched and arid place it looked from 22,000 feet, much the same as Malta and of the same colour.

We were still operating from Hal Far, journeying to and from Ta Kali by jolting, rattling bus each morning and afternoon. It was my fourth trip from that airfield and in the same aircraft – Z4043 – a tropicalised Mark I, the engine tolerably smooth at 2,600 revs but with a slightly worrying oil temperature which was consistently higher than the normal 60-65 degrees. After my first engine failure three days earlier, I had watched my gauges like a hawk, looking and listening for the smallest deviation of the pointers or sound of trouble. Never before had I cause to doubt the old and trusty Merlin – not until now, that is!

We flew around in wide figures of eight. On guard. Watchful. With gradually lessening suspicion. Until finally, the pancake instruction.

Tilting towards the south, we dropped our noses, the roar of the slipstream rising to a hissing scream as our descent quickened, until we jolted finally and very uncomfortably into the hard-edged eddies of rising heat some 3,000 feet above the glistening ochre of the sandstone. My Hurricane lurched and shuddered as the waves of convection pummelled and snatched at it. God Almighty, what bumps! Always the same in summer, we had been told.

Then, everything much quieter and, with the hangars drifting past on our left, we landed. And taxied in. I glanced into the mirror above my cockpit hood. Our airscrews were whipping up vast clouds of dust which followed us about in dark, drifting curtains. Thank heaven I was the leader and ahead of all the others. How the engines were expected to keep going in these conditions I would never know. I looked quickly down to check that the shutter of my Vokes filter was correctly positioned.

Another trip completed. It was 31 May, my ninth day in Malta, and my eighth flight in anger. And I was still in one piece, thank God, which, after our rude welcome the week before, was something of a surprise.

There had been bombers overhead throughout the previous several nights and much waving of searchlights and tonking of guns. If there were bombs dropped, none had come near to us at Ta Kali so that we viewed it all with little more than casual interest. That was one thing about Malta; there was a performance laid on every night – better than going to the theatre. A little less comforting was the news that we would be expected to take our turn at night flying almost immediately; which concerned me more than a little as I didn't trust some of our aircraft even in daylight!

First of June, which was a Sunday. The weather hot and sticky still, the Sabbath's silence almost tangible, the black-robed, flat-hatted priests more than ever in evidence.

Having been bitten miserably by mosquitoes the previous night, I awoke, covered with red bumps and scratching like a terrier. As we slept naked, after their aperitif of Flit, the brutes had masses of warm, damp flesh on which to disport themselves. Positively bloated with blood, they would then hang on the sides of the net like bats, so that the first five minutes of consciousness were always devoted to swiping them vengefully to the accompaniment of muttered curses, after which the place looked like a miniature slaughter house. After that, the next five minutes were spent looking for the holes in the net where the little blighters had made their entry.

My flight was on duty that day and when I had struggled into my thick black flying overall, I found it unpleasantly pongy and clammily cold with congealed sweat. Did the dhobi deal with overalls? I would have to find out.

I was scrambled almost immediately but brought down after twenty-five minutes. In fact, we were seldom kept up longer than that. There was a lot of enemy activity over Sicily, it appeared, but after drawing us into the air, the Huns, or whoever, seemed always to lose interest. Or was it control being hypersensitive because of our harsh words following the massacre at Ta Kali on the 25th? Whatever the reason, we seemed to get masses of scrambles but no interceptions. Apart from looking into the business-end of those 109s during their strafing run, thus far I had not seen a single enemy aircraft.

On 3 June, we were back at Hal Far for the day, this time going by air. If on the dawn stint, we usually left our aircraft there for 'Butch's' half of the squadron to use, before coming back by bus. That ten-mile rattling, bone-shaking return journey in the midday heat and behind those lunatic drivers, I found far more wearing than flying the clapped-out Hurricanes.

By then I was beginning to know the geography of the island quite well, including the names of the places. Kalafrana Bay, next door to Hal Far, was a very picturesque area; the Sunderland flying boats operated from there on their nocturnal comings and goings, but even when they didn't, a dummy flare path was usually laid down in the bay to confuse the enemy. Whatever its effect on the enemy, it certainly confused some of our own heavy boiler chaps, as more than one had already landed in the water by mistake – and others would continue to do so. Mostly inexperienced OTU boys and freshly out of England, it must have been a great surprise for them to be dunked in the water, having spent hours creeping around the Mediterranean in the darkness.

Flying across that day, I had looked down on the new air-strip being created at Safi, situated half-way between Luqa and Hal Far. We were told that we were likely to disperse our aircraft there in the future, anywhere to get them away from the three airfields where the enemy could blitz them.

There were some Swordfish and other naval aircraft in evidence at Hal Far that day. The night before, apparently, one of them carrying a mine – an Albacore, I was told – had hit a wall on take-off and had exploded. Instant dispersal! A terrible way to go, though.

I did not fly for the two days between 3 and 6 June, my flight being on duty for only half of that period. However, 'Butch' Barton, flying Z4043, the aircraft we often shared, was vectored onto an Italian Savoia 79, a three-engined bomber and multi-purpose aircraft which, having taken off from Sicily, was apparently en route for Libya. No doubt believing that the ardour of Malta's defending fighters had been sufficiently cooled by the attacks of previous weeks and perhaps a little over-confident as a result, the Italians chose to fly too close to the island, enabling 'Butch' to make an interception a little to the north and west of Gozo. Almost predictably, the little man, with his usual zeal and efficiency, shot it down into the sea where it fell a blazing wreck. None of the crew was seen in the water, nor were any bodies found later when the air-sea rescue launch reached the spot. Feather number one in 249's cap, the first of many in the months to come.

It was about this time, too, that on one of our afternoons of freedom, a group of us went swimming at Ghajn Tuffieha, our first such party in Malta. On the south-west side of the island and pronounced, we were advised, 'Ein Tuffewer', it was the only place where there was any sand.

'Butch' drove us there in the ochre-coloured Austin and six of us had the elderly springs well and truly bottoming as we crept along the lonely cratered lane that led down to the beach. The bay, at the bottom of a steep decline, was a small and almost deserted curve of sand, the water uninvitingly grey and tepid. Not exactly Torquay!

As we descended with our swimming trunks and towels, I saw in the middle distance several people in a huddle, one of them bending over what appeared to be a seal lying on the sand. I wandered over to look, and others followed.

It was no seal, unfortunately, but a large man who was leaking water and very dead. Drowned. A worried-looking Maltese in shorts and with dark curly hair was applying artificial respiration but to no avail, and two youngish women were weeping quietly and plainly in shock.

I spoke to them. The victim was English and the captain of one of the visiting merchant ships, the ladies local 'companions'. Against advice, apparently, he had ventured too far out and got into difficulties, the rest being obvious. He was bloated, green and very unpleasant looking. I turned away, feeling slightly sick.

Later, after we had moved away, the body was carried off on a stretcher, a large lolling mound, an arm hanging. The ladies, still weeping, followed at a discreet distance and I was sombrely reminded of the two Marys at the Crucifixion. And we hadn't even started our swimming!

Even so, we took to the water, which felt much as it looked, like warm, grey glue, and after splashing about for several hours, towelled ourselves dry and moved off, our feet gritty with sand. Not a very joyful afternoon. I felt miserable and never wanted to see Ghajn Tuffieha again. Nor did I throughout my seven-month stay in Malta.

The days limped by, hot and breathless. Several more frantic scrambles, one of them on 7 June to the far end of the island in pursuit of a mob of Macchi 200s which had attacked Hal Far. We raced down full of the offensive spirit but by the time we had reached there, the birds had flown. I

was in Z4043 again, the aircraft in which 'Butch' had shot down the Savoia
a few days earlier; I did not like it particularly but felt that a little of its good
luck might rub off on me. But, we saw not a thing. Even so, we chased out
to sea in pursuit, ending up some thirty miles north of the island, in all fifty
minutes of near full-throttle flying. Only later did the penny drop; they were
probably after a large batch of reinforcement aircraft which had flown in
the day before.

We had had news of the newcomers several days earlier. More Hurricanes,
we were told, some Mark IIs this time, at least half of them going on to
the Middle East. Included in the group, we were surprised to learn, was
46 Squadron, which was to remain in Malta. 46! Our old mates from
North Weald, with 'Rags' Rabagliati, Pete LeFevre, 'Bert' Ambrose, 'Chips'
Carpenter, MacGregor, and the rest; it would be nice to share the burden of
defence with some old and trusted companions.

I did not see them arrive; escorted by Blenheims, they were mercifully
spared the problems caused by the decrepit Fulmars and all of them landed
unscathed. But, like 249, in no very cheerful frame of mind; their airmen,
too, with their luggage and some of their pilots, were traipsing around the
Cape, never to be seen again. Why, oh why, did the powers that be do such
things? Wasn't there anyone who understood that a squadron was like a
family, that squadron spirit was a delicately nurtured plant, and that to
disregard it was to deal the unit a body blow from which it could take ages
to recover?

It seemed that we were flying constantly, but for every hour we spent in
the air, we spent five on the ground, fanning ourselves in our no-sided tent
and blessing Malta, its noisome discomforts and its sweltering heat. And a
particular source of irritation – very much a personal hate, this – were the
chattering chore-horses which recharged our trolley-acks.

Our Hurricanes were normally started using external accumulators
which were moved about in wheeled trolleys and plugged in when required.
In order to keep them properly charged, a petrol motor was attached to
each and kept running as long as was necessary. During the interminable
hours of 'Readiness', there could be up to half-a-dozen of these abominable
manufacturers of noise clattering away incessantly within yards of us. For

an hour it was tolerable, after two the nerves began to jangle, but after four to six, everyone within twenty paces was contemplating murder. Moreover, with the chore-horses in full voice, very little else could be heard, which in Malta could amount to a death sentence.

It was on one such occasion, with the chore-horses chugging and rattling remorselessly, that someone chanced to look up to see a twin-engined Junkers 88, about 50 feet up, bearing down on us from the shallow valley alongside M'dina and Rabat. As it was less than ten days since the Hun 109s had attacked us with catastrophic results, we were in no mood to treat the matter lightly. In an instant we were all on our feet and running like stags in as many directions as there are spokes in a wheel, expecting all the time to hear the ripping, pulverising chatter of cannons and machine-guns, everyone frantically seeking some place of sanctuary – hole, wall, equipment, anything in, or behind which to hide.

In the space of seconds and with a shattering roar, the aircraft had swept over our heads, revealing itself to be not an 88 but a Maryland. From 69 Squadron at Luqa. That bloody man Devine!

With a mixture of relief and anger, we rose to our feet, dusted ourselves off, and congregated, presently to be joined by the crumpled, bloodied and sorry-looking figure of the tall and usually immaculate Flying Officer Harrington – Harrington of the Bank, the pilot of one now burnt-out Hurricane and the late owner of a pair of apparently priceless Polaroid spectacles. His face was a picture. 'I say, old boy' – the usual preface – 'who was the stupid bastard who did that? Did you see who it was?' There was more, but unprintable, and murder in his eyes. And for a good reason. Covered in scratches and blood, he had flung himself head-first into a rectangular hole in the ground – crammed with refuse and a mass of barbed wire!

That was it! I ordered all the chore-horses to be switched off immediately – we couldn't hear the approach of fifty Huns with all that din. But barely had the noise of them died away when a newly-commissioned engineer officer appeared from the far side of the airfield, in high dudgeon, wanting to know who had had the temerity to interfere with his chargers. In a savage mood, I was not about to be lectured by anyone, least of all a junior I regarded as a non-flying, paper-qualified, ex-university nonentity, and we nearly came to blows. But the chattering was silenced, at least for a time, although finally, because even I recognised the need to keep the batteries charged, we came to an arrangement.

It was around the dispersal tent, too, that we had a drains problem, or so we thought. For several days we wandered about, complaining of the terrible smell and rooting around for the cause. But there were no drains, it seemed, or not in the immediate vicinity. What on earth was it? A dead rat? Another rotting animal, perhaps?

On about the third morning, the answer was provided by the slightly truculent airman-of-the-watch who had joined me on the floor of the tent at the speed of light when the 109s had attacked us a fortnight earlier. He had just come on duty and was listening to our conversation.

He turned and faced us, his mouth working. 'It's that other bloke's feet, sorr. He stinks us out in the billet.'

We all looked up, stunned. 'Whose feet?'

'That bloke I've just relieved, sorr. The other feller. It's his feet a'right. He never washes 'em, or his socks. Drives us all mad in the billet.' He pulled an agonised face. 'Terrible it is, sorr.' The boy's Glaswegian voice was thick with pent-up indignation.

Amused, faintly shocked but happy to have the matter resolved, the airman with the cheesy feet was dealt with the following day, after which there were no more 'dead rats' or searches.

It was early in June, too, that our new AOC, Air Vice Marshal H. P. Lloyd, arrived at dispersal to meet us all.

Referred to familiarly as Hugh Pughe, the Air Marshal was a middle-sized man of stocky build, who cultivated a rather Cromwellian sternness and brevity of speech. With bright blue eyes, he also had the slightly disconcerting habit of thrusting forward his face until it was within inches of one's own, and staring wordlessly, a fire-eating affectation I found rather childish. After all, we didn't need to be impressed by such theatrical mannerisms; most of us had been fighting continuously for almost a year and knew only too well what was required of us.

But the Air Marshal was friendly enough. We subsequently learned that he had been briefed to bolster morale and to be a thorn in the side of the enemy by cutting Axis supply lines to Africa, using every air resource at his disposal, which he seemed determined to do. Needless to say, we expressed our willingness to play our part, adding vehemently that we wished we had something more serviceable and with a better performance than the lame-duck Hurricanes we had been lumbered with. The poor quality of our aircraft and the need for something better, was our theme on that occasion and indeed on every occasion for the duration of my stay in Malta.

Then, on 8 June, more unproductive scrambles during the day followed by night flying, 'Butch', several others and I being called upon to defend Malta in the dark. Despite the uncertain quality of our mounts, I actually found myself looking forward to the event.

Ta Kali airfield being merely a flat dust-bowl of worn grass, the flare path was laid out by hand and consisted of about a dozen glim lamps, which could barely be seen above 2,000 feet. There was also a Chance light – when it could be persuaded to work – but no such luxuries as lead-in, exit, or other perimeter lights. In fact, they were seldom needed as in full moon conditions one could almost read a newspaper, and even on the darkest nights – and they could be very dark in Malta – the searchlights proved a useful means of orientating oneself.

Over an area approximately fifteen miles by eight, our system of defence was simple and effective. The bombers usually arriving singly and invariably aiming at Grand Harbour or one or other of our three airfields, the searchlights could normally be expected to illuminate each one as it approached from the north. Meanwhile, up to two Hurricanes, patrolling to one side, would wait for the tell-tale grey- white object to be revealed. Thereafter, a single fighter would scuttle swiftly into the line-astern position and let fly – very straightforward and usually very effective. Or, on an order to us to get out of the way, the guns would take over, Valletta would shake with the crash and crump of a hundred salvos and the sky would be filled with flying shrapnel. In the strictest sense, we were never controlled onto the target, although there were few occasions when we were not given a height and vector, after which we just followed the searchlight beams like cats waiting to pounce.

As good fortune would have it, on that first night we had instant success, 'Butch' Barton – who else? – being lucky enough to be on patrol when a BR

20 was illuminated. Sliding quickly into position, he opened fire and was rewarded immediately when the Italian aircraft was set alight and plunged into the ground, killing those of the crew who were unable to bale out. Despite flying for several hours, however, and positively willing an Eyetie to be illuminated, I had no luck, a particular disappointment as, later, another BR 20 was attacked by two of our aircraft, flown by John Beazley and the diminutive 'Titch' Palliser, and claimed as a 'probable'.

On the whole, a most successful night; if this was night-fighting, it was dead easy. Not only was the target area small and the searchlights more than adept, but the BR 20s were most obliging, catching fire almost at the first strike. Not a bit like England, where one flew endless sorties with hardly a sniff of a Hun, and even when an interception was made, the Junkers 88s especially being as tough as boots and seemingly impervious to scores of strikes.

I was on duty again at dawn but having just flown for almost two hours and been up most of the night, I elected not to lead the first section off, to my everlasting regret. It was a hazy morning with the promise of a blazing sun and scorching day.

Fairly early on, we received a scramble order but with little information of what was afoot. The stately Harrington, who had never before seen an enemy aircraft, took off with three others, Sergeant Rex, formerly a member of 3 Squadron in England, the young and inexperienced Sergeant Lawson, and a recent addition to 249, Sergeant Livingstone, a fair-haired non-smiling Scotsman who had been with 261 and had only recently moved across to us via 185 Squadron. Off they roared in a vast pall of dust and fled away to the south. After which – silence.

About fifteen minutes later the telephone rang and I was informed in a terse sentence that the section had intercepted some forty miles south of the island and that there were people in the water. Some Savoias had apparently been skirting Malta en route for Libya and at least one had been shot down. One of our Hurricanes had also gone in.

I immediately arranged for a further section to take off and search, and hardly had my instructions been given when a single Hurricane approached from the south and landed without ceremony. It was Harrington, as animated as ever I had seen him.

They had suddenly come upon four Savoias low down, he explained. One of the Eyeties had been shot into the sea and Sergeant Rex had also gone in – whether shot down or due to some sort of engine failure he didn't know. At the moment Rex was swimming about in his Mae West, with the others marking the spot.

A long way south, unfortunately, it would take ages for a boat to reach him. The adrenalin still racing, 'Harry' was walking round in circles. How he wished I had been leading; probably have done things differently. He was more excited and concerned than I ever imagined he could be.

Amid a welter of questions and answers, we sorted ourselves out, news being received that the air-sea rescue launch had already left.

After which, we waited.

Shortly after, the remaining Hurricanes returned and with the assistance of several more, the rescue launch buffeted its way towards Africa.

Two hours later and almost fifty miles south of the island, Sergeant Rex was picked up, not too unhappy with life apparently, having been swimming powerfully in the wrong direction. Also hooked out of the sea was a single burnt and bedraggled Italian, who was clinging to what remained of one wing of the Savoia. Wrapped up and cosseted, Rex and the Eyetie spent the next two hours sitting in the launch, commiserating with each other.

Later, we talked it over. It seemed that everyone had shot at the Savoias but only one had gone in. What about the others, I asked sternly? Shaken heads; they had just flown on, it seemed, one being as many as they could cope with, the Hurricane ditching and all that. Livingstone was claiming it, although others had shared in its destruction, including Rex who was admitting that he did not know whether he had been hit by return fire or had suffered a straightforward coolant leak. Coolant leak! Another engine problem? But, what did it matter; aircraft and offending engine were down among the dead men now!

Later we heard that the little Italian had been taken to Imtarfa hospital, where he was recovering. As for me, I was kicking myself; having missed out on a BR 20 the night before, I had allowed Harrington to lead the first section off, which was something I would never have permitted in normal circumstances. Still, it could have been me bobbing about out there like a cork. No, I would have to learn to be patient and take things as they came.

Everyone seemed very pleased; it was a long time since Malta's Hurricanes had had a success so far away south. Good old 249, was the verdict.

A day or so later, several of us, including Crossey and Harrington, visited the Italian in hospital, having bought him a razor and other odds and ends. We found him in one of the wards, looking very apprehensive. With the assistance of one of the Maltese doctors, who was known to us and spoke Italian, we calmed his fears and tried to cheer him up, until, eventually, he was so overcome by our good nature that he came close to breaking down. Poor chap, he was the only survivor apparently, although he did not seem too upset about it. Pouff, they had gone, he said, dismissing his erstwhile companions to purgatory, or wherever Italians went, with a few eloquent hand signals and a Latin lift of his shoulder. We parted finally, with the little man waving like a child and declaring undying gratitude and friendship. As we left, I wondered what would become of him. A pathetic little chap, and very lucky to be alive.

Although, with others of 249, I was scrambled on both the 10th and 11th, I made no contact. More fortunate were some members of 46 Squadron, who, on the morning of the 11th and during their first flight in anger from the island, intercepted a force of Italian fighters who were escorting a single Savoia reconnaissance aircraft. A ragged engagement ensued after which all sorts of claims were made. Good luck to them, we thought; for us, it had been a nothing day. Thus far, I had not even seen an Italian aircraft.

The following day, which was the 12th, was different, however.

Being scrambled mid-morning, I climbed away towards the south and east with my ragged formation of eight, turning north then west around Hal Far, by which time we were at about 17,000 feet. Receiving definite news of incoming aircraft, I soon saw moving ack-ack fire slightly below me and in the direction of Valletta.

I hardly had time to weigh up the situation, when a mob of aircraft in close formation emerged from the splatter of bursting ack-ack, slightly below us and heading in the opposite direction. Then, as they passed quickly underneath, I reared up and dropped down on them, my retinue streaming in pursuit.

I just had time to recognise a three-engined Savoia bomber in the middle of the enemy group surrounded by fighters, the closest of which I identified as an Me 109 with a light-coloured nose. Then, as we charged among them, aircraft began to scatter in all directions, like leaves whirling in a sudden gust of wind.

Hanging on to the one I had perceived to be a 109, I was thwarted momentarily when it reared up and pointed its nose straight to the heavens. I attempted to follow but was losing ground when, to my surprise, it did not pull away as expected but turned over and in the act of so doing, presented itself as an almost stationary target. I fired. My tracer with its familiar flecks of curving, whipping red, reached out and clutched both fuselage and wings in a brief rippling embrace. After which it was gone. Below my tipping wing. Downwards. Turning. Diving steeply.

I followed, violently, keeping it in sight. I was aware of the sea directly beneath and the coastline behind me, Filfla somewhere adjacent to my forehead, looking on impassively. The enemy turning slowly but going straight down. The slipstream screaming, I flashed worried glances to my sides and rear. Nothing. Going like mad now, left foot extended to the limit, everything roaring and shaking. Firing! Then a sudden small blob that was a parachute, detaching, a white streak at first, then developing, finally drifting sideways before rushing quickly in my direction and vanishing to my rear. Further below me still, a diminishing silhouette and a sudden slow-motion eruption of water which died quickly into a disc of pale green as the aircraft went in. I pulled away, staring, everything bending and draining. Then climbed, breathlessly elated but vibrantly tense. Isolated aircraft in the distance, flying in all directions, seemingly unconcerned. And the enemy? Gone!

Back on the ground there was lots of excitement but differing stories. Several, including Crossey, were able to confirm the crash of my victim into the sea off Filfla, together with the parachute. Hamish Munro, who had joined the squadron at North Weald in the spring, was one of several who appeared to be missing and someone was explaining how he had been attacked by Macchi 200s. Macchi 200s! What on earth was he talking about? The aircraft I had encountered alongside the Savoia had been a 109; I ought to know as I'd been shooting at the blighters for the last nine months! One or two, including Crossey and Sergeant Etchells, agreed, but others were doubtful. I heard my voice rising. You couldn't confuse a 109 with a Macchi 200, for heaven's sake; one had an in-line engine and the other a ruddy great radial. Then everyone was admitting that there might have been two formations, the second being the Macchis. Macchis! I hadn't seen any Macchis. We went on talking hotly. Arguing, but finally coming to a reluctant consensus. Still one or two chaps missing, although someone was said to have force-landed at Safi. I gave up; nothing was more confusing than air combat. Later, we heard that 46 had also engaged some Macchis. Had they? Well, bully for them!

When we had been relieved and were back in the courtyard of Torre Cumbo, the Station Commander, John Warfield, congratulated me. Thanking him, I added a little peevishly that there had been so much confusion, I was now not sure what had happened.

I found myself hoping that the chap in the parachute would be picked up, but by the late afternoon there was no news. I hated the thought of anyone being left in the sea, imagining myself a victim and being drowned by degrees. However, because it was twenty miles away and I had other things to think about, I soon forgot about it. A not too satisfactory morning in spite of our success. Poor old Ham Munro; he hadn't lasted long.

Sometime after lunch, because there was so much to-ing and fro- ing from the airfield, I walked the mile or so back to dispersal to watch scattered remnants of 'Butch's' flight who were landing and taxying in, surrounded by the usual clouds of dust. Around the pilots' tent there was a babble of excitement and a number of chaps were pointing fingers at each other and claiming that he or they had done it. On the fringe of things, I was soon to learn why.

Following the morning's activity, a number of Italian air-sea rescue planes had apparently been sent out from Sicily to pick up those of the enemy who had been shot into the sea, and 'Butch' and his men had run into a Cant seaplane low down over the water some forty miles north of the island. As the red crosses were plainly visible, they flew around but did not attack, reporting the interception meanwhile.

Back came the instruction: 'Shoot it down!' But none of them wanted to, and remonstrated. Back came a further instruction: 'Shoot it down – or else!' So, they shot it down – as gently as they could, and it collapsed into the water.

Back at Ta Kali no one wanted to claim it, hence the pointed fingers and protestations of innocence. Listening to the quite lively exchange and watching the flushed faces, I found it all rather amusing. Finally, several were ordered to put in combat reports, although I don't know even now whose names were eventually associated with the foul deed. It had been a direct order from the AOC, apparently; not a very nice thing to have had to do – or decide.

It had been quite a day for aircraft falling into the water. 46 Squadron had lost several and some time later, over a drink in Valletta, I learned that another of the clapped-out Fulmars from Hal Far had had an engine failure that day and had been obliged to ditch; their aircraft were as bad as ours, if not worse. Were their Lordships, or 'Airships', aware of the strain it was flying over the sea continually, all the time waiting for the engine to conk out or spring a leak? It seemed not.

The 14th June dawned cloudy and continued that way, which was most unusual. My part of the squadron came to 'Readiness' at 1 p.m.

Several large formations of Hurricanes were expected to land in Malta, bound for the Middle East, our journey of 21 May repeated yet again. They were unlikely to affect us, we were told, except that we should be prepared to ward off any attempt to attack them on arrival, as indeed we had been attacked. I discussed arrangements with control and we sat there, waiting.

And scrambled we were, but not to repel the enemy. The controller had spoken to me briefly before take-off. Apparently, the Hurricanes, in several formations, were being led by a group of twin-engined aircraft which had taken off from Gibraltar prior to rendezvousing with the carriers *Ark Royal* and *Victorious*. Unfortunately, RDF plots now indicated that one of the escorting aircraft, with its Hurricanes, was well north of Malta and showing every sign of missing the island altogether. Panic stations! We were to intercept them as quickly as possible and bring them back.

There followed a quite extraordinary series of events. As we raced northwards below cloud, it appeared that the guiding Hudson was ignoring all vectors and instructions passed to it by control, the usual RT silence being thrown to the wind. Soon we were more than forty miles north, at which point we were informed that the formation was then to the east of

Malta and heading south. That sounded more like it; it looked as if they were now on the right track. Round we turned and headed for home, soon to be told that escort and formation were heading away from Malta again. The half-wits! What had got into them? We turned and, for the second time, set off in pursuit.

After about forty minutes of chasing about below cloud, much of it closer to Sicily than Malta, we had still not intercepted them. However, on being told that they finally seemed to be heading towards the island, we were brought back to land. Panic over.

But it wasn't! Hardly had we landed when it became clear that the whole formation was once more in difficulty, with the Hurricanes now in despair and telling anyone who cared to listen that they were fast running out of fuel. At their wit's end, control ordered us off, this time sending us south-east in order to reach them, hopefully before they fell into the sea, after which we were to assist the air-sea rescue boats. Racing out over Kalafrana Bay, Crossey and I headed in the general direction of Egypt, little more than 30 feet above the waves, each of us with the unpleasant vision of a dozen or more aircraft dropping into the water one by one.

Although we were not to know it at the time, most of the Hurricanes passed us unseen and scraped in on their last dregs of petrol, two pilots crashing, even so, and one being killed, when their aircraft ran out of fuel before they could land.

Meanwhile, some forty miles south-east and barely above the waves, we had the good fortune to find one of the two pilots who had already ditched. Leaving Crossey to circle the tiny yellow dot in the water, I returned and made contact with the rescue launch, which was crashing and bouncing its way towards us at maximum speed, and after pointing it in the right direction, flew backwards and forwards endlessly, acting as guide. After hours, it seemed, we watched it successfully make the pick-up, after which we left, full of warm feelings. It was nice to be able to save a life for a change!

Just before sunset that evening, with others, I flew across to the new strip at Safi to disperse my aircraft in the fields there, the first of a score of occasions. It was blissfully pleasant as I strolled back the half-mile towards our waiting transport – calm, quiet, balmily warm, and with the now familiar and quite appealing perfume of Malta. Even in war there were moments of utter peace and deep, sensual tranquillity. Greatly moved by the occasion, I wrote of it in detail to my parents.

In the next several days, more scrambles but no sightings. Someone was saying that it looked as though the Huns had left Sicily. Had they? That would account for the dearth of activity, but we would need to be convinced. There was no confirmation, however, only speculation. Then, on 18 June, a sad event.

By this time 249 had been in Malta three weeks and at best could muster on average about ten aircraft – eight Mark Is and a couple of Mark 2s. Most of the Mark Is were tropicalised but the Mark IIs were not, their open air-intakes, situated under the engine and between the undercarriage legs, ideally placed to suck in every particle of dust and filth whipped up by our whirling airscrews during take-off, landing, and even taxiing. Mr Sidney Camm, in his moments of inspiration when designing the Hurricane, clearly did not have deserts in mind – nor Malta!

I never flew the Mark IIs for the most obvious reason; as leader, had I used the faster type of aircraft, the rest of my formation would always have difficulty keeping up. Reluctantly, therefore, but as a matter of course, I led in a Mark II, and on the first scramble of that day, I was flying Z4048.

As our dispersal was at the southern end of Ta Kali, we mostly took off south to north, which reduced taxiing – and the filth – to a minimum. In this direction, we were faced with rising ground at the end of the airfield and a mass of ridges and stone walls. Every time my wheels left the ground, I prayed; prayed that my engine would keep going and that I would not end up ploughing into the hill or crashing through a score of obstructions. There were very few places to force-land in Malta and to bail out was considered to be the only sensible course of action. But, below 1,000 feet, even baling out was a hazard.

On that occasion, as I roared off in the usual panic, I sensed that there was something wrong with my engine, but in the excitement of the moment, I pressed ahead and committed myself to the air with everything shaking and banging. Twenty feet up, I knew it was going to stop. This was it! The hill and the walls clutching at me, I did the unforgiveable – I took a chance on turning back towards the airfield. For some moments, and with my heart in my mouth, I thought I would not make it. However, popping, lurching and banging, the Hurricane dragged itself around, and in the space of seconds I was back again on the ground, limp with emotion and breathing thanks to the Almighty that things had turned out as they had. Away in the distance, my companions were climbing away and turning north.

Relief soon gave way to annoyance, however, and whilst the engine panels were being removed and the cause of the trouble investigated, I stood and watched, seething and fulminating. Bloody hopeless aircraft! It really wasn't good enough; what was a formation without a leader? And I was still in a black mood when, an hour or so later, all the others were back and 4048's problems were still being rectified.

As there were hints of further action from control, I suddenly came to a decision; I would fly the only Mark II and someone else would have to go without, or fly 4048 if and when it became serviceable. Then, as the new boy Sergeant Livingstone was the weaver and had his kit in the only Mark II, I instructed him to remove his belongings, which he did, reluctantly, his face registering surly disapproval.

After which we sat. And waited.

Eventually, the scramble order came. We all raced to the point of take-off, rudders wagging. Then turned, facing north. Clouds of dust billowing and rising behind us, the whole formation roughly line abreast to avoid each other's slipstream and dirt. Then – off! As leader and marginally in front, I opened my throttle firmly and we surged forward.

Well – not quite! Everyone else surged, I merely trickled. With my throttle lever up to the gate, then through, I should have been getting first 9 lbs, then 12 lbs boost. Instead of which I achieved barely enough power to set me jog-trotting across the airfield at around 20 mph. What on earth – ? Covered in a cloud of filth from the remainder of my roaring formation which had overtaken me for the second time that morning, I gaped at the throttle lever in my left hand. It was at maximum stretch and I had no power – an engine malfunction, twice running! I stopped at the end of the airfield and taxied slowly back. Not fuming this time, just apathetically resigned.

Back in dispersal, my Flight Sergeant was almost jaunty.

'Never mind, sir. It's only the boost capsule stuck. Happens all the time. With all the sherbet (a nice euphemism, that) being sucked into the engine, it's a wonder they ever work at all. It'll only take an hour or so to fix.' And as he spoke the engine cowlings were being stripped off and discarded. Boost capsule! I'd never heard of any such device – boost capsules, thermostats, aneroid thises and thats, such technicalities left me cold. All I wanted was the engine to go, and to keep going!

For twenty minutes or so I stood around with my hands in my pockets, watching a couple of fitters, naked to the waist and streaming with sweat, tinker with the innards and call out to each other. Finally, when they had doctored it to their satisfaction, the engine was restarted and run up, the noise and whipped-up sand a deafening and abrasive whirlwind.

Then, amid the turmoil, the telephone. I ran to answer. Excitement! My flight had intercepted, apparently; there had been an engagement, although the result was uncertain. They were now on their way back.

As we all stood outside the aircrew tent with shaded eyes looking towards Valletta, a pair of Hurricanes appeared in the distance, then another, and finally more. One, however, was on its own and approaching slowly. With something wrong, too, a wisp of white trailing in a tiny feather from its rear. We all watched – wondering. Then as it entered the circuit at about 800 feet and half-a-mile from where we stood, I saw a black dot detach itself from the cockpit. The pilot! As the aircraft fell away downwards, I watched the tiny dark figure drop behind. Oh no! A small sliver of white as the parachute streamed, but all too slowly. Everything in slow motion. Come on! Come on! Open! It did – partially, but not quickly enough. The dot, larger now, fell . . . fell . . . then thudded into the ground, bounced minutely, and lay still, the parachute, a white fluttering shroud, gently subsiding alongside like a cuddling animal seeking affection. Meanwhile, only several hundred yards away, the crashed Hurricane burned in a frenzy of flame and black smoke.

With others around me, I stood and watched – helpless, wordless, and faintly sick. Then, wearily: who was it? In moments, we knew. It was Sergeant Livingstone. In 4048!

There had been a brush with Macchi 200s, apparently, and Palliser and someone else were claiming a 'probable', a 'damaged' – something. But, what did it matter? A man was dead; the poor, sad, unsmiling Livingstone. In that bloody aircraft, too! Had he been hit, or was it just an engine problem? No one could be sure.

The day dragged on. Blighted.

For the next week we seemed to do little other than deliver then collect our aircraft to and from Safi and be scrambled against raids which either did not materialise or were too high for us to do anything about. Between 19 and 28 June I flew on nine interceptions only, being airborne for little more than twenty minutes on each occasion. Except, that is, for the first sortie on the 27th when, leading ten aircraft, I saw ack-ack fire high above Grand Harbour. A little to the north of Hal Far at the time, we were climbing through 17,000 feet with the enemy several thousand feet above us. Turning towards them we gave chase, but the mass of them, mere dots, fled away northwards towards Sicily. They were Macchi 200s apparently, although we did not get close enough to identify them. Escorting a single Savoia reconnaissance aircraft, we were told, which seemed a disproportionate amount of fighter effort in the circumstances. With the Huns clearly gone from Sicily, the Italians did not seem keen to bomb us by day, preferring to do so at night. What then did they hope to achieve, apart from taking pictures of Grand Harbour?

After chasing them almost to Sicily, we returned having spent eighty minutes in the air. Later, we did a second trip with much the same result. Other than in manoeuvrability, the Macchi 200, which was an open-cockpit aircraft (some had hoods but, apparently, the Italian pilots preferred an open cockpit with a wind deflector), appeared to be slightly inferior in performance to even our older Hurricanes, their pilots seldom keen to fight other than over their own backyard. Having the initiative, and height, they habitually made a shallow dive when approaching Malta so that they were moving fairly quickly when they came within our orbit. When caught unawares, mostly during their return journey, they could be dealt with quite easily, in marked contrast to the Hun 109s which were the most difficult brutes to cope with whatever the circumstances, being able to dive or climb away from us almost at will. I was quite happy to chase Eyeties all day long, but knowing they were merely fighters flying at altitude and not intending to bomb or strafe us, somehow there was not the same degree of urgency about our interceptions, although I doubt that any one of us would ever have admitted harbouring any such thought or attitude. With the departure of the Luftwaffe, a little of the hard edge had gone out of our determination to pursue the enemy to the death; combat, now, was more of a dangerous game.

More Hurricanes from the *Ark Royal* arrived in Malta that day, Mark II Cs apparently, each tropicalised and with four cannons, although for some reason I did not see them land. There was talk that we would all be re-equipped with the Mark II pretty soon – they seemed to be turning up regularly now – which pleased me more than a little as I was still flying one of the old Mark Is, usually 4380. In spite of my prejudice against the tropicalised version of the Hurricane, there was no doubt about it, the untropicalised ones just didn't work. We were constantly having engine problems on all our aircraft but especially the few Mark IIs, so that scarcely a day passed when I didn't sit there during take-off, stiff with apprehension, waiting for the loss of power or stoppage that would pitch me into the hill ahead or the endless rows of stone walls. And, as if to further reduce my confidence in our equipment, on 30 June, when engaged in a hectic scramble in 2815, the Mark II which had previously let me down and which, even indirectly, was a factor in Livingstone's death, I had a repeat performance of the engine's intractability. Once more, with the throttle wide open, all I could achieve was a gentle 20 mph trot to the far end of the airfield. On that occasion, however, my feelings were less of anger and more a mixture of despair and relief, despair that we would ever get the aircraft right, and relief that something worse had not happened and that I was still in one piece. When I had taxied back to dispersal and met the enquiring looks of my Flight Sergeant and crew, my advice to them was tersely abrupt: 'Burn the bloody thing!'

It was also during the last week in June that we learned of Germany's attack on Russia and that the Russian Air Force had been almost wiped out. So, that's where the Huns from Sicily had got to! Discussing this development in the mess, the general view was that Hitler was out of his mind but that it was a godsend; what had possessed the man to do such a thing, to make the most elementary mistake of all, that of waging major war on more than one front? We had been jolly glad to see the back of those Huns in Sicily though; with the Hurricanes we had to fly, anything might have happened!

21

Summer Sets In

1 July was a Tuesday. It was still unpleasantly hot and humid, although we were becoming accustomed to the extremes of temperature and the discomfort of being alternately kippered in the cockpit low down and frozen high up. I found that temperature alone did not affect me greatly although the sun did; being very fair-skinned, my hide took every opportunity to come off in strips, obliging me to keep myself covered whenever possible.

Before dawn on that first day, we all took the bus to Safi to collect our aircraft dispersed there, and minutes later I was kicking myself when I found that I had so organised things that I had left myself to fly 2815. 2815! Two engine failures in three flights! Would this be the third? And at Safi, too, a make-shift strip, surrounded by natural and man-made hazards, the area being littered with explosive devices laid down to thwart any parachute or glider attack. Happily the aircraft behaved perfectly and I landed at Ta Kali without incident. Even more happily, it was to be the last time I ever flew 2815; in fact, I flew neither it nor any of the old Mark Is ever again, a brand new set of Mark IIs being delivered to us. Yes, things were definitely looking up. Even the fresh paintwork cheered us up although we were still without our squadron markings which, strangely, I missed most of all, finding that they gave me a sense of belonging and were a powerful link with past successes.

For three days after, we were not called upon to fly. I sorted myself out a new aircraft, Z3498, had its spinner painted red and felt altogether better as a result. There were a number of new officers and NCOs posted to the squadron, too, one of them, Graham Leggett, being known to me in England. Otherwise, the newcomers were totally inexperienced and seemed terribly young, although they were barely younger than myself. I thanked God that there was a lull in activities; had the Huns been in Sicily there would have been slaughter on a grand scale. With so many experienced fellows available at home, why did they keep sending out these green apprentices? And to Malta, of all places!

It was about 1 July, too, that 46 Squadron, who were now sharing Ta Kali with us, learned that they were to forfeit their squadron number and be known henceforth as 126 Squadron. They were stunned – absolutely – as were the rest of us. What a thing to do! Here they were, one of the oldest squadrons in the Air Force and among the most famous, being instructed at a moment's notice to lose their identity. There was near mutiny. Even I was horrified; to me 'Rags' Rabagliati, Pete LeFevre, and all the rest, colleagues throughout the Battle of Britain and after, were 46, as were then-illustrious forebears, MacLaren, one of the big aces of 1918, and Victor Yeates, who had written Winged Victory in 1937, a book I had grown up with and one which I considered to be the best description written of aerial warfare during the Great War. We, too, had lost our airmen and others in process of journeying to the Middle East, but we, at least, had kept our name and number. Now they had lost everything. The Air Ministry, or whoever, must be mad. In the mess, we all exchanged furious and recklessly undiplomatic comments on the stupidity of those in control of our affairs. Fools! They just didn't understand!

But whatever these distractions, we were all settling down in Malta; letters from home were arriving spasmodically, but arriving; the food and conditions in the mess were improving; there was talk of a proper dispersal building being constructed on the airfield to replace the tent; and in our constant battle with the mosquito and flea population, we seemed to be gaining ground, although the amount of 'Flit' expended in and around my shared bedroom could have floated a ship.

Crossey and I were also in process of providing ourselves with a new wardrobe, a tailor in Valletta producing an elegant line in shirts and shorts in a rather fetching curtain material which, whilst its qualities of lightness and ventilation might be lacking, at least enabled us to feel comfortable and look like officers, thereby heightening our morale.

Our knowledge of Valletta, too, had widened considerably, but, alas, not always to our advantage. Earlier in June, 'Butch' Barton's half of the squadron had sallied forth into the town-centre and embarked upon an afternoon and evening of good fellowship. Towards midnight and then in the company of Wing Commander 'Bull' Halahan, they had created such a disturbance, in first a bar and then an hotel, that the police had been summoned. Unhappily, the upholders of the law had not much relished the task of either reasoning with, or subduing, a dozen or so rowdy Air Force officers in full voice, and had unfortunately shown their timidity. The outcome was, reinforcements were called for and about half the fighter defence of Malta was eventually marched cheering through the streets and into gaol, where several of the more uninhibited among them began running up and down the bars of the cell like caged monkeys, making the appropriate gestures and noises and frightening the police half to death.

And there they stayed.

The following morning, authority's dilemma was plain to see: who was going to defend the island? Without further ado, the squadron was released and arrived back at Ta Kali with thick heads and dry mouths but still enjoying the joke, although Squadron Leader Barton's smile was observed to be more than a little strained. As indeed was 'Bull' Halahan's. Summoned to the Air Officer Commanding's presence that very morning, within hours he had been banished from Malta, his career blighted for all time.

Altogether, a sad and tragic ending to a harmless prank and a reminder that hooliganism did not start in the football stadiums.

On 7 July, feeling full of bounce in my new Hurricane II, I led my half of the squadron against a large, fast-moving raid of which we heard a good deal but saw nothing. After racing northwards to within gliding distance of Sicily, we returned in fine fettle, despite encountering nothing other than a wilderness of sea. For a change, it was nice to fly behind an engine which sounded reassuringly healthy.

On my way home, watching the distant sand-coloured slivers that were Malta and Gozo develop slowly into the island's familiar inlets, bays, and ridges and finally the white-brown congestions of Valletta and distant Rabat, I mused on the difficulties of intercepting anything in this vast arena of glaring sun and sea – unless one ran full tilt into the enemy, that is, or we crossed paths within a mile or two and several thousand feet. Knowing that we were dealing with the Italian Air Force only, I found myself in a comparatively relaxed frame of mind; at least we did not have the constant dread of being jumped from the rear by 109s which dived and zoomed much faster than we were ever able to cope with. We had heard that all the Hun fighter squadrons were re-equipping with the 'F' version of the 109, which had a considerably better performance than the 'E', whose potential for mischief we knew only too well; if that were so, even with our improved Hurricanes, we would be back to square one. Moreover, there was news, too, of the Eyeties getting something called a Macchi 202, which had the same in-line engine as the 109 and was supposed to be about as fast. None of us had seen any, but we were not too concerned about the prospect of meeting them; Eyeties were Eyeties, when all was said and done.

Commencing 8 July, 249 spent the next fortnight operating mainly at night, although the change of role did not mean that we had the hours of daylight to ourselves. Apart from being called upon to make the occasional scramble – fruitless, needless to say – it did enable us to indulge in a little practice flying and interception training, the latter exercises being mainly for the benefit of the controllers 'down the hole'. After the tensions of the first several weeks, this interlude, together with our new and more reliable aircraft, brought about a comparatively relaxed atmosphere. Even the mosquitoes, the fleas, and the everlasting 'Flit', seemed lesser irritants.

And on the night of the 8th, we had some success.

Flying Z3498, I took off well after dark with the message ringing in my ears that bombers were on the way. Climbing up to 15,000 feet, I took up my patrol line a few miles to the east of Valletta, and waited, flying meanwhile in wide figures of eight.

For some time, nothing – no word, no searchlights, no activity of any sort. The night pretty dark but with a well-defined horizon which made instrument flying easy, I wandered about, not in the least perturbed or even excited. In my opinion night fighting did not have much to commend it as it was so seldom rewarding; the enemy hardly ever turned up when, or where, expected and most of one's time and effort was spent establishing one's position and getting back to base in conditions of complete black-out. After about forty minutes, though, a terse sentence with news that one – two – bogeys were 10 miles north, angels 14. And almost immediately, searchlights.

The beams materialised out of nothing, blue-white fingers in the darkness, feeling around, sightless, exploring. This was more like it! Suddenly alert, I sorted out my cockpit by feel, dimmed everything – including the graticules in my gunsight – to the faintest minimum, twisted my gun-button to 'FIRE' and surged up alongside a clutch of around six beams which were crossing experimentally like pale scissoring lances. About a mile distant and following them as they probed, I watched carefully. On edge. Expectant.

Then more searchlights, a dozen or so now, concentrating. Over Valletta, about – I found myself praying that they would keep their itching fingers off those triggers far below. The beams now in a steep pyramid, solidly together. They had something, or had they? Unable to see, I dropped down below the cone and looked up. Nothing. Nothing yet, and the thin moving columns of light falling behind – I was going too fast, damn it. I curved away to the left and made a complete turn, picking up the beams again and focusing hard. Still nothing. Then . . . something! Fleetingly. Was it? I looked again. Yes! I could see it.

As the beams caught the bomber, I had a glimpse of the pale under surfaces of a largish aircraft. A surge of excitement. I turned hard in its direction, flying by feel and instinct in the darkness. The lights moving quickly now and together, but with no bomber in the cone, or none that I could see. Hang on! Hold him! Don't let him go! I hurled my Hurricane in pursuit. Where was it! Line astern now and about 500 yards behind but with nothing visible ahead. The lights moving still as though they were seeing the enemy aircraft from the ground, whereas from directly behind I could see nothing. I dropped down again and looked up hoping to see the pale reflection. Nothing. The fingers wandered about uncertainly, searching again. Then, in a searing blaze of blue and white, they caught me. Oh, no! Not me, you clowns! I ducked down into the cockpit – for one, two, three seconds – before the brilliant eyes beneath, recognising their error, shifted their glare and I was straining my own eyes into the red darkness of light-scarred blindness. Damn and blast the stupid . . . ! The beams ahead of me now, but there, to the left of the cone, a small dark shadow that was the bomber. Eureka! I could see it, but those below couldn't! To the left, I felt like screaming. Your left! But the beams moved away to the right, missing it, as I followed closely. After which, in a flash – inspiration! I would fire and whoever it was would fire back at my tracer, giving away their position. I did so and my cannons thumped and shook – a short burst, but not a sign of tracer. And nothing in return, either. My aircraft had cannons, hadn't it? – loaded with ball and armour-piercing; no tracer and certainly no de Wilde. What a time not to have machine-guns!

I found myself curving to the right in a fast dive but well behind the moving cone of light. Somewhere in the centre of the island, I imagined. I'd missed it! Missed it, after being so close, too. Still searching hopefully, I followed the searchlights like a cat. But they were clearly uncertain now – splitting, moving this way and that, and finally – one by one, being doused, the pin-prick sources of light far below spluttering minutely and fading, until, after a time, I was left in total blackness. Heading – which way? I straightened up and, my DI having toppled, strained my eyes into the gloomy bowl of the compass between my knees. Faintly, the petulantly wandering needle eventually indicated that I was flying north. North! I was way out to sea again, probably. Hell! All over and yet again I had missed a sitter. I turned around and climbing back to 14,000 feet, informed control I was resuming my patrol. They acknowledged my remark dispassionately, adding that there was no other business at the moment. Thereafter, everything went quiet and I had the night – and the blackness beneath that was Malta – all to myself.

Twenty minutes later, I landed. I had been airborne seventy minutes.

Back in dispersal and in the shaded glimmer within the tent, someone was saying he knew he had heard gunfire, after which I was voicing my annoyance and 'Butch' was commiserating with me in his quiet Canadian voice:

'Hard luck, Ginger!' He even reached out a hand to touch my arm, which was about the most demonstrative act I had ever seen my squadron commander perform.

Hard luck! I was seething inside. Fancy letting that blighter get away.

Somewhat later, and whilst I and several others were still in dispersal awaiting developments, Flying Officer Cassidy took off to man the patrol line.

Cassidy, variously referred to as Cass, Casserole, or Hopalong, was a small, doe-eyed young man of Catholic Irish ancestry, who had transferred to 249 from 25 Squadron at North Weald the previous autumn. Formerly on fighter Blenheims, during his early weeks with 249 he had mainly impressed himself on my mind as having run foul of his then Station Commander who was himself a devout Catholic and who constantly demanded to know why Cassidy had not been to Mass. With members of the Roman church thin on the ground, I sensed that although Cass always referred to the Station Commander's strictures as rather a joke, there was just that hint of outrage in his description of events which suggested they were not quite the joke he alleged them to be.

After the sound of Cassidy's Hurricane had faded into the darkness, I stood around enjoying the mellow warmth and scents of the Maltese night. Other than the dim illumination within the tent, everything was black and silent with only the occasional sound of laughter from the small groups of airmen who formed the first-line servicing party. Stretching away to the north was the flare-path, a dozen or so pin-pricks of light at the head of which was the black stump of the Chance floodlight, its beam extinguished. Everybody waited. Patiently.

After a time, the telephone. At least one bogey approaching from the north. Expectantly, we all looked towards the north and presently the searchlights flicked on – one, three, six, then many more – waving experimentally like the antennae of some giant insect blindly seeking out its prey. Then, as the drone of engines high up drifted in our direction, they began to focus, pencils of pale grey moving in tall pyramids, purposefully now, catching the underside of the occasional small patch of cloud in sudden splodges of reflected light. Had they caught it? We couldn't see. I found myself holding my breath. They should, though. Any moment. And as we strained our lifted eyes into the darkness, the additional sound of Cassidy's Hurricane, an all-too familiar sound. Everyone tense. Come on! Come on! Pick the blighter up!

And they did. A sudden flick of something extra and the beams caught the underside of a twin-engine aircraft. They'd got it! Immediately, every lance of light moved quickly onto the target. And held it. They'd got it all right! Now for it!

I estimated the Eyetie bomber to be something over 10,000 feet, the noise of its thrumming unsynchronised engines clear in our ears. It moved across Valletta in our direction then turned away towards the south. Hell!

Normally, the night bombers turned north, which would have brought it right across Ta Kali. Now we wouldn't see the interception, unless Cassidy caught up with it in seconds. Where was he, for Pete's sake? Anyone see him? But no one had done.

Expectant still, we watched the beams follow the now fading sound of engines until they, too, were only dim shafts in the far distance. Probably in the Hal Far area, we estimated. And no interception. Cass must have seen it, surely, or been told. What a shame. Another disappointment. We continued to watch. And listen. Until everything died away into silence. And darkness.

Then, just above the horizon and far to the south a sudden flicker of light. Followed by a tiny shifting flare. Moving. Dropping. Falling. Not unlike a star, but much more slowly. He'd got it! Cass had hit it!– it was on fire! His first aircraft at night, too! Voices raised in a thin, ragged cheer. Yes, the blighter was a goner, all right. We continued to strain our eyes. The noiseless moving light fell away downwards . . . downwards . . . until, finally, it disappeared. Totally. Extinguished in a second by rocky earth or water, what did it matter? After which, and for the second time, there was only silence. And the mellow, sweet-scented darkness that was Malta.

In less than ten minutes, Cassidy's Hurricane was back in the circuit, an invisible noise. Moving around. Then, much quieter now, we heard the whisper of his engine over M'dina. On with the Chance light! The din of the generator rose to a dull roar as the broad flat beam developed into a pool of light extending down to the fourth or fifth flare. An aircraft emerged suddenly, almost silently, out of the darkness and into the beam, before floating to the ground and disappearing into the black void of the airfield beyond. He'd made it. He was down. Well done! A real hero!

Within minutes, Cassidy was being carried shoulder-high around dispersal, grinning, but feeling such as he looked, totally embarrassed. A BR 20, he thought. Into the sea south of the island. Easy really. Caught fire so quickly, at the first touch, it seemed. Obviously no self-sealing tanks or armour plate. Incredible! None of us gave the Eyetie crew a single thought – dead or alive!

Talk and more talk. A good night, in most people's opinion. Not in mine, though. To think, we might have had two! Two in a single night! Sometime later, I wrote in my logbook: '8th July. Fired at Italian aircraft; must have missed!'

The following day, we heard that a section of 185 from Hal Far had intercepted a small group of Macchi 200s and a couple of Air Sea Rescue float-planes, which were presumably looking for survivors. Being vectored onto them somewhere to the east of the island, they had attacked, apparently, but to no great effect, although claims of a sort had been made. We all reckoned they couldn't have been trying very hard. Shooting down ASR float-planes didn't come easily to any of us, although the policy was to do so.

What a thoroughly nasty war!

There was nothing much doing for 249 over the next several days. I mucked about in dispersal, was involved in a few abortive scrambles, most of them of less than twenty minutes duration, and went into Valletta, fighting off the fleas en route. In the bars there, we heard that a few of 126 and 185, 'Rags' Rabagliati and 'Boy' Mould included, had made a low level attack on Syracuse harbour and had claimed all sorts of flying boats which had been moored there. Terribly daring, as Syracuse, well up the east coast of Sicily, was very well defended and more than 100 miles distant. 'Rags', with his slow smile, told me about it in his quiet drawling voice, his explanation all the more appealing as he had a slight lisp. 'Boy' Mould, whom I had met several times at Hal Far, was the commanding officer of 185 and had been with No. 1 Squadron in France at the beginning of the war. A most charming, pleasant-faced young man, he was about four years older than myself and had achieved great fame when he was credited with shooting down the first enemy aircraft to fall to the British forces in France. Syracuse! With some of the engines I had flown behind, venturing anywhere beyond gliding distance of Ta Kali was apt to give me the willies!

My twenty-first birthday being on 14 July, as I thought it would be doubly upsetting for my parents were I to be killed on that day, I arranged not to fly. I need not have worried, however, as nothing much happened. I learned subsequently that to celebrate the occasion, my parents had sent me a greetings telegram – which arrived a fortnight later! The mail, too, was hopeless. At one stage, my family did not receive a letter from me for nearly two months and became almost demented with worry, speculating that I might even have been sent off to Russia. It was terribly cold in Russia, my mother observed in one unhappy letter – forgetting no doubt that it was mid-summer – adding that she did hope I wouldn't be sent there as I hadn't the proper clothing. I had a hollow feeling that she might decide to complain to Air Ministry.

To all of which I eventually replied that I wasn't in Russia and, as regards correspondence, I was doing my best. Malta was a bit isolated at the moment, didn't she understand, and I wasn't really responsibly for my letters turning up in batches of five and six. In England, press reports were suggesting that we were having a terrible time, which was far from the truth. Now that the Huns had departed and our engines and aircraft were newer and rather more reliable, I was moderately happy. There was the nightly, ever present threat of being hit by a bomb, of course, and there were more sea and stone walls than I would have wished for, otherwise things were more than tolerable.

For the next several days I continued to race off the ground on half a dozen dust-streaming interceptions, all of them abortive as we saw not a thing. Then, as luck would have it, on the 17th, a day when my half of the squadron was not on duty, 'Butch' and seven others ran full tilt into a minor swarm of Macchi 200s a little north of Valletta, a group which had become separated from the main Italian formation of something over forty. In the brief, running fight that ensued, 'Butch', with his usual combination of skill and good fortune, disposed of one, and a further Macchi was shot down by several other members of his flight. Unhappily, one of our own Sergeants was lost, a young man called Guest, who had joined the squadron just before our departure from England and of whom I knew only a little.

With the squadron still operating in two parts, some of the family feeling so carefully nurtured over the past twelve months and so splendidly evident during the summer and autumn of 1940, seemed to be slipping away. I was barely acquainted with half a dozen of the pilots in 'Butch's' group and even in my own, there were several who were merely names and faces. A sad business, as I always felt that morale, to a large degree, was founded on example, continuity, and personal association, none of these elements being able to flourish in an atmosphere of constant change and uncertainty. The incident resulting in the death of Livingstone remained poignantly in mind; as his flight commander, I wished I had known him better, Sergeant Guest, too, for that matter.

The AOC, Hugh Pughe Lloyd, came to visit us again about this time, treating me, as leader of those on duty, to his now-familiar stern, Cromwellian glare from a distance of about nine inches. Our conversation was pleasant enough, however. I pointed out that in spite of a substantial number of reinforcement Hurricanes arriving in Malta, 249 could seldom put up more than eight aircraft, our serviceability state remaining deplorable as we still possessed a few clapped-out Mark Is and untropicalised Mark IIs, whose engines seemed only to function when the spirit moved them. In terms of performance, whilst we could cope with the Macchi 200s, Savoias and other Eyetie aircraft, if the Huns returned with their 109s and 88s, or if the new Macchi 202s put in an appearance, we would be hard put to hold our own. Were there no Spitfires available? Or Tomahawks, even?

Fixing me with a fierce stare, Hugh Pughe explained that we should all be more offensive-minded. Carry the fight to the enemy! Strike them everywhere! Bomb them out of their stride, that was the ticket! And that was what we would have to do.

I listened to his fierce exhortations in mild wonderment and dismay. Somehow there seemed to be a credibility gap between my AOC's expectations and our own capabilities.

Meanwhile, in addition to our daylight activities, we were still operating at night and on 24 and 28 July, I was airborne again, the first occasion being especially memorable.

On a moonlit night, it was a joy to fly in Malta; one hardly needed a flare path even for landing. Moreover, from 15,000 feet, with the horizon a firm line in every direction and the whole island clearly visible, navigation, even without the searchlights, was a simple enough matter. Sadly, my flight of 24 July was not one of those occasions.

Being scrambled shortly before midnight, I found the night sky as black as ever I had known it. For the first time I could recall, I was obliged to climb away entirely on instruments, my head buried in the office not only until I was at height but also as I was wandering about on my supposed patrol-line somewhere in the area of Kalafrana Bay. There was no horizon, no searchlights, not a candle's flicker anywhere, just impenetrable, velvety blackness, a blackness accentuated by the magenta flare of my engine exhausts, visible evidence of the struggle being waged to keep my

Hurricane and me in the air. Uncomfortably alone and with only a vague notion of where I was, I kept in touch with control with plaintive enquiries as to what was going on, the reassuring voice from below establishing a welcome link between me and the earth in an otherwise dark and hostile wilderness. At that very moment, my parents would be comfortably and obliviously asleep in far away England; if only they could see me now, I mused. I cruised around at 14,000 feet, watching my instruments like a hawk. If I ran into a bomber tonight, in the excitement of manoeuvring and shooting, I was going to have my work cut out deciding which way was up!

Then, the voice from below. Bogey approaching from the north. Vector three-five-zero. I turned in that direction, straightened up, and flew off to greet the enemy. After which, I waited. And searched. And waited. In every direction, nothing but a blank, black wall.

After a time, but behind me – miles behind me! – a sudden clutch of searchlights. I turned, very circumspectly, and flew back towards them, my eyes darting in rapid glances away from my instrument- panel. I followed the hesitant beams expectantly, about a mile behind. Cautiously and on edge. Nothing to see, though. The tall pencils of light moving indecisively this way and that, then more in concert. Drifting. Searching. Moving off to my right. But nothing still. I watched carefully the apex of the minutely waving cone of wands. Stalking. Following. Turning with them.. More. Then more. Now straightening. Close, very close, almost within touching distance. I began to lose patience. Come on, for God's sake, show something! Now, going north again, I sensed. I fell into line astern. Whoever it was was now going home, surely? Then, after some apparent indecision far below, in an instant – nothing! The lights disappeared at the snap of a finger, leaving me in eye-searing blackness.

For a full minute, I remained glued to my instruments but after some anxious moments of reorientation, I looked up to see a reddish flare ahead of me. The glow of an exhaust! An exhaust! Eureka! A bomber, ahead but slightly higher. A Hun – Eyetie – or whoever, going away northwards. About 500 feet higher, I judged, a distinct exhaust glow, something I had seen at night several times before. Careful though. Didn't want to scare the blighter and provoke a shower of sherbet from the rear gunner.

I opened up and felt my engine and airframe tighten as the throttle lever was thrust forward to the gate and my airscrew fined to a shrill, 2,850 revs. Then everything right forward to obtain maximum power. My gaze raptly focused on the spot of light ahead – mustn't lose it!

I climbed hotly in pursuit, tensely oblivious of the endless void of blackness all around me.

A minute or more of urgent, vibrating flight. A quick glance at my instruments – 250 on the clock at something approaching 14,000 feet– getting on for a Hurricane's maximum speed on the level (true airspeed increases with height; I was actually flying at a little over 300 mph). My aircraft drumming and shivering in tune with my excitement. Ought to be catching up by now. The Hun, or whoever, still ahead and a bit above, which was rather odd. Going like hell, too! Press on, though.

I urged my Hurricane forward. Faster! Faster!

The adrenalin surging, I raced northwards for perhaps five trembling, raging minutes. Until, reluctantly and with a gradual dawning of comprehension, I began to realise that I was not chasing an enemy aircraft at all but one of the Lord's own cosmic creations – a star! Low on the horizon and reddish in colour, was it Mars? Venus? Something to do with the Plough? My astronomy negligible, I didn't know, nor did I care very much.

Closing the throttle – to my Hurricane's immense relief, I sensed – I turned carefully towards the south and after straightening up, called for a fix and homing vector. The now familiar voice came up from below: 'Any luck?' And, after some moments, the same voice: 'Steer, 175 degrees, distance 38 miles!'

I sagged back with relief. Thank God for that! Just the sort of night for me to have an RT failure as well! More composed now, I headed south into the blackness.

Glued to my instruments, I let down gradually, carefully, praying for the companionable sight of the searchlights which, thus far, had seemed eager to give assistance only to the enemy. But, for me, not so much as a flicker. I thought of asking control to have them switched on but decided against it. Having behaved like a half-wit, it was best to keep quiet about it!

That night, I saw nothing whatever of Malta until I was back again in the circuit at Ta Kali, at which point and almost by accident, I caught sight of the thin line of pin-pricks which were the flare path lights. I had been airborne a mere forty minutes, which had seemed like hours. And all for nothing.

I wrote home that night, apparently at peace in the remaining period of cool, silent darkness. A very tired letter, though, and a little disheartened and peevish. What was the use of all this harrying and chasing about, I asked querulously? More than two months in Malta, and I had hardly fired a shot.

Having flown three times on the 24th and been up most of that night, I was not on duty for the next two days, 'Butch's' half of the squadron together with 185, across at Hal Far, taking over the responsibility of defending the island. We had heard earlier, via the grapevine, that there was a big escorted convoy of ours somewhere away to the west, but as it was not yet within our orbit, we gave it little thought.

Despite my lack of sleep, I was sufficiently alive and active – most unusual for me! – to be out and about in Valletta during the morning of the following day and was witness to a part of my own squadron in action. The air raid siren having sounded and with people in the streets either scurrying for shelter or gawping into the sky, I joined the watchers and heard the thin, angry drone of invisible engines high above, followed by the faint 'brrrr' of distant machine-guns and soon after, the white, pencil-thin trace of an aircraft heading rapidly earthwards. My vision obstructed by the building next to me, I lost sight of it for a time, but seconds later I saw it again and immediately sensed a plunge to destruction. One of ours? I shaded my eyes. Impossible to say; no flames or anything really dramatic, only faint, minute puffs of white from an aircraft now over the vertical, screaming like a banshee and looking as though it would dive right into the middle of Valletta. Which it did, with a terrible bang, not too far away from where I was standing.

Immediately, there was excitement and shrill hysterical chatter, with people running in the direction of the crash, no doubt wishing to dip their handkerchiefs in the blood. I halted in disgust. The ghouls! Well, there would be no blood with that one, and very little of anything else. I just hoped it had not been one of ours.

In fact, it was a Macchi 200, the victim of Bob Matthews, a pilot officer in 'Butch's' flight who had joined 249 shortly before our departure from England, the Eyetie fighter being one of several destroyed as the result of an interception made a little north of Valletta. Even more horrifying, the Italian pilot had apparently baled out but his parachute not functioning properly, the unfortunate man had followed his Macchi down to disaster, a pathetic curving stone. Poor chap! Although it was about the fifth such incident I had either witnessed or knew of over the previous twelve months, the latest being Sergeant Livingstone, the stomach-churning unpleasantness of it never diminished. Plenty of time for each wretched victim to watch and wait for his inevitable pulverising and bloody end. Did nature anaesthetise the mind on such occasions? I hoped I would never be in the position to find out.

But, whatever its immediate effect on me, the memory of the incident soon evaporated. It had been the usual reconnaissance aircraft, apparently, a twin-engined Cant this time – it too being shot down – escorted by a mass of Italian fighters. Silly people; why did they insist on doing the same thing day after day? If all they wanted were pictures of Grand Harbour and Luqa, surely they could achieve their ends more economically. We supposed they had come to photograph Valletta, which was bulging with ships, the convoy we had heard about having reached its destination if in somewhat depleted numbers. Now what? we wondered.

Within hours we were to find out.

It was still dark the following morning when I was awakened by bumps, but bumps with a difference. With bombs, one's sleeping ear was cocked first for the drone of the bomber, then the whistle and thump of bombs in the middle distance, until finally, when the whistles became the briefest of shrieks and the ground began to shake, it was over the side and under the bed in a single liquid movement. How I – and others – achieved this magical transfer of more than eleven stones of flesh and blood, was always a mystery as my mosquito net was always tucked in tightly, yet never once did it impede my lightning progress. Perhaps surprisingly, I was never greatly upset by enemy bombing in Malta, even when the 500 pounders fell within yards of the Mess; quite without evidence or reason, I was always confident that the bombs were destined to drop on someone else.

It was against this background that I interpreted the thumps in the early morning of 26 July as something other than bombs, although earlier there had been the usual noise of bombing in the distance. Naked except for a towel round my middle, my bare feet smacking on the cool flagstones of my shared bedroom, I joined Crossey and several others who were outside, talking in quiet tones on the elevated walk-way that ran one side of the courtyard. It was still quite dark.

'What's up?'

Crossey replied that he didn't know in hushed tones that suggested that he didn't want the enemy to hear. An attack of some sort. Out to sea, he thought. The continuous series of bumps in the distance were clearly more in keeping with naval guns than the anti-aircraft fire with which we were so familiar.

'D'you think we're being invaded?'

'Invaded! I hope not!' An unsteady laugh.

'Have you got your gun?'

'Gun! I think so. Somewhere. It might be an idea to dig it out.'

I agreed – profoundly; the prospect of Max Schmeling's (former World Heavyweight Champion; in 1941 a German paratrooper) face appearing around the door-jamb behind a Tommy-gun was not in the least appealing.

The first streaks of dawn in the east, there soon came the distant noise of aircraft engines bursting into life and after some minutes, several pairs of Hurricanes rose out of the night and, dark silhouettes, roared across our front, climbing towards the lightening grey beyond St Paul's Bay. Far away to our right, searchlight beams slanted obliquely across the sky and out to sea. Yes, something was most definitely up!

For half an hour or so, we hung about on the stone parapet in the cool dampness of dawn, speculating, listening, and watching as aircraft left and reappeared with the urgency that suggested battle, the distant noise of guns continuing spasmodically meanwhile. Then, word began to filter through that there had been a seaborne attack on Grand Harbour but that things were now under control; some 'E' boats, or their Italian equivalent, had apparently made a suicide attack but had been beaten off. The Hurricanes of 126 Squadron we had seen taking off from Ta Kali had shot up a number of the MTBs and there were Eyetie fighters about too.

Things not being quite as desperate as we had feared, the tension subsided and I suddenly found myself shivering. As it was still well before 6 a.m. – still time for a couple of hours' zzzz before breakfast – I padded back to my bed. No point in hanging about, catching pneumonia.

By mid-afternoon the following day, the picture was more or less clear. Several Italian MTBs and up to a dozen smaller vessels, including one-man explosive craft and human torpedoes, had been escorted to within 20 miles of Malta by a mother ship and launched against Grand Harbour in a do-or-die attempt to breach the defences and get at the ships within. The attack had started, as we well knew, considerably before dawn, to the accompaniment of a diversionary bombing attack, the sounds of which we had faintly heard. Then, when the light was sufficiently good, a force of Macchi 200s had flown south in order to cover the withdrawal of the seaborne force.

249 Squadron not being on duty that morning, it fell to 126 and 185 to scramble against what was for them a quite unusual target and also brave the hail of shell and shot that was arcing luminously from the now wide awake shore defences. In fact, those on shore had never been other than wide awake, being forewarned, apparently, of the Italian attack (from our own intelligence via the captured ULTRA decoding equipment).

Scarcely believing their good fortune, the Hurricanes had attacked the MTBs and other craft and were in turn attacked by the Macchis. On balance, however, our own side had triumphed handsomely, almost all the MTBs and other craft being disabled or sunk and several Macchis being shot into the sea. However, during the fracas, Denis Winton, who had been part of my flight in 249 during our first days in Malta and had later joined 185, was hit – whether by fighter or ship was unclear – and forced to bale out. Plopping into the sea, he inflated his dinghy and climbed aboard, thanking God for his deliverance.

Sometime later, he became aware that he was fairly close to one of the larger vessels he had attacked and put out of action. As the MTB appeared to be harmlessly adrift and deciding that it represented a more secure sanctuary than his bobbing dinghy, he swam and otherwise urged himself towards it and finally clambered aboard only to find himself faced with the product of his own handiwork – eight mutilated and bleeding corpses. Mildly revolted by the carnage around him, he was obliged to stay there for several hours, praying that some other belligerent Hurricanes would not attack the Italian vessel of which he was now the sole occupant. Sometime later, after waving an improvised white flag in an effort to convince the crew of a cautiously circling British rescue craft that he needed rescuing, he was picked up by a Swordfish floatplane, a type of aircraft I never at any time saw on the island. Later, displaying his trophies, he was able to regale us amusingly with the tale of his macabre adventure. The MTB was also retrieved, being towed back to Malta with its eight uncomplaining occupants.

A successful day for those of us in Malta, a gory and tragic one for the Italian attackers, their casualties being fifteen dead and eighteen captured. Such glorious, flamboyant but foolhardy bravery, so typical of the Eyeties; given the circumstances, what did they hope to achieve? All the same, I was glad it had not been Max Schmeling and his mates! Which rather begged the question: what would I have done in the event of a German parachute invasion? Despite the recent airborne assault on Crete, which had had such bitter consequences for us British, none of us at Ta Kali was in the least prepared for any such happening in Malta, nor had we even talked about it – seriously that is. I wasn't even sure of the whereabouts of my revolver!

July drifted to a close with a searingly brilliant sun and humid and oppressive heat. In our primitive dispersal tent, we gasped and fanned ourselves and prayed for rain as we waited for the next scramble instruction, blessing the talcum powder dust that insinuated itself into mouth, eyes and hair whenever a whirling airscrew lifted it in twisting devils from the baked earth and set it in motion as a malevolent wandering cloud. On the track that ran close to dispersal and across the landing run, the occasional horse, cart, and somnolent peasant would wander disconcertingly in front of aircraft in the final stages of touching down, producing screams of invective from outraged pilots who were obliged either to veer away or go round again. There were dire threats uttered about 'giving the idle buggers a squirt' – with eight or twelve Brownings, naturally – but no one was ever driven to such an extreme. Notices, threats, and even cajolery had little effect; the peasantry grinned, nodded, then went on doing exactly what it had been doing for two thousand years.

On the 27th, I was off on a longish scramble in 612, a Mark II I had never flown before. Some 60 miles north and west of the island, we were kept at a low altitude and warned to look out for low flying Savoias en route to Libya. But, either the Eyeties had come and gone or were a figment of the controller's imagination; whatever the reason, we saw nothing. Later, we learned that a section of 185 had had some success earlier in the day, shooting down two of the selfsame Savoias. Perhaps it was their success that had prompted control to send us off.

It was more of the same the following day with a long night at 'Readiness', my dreary vigil broken only by a single scramble and a brief but uneventful trip of fifteen minutes during which the searchlights did not even deign to put in an appearance. Our own comparative inactivity that day was, however, in marked contrast with the pulsating comings and goings of the Beaufighters based temporarily at Luqa.

Hugh Pughe, our belligerent AOC, not for the first time and certainly not for the last, had contrived to prolong the stay of one of the Beaufighter squadrons in transit to the Middle East, for the purpose of carrying out a series of low-level attacks on airfields and other targets in Sicily. For this particular duty the Beau was well suited as it had a good turn of speed low down – slightly better than that of our Hurricanes, in fact – and having two whopping great aircooled radial engines, was far less likely to be crippled by-light flak than were our own aircraft with their single engines and exposed radiators. Furthermore, the Beaufighter was an unusually quiet aircraft, particularly at high speed, and had a formidable armament of four cannons and six machine guns. To the enemy, it eventually became known as 'whispering death', a description well merited as it dealt fearful damage on a number of occasions during the summer of 1941, one of the most notable being that of 28 July when about twenty enemy aircraft were destroyed and damaged on the ground in addition to a considerable number of troops on the move and some small craft at sea. Having been on the receiving end of the Hun 109s some eight weeks earlier, my imagination had no difficulty in visualising the chaos likely to be inflicted by four times as many aircraft, each with massively greater fire power than the Me 109.

The following day, even I thought I was in for some success. Being scrambled with only the briefest information of what was ahead of us, four of us fled westwards at lowish altitude, in search, we thought, of a batch of juicy Savoias en route for Libya. Some fifty miles out and at less than 1,000 feet, I suddenly saw them a long way off, skimming across the wave tops. A wild surge of exultation. 'Tallyho!' Four of them! This time we'd got the blighters! Open with the throttle and up with the revs; a brief and feverish glance at my gun button and gun sight, the former properly on 'FIRE' the range bars on the sight set at forty feet. Forty feet! That was no good. A twist by feel to sixty, click, click – to me, all bomber aircraft had a wingspan of sixty feet, Dorniers, 88s, BR 20s, the lot.

We curved towards them, the blood draining. At about a mile range now, pulling hard in a tightish turn, and with memories of past engagements with Dorniers and 88s vividly in mind, I resolved to attack the far outside aircraft, noting with mild disapproval that I would be unable to take up the comparatively safe position under the tail. Half a mile! I pulled up sharply before diving – at which point my heart sank and all the emotion ebbed away. They were Blenheims. Four ruddy Blenheims!

Like predators thwarted of their prey, we veered away, still tense, resentful and scowling. And spread out, two of us either side. What an anticlimax! Still, no point in frightening these chaps to death, they had a hell of a life anyway carrying out their mast-height attacks and suffering terrible casualties; we would give their morale a lift and escort them home. Which we did. Our one good turn for the day.

The next day, too, more fruitless haring about, this time without even a sight of an aircraft. What had happened to the enemy? – they certainly didn't seem to be trying very hard these days. It was a Thursday, I noted; the last day of July.

My letter home that night was cheerful if circumspectly phrased in order to avoid the censor's black ink. I was always vaguely resentful about having my letters read and censored; if as Flight Commander I was allowed to censor other people's, why couldn't I censor my own? A silly business, the system probably starting at Agincourt!

Making up my logbook for the month, I saw that I had made forty-four operational flights since arriving in Malta; masses of adrenalin expended for remarkably few results. I was becoming accustomed to flying over endless tracts of sea and operating from an island on which it was almost impossible to force-land safely. On the other hand, having had five engine failures in eight weeks – euphemistically termed 'malfunctions' – I still did not have complete confidence in the Hurricanes I was flying. Even the dinghy, which had contributed so much to my peace of mind and on which I had sat so painfully during my initial trip from the *Ark Royal*, had proved to be suspect. Shortly after our arrival, when a group of us had gone down to Sliema to try out our new life-saving equipment, my dinghy had not only refused to inflate, the carbon dioxide bottle choking to an immediate stop with a strangled 'fizz', but had sunk dismally with scarcely a splutter when I attempted to use the little concertina handpump, there being a six-inch gash in the yellow rubber.

But, in spite of everything, I was alive, wasn't I? And moderately happy. For all of which I thanked God!

And as a sign that the Lord was indeed on my side, the following day, 'Butch' Barton had an engine failure on take-off flying Z3492, the aircraft I had used on its previous flight to intercept the Blenheims. His engine stopping at several hundred feet, quite properly he did not attempt to turn back but crashed straight ahead, his Hurricane ploughing through several of the stone walls I had been eyeing so jaundicedly over the past eight weeks. His aircraft wrecked and trapped in the cockpit, the little man was nastily burnt about the face when the aircraft batteries came loose and doused him with acid.

Crossey and I visited him in Imtafa hospital the day after and found him disfigured, shocked and trembling but profoundly thankful that things had turned out as well as they had. Few people had survived such an experience and with so much operational and other flying behind him, he felt that an engine failure of some sort was long overdue. And now it had happened, in Malta of all places, and he was still alive and kicking. Looking tiny and waif-like in his hospital bed, he was childishly relieved at his deliverance.

As we left him behind, I was all too conscious of the squadron's debt to the little man. Small and slight in stature, in no way a heroic figure and unassuming almost to a fault, he was one of the best leaders and fighter pilots it would be my good fortune to meet. Having flown together for more than a year, including the whole of the Battle of Britain, my admiration for his ability and devotion to duty was unbounded.

As he was expected to be in hospital and out of action for some time, it fell to me to command the squadron. And of more immediate satisfaction, to be the guardian of our single most cherished possession – one clapped-out Austin 16!

22

August 1941

August, a month of comparative tranquillity, was also one of change and uncertainty. It was a time, too, when, with a considerable reduction in the demands made upon our services, the more amorous of us were enabled to widen our experience in an area delicately referred to as poodle-faking. Now that we were guests of the Maltese people – more or less – it was incumbent upon us (we considered) to keep ourselves in the mainstream of social intercourse, a duty which inevitably involved the civilian population, or, more precisely, the civilian population's daughters.

It had all started early in June when a number of 249 were invited to a swimming party at the Dragonara Palace, a place noted for its magnificent scenic position, its private swimming pool, and the largesse and munificence of its owner the Marquis Scicluna. In addition, as fringe benefits so to speak, there were two plump but pleasant daughters – and a model railway in the basement! Alas, the daughters didn't stand a chance; on the two occasions I was a guest there, the model railway claimed my attention entirely.

At about the same time, I chanced to be in dispersal at Ta Kali when a gharry, with the statutory straw-hatted nag, creaked past in a swirl of dust. At the reins and dextrously flicking a whip with Beau Brummell aplomb, was a pilot of 261 Squadron, whom I knew would shortly be leaving, and alongside him a delectable dark-eyed girl of about twenty whose name I later discovered was Patsy. Patsy was the second daughter of the Chief Justice of Malta, Sir Phillip Pullicino, one of five daughters, in fact, two of whom were later to marry Service colleagues of mine. I also learned that she lived in Rabat, her parents having had the good sense to evacuate their former home in Sliema when the bombs had begun to fall.

Sometime later, Crossey, Palliser, Mills, and I, under the guidance of Pilot Officer Cavan, who had earlier been with 261 Squadron and therefore knew the ropes, made our way up to Rabat for the purpose of inveigling our way into the small community of evacuated families who were living there in cool and isolated security. A rendezvous with a bevy of daughters having been arranged, the vivacious Patsy among them, we assembled on that first occasion at a down-at-heel estaminet with leaning, paint-flaked shutters, called the Point de Vue. Shyly and on our best behaviour, we drank John Collinses and tepid soft drinks amid the long dark shadows of the medieval churches, our adolescent conversation and laughter piercing the breathless afternoon silence and echoing among the sombre walls and deserted, narrow streets. On that first afternoon, too, we picked loganberries on the unkempt slopes of a nearby garden with all the playful simplicity of children on a Sunday-school outing. It was an enchanting occasion, utterly at odds with the grim and deadly business on which we were normally engaged, serving to provide us all with a brief interval of normality.

In the weeks that followed, on such free afternoons as we had, a small group of us, limp and panting in the blistering heat, would tramp the dusty two-mile hill to Rabat, arriving at the Point de Vue exhausted, to sink dripping into the rickety cane and iron chairs on the forecourt before being welcomed by the young ladies of Rabat. Their names live on in my memory: Patsy, Ena and Anne Pullicino, Liliana di Georgio, Florence Testaferrata, the delightful 'Janey' whose other name escapes me, and others. Later, when we spread our wings, there were other daughters just as speciously prim, as well-mannered and as appealingly flirtatious. At various venues in Sliema and Valletta, there were the occasional formal parties, with evening frocks and sipped drinks amid the whistle and thump of bombs; decorous dances with foreheads beaded with perspiration and damp palms on virginally slim waists and exposed shoulders; visits to the only cinema in Valletta to hold hands in the half-light and be eaten into a lump by battalions of fleas hopping about like gazelles in the thick plush of the red seats; and breathlessly hurried journeys home to Rabat and elsewhere by gharry – mustn't be later than ten o'clock or else! – with chaste kisses on the doorstep, the occasional parent in some shadowy offing, keeping an eagle eye on what the daughter of the house was up to and praying, no doubt, that their offspring's experience was not advancing at too rapid a pace.

Those were simple, uncomplicated meetings, as refreshing as they were uncorrupted by crude thoughts of anything even approximating to sex; indeed, had such vile intentions lurked in our minds (and they probably did from time to time), the opportunities for fulfilment were sadly lacking. In Malta, there was neither the time nor the place to do anything!

Over an interval of years, our activities might now appear to be juvenile, but near-juveniles we were, each one of us in his way in need of a little love and gentleness as a relaxation from flying and fighting, engine failures, flak, tracer, the endless wastes of inhospitable sea, and the harsh realities of living in a sometimes coarse and turbulent all-male community. The young ladies of Malta played their part in the defence of their island to a greater extent than ever they realised. Moreover, they provided an additional service; as all of them spoke fluent Italian, we heard more from their reports of what the Italian radio had to say about our day-to-day battles over and around Malta than ever we received from our own intelligence sources. If we had shot at a Macchi, a Cant or a Savoia, we simply asked the girlfriend the following day for news of its fate. And usually they were able to oblige.

There was so little doing that August, we decided that the Eyeties had gone on holiday, and good luck to them – unlike the Germans, a most civilised enemy. With the temperature constantly in the 80s and 90s amid a wilting humidity, the respite was more than welcome. Grouped at the end of the airfield in a scattered clutch and all hooked up for action, our Hurricanes hung their heads and almost visibly shrivelled in the sun, their wings so hot that on several occasions, 20mm cannon ammunition exploded within the stifling confines of the baking metal.

The month had started off inauspiciously. In the last days of July, it had been decided to form a new flight, the Malta Night Fighter Unit – MNFU, as it came to be known. Moderately cheered by this decision, as I had been one of a small group who had been flying by both day and night, I was less happy to learn that 249 would be required to provide the bulk of the pilots. In the event, some of our long-serving stalwarts – Cassidy, Thompson and Mills – all of whom had been with 249 since the autumn of 1940, together with Robertson and the experienced and doubly decorated Donald Stones, two more recent additions, left to become part of the new unit. Squadron Leader Powell-Sheddon, a pleasant, rather bulky young man with a slight but most agreeable stammer, arrived from parts unknown to take charge, and around a dozen officer and NCO pilots took possession of a group of the better Mark II Hurricanes and went into business, initially at Ta Kali. Thereafter, I was not called upon to fly at night except in an attacking role, which turned out to be a good deal more hazardous than defending the island, our only targets being 100 miles away in Sicily.

This further reduction among the old hands of 249 depressed me not a little, so much so that I wrote of it in a dismal letter to my parents. The squadron was disintegrating, I lamented; only about six of us left of the original group of the summer and autumn of 1940. Why did they keep mucking us about? The spirit of a squadron was the thing, and ours was dying. And indeed it was; and so was I – in terms of fervour, anyway. 'Butch's' accident had marked the beginning of the end, although during that hot and humid August, I suspect that it was then only a subconscious thought. Things just weren't the same any more, which, after more than a year of incessant fighting and flying, was more than understandable. But 'Butch' and Pat Wells, though temporarily incapacitated, were still with us, plus the imperturbable Beazley, my particular mate, Crossey, and the irrepressible little man, Palliser. Were they as jaded as I was beginning to feel? On the other hand, there were brighter, fresher faces, too, new chaps who had joined us in England: the smiling, even-tempered Davis, a little older than most and a David to Beazley's Jonathan; Bob Matthews, with the wry grin and the equally wry sense of humour, who had shot down the Macchi I had so recently seen plunge into the centre of Valletta; the fair-haired Graham Leggett; the tall, aesthetic-looking but mischievous Harrington, the squadron's acknowledged 'character' with the cards; 'Tony' Morello, with his dark Italian looks, who was part of us yet somehow never quite appeared to be so; and the newer boys still, Cavan, Moon, 'Jack' Hulbert, the gentle and burly Stuart, nicknamed 'Horse', plus a batch of NCO pilots, new, expectantly enthusiastic but to my critical eye, pathetically inexperienced – all these now formed the bulk of the squadron. Thank God there had been a lull. If the Huns with their new 109Fs suddenly returned – it was all too grisly even to contemplate!

Of those in the other squadrons, 126 and 185, there were some I had known from my North Weald days and others I knew by reputation and casual acquaintance. 'Boy' Mould, the commanding officer of 185, was an affable young man with dark, wavy hair and an infectious grin; a most engaging person, I had warmed to him immediately when we had first met at Hal Far in May. And some others of 185, too, had left a lasting and most favourable impression – Jeffries, Eliot, Thompson, and more.

Of 126, formerly 46 Squadron, there was the seemingly indestructible partnership of 'Rags' Rabagliati, Peter Le Fevre, 'Chips' Carpenter, 'Bert' Ambrose, and MacGregor. Also in the squadron was a comparative newcomer, Pat Lardner-Burke, a no-nonsense Rhodesian who was as laconically tough as his appearance suggested and was to do very well in the weeks to come, together with a Pilot Officer Anderson. He was tragically killed later in the war, as were Rabagliati and Le Fevre. Although Anderson and I did not take to each other at first, I came to admire him as an artist of considerable talent, a common interest which drew us together, enabling us in the weeks ahead to indulge a shared recreation. Remarking, though not complaining, that the war had rather upset his career, he spent a lot of his time sketching aircraft and producing vividly realistic portrayals of combat, the victims always being the enemy, needless to say.

Another newcomer to Malta who made a special impression on me, was Pilot Officer David Barnwell, whose father was responsible for the design of the Bristol Blenheim bomber, the aircraft type which was having such a thin time of it at Luqa, several miles to the south of us. Initially at Ta Kali and later with the MNFU at Hal Far, Barnwell positively radiated a Boys Own brand of enthusiasm besides having a most lively and attractive personality. A gilded youth in almost every respect and part of a gallant family which was almost wiped out by the war, his star was to burn brilliantly but, alas, all too briefly.

Concurrent with the flying, the fighting, and our own and the squadron's developing affairs, a whole series of minor happenings occurred during those breathless summer days.

We had learnt on the grapevine that it was the intention to build a dispersal building to replace the miserable tents which formed our only accommodation on the airfield. It was no surprise, therefore, when a small gang of Maltese workmen turned up one morning and set about marking out the site. What did surprise us, however, was that they didn't arrive with bricks, hods and the usual impedimenta of building, but with a cart and straw-hatted horse and little more than a half-dozen saws, iron bars, and hammers. Being a handyman from way back and for most of the time bored with hanging about at 'Readiness', I stood around in full flying kit and Mae West, mildly curious to see how it was done.

The workmen themselves were unique; all had bare feet and large flat caps, the type seen at soccer matches in England during the early '30s. In colour, they were all the shade of the dust – ochre-grey – and each had his trousers rolled up to the knee. From sun-cracked faces the texture of crocodile skin, issued not so much as a single word or smile. Clearly, building dispersal huts was pretty routine stuff.

Within minutes they had retired some thirty yards distant and commenced to dig holes in the ground with picks, jemmies, and hammers. Then, when they had levered out vast chunks of the whitish sandstone, they set about sawing it up with handsaws. Sawing up Malta! I had never seen anyone do that before. Finally, after fashioning the quite sizeable boulders into rough but formidable oblongs, they produced primitive planes, which looked as though they had originated at the time of pyramids, and planed everything into smooth, rectangular shapes. Thus busily engaged for about three days, they collected a huge mound of blocks, all regular and of the same dimensions, with barely the flick of a ruler or square. Fascinated by now, I watched in awe and admiration.

After that came the business of constructing the building itself, a long, low bungalow affair with a kind of veranda with pillars, designed to enable us to sit outside but out of the sun, a not unwelcome arrangement bearing in mind the need to keep a beady eye cocked for low-flying attackers.

Finally, over a period of several weeks, the heavy blocks were humped into position by hand, mortar consisting of ingredients that could only be guessed at, was heaped and slopped on the ground, the mixers squatting like Arabs meanwhile, using their hands occasionally and spitting majestically into the goo to give it that extra bit of 'stick'.

And up it went, until we had a dispersal building to be proud of, spacious and coolly white within, a place in which to shelter in the event of a strafing attack and to abandon with all haste at the first whistle of an adjacent bomb, although despite heavy bombing attacks later, this building survived the war. I examined the walls and ceiling with a critical eye. Everything was dead straight, plumb-line vertical, and (quite unlike my own wooden creations) exactly square, the workmanship exemplary. Moreover, where the stone had been dug out of the ground, we had yet another natural and perfectly good air-raid shelter on our doorstep.

But, whatever our surprise initially at the versatility and craftsmanship of the Maltese workmen, we were in contact daily with other examples of their expertise.

Although there had been several reinforcement flights of Hurricanes into Malta since our arrival in May, spare parts were always a problem and it was often necessary to cannibalise – strip one aircraft to make serviceable another – one especially vulnerable item being the propeller.

All the Hurricane Mark IIs and some of the remaining Mark Is were then equipped with Rotol airscrews, the blades of which were constructed basically of laminated wood, covered in a reinforcing metal and plastic sheath. In the event of a crash, forced-landing, or taxiing accident, the airscrew blades were invariably chopped off at the roots and damaged beyond repair. Some were not beyond salvaging, however, and although in Britain they would probably have been scrapped, in Malta, where the need was great, they were sent for repair.

Such work, indeed most of the repair work on any Service item, from ships to shoes, was carried out in the naval dockyard in Valletta or in the primitive workshops in the complex of narrow streets bordering the dockyard. There, miracles were worked and airscrews which needed the skills of Houdini and a watchmaker combined, were reconstructed, using the most basic of tools, from substitute materials and with all the elaborate twists and curves that were necessary, so perfectly that not even an experienced eye could detect a flaw. Over the months, we used several such airscrews in 249 and I never ceased to be humbled by the skill of those who had rebuilt them.

It was in Malta, too, that I learned a little about the armour-plate I had been carting about in and around my cockpit for the past eighteen months, how brutally heavy it was and how nearly impossible it was to bend, cut, bore, or otherwise modify, a fact which was to exercise our minds considerably in the weeks to come.

Clearly, there was much more involved in going to war than sitting in the cockpit and firing the guns now and then. The importance of those who supported us with equipment, know-how and nimbleness of finger and hand, was beginning to seep through even to my arrogant, prejudiced noddle.

We had been hanging about at 'Readiness' for most of the morning.

It was blisteringly hot at dispersal and we were bored and sweating.

I looked up to find two figures approaching through the eddies of heat and dust, one the station commander, the other a small anonymous person in side-cap and long khaki trousers. Khaki trousers! Unusual that; everyone wore shorts in Malta. I rose and went out to greet them.

The visitor, who came only a little higher than my shoulder, was introduced and to my mild surprise I saw that he wore an Air Vice Marshal's stripes on the tabs of his rather crumpled shirt. His name going right over my head, I imagined him to be some 'equipper' or 'plumber' out from Air Ministry. Would I show him round and explain things? Of course – I smiled the patient, rather superior smile I reserved for high-ranking penguins.

For about fifteen minutes we strolled between the aircraft in the sun and dust, my companion uttering not a word. I told him about the squadron, our role, and what we had achieved in the past three months, adding that although we mostly had Hurricane IIs now, our serviceability rate remained pretty awful; we were still having all sorts of engine and other problems and, as if that wasn't enough, just recently even the cannon ammunition was exploding prematurely in the wings. Hurricane Is were worse than useless, of course, and even the Mark IIs were only acceptable for as long as we had Macchi 200s, BR 20s and Savoias to deal with. Why did those of us overseas always have to fly the junk? There were masses of Spits at home and we really ought to have some in Malta if we were to do anything worthwhile – tropicalised, mind you, the ordinary sort would be no good. Or perhaps Tomahawks, even; anything that would enable us to catch the Eyeties or Huns more easily. I warmed to my favourite subject.

When I had just about exhausted the topic, my companion put in a few quiet questions, nodding in response to my replies, otherwise he said nothing that sparked my interest. Odd little blighter, I thought, no decorations or anything like that; still, equippers and plumbers didn't really need that sort of thing I supposed. The little fellow was very courteous, however, and after a time, he thanked me pleasantly and we parted. Back among the lounging pilots, someone asked me who our visitor had been and I had to admit I didn't know. Later, however, I spoke to someone who did.

'Who was that little chap who came round today?' I asked.

'Tedder.'

'Who?'

'A bloke called Tedder. He's just been appointed something or other in the Desert. Can't remember what, exactly.' (As Tedder was then commander-in-chief of the Middle East Airforce, he must have been an Air Marshall).

And there it was left.

With more time on our hands, there was the opportunity for leave and the right place to go, apparently, was the RAF rest camp at St Paul's Bay.

Strangely, I did not avail myself of the facilities there initially as the main diversions were sunbathing and swimming, neither of which appealed to me much. Although very little affected by extremes of heat and cold, being very fair-skinned, I burned badly in the sun, after which it was pure hell wearing a parachute harness and Mae West and buckling on my cockpit straps.

To a less jaundiced eye, however, the rest camp had much to offer. St Paul's Bay was then (unlike now) a comparatively deserted and very beautiful deep water inlet on the north side of the island, and the rest-centre a pleasant villa whose garden led down to rocks from which one could dive into water that was sparklingly blue and unpolluted. To the water-babies, it was paradise.

There usually being at least six officers from the various squadrons in residence at any one time, the air was invariably filled with the sound of music and song, there being a vast and comprehensive collection of Bing Crosby, Andrews Sisters, Glenn Miller and other big-band records, most of them scattered in chaotic disarray around the various rooms. This constant background of sound plus cheerfully profane conversation and quite decent messing – the food a distinct improvement on that at Ta Kali – proved to be a great attraction for most of my colleagues, though less so for me. Invariably restless after a day or two, I seldom stayed for my full entitlement of leave and was soon to recognise that what I wanted most was solitude –

an absence of people, war-talk and din and a quiet haven where I could read without interruption and draw and paint. In spite of its name, the rest camp was not one of those places.

August drifted to a close, though not uneventfully. I made only nine operational trips that month and most others in the squadron did less. At night, there was a fair amount of bombing with constant whistles and thumps far and near, causing me to sleep with a permanent half-open eye, mentally if not physically prepared to vanish under the bed if things got out of hand. MNFU were often in action during the hours of darkness, shooting down two or three BR 20s that month – at the time, everything to us was a BR 20, in much the same way as, during the Battle of Britain, everything the enemy shot at was a Spitfire.

I ran into 'Rags' Rabagliati one evening who said with mild amusement that he had just been on an air-test and had suddenly run into an Eyetie bomber, which he had managed to shoot into the sea. Surprised, I replied that it sounded a pretty rum sort of air-test, to which, with his slow smile and drawling lisp, he admitted it had been – he had been flying alone at 1,000 feet along the southern coast of Sicily, some 80 miles away to the north. I couldn't conceal my astonishment. Since his squadron had joined us in Malta, 'Rags' had never failed to amaze and amuse me. Being a squadron commander, he had rather more freedom of action than the rest of us; even so, he was clearly taking full advantage of his good fortune and opportunities and was not only quite fearless in action but never seemed the least concerned when wandering about over endless wastes of sea in aircraft that were anything but reliable. Days later, with several others of 126, he made a dawn attack on the Italian seaplane base at Syracuse in Sicily, destroying, or damaging, about six of the enemy. We were all full of admiration for his performance; a great morale raiser, was 'Rags'.

Meanwhile, we continued to have engine problems with painful regularity, yet another pilot from Hal Far being forced to bail out over the sea when his engine stopped. There were several other failures, too, details of which we only heard of later.

About mid-month, being invited to give my opinion of an aircraft – not of 249 Squadron – which appeared to be giving trouble, I walked across to 'Maintenance' at Ta Kali to be confronted by an irate engineer officer, a diffident and apologetic-looking sergeant pilot, and between them, one rather haggard-looking Hurricane equipped with long-range tanks. Their story was simple enough; the sergeant had been one of a group of four who had been instructed to fly to Egypt, a distance of more than 800 miles, all of it across open sea and skirting hostile territory. After setting out, the sergeant, who looked about sixteen years old, didn't much like the sound of his engine and turned back. On his return to Ta Kali, the engineer officer ran the engine and almost abusively pronounced it serviceable, whereupon the sergeant, not too confidently, disagreed. Stalemate; there had to be a third opinion.

I took off and flew the Hurricane around for about fifteen minutes, testing all the bits and pieces. The engine unpleasantly rough and the airframe certainly not among the best I had ever flown, I had to admit, even so, that there appeared nothing fundamentally wrong with the aircraft. Nevertheless, my sympathies were all with the sergeant; he, not the irate engineer, who by this time was hinting darkly at lack of moral fibre, was the one who would have to negotiate the 800 miles of sea and run the gauntlet of the Huns in Crete and North Africa, this time all on his own. I was desperately sorry for the youth; I felt I was issuing a death sentence.

Sometime later the Hurricane took off– and disappeared without trace. In fact, three of the group of four aircraft which set off for Egypt that sorry day, were never seen again. But all this I only learned much later, otherwise I would probably have felt a good deal worse than I did at the time.

Feeling that 249 was being discriminated against as regards opportunities to attack Sicilian targets and being aware that there was a considerable force of enemy aircraft on Comiso airfield, I asked control's permission to make a dawn strafing run. Everyone in my flight full of enthusiasm, we even wrote an insulting note to the Italian Air Force which we planned to drop on the airfield via the flare tube of one of our Hurricanes.

Unhappily, or perhaps fortunately, control would have none of it. We hadn't enough up-to-date intelligence, they said; furthermore, it was too dangerous; Malta couldn't risk losing half a dozen Hurricanes on so uncertain a venture. What about an ordinary sweep over the area? That would cool our ardour besides giving us at least an even chance if a fight developed. Meanwhile, I was to do nothing.

The following day, they came back with grudging approval for a sweep, coupled with telephone instructions which I wrote down in pencil on a piece of paper I still possess. These allowed us to fly over Sicily but forbade us absolutely to attack any targets on the ground.

We were totally deflated; if a strafing attack was ruled out, what was the point? – as we had difficulty in catching the Macchis in the air, the object was to catch them on the ground. But, although everyone confessed to being disappointed, I sensed that after so much discussion and argument, the fire in our bellies had died to a smoulder.

In the event, nine of us took off and carried out a long sweep from Cap Passaro to a point some thirty miles north. At little more than 9,000 feet, we were over Sicily and within sight of Comiso for almost half an hour, which was simply asking for trouble. But of that there was none; we saw not an aircraft, a single ack-ack burst, nor any other type of target. As I gazed down on the parched and lifeless undulations of Sicily, I felt inclined to agree that the risks of such sorties far outweighed the likely advantages. We didn't even have the opportunity to drop our rude note!

Then, some days later, a most extraordinary incident.

At 'Readiness' as usual and being called to the telephone, it was explained to me by the controller in conspiratorial tones, that they were expecting a 'visitor' from the north-east – I visualised him glancing over his shoulder as he spoke. Mildly perplexed, I asked what kind of 'visitor', being further informed that it was part of a – er – clandestine operation, if I knew what he meant. By this time a little amused as well as surprised, I tried to pump the man, but to little effect. The aircraft would be coming roughly from the direction of Greece, he explained; it could be any sort of aircraft and at any height and they hoped they would have sufficient warning to send me off with a section of four to intercept. After that, we were to escort it safely back to Malta. All right? Quite straightforward, really.

I was intrigued. Who could it possibly be? Some exiled head of state? King Zog of Albania? Peter of Yugoslavia? Some leader vital to the allied cause? Someone pretty important, obviously, to merit all this fuss. I even had time to fantasize; would I be in line for some exotic foreign decoration – the Order of the Golden Goat, that sort of thing?

There were several comings and goings before we finally received the word to go, after which we were vectored almost due east, which seldom happened in Malta. I was flying 'B' on that occasion, the Hurricane I had used on the sweep over Sicily several days earlier, and I had with me new boys Hulbert and Stuart plus one of the sergeants.

Right at the start, however, a most irritating development. Shortly after leaving the ground, my windscreen began to show the tell-tale sign of a Git's oil-seal leak, a long-standing and apparently incurable fault on the Hurricane which had required a modification in the form of a rim fitted behind the propeller to catch oil which emerged from that area in a fine, yellow spray. On this occasion, alas, my leak was much more than the rim could accommodate, so that by the time I had reached the far end of the island, I could barely see forward. However, as the other members of my section were fairly new and as I didn't want to miss the occasion, the thought of turning back never crossed my mind.

At about 5,000 feet we headed out a little north of east and after about fifteen minutes flying were some forty miles away from Malta with nothing in sight but open sea and an endless horizon. By this time, almost totally blind ahead, I had my hood open and was looking forward as best I could from the open cockpit and the rapidly yellowing side-panels of the windscreen. Meanwhile, the vectors kept coming up to us fairly regularly with our target apparently dead ahead of us and approaching. I was quietly content; except for being smothered in oil, everything was fine.

Then, I spotted it, a twin-engined aircraft of some sort, low down, dark against the sea and flying in the opposite direction. I gave a rather low-key 'Tallyho' and, crossing over the top of it, all four of us turned and took station, two either side, before straightening up. Then, dropping down a further 1,000 feet or so, we headed back towards Malta.

With yellow goo now completely obscuring my vision, I didn't choose to get any closer, nor was there any need; from where I was, I could see the other aircraft quite distinctly, below and slightly ahead. Down there, I mused, the important personage was probably relaxing for the first time and thanking God for our presence. And sorting out our decorations, too, I shouldn't wonder!

For around ten minutes we flew back together, the four of us providing what was no doubt a comforting escort to the aircraft beneath, control being advised of our progress from time to time and everyone in good heart. In the distance, Malta hove into sight, then as details became clearer, Delimara Point and Kalafrana Bay.

As we neared the island, I found myself drifting lower until all four of us were barely several hundred feet above the target aircraft which by that time was just above the waves. And heading straight for Kalafrana Bay, which I thought was a bit odd as I was expecting it to land at Luqa. Still – .

At this point, although I had no grounds for suspicion, the faintest shadow of doubt crossed my mind, causing me to look more closely at the aircraft beneath. I couldn't immediately recognise the type, on the other hand I hadn't needed to, the information we had been given, both on the ground and in the air, being so specific. All the same – ! Then, whilst I was still toying with my doubts and with the 'visitor' entering the jaws of Kalafrana Bay, something splashed down into the water and the aircraft upended itself in a steep turn to the right so that it passed directly beneath me.

My mouth literally fell open, because I recognised at once the nature of the bounding splash – it was that of an air-launched torpedo. A torpedo! This chap was an Eyetie and had just dropped a torpedo! And we had escorted him all the way to Malta to do it! Well, would you credit it? The cheeky . . . ! Words failed me.

Right down on the water now, our erstwhile 'visitor' was heading hot-foot in the direction of Sicily; however, having turned with it, we remained 1,000 or so feet above, all of us still unbelieving and in two minds.

In one outraged sentence, I then informed control that their so- called 'visitor' had just dropped a torpedo in Kalafrana Bay, a message which stopped conversation entirely. Then, an uncertain voice: was I absolutely sure? Of course I was sure, we had just watched it happen, hadn't we? Silence and more confusion the other end. After which: 'All right. If you're quite sure, engage it! Shoot it down – immediately!'

It took us several minutes to catch the Italian aircraft, and with my hood open and unable to see forward, I dived to sea-level in no easy frame of mind. Irritated but excited and aware that the others were somewhere off to my right, I thought about cleaning my windscreen but saw immediately that my straps would prevent me from reaching forward sufficiently. For this reason, I pulled away to the left and instructed the others to attack without me; unlike me, at least two of them were flying Mark II Cs, equipped with cannons, so that even a few hits would suffice. After which, I undid my straps, half-rose in my seat, and tried to insinuate my right hand around the windscreen. But only for a second; the 260 mph slipstream immediately snatched at my arm and nearly took it off, causing me to recoil and jerk the controls so violently that for one horrifying moment, I thought I would be pitched out. Momentarily unnerved, I pulled away, regained my composure, then dropped down again to sea-level and to within 400 yards of the enemy aircraft, feeling as I did so the twist of the Eyetie's slipstream. But of the aircraft ahead I could see not a thing, only the pink lines and dot of my own reflector-sight against the brown. Damn it! I would have to leave it to the others.

Pulling up again, I then sat above and alongside the Italian aircraft, watching my companions approach in turn and shoot. They did so several times but I could see only the splash and ricochet of their shells in the water, the Cant – for we had all recognised it as such – now so low that its airscrews were whipping up a feathery trace from the waves.

In despair and almost beside myself with frustration, I watched the tragi-farce drift to a conclusion. The Eyetie, certainly hit, began to trail enough smoke to suggest that it had been damaged quite seriously, but there it remained, flying still and heading for home.

Eventually, some thirty miles north of Malta and my section out of ammunition, we all turned and headed back, our 'visitor' meanwhile still limping off towards the north. Almost sick with feelings of failure and defeat, I was hardly aware of the return journey and landing.

Back on the ground, I learned that Stuart had also suffered a malfunction and had hardly participated in the fight. Hulbert and the sergeant were jubilant, however, being convinced that the Eyetie would never be able to get back, a view supported by a later report from other aircraft which had sighted oil and wreckage in the area. A claim was therefore made for one Cant 'destroyed' which I allowed to go forward though with some reluctance, persuading myself that even if the outcome were doubtful, if it boosted the morale of my chaps, perhaps it was permissible. Privately, however, I later confided in 'Butch' Barton that I thought the claim was overstated.

The following day, I heard from several of our lady friends in Rabat that the Italian wireless had reported that one of their aircraft had returned from a daring attack on Malta, in a heavily damaged condition and with the crew wounded. Although hailed by the Italians as an heroic victory, I was comforted by the thought that if the action had been that heroic, the Cant and its crew might well have been put out of action, if not permanently, for a considerable time. Which, I supposed, was a victory of sorts.

Strangely, the circumstances relating to the incident were never discussed nor even mentioned thereafter, a discreet veil being drawn over the whole affair. For my part, I was so furious with Hurricane 'B' that I determined never to fly the damned thing again. And I never did.

23

A Quiet Autumn

September nudged August slowly into the past, the weather unremittingly hot and sticky. Although we did not know it at the time, for the next several weeks, those of us in Hurricanes would do very little, the war from Malta being waged by the Blenheims, the Wellingtons, the Fulmars and Swordfish.

In the Western Desert, elements of our ground forces yet to be formed into the famous 8th Army, were still resisting attempts by Rommel's German and Italian divisions to move forward to the borders of Egypt, and having failed to retake Tobruk, the brilliant Wavell had finally lost the confidence of the Prime Minister and others and had been replaced by General Auchinleck. In a further hotch-potch of advances and retreats, Free-French and British troops had moved into Syria, so that with these and other movements and actions, it seemed that our forces were either fighting or engaged almost everywhere, even in the Far East where the Japanese were already on the move. But by far the most serious news came from Russia, where the Germans were apparently making hay of our new allies, who had suffered astronomical casualties, the invaders moving ominously towards Moscow, Leningrad, and the Crimean peninsula.

All of which made dismal reading in the *Times of Malta* although, with touching faith in Britain's invincibility, it worried me not a jot. At Ta Kali, we were doing all right, we were getting masses of time off, and even if our engines did stop occasionally, things would sort themselves out. Still turning up regularly in Valletta for my hot pork sandwiches at Monico's and my hair-cuts and more refined snacks in the Union Club, I only wished I could get a decent cup of tea. What on earth did the Maltese do to their water?

I had a week's leave in September, which I spent mostly at the rest camp at St Paul's Bay, a period so forgettable that I made only the briefest mention of it in my letters home and diary. Otherwise, I flew barely a dozen sorties that month, although one was to cause me concern. Prior to roaring off on one of our dust-streaming scrambles, I had become aware of a nasty smell when taxiing out. Then, barely had I become airborne and closed the hood than the whole cockpit was filled with a cloud of pungent white smoke. In a near-panic, I turned for home and almost threw my Hurricane at the ground, expecting all the time an eruption of flame. However, to my considerable embarrassment, it proved to be far less than an emergency. Having removed the side panels, it was found that one of the ground-crew had spilt a gallon can of glycol in and around the cockpit, most of which had percolated down onto the pipes that ran between engine and radiator, producing something akin to a smoke-screen when everything heated up. A great joke after the event, it was not so funny at the time.

Although there were the routine nocturnal dronings and thumps throughout the early part of the month, there was little action for us day fighters, the only serious engagements occurring on about the 4th, when 126 and 185, who happened to be on duty, ran into a flock of Macchis high up over Grand Harbour and shot down several. Later the same day, 'Butch' Barton, with the other half of 249, chased a minor swarm of Macchi 200s towards the Sicilian coast, at which point, to 'Butch's' considerable consternation, the Eyeties suddenly turned and fought like tigers. This development not being at all according to the script, the Italians usually preferring to run for home, 'Butch' and his men were caught on the hop, low down, a long way from home, and against aircraft capable of out-performing the Hurricane in close combat. At a disadvantage and having to run for it, almost inevitably 249 lost two aircraft, those of Pilot Officer Smith, whom I hardly knew, and Sergeant Kimberley, 'Butch' himself being quite shaken by the severity of the engagement. His description of events normally so lacking in emotion, I had seldom seen him so affected; he really had thought his number was up.

Thereafter, action around Malta was mainly by night, so that for us, the next period of excitement occurred mid-month when two further batches of Hurricanes arrived from our old friends, the carriers *Ark Royal* and *Furious*, only half of which were to remain on the island.

On leave at the time, I was in the mess at Ta Kali when the second group of Hurricanes appeared and having nothing much else to do, walked up to dispersal to watch them touch down. It was not exactly an encouraging spectacle as, landing north to south on that occasion, several of them overshot hopelessly, two or three careering past us, one at least finishing up on its nose. It was quite heartbreaking to watch brand new aircraft we were so much in need of, broken by inept and inexperienced pilots, and there were loud groans and unflattering remarks about the legitimacy of several of those involved.

Included in the new group were four Americans who had apparently come to Britain via the Royal Canadian Air Force. I had never seen Americans in RAF blue before despite there being a publicity stunt involving a so-called Eagle Squadron in England, so that their arrival created some interest. Two of the four, Steele and Streets, were the long and short of it, one being tall and thin and the other positively wee. Chatting with them in the mess shortly after, I gathered that on reaching England, they had been entertained at Buckingham Palace, on which occasion the small one had apparently asked the Duke of Kent's wife, Princess Marina, for a 'date'. I was wryly amused. What next, for heaven's sake? Were they not aware?

The latest influx of aircraft and the dearth of operational activity enabled all three fighter squadrons on the island to be brought up to established strength; in fact, in 249 we had more Hurricanes than we could use. Moreover, it did enable each of the more senior of us to have a personal aircraft, besides giving us sufficient time to paint on our squadron identification letters. Back again came the old grey markings GN, I laid claim to a brand-new Mark II B, GN-R, and I had my flight's airscrew spinners painted red. After the wrecks we had been flying over the past several months, here were aircraft we could now fight in with confidence. Moreover, they were beginning to look the part, which was so important. My morale positively soared.

But not for long, alas. Word came through that we would shortly be fitting bomb-racks to accommodate eight 40 lb bombs, and that our old 44-gallon long-range tanks would be re-fitted, enabling us to carry out three-hour patrols in search of low-flying Axis aircraft en route to North Africa. Bombs! Long-range tanks! What next, mines and torpedoes? What were we, fighter aircraft, or one-engined Blenheims?

Then, in the latter half of the month, a lot of excitement. With the *Ark* and *Furious* bringing in the Hurricanes and, later still, with the approach of a large convoy accompanied by the *Ark Royal*, the battleships, *Nelson*, *Rodney* and *Prince of Wales*, together with a clutch of cruisers and a mass of destroyers as escort, not only were the Italian naval and air forces drawn from their lairs in Sardinia and Sicily, but Malta itself was reinforced by Beaufighters from the Middle East.

Much of the action during that two week period was well beyond the range of our Hurricanes; even so we became aware of all the activity elsewhere on the island, word filtering through of what the fleet Fulmars were up to, poor things, plus our own Malta-based naval aircraft and the intrepid Blenheims. Apparently, the Italian navy, perceiving the size and strength of the British fleet, wisely turned about and tip-toed to the rear, but their air force pressed home its attacks with torpedoes and bombs, so that many fierce and bloody engagements took place somewhere south of Sardinia. Between the 26th and 28th, however, the whole convoy and escort came within our orbit and most of us in Hurricanes were sent off in sections to act as look-outs and escort.

My first sorties were strictly defensive, however; being warned of possible air attacks on Hal Far and Luqa, with members of my flight, I roamed about over the sea north of the island for hours on end. But none of the enemy appeared and we returned shrugging our shoulders. Why all the trouble and fuss?

Then, on the 28th, flying my new aircraft, GN-R, I was vectored westwards to meet the convoy and escort, and having arrived was promptly shot at, the flak bursts appearing magically in the sky directly ahead of me, though fortunately not too close. Thinking there were enemy aircraft around that we had not seen, we fairly hopped about for a minute or two until it became clear that the shots were aimed at us. However, they proved to be no more than a greeting as we were able to continue our patrol for more than an hour, the fleet spread out in long lines some 4,000 feet beneath, white moustaches creaming from their bows – a truly magnificent sight.

Later, I defended Luqa again, patrolling the area in wide, bored curves. None of the enemy appeared, however, which left me reflecting that a fighter pilot's life, even in Malta, was much like that of the ordinary bloke in the army – ninety-five per cent boredom and five per cent blistering, blood-curdling excitement.

The month slid to an undramatic close. Pat Wells, who had rejoined us briefly having recovered from his wounds, left in company with Tony Morello, bound, it was said, for Khartoum. Khartoum! None of us wanted to go to Khartoum, which was the current dirty word, an Operation Training Unit being located there. Everyone thought in terms of England – and Spitfires! Oh, for some really decent aircraft and somewhere to make a forced-landing without either being drowned or breaking one's neck. I was getting bored with Malta and didn't think I wanted to stay much longer.

Earlier in the month, a fellow called Barnes of 126 Squadron had had his engine stop and had ploughed through a couple of stone walls, miraculously surviving, someone jocularly remarking at the time that he had discovered the quickest possible way of slowing down. Such macabre humour was always in vogue at Ta Kali.

It was also towards the end of September that a PRU Spitfire arrived with a Flight Lieutenant Messervy at the helm. Messervy was a ginger-haired, balding man, rather older than myself, who, though pleasant enough, did not give very much away. His journey of 1,250 miles from England, straight across Hun-controlled France, had taken almost five hours and he was in Malta to carry out some rather special reconnaissance flights, it appeared. His unarmed Spit, painted a light blue, looked delicious, provoking nostalgic recollections of our own Spits in May and June of the previous year. As we chatted, I decided against ever applying to be in the PRU business; the flights were far too long and the whole thing too coldly and calculatingly brave for me.

October, and a dismal beginning.

We had been scrambled and were climbing up southwards along the coast towards Hal Far. It was a dull day with a fair amount of medium cloud in layers so that we were kept fairly low. After a time, control appeared to lose interest in us, leading me to conclude there was nothing much doing. Then, after a little more than thirty minutes in the air, we were instructed to land.

Back on the ground little was said, so that later it came as a complete surprise when I learned that 185 Squadron had been in action and that their commanding officer, 'Boy' Mould, had been shot down and killed. I was very unhappy, not only because of 'Boy's' sad and tragic death, but because of our own non-involvement; if there had been that much action, why hadn't we been allowed to take part, or even been told? The Eyeties had been in their new Macchi 202s, apparently, and had moved around pretty smartly.

For the following two days, I found myself north of the island flying first at 22,000 feet, then at 27,000, on each occasion watching the enemy stream overhead in silent, pencil-white curves, always much faster than us it seemed and well beyond our reach. Finally, on 6 October, smarting with frustration, we paraded at full squadron strength at 31,000 feet, whereupon the enemy, either prudently or because they never intended to come anyway, turned back. I heard this information from control with some relief; I never liked fighting in a Hurricane much above 30,000 feet; it was so cold up there and the aircraft tended to fall away and stall in anything more than a gentle turn.

Then, the following day we heard that we were to bomb Sicily – at night!

Never having bombed anything since FTS, when I had thrown 8 lb smoke bombs from Hawker Audaxes in the general direction of the Montrose basin, I didn't rate my chances of hitting anything as very high. In fact, there was a story, apocryphal no doubt, that when the farmers living on the borders of the Montrose basin became aware that it was our day for bombing, they would take the day off and disappear into the foothills.

My target being the railway station at Gela, I took off towards midnight and flew northwards, expecting to find the place without too much difficulty on a night that was dark but clear.

Fondly hoping that the Italians would reveal their known defensive positions by shooting at me with their red balls, they did nothing of the sort, obliging me to wander about endlessly over Sicily trying to discover where exactly I was. In fact, I never did find the railway station but, by sheer good fortune, came across the railway line that presumably lead to it, which I saw dimly beneath me from a height of 1,500 feet. By this time, remembering the thousands of tons of bombs that had been dropped on London to such little effect and deciding that dropping my eight insignificant bangers was a howling waste of time, I did a gentle dive in that direction and disposed of my load. Observing one faint flash in the blackness below, I flew the 100 or so miles back home.

Two days after, for reasons I cannot recall, I was obliged to make an emergency landing at Luqa, my first time on that airfield since the day of my arrival in May. There seemed lots of aircraft parked there which was probably the reason for the low level dawn attack on the 14th, carried out by a small formation of Macchi 202s, which raced across the airfield at first light with banshee screams and glistening beads of tracer. One of several of 249 who were scrambled in pursuit, I was too late to catch the Macchis, which, by that time, were halfway back to Sicily. Several aircraft of MNFU were, however, more fortunate, having taken off before us, and an interception was made some miles north of the island by David Barnwell, who gave a 'Tallyho' then apparently made a successful attack. Shortly after, he was heard to say that his engine had failed and that he was baling out – after which, nothing. Dispatched immediately, the air-sea rescue boat combed the area for the rest of the day, but without success.

So perished one of the golden boys of Malta, like so many gifted airmen of the past, disappearing in circumstances that were never entirely clear, although the Italians were subsequently to claim a victory during the course of that attack. But, as so often happened in air combat, although on the verge of being an active participant, I knew little of what had taken place until later.

In all, a sad, sad day. David Barnwell had been in Malta only a matter of weeks but even in that brief period, he had distinguished himself greatly. We all felt the chill of his passing, which was not usually the case.

The day was also something of a landmark for me in that, two days before the Barnwell incident, I received what I regarded to be the ultimate insult. Scrambled in pursuit of a small group of Macchis approaching from the north, I climbed hard with my section towards Grand Harbour, eventually crossing out to sea at about 20,000 feet. Then, as we continued to claw for height, I saw several bursts of ack- ack in the distance, after which came the instruction, 'Clear the area to the north. The guns have been ordered to engage.' Or, as I chose to interpret the message: 'Hop it, you useless creatures, and let someone else have a go!' Outraged initially, I had half a mind to ignore the instruction, but not wishing to confuse the gunners below, with my three followers, I slunk off in the direction of Gozo. My God, things had come to a pretty pass when ack-ack was considered more effective than fighters!

I landed that day in a bitter frame of mind, although I was soon to realise that my anger was wasted; in the weeks to follow, there were many similar instructions which various members of 249 were only too glad to carry out to the letter.

The next day, I was involved in three more such scrambles, all inconclusive, one being just that little bit different.

I was at about 2,000 feet, climbing hard, when there was a bang somewhere to my left and something whipped past in the air. Not knowing quite what had happened, I pulled away and returned to Ta Kali to find that the landing light had disappeared, leaving a sizeable gap in the leading edge of my port wing.

It was quite extraordinary; for a whole year in England, I had frequently flown the Hurricane at more than 450 mph throughout one of the most intensive periods of fighting ever known, and apart from the occasional oil leak, never had cause to complain about my engine or my aircraft. But in Malta, in less than five months, I had suffered five major engine malfunctions, any one of which could have resulted in my death, plus sundry other leaks, failures and difficulties, the latest being the loss of the landing light, which had broken away from a newish aircraft at something less than 150 mph. Moreover, my experiences were not untypical – the evil eyes were certainly hard at work, it seemed, and not only around Ta Kali!

In line with our instructions to 'take the offensive', the second half of October saw 249 engaged in lengthy flights in search of transport aircraft en route from Sicily to Africa. As the chosen path for these aircraft appeared to be some fifty miles to the west of Malta, this was regarded as being the most fruitful area in which to operate. There was no question of our being controlled onto known targets, it was all a business of guess and hope. Four of our Hurricanes being fitted with two 44-gallon wing tanks each, Crossey and I were the first to go.

I had mixed feelings about the arrangement. The prospect of shooting down a few juicy Savoias or Cants was appealing enough, but going into action carrying what amounted to a primed bomb under each wing was less attractive. Our long-range tanks were simply not meant for fighting:

they could not be jettisoned, they reduced the Hurricane's performance very considerably, and even when empty, contained a lethally explosive mixture. Were we to encounter enemy fighters, our number would almost certainly be up as we could neither fight nor run, dire possibilities which sharpened our minds considerably when making plans.

In the event, nothing much happened on that first trip. We took off in fine weather with just a little cloud at around 4,000 feet and flew low over the sea until we reached Linosa then Lampedusa, after which we wandered further south and west until we were almost within sight of the African coast. I was not too keen on going in the direction of Pantelleria, knowing full well that Macchi 200s and CR 42s were based there; I had never encountered a CR 42, a biplane admittedly but a remarkably nippy in-fighter, and in a Hurricane with long-range tanks, I didn't particularly want to.

After almost three hours we returned, our concentration flagging and our backsides numb from the malicious pressure of our cushionless dinghies, having seen neither enemy aircraft nor vessel.

Three days later, on 19 October, 'Butch' Barton and Palliser, flying exactly the same route, ran into a single Savoia 81 transport aircraft which they promptly shot into the sea, the aircraft exploding in a huge ball of flame and smoke. A very ugly sight, 'Butch' reported with a sad shake of his head, but with the heartlessness of youth, I can't say that the plight of the victims worried us very much. Cheered by yet another success for 'Butch', I couldn't help being a little envious even so; where was the enemy when Crossey and I were around?

On 30 October, Crossey and I tried again, this time taking the bull by the horns and flying directly to Pantelleria. Initially beneath a friendly bank of cloud, by the time we reached Pantelleria the sky was completely clear. Not too happy with this development, we skirted the island on tip-toe – Savoias were one thing, fighters altogether another! Suspiciously on edge, we drifted slowly to the south then east until we were back in the area of Linosa and Lampedusa, once again seeing nothing but a wilderness of open sea.

Thereafter, our long-range trips in that area petered out, our efforts being mainly concentrated on attacking targets in Sicily and on defending Malta. In fact, it was the last long-range sortie I was to make in the Mediterranean war zone.

In the intervals between these offensive exercises, we were back on the treadmill of scramble, climb and patrol as the carrier *Ark Royal* plus the cruisers and destroyers of a reinforced Force 'K' approached the island from the west. Leading a section of four, I flew out to protect them, being shot at once again for my pains, the end result being masses of flying but no Eyeties. In spite of this lack of success, however, I was not at all unhappy; my new aircraft, GN-R, was pleasant to fly, with the smoothest of engines and a reassuringly tight airframe. Then, on 22 October, which was a Wednesday, I had the first of two days off.

It was on that morning that I went into Valletta but finding myself at a loose end by lunch time, on impulse I suddenly decided to spend the rest of the day at the rest camp at St Paul's Bay. There being no transport available, I ran the whole eight miles at a jog, reducing myself to a grease-spot but thoroughly enjoying the unaccustomed exercise.

Arriving in the early afternoon and finding Crossey and several others in residence, I joined them on the rocks alongside the water. It being a beautiful scene, peaceful and bright, we all lay back and relaxed. Super! Malta wasn't such a bad place after all.

After a time, we heard the thin sound of aircraft high up and straining our eyes against the glare, caught the occasional glimpse of wings flashing in the sun. 249, probably. Doing what? we wondered.

Then faintly, the noise of engines wailing and the distant 'burrrr' of machine guns. A fight, by George! Right above our heads, too. We all sat up and took notice. Twenty seconds or so of noise and unseen movement aloft, then a blink of light followed by a thin trail of smoke. Someone hit!

We watched the dot that was the doomed aircraft begin its dark pencil-line trail towards the sea – it would crash somewhere towards the entrance to the bay, we decided. And following the aircraft, the tiny white canopy of a parachute, moving slowly sideways, far, far away. Silently, we all followed the aircraft's progress as it fell towards the water. Until it disappeared. No noise. Just a small eruption of white and silent oblivion. High above, the parachute continued its feather-like descent. Poor bloke, we all commented comfortably from the safety of our ringside seats, someone in for a ducking.

As we sat there gazing through shaded eyes, it never for a moment crossed my mind that it might be my new aircraft, GN-R. But it was, flown by Sergeant Owen on that occasion, who was later picked up – the third personal aircraft I had lost when being flown briefly by someone else.

Back at Ta Kali on the 24th, I chose another aircraft, GN-J, of unhappy memory (I was forced to bail out of GN-J on 7 November, 1940, after a mid-air collision), persuading myself that I couldn't possibly have two mid-air collisions in aircraft similarly marked. With Grand Harbour full of the 'grey funnel line', we carried another long patrol over the sea north of the island then a panic scramble in the defence of Luqa, nothing being seen on either occasion.

It was also on the 24th that six aircraft of 126 bombed the Eyetie airfield at Comiso, escorted by 'Butch' leading half of 249 at 12,000 feet, and me with the rest at 21,000.

The trip was almost a bore. I was far too high – and preoccupied – to see the bombs delivered and roamed about miles into Sicily, mostly above cloud. But not one single enemy aircraft did we see. Or flak burst. Or anything else, in fact. Just massive banks of white beneath us and rolling brown countryside through the occasional gap. I recall thinking: if I had to force-land in Sicily, which part of me would the Mafia cut off? But not even such sombre speculations succeeded in livening me up.

After which, suddenly, it was November.

24

The Year Dies

The Air Force normally went into blue in November; the weather was cool enough and although some did, most didn't. Also it was cloudy, which encouraged the warlike to think in terms of 'mosquitoes' – low level strafing attacks on targets of opportunity in Sicily. Plus bombing, of course. Bearing in mind the minute size of our bombs and the lack of penetration of our Brownings, I thought it all a waste of time. Still – if this was what our masters wanted.

Between the 1st and 4th of the month, I did four trips over Sicily, roaming around at nought feet or in the fringes of the cloud, looking for something to shoot at but with only trifling success. Sicily, at close quarters, being more of a brown desert than ever I had imagined, on the first of the trips, my section of two was intercepted four times by – I judged – the same pair of Macchis. Fortunately, with enough cloud about for safety, they did not get close enough to do any damage and I was not in the least interested in fighting Macchis at 500 feet over Sicily with 100 miles of enemy territory and water between me and home. On the fourth trip, when I was carrying eight 40 lb bombs, the weather became so miserable in my particular area, that after wandering round for what seemed an age, I became fed up and dropped all eight of them on a man with a lorry a little to the north of Cap Passaro. I doubt that he enjoyed the experience.

The day following, feeling the need to do something a little more constructive with my bombs, I ordered a programme of dive-bombing, which my flight and I carried out off Filfla Rock. With happy memories of Montrose, it turned out to be rather fun, all of us diving steeply from about 8,000 feet and letting go when our noses were lifted through the target smoke-float we had dropped in the water. Moreover, with electrical releases, it was a good deal easier than struggling with the mechanical toggles and pieces of bent wire, as we had been obliged to do on the old Hawker Audaxes.

But my rising spirits were firmly depressed when, the same day, one of the new De Havilland Mosquitos flew into Ta Kali from England and I was persuaded to test the performance of my Hurricane against it. I should have known better!

The Mosquito, a Photographic Reconnaissance Mark I, was a visitor from Benson and, lightly loaded, was by the standards of the time incredibly fast and agile. Having taken off together and sorted ourselves out, the fight thereafter developed into a chase, with me desperately but unsuccessfully trying to remain in the same piece of sky. Unable to hang on to it and with my engine raging away at maximum boost and 2,850 revs, I finally retired – gracefully, I hope. Clearly, the 'Mossie' could walk away from me any time it liked, my ability to turn inside it meaning very little as I could never get sufficiently close to initiate a dog-fight. I had long suspected that our Hurricanes were clod-hopping carthorses, my flight that morning merely confirmed my suspicions.

The following day, 8 November, I wasn't required to fly but on hearing sounds of activity on the airfield around noon, walked up to dispersal from the mess. 126 Squadron were on duty and the majority of their aircraft had already been airborne for some time. Then, high up and in the direction of Valletta, the splattered smudges of ack-ack and the usual signs of activity although the aircraft themselves were invisible. Then, as I stood and chatted, a number of Hurricanes returned and I idly watched them approach then circle the airfield, first one, then several, touching down and taxiing in, dust streaming.

My interest quickening as I saw that the gun patches were missing, I found myself attracted to one Hurricane which was moving slowly and rather aimlessly in my direction. Then I noticed the battle damage and began to run.

The propeller was still turning as I pulled down the retractable step and climbed onto the wing-walk, the slipstream clutching at my face and hair. The pilot still had his face mask attached but I recognised him immediately as Pat Lardner-Burke.

I heard myself shouting, 'Are you all right?' – then knew immediately that he wasn't.

Pat's head was bowed and his shoulders slumped. He undid his mask, clumsily. 'They've got me in the back.' He was obviously in shock and pain.

I sought to comfort him. 'All right. Don't worry. Just hang on and we'll get you out.' I shouted to those beneath. 'Get the ambulance and a stretcher.' After which I began to consider how best to extricate him.

Whatever its virtues, the Hurricane was not designed to enable a damaged pilot to be evacuated easily. About ten feet in the air, the cockpit did not have a side-flap, as did the Spitfire, so that to dismount, the pilot was obliged to climb out backwards, using first the cockpit rim then one of the steps, before walking down the wing-root and jumping to the ground. Needless to say, such gymnastics were beyond anyone crippled by wounds.

Aware of the need to act quickly, I tried climbing onto the rim of the cockpit myself but found nowhere to put my feet. Then I thought about sitting on top of the open hood but saw immediately that I would not be able to reach down sufficiently to heave him up bodily. A pox on the man who designed this aircraft, I thought wildly, we would have to get a crane and winch him out. But there was no crane, or none that wouldn't take hours to find and fetch.

I said urgently, 'Pat, can you stand? Or climb out yourself? Otherwise we can't get at you.'

He said wearily, 'I'll try,' and painfully pulling himself to his feet whilst I grasped his shoulders, he croaked an entreaty which would remain with me always: 'Don't shake me, Ginger . . . for Christ's sake don't shake me.'

Somehow we all reached the ground, to be faced with two airmen with a collapsible canvas stretcher. Uncertain and a little shocked, they laid it down in the dust and we all stood looking at it.

I said tightly, 'Pick it up, for God's sake; he can't get down on his hands and knees.'

They did so but I sensed that as soon as he put his weight on it, they would drop him. Impatiently, I waved for several others to come forward and he eventually laid himself down and was lifted into the ambulance. It looked as though the bullet, or whatever, had gone clean through his left lung.

When the ambulance had moved off in the direction of Imtafa, I climbed back onto the aircraft. There was not much damage but what there was was frightening. Several bullets – point-fives from a Macchi 202 – had hit the side of the aircraft behind the cockpit and one had punched a hole in the armour-plate as though it had been nothing more than a sheet of aluminium. After that it had penetrated the back of the seat, gone completely through the pilot, before continuing through the dashboard and into the armour-plate and darkness beyond. I was shaken. I had seen German bullet and cannon-shell strikes on armour-plate before and they had never done more than raise small dimples in the rock-hard metal. But this one had ploughed ahead as though there had been no armour. Several other pilots joined me and breathed their horrified astonishment. Crikey! And we'd always thought – !

Pat Lardner-Burke never flew again in Malta and those of us who did discussed the possibility of fitting an extra thickness of armour behind our seats. But such a modification would be impossible, we were told; the stuff would weigh a ton, its installation would have to be a dockyard job, and it wasn't available anyway. No, the only solution was not to get hit!

For several days thereafter, I was to remember that hole – vividly! Who would have thought it?

There being masses of pilots and aircraft, I had a week off until 13 November, spending my time drawing, painting and mooching around Sliema and Valletta. Life was seldom dull, however, as scarcely a day passed without the whooping dirge of the air-raid sirens heralding the inevitable thumps and crumps of ack-ack, bursting shells, and bombs. Hulbert, Stuart, and several others had rented a splendid four-storey furnished house on the front in Sliema for the grand sum of £5 per month, and I was able to take advantage of their hospitality and lodge there occasionally. There was neither linen nor blankets on the beds but that didn't matter; the fleas were there in abundance, lining up for their ration of succulent English blood, and to me, a bed was less a place of repose than a handy refuge in the event of an adjacent bomb.

It was during that week in Sliema that an air-raid occurred one evening when I was escorting Patsy from a function we had attended together. As the bombs began to come unpleasantly close, she insisted on our taking shelter in the crypt of a nearby church, an area the size of a tennis court already accommodating a hundred or so local inhabitants whose rolling eyes and shivering fear verged on the comical. As we stood a little self-consciously among the crowd, I put on the special face I reserved for such occasions and was assuring Patsy that there was nothing whatever to worry about, when there was a thunderous explosion nearby and the building almost took off. Instantly, with a moan of horror and no doubt believing that the gates of heaven were rolling back to greet them, the entire congregation sank to their knees, crossing themselves meanwhile, so that in a moment I found myself the only person standing amid a sea of prostrate forms and wailing incantations. From a height of six feet three inches, I looked around in acute embarrassment; all I could see were foreheads against the floor – and bums! What did I do now, show the flag or join them? Then I began to giggle. Patsy looked up, more nervous than amused, then held out her hand. I took it and sank grudgingly to my knees. Ah, well! Not exactly British, I supposed, but when in Rome – !

It was during that week, too, that a Wing Commander Brown arrived to lead the Ta Kali wing, which was something of a joke as 249 had only recently been able to field more than nine aircraft. The newcomer, a Canadian, was a pleasant, rather stiff little man who wore a small military moustache. Known familiarly as 'Hilly', he had been in No. 1 Squadron in France at the outset of the war and had done very well. Earnest-faced, he appeared to be very serious about his new job.

On the night of the 11th, we all gathered in the ante-room of the mess around dinner-time to discuss an attack on Comiso airfield in Sicily to take place at dawn the following day. Both 249 and 126 would be involved but because I was still on leave, I was unable to include myself among the twelve members of the squadron taking part.

The new Wing Commander was full of quiet resolve. A strafing section would go in initially to divert the defending guns, then a dozen or so Hurricanes with bombs would follow, escorted by a further twelve acting as fighter escort. Tactics were discussed and precise targets identified. Surprise was a key factor – with so many enemy fighters based at Comiso and Gela, the possibility of a knock-down-drag-out fight if things went wrong was more than just remote. From my seat in the stalls, it all sounded very exciting and I began to feel quite enviously deprived.

The following morning, with lots of noise and fuss, all twenty-four Hurricanes took off in the half-light and disappeared towards the north. Shivering and in my bare feet, I watched them from the stone balcony beside my bedroom, still more than a little miserable at not being part of the show.

An hour or so later they were back – most of them, anyway. Some Eyetie aircraft had been caught on the ground, it appeared, and a few others attacked and dealt with in the air. But the first Hurricanes had run into trouble, our new Wing Commander being hit squarely by one of the defenders' first bursts, causing his aircraft to pull up steeply, stall, then dive straight into the ground. For several who had witnessed the incident, there was no question but that he had been killed instantly.

Poor old 'Hilly' Brown. Such an experienced and highly decorated officer, and on his very first operational sortie from the island, too. Although we had known him only a matter of hours, we were all shocked by his passing. It seemed so unfair.

Later, the Italians generously dropped a message on Malta with confirmation of 'Hilly's' death and his burial with full military honours, although I knew nothing of it at the time. There was news, too, of one of 126's sergeants who had been shot down into the sea and taken prisoner. In all, a rather confused and bitty operation which had hardly been a success. I was almost glad that I had been obliged to stay at home.

Later the same day but far away to the west, three more Hurricane squadrons were taking off from several aircraft carriers and flying towards the island. As occasionally happened with reinforcement flights, their journey was dogged by misfortune, one pilot landing in Sicily, two in North Africa, a fourth damaging his aircraft when taking off from the carrier Argus, and a fifth crash-landing at Hal Far. And it was on the following day, 13 November, that the *Ark Royal*, which had been part of the supply fleet and from which I myself had flown some six months earlier, was torpedoed on its return journey to Gibraltar.

We were all desperately sad to learn about the *Ark*, a German submarine finally putting paid to her after so many false claims. I recalled only too well her massive size and splendour, the courtesy of her officers and crew, the wardroom bright with lights and the mess kits, pink gins and wonderful food, my iron-hard bunk with the ridge down the middle, and that ghastly dawn when we had taken off into the endless void of hostile sea and cloud. And now she was sitting on the bottom somewhere, a silent rusting hulk. With most of her Fulmars and Swordfish, too, apparently. Well, perhaps they wouldn't be missed too much!

I was to be very busy until the end of November, although my hectic activity did not produce much in the way of results.

From 15 to 17 November, we were obliged to operate from Luqa as Ta Kali became flooded, a seemingly odd occurrence in a semi-desert country but understandable when it was explained that there were no drains in the area of our airfield and that it had at one time been a lake. Whatever the reasons, torrential rain forced us to do what the Germans and Italians had signally failed to accomplish – leave the place! However, although the Blenheims and Marylands remained fairly active, 249 was not called upon to operate. There was news that our forces in the Western Desert were on the move again, obliging everything in Malta – apart from ourselves – to search for and attack seaborne supplies en route for Axis forces in North Africa.

Back at Ta Kali on the 19th, we embarked on a series of scrambles and shortish trips, mainly in pursuit of Macchi 202s which either whipped across the top of the island beyond our reach or dived down to strafe Hal Far and Luqa. As they appeared to be ignoring us at Ta Kali, we concluded that the Blenheims, Swordfish and Albacores were doing rather more damage than the Huns and Eyeties were prepared to accept.

On the 22nd, when I was not on the 'state' unfortunately, there was a major mix-up in the Gozo area when 126 and 249 encountered about twenty Eyetie 202s at heights varying between 25,000 and 35,000 feet. As the top elements of Macchis dived down to attack, a streaming fight ensued, the mass of aircraft descending upon 249, which happened to be the bottom squadron. Finally, with the Italians racing away to the north, there were many individual engagements, most of them inconclusive. Back on the ground there were widely conflicting stories regarding numbers of aircraft, types, who did what, and how things had developed. It was the same old business; those in the middle of a fight usually knew least about it.

In the calmer atmosphere of Monico's, Maxim's and the Phoenix Hotel in

Valletta, and mightily fortified by John Collinses and hot pork sandwiches, the news was exchanged. The Blenheims and Swordfish chaps had suffered terrible casualties, apparently; Force 'K' had played havoc with the Axis convoys, about three-quarters of which had been sunk; the Wellingtons were bombing everything within range into a pulp; and the Marylands, assisted by a few PRU Spits from Benson, had been combing the Med, north, south, east and west, in search of Rommel's seaborne supplies and reinforcements. The war had obviously started again in earnest; there were even dark rumours that the Huns were on their way back to Sicily.

In the convivial atmosphere of the Valletta bars, the prospect of once more being inundated with Ju 88s and Me 109s – not Es this time but Fs! – was little more than a grim joke, the general response being, so what? – we had clobbered them in England, so we could do so again. But could we? With the grog beginning to talk, my own confident assertions sounded suspiciously like bravado as more than most I was aware that our Hurricanes just did not have the performance to compete. Moreover, even with our newer aircraft, we were still having more than our share of engine failures; apart from others we didn't know about, Don Stones of MNFU had recently been forced to bail out when his engine had stopped and 'Polly' Sheddon had suffered a failure on take-off only a day or so earlier. Everyone had been bellyaching for Spitfires for months past, but to no effect; couldn't their Airships understand? Or even the AOC for that matter: Hugh Pughe kept stamping around breathing fire and brimstone but he didn't have to fly the wretched things, did he? I recalled only too well an incident some weeks before, when immediately following a particularly trying engagement, he had turned up at Ta Kali and loftily informed those of us present that 'it wasn't the aircraft, it was the man'. I recalled, too, the ugly silence that had followed, a silence in which, for one wildly absurd moment, I actually thought that someone might strike him. Even so, our problems were trifling compared with those of the Blenheims boys. How they kept going, with casualties sometimes as high as 50 per cent, was beyond comprehension. Thank God I was on fighters – Hurricanes even!

It was towards the end of the month, too, that 'Butch' Barton and I heard that we would shortly be moving on. Though 'Butch' seemed glad to be leaving, rather to my surprise I found myself limply apathetic. Go or stay, I didn't give a damn; what did arouse my interest was the news that I would be returning to England and not travelling further east to the Desert and beyond. Hugh Pughe had confronted me in dispersal with his blue-eyed stare, then had winked and jerked his head towards the west. Home! I recall feeling profoundly relieved; another year in Khartoum, or wherever, would have just about finished me off. 'Butch' would be succeeded by a chap called Mortimer-Rose whilst my replacement was to be a Flight Lieutenant Sidney Brandt. The dates of their arrival were uncertain.

For the last five days of November I flew fairly hard and mostly over Sicily where, I observed in my letters and logbook, there seemed to be a dearth of enemy fighters on or around Comiso and Gela despite the recent flurries of excitement over Malta. Against the last entry for the month, I penned a note: 'searched 25 miles east Kalafrana Bay; one dinghy found.'

I have no recollection of the flight, the dinghy, or who it was I was instrumental in rescuing.

25

The End in Sight

December started quietly, the lull before the storm as it proved to be. The weather dull with rain and plenty of cloud, the Eyeties stayed away and only the Blenheims and Wellingtons from Luqa seemed active.

At Ta Kali, there was an atmosphere of uncertainty and change; 'Polly' Sheldon appeared with another half-stripe on his arm and became Station Commander and 'Butch' Barton slipped away one night to board a Sunderland in Kalafrana Bay bound for Gibraltar and home. There was no departing binge or palaver, he just went. Quietly. Without fuss. Disappearing as he had always fought, with unassuming distinction. I suspect he was glad to leave; he had been on the go since September 1939 and was beginning to believe that his luck would shortly run out. At about the same time, the new man, Mortimer-Rose, turned up, smallish, agreeable, a little younger than 'Butch', but with much the same background.

On 7 December, I took off for Sicily and, in and out of cloud most of the way, dropped my eight 40 lb bombs on Ragusa railway station. As my target was within spitting distance of the Eyetie fighter base at Comiso, I half expected to run into a clutch of hostile Macchis, or 109s even, but in the event I saw nothing, not even a burst of flak. Although I was not aware of it at the time, it was to be my last sortie over Sicily and with repatriation at least a subconscious thought, found myself thinking and acting a good deal more circumspectly than usual.

It was on that day, too, that the Japanese attacked Pearl Harbour with horrifying casualties to the United States Navy, although we did not hear of it until the following morning. Discussing the attack over dinner, apart from the general belief that America's entry into the war was a good thing, most of us felt that someone must have boobed. Surprise? The Americans ought to have known something, surely! And if not, why? We all recognised it as being a most significant event although more of a disaster than a turning point in the war. In fact, we were to be rather more concerned about the loss of our own battleships, *Repulse* and *Prince of Wales*, which occurred a few days later off the coast of Malaya. On that occasion, I found myself in a furious debate with several around the dinner table who were taking what I considered to be too pessimistic a view of events. After the Battle of Britain, of course we couldn't be beaten, I proclaimed passionately, and to suggest otherwise was pure defeatism. However, despite my vehemence, there were some gloomy faces around the table that night and it was clear that not everyone agreed with me.

Then, down at dispersal on 11 December, news that was both good and bad; my replacement, 'Butch' Brandt, was on his way from Gibraltar; however, at that very moment, the Wellington in which he was travelling was heavily under attack in the area of Pantelleria. With a horrifying vision of him being plucked from my grasp, I scrambled as quickly as ever I had done and, with Crossey and several others, fled out towards the west like an avenging angel.

I would like to think that it was our intervention that enabled the Wellington to escape, although I suspect that by the time we had raced the hundred or so miles, the die had already been cast. Whatever the reason, the Wellington survived although two of its several companions did not. When we arrived, swords bared and grimly prepared to murder every Macchi and CR 42 in sight, we encountered nothing other than wide open seas, scattered cloud at 4,000 feet, and the most brilliant and empty of autumn days. Still seething with hostility, we skirted the hump of Pantelleria looking for birds that had long since flown.

On the way back, we overtook the Wellington as it was approaching Malta and shepherded it into Luqa, returning ourselves to Ta Kali. Later, 'Butch' Brandt arrived at Ta Kali in a very sombre frame of mind. His Wellington had been attacked by a group of CR 42s, apparently, and although a passenger, he had manned an extra machine-gun from a makeshift position in the waist of the bomber, firing furiously in its defence. The Wellington had been hit, even so, and one or more of the crew wounded; a very close-run thing, in Brandt's opinion.

A small rather stocky man with dark hair, I found him amusingly matter-of-fact. I said that for four Wimpeys to fly past Pantelleria in broad daylight and at a few thousand feet, was simply asking for trouble, and he agreed. We both decided that bomber pilots were pretty odd people anyway, although on this occasion they were probably only acting on instructions. He then asked when he was likely to take over my flight, to which I replied that as far as I was concerned he had already done so. At that, his face fell so comically that I agreed to hang on for a time, and did so for the next four days, although nothing much happened during that period.

As we had all been warned that the Germans were back in Sicily, I was only too aware that sooner or later the axe would fall and that against Ju 88s and the new 109Fs, our Hurricanes were going to have a pretty thin time. Not only were the bombers themselves as tough as boots – as well I knew – but the initiative would always be with the enemy, our own aircraft doomed to be climbing into groups of fast- moving 109s, the Hun fighters being at least 50 mph faster than the Hurricanes on the level and infinitely more nippy in the climb and dive. It was the Battle of Britain all over again, only more so. The Huns would have us on toast!

With these thoughts very much in mind, for several days I went to dispersal and watched my successor and his new command prepare themselves for the onslaught with mixed feelings of sympathy and regret, regret that for the first time in eighteen months I would not be taking part, and sympathy for Brandt who, clearly an innocent abroad, was just about to learn what it was like fighting in an aircraft vastly inferior in performance to that of the enemy and with no immediate expectation of replacements or spares. Having already handed over, did I offer to help or let him get on with it? Rightly or wrongly, I chose the latter course of action and was to suffer sharp pangs of remorse as a result.

My worst fears were soon confirmed. On 19 December, the Luftwaffe made its first appearance in strength, although it was 126 Squadron which bore the brunt of the attack, one of its new Americans, Steele, being shot down into the sea. Although he was observed to be in, or near, his dinghy, when the rescue craft arrived he was nowhere to be seen. The Huns, too, suffered losses, but the significance of this their first attack was ominous. The remaining Americans took Steele's death very gloomily.

The following day, a mixed bag of Ju 88s, Macchis and 109s appeared in even greater strength and this time 249 was heavily committed, claiming several 88s shot down or damaged but losing Sergeant Moran and the pleasant-faced Pilot Officer Cavan, both of whom were killed. I was especially unhappy about the youthful Cavan as he had been our guide and mentor on that first and memorable poodle-faking expedition, seven months earlier.

Then, for the next three days it was more of the same, with constant scrambles and breathless full-throttle climbs, the new 109Fs not only escorting their bombers with complete and obvious assurance but even sweeping down to sea level with the utmost disdain and attacking fishing boats off Grand Harbour. During this period a number of Hurricanes of 126 and 185 were lost in addition to two of 249, Graham Leggett being forced to bale out and the wry-smiling Robert Matthews being killed in dramatic circumstances when his aircraft, pursued by a 109, flew full-tilt into the sea wall in Valletta. With a number of other Hurricanes damaged in the various combats, 249 had lost more than half its complement of aircraft in three days, the Huns and Italians combined having made twenty raids in less than a week.

Most of this I witnessed dolefully as I hung about dispersal, fretting over my enforced inactivity and saddened by the damage inflicted on my old flight and squadron. Beazley, Palliser, Crossey, Davis et al, continued in the thick of things and I was playfully encouraged to 'come back and have a go'. My successor, Brandt, clearly taken aback by the maelstrom into which he had been pitch-forked and desperate to find serviceable aircraft, wore a funereal expression. Was this as it had always been? I tried to be encouraging, fearing the worst but keeping my apprehensions to myself; in my bones I knew it to be only the beginning.

Christmas Day came with no celebrations and an ominous silence; everyone waited on tenterhooks but there were no raids (apparently, the Germans made known their intention not to attack us on Christmas Day, but we were never informed).

That morning in our room in the mess, Crossey and I talked of the future. He was thinking of getting married, he confided. Married! My mouth fell open. To whom? The delectable Liliana di Georgio, apparently. I fell silent, amazed and suddenly sensing a new distance between us, between myself and someone I had known, lived with, and fought alongside for almost two years. Yes, the squadron was changing, disintegrating almost, the old faces moving slowly out of focus as though in a mist.

Later that day, I made up my logbook and added up the various columns and totals. Since arriving in Malta on 21 May, I had made eighty-nine flights against the enemy and, in all, flown 320 operational hours since July 1940. Willing to admit to staleness, I did not feel spent exactly nor in any way unhappy about fighting; never having been badly mauled by enemy aircraft, I could honestly say they had never held any terrors for me; flak and those loathsome red balls, yes, but never aircraft. I was just less enthusiastic, without that extra edge that made the difference between success and failure, between surviving and being killed. But more than that, I was fed up with engine failures, fed up with flying over endless miles of sea in lame- duck aircraft that sank like a stone as soon as they were forced to ditch, weary of the terrible sameness of scramble, climb, and the pursuit of an enemy who seemed always to be out of reach. Fed up, too, with sitting about for interminable hours at dispersal, limp and greasy with sweat, dust in my mouth and in my hair and in my indifferent food. And with the eternal mosquitoes, the man-eating fleas, trotting off to the bogs once a month with a churning, liquid stomach, and the poisonous 'Flit'! With Malta, in fact, although God knew, there were many worse places. Yes, I was probably due for a change. And another type of aircraft, please, please God? With any luck I would never have to fight in a Hurricane again.

There being nothing much doing in the mess, I went into Valletta on my own and eventually found myself mixed up in a party of pongos (one of the RAF's less objectionable names for the Army) who were celebrating riotously. An age and a Niagara of drink later, my head reeling and infinitely weary, I slept in my clothes on a strange bed in some Army barracks I never knew existed. Cold and restless throughout the night, I awoke at dawn, dry of mouth and with a splitting head, my memory weakly recalling the crescendo of enforced jollity the previous night and my own flagging, half-hearted contribution.

And now it was Boxing Day. Boxing Day! I recalled all too clearly Boxing Day, 1940. At North Weald. Waiting for that first flight over France, the one that was postponed. A thousand years ago now, or so it seemed. But I wasn't a member of 249 anymore, was I? After almost twenty months of flying and fighting. No, things would never be the same. There was no one left – or very few. It was time to go.

I was still in Valletta when the air-raid sirens began their whooping dirge and in the distance heard the first thudding 'tonk-tonk-tonks' of the ack-ack. But, gingerly treading some anonymous pavement, I was barely interested and did not even bother to look up. What the hell! If the Huns wanted to drop their bombs, let 'em get on with it; knock the whole place down for all I cared.

By degrees and by some means, I found my way back to Ta Kali and retired to bed. Crossey being on duty, our shared room was coldly empty. Hurricanes were racing off the ground again, the muted noise of their engines dying away into silence. Then more distant thuds and rumbles, but who cared? I closed my eyes. I wasn't part of it any more.

After a time – was it hours or minutes later? – I came to to the sound of my name being called. As I surfaced slowly, I recognised the voice of the very courteous Maltese youth with the khaki shorts and Rudolph Valentino moustache, who manned the telephone in a room the far side of the courtyard.

'Flight Lieutenant Neil?' His faintly Maltese accent. 'Mistair Neil? Sir? You're wanted on the telephone. Flight Lieutenant?'

I rose and, in my bare feet, padded sleepily to the half-open shutters. The little fellow was down below, shouting upwards in my direction.

'You're wanted on the telephone, sir. Air Headquarters. You must go to Valletta as soon as possible. Please come and speak to them. I think you are to go home, sir.'

Home! The little chap was smiling up at me. Home! As soon as possible! By ship, presumably! And on Boxing Day! It was all too much to take in.

When I arrived in Grand Harbour, the afternoon was well advanced and with a low and threatening overcast, the light was already beginning to fade. To my surprise, I found myself one of a small group, Harrington having accompanied me from Ta Kali, and Cassidy, late of 249 and now with MNFU, turning up with Peter Le Fevre of 126 Squadron. With our combined baggage in a sad and trivial heap among the bollards, ropes and general impedimenta of a busy dockside, we stood surveying the scene with quiet interest.

There was much to see. The harbour was crowded; apart from several cruisers, at least six destroyers, and, in a far corner, a clutch of submarines nestling snugly together like vipers in a nest, there were some half a dozen merchantmen of various sizes. Everywhere a hive of industry, there was a vibrant air of tension and preparation, a new experience for me, as, although I had been to Valletta many times before, I had never been in the centre of the naval dockyard and so close to the business-end of Grand Harbour. All the vessels looked worn and tiredly travel-stained with peeling paintwork and rust streaks everywhere, their guns starkly in evidence and already elevated skywards like a thicket of grey sticks.

From several Service informants who had turned up to assist in our departure, we learned that four merchantmen, one of which would be our home for the immediate future, were refrigerator ships normally employed on the London-New Zealand run. These would form the nucleus of a convoy and, accompanied by at least the bulk of Force 'K', would be making a swift and desperate dash for Egypt, the passage likely to take three or four days. The omens were not good, however; the enemy, having sustained enormous shipping casualties of their own, were in a vicious mood and only the immediate crisis had forced this break-out on a reluctant navy and the even more reluctant merchantmen. If they did not get through, the consequences for Malta could be serious. Not get through! We exchanged doubtful glances. Now they tell us!

Within minutes we were being ushered aboard SS *Sydney Star* and I was taken below to the usual seven-by-seven cabin, furnished in the heaviest of mahogany, which set me speculating wryly that if the ship were torpedoed, my part of it, anyway, was likely to float! I noted with mild dismay, however, that not only was I situated in the middle of the ship and without either scuttle, fresh air or daylight, but, as in HMS *Furious*, I seemed to have more than my fair share of the hissings, suckings and blowings being manufactured in some devil's cauldron below. Even so, counting myself lucky to have a cabin to myself, I returned to the deck to see what was going on.

I had not long to wait. Within minutes, several of the destroyers (I remember the names of all of them: H.M. destroyers *Arrow*, *Lance*, *Lively*, *Gurkha*, *Foxhound* and *Nestor*) alongside us began to glide slowly towards the entrance of Grand Harbour and tremors beneath the deck indicated that we were about to follow. We were off. After seven months in Malta, of my route and what lay ahead of me, I had not the slightest idea, nor did I care very much. I was going home. Home! Nothing else mattered.

My rose-tinged euphoria was to last barely a minute, however, as suddenly and without warning, the nearest of the destroyers fired several of its four-inch guns, as did other naval ships further afield, the violent reports coming so unexpectedly that I, and everyone near me, almost literally took off. Then, as we gave startled glances upwards to the ragged clouds above, strings of red balls began to climb away into the murk and a Ju 88, at not more than 800 feet, appeared as though by magic and flew directly overhead, tracer and ack-ack of every sort curving in its wake in a drifting veil of hate as though magnetically attracted by its presence. Weaving, banking and desperate to escape, the Hun aircraft lifted finally into the cloud and disappeared, the defending guns still barking furiously like maddened guard-dogs frustrated by their chains.

A voice sounded wearily in my ear. 'Christ! That's done it. Now we won't get a moment's peace 'til we reach Port Said.'

I looked around. The face of one of the ship's officers was a mask of dismay, his expression indicating all too clearly that he had seen it all before. Still, it was comforting to know that at least he expected us to get there!

26

Voyage to Egypt

That first evening at sea was uneventful, the weather overcast and damply miserable. I went on deck once and was greeted by a chilling wind and impenetrable darkness. Somewhere within yards of where I shivered was a cruiser, six destroyers and three other merchantmen. How on earth were they to avoid each other in the darkness? Mildly unsettled by the possibility of a collision, I left them to it and retired.

Nothing much happened that night nor even the following day, much to my surprise and, I suspect, the surprise of everyone else. There was the drab, wet greyness of an endless, white-flecked leaden sea; cloud, which sat above our heads in a solid layer, and ships everywhere, swaying and dipping in slow motion. To our left, about 400 yards away, sat the cruiser HMS *Dido*, its 5.25 inch dual-purpose guns pointing almost comically backwards and to the sky, whilst ahead, on either side and behind, the half-dozen destroyers sat placidly on station, at long intervals seeming to lose patience, at which times they would race about like grey whippets, leaning outwards on their curving turns with bow waves creaming majestically as they changed direction and position. Everything and everyone looked towards the north. In the direction of the enemy. Towards occupied Europe – and Crete!

Normally a good sailor, I found my tiny cabin oppressively claustrophobic, the lack of daylight and fresh air especially dispiriting. I tried reading, then drawing and painting, but could not settle to anything as the ship shuddered and pitched, the heavy mahogany furniture tilting, creaking and groaning in sympathy. Mealtimes were welcome breaks during which all four of us RAF officers dined at the Captain's table, the latter a worried little man who was only occasionally joined by the Chief Engineer and one or two others, their empty chairs serving to cast an additional shadow over our halting conversation. From time to time, the four of us would inject a little light-hearted banter into the proceedings but our witticisms fell mostly on deaf ears.

The following day, however, turned out to be somewhat different, by which time I judged we were somewhere south of Crete.

We had barely finished breakfast when the air-raid alarm sounded and we rushed on deck to find the guns barking away and the sky filled with bursting ack-ack. A Ju 88 was crossing overhead at about 4,000 feet and moving away westwards leaving a trail of ack-ack puffs in its wake as our guns strove unsuccessfully to keep pace with it. Within minutes it had vanished but the significance of its appearance was all too clear; we had been spotted and our course and speed estimated; from now on we could expect the worst.

Within the hour, there came a second alarm, at which we all raced on deck once more, this time to see another Ju 88, at about the same height, begin a shallow dive in our direction and, breasting a flurry of ack-ack bursts, drop a stick of bombs which curved swiftly downwards to explode in the sea within 100 yards of where we stood, slow- moving columns of white rising magnificently from the several muted eruptions. After which, the Hun aircraft scuttled away, weaving and banking, as the guns of the whole convoy went mad.

I was delighted. This was exciting stuff; and how lovely to see someone else being shot at for a change! It had not occurred to me for a moment that my life might be in jeopardy, the bombs had looked so innocuous, the incident simply adding spice to what had thus far been a fairly hum-drum voyage. Our good spirits restored, we retired for lunch talking animatedly about the attack and the uselessness of the ack-ack.

The Captain and several of his officers having joined us for the meal, it was obvious that the head-man was in a nervous and unsociable mood, as well he might be! Much less concerned, we joked about the attack, pointing out that the bombing had been about as effective as the gunfire, which seemed to us all bark and no bite. The gunners were hopeless, we opined; how could they expect to hit anything if they were ignorant of even the rudiments of deflection shooting? Being fighter pilots we knew all about such things, naturally; it was a pity the gun crews weren't similarly competent. We laid it on pretty thick, aware of our hosts' frowning and slightly injured silence.

Finally, the Captain stood up and blotted his lips. Did we think we could do any better? We all exchanged exaggerated glances of surprise. Of course we could; it was just a matter of know-how and practice, wasn't it? He nodded then turned away. In that case, when the next attack came, we could show him just how it was done. All right?

It was about 3 p.m., when, having retired to my cabin, I was jerked into wakefulness by a rap on the door. It was one of the ship's officers in a tense mood. The Captain's compliments and would I please report to the bridge; another air attack was imminent. A little taken aback, I followed the man with urgent steps, soon to be joined by Peter Le Fevre, Cassidy and Harrington. There we were told that radar plots suggested that a major attack was brewing. The Captain turned and pointed. There were two gun positions, one on each extremity of the bridge; perhaps we might like to get out there and man the machine-guns. We agreed, readily, and sorting ourselves out, Peter Le Fevre and I chose the one on the starboard wing and Cassidy and Harrington the other. We were fairly light-hearted about the whole business.

The small cupola to which Pete and I were introduced was on a projection high above the bridge itself and over the water. Climbing inside, where there was barely room even for one small person – and neither of us was small! – I looked down on the sea streaming beneath with a powerful feeling of insecurity. Thus far, our involvement had been a bit of a joke; now, for the first time, the ugly reality of what we had let ourselves in for was beginning to dawn. Besides ourselves in the cupola there was a mounting, a single American machine-gun called a Marlin, and yards of ammunition in a belt. Bullets! Real live bullets! And a man was showing us how it all worked.

Did we know anything about Marlins? We said that we didn't. All right then, this was the way it was loaded, and this was how it was fired. Okay? We replied that we thought so and the man climbed down hastily and disappeared. I fingered the weapon a little uncertainly and caught sight of Cassidy and Harrington in the distance, grinning and waving like children on a Sunday-school outing. After which it was decided that I should do the firing and Pete should feed in and generally be in charge of the ammunition. I swung the gun around experimentally but not without difficulty as there was hardly space to breathe. Then, with nothing much else to do, we waited. For about ten minutes. Looking around to see what else was going on, and where.

From our eyrie, we were able to look down into the glazed bridge where the Captain was pacing up and down with all the anxiety of an expectant father in a maternity wing, and spaced at intervals along the main deck were several gun positions where small knots of men grouped themselves around long-barrelled 20 mm cannons. Immediately to our rear and almost within touching distance, was the funnel, a single dark column rising steeply upwards, and beyond that an abundance of lifeboats, railings and air vents, plus all the paraphernalia of an ocean-going vessel.

The four merchantmen in a rough line, I could not see much of the one ahead but the one following was about 300 yards away and a little off to our right. With more than casual interest I noted that if I fired my gun, it was likely that I would rake the decks of the next ship and, more to the point, that its guns would do exactly the same to us. Deciding that this seemed to be a silly arrangement, I resolved to keep the matter in mind.

Alongside and some 400 yards to my left ploughed the cruiser *Dido*, plunging and rearing magnificently, its guns all turned upwards and backwards towards the north, whilst further afield, the six destroyers – or was it now eight? – formed an inner and outer screen, some fairly close, others as far away as the near horizon, all of them radiating a vibrating awareness of impending battle.

Then without warning, a rapid series of sharp cracks, about eight of them. And smoke. The destroyers were firing. After which, and before I had time to sort out who was doing what, a salvo from the cruiser, which made me almost jump out of my skin, the guns themselves hurling out smoke and recoiling like snakes recovering from a strike. I then saw that the *Dido*'s main weapons had been dipped so that they were almost level and that the Captain just below me was jumping up and down, mouthing something in my direction, and pointing. I peered northwards and saw what he meant – aircraft low down and on the horizon. About a dozen of them. Not flying towards us but moving left and right, which I thought rather odd. Big ones, too! The guns now going mad and masses of ack-ack bursts in the far distance. It was the start of an attack all right, but of what I could not see. Torpedo bombers probably.

For some minutes there was something of a hiatus, the bigger guns banging away spasmodically and the aircraft still several miles away, wandering back and forth on the horizon. Peter Le Fevre and I, all keyed up by the prospects of action, exchanged slightly hysterical jokes in our tiny cupola. If the bombers were Eyeties, they were probably jugging up with Chianti to bolster their spirits; anyway, what did it matter if they did drop a few 'fish', they would only hit the other side of the ship, wouldn't they? – I was happy to harbour the quite ridiculous notion that only the port side of the vessel was then likely to sink! But as we continued in this lighter vein, things took a turn for the worse; the bombers all began to head west, then, skirting the rear of our convoy, made a wide circle towards the south. After which they began to deploy themselves – on our side of the ship!

With about half a dozen of them some fifty feet above the waves, the Italian Savoias – we had now identified them as such – began to approach with quite ominous method and discipline and for the first time I felt a chilling spasm of naked fear. It looked as though we were going to be torpedoed and there was nothing whatever we could do about it.

Then it started, three of the noisiest and most hair-raising minutes of my life, the engagement introduced by the crack of countless guns, the shriek of four- and five-inch shells as they ripped through the rigging above my head, the thud-thud-thud of the Bofors, the tearing rattle of cannon and machine-gun, the soaring curve of flaring incendiaries and the white streaks of smoking tracer as it whipped across the waves. But through it all, seemingly unscathed and with magnificent, even foolhardy, bravery, came the Savoias. Line abreast, a terrifying phalanx. Eight hundred yards – five hundred – three hundred.

Remembering the 'whites of their eyes' dictum, I began to fire, the Marlin gun juddering and rattling like a mad thing in my hands, the belt of bullets jerking then dissolving into nothing as the empty cases flew away beyond and into the cupola. One Savoia directly in front of me now, two hundred yards distant and coming my way: I could see the three engines and cockpit quite clearly, the pilot almost. Then Peter Le Fevre's voice, a single strangled cry: 'I'm off!' And in a flash he was gone, all fourteen stone of him over the side of the cupola like an eel, and away. Still everyone firing like madmen. Deafeningly. The sharp stink of cordite everywhere. My own gun shaking crazily, the belt jumping, heat and stench rising into my face. The Savoia almost within touching distance. And something falling, rearing up in slow motion, before finally splashing into the water. A torpedo! Aimed straight between my legs. It couldn't miss. I was going to die. Die! In five seconds, I was going to die!

There are very few occasions even in wartime when one knows that death is inevitable and that there is nothing whatever one can do to halt the process. Chaka's warriors ordered to march over the cliff must have experienced roughly the same feeling as I did when I watched that torpedo enter the water less than 100 yards away. I had five seconds, I estimated, before the explosion came that would take me into eternity, and with half my conscious thoughts – I was then otherwise engaged – I began to count, one, two, three . . . !

When I had reached five, I remember cringing. Then six – seven– eight. Eight? I was still alive! Nine – ten! Glorious, unbounded relief! What had happened? I had no idea, nor did I care. The gun still clamouring in my hands, I was following the Savoia closely as it careered towards me then roared, deafeningly, a mere fifty feet over the stern of the ship, everything visible, engines, cockpit, the insignia on the wings and side, the whirling propellers, even. Meanwhile, the whipping smoke-trail of my bullets streaming in pursuit, with a stab of dismay I realised I had just fired directly into the bridge of the following merchant ship. But my mind almost unhinged with excitement, I continued, following the Savoia across the rear of my own vessel, my bullets splashing through the funnel in a single perforating line, then out again amid the rigging and beyond. The din incredible, the sheer bloodlust unbelievable. Down below, half of one eye caught sight of the Captain racing madly from one side of the bridge to the other, shouting. On and on. Would it never end?

Then, two incredible incidents. A thin scream, a new noise. A small winged object streaked over my head and flew straight into the path of my stream of tracer. A Wildcat, coming to rescue us. A naval Wildcat, presumably from one of the Fleet Air Arm squadrons based in North Africa; one of several that were hurling themselves with incredible courage into the fray, through all the bullets, the cannon-shells and bursting ack-ack. And I had hit it! I had hit it! I heard myself screaming: 'Stop! Stop! Stop!' I released my own trigger, appalled by what had occurred. But to no avail. Every other gun, it seemed, kept firing, the clamour beyond the power of words to describe.

But the Savoia that I and a score of others had shot at and behind which the Wildcat was now racing into position, was staggering. Reeling sideways like a wounded animal, then falling. A brief picture of the aircraft in plan view as it cart-wheeled downwards, followed by a huge eruption of spray, and flame, and smoke as it hit the water some 800 yards away. And the Wildcat . . . was it going in too? It couldn't be! But it was! It was! Oh Christ: No! No! No! (The Wildcat was in fact shot down into the sea).

But there were other goings-on to claim my attention, aircraft everywhere, low on the water, streaking away northwards – big ones, small ones, guns barking and kicking, smoke drifting, the cannons and machine-guns going mad, the sky pock-marked with puffs of ack-ack and criss-crossed with tracer and soaring red balls. On and on! Would it never end? How did one put an end to this inferno?

Finally the battle moved away and, limp with emotion, I was left surveying the globules of flame and the column of billowing black smoke that were the remains of the Savoia. Then, to my surprise, a destroyer with a flaring bow-wave, headed back towards it and stopped. Stopped! To search. I found myself protesting, incredulous but silent. Why there, for God's sake? Why not further afield for the remains of the Wildcat? I prayed that it would move on, but it didn't, after several minutes racing away to its former position in the screen. Why not, I felt like screaming. Our own man! Do something!

I felt stricken. How crazy was war, and more particularly war as waged by the British. Here we had been, hell-bent on destroying every vestige of the Italians and their wretched bombers; then when we had partially achieved our aim, the Navy rushes back and stops to pick up Italian survivors but not our own. Stops, jeopardising the safety of an entire ship and its crew in submarine-infested waters when there were obviously no enemy survivors. In Malta we had been shooting down Italian rescue aircraft daubed with red crosses for the last seven months – under instruction, needless to say. And now this! War was crazy, all right!

By degrees the emotion ebbed away until finally the guns were silent, the sky clear and with every ship back in position, we were streaming ahead, rising and falling with the swell, seemingly as though nothing untoward had happened. By degrees, too, I regained my composure, tidied up the cupola and looked up at the line of holes in the funnel. Crikey! I supposed I ought to apologise about those!

That evening we talked a good deal about the attack and the fate of the Wildcat. Everyone seemed convinced that it had been shot down but with so much else falling in the water, no one could say definitely that he had seen it crash. I felt very unhappy about the whole affair; it seemed that once the guns had started to fire it was almost impossible to get them to stop. The noise had come as a great surprise to me; how could any order be transmitted through all that din? Limp with so much discussion, I finally retired to my mahogany box in a depressed frame of mind.

The following day dawned bright and clear. Up on deck we welcomed our first sighting of the sun and were treated to a series of performances by the destroyers which kept racing about most spectacularly dropping depth charges; there were submarines in our area, it appeared, and the Navy was taking no chances. Then, after a time, a 'Granny' (Short Sunderland four-engined flying boat) turned up and wandered around for much of the day, suggesting to us all that we were pretty close to the North African coast and clear of Hun fighters. I had never seen a Sunderland flying boat in action before and was surprised by its lack of pace. I decided that flying around endlessly in circles at about the speed of a Tiger Moth would not have suited me, although it probably had an automatic pilot, enabling the crew to concentrate on the important things – such as frying their eggs and bacon! Imagine, eighteen hours of that on the trot! Well, it took all sorts to make an Air Force, I supposed.

Now about twelve hours sailing from Port Said, much of the tension had disappeared; it looked as though we would make it after all and even the Captain's face was seen to crack into the occasional bleak smile. The weather was warmer, too, which was a joy. Dinner was quite a chatty meal that night and we all retired to bed in a happier frame of mind – until I allowed myself to think of the Wildcat. What if I had shot it down?

Somewhere in the small hours, I awoke, aware that everything had stopped – no engine beat, no noise, no tremblings, no movement. I arose, slowly, and went up on deck. There were few people about and it was dawn – the most beautiful, silent, heart-stirring dawn I had ever beheld. And the smelliest!

We were stationary, a mile or two from a low-lying jetty, the sea mirror-smooth, the early morning sky an endless expanse of pastel yellows, blues and greens, softened by the almost transparent milk of a dawn mist. It was cool but pleasant, without even a breath of wind. Egypt! For the first time in my life I could see it – and smell it! The scent of the east – plus the stench of 4,000 tons of rotting potatoes! The local peasantry were on strike, apparently; I recalled hearing it on the news.

Beside me on the bridge, the Captain had lost his smile and was pacing about irritably. What the hell were we doing hanging about out here? We could be torpedoed any minute. If they couldn't accommodate us in the Canal, why didn't they tell us to extend our voyage? Sheer bloody stupidity, that's what it was! On the horizon, two destroyers slunk about like grey wolves on the perimeter of a camp. I remember smiling. How nice to know that other people had their problems.

It was a Tuesday 30 December 1941. We were to reach Cairo the following day, New Year's Eve.

Although I was not to know it at the time, as I leaned over the rail of the ship that day, rejoicing in the still, silent beauty of a Middle Eastern morning, my successor in Malta, Flight Lieutenant Sidney 'Butch' Brandt, had already been dead some twelve hours.

Scrambled in the late afternoon of the 29th, he had rushed out to the north of the island where some 109s were attacking the Malta–Gozo ferry and, together with the youthful, fair-faced Sergeant Lawson, had been shot down and killed. Poor, inexperienced 'Butch'! He hadn't lasted long; little more than a fortnight, in fact. And it could have been me. Anyone. He was to be the first of many.

By that time, too, 249's new commanding officer, Mortimer-Rose, had already been wounded, command passing to my old friend 'Beazle' (Flight Lieutenant John Beazley), who himself would remain only several weeks before being posted away.

Among others, the casualties mounted rapidly. The amiable 'Horse' (Pilot Officer Stuart) was killed when he suffered the almost inevitable engine failure on take-off; 'Jack' Hulbert was shot to death by 109s, together with Sergeant MacDowall, and there were others – all of them lambs to the slaughter. Palliser, Crossey, Davis and the rest were also soon to move on – a chapter had been completed, the remnants of the old squadron wiped away like chalk from a slate.

In those early months of 1942, it was to be a grossly unequal contest. The Hurricanes, totally out-performed, were soon reduced to impotence. Harried relentlessly in the air and attacked on the ground by a far superior fighter force – the Hun 109s eventually patrolling the Maltese airfields as if they were their own – they took to the air in reducing numbers, often being vectored away from the island for their own safety, until by March 1942, so few of them remained that some of the pilots of 249 were deployed on the rooftops in Valletta to act as aircraft spotters.

Sadly, although this unhappy situation had been predicted, the warnings had been ignored by those who, earlier, might have strengthened the fighter force in Malta with Spitfires. Eventually, when driven to it, they did, the first Spits arriving in March of that year. By which time, alas, for some it was too late! Needlessly so, in the opinion of many.

27

The Final Stage

After our difficult journey of almost four days as passengers on the SS *Sydney Star*, during which we had been bombed several times by the Luftwaffe and subjected to a very nasty attack by twelve Italian Savoia torpedo bombers just south of Crete, our small party from Malta finally reached its destination, Port Said.

I was not in the least impressed. Shivering and standing alone at 4 a.m. on the deck of the then silent and stationary *Sydney Star*, I became aware of several destroyers prowling suspiciously in the distance. At the same time, a further half a dozen ships lay motionless nearby , either waiting to draw up to the adjacent quay or proceed through the Suez Canal – which I couldn't see but which apparently lay directly ahead.

I remember, too, the morning being utterly silent and the weather brilliant beyond belief, with a brassy sun overhead amid the faintest wisps of pink and white cloud in an endless sky of steel-blue. This was the Egypt I had read about! What was less impressive, were the lines of dark, low-lying shed-type buildings I could see a mile or so away.

Later, it was about noon I recall, when all four of us passengers were deposited like luggage on the quay and I found myself sitting listlessly on a bulging parachute bag, waiting for someone to tell me what was in store for us.

I had been told by Hugh Pughe Lloyd in Malta that I was 'going home'. But in Malta, home had been a mere 1,500 miles distant, and here I was four or five days later, another 2,000 miles further on. What an earth was happening? If we were due to continue our journey by ship, there were heaven-knows how many miles and weeks ahead of us, travelling round East Africa, South Africa, West Africa, Timbuktu, and who knew where else! England, Spitfires, and decent aircraft to fly, were suddenly almost out of sight; the war might even be over before we finally landed in England! (In my defence, I was still only an impatient twenty-one years of age and life ahead of me sometimes appeared more sombre and complicated than it really was.)

In the near distance a clutch of officers and NCOs in khaki were speaking to my companions from Malta. A sergeant detached himself from the group and came in my direction. I was encouraged to see he was smiling and our subsequent conversation is worth repeating.

He started. 'Hello, sir. I'm the movements chap round here. I have called for some transport and am hoping to get you on your way to Cairo before too long.'

'Cairo? How far away is that?'

'Five or six hours away – around 200 miles. Down south at first, alongside the Canal to Ismailia, then west through Abu Sueir and beyond to the big city. Not too bad a road but I'm afraid you may find it a bit uncomfortable sitting on your bags in the back of a lorry.'

'And where do we go in Cairo?'

'You'll be going to Air Headquarters first, where they will sort out your accommodation for the immediate future and I dare say deal with any problems you have about money.'

A hollow laugh from me. 'Money! What's that? I don't think we have a penny between us. Anyway, what do they use round here?'

'Egyptian pounds and piastres, or 'ackers', so called. But don't worry; they'll see you alright.'

'And how long do we expect to be in Cairo?'

'Could be anything, sir. A week, a month, six months even! They may even change your posting depending on the situation in the desert. Many of you chaps from Malta finish up in the OTU in Khartoum. There is absolute chaos in the Far East at the moment. Singapore is under attack and there are masses of refugees – women and children – sailing for home. Ship transport is like gold dust. I have no idea what or when shipping may become available.'

I remember shaking my head in despair. Spitfires were fast disappearing over the horizon.

An hour later, as we passed through the town of Port Said in our several open-topped military trucks, I had my first sight of Egypt and some of its people.

To me, most of the town looked like a refuse tip, with low mud-coloured buildings between which a host of ragamuffin figures clad in white night-shirts, and headclothes, whipped into motion sad-looking donkeys or emaciated horses, most of which appeared to be on the verge of collapse. And between all this primitive dust-laden activity ran barefooted urchins waving and screaming, accompanied by yellow pi-dogs – plus camels, which, between thunderous belches, lumbered carefully around the place as though treading on hot bricks.

The road, which was quite modern and smooth, ran south alongside the Suez Canal, which was on our left and I judged it to be about 150 yards wide. To the right was a wide strip of pleasant looking green and brown vegetation and a thin line of palm trees, but beyond that, there was nothing but an endless expanse of sandy desert, interspersed with occasional groups of mud-coloured buildings. The weather being tolerably cool, I sat on my bulky parachute bag and for the first hour or so, quite enjoyed the ride. Surprisingly, there were no ships to be seen – or none that I can remember.

Although I was not to know it at the time, the desert to my right continued to the Nile delta, seventy or so miles away to the west, and was referred to in the Old Testament as the Land of Goshen, from which the Israelites made their escape from slavery in Egypt before crossing the Red Sea, which, with a little heavenly assistance, conveniently parted for them, enabling them to pass into the Sinai Desert, to our left. The crossing, apparently, was made at a place called Lake Timsah, about fifty or so miles south of where we were at the time, and is a lake which still exists.

After several hours, another large scattering of low buildings appeared ahead and I was told that this was the important town of Ismailia and the homes of many of the mainly British and French pilots, who shepherded the ships as they passed through the Canal. This, apparently, was a very onerous and important duty – according to those so employed, anyway – but observing the placid surface of the waterway was a duty which seemed pretty straightforward to me.

After a brief stop, our little convoy turned right and we began to follow another canal which looked quite civilised, fringed as it was with lines of palm trees, but took on an altogether different aspect when I observed the dead bodies of several donkeys and a dog or two, floating about on the surface, their legs sticking up grotesquely from bloated grey carcases. Again, the local vegetation was pleasantly brown and green and little gatherings of habitation were strung out along the far side of the water. The white nightshirts of those living there became increasingly in evidence as we drove along and it seemed clear that they used the canal not only for irrigation and probably drinking purposes but also as a sewer, the local name, our drivers informed us with cheerful disgust, being the Sweetwater Canal!

Halting for a time at a village named Abu Sueir, we were told that an RAF station lay off to our right and that 249 Squadron's heavy baggage, which had 'gone round the other way', was held in the Maintenance Unit there. If we so wished, we could delay our journey and pick it up. As this seemed to be a sensible thing to do, my particular vehicle pulled into a narrow alley of stone-built dwellings, and Harrington and Cassidy were elected to visit the MU and find our various possessions. Immediately thereafter, there followed two trivial incidents, one screamingly funny, the other not so hilarious.

When my two Malta companions had departed, I took a front seat in my truck and sat there for some time, idly watching the world go by. The narrow alley in which we had parked, was crowded with people, animals and carts, all noisily pushing their way through. In front of me and to one side, stood an Egyptian policeman clad in his black uniform and red fez and immediately behind him was a camel with a man on top. As the policeman stepped several paces to the rear to avoid the crush, he inadvertently trod on the animal's foot. The camel, clearly surprised and outraged, uttered the camel equivalent of 'Ow!', before baring its very considerable row of teeth, and with a belch and a roar, bent down and bit its assailant in the neck. The policeman's fez flew off into space, and its owner fell with a cry between the many wheels and dusty feet of the multitude, before rising in a fury and beginning to punch the animal with his fists.

The whole incident was so bizarre, I nearly fell off my seat laughing. Then, with the shouting policeman continuing to belabour the camel, my companions returned carting our various pieces of luggage. The large, packed suitcase, which I had bought in Scotland when I was at Flying Training School in 1939, seemed very light. When I opened it up, it was almost empty. Some light-fingered character had stolen almost all my possessions.

I have no recollection of the rest of our journey other than our arrival in Cairo and our brief visit to some vaguely remembered headquarters where there were many chaps in very smart khaki uniforms (I was later to refer to them as the 'Gaberdine Swine') who finally gave us some local money and despatched us in the direction of the Metropolitan Hotel. I was so tired at this point, I just didn't care anymore and could have slept on a clothesline.

The Metropolitan Hotel was a very grand affair and I well remember sinking into a very plush bed, the like of which I had seldom before experienced, in a room almost as big as a small aircraft hangar. Looking back, I doubt that I slept at all well that night, worrying, I imagine, about the cost of my splendid abode, and who was going to pay the bill.

Indeed, I was to harbour similar thoughts when I sat in the entrance hall of the hotel later that day and watched, open-mouthed, as a dozen small, fat, Egyptian gentlemen, impeccably attired in dinner jackets, led streams of very pretty, scantily-clad young dark-eyed ladies past me into the magnificently chandeliered dining room. I could scarcely believe my eyes. Even in the best uniform I possessed, I felt like a poor relation. And all this in a war that was on our doorstep and was not going at all well for us British, and presumably, our Egyptian allies, whose country was at present being invaded by Rommel's seemingly invincible German army.

I was to remain in the Metropolitan hotel for the next four days, during which time I was to 'encounter' life in that strange but fascinating city. And my experiences are worth recording.

First, Cairo itself – a colourful maelstrom of modernism, minarets and medievalism and noisy beyond belief, with enormous American cars jostling with camel and horse-drawn vehicles of every description, the car-drivers and cart-jockeys shouting, waving their arms and hooting their horns continuously as though their lives depended on it. Never in my life had I ever heard such noise.

And the seething crowds! Tens of thousands of khaki-clad servicemen, mingling with an equal number of local citizens, all of them, from the rich to the ragged, clad in accordance with their trade, calling or profession. Such a bewildering confusion of animals, vehicles and people, I often later found it too difficult to cross a road on foot, forcing me – but only after taking a very deep breath – to use the madly driven taxis.

Later, having ventured forth into the town, with several newly found friends who had flown Wellingtons in the Middle East, I decided to visit Shepheard's Hotel, the mecca for all decent-minded chaps from Britain, then Groppi's Café, where they sold pastries and cream cakes to die for. Each was a revelation, Shepherds because of its excellence and its widely held reputation as being one of the few remaining icons of the British Raj, and Groppi's Café because of its fame and the richness of its products

As we sat in each splendid venue, over many meals and coffees (so utterly different from home and Malta!), my friends and I talked endlessly of the state of the war in the desert and the various opinions held locally, not only of our leaders, troops and equipment, but also the effectiveness of the German and Italian enemy. And in so doing, I am bound to add, a new picture emerged in my mind.

A small group of us also did a little private sight-seeing, visiting the Pyramid and Sphinx at Giza, where we rode on the back of camels and watched the local lads in their nightshirts race to the top of the pyramid to earn themselves a few hard-earned pennies.

As regards the state of the war, I was well aware that the battle for the Suez Canal had been successful for the British for the first months of the desert war. The Italian army's first thrusts from Libya had been beaten back by General Wavell and tens of thousands of prisoners taken. However, when Hitler had sent his favourite General, Erwin Rommel, with an army to assist the Italians, the position had deteriorated rapidly. The Germans had better aircraft, tanks and other equipment than the British and our forces had been pushed back repeatedly. Indeed, when we arrived in Egypt from Malta at the turn of the year, our army's to-ing and fro-ing in the desert had become almost a matter of amusement and referred to as 'The Benghazi Handicap'.

By mid 1941, General Wavell had been replaced by General Auchinleck, but the new leader's plans and methods were fast losing favour with the Prime Minister, Mr. Churchill, with the result that about the time of our arrival in Cairo, 'the Auk' was reported to be under pressure to take more positive action and be under something of a cloud.

The reputation of some of the various forces under his command varied greatly. The New Zealanders were considered to be splendid troops, as was the 1st Division of the Australians, the latter being composed of units of the regular army. Sadly, the 2nd Australian Division, having, it was said, to have been recruited from the 'dregs of the Australian docksides' were sometimes described as 'an undisciplined rabble' – and, my goodness, I was soon to learn why! The South African special forces (their Air Force and Tank Units) were also regarded as first class, but their infantry less so, being mainly composed of Afrikaners, of whom it was said 'they didn't know what they were fighting for and were deeply unhappy to be up here anyway'!

Among the British, the Foot Guards and some other well known regiments were said to be splendid, as was the 7th Armoured Division, (the 'Desert Rats'), although their Matilda tanks were unpopular, being slow, cumbersome, and completely outgunned by the German Mark 4s with their massive 88 mm weapons. In the air, the Germans were also much better equipped. Our Hurricane fighters were altogether too slow and outdated; although they could cope with the bombers, they could not really compete with the new 'F' version of the Me 109. The American Tomahawk, too, was described as a 'bit of a brick' and its Allison engine prone to exhibit bearing difficulties. As for our light and medium bomber aircraft, they were regarded as no more than adequate, although new types were said to be 'coming along'.

On about our fifth care-free day in Cairo, our small party was told that it would shortly be moving to Helwan, an RAF airfield some fifteen or so miles to the south. That particular day remains in my mind because of two small incidents that took place shortly before our departure.

Walking somewhere in the centre of Cairo, I was faced with a long column of about 500 soldiers in tropical kit wearing rather unusual peaked forage caps. They were standing quietly in line and I recognised them immediately as German prisoners of war, guarded by several of our own soldiers carrying rifles with fixed bayonets. They were notably different from some Italian prisoners I had already seen who were usually much more animated, many of them pulling faces and making rude gestures of some sort. The difference was most noticeable. The Germans, I was told, were mostly of the 90th Infantry Division, some of Rommel's most successful troops, and their quiet discipline and composure was plain to see and almost a cause for admiration.

My second experience was less pleasurable to record. Almost every night, there had been noise and confusion outside my hotel. My bedroom being on the second floor, although irritated by all the din and the glare of lights, I was not much concerned. However, when I was told that some riotous and drunken troops – Australian, it was alleged – had rampaged through the hotel late at night, broken into bedrooms, dragged one sleeping officer out of bed and thrown him out of the window, with others I was more than a little on edge. The result being, for at least one night, I had slept with a loaded revolver in my hand, prepared to shoot anyone – drunk or sober – who threatened me in such a way. It was all quite upsetting at the time.

I was glad when our small Malta party moved down to Helwan – I was tired of all the noise and bustle in Cairo, despite the cream cakes and rich living, although the biblical history of that area of Egypt fascinated me. The RAF had apparently been based at Helwan for many years and had sited there an aircraft park and a Maintenance Unit, which almost entirely dealt with fighters – Curtiss Tomahawks, in the main, and Gloster Gladiators, a few of which had served in Greece.

I was granted a quiet and secluded bedroom with the usual furniture and trappings of the Middle East – mosquito nets, water chatties, rugs, bamboo chairs and similar equipment. I also inherited a bearer, a tall, grave, elderly man with a beard, who did not speak a word of English. Even so, dressed in his full-length white djellaba and turban, with quiet dignity he anticipated my every requirement and served me so well that I was very sad, finally, to leave him.

I remember my week's stay there with great pleasure; I was able to read books on biblical history, write a little, and spend some time drawing and sketching, besides strolling round the airfield and touring the hangars where the aircraft were being inspected and serviced. I noted with interest the quite extraordinary degree to which the dismantled aircraft engines had been affected by service in the desert, many of their inner parts stained yellow by the sand. On several occasions I travelled into Cairo by electric train (as though I were on the tube in London!) and spent some time with the young test pilot who flew one of the Gladiators twice a day, entertaining us all with his excellent aerobatics. Altogether a most restful and delightful several days.

After being warned that the four of us from Malta would shortly be moving on, first to Port Tewfik on the Red Sea coast, then by sea, probably to South Africa, after about a week, we were taken back to Cairo and, with our trivial heaps of baggage, loaded on to a train.

Our journey uneventful, we arrived at our destination at dead of night and, weary with the long uncomfortable journey, were directed to some anonymous place in the desert where there was a clutch of empty tents in which, it was explained, we would spend the rest of the night. There being no furniture in sight, when I asked on what we expected to sleep, I was told by a harassed NCO that he might be able to find a few wooden trestle tables but, the choice was mine, either I slept on a table or spent a night on the floor.

The next five hours were miserable beyond words to describe. I tried sleeping on my personal rock-hard table then on the sandy floor, scraping a hollow to accommodate my hip bone. The night being bitterly cold and still fully clothed, I rose next morning, aching in every joint. Breakfast was a mug of stewed tea, looking and tasting like bull's blood. It was an utterly forgettable occasion!

In the half light, I have no recollection of the manner in which we arrived on the vessel which was to transport us 'in a southerly direction'. As it was a sizeable liner and moored in mid-stream, we must have been taken there on a lighter. All I remember is that our ship was big, had two funnels, bore the name *Nieuw Amsterdam* and that it was Dutch.

In addition to our small group of four from Malta, there was a mixed collection of twenty or thirty other passengers, male and female, from the RAF and Army. All a little bewildered by our change of circumstances, we were further surprised by the obvious opulence of our new surroundings and the space we were afforded – large cabins, each with comfortable beds, and beautifully furnished dining and living rooms, with civilian stewards serving food we had not seen for an age – in short a minor Shangri-La, for all of us a new experience only slightly marred by the news that our ship would also be carrying 1,000 Italian prisoners of war about to be transported to somewhere in East Africa.

For two days, for me it was sheer bliss. I slept in a comfortable bed without the nightly fear of being bombed, torpedoed, or being thrown out of my hotel window by drunken Australians. As the *Nieuw Amsderdam* sailed majestically but slowly down the Red Sea, with all of us watching the dolphins and flying fish besport themselves beside us, I had seldom been so relaxed. Until on the third day, I went down with what was first described as a tummy bug!

As I lay in bed, rolling about with pain and vomiting at both ends, I was visited by an Army doctor, who patted my head and comforted me with the prognosis that I was unlikely to die but that I might have a day or two's misery ahead of me. However, it turned out to be rather more serious than that as I was eventually declared to be the victim of food poisoning, and was racked with pain and sickness that lasted for almost the rest of our voyage to South Africa.

During my confinement, our ship apparently put in at one of the Somaliland countries on the African east coast – which one I never learnt --and offloaded our Italian prisoners of war. At this point in the voyage, I was past caring and just wanted to die, thinking at the time how unfortunate I was that, after two years of hard fighting in lame-duck Hurricanes, I might die painfully as the result of eating some wretched pieces of salad or chicken. In fact, it was not until only a day or so before our arrival in Durban in South Africa that I finally surfaced and was able to totter limply about on deck and gaze in wonderment at an unending blue sea and a cloudless sky. A day or two later, I had recovered sufficiently to walk with others from the Durban dock area, where the *Nieuw Amsterdam* had finally tied up, into town.

Having at this point been told that we would be changing ships, we also learnt that our future transport, coming from Singapore and carrying 'thousands of refugees', was still at sea.

Rather than being depressed by the news of the poor unfortunates who were refugees, we were uplifted by the prospect of spending a few extra days in Durban, which, we were well aware, was still untouched by war, with its associated miseries of food-rationing, blackouts, plus the sight and noise of combat on the ground and in the air. Not only that, the South Africans, in that part of the world being mainly of British origin, had long held the reputation of being welcoming and hospitable. How lucky could we get? After more than two years in war-torn, blacked-out Britain and Malta, this was surely the place to be!

Our optimism was proved to be well founded. In the town, we used public transport without having to pay so much as a penny. There were lights and colours everywhere. Like children, we went up and down the high-rise buildings, just for the joy of riding in the lifts. We were stopped in the streets by smiling young women who, noticing our uniforms, invited us to tea or drinks, or even to their homes for a family meal. We seemed to be welcomed everywhere. However, we observed, with some surprise, the lack of young men in the shops and streets, it then being explained that most 'fathers, sons and boyfriends were up in the desert, fighting' – which, I recall, brought from me a rueful, apologetic smile. With their men-folk away, were we not taking advantage of these kind, companionable ladies?

On about our third day in Durban, our ship from the Far East quietly and almost apologetically limped in. Camouflaged and rusty, the SS *Oronsay* was not an impressive sight. About 20,000 tons and about half the size of the *Nieuw Amsterdam,* it had two rather tall, ancient funnels, two masts, (fore and aft), an open bridge, and positively seethed with men, women and children. At the time, we were all told that, including the crew, there were almost 2,000 people on board, but there may have been more. Both the ship and everyone on it looked very weary indeed.

Still in our small group of four from Malta, we were joined by other RAF personnel, some from bomber squadrons serving in the Middle East, and others I can only now describe as 'not aircrew'. With many new faces around – Army, Air Force and a few Navy – plus a mass of civilians, it was a period of utter bewilderment, during which time we were all sorted out – two, three, or four to each small cabin – and spent most of the first day tripping over each other and trying to locate the living areas, the dining room and other important parts of the crowded vessel.

In one respect, I was on home ground as the ship was of the familiar Orient Line and registered in Liverpool. Most of the crew members, too, I discovered, were worldly 'scousers' who soon exhibited their own particular brand of sardonic humour. During our first meal, as my soup was being served, when I jokingly asked our dining-room steward whether our ship had ever been bombed or torpedoed before, the man nodded and replied with a straight face, 'Just a coupl'a times, whack! Everything usually came in through that scuttle just over your napper.'

Sadly, we were only to remain in Durban for a further two days before pulling out and sailing south, bound, we were told, for Cape Town. By degrees, order was restored out of chaos. An RAF Orderly Room suddenly appeared out of nowhere and various types of Routine Orders were produced by a person, or persons, I was never able to identify. However, as the ship was behaving itself, the food was good, the sun shone in a cloudless sky and as we bowled long at a steady fifteen knots in roughly the direction of England and home, everyone was tolerably happy with life despite our cramped conditions.

On our second day at sea, I suddenly found my name on a list which informed me that I was to take a spell as 'Aircraft Spotter' – in two hour periods each day, I was to identify and give early warning of the approach of any aircraft, friend or foe.

I read the instruction with complete equanimity; I was quite willing – indeed happy, to sun myself on the bridge, drink gin and tonics, and watch for enemy aircraft, none of which were ever likely to appear in our neck of the woods. However, in the event, my time there turned out to be most instructive.

I learnt almost at once that it was almost impossible to hear the engine (or engines) of any aircraft against the background hum of a fifteen-knot wind and other mysterious noises made by the ship. This was soon made apparent when, during my first hour of duty, one of the ship's officers confronted me, screaming abuse and waving his arms.

'Can't you see that aircraft over there, you dozy bastard?'

Instantly affronted by the man's manner and tone of voice, whilst shouting a coarse reply in his direction, I looked up to see a twin-engined 'something' bearing down on us. A friendly aircraft I never did recognise then swam silently alongside at about 2,000 feet, before disappearing astern in minutes. A trifle shamefaced, I renewed my search more rigorously, realising that my eyes were much more important than my ears when engaged on spotting duty, and that it was almost impossible to detect an approaching enemy aircraft without using specialized equipment or by sheer luck.

It was also during my periods of watch on the bridge that I became aware of another, rather elderly, gentleman who turned up now and then to join me. Having nodded to him occasionally, when I quietly asked a third party who my occasional companion might be, I was informed it was a 'chap called Brooke-Popham'.

'Brooke-Popham!' I almost genuflected in surprise as knew of him all too well. A famous pre-war airman, Air Chief Marshal Sir Henry Robert Brooke-Popham had been Commander-in-Chief, Far East Command, for some years, only to be relieved of his post a month or two before. Aware that he was probably on his way home and no doubt deeply distressed by the turn of events in and beyond Singapore, I resolved to speak to him if only to be friendly, to offer sympathy and to learn more about the rapidly deteriorating war situation in his former command.

I found him a delightful man, quiet, articulate, full of remorse, but not at all bitter about the desperate situation he had been faced with towards the end of his period of tenure and the criticism that had since had been levelled at him personally. He spoke to me quietly and unguardedly for many hours and I began to realise the almost intolerable pressures – military and political – that senior officers in the Services often encountered and the effect it had on their minds and bodies.

I do not recall exactly the dates of the several long occasions during which we spoke, but it must have been only days before Singapore finally fell to the Japanese on 14 February, 1942. Such a terrible loss for Britain, for the servicemen who lost their lives, for those who became prisoners of war, for their families, and for the poor unfortunate man who had to bear to bear at least some of the acrimony that resulted from poor planning and Britain's ignominious failure and defeat.

We reached Cape Town without mishap and found it as welcoming as Durban but in a somewhat different way. Durban was more 'British', Cape Town more cosmopolitan, the Afrikaner and Huguenot elements more obvious in the language and accents. Even so, the welcome was genuine, from the British element especially, but I found it disturbing that so many well-to-do British of fighting age were still living the high life, driving about in big American cars, and apparently taking very little part in the war.

Our initial stay there was brief and we set off again after a day or two, steering a westerly course, and mentally prepared for a long detour through choppy waters into the South Atlantic, with all the terrors it held from being a lone ship and an easy target for enemy submarines.

Our apprehensions, however, were short-lived as our ship developed propeller trouble and after a day at sea, we turned about and docked for a second time in Cape Town to enable repairs to be carried out. This, of course, was gleefully welcomed as our stay in that beautiful town and area was extended by another three days – three days in which we continued to be entertained royally and were able to visit local beaches and beauty spots and take the cable car to the top of Table Mountain to enjoy the magnificent scenery.

With our ship declared sea worthy again we set off a second time and after a fairly sick-making several days, found ourselves alone in Mid Atlantic, steering a regular zig-zag course (to confuse the enemy) and, taking out the kinks, progressing northwards at the very moderate rate of about twelve knots.

On board, we ate reasonably well and lived adequately if not comfortably in our small cabins. New faces and voices became familiar and I especially recall those of four naval officers who had survived the sinking of the two battleships HMS *Prince of Wales* and *Repulse* a few months earlier.

In the crowded staterooms, we, the passengers, played bridge, watched the occasional film and amused ourselves as best we could. The refugee families, in the main deeply unhappy with their lot, gradually began to smile a little and a few relationships were formed. The children became fractious from time to time, but on the whole there were no personnel disturbances or problems I can recall. I spent a lot of time writing in an oversized Smith's diary and drawing portraits, none of which were worth keeping.

As the days went by, life became very boring, the only pleasing aspect of the voyage being the recognition that we were still on top of the water and not underneath it! This remark is especially pertinent as in August, about six months later, making a similar voyage in roughly the same area, our gallant ship, the *SS Oronsay*, was torpedoed by an Italian submarine and sunk with considerable loss of life.

On a date I do not exactly recall, our ship then turned right, and made for the port of Freetown in Sierra Leone, for a reason that was never explained but assumed by most of us, to replenish our supply of water and provisions.

Whatever the reason, we all remained on board and observed the miserable looking coastline from a distance, our ship remaining there for little more than a day. Suitably replenished, it then headed out into mid-Atlantic, and, returning to its normal twelve-knot, zig-zagging routine, headed for the frozen north.

By this time it seemed that we had been at sea for months and the wish and desire to reach home was plainly evident. However, everyone was aware that we would be sailing into known U-boat hunting grounds where recent shipping losses were still massively high. Anxious to avoid the main convoy routes and the enemy submarine packs, our lone ship, still zig-zagging its heart out, then steered a north-westerly course, which had many of us believing that the aim was to land us all in Canada. And it was at this point that we ran into a massive and quite fearsome hurricane which had apparently come up the American coast from the West Indies.

First, we encountered high winds and massive waves. Then, our ship having entered the eye of the storm, the sea developed into mountainous swells, which had it plunging and rocking like a child's toy in a bath. Finally, having reduced speed to an absolute minimum, our vessel, still pitching and wallowing in a quite frightening manner, turned its prow into wind – and just stayed put!

At this stage everyone aboard was genuinely frightened. The ship, we were told, was heeling over, left and right, well beyond allowable safety limits. Some of the lifeboats had already been smashed or carried away, all passengers had been instructed to remain, day and night, in their clothes and life jackets. Hot meals, having long since been discontinued, the few of us still capable of eating, existed on hastily prepared cold snacks.

Finally, the storm, having lasted for two days, gradually moved away, allowing the ship to shake itself, recover, and after taking stock and a very deep breath, turn onto its original heading and slowly limp away.

For the following several days, we seemed to wander around a very miserable, icy, hostile ocean, continuing north almost as far as Greenland before turning towards the east, and Iceland. The weather miserable beyond belief, we never saw land or another ship. Nor did we ever learn exactly where we were. Until, one day, some of us felt and sensed our ship was turning south. South, for heaven's sake! South, towards England and home!

As we sailed down the Irish Sea and finally docked in *Oronsay's* home base, Liverpool, it should have been a *Grand Finale* for me – but it wasn't! Two days earlier, I had gone down with a vicious head cold which had developed into 'flu.

Sick and miserable, I was confined, sniffing and dribbling, to my tiny cabin bed when the same Army doctor, who had tended to me in the *Nieuw Amsterdam* reappeared, to pat me on the head again and announce that although I was unlikely to die, I should remain where I was for at least three days before even attempting to leave the ship. For this reason, when the vast multitude on the ship departed in the highest of spirits, I was left in my cabin, not in the best of tempers and was less than courteous when of one the ship's officers, with whom I had become friendly, arrived grinning at my bedside to offer me a bag of oranges.

I remember looking at it in dismay. A bag of oranges, for heaven's sake! That was all a chap needed when just at the point of death!

However, this most unusual gift ought properly to be explained. Few people in food-rationed Britain had *seen* an orange since the beginning of the war, so it was similar to my being offered an ingot of twenty-four carat gold.

When I enquired about why I was so favoured and where it had come from, my ship's-officer friend explained that the ship normally carried about a million boxes of them as ballast and that, looking and feeling so miserable, I qualified for at least a bagful.

Which was the reason that when, four days later, I finally arrived at my parents' home in Northwick Park, London at 2 a.m., on a day in early March, having travelled down by train from Lime Street, Liverpool, and found them in their pyjamas, the three of us were able to share a bagful of juicy oranges amid tears of joy.

Their only son, still only twenty-one years of age, having fought in Spitfires and Hurricanes since May, 1940, but now safe at least for the moment, was back home again. For the two of them, it was a present even better than a bag of oranges.

What Happened After the Battle of Britain?

In 2015, the year in which this reprinted book will be published, the Battle of Britain will be seventy-five years old and I, the author, will be in my ninety-sixth year.

Of the original twenty or so pilots of 249 Squadron, formed on 15 May 1940, I am now, I believe, the only pilot still alive.

I have, moreover, many times over the years, considered it extraordinary that, although I lived alongside and fought with those early colleagues and friends for so short a time – some for no more than a few days or weeks – after seventy-five years, they all remain vividly in my memory.

I still recall their voices, their laughter, their juvenile jokes, and their many idiosyncrasies. I remember especially the pipes and cigarettes they smoked, their fondness for the local pubs and beer, the violent and destructive games they seemed to enjoy in the Mess, and their childish habits of collecting trophies from the outside world to adorn their private rooms in the Officers' and Sergeants' quarters. And, yes, I freely recognize them now to be twenty-one-year-old adolescents – because that is what they were! – and at nineteen years of age, I was probably among the most juvenile of them, if a mite less worldly than some. Such memories I recalled most poignantly, when attending the Battle of Britain Memorial Service at Westminster Abbey on 20 September 2009, and heard a young officer of the modern Royal Air Force, read one of the lessons taken from the Book of Samuel. It ran:

In life and in death, they were not divided; they were swifter than eagles, they were stronger than lions.

Such sentiments persuaded me to add, with reverence and humility, the following passages.

Wing Commander Victor Beamish

Victor, one of three Beamish brothers in the Royal Air Force, was Station Commander at RAF North Weald when 249 Squadron operated from there for most of the Battle of Britain.

Aged thirty-eight, and much older than many who took part, Victor, like Admiral Nelson, was a person completely without fear. An aggressive warrior in battle, he was, even so, a brilliant but thoughtless nuisance in the air. He observed no rules, and although frequently part of our squadron formations, he was apt to leave or join us whenever he felt inclined.

Always following and never leading, he was a constant threat to everyone when flying in our midst. Indeed, on 7 November 1940, after one of his mindless forays, he collided with me at 16,000 feet, obliging me to bale out, miraculously landing his own badly damaged Hurricane near Detling airfield in Kent.

Even so, we all admired and venerated him not only for his combat successes but also for his smiling and abject apologies when he brought us to the point of murder when breaking the rules so blatantly and so often 'getting in the way'. However, in spite of everything, his aggressive fighting spirit was an example to us all.

In March 1941, he left North Weald and a year or so later became Group Captain commanding RAF Kenley, where he continued his violent personal battle with the Luftwaffe, this time flying Mark V Spitfires.

Returning from Malta in the spring of 1942, I wrote to him from No. 81 Group Headquarters, where I was languishing as a so-called staff officer, suggesting that I might join one of the squadrons in his Wing. He wrote back a charming letter, which I still posses, inviting me to visit Kenley to discuss the matter.

Sadly, it never happened! After being a prime mover in the German battleships Scharnhorst and Gneisenau debacle, and their escape up the English Channel, Victor was shot down shortly after and was lost.

Thus died the bravest of men and another twist occurred in my own career.

Squadron Leader John Grandy

John was a handsome young man of twenty-seven when he first took command of 249 Squadron.

By his own admission, he was not the world's best fighter pilot and, as he later admitted, it was entirely his own fault that he was shot down on 7 September 1940, at which time he baled out and sustained the leg injuries that prevented him from taking any further part in the Battle.

However, a person of considerable charm and a most capable administrator, he went from strength to strength, aided by an equally personable young wife, Cecille, rising apparently without effort over the years to the final supreme rank of Marshal of the Royal Air Force.

A commanding officer who 'collected' – mainly from the universities of London, Oxford and Cambridge – his own type of people to serve under him, as a very young officer straight from Flying Training School in Scotland, and initially not one of his favoured few, I was only cautiously tolerated at first. However, by mid-June 1940, when I had successfully flown a Spitfire for almost 100 hours over a four-week period, he warmed to me and our relationship blossomed. Thereafter, I was always 'Ginger' to him, a nickname that was to continue for the rest of our long acquaintanceship.

I met him many times over the years and was in India when he landed a Dakota at Rangoon, when it was uncertain that the Japanese in Burma had finally surrendered. For this he was awarded a well merited DSO, the first of many decorations he was later to receive.

Later, having more or less retired – Marshals of the Royal Air Force never actually retire! – he was living on the outskirts of Windsor Park and shopping in Windsor town when he was struck down by a stroke. Tragically, only months later, his lovely wife Cecille died, after which John became like a man without arms, as he greatly depended on her.

From time to time and living alone, he would ask to see me and I would drive down from Norfolk to visit him, but conversation eventually became difficult when his short-term memory failed and his emotions were apt to take over.

Finally, in 2006, he died, aged ninety-three, a very successful officer, but, at the end, a very lonely one.

Flight Lieutenant Ronald Kellett

Ronald Gustave ('Boozy') Kellett, at thirty-one years of age, was the oldest pilot in 249 Squadron when he joined us, shortly after my own arrival on 15 May.

From the outset, he was 'different'! Small, rather portly, completely non-athletic, with a florid complexion and permanently irascible, he was the antithesis of the popular image of the dashing young fighter pilot.

My first flight commander, during the several summer months I served with him, I never once saw 'Boozy' laugh or even raise a smile. He always gave the impression of disliking everyone on sight, so that it was a complete surprise for me to discover later that he could be a very kind and generous man.

As is described earlier in this book, he introduced me to low-winged monoplanes and to my first Spitfire, making no effort to conceal the fact that he thought me pretty ordinary stuff and that I might not meet the required standard.

Although our relations improved after I had flown fairly intensively and without an accident over the following seven weeks, when he was suddenly promoted and posted away in early July, I did not exactly burst into tears.

Kellett went on to command No. 303 Polish Squadron, flying from Northolt, and did wonderfully well with them, moving on to No. 96 Night Fighter Squadron at the end of the Battle of Britain. Later still, after a further promotion, he joined us at RAF North Weald, taking up the new appointment of Wing Commander Flying.

At that point, a rather extraordinary development. A few days after his arrival, I informed him that I intended leading a high-level offensive sortie of six aircraft of 249 Squadron over France. When I invited him to take part, he agreed but elected to fly, not as leader but as the tail-end weaver.

When we reached our patrol-line in France, our six aircraft were at 33,000 feet, where the temperature was minus 65 degrees Centigrade. However, 'Boozy', in the seventh aircraft, and for reasons of his own, decided to fly above us at 34,000 feet.

After less than an hour, the cold was such that we were all 'fit to die' – the Hurricane had holes everywhere around the cockpit and possessed no heating of any kind – and only began to thaw out when we were back on the ground almost two hours later.

Expecting 'Boozy' to turn up at the debriefing, I was somewhat surprised to learn that after landing, he had gone straight to sick-quarters – and after that to hospital! So affected was he by the cripplingly low temperature, we never saw him again, and as far as I am aware, ours was the last operational flight he ever made.

I met him once in 1942 when he was a staff officer in the Air Ministry and I had just returned from Malta, but lost sight of him for the remainder of the War. Later still, I learned that he had retired from the Air Force in 1945 and had gone back to stock-broking in the City.

Fifty-odd years after, I was very surprised to receive a communication from a married daughter of his who lives not far from me in Norfolk. Apparently, 'Boozy' had read my book, *Gun Button to Fire*, and, delighted with what he described as 'my kind remarks' about him, had asked that I visit him to discuss 'old times'.

Driving south, I found him living alone in a small village on the Kent/ Sussex border. Very much the 'Boozy' I remembered him to be, he had mellowed a little – but not very much!

After pressing on me a number of very stiff gins, he took me to lunch at the local pub and insisted that I join him in a large meal of liver and bacon – much of which neither he nor I were able to eat. In the tap room, whose walls displayed pictures of him as a wartime hero, he seemed just an elderly and rather lonely old gentleman, although a nearby daughter apparently looked after him more than adequately.

Finally, after an interval of many months, I heard, very sadly, that he had died in 1998. He was eighty-nine.

A strange, unusual man, he served his country well.

Flight Lieutenant/Squadron Leader R.A. Barton

'Butch' Barton, in my view, was one of the best RAF fighter pilots of the Second World War. Which was surprising, as he did not look or sound like a hero.

A Canadian from British Columbia, who joined the RAF on a four year short service commission in 1936, he was small, had little dress sense, could never be described as eloquent, and his hand-writing looked like the trail of a fly with ink on its feet, crawling across an empty page. Moreover, and to my personal distaste, he smoked vile-smelling Canadian cigarettes called 'Sweet Caporals'. In short, although never in the slightest degree objectionable, he was not a particularly appealing young man.

Formerly with 41 Squadron, he joined 249 as a flight commander in May 1940. Later, in November 1940, when, somewhat to *his* surprise, he was appointed squadron commander, he became transformed. He was brave and calculating in battle and, like many Canadians, was an excellent shot, both with a twelve-bore shotgun and a Hurricane's eight Browning machine guns.

Always calm and fearless in the air he was a determined, self-effacing leader, who, after being shot down several times in September 1940 and obliged to use his parachute, was finally credited with about eight victories during the Battle of Britain and another eight during the squadron's difficult period in Malta, when the unit was obliged to defend the island with poorly maintained and obsolete Mark I Hurricanes.

Halfway through his tour of duty in Malta, he survived an engine failure on take-off and a nasty crash in which he was injured and also disfigured by battery acid.

It was at this point, I believe, he felt the time had come to take a long rest. He had been on operational flying since September 1939, and his old enthusiasms seemed to have ebbed away.

Back in England, he was first with the Spitfire OTU at Aston Down in Gloucestershire, before moving up to Grangemouth in Scotland, where we met from time to time and yarned endlessly about how we were going to change the world when the war ended.

In 1945, when the fighting finally came to a halt, 'Butch' remained in the Air Force for a time in a non-flying capacity but retired in 1959 and went back to Canada in 1965.

Later, after his wife Gwen had died, he married for a second time – a New Zealand lady – and for a period travelled to and fro between Canada and New Zealand.

Hearing that he had at last settled down in British Columbia, I wrote to him seven or eight years ago, promising to visit him when next I was passing through Vancouver. Surprisingly, he replied in his barely decipherable hand writing, explaining that he was now something of a hermit and spending much of his life fishing in the mountainous interior of British Columbia. When the opportunity finally arose, however, I found myself unable to make such a long journey and was obliged to call the visit off.

For a long time, I did not have news of him, but have since learned that he died in 2010. So splendid a warrior, I am unhappy that he is given so little credit for his considerable contribution to 249's success during the Battle of Britain and beyond.

Flight Lieutenant James Nicolson

Nicolson became flight commander of 'A' Flight, 249 Squadron, when 'Boozy' Kellett left in mid-July 1940.

I was delighted with his elevation as 'Nick' was a close friend of mine and, at twenty-three, only three years old than me. However, his seniority did not prevent him taking full advantage of our close relationship, as, through him, I was involved in a several 'playful' air incidents, as the result of which I found myself incarcerated as Duty Pilot in Flying Control – as Air Traffic Control was then called.

'Nick', a self-confessed expert on pretty well everything, was an endless talker and mimic, causing some of us to speculate that one day he would become a politician, as indeed he was invited to consider in later years – the Nicolson family had literary and political connections.

When on 16 September 1940, flying from Boscombe Down and in his very first engagement with the enemy, he was shot down and badly burned, being awarded the Victoria Cross the following November, which came as big a surprise to him as it was to us. Indeed, his wife Muriel several times confided in me that 'Nick' spent the rest of his life trying to live up to the honour he had been so surprisingly gifted.

I saw him from to time in England but lost touch with him later when he was posted to Burma. There, he did well on Mosquitos and was awarded the DFC.

In the early spring of 1945, I met him again when he was a Wing Commander in Eastern Air Command, a mixed British and American Headquarters on the outskirts of Calcutta. I was on my way to Burma and we had a riotous weekend together, during which he was his old very noisy but appealing self, telling enormous 'whoppers' and keeping his American colleagues vastly amused.

It was during my brief stay with him that he mentioned that he was under 'a bit of a cloud', having been involved in a road accident in which an Indian civilian had been killed. Anxious to 'get out of the way' – to quote his own expression – it seems that he may have volunteered to fly as a supernumerary member of crew on a Liberator of 355 Squadron, engaged on a bombing mission.

Over the Bay of Bengal and about an hour into the flight, an engine caught fire, the aircraft was ditched and Nicolson was lost, only two of the crew surviving.

I kept in touch with Muriel his wife for many years until she finally died quite recently. She would never reveal her age but it appears she was about 100 years old when she passed away. Very sadly too, their only son was also killed in a road accident when in the prime of life.

'Nick' was a most likeable, even-tempered and capable officer – a very bright star which suddenly went out!

Flight Lieutenant Denis Parnall

Denis Parnall assumed command of 'A' Flight, 249 Squadron, when Nicolson was posted away.

Despite first meeting him in 1938, when I was in the Volunteer Reserve and he was Personal Assistant to a visiting Air Marshal, when he was finally lost in September 1940, I probably knew less about him than of any of my 249 Squadron colleagues.

Denis was a very handsome young man and having been through Cambridge University before the war, would probably have ascended to higher things in the Air Force had he been spared. The fairly affluent Parnall family were part of the well known Parnall Aviation Company, which produced the Parnall Plover and other similar aircraft during the 1920s and Denis, although with a permanent commission in the General Duties branch of the RAF, had studied engineering.

During the early weeks of the Battle of Britain he was fairly successful and had claimed, in part, several victories. In our dispersal hut, he occupied the bed next to mine and I remember him as a slightly older, well organized, but slightly aloof young officer who was very earnest about all aspects of his job as flight commander.

Around noon on 18 September, Denis was part of our full squadron, who had taken off to intercept a major enemy formation approaching from the area of Deal, north of Dover.

After successfully meeting the enemy in the Canterbury area of Kent, we took our toll of the invading formation of Heinkel 111s and returned to North Weald, dispersed and in sections, but reasonably content – to find Denis Parnall missing! Apparently, with his Hurricane giving trouble, he had returned to the airfield but had taken off again shortly after, intending to join up with the rest of us in the air. Sadly, he never made contact.

For several days there was no news of him. Then, fragments of a Hurricane were discovered fairly close to North Weald, the aircraft having totally disintegrated and only identifiable by the numbers on its Browning guns.

The Hurricane having 'gone in' at high speed, the pilot's body parts were strewn over several fields. Initially, the human remains were gathered up and interred in the local cemetery at North Weald. Later, however, they were taken down to the north coast of Cornwall, where, having been identified as belonging to Denis, they were re-interred beneath a memorial erected by the Parnall family.

For years there was no answer as to how, or why, Denis's aircraft should have been lost so close to North Weald – our main engagement had been miles to the south over central Kent, and German Me 109s seldom ventured north of the Thames.

Then, a breakthrough! A local youth, by this time having grown into manhood, had reported that, on 18 September 1940, he had witnessed a battle right above him, in which a Hurricane had been shot down by German fighters. He remembered seeing the bullet holes in small bits of the Hurricane wreckage, and had helped collect the pilot's remains from several fields close to Kelvedon Hatch.

More than fifty years later, a great-nephew of Denis's – himself a Cornwall solicitor – contacted with me with a request that he might visit and have me read some letters and records belonging to Denis and his brother, the latter having also died. Could I cast any light on Denis's death and which records belonged to whom?

We had a long and pleasant chat, and although I doubt that I helped him very much, I felt I was at least able to paint a picture of what actually occurred on that fatal day.

Pilot Officer John Beazley

John Beazley joined 249 Squadron within hours of me on 15 May 1940. The son of a High Court judge, he was an Oxford graduate and at about twenty-three years of age, was rather older than most of us. Always a reserved person, he had a great, if quiet sense of humour and an attractive chuckle.

John was among the first of the squadron to claim shared victories when at Leconfield, Yorkshire, and later when flying from Boscombe Down. He was also involved in the first interceptions from North Weald but was soon shot down over Kent, taking to his parachute but landing unharmed.

He did not fare so well on 27 September, however, when he, with the rest of the squadron, intercepted about a dozen twin-engined Me 110s in the area of Gatwick. Initially in a defensive circle, the German fighters suddenly broke ranks and dived to ground level in an attempt to escape.

At this point, at tree-top height and in close pursuit of one Me 110, I became aware of a second Hurricane immediately to my left. I recall very clearly, instinctively ducking as tracer from the rear gunner flew towards my face and then observing the other Hurricane suddenly pull away and disappear. Following the then severely damaged enemy aircraft on my own, I also had to break off soon after when a massive oil leak obliged me to make an emergency landing at Detling.

Landing back at North Weald later in the day, I learned that the second Hurricane had been that of John Beazley, that he been hit and nastily wounded in the foot, and been taken off to hospital.

John was able to rejoin the squadron some months later and fly with the rest of us to Malta. There, like every other member of 249, he had to suffer the indignity of being obliged to fly outdated Hurricanes for a period of nine months and finally witness his squadron being totally outclassed and outfought by the Luftwaffe.

With most of the original members of 249 drifting away towards the end of 1941, John remained to command the squadron for a few weeks in early 1942, before being posted to the Middle East on 16 February, finally completing his stint of overseas service in Egypt, Libya and Sudan. Then, after returning to the United Kingdom in 1944, he served with 89 Squadron, flew Beaufighters, and eventually left the service in 1946.

John spent the first years of civilian life in 'shipping' – the Beazley family had shipping interests – after which he joined the Colonial Office and, with his charming new wife, went to Nigeria where he worked as 'Administrator' for some twelve years, rising eventually to the senior rank of 'Resident'.

Back in Britain, he took up accountancy and applied his new skills to various worthy causes besides earning himself an honest crust, at the same time raising a family and setting up home in Hertfordshire.

Our paths did not cross for many years following the end of the war, so that when we did meet again, I found him far less than the virile person he once was. However, in 2011, aged ninety-four, yet still with an active mind, his failing eyesight caused him great difficulties and physical problems became a formidable burden. Finally, life became insupportable and he died that year, with his lovely wife, Mary, dying in 2013. It is also a sad fact that, unbeknown to me until quite recently, all his life John had recurring nightmares of fire in the cockpit of his aircraft, and his wounded foot caused problems until his final hours.

A most gallant and pleasant friend for seventy years, a picture I will always retain in my mind's eye is of him, fully dressed and with shoes on, lying on his bed in dispersal at North Weald, quietly engrossed in an improving book, and smoking the most revolting pipe I had ever seen.

Pilot Officer George Barclay

George Barclay, a clergyman's son and about a year older than me, was a Cambridge undergraduate and one of the young men 'collected' by John Grandy.

Tall, dark and handsome, George was somewhat noisy in a 'frightfully decent' way – when George Barclay was in the room everyone knew about it! Moreover, I always felt him to be a trifle overly ambitious and, in my opinion, just a little bit odd! I am sure, however, that had the fates been kinder to him, he would certainly have prospered in the Air Force.

Joining 249 in mid-June 1940, George was an enthusiastic fighter pilot, if a little accident prone. Quite successful in the early weeks of September, he was shot down in the latter part of the month but made a successful crash-landing.

During the following weeks he and I flew together many times, sometimes as a pair, at other times as members of the complete squadron. Unusually distinctive when flying, he always sat low-down in the cockpit and habitually 'peeped' above his cockpit coaming. He mostly insisted, too, on flying with his hood open, until the added threat of it encouraging fire in the cockpit made him change his mind.

In November, he was shot down yet again, this time being both wounded and burnt. After taking to his parachute, he spent several months recovering and did not return to 249, being posted instead to the new OTU at Debden.

249 Squadron having moved meanwhile to Malta, George was made a flight commander in No. 611 Squadron, then based at Hornchurch, and was again shot down when flying a Mark V Spitfire over France. On that occasion, he managed to avoid being picked up immediately by the Germans and, with the aid of the French Escape Organization, made his way back to England after a long and difficult journey through France and Spain.

It was when I had returned from Malta in the early summer of 1942, that I met him again. This time he was in high spirits as he was in process of taking No. 601 Squadron to the Middle East – among the first Spitfire units to be employed in the Western Desert area.

I heard later that he had, in fact, sailed first to West Africa, then flown his squadron across Central Africa to Egypt, where he was in the act of finishing off their final training before leading them into battle. However, he was suddenly summoned to Cairo and instructed to leave 601 and take over No. 238 Squadron, then equipped with outdated Hurricanes.

Deeply unhappy about this new arrangement, he did so in early July 1942 and, on 17 July, was shot down and killed over El Alamein.

In 1958, I was back again at RAF North Weald as a Wing Commander when

I was invited to visit the Barclay family at their home in Hertfordshire. There I was asked by George's father to read a mass of George's letters and diaries and give an opinion as to whether or not they were worth publishing. After studying them for many hours, I decided that they were, although needing editing. Hearing little more about my suggestion, I was a little surprised when a book was published many years later entitled *Fighter Pilot – A Self Portrait by George Barclay* – which was indeed an edited version of his recorded thoughts.

When I remember George Barclay, in my mind's eye I see him enthusiastic in all things, noisy in a refined way, always vehemently expressing a point of view – and, heavily into tobacco at the time, constantly puffing away at his small student pipe, one of his most treasured possessions.

Much more recently, I asked a friend visiting Egypt to find George's grave in the War Cemetery at El Alamein. He did so and I now have a photograph of his headstone in my study and a small phial of desert sand from his burial site.

A sad end for so gifted a young man. Was his sudden transfer to 238 Squadron the result of some underhand conspiracy and the cause of his death? It has since been rumoured that it might well have been.

Pilot Officer Bryan Meaker

Bryan Meaker came from southern Ireland and joined 249 in late June 1940. Slight in stature and always quiet and smiling, Bryan gave no hint that he might develop into a most determined and capable fight pilot. He was about a year older than me but gave me the impression of being rather younger. He and 'Butch' Barton became great friends and enjoyed flying together.

Meaker did especially well during the last weeks of August 1940 and into September, and was one of the first of 249 to be decorated with the DFC after being credited with the destruction of at least seven enemy aircraft.

His success continued on the morning of 27 September, when he claimed his final victory, an Me 110 fighter in the area of Reigate, Sussex.

During the afternoon of the same day and a member of the whole squadron, he took part in an attack on a large force of Ju 88 bombers in the area immediately south of Maidstone in Kent.

It was an engagement I was to remember all too well as I briefly recall recognizing his aircraft flying within yards of me on my left, as I opened fire on a bomber on the right of a formation of about six.

I remember, too, twisting lines of tracer coming in our direction from the rear ends of the Ju 88s and almost immediately becoming aware of the Hurricane beside me falling away and disappearing. Thereafter, I had problems of my own and did not see or hear of Bryan or his aircraft until some hours later when we were attempting to piece together the events of a very dramatic afternoon.

The news was distressing. Several other squadron members had seen a Hurricane fall back during our attack, after which a parachute was seen to develop but become entangled in the tail of the aircraft, dragging the pilot downwards and, it was presumed, to a horrible death.

Much later, it was confirmed that Bryan Meaker had, indeed, fallen to his death near a village called Dallington, and, later, that he was buried at West Dean Cemetery, Sussex. But it was nearly fifty years after, that a memorial was placed on the spot where he fell.

Poor unfortunate Bryan. A tragic way to die for such a brave and capable young man.

Pilot Officer Percy Burton

Percy Burton at twenty-three was older than he looked. Born and brought up in South Africa, he was the son of a prominent Government Minister and a member of a family which, although always prepared to extol the glories of their homeland, vehemently affirmed their British connection and considered themselves above all else to be King George's loyal subjects. Small and slight in stature, amusingly off-hand, and constantly smoking the inevitable student pipe, he was at Oxford studying for his doctorate in jurisprudence when he was caught up by war. Another of John Grandy's 'collection' of selected officers, he joined 249 in July 1940.

I have no clear recollection of Percy's involvement in the squadron's daily activities, except to recall that he was flying alongside me when we watched helplessly from a height of 14,000 feet, our airfield at North Weald being heavily bombed on 3 September. Other than on that particular occasion, for me, he was merely one of the newer officers who occupied one of the two rows of beds in our dispersal hut.

However, for him, 27 September was a day of tragedy. With the rest of us in 249, he had attacked a formation of twin-engined Me 110 fighters at around 15,000 feet in the area of Gatwick and had followed one down to ground level as it strove to escape. Thereafter, during a running engagement over a distance of about forty miles, he had apparently been severely wounded and, it was later alleged, anticipating his own death, had then rammed the enemy fighter in a final act of defiance, causing both aircraft to crash near the Sussex village of Hailsham, bringing about his own death and that of the German crew of two.

The local population, having witnessed the drama at ground level, were loud in their praise of Percy's heroism, not only for destroying the German aircraft but also for his selfless act in deliberately preventing the devastation of their village.

Later, on the basis of their recommendation and the reports of other witnesses, his name was put forward for the award of the Victoria Cross, an honour that was rejected when, some six months later and to the disgust of all of us in 249, Percy was eventually granted a 'Mention in Despatches'.

Some fifty years later, during a visit to South Africa, I met Percy's sister, a tiny, bird-like lady of ninety-two who, as active and as bright as a wren, informed me that she had visited her brother's final resting place in Tangmere, Sussex and had met many of the villagers of Hailsham in whose arms he had finally died.

After our meeting, and still stoutly averring her devotion to Britain, she drove off in her small car in the proverbial cloud of dust – only for me to learn a month later that she had been killed in a road accident when her car, standing at a red traffic-light, had been shunted into the path of a line of oncoming vehicles.

Such a loyal and splendid family. So tragic a series of events. And so shameful an official misinterpretation of protocol that denied a gallant young man his rightful place in history.

Pilot Officer Robert Fleming

Robert 'Boost' Fleming, was barely twenty years of age when he joined us in 249 Squadron during the last week of July 1940. An undergraduate at London University and a member of the University Air Squadron – of which

John Grandy was then the Adjutant and Chief Flying Instructor – he became an obvious choice for his future squadron commander.

Small, gentle and unfailingly polite, Fleming always reminded me of a sixteen-year-old choirboy, an appearance greatly at odds with his nickname 'Boost', which arose from his predilection for noisy, high-speed flights in a Spitfire during his training at OTU. However, as we were members of different flights in 249, I was never given the opportunity to know him intimately, although we flew together regularly when the squadron operated as a single formation.

Sadly, the events of 7 September were to bring about a minor disaster within the squadron as a whole and the horrifying termination of his short career.

At about noon on that day, 249 intercepted a large formation of Dornier 17s over Kent and in the act of engaging the bombers from the rear, were themselves attacked from behind by escorting Me 109 fighters. Within minutes seven Hurricanes out of twelve had been shot down or severely damaged, several of them in flames.

Fleming, his aircraft on fire, had baled out successfully in the area of Maidstone but was seen by other squadron members running around on the ground, attempting to beat out flames from his blazing clothing, a picture which to some of us not involved in the affair and possessing the type of gallows humour peculiar to the young, resembled little more than a Laurel and Hardy pantomime joke.

Sadly, it was no joke as the young and gentle 'Boost' Fleming collapsed soon after and died from burns and shock.

My logbook shows that I flew against the enemy four times that day and that the squadron finished up with five serviceable aircraft out of an established strength of eighteen.

And as one who admits to being amused – if only faintly – having been told of 'Boost's' tragic incident, I have spent my life regretting the fact that I so lightly and unfeelingly regarded the death of a colleague in such horrible circumstances.

Pilot Officer Patrick Wells

Pat Wells, although from a fairly affluent Midlands brewing family and educated at Bedford School, was mainly raised in South Africa. Later he studied mining engineering at London University and joined the University Air Squadron. There he met and was instructed by John Grandy, who was instrumental in his joining 249 Squadron in July 1940.

A few years older than me, he was shot down on 7 September over Kent and taken to Faversham hospital, where he recovered sufficiently to rejoin the squadron several months later, only to be shot down again in November, this time being injured and burnt quite badly, by no less a person than Adolf Galland, the celebrated Luftwaffe pilot.

After recovering in East Grinstead hospital, where he underwent extensive plastic surgery, he returned to 249 in time to accompany the squadron when it left for the Middle East by aircraft carrier in May 1941.

In Malta, Pat had not even taken off from the airfield of Ta Kali, on the squadron's first flight in anger, when a small section of three Me 109s, based in Sicily, carried out a strafing attack and destroyed, or seriously damaged, five of the nine Hurricanes standing at Readiness. Hit nastily in the foot by a cannon shell, Pat was carted off to hospital and although declared fit enough to fly in early August, did not take an active part in the squadron's affairs and was posted to the Middle East in September.

For the next several years, he instructed at the fighter OTU at Khartoum and served in Nos. 73 and 255 Squadrons in Libya and Italy, before returning to the United Kingdom and converting to Beaufighters, having, meanwhile, been decorated with the DSO.

Pat left the Service in 1946 and for a time tried his hand in the brewing industry, toyed with mining in both South Africa and Cornwall, and finally settled into the aircraft consultancy business in South Africa.

After he left Malta in 1941, I did not come across him for many years, although I had news of him from time to time. However, we were thrown together by chance in the late 1980s, since when we became close friends throughout his remaining years.

I met his wife and him in South Africa, where he lived in some opulence at Constantia, near Cape Town, and he stayed with my wife and me in Norfolk several times in the late 1990s, on which occasions, having learned that he had been shot down by Adolf Galland in 1940, he used my Norfolk home as a base before making annual trips to Germany as Galland's guest.

Pat was a complex and, in some respects, a sad man. As brave as a lion in the air, he was plagued by uncertainties and fears for much of his life after the war. He seldom saw his two children, who lived abroad, and when his wife, Jessica, died he seemed to descend into something of a depression.

Pat died in South Africa in 2002, aged eighty-five. A brave but complicated person, he served his country well and I miss him.

Pilot Officer Terence Crossey

'Ozzie' Crossey – 'Ozzie' because he habitually wore a black, roll-necked jersey beneath his flying overall, in the manner of Sir Oswald Moseley – was a South African short-service officer who joined No. 249 Squadron in early June 1940.

About two years older than me, he was a quiet, well-organized young man, who seldom had much to say for himself, seemed for ever on the periphery of things, but always knew what was going on. A colleague later described him as, 'never doing very much, but always doing it very well!'

Never a spectacular achiever, James Terence Crossey flew regularly and without complaint throughout the entire Battle of Britain, being damaged in his Hurricane several times and notching up a few shared victories.

With his bed in our dispersal hut situated just across the room from mine, I see him even now in my mind's eye, opening his slim, gold cigarette case, decorated with an etched outline map of England, and tidily extracting a cigarette which he always lit and smoked with consummate care.

In the officers' mess, he invariably beat me at snooker, and when playing 'L'Attaque' or 'Totopoly', concentrated on every game with the same quiet attention to detail he applied to the business of flying his Hurricane.

In Malta, we shared a bedroom and flew our outclassed Hurricanes together for eight rather trying months, neither of us achieving very much but staying alive.

Towards the end of our time together at Ta Kali, it seemed to me that he went carefully through the process of selecting an attractive young Maltese lady of substance, marrying her, and then being posted to the Middle East in February 1942, moving on almost immediately from there to South Africa where he served for several years as a flying instructor.

In 1945, on my way to Burma, I met him very briefly when he was passing through India. Apparently he had been flying Dakotas from squadrons based in Egypt and Burma and was returning to England.

After that, it appears he left the Service in 1946 and returned to Malta where he became a leading figure in Malta Air Lines, an enterprise controlled by his Maltese father-in-law.

I met him and his wife several times in Malta in the 1970s and 1980s. With a growing family of two he was living with his wife in Rabat and clearly very prosperous. So it was very sad to hear that in the mid 1980s, having gone into hospital for no more than a check up, he had apparently collapsed and died.

'Ozzie' Crossey was a good friend. We flew together regularly in battle for almost two years. He was always around. He never let me down.

Pilot Officer Gerald Lewis

Gerald Lewis was another South African, a short-service officer who came to 249 in September 1940. A splendid looking young man, he was 6ft 3in, had a mop of flaxen hair and a very engaging grin.

He had also been very successful during the early months of the war, serving in France with No. 85 Squadron and earning a DFC after being credited with the destruction of at least five enemy aircraft and himself being shot down, though uninjured.

Continuing his good work with 249, he claimed another nine enemy aircraft before he was again shot down on 28 September, this time baling out after being badly burnt.

Recovering in Faversham Hospital, he rejoined 249 in January 1941 and, having being awarded a bar to his DFC, he joined my own flight and flew with me on several offensive sorties over France.

On 10 February, 249 Squadron was acting as high cover to a bomber attack on Dunkirk, with my own section of four, consisting of Lewis, Crossey and Davis, flying as rear-guard at 20,000 feet.

Over the target, we were attacked by a large force of Me 109s, Davis being shot down almost immediately and Lewis badly mauled. Landing back at North Weald, the cockpit of his aircraft a wreck, I found Gerald profoundly disturbed by the incident and unusually critical of the manner in which such sorties were being carried out. It was this engagement, I believe, that was a tipping point for him, as he never felt entirely comfortable on any such operation again.

When in April 1941, the squadron was told that it was to move to the Middle East, as a married officer, Lewis was informed that he would not be making the journey and that he would be posted to the new OTU then being formed at Debden. So, his departure from the squadron, sadly, was to be the last time I was ever to see him.

Although we only served together for about five months, I grew to be very fond of Gerald. A shy and retiring young man, he was never at ease in mixed company especially and, despite his splendid physique, seldom took part in any overt display of horseplay. Inordinately fond of his home country he would talk at length – usually after dinner in the mess – about the glories of South Africa and how important it was for me to emigrate to the Drakensburg mountains in Natal after the war.

Later, I was told by friends serving with him, how he had gradually lost confidence in himself and that he was then keen 'to get away from it all'. So that when he was posted to command No. 261 Squadron in 'out of the way' Ceylon, it must have come as a great relief.

But the fates were against him as he was to move east *into* trouble! Only weeks after arriving in Trincomalee, a Japanese carrier force attacked the island and he was shot down and wounded yet again, when in the act of taking off to intercept.

I believe he returned to the United Kingdom several months after the Ceylon incident, but I lost track of him until many years after the war. It was only in the 1990s, in fact, that Pat Wells informed me that earlier he had met Gerald in South Africa and that our late colleague had 'taken to religion in a big way', and was 'trying to convert everyone'.

I had long been aware that even before his arrival at North Weald, Gerald had married, but I never heard mention of any children. It came as a great surprise, therefore, when many years later, I learned that he had been a father to eight and that he and his wife had passed away in the 1980s. Whatever the size of his family, they could be proud of their father's achievements as he gave a great deal for Britain and also for South Africa.

Flying Officer Keith Lofts

Keith Lofts suddenly appeared in our midst during the second week in September, an ex-member of No. 615 Squadron, Auxiliary Air Force.

A nice enough young man – he was about two years older then me – I did not take to him a first as he seemed a little distant and, being an Auxiliary, I think most of us regarded him as slightly different and not exactly a member of the 249 family.

But he seemed enthusiastic enough and was obviously experienced, with several victories to his credit as the result of previous service in France. I flew with him several times as one of a pair and we operated together quite comfortably. Even so, when on the ground, I remember feeling that at North Weald he was altogether too close to the fleshpots of London as he did not mingle with the rest of us and we saw rather less of him around the ante-room of the officers' mess than might have been expected.

However, operationally, Keith performed very well throughout the remainder of September and October and, with Denis Parnall killed on 18 September and John Beazley wounded and put out of action on 27 September, he soon became flight commander of 'A' flight.

In mid-October he was hit by return fire when attacking a Dornier 215 over Kent, forcing him to crash-land his Hurricane at Tenterden. He was damaged once again when taking off from North Weald on 29 September, as a strong force of Me 109s carrying bombs carried out a major attack on the airfield.

In February 1941, Keith was posted away and joined the new OTU at Debden, several months before 249 Squadron left for the Middle East. Our paths parting at that point, I did not see anything of him until the end of the War, although snippets of information about his movements filtered through to me now and then.

In fact, it was not until 1948 that I encountered him once more, at which time he had left the RAF proper and was back again, this time commanding No. 604 Squadron RAuxAF. After that, I came across him from time to time, on several occasions meeting on our old airfield of North Weald.

Then, in 1951, came the unhappy news that he had been killed flying a Vampire jet, when practising for the Cooper Trophy Air Race – a low level 'round the pylons' event involving squadrons of the RAuxAF.

After that, not a word! Until, almost forty years later, when I received a communication from a close relative of his living not far from me in Norfolk, suggesting that I call on him to examine some of Keith's diaries and documents. I did so, and it was a revelation.

The young man I had regarded so suspiciously and with such little regard, was revealed in his writings to be a most patriotic, thoughtful and sensitive person, devoted passionately to the task he was engaged upon and his responsibilities as a officer.

And I had so misjudged him! I felt humbled and needing to apologize.

Pilot Officer Richard Wynn

'Dicky' Wynn joined us when we were at Church Fenton, Yorkshire, in early August. A handsome, powerfully built, delightful young man, he was the son of a serving senior officer in the RAF, and had been partially educated in America. He also turned out to be one of the most unfortunate pilots in 249.

Shortly after joining the squadron, he suffered an engine failure in his Hurricane when flying from Boscombe Down, necessitating a rather precarious force-landing. After which, having moved with us to North Weald, and being involved in one of the squadron's first major engagements over northern Kent, he was hit by return fire from a Dornier 215 bomber, the incoming bullets piercing the side of his windscreen and striking him in the neck.

Bleeding heavily and very seriously injured, he managed to crash-land his aircraft a little south and west of Canterbury, after which he spent three months recovering in Chartham hospital.

Around Christmas time 1940, Richard Wynn returned to the squadron and flew with me in 'B' Flight, which I then commanded, taking part as normal in most of the operations that came our way. Until 7 April 1941, that is!

It was on that day that we were engaged on a series of convoy patrols which had us flying in pairs up and down the east coast, escorting lines of ships sailing between Clacton and Southwold.

Leading a formation of six, on what I recall was a final 'showing the flag' exercise during the late afternoon, after spending ninety minutes in the air, we were returning to North Weald and preparing to land.

At which point, and approaching the village of Ongar some five miles away from the airfield, 'Dicky's' Hurricane just fell away from the formation and from 2,000 feet, dived straight into the ground, killing him instantly.

Discussing the accident immediately afterwards, no one could offer any explanation. There had been no hint of mechanical failure and not a word said on the RT. The only possible cause was that the old wound in his neck had suddenly opened up, bringing about an almost instant blackout and unconsciousness.

A sad and unexpected end to such a splendid young man.

Flying Officer Ewart Lohmeyer

Ewart Lohmeyer was not a pilot but the Adjutant in 249 Squadron. Although he did not fly, his contribution to the squadron's success was enormous.

Known as 'Loh', or 'the Adj', he was in his mid-forties when he arrived at Church Fenton in May 1940. Having served briefly in the RAF during the First World War, he wore an observer's brevet on his tunic and the ribbon of the DFC. He would admit, now and then, that he had flown in the back cockpit of a DH4 and had fired the rear gun occasionally and dropped a bomb or two. He was never heard to mention his decoration.

The 'Adj' was a great guiding influence on John Grandy, our first commanding officer, and a considerable help to me personally, without which I might not have lasted beyond my first weeks with 249 Squadron. He was also a significant factor in my being promoted to flight commander in November 1940.

Loh's calming influence and gentle guidance, together with his administrative skills, all helped to sustain the whole squadron when casualties and the strain of combat resulted in short tempers and occasional bouts of adolescent behaviour. In short, his contribution was enormous, so that when the squadron was ordered overseas in May 1941, there was deep and genuine regret that he would be obliged to leave us. However, for him it meant advancement and he did, indeed, go from strength to strength, being promoted and moving with distinction around the main stations of Fighter Command.

In civilian life, the 'Adj' was in 'Malaysian rubber' and had a successful business in the City. He lived, I remember, in Kingston-on-Thames, although I never knew much about his family.

In 1958, not having seen him for seventeen years, I telephoned him at his suburban home, as the result of which he invited me to his office in the 'golden mile'.

We met and after a glorious reunion and a considerable lunch, he guided me on a fascinating journey around the labyrinths of Dickensian London.

As we shook hands and parted, I sensed that we would never see each other again – which was indeed the case. Within days, I had left for America, and Ewart Lohmeyer would remain little more than a happy memory – of a man, his powerful influence in No. 249 Squadron, and his considerable contribution to our success.

The NCO Pilots of 249 Squadron

I have long felt that the NCO pilots engaged in the Battle of Britain were never given sufficient credit for their achievements.

This is perhaps understandable as it is an officer's duty to command and lead, resulting in their being at the forefront of any engagement, with the NCO pilots tending to follow from the rear of any formation, large or small, and be allowed their opportunity to shine when their senior colleagues were, for one reason or other, unsuccessful. Perhaps, somewhat ignobly, historians have long tended to laud their officer heroes but not those who were NCOs.

In any fighter squadron during the early summer of 1940, the ratio of officer aircrew to NCO pilots, was about 60:40. As the Battle proceeded, however, and the squadrons reinforced, the majority of new arrivals were from the Volunteer Reserve, who were largely NCOs, lacking in experience, and regarded by some officers-in-charge as slightly lesser mortals.

This differed from the situation earlier on when NCO pilots were drawn from the regular element of the Air Force and had gone through the tortuous business of advancing step by step through the ranks and selection at many levels.

These ex-regular airmen were very good indeed, and almost without exception did excellently, Frank Carey of 43 Squadron, James Hallowes of 41, and 'Taffy' Higginson of 56, being notable examples – among many others. Even so, they all started at the back, so to speak, before their experience and success took them to the front and enabled them to take the lead and eventually take command.

On the social front, too, there were undoubtedly differences early on. Officers and NCOs usually followed different life-styles, used different pubs and means of recreation in their off-duty hours, and generally did not mix except when on duty and in the dispersal huts. All this was done mostly without embarrassment, each group feeling more at ease in its own environment.

This, however, tended to disappear as the war progressed and Volunteer Reservists virtually took over the Air Force. Education requirements were largely the same for pre-war short-service commission candidates and for those applying to join the Volunteer Reserve. Moreover, most NCO pilots serving in the Battle of Britain, regular airman or Volunteer Reservist, were commissioned within a year or two thereafter, and the more obvious signs of segregation gradually disappeared. All of which was especially true in 249 Squadron.

Among those I served with in 249, the following are especially remembered.

Sergeant Richard Smithson

Sergeant Smithson was one of the first members of 249 Squadron when it formed at Church Fenton on 15 May 1940. Having joined the Air Force as an Air Mechanic in 1935, he had finally obtained pilot training and was one of three of us flying Hurricanes who intercepted the squadron's first enemy aircraft off the Yorkshire coast on 4 July.

A small, smiling boy, I remember him as quiet, disciplined and always willing to help. An able and agreeable colleague, we flew together many times, first in Spitfires then later in Hurricanes.

Later, at Boscombe Down and at North Weald he made his small contribution in his usual unobtrusive way but on 7 September, was one of seven squadron members who were shot down from behind by Me 109s when closely engaging a formation of Dornier bombers over Maidstone.

Badly injured and with an arm covered in blood – which he displayed to a colleague flying briefly alongside him – he crash-landed his Hurricane at

Eastchurch in Kent and spent more than a month recovering in hospital.

In mid-December, I well remember him arriving at dispersal to say goodbye, having been posted to 96 Squadron, the newly formed night fighter unit, then commanded by 'Boozy' Kellett and equipped with Hurricanes.

In July 1941, he apparently received a commission but, tragically, a few days later, was killed when flying a Hurricane.

For many years I did not hear anything of either him or his wider family. However, after a silence of more than sixty-nine years, I received a letter from a distant nephew living in the Newcastle area, asking for details of his service and accomplishments, together with a brief description of him as a person.

I was happy to oblige, describing him as a brave and splendid companion who met all his responsibilities courageously and in the most competent way possible.

Sergeant Frederick Killingback

Although he did nothing spectacular, Sergeant Killingback deserves a place in this story of 249 as, like Smithson, he joined the squadron early on and rose from being an Aircrafthand in 1935, to becoming a competent pilot on both Spitfires and Hurricanes.

We flew together many times throughout the summer and autumn of 1940 and he was one of the unfortunate pilots who was shot down and injured on 7 September, when 249 lost almost half its aircraft and pilots during one engagement. Baling out over Maidstone, in Kent, he spent some time in hospital and only returned to the squadron shortly before Christmas 1940.

I have no recollection of precisely what he did until the early spring of 1941, when I recall him being posted away, with others, first as a stand-in ferry-pilot, then to the OTU at Debden, where he became an instructor.

A quiet, friendly and diligent man, he was commissioned later in 1941 and, for me, he just disappeared into obscurity after being released from the Air Force in 1948.

Sergeant Harry Davidson

Davidson and I became good friends as early as 1938, when we trained together as student pilots in the Volunteer Reserve.

A 'Lancashire lad', with his broad northern accent, his machine-gun laugh, his bright blue eyes and his flashing white dentures, Harry Davidson became everyone's favourite in 249.

In the air he was more than just competent, as he was credited, wholly or in part, with about six enemy bombers and fighters while flying with me as one of a pair, in my section, or finally in my flight when I was promoted. In fact, we flew together so often throughout much of that summer, autumn and winter of 1940, that I grew to feel totally dependent on him flying alongside, or behind me.

In March 1941, he was commissioned and it was only a little later that relations between us became a little strained. Believing, quite wrongly, that I had had a hand in 249 Squadron being ordered overseas, he became upset when being told that, as a married officer, he would not be flying with us and be posted away.

In the event, he did indeed leave 249 in April 1941 to join the newly formed Merchant Ship Flying Unit – referred to at the time as the Merchant Ship Suicide Unit – and it was at that point, very sadly, that we parted for ever.

Later, although flying with the MSFU and taking part in at least one desperate sortie out at sea, he survived the ordeal and moved on to No. 285 Anti Aircraft Cooperation Unit. And it was with them, unfortunately, that in October 1942, he was involved in a flying accident and was killed.

Born in 1915, Harry Davidson was twenty-seven when he died, and to this day, I have always had a suspicion that, in some minor way, I might have been responsible for his death.

Sergeant Charles Palliser

Palliser was stocky young man from the north-east. A year or so older than me, he joined 249 in late September 1940, having been with several other squadrons before arriving at North Weald, although only for short periods.

In 249, he soon began to make himself heard as he was a forthright young man, whom I christened 'Titch', because of his lack of inches. It was only very much later that I learned that he did not entirely approve of his new nickname.

He was immediately productive, with several victories and other shared successes in September and over the following weeks and months, his good fortune continuing into the New Year, although he fought a losing battle over the Channel coast with a formation of Me 109s on 5 December, and was obliged to force-land away from North Weald, damaged and short of fuel.

Commissioned in April 1941, and for ever wearing his new service dress hat at a jaunty angle, he continued to make his presence felt at North Weald and, with the rest of the squadron, set off in early May for the Middle East on the aircraft carriers HMS *Furious* and *Ark Royal*.

In Malta, where the squadron, en route for Egypt, came to an unplanned halt, he continued to be successful against the Italians, and, beyond November 1941, against the Luftwaffe.

After being awarded the DFC and being promoted to flight lieutenant, he left Malta in February 1942 and moved down to South Africa, where he served for some years as an instructor.

After returning briefly to the United Kingdom, and engaged once more on instruction duties, he was posted to Southern Rhodesia for a spell, before finally emigrating, with his new South African bride, to Australia.

After leaving Malta myself at the end of 1941, I did not see Charles Palliser again until we met briefly at a 249 Squadron reunion at North Weald in the 1990s.

Still his same old self, he had lost none of his power of speech, and looked very much the same, if a little bit sleeker.

A perky, confident young man, he was a courageous fighter pilot and made a splendid contribution to 249's success story over the years. Eventually, he lived in Australia with his wife and two daughters until his death in 2011.

Sergeant John Beard

John Bentley Beard was a year or two older than me and among the first group of pilots to join 249 Squadron in May 1940. A quiet retiring person, he had been in the Volunteer Reserve for some years before the war started and always gave me the impression of being more experienced that the rest of us, having been with 609 Squadron since December 1939.

With 249, he started well with about six victories in September 1940, achieving minor fame, too, by being shot down by British anti-aircraft fire on 7 September. I well recall wearily climbing up alone between North Weald and London that day, and watching a parachute float past my wing at about 8,000 feet, little knowing that the person dangling at the end of it was John Beard.

He was also shot down over Kent by Me 109s on 25 October, and obliged to bale out. Nastily wounded, he spent some time recovering in Pembury Hospital before returning to the squadron in December, at which time he was delighted to discover that he had been commissioned.

John left 249 Squadron at the end of April and after a time at the OTU at Debden, moved on from there to the Central Gunnery School at Sutton Bridge in 1942.

Thereafter, he concentrated on teaching marksmanship and became something of a gunnery expert, both at Sutton Bridge and later at Catfoss, starting up various armament boards and test units in several parts of the country.

Already holding the DFC, he was awarded the Air Force Cross for his work in the armament field, after which he did various jobs at home and abroad before leaving the Air Force in 1946.

I did not meet him again for many years, until the Battle of Britain became fashionable again in the 1980s. After that, we began to meet now and then at various museum functions, displays and signings.

Always a quiet, smiling person, he never had much to say for himself, and over the years I watched, very sadly, the hands that were such a part of his expertise as a marksman, become distended and crippled by arthritis.

John Bentley Beard died in 2006 and 249 Squadron was much the more successful for his service with them.

Sergeant William Davis

I have long described Davis as a P.G. Wodehouse figure. Very tall and thin, and for ever smiling, he joined 249 in August and, with him being part of 'B'

Flight for some months, I saw him only from a distance.

He flew constantly during the heated combats of September but was shot down on 11 September when his aircraft was hit by return fire when attacking a formation of Heinkel 111s. Wounded and obliged to bale out when his aircraft caught fire, he landed at Benenden in Kent, where he spent some time in hospital.

I do not remember seeing much of him until he returned to the squadron and joined me in 'B' flight, which I then commanded.

Then, on 10 February 1941, I was leading the top cover section escorting a bomber formation of six Blenheims, attacking Dunkirk. My four, consisting of Lewis, Crossey and Davis, plus me, were intercepted over the target by a strong formation of Me 109s, and during the brief combat that followed, Lewis was badly damaged and Davis suddenly disappeared.

We knew nothing of his fate at first, but then discovered that he had been shot down and was a prisoner of war. Which was a minor tragedy for him as he had been told that very morning the he had been commissioned.

Which for me, of course, signalled the end of 'Bill' Davis – until about fifty years later, I received a letter from a relative, asking for details of his service with 249 and a description of his final flight.

Apparently Davis, who had come from the north Midlands area, had died in 1984, and the local community, like the family, were interested in the history of the engagement, and the manner of their hero's demise. All of which I was happy to provide.

I will always remember 'Bill' Davis as a delightful, smiling boy – and an unlucky one!

Sergeant George Stroud

I am bound to say that I never knew George Stroud very well during his time with 249 Squadron, but the incident over the Channel coast on 5 December 1940, in which he was principally involved, will always remain vividly in mind.

Stroud joined 249 in early September and I remember him as a small, rather untidy young man with a mop of tousled hair.

On 5 December, the whole squadron, under instruction, had paraded up and down the south coast in the general area of Dungeness. Kept up for far too long, we were becoming short of fuel and dangerously vulnerable, when we were attacked by a large force of Me 109s, who played us like fish, diving down then climbing away steeply when repulsed.

Moments later, when spiralling down in order to escape, I was suddenly overtaken by a Hurricane enveloped in a vivid ball of flame. Concerned that I might be the next victim, I dived away without discovering whose Hurricane it was.

Back at North Weald, we discovered the unhappy victim to be Sergeant Stroud, who, badly burnt, had baled out and been taken to hospital. Moreover, five other pilots had run out of fuel and been forced to crash-land their aircraft in various parts of Kent and Essex.

Returning to the squadron later, the next incident of moment for Stroud was, when planning for our flight from the aircraft carrier HMS *Furious*, that was to take us to the Middle East in May, we found there were too few aircraft available for the whole squadron. Unhappily for him, George then drew the short straw and had to make the long sea journey alone around South Africa.

After that, there was a gap of fifty years before I met him again. Engaged to give a series of talks in Lancashire, I came across him at Woodvale airfield, near Southport, where he was then involved in instructing some RAF Cadets.

I hardly recognized him. The tousled hair had been replaced by a splendid expanse of skin, and his features seemed strangely different, no doubt because of his burns.

But, he and his wife entertained me magnificently, showing me proudly around their immaculate house and garden. After which, his wife wrote to me regularly, keeping me abreast of family news.

Until suddenly, the letters ceased and the news reached me that she had unexpectedly died. As indeed did George, a year or two after.

A lovely pair. And such rich memories of ex-Sergeant Stroud.

Sergeant Alistair Main

I have left comments about Sergeant Main until the last, as his inclusion in this list of squadron colleagues is, to me, very important.

Of all the pilots in 249 Squadron, I probably knew less about him than about any other colleague. First, because he was with us for so brief a period. Second, because he was the first in the squadron to lose his life when flying on an operational sortie. And last, being killed on 15 July, for some unaccountable reason, he has never been granted the title, Battle of Britain pilot.

Although one of the first pilots to join us, at Church Fenton he was in 'B' flight and flew from the far side of the airfield. And because at the time we did not use a central dispersal hut, he and I seldom had the opportunity to meet or speak to each other.

Even so, he lives in my memory as someone sporting a large black moustache – very fashionable at the time – speaking with a Scottish accent, telling very amusing stories, and being pretty good at card games. All of which distinguishing details I only discovered after spending just a few hours with him on that night of 15 July.

It was on that occasion that six of us were programmed to take off into stygian blackness to counter an enemy bombing attack on Leeds, about which we had been warned by Sector Control. Sergeant 'Masher' Main was number four in line for take off and I, number five.

A little before preparing rather apprehensively to leave, I was standing outside in the darkness assessing the weather, when an enemy bomber droned overhead and dropped a mass of incendiaries. In the near distance, they all burst into a huge fireball of crimson flame before dying away to a muted glow, leading us to believe that the Hun overhead had aimed at us, but had missed.

A little later I took off and spent the most miserable two hours of my life, flying through absolute blackness, cloud and rain, before returning to base and landing.

Once again in our darkened dispersal hut, I was informed that the incendiaries most of us had seen dropped a mile or so away, were not enemy bombs but Sergeant Main crashing to his death.

Later, it was said that his Hurricane had suffered an engine failure, but I have always had my doubts. Rolls Royce Merlin engines seldom stopped without reason or warning, leading me to believe that 'Masher' Main had become disorientated in the darkness and had lost control.

He and I had spent less than three hours together before he had taken off and I have always regretted knowing so little about him when he died.

Within hours, his remains had been gathered up and taken to his home in Dundee where they were buried.

Abbreviated List

Some more perceptive readers may conclude that the names of some of my former colleague are missing from my list. This is true, and for several reasons.

The eventual movements of some, I simply do not remember. One or two others remained in the squadron for so short a time that their involvement is hardly worth recording. And several others still, are not included for reasons I shall simply describe as 'delicate and personal'.

Almost all, I imagine, are now dead, but if there are any relatives or friends offended by their non-inclusion, may I now apologize and explain that it is not because I harbour any malicious feelings towards them, but for one or more of the reasons I have already described.

Throughout the sixteen-week period of the Battle of Britain, there was a constant interchange of aircrew within the squadrons of Fighter Command, some pilots being disposed of because they were incompetent or unable to fit in, and a few who were considered better suited to other roles in the Air Force. Very few were totally discarded. Many just did better elsewhere.

Some Final Observations

When I first joined No. 249 Squadron, I was just nineteen years of age, and the Spitfires and Hurricanes I first flew in battle were, in my opinion, second to none.

Later, when somewhat older and with more experience, I came to the conclusion that both our aircraft and our tactics of the time, fell far short of being superior.

However, in the heat of combat, when there was usually no time to think, consider and adjust, errors and shortcomings were simply compounded, so that during the Battle of Britain, many pilots lost their lives because of poor or inadequate training and the bad design of their aircraft.

The Hurricane, for example, which is always lauded by the uninformed as uniquely 'the best', was indeed responsible during the Battle for the destruction of more enemy aircraft than all the Spitfires, anti-aircraft defences and any other method of defence combined. However, the aircraft itself was almost obsolete by the summer of 1940, and a downright handicap for all those who had the misfortune to fly it during 1941 and the years following.

Designed well before 1936 – and some would say, before 1930! – it was little more than an old Hawker Hart medium bomber without a top wing or fixed undercarriage, but with a somewhat larger engine. Furthermore, two of the three fuel tanks in the Hurricane were in such exposed positions left and right of the pilot's feet, that the fire risk was enormous, so that at least half the pilots flying Hurricanes, and considerably more than those flying Spitfires, were hideously burned when damaged in combat.

The early Spitfire, too, had its disadvantages, as both it and the Hurricane employed the Rolls Royce Merlin engine of only 27 litres capacity. Incorporating a carburettor, the engine would flood whenever the nose of the aircraft was suddenly depressed, resulting in a gush of black smoke emanating from the exhausts and engine power being shut off for several seconds.

The fire power, too, was sadly lacking in all our fighters, both the early Hurricane and Spitfire using eight rifle-calibre machine guns. Carrying less than fifteen seconds-worth of ammunition, the hitting power of all eight guns was often totally inadequate when attempting to bring down a well armed bomber, such as a Junkers 88, which frequently could absorb hundreds of bullets before being critically damaged.

The German Messerschmitt 109, on the other hand, was far less pleasant to fly and had its disadvantages, but it was a splendid aircraft, nevertheless. First, it mounted a much bigger engine – 39 litres – had a better supercharger, and a direct fuel-injection system rather than a carburettor, enabling it to put its nose down in a trice and dive away from any of our aircraft, or climb steeply clear if threatened.

In short, I believe the 109 to have been superior to the early Spitfire which, though marginally faster, had to work up speed in order to compete.

Moreover, being smaller than either the Hurricane or the Spitfire, the German aircraft could usually dictate tactics when engaged in fighter versus fighter combat, having, too, the enormous advantage of mounting two 20mm cannons in the wings, besides several machine guns in the fuselage and carrying twice as much ammunition as our own fighters.

Very interestingly, conversations with German fighter pilots who had fought against us at that time, have long revealed that even one or two hits with their explosive cannon ammunition was sufficient to bring down any of our fighters – or even our light bombers.

In short, our defending Spitfires and Hurricanes were less that perfect during the Battle of Britain, and many of my colleagues and friends were killed or damaged for life, because of their design and unfavourable performance, or because of other training deficiencies. How then did we ever win the Battle of Britain? If indeed we did win it!

My personal opinion, as one who was involved from first to last, is that we might now be allowed to regard it as something of a win, if only because Hitler, at the head of his magnificent, overwhelming army, was prevented from invading Britain because the RAF denied him the conditions enabling him to do so. There were many other factors involved, of course, not least Hitler's personality and beliefs, and, some would claim, the influence of Divine intervention.

Whatever the reason, had the Germans been allowed to invade on 15 September 1940, it is more than likely that they would have won, as the British Army at the time was a spent force, and not everyone in the United Kingdom was that keen to fight, despite Mr Churchill's rhetoric.

In one of his books the Prime Minister referred to 'The Hinge of Fate'. The Battle of Britain was indeed, such a 'Hinge'. Had 249 Squadron and other units in Fighter Command not prevailed, Europe and indeed the world, would now be a greatly different place.

Such thoughts, however, were never in my adolescent mind in 1940, as I was always confident that Britain and the RAF were indestructible. Moreover, never once in 249 Squadron, even when under the greatest stress, did I ever hear the word *defeat* ever mentioned.

Such was the spirit in 249. Great, too, were the sacrifices made by my long-dead colleagues and friends.

Battle of Britain Log Book

YEAR 1940	AIRCRAFT		2ND PILOT, PUPIL OR PASSENGER	DUTY (INCLUDING RESULTS AND REMARKS)	SINGLE-ENGINE AIRCRAFT				MULTI-ENGINE AIRCRAFT						PASS. ENGER	INSTR/CLOUD FLYING (incl. in cols. (1) to (10))	
MONTH DATE	Type	No.	PILOT, OR 1ST PILOT		DAY Dual (1)	DAY Pilot (2)	NIGHT Dual (3)	NIGHT Pilot (4)	Dual (5)	DAY 1st Pilot (6)	2nd Pilot (7)	Dual (8)	NIGHT 1st Pilot (9)	2nd Pilot (10)	(11)	Dual (12)	Pilot (13)
				TOTALS BROUGHT FORWARD	58.10	187.6	3.00	9.16							1.20	4.40	3.55
July 1	HURRICANE P3616		SELF	NIGHT FLYING TEST.		.35											
"	" P3616		SELF	FORMATION				1.00									
"	" P3616		SELF	PRACTICE ATTACKS				.50									
July 2	HURRICANE P3616		SELF	To LECONFIELD - BAD WEATHER		.20											
July 3	HURRICANE P3616		SELF	To LECONFIELD		1.30											
July 4	HURRICANE P3616		SELF	(o.P.) INTERCEPTION. DORNIER 17 (NO RESULT)		1.00		.40	SAW US ALMOST IMMEDIATELY AND DIVED BELOW OUR LESS INTO A CLOUD								
July 5	HURRICANE P3616		SELF	INTERCEPTION of (NO CONTACT)		.05											
"	" P3616		SELF	INTERCEPTION of (NO CONTACT)		.15											
					27.10 91.20 1.00												
July 6	HURRICANE P3616		SELF	NIGHT OPERATIONS (NO CONTACT)				1.16									
July 9	HURRICANE P3616		SELF	R.R. CO.O.		.60											
July 10	HURRICANE P3616		SELF	NIGHT FLYING TEST.		.10											
July 12	HURRICANE P3616		SELF	N.F.T.		.25											
July 15	HURRICANE P3616		SELF	N.F.T		.15											
15	" 2		SELF	NIGHT OPS. NO INTERCEPTION				1.25									
				TOTALS CARRIED FORWARD	58.10	193.10	3.00	12.35							1.20	4.40	3.55

GRAND TOTAL [Cols. (1) to (10)] .... Hrs. .... Mins.

The author's log book for 1-15 July 1940.

| YEAR | | AIRCRAFT | | PILOT, OR | 2ND PILOT, PUPIL | DUTY | SINGLE-ENGINE AIRCRAFT | | | | MULTI-ENGINE AIRCRAFT | | | | | | | PASS-ENGER | INSTR./CLOUD FLYING [Incl. in cols. (1) to (10)] | |
MONTH	DATE	Type	No.	1ST PILOT	OR PASSENGER	(INCLUDING RESULTS AND REMARKS)	DAY Dual (1)	DAY Pilot (2)	NIGHT Dual (3)	NIGHT Pilot (4)	DAY Dual (5)	DAY 1st Pilot (6)	DAY 2nd Pilot (7)	NIGHT Dual (8)	NIGHT 1st Pilot (9)	NIGHT 2nd Pilot (10)	(11)	Dual (12)	Pilot (13)
				—	—	TOTALS BROUGHT FORWARD	58.10	193		3.00	12.35							1.20	1.20	3.55
JULY	16	HURRICANE	P3616	SELF		To Sherburn		.10												
JULY	18	HURRICANE	P3865	SELF		LOW FLYING P.		1.00												
JULY	19	HURRICANE	P3616	SELF		CLOUD FLYING + PRACTICE		1.15												
JULY	21	HURRICANE	P3666	SELF		N.F.T		.25												
JULY	22	HURRICANE	P3660	SELF		A.A. COOP		.30												
JULY	24	HURRICANE	P3616	SELF		FORMATION + DOGFIGHTING		1.10												
	"	"	"	SELF		PATROL	58.10	177.2		.10										
JULY	27	HURRICANE	P3616	SELF		TO ACKLINGTON, RET. FOR BAD.W		.10												
	"	"	P3616	SELF		TO ACKLINGTON		.40												
	"	"	P3616	SELF		AIR FIRING		.35												
	"	"	P3616	SELF		AIR FIRING		.10												
JULY	29	HURRICANE	P3616	SELF		FROM. ACKLINGTON	58.10	1.00	13.45 und 3.00	13.45										
JULY	29	HURRICANE	P3616	SELF		FORMATION + FIGHTER ATTACKS		1.30												
JULY	30	HURRICANE	P3616	SELF		To Sherburn		.10												
						TOTALS CARRIED FORWARD	58.10	201.25	3.00	13.05							1.20	4.40	5.55

GRAND TOTAL [Cols. (1) to (10)] .... Hrs. .... Mins.

The author's log book for 16–30 July 1940.

| YEAR | | AIRCRAFT | | PILOT, OR 1ST PILOT | 2ND PILOT, PUPIL OR PASSENGER | DUTY (INCLUDING RESULTS AND REMARKS) | SINGLE-ENGINE AIRCRAFT | | | | MULTI-ENGINE AIRCRAFT | | | | | | PASS-ENGER | INSTR/CLOUD FLYING [incl. in cols. (1) to (10)] | |
MONTH	DATE	Type	No.				DAY Dual (1)	DAY Pilot (2)	NIGHT Dual (3)	NIGHT Pilot (4)	DAY Dual (5)	DAY 1st Pilot (6)	DAY 2nd Pilot (7)	NIGHT Dual (8)	NIGHT 1st Pilot (9)	NIGHT 2nd Pilot (10)	(11)	Dual (12)	Pilot (13)
						Totals Brought Forward	58.10	201.25	3.00	13.45							1.20	4.40	1.37
July	31	HURRICANE	P3616	SELF		To Church Fenton		.10											
"	"	"	"	SELF		N.F.T.		.20											
"	"	"	"	SELF		To Sherburn		.10									1.20	4.40	5.35
						SUMMARY FOR JULY 1940	58.10	202.05	3.00	13.05									
						UNIT — No 249 Sqn — 1 HURRICANE	14.50			4.35									
						DATE — 3 Aug 1940													
						SIGNATURE — Tom Neil													

D.G. Parnall
F/Lt
O.C. A FLIGHT

Tom Neil
P/O?
O.C. 249 SQN

GRAND TOTAL [Cols. (1) to (10)] .... Hrs. .... Mins.   TOTALS CARRIED FORWARD

The author's log book for 31 July 1940.

YEAR 1940		AIRCRAFT		2ND PILOT, PUPIL OR PASSENGER	PILOT, OR 1ST PILOT	DUTY (INCLUDING RESULTS AND REMARKS)	SINGLE-ENGINE AIRCRAFT				MULTI-ENGINE AIRCRAFT							PASS-ENGER	INSTR/CLOUD FLYING (Incl. in cols. (1) to (10))	
MONTH	DATE	Type	No.				DAY Dual (1)	DAY Pilot (2)	NIGHT Dual (3)	NIGHT Pilot (4)	DAY Dual (5)	DAY 2nd Pilot (6)	DAY 1st Pilot (7)	NIGHT Dual (8)	NIGHT 1st Pilot (9)	NIGHT 2nd Pilot (10)		(11)	Dual (12)	Pilot (13)
						TOTALS BROUGHT FORWARD	38.10	201.25	3.40	13.05								1.20	4.40	5.40
Aug	1	HURRICANE	P3616	—	SELF	To Church. Fenton.		.10												
Aug	2	MASTER	—	F/O. YOUNG	SELF	BLIND TAKE OFFS		1.25				HE TOOK OFF IN THE 12th HE LEFT FLAPS DOWN MY LAST FLIGHT			VERY NEARLY		
Aug	4	HURRICANE	P3616	—	SELF	FIGHTER ATTACKS		1.20												
Aug	"	"	P3616	—	SELF	To SHERBURN		.10												
Aug	5	HURRICANE	P3860	—	SELF	To G. FENTON		.10												
Aug	6	HURRICANE	P3860	—	SELF	DOG FIGHTING		.55												
Aug	8	HURRICANE	P3616	—	SELF	FIGHTER. ATTACKS		1.05												
Aug	"	"	P3616	—	SELF	"		1.15												
Aug	11	HURRICANE	P3616	—	SELF	CLOUD FLYING. AIR DRILL		.55												
"	"	"	3902	—	SELF	INTERCEPTION. PATROL. CONVOY		1.55												
						No. CONTACT WITH E.A.														
Aug	12	HURRICANE	P3616	—	SELF	R.T. AIR DRILL		1.00												
Aug	13	HURRICANE	P3616	—	SELF	To SHERBURN		.10												
Aug	14	HURRICANE	P3616	—	SELF	To BOSCOMBE DOWN.		1.15					CASTING ON LEAVE To				
Aug	15	"	P3861	—	SELF	SCRAMBLE. PATROL. BASE		.35				SAW 2 SEC ABOVE ras OF CLOUD Didn't recognise him				
Aug	15	HURRICANE	P3861	—	SELF	SCRAMBLE. A.FT PATROL WHYMILL No CONTACT		1.20				ad E.A.					
						TOTALS CARRIED FORWARD	38.10 215.05		3.40	13.05								1.20		

The author's log book for 1-15 August 1940.

The author's log book for 15–27 August 1940. Note remark on the 16th, 'Nick shot down', this refers to James Nicolson and the incident which earned him the only VC of the Battle of Britain.

YEAR 1940 MONTH	DATE	AIRCRAFT Type	No.	PILOT, OR 1ST PILOT	2ND PILOT, PUPIL OR PASSENGER	DUTY (INCLUDING RESULTS AND REMARKS)
						TOTALS BROUGHT FORWARD
SEPT	2	HURRICANE V7401		SELF	—	TO HENLOW
"	2	MAGISTER R1836		SELF	SGT SMITHSON	FROM HENLOW
"	3	HURRICANE	V7313	SELF	3	X. RAID — MY FIRST FIGHT. NEARLY DIED OF SHOCK. N. WEALD
"		"	"	SELF		X. RAID — HEAVILY BOMBED: AIR NOT FUN. WHOA GAINED.
"		"	V7313	SELF		X. RAID — WEAPON LOVED! ME 110's: VERY FIERCE
"	5	"	V7313	SELF		X. RAID — 2 ENG. AIRCRAFT SHOT E.A. OPEN FIRE GUN
"		"	V7313	SELF		X. RAID — WHO CARES? A/C ROUNDED SKY BY ME 109's.
"	6	"	V7313	SELF		X RAID — 1 Me 109 DESTROYED
"		"	V7313	SELF		X RAID — VICINITY MAIDSTONE 18000'
"	7	"	V7313	SELF		X RAID — GOT HIM IN BAYEUX; FINALLY MADE HIM JUMP OUT
"		"	V7313	SELF		X RAID
"		"	V7313	SELF		X RAID — WE LOST HALF SQUADRON. BOOST FLEMING.
"		"	V7313	SELF		X RAID — KILLED, WELLS KILLING-BECK, SMITHSON, GODFREY,
"		"	V7313	SELF		X RAID — BARTON SHOT DOWN. I WAS VERY, VERY SCARED.
"	9	"	V7313	SELF		X RAID — RESULTS NEGLIGIBLE
"		"	V7313	SELF		X RAID
"		"	V7313	SELF		X RAID
"		"	V7313	SELF		X RAID
"	12	"	V7313	SELF		X RAID — 1 Me 111 DESTROYED
"		"	V7313	SELF		X RAID
"		"	V7313	SELF		X RAID
"	14	"	V7313	SELF		X RAID
"		"	V7313	SELF		X RAID
"	15	"	V7313	SELF		X RAID — 1 Do 215 DESTROYED, 1 Do 215 DESTROYED, 2 Me 109 DESTROYED — STARTED OVER LONDON DOCKS. E/A CRASHED BY KINGLEY STATION 30 MILES SOUTH OF LONDON
"		"	V7303	SELF		X RAID
"		"	V7313	SELF		X RAID — 1 destr. 1 probable originally claimed 2 destr. Confirmed later would probably by Polish — over London at 15000
"	16	"	V6665	SELF		X RAID — Do. Se.

SINGLE-ENGINE AIRCRAFT				MULTI-ENGINE AIRCRAFT					PASS- ENGER	INSTR/CLOUD FLYING
DAY		NIGHT		DAY			NIGHT			
Dual (1)	Pilot (2)	Dual (3)	Pilot (4)	Dual (5)	1st Pilot (6)	2nd Pilot (7)	1st Pilot (8)	2nd Pilot (9)	(11)	(10)
68.10	266.30	1.00	13.00							5.038
	.15								1.20	2.00
	.15									
	1.05									
	.55									
	1.40									
	1.45									
	1.15									
	.55									
	1.20									
	.15									
	1.20									
	1.25									
	.45									
	1.35									
	1.20									
	1.35									
	.55									
	.15									
	1.00									
	1.03									
	1.10									
	1.10									
	1.20									
	1.25									
58.10	257.25	3.00	13.45						1.20	4.40 5.55

GRAND TOTAL [Cols. (1) to (10)] .... Hrs. .... Mins.

The author's log book for 2–16 September 1940. Note the swastikas, each denoting a 'kill'. 15 September 1940 was a critical date in the Battle of Britain. Two massive waves of German attacks were decisively repulsed by the RAF, with every single aircraft of 11 Group being used on that day. The total casualties on this critical day were 60 German and 26 RAF aircraft shot down. The author shot down 4 of this total. the German defeat caused Hitler to order, two days later, the postponement of preparations for the invasion of Britain. Henceforth, in the face of mounting losses in men, aircraft and the lack of adequate replacements, the Luftwaffe switched from daylight to night-time bombing.

The author's log book for 17-30 September 1940.

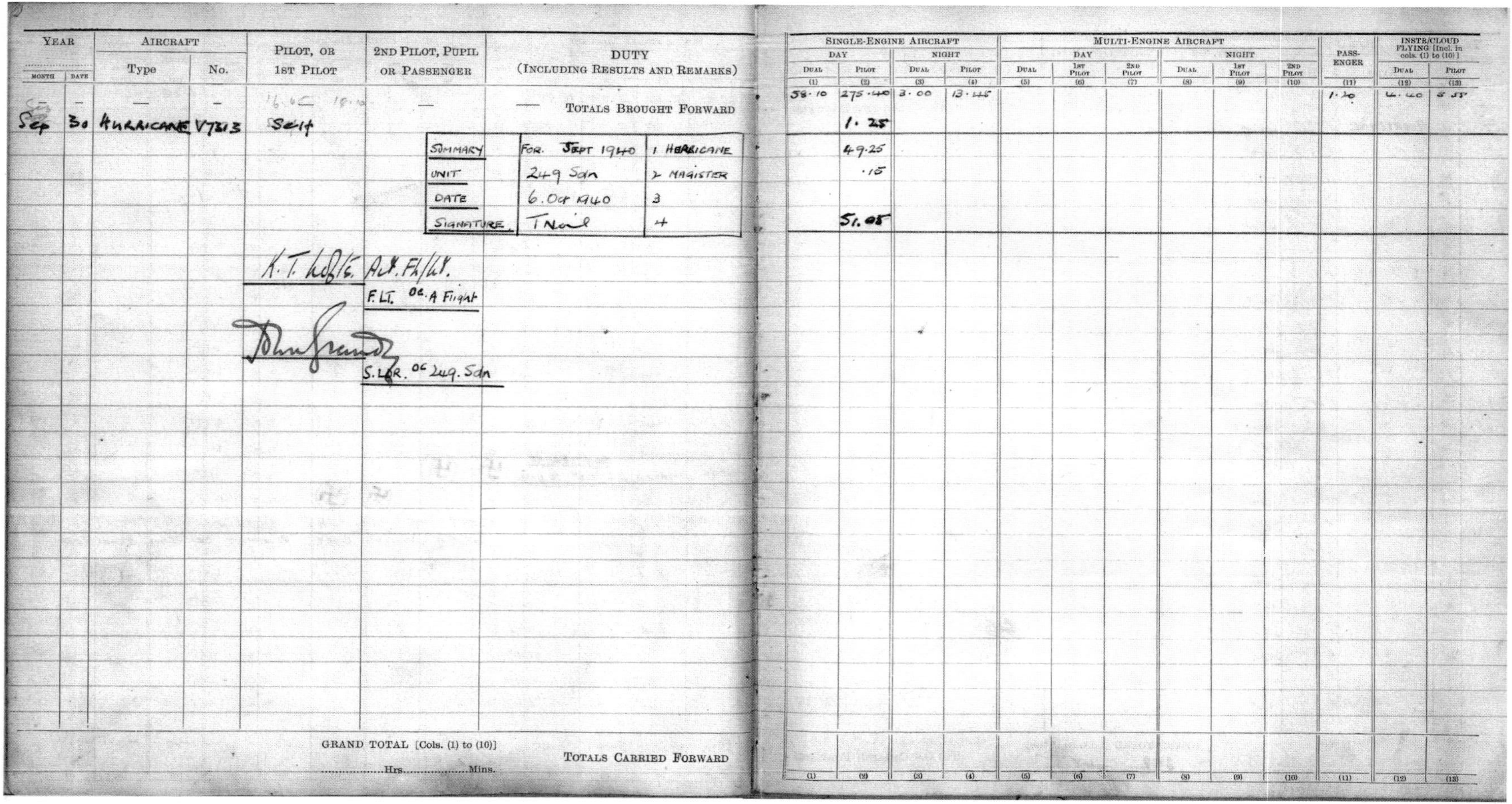

Year Month	Date	Aircraft Type	No.	Pilot, or 1st Pilot	2nd Pilot, Pupil or Passenger	Duty (Including Results and Remarks)
—	—	—	—	—	—	— Totals Brought Forward
Sep	30	Hurricane	V7313	Self		

Summary	For. Sept 1940	1 Hurricane
Unit	249 Sqn	2 Magister
Date	6. Oct 1940	3
Signature	T Neil	4

K. T. Lofts, Act. Flt/Lt.
F. Lt. OC. A Flight

John Grandy
S. Ldr. OC 249. Sqn

	Single-Engine Aircraft Day Dual (1)	Day Pilot (2)	Night Dual (3)	Night Pilot (4)	Multi-Engine Aircraft Day Dual (5)	Day 1st Pilot (6)	Day 2nd Pilot (7)	Night Dual (8)	Night 1st Pilot (9)	Night 2nd Pilot (10)	Passenger (11)	Instr/Cloud Flying [Incl. in cols. (1) to (10)] Dual (12)	Pilot (13)
Totals Brought Forward	58.10	275.40	3.00	13.45							1.20	4.40	5.55
Sep 30		1.25											
Summary		49.25											
		.15											
		51.05											

Grand Total [Cols. (1) to (10)] ....Hrs..........Mins.

Totals Carried Forward

The author's log book for 31 September 1940.

The author's log book for 1-25 October 1940.

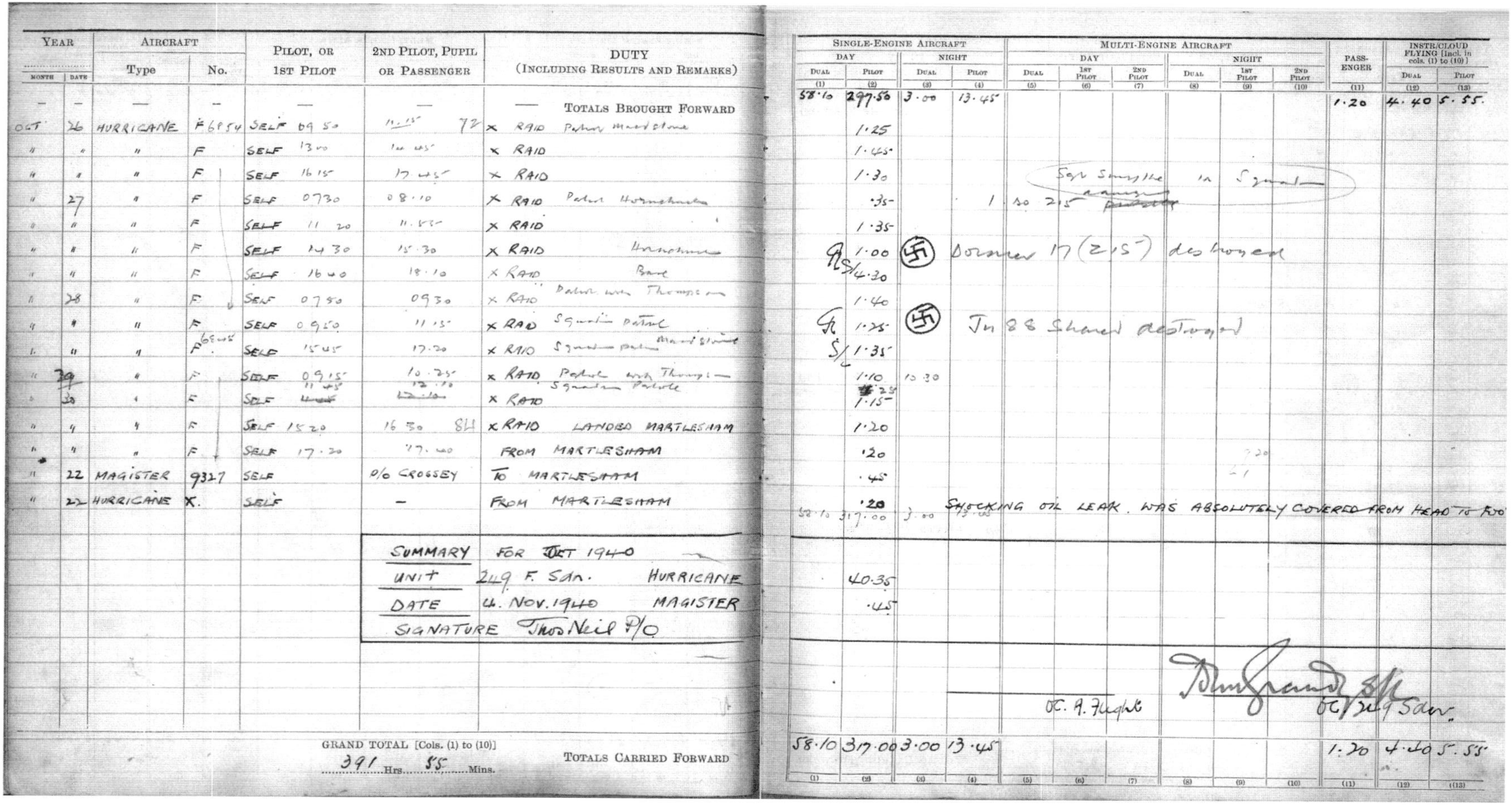

The author's log book for 26-30 October 1940.

The author's log book for 1–28 November 1940. Note the author's doodle in the remarks section on his second sortie of the day of 7 November of a parachute and '.01½', this records the author bailing out and the descent taking one and a half minutes!

YEAR		AIRCRAFT		PILOT, OR	2ND PILOT, PUPIL	DUTY
MONTH	DATE	Type	No.	1ST PILOT	OR PASSENGER	(INCLUDING RESULTS AND REMARKS)
					—	TOTALS BROUGHT FORWARD
Nov.	29	HURRICANE	D	Self 08.35	10.30 107	× R/P/O
"	"	"	D	Self 11.10	12.30	× R/P/O
"	30	"	F	Self 11.05	12.05	× R/P/O
"	"	"	F	Self 13.45	14.15 110	× R/P/O
						Summary for NOVEMBER 1940	1. HURRICANE
						Unit 249 Fighter Aircraft	2. —
						Date 2 DEC 1940 Types	3. —
						Signature Tom Neil	4. —

GRAND TOTAL [Cols. (1) to (10)] 426 Hrs. 20 Mins.   TOTALS CARRIED FORWARD

H. T. Duffie Flt. oc. A. Flt.

... Barton Flt. Lieut. C.O 249 Sqn.

SINGLE-ENGINE AIRCRAFT				MULTI-ENGINE AIRCRAFT							PASS-ENGER	INSTR/CLOUD FLYING (Incl. in cols. (1) to (10))	
DAY		NIGHT		DAY			NIGHT					Dual	Pilot
Dual	Pilot	Dual	Pilot	Dual	1st Pilot	2nd Pilot	Dual	1st Pilot	2nd Pilot		(11)	(12)	(13)
(1)	(2)	(3)	(4)	(5)	(6)	(7)	(8)	(9)	(10)				
58.10	341.40	3.00	13.45								1.20	2.20	5.15
	1.55												
	1.20												
	1.00												
	1.20												
58.10	347.25	3.00	13.45								1.20	4.40	5.15
	34.35												

F. V. Beamish W/CMDR
C.MDG R.A.F. STN.
NORTH WEALD

The author's log book for 29-30 November 1940.

Also available from Amberley Publishing

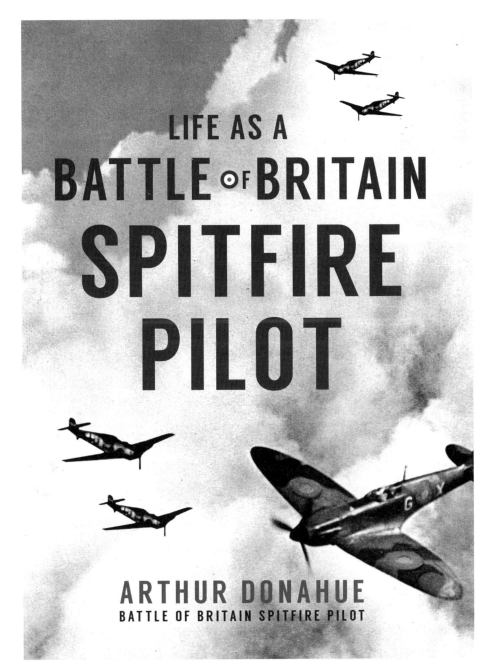

LIFE AS A
BATTLE OF BRITAIN
SPITFIRE
PILOT

ARTHUR DONAHUE
BATTLE OF BRITAIN SPITFIRE PILOT

Also available from Amberley Publishing

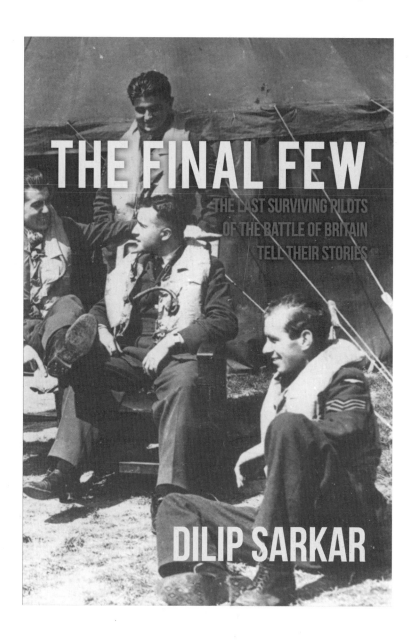

THE FINAL FEW
THE LAST SURVIVING PILOTS
OF THE BATTLE OF BRITAIN
TELL THEIR STORIES

DILIP SARKAR

Available from all good bookshops or to order direct
Please call **01453–847–800**
www.amberley-books.com